RAJPAL
DICTIONARY OF ENGLISH IDIOMS & PHRASES

RAJPAL
DICTIONARY OF ENGLISH IDIOMS & PHRASES

Compiled by

G.D. Sharma

Edited by

Brig. A.K. Shori

rajpal

₹ 595

ISBN : 9788170288572

Edition : 2019 © Brig. A. K. Shori

RAJPAL DICTIONARY OF ENGLISH IDIOMS & PHRASES

Edited by Brig. A.K. Shori

Printed at Deepika Enterprises, Delhi

DICTIONARY OF IDIOMS & Phrases

RAJPAL & SONS

Rajpal & Sons 1590, Madarsa Road, Kashmere Gate, Delhi-110006

Phone : 011-23869812, 23865483, 23867791

website : www.rajpalpublishing.com

e-mail : sales@rajpalpublishing.com

www.facebook.com/rajpalandsons

Dedicated to

(Late) Sh. Guru Dev Sharma, my father-in-law

A legend of simplicity and sacrifice

&

Sh. Dharam Pal Shori, my father

A living legend of courage and self-confidence

Preface

The first thought of getting this book published occurred sometime before 2001, though I had toyed with the idea whenever I saw my father-in-law, the late G.D. Sharma, deeply engrossed in jotting down phrases, quotations and idioms from newspapers, books and periodicals on every bit of paper that he could lay his hands on. A curious enquiry led me towards a huge collection of written material piled up and stacked in sacks, as if waiting to perish with time.

On flipping through some of the sheets, I noticed a goldmine of knowledge, which, if left unattended, might go waste. My curiosity prompted my father-in-law to open up and explain how he was fascinated by idioms and phrases. To learn that since the last more than four decades he had been jotting down, compiling and penning alphabetically the idioms initially with a pen on a piece of paper, then typing on a manual typewriter, was nothing short of mind-boggling. That a person could be so patient, dedicated and committed to a passion was simply unbelievable!

The initial study of paper immediately revealed a treasure-trove of diaries, notebooks, papers, registers, clippings and what not. Some of the papers had already become brittle and hand-writing illegible, yet the stuff had been stored and transported since the last 40 or 50 years from one place to another, from one house to another. While I debated in my mind what to do with the material, he looked expectantly at me. I asked him, "Why not get this published in book form?" His reply displayed a mixture of hope, a hidden desire and an element of doubt. I decided to go in for it.

A study of the material made me aware of what a stupendous task lay ahead of me. The compilation could be worth its money only if the idioms were explained in a sentence or two to make them comprehensible to the reader. This entailed a massive task as some of the alphabets carried more than 700 idioms, with a sizeable number having more than one meaning. By the time I resolved to do it, the old man, now 80 years of age, a heart patient and with a leg lost some 20 years back, showed some glimmer of life. He knew he had to undertake a task which required a lot of concentration and hard work.

Work Begins

The task was not easy as the contents were in more than one place and had to be arranged alphabetically. The construction of sentences was a new and more challenging task. I started feeding the data into my laptop and the first printout was a great source of excitement. My father-in-law set himself to revising the text and the work started flowing. My mother-in-law stood behind him day and night, looking after his health, taking care of his medicines and ensuring that he took proper rest. It soon became clear that in a year's time we could complete it. In between, I was posted out from Udhampur to Delhi. My father-in-law's health was not very good and I was bogged down with office work. The time available was limited. As a result the pace was slow but our determination and resolve strong.

By mid-2005, a considerable amount of work had been done and we were hopeful to complete it by Diwali. In between, the hard disc of my laptop crashed. A considerable amount of data got lost; luckily the backup was there but it was not up-to-date. Though not much data had been lost, it led to delays. Despite things slowing down a bit, we hoped to finish the work by year end. However, fate had something else in store for us. My father-in-law's health deteriorated suddenly and on 3 November 2005, he left this world, leaving us lonely and depressed.

He had worked on the book till his last day as the pen, diary and other material lay on his table when he suffered a stroke. We rushed him to the hospital. He had almost finished his work and was midway on the alphabet 'S'. The unfinished task was awesome but I had to complete it at all cost. It took me almost another year to get the first draft ready.

I never knew that proofreading could be such a tedious and cumbersome job. I looked around for help and my wife was more than willing to oblige. Her passion proved so encouraging that it lifted my spirits to the peak level till the mission was achieved ultimately.

Aftermath

The more I thought about the events following the birth of the idea, the more I felt determined and strong. If a man of 80 years of age, having lost his leg and with a weak heart could be so dedicated and committed as to share his treasure of knowledge with others, then why not a man younger in age be equally determined and motivated to achieve the goal which the older man could not? This book is a tribute to him. Here I would like to mention the name of another person who was a source of inspiration, a rock of Gibraltar, deserving much more than what he got in his life. He was my father, Dharam Pal Shori, a man of strong will power and undaunted moral strength capable of facing any problem in this world.

Brig. A.K. Shori

A

A bad egg: *A rotten or a worthless person* * A bad egg is sufficient to spoil the whole lot * A responsible job cannot be offered to a bad egg

A bad hat: *A rascal; a bad person* * A bad hat brings a bad name to the family and society

A bad job: *A piece of work not done properly* * A person who does a bad job cannot be paid his salary

A bad lot: *A group of persons whose company is bad* * The boy is part of a bad lot and thus should be avoided

A bad man is better than a bad name: *It is advisable to preserve one's reputation even if it means keeping wrong company* * Friendship with a bad friend can be broken off but a bad name cannot be washed off

A bad workman quarrels with his tools: *A person who is not a good worker tends to blame his tools for doing a bad job* * A carpenter cannot cover up his inefficiency by quarrelling with his tools

A bare living: *Survival on a paltry sum* * Minimum wages are a prerequisite for a bare living

A bare majority: *A very small majority* * The politician won the election by a bare majority

A bed of roses: *Comfortable and convenient* * Life is not a bed of roses as it seems to you

A bee in one's bonnet: *A whimsical or a crazy fancy for some object or person* * The boy has a bee in his bonnet about chess because he keeps on talking about it the whole day

A belly full of complaints: *Having many complaints against somebody; being dissatisfied with things in life* * The labourers came out with a belly full of complaints against the management during the meeting

A big gun: *A person of repute or an important person* * It requires hard work and dedication to become a big gun in society

A big noise: *An important person* * The former minister is still a big noise even after leaving the ministry

A bird in hand is worth two in the bush: *Treasure what you possess than to run after something which is not yours* * The girl should be satisfied with her boyfriend rather than running after other boys as she should realise that a bird in hand is worth two in the bush

A bird of passage: *A person staying temporarily in a country or place* * A person going abroad for earning his livelihood is a bird of passage in that country

A bird's eye view: *A general view* * We had a bird's eye view of the Mansarovar lake while flying above it

A bit longer: *A little while longer* * We stayed away from school a bit longer than the allowed time

A bit of all right: *Very attractive* * The woman at the party looked a bit of all right in her new dress

A bit of a nuisance: *Something unpleasant or troublesome* * The loud music at the party was a bit of a nuisance

A bit thick: *More than what one can put up with* * Apart from insulting me he was a bit thick to abuse me, so I gave him a sound thrashing

A black-sheep: *A person who does something bad* * All his siblings are doing well in life; he is the only black sheep in the family

A blank-minded person: *Forgetful* * He has to be reminded of the work he has to do because he is a very blank-minded person

A blazing row: *A violent quarrel* * There was a blazing row when all of them got drunk last night in the pub

A blessing in disguise: *Some unfortunate happening which eventually turns out to be something good* * Poverty turned out to be a blessing in disguise as it prodded Lal Bahadur Shastri to study hard and earn money

A blot on the escutcheon: *A stain on one's good name* * He was a blot on the escutcheon as his bad activities sullied the fair name of his family

A bolt from the blue: *A sudden shock or calamity* * The sudden demise of his only son was like a bolt from the blue for the father

A bona fide offer: *Offer made in good faith* * A bona fide offer should never be refused

A bone of contention: *Something that is a cause of*

disagreement * Kashmir has been a bone of contention between India and Pakistan

A bone to pick: *Something to occupy one's mind; differences over an issue to be cleared with somebody* * His quarrelsome nature incites him to pick a bone over flimsy issues * To bridge the relationship between two rival groups, it would be advisable to have a bone to pick through a peaceful discussion

A born actor: *A person who has the gift of acting well* * Meena Kumari was a born actor who could act any scene without any effort

Abound in: *To have in a great amount* * I think I abound in all good qualities

A bowing acquaintance: *A mild acquaintance* * A bowing acquaintance with a politician will not help me in getting the work done

A breakdown on the motorway: *A motor car stops working* * We got a lift and reached on time despite the breakdown on the motorway

A breath of wind: *A slight breeze* * Even a breath of wind during the summer is very soothing

A broken home: *A family where the parents have separated* * It is the children who have to suffer the most in a broken home

A broken reed: *A person who cannot be depended upon* * Do not count on his support as he is a broken reed

A broth of a boy: *A quintessence of a good person* * Innocence and sweetness could be seen in the broth of a boy

A brown study: *Dreaming or going into a reverie* * I called out to him loudly but my teacher did not hear me as he was in a brown study

A built up area: *An area which has many buildings* * The vacant land on the outskirts of the city is now a built up area

A bull in a china shop: *One who lacks delicacy that a situation calls for; a reckless person* * She was behaving like a bull in a china shop, little realising that the family had suffered a loss

A burnt child dreads the fire: *Once bitten twice shy; one who has burnt his fingers once will not go near the fire again* * After suffering a major loss in the new venture, I will not like to invest in it again as I am now like a burnt child that dreads the fire

A But and Ben: *A two-roomed*

flat * Who could imagine that a person living in a But and Ben would one day become the President of USA

A capful of breeze: *A slight breeze* * A capful of breeze is always welcome in summer

A case in point: *Say something to suggest that it is true* * Lack of communication has been a problem and their breakup is a case in point

A cast-iron excuse: *A perfect excuse* * He was granted leave from school because his broken arm provided a cast-iron excuse

A cat's paw: *One who serves as a tool* * A minister's role in the cabinet is like a cat's paw for the Prime Minister when he wants to get cabinet approval

A change of heart: *A change of opinion* * The members, who hated their leader, had a change of heart and started liking him on hearing his side of the story

A chapter of accidents: *A series of accidents* * There is a chapter of accidents when droughts follow floods as the daily reports reveal in the newspapers

A chicken-hearted person: *A cowardly man* * A chicken-hearted person cannot fight in the boxing ring

A child's play: *Very easy* * It is not a child's play to pass in the civil service examination

A close-fisted man: *A miser* * We could not extract even a single penny from that close-fisted man

A cock and bull story: *Imaginary or false story* * The cunning student tried to justify his absence from class by telling a cock and bull story

A colt's tooth: *Addiction to youthful pleasures* * Many adults fall prey to a colt's tooth and spoil their career

A common sense: *Practical intelligence* * A person deprived of common sense cannot acquit himself well in any job

A compound fracture: *Fracture of the bone into small pieces* * The car accident caused a compound fracture in his leg, making it very painful for him to walk

A confirmed bachelor: *A man who does not get married till late age* * A confirmed bachelor lives a longer life than a married man

A conscious decision: *A deliberate decision* * He took a conscious decision to quit smoking

A cool head: *A calm judgement* * Most of the knotty problems can be solved by keeping a cool head

A coronary: *A heart attack when the artery gets blocked* * A coronary trouble is the outcome of modern-day life of tension and competition

A crook in the lot: *A very crooked person* * As a politician he is a crook in the lot

A crown of laurel: *Honours gained* * He richly deserves a crown of laurels for his honesty and hard work

A cry for the moon: *Unaffordable desire* * A person who cannot make the two ends meet cannot think of buying a car as it would be like crying for the moon

A cry in the wilderness: *Useless demand which will not be heard* * The worker's protest for a raise in wages proved to be a cry in the wilderness

A curtain lecture: *A lecture or rebuke* * He has annoyed his wife and will have to face a curtain rebuke from her on reaching home

A cut above: *Distinctly better* * The new piece of essay is a cut above the ones you had written earlier

A dare-devil: *A very adventurous fellow* * It was a dare-devil stunt that you performed in the circus

A dark horse: *One whose capabilities are not known; a person with undisclosed abilities* *In the horse race I am depending heavily on my dark horse to lead me to victory * Bravo is like a dark horse in the West Indies cricket team for the Test Match * The opposition party has not disclosed the name of their nominee and is keeping the dark horse undisclosed * India is the dark horse as it may win the next World Cricket Cup

A day after the fair: *Too late* * It was a day after the fair to amend for his mistake

A dead duck: *Unlikely to succeed because of some mistake* * This project will be a dead duck because he has not done any research on it beforehand

A dead language: *A language no longer in use* * Latin has become a dead language in most countries of Europe

A dead letter: *Something fallen into disuse* * Honesty has become a dead letter these days

A dig in the ribs: *To nudge someone with the elbow* * A dig in the ribs by my wife alerted me to the danger of speaking out my mind

A dim recollection of something: *Remember something vaguely* * I have a dim recollection of having seen this man somewhere before

A disincentive to work: *Not encouraging for work* * The low wages are a disincentive for the labourers to work

A disreputable character: *A wicked person who cannot be trusted or respected* * Everyone keeps him at a distance as he is a man of disreputable character

A distant relative: *A relative, not from a close family* * A distant relative helped me financially when I was in need

A dog in the manger: *A person who does not want something but spoils it so that others too cannot get it* * Don't be a dog in the manger just because you have not been given the gift

A dog's life: *A hard and unhappy life* * She is leading a dog's life since her husband left her behind to fend for herself

A doodle: *A scribble or a sketch* * When the teacher saw her doodle in her book he knew that she was bored

A drop in the ocean: *A thing of no consequence; something which is very small* * My contribution to the earthquake victims is like a drop in the ocean

A drowning man catches at a straw: *A small thing to use as a support when in a difficulty* * When the floods arrived, he held on to a branch because what else could a drowning man do but catch at a straw

A dry eye: *Not crying even when a situation demands* * The man showed a dry eye even when there was a death in the family

A face like a fiddle: *A long or dismal face* * The expression on the face of the tennis coach made his face look like a fiddle

A fair-weather friend: *A friend only in favourable circumstances* * I do not keep the company of fair-weather friends because they are not there when you need them

A far cry: *A long way off; a great distance* * It is still a far cry for man to land on the moon

A fast buck: *Make money easily* * He has made a fast buck through illicit trade

A fat lot of good: *Hardly any good coming out of something* * The new drug without being tested will do a fat lot of good to asthma patients

A feather in one's cap: *To earn a distinction* * By winning the Champions Trophy, our cricket team has added a feather in its cap

A few: *A small number* * Only a few spectators came to watch the game * A few persons will do the job of pruning trees in the garden

A few words: *To speak very little* * As he is a man of a few words it becomes difficult to carry on a conversation with him

A figure among ciphers: *A person of little knowledge among those with no knowledge at all* * He seems like a figure among ciphers when you hear him speak among his friends who know even less than him

A finger in the pie: *To get a share in some work* * A finger in the pie in terms of profit motivates him to work more * Avoid having a finger in the pie to guard against ugly consequences

A first in physics: *A first-class degree in physics* * It becomes difficult to get admission in a good college unless one is a first in physics

A fish out of water: *Out of place; out of element* * He felt like a fish out of water at the gala party where the elite of the city were present

A fit of distraction: *A confused state of mind* * He could not give his true opinion as he was in a fit of distraction

A flat refusal: *To refuse outright* * She annoyed her parents by giving a flat refusal when they asked for help

A flesh wound: *A superficial wound; not a deep wound* * Thank God, it is only a flesh wound and not a fracture

A fly in the ointment: *Some slight flaw which corrupts a thing; a minor disruption when deeply engrossed in work* * The presence of my aunt when I am working will act like a fly in the ointment and spoil my mood

A fog cannot be dispelled by a fan: *An impossible effort to serve a purpose* * One has to plan meticulously in before starting a new venture since a fog cannot be dispelled by a fan

A fool's bolt is soon shot: *A fool loses the initiative, leaving himself unprotected* * A fool's bolt is soon shot when he starts arguing with a trespasser little realising that a car is coming from behind

A fool's errand: *A futile effort;*

a futile journey *Despite all the effort put to search for the ring, it turned out to be a fool's errand * It will be a fool's errand to go deep in the sea at this time of the year when the monsoon has set in

A fool's paradise: *To live in a dream; far from reality* * To dream about winning a lottery is nothing short of living in a fool's paradise

A foregone conclusion: *Result is known beforehand* * The result of the match was a foregone conclusion as he was no match for his opponent

A free fight: *A fight without rules* * A free fight broke out among the spectators when two teams were playing a match

A Freudian slip: *Saying something contrary to what is intended and which reveals the true thought* * A Freudian slip by the orator placed him in an awkward situation

A friend in need is a friend indeed: *One who helps in time of difficulty* * The timely blood donation by my friend to save me proved that a friend in need is a friend indeed

A gathering storm: *Imminent; a likely trouble about to happen* * Advance information on a gathering storm can be helpful in being prepared for it

A ghost of a smile: *A very light smile* * A ghost of a smile appeared on his face though he was far from pleased at the incident

A ghost writer: *One who writes articles, speeches or books for others* * A ghost writer can earn money but not a name

A gift of the gab: *Ability to speak in a persuasive manner* * The foremost prerequisite for a politician is to acquire a gift of the gab to win the hearts of the general public

A golden key opens all the doors save that of heaven: *Abundance of wealth may help to entice friends and foes but not God* * Wealth acquired through illegal means can help to win friends but not God

A good bet: *An action that is most likely to be successful* * It is a good bet that the rapist will be hanged for his sinful act

A good buy: *A bargain* * We made a good buy in the exhibition as it was cheaper than what you get in the market

A good catch: *Be a good prospec-*

tive husband/worker; to catch a lot of fish * He is a good catch as a husband for he is well-off and well qualified * While fishing, we made a good catch last evening

A good few: *A considerable number* * A good few people gathered to help the earthquake victims

A good half-hour: *Not less than* * I waited for my friend for a good half-hour before he emerged from the room

A good job: *A piece of work well done* * The conversion of a penalty corner into a goal was a good job done by the hockey player

A good many: *A large number of* * I have a good many things to do today and I hope to complete them all

A good many people: *A lot of persons* * A good many people attended the funeral of the leader

A good name: *Fame* * He earned a good name because of his good deeds

A good nose: *An instinct for finding something valuable* * The scientist has a good nose for finding gold in the river-bed

A good Samaritan: *One who does charity in time of need* * To help the flood-affected victims, the rich man should act as a good Samaritan and donate money

A good sort: *A decent fellow* * I love him very much as he is a good sort and means no harm

A good track record: *Very successful* * He has a very good track record as a servant and should be promptly employed before he finds employment elsewhere

A good while: *A fairly long time* * It will take a good while to complete the job in hand

A good word: *A recommendation; a favourable mention; praise* * As I am very keen to work in that office, could you please put in a good word for me

A grating sound: *An irritating sound* * A grating sound coming from the neighbourhood disturbed his sleep.

A great many: *A large number; as many* * A great many people gathered to listen to their leader's speech

A great song and dance: *A great fuss* * The father made a great song and dance when his daughter came home late

A guilty mind: *A person who has done something wrong and is suspicious of being caught*

* A person with a guilty mind cannot live in peace

A hair-breadth escape: *A narrow escape* * My car hit a tree at full speed but I had a hair-breadth escape from death

A hair of the dog (that bit him): *A small dose which causes trouble; a homeopathic dose* * It required a hair of the dog to recover from illness * It proved to be a hair of the dog that bit her when she began to vomit on swallowing a tiny tablet meant for killing germs

A handle to one's name: *A title* * Addressing the queen as Your Excellency is a handle to her name

A hard bargain: *A tough negotiator* * To get the deal through you have to drive a hard bargain

A hard nut to crack: *A tough problem to solve* * She played very well and reached the final round where she found her opponent a hard nut to crack

A hard way: *A way of doing things which is difficult* * She has the habit of doing things the hard way instead of doing them simply

A haunted house: *A house wherein spirits or ghosts are supposed to reside* * Nobody can sleep even a single night in a haunted house

A heart condition: *A weak heart* * A patient having a heart condition should not be given a cause for tension

A heart of stone: *Not easily moved; unfeeling or cruel* * The brutal killer of a child must be having a heart of stone

A hell of a noise: *A very loud noise* *A hell of a noise was made when the bus overturned

A Herculean task: *Work requiring immense effort* * To restore world peace is certainly a Herculean task

A high-powered: *Very powerful* * The new car is having a high-powered engine * A high-powered committee was constituted to look into the problem

A hit or a miss: *A case in which either success or complete failure is possible; depend more on chance* * The bus is usually late and so reaching office on time is a case of hit or miss

A hole in the wall: *A small place or joint* * I went to eat at a hole in a wall but the food was delicious

A hollow promise: *False promise* * He made a hollow promise to complete the work which he could not

A honeyed tongue: *To speak nicely to deceive* * The girl spoke in a honeyed tongue when she did not mean what she said * Innocent people fall prey to crooked persons who speak with a honeyed tongue

A host in himself: *One with great strength, skill or resources within oneself* * Muhammad Ali, the great boxer, was a host in himself * Riches have made the politician a host in himself

A house with a sitting tenant: *With someone living in a house and paying rent* * He bought a house with a sitting tenant and could not get it vacated

A kettle of fish: *Something very different* * He knows all about operating a computer but to set it right is a different kettle of fish

A leading light: *A very important person* * The girl is a leading light in her office because of her good work

A lead towel: *A bullet* * He was injured by a stray lead towel

A leap in the dark: *An act whose consequences are not known* * It will be a leap in the dark to appear in an examination for which you are not prepared

A lick and a promise: *A perfunctory wash* * The police adopted alick-and-a-promise policy to search for the kidnapped boy

A lie-in: *Stay in bed longer than usual* * You can have a nice lie-in on Sunday morning

A line of sight: *The direction in which one must look to catch sight of* * The shooter must aim his rifle in a line of sight to hit the target

A little: *A small amount* * It will require a little more to give a finishing touch to the work in hand

A little bird told me: *To hear a secret so as not to reveal* * I know she is going to the movie because a little bird told me so

A little knowledge is a dangerous thing: *Incomplete knowledge is a dangerous thing* * Please study the issue thoroughly well because a little knowledge is a dangerous thing

A little way: *Short distance* * You will have to cover a little way to reach my village

A load off one's mind: *Feel much relieved and relaxed* * By agreeing to help me you have taken a load off my mind

A long way off: *At great dis-*

tance * The ship is now a long way off the shore

A lot: *Considerably; to a great extent* * I had to put in a lot of effort to pass the exam.

A lot of: *Many* * A lot of reading material is available in this book

A lucky break: *Change from bad luck* * He was losing the match but by winning this point he has got a lucky break

A man of discrimination: *Of good taste* * He is a man of discrimination as he has very high tastes

A man of few words: *Someone who says very little* * He rarely expresses his feelings to others as he is a man of few words

A man of letters: *A scholar having literary taste* * Nehru, apart from being a politician, was a man of letters

A man of parts: *A man of uncommon qualities/abilities* * Our college principal is a man of parts as he has varied interests

A man of rank: *A man of high birth* * Jawahar Lal Nehru was a man of rank

A man of sense: *Sagacious man* * A man of sense is held in high esteem by all those around him

A man of spirits: *Very courageous man* * Napoleon was a man of spirits as nothing frightened him

A man of straw: *A person without substantial means; a person who can be easily overcome; a person with no will or voice of his own* * A man of straw can be easily twisted around one's fingers

A man of substance: *A wealthy and powerful man* * A man of substance is respected everywhere

A man/woman after one's own heart: *A person whom one likes very much* * One who implements policies for the welfare of the poor is a man after one's own heart

A matter of course: *Something to be expected in the natural course of events; usual affair* * It is a matter of course for me to go to bed early

A meal of sorts: *Not a very good meal* * The hotel charges are very high even for a meal of sorts

A menace: *Very troublesome and naughty* * Stray dogs have become a menace on the road

A mint of money: *A great deal of money* * The way she spends money makes it appear as though she has a mint of money

A mixed blessing: *Both sorrow*

and pleasure; something that has both advantages and disadvantages * Children can prove to be a mixed blessing for they can behave well at time and be a nuisance on some occasions * Excess of wealth is a mixed blessing because it helps you buy what you want but it may also spoil your habits

A mixed marriage: *Marriage between two people of different races* * A mixed marriage helps in bringing about national integration

A modest flat: *One which does not look expensive* * The newly married couple is in search of a modest flat as they do not have enough funds

A moonlight flit: *Escaping quietly at night* * The prisoners performed a moonlight flit by escaping from behind the prison walls

A narrow escape: *A miraculous escape from death* * The passengers had a narrow escape when their bus overturned causing injury to some

A natural bent of mind: *A natural instinct* * Sania has a natural bent of mind for playing tennis

A net profit: *Actual gain after incurring expenses* * My first deal has given me a net profit of a thousand rupees after deducting my expenses

A new departure: *A new course or procedure; a change of purpose or method* * The new taxation procedure is a new departure from the old method

A new lease of life: *A fresh start in life* * After undergoing medical treatment at the hospital she received a new lease of life

A nine day's wonder: *Something that is short-lived* * A youthful life is a nine day's wonder

A nip in the air: *A bit of cold weather* * Wear a shawl as there is a nip in the air and you may catch a cold

A pain in the neck: *A troublesome person/thing* * I have broken my friendship with her since she was becoming a pain in the neck with her rude behaviour

A past master: *An expert in doing wrong things* * Your friend is really a past master in telling lies

A pat on the back: *Expression of approval* * The principal gave me a pat on my back when I fared well in my class

A peg to hang on: *Pretext; excuse* * He decided to celebrate his birthday as a peg to hang on since he wanted to meet his friends

A piece: *One; each* * The bananas are being sold at Rs 2 a piece

A piece of my mind: *To give advice in anger; to express displeasure* * I gave him a piece of my mind when he irritated me

A piece of furniture: *An article of furniture; a thing or a person to be used and ignored* * He does not attend to the household problems and treats me like a piece of furniture

A pig in a poke: *A blind bargain; something bought without seeing* * It was something like a pig in a poke when I purchased a piece of barren land

A pleasant surprise: *A surprise that is pleasurable* * It was a pleasant surprise to see her after a long time * It was a pleasant surprise to see the police recover the stolen goods so soon

A pretty penny: *A considerable sum of money* * I could save a pretty penny after two years of hard work abroad

A quantity of waste paper: *A lot of waste* * The yard is full of a quantity of waste paper

A queer fish: *A strange person* * Our new manager seems a queer fish as he behaves in a very officious manner

A quick one: *A small quick drink* * The soldiers left for the battle-field after having a quick one

A quick temper: *One who loses temper easily* * It is better to talk to her softly since she has a quick temper

A rainy day: *A bad period* * Wise men save money for a rainy day and not spend it recklessly

A raw deal: *Unfair treatment* * The dismissed official got a raw deal since he alone is not to be blamed for the mistake

A ready reply to: *Always has an answer* * He has a ready reply to anything that you tell him

A recipe for disaster: *Bound to fail* * If the government introduces the law it is bound to be a recipe for disaster

A red letter day: *Auspicious and important day* * 15th August is a red letter day in Indian history

A red rag to a bull: *A cause of anger* * To tell him the bitter truth of his inability to handle the job professionally is like showing a red rag to a bull

A resort: *A place for enjoying a holiday* * A resort opened recently on the outskirts of the town has become very popular

A right hand man: *Useful person who can be relied upon* * Our Vice-Principal is the right hand man of the Principal

A ripe old age: *Till a very old age* * A man acquires more sobriety at a ripe old age * You cannot expect him to do physical work at such a ripe old age

A roaring trade: *Successful business* * On a hot day the ice-cream sellers were doing a roaring trade

A rod in the pickle: *Punishment yet to be given* * The culprit is still in jail because of a rod in the pickle

A rolling stone: *Not constant at work in one place* * He does one job in one place and then takes on another in another place like a rolling stone

A rotten apple spoils the lot: *One bad thing infects the whole thing* * He is a jail-bird so keep him away from your children as a rotten apple spoils all around him

A rough diamond: *A crude and rustic person but who is worldly wise* * The farmer is a rough diamond but he knows his job alright

A rough sea: *Turbulent weather* * The fishermen were caught in rough sea and had to rush back to the shore

A round peg in a square hole: *A misfit* * Even a talented carpenter can be a round peg in a square hole if given the job of a mason

A royal road: *An easy way for being successful* * Dedication or hard work is a royal road to success in life

A rumour is afloat: *A hearsay that is in circulation* * A rumour is afloat about some deadly virus spreading brain fever in the city

A run on: *Sudden demand by many people; a rapid demand for something* * There has been a run on for the tickets to the Indo-Pakistan cricket match

A runny nose: *A nose that runs due to cold* * He got a runny nose due to bad cold

A safe bet: *Extremely likely to happen* * The dark clouds indicate a safe bet that it will rain today

A screw loose: *Something defective, especially mentally* * The way he continued talking endlessly about his hobby that it seemed he had a screw loose

A screw with a left-handed thread: *Something which you*

have to turn to the left to tighten * At times, a mechanic has to use a screw with a left-handed thread for fixing up fittings

A secret ballot: *Election where the votes of the individual voters are not disclosed* * The speaker has the power to cast a secret ballot during the Parliament session

A sharp tongue: *A bitter tongue* * A sharp-tongued person is derided by one and all

A sheet anchor: *A chief support* * Rahul Dravid is a sheet anchor for the Indian cricket team

A sheet in the wind: *Half drunk* * K.L. Sehgal occasionally used to be a sheet of the wind before recording his songs

A shot in the arm: *An injection to revive; provide help and encouragement* * The injection given to the patient proved to be a shot in the arm as it relieved his pain * The latest rise in the interest rates has given the industry a shot in the arm

A shot in the locker: *Something kept in the reserve; to be still potent* * He still has a shot in the locker in case he runs short of money to run his business

A shrewd move: *A smart action; a timely move* * It was a shrewd move to buy shares of the company just before their prices began to rise * A shrewd move by my friend put me in a comfortable situation

A sight more: *A lot more* * You deserve a sight more from the boss than what he gives

A slate loose: *A slight mental derangement* * Due to a sudden shock he fell prey to a slate loose and is under treatment

A slip of pen: *Mistake in writing* * It was a slip of pen when the journalist wrote that Marie Curie was a famous writer.

A slip of the tongue: *Mistake when talking* * It was more a slip of tongue by the speaker that Kalidas was a great mathematician

A slow coach: *A lazy person* * Harry can never complete his work as he is a slow coach

A split personality: *Quite different behaviour at times* * It is difficult to understand him as he has a split personality because of which he keeps changing his stance

A square deal: *A fair bargain* * I do expect a fair deal from my friends and relatives

A square peg in a round hole: *Misfit* * Making a child do the work of an adult is like making a square peg fit in a round hole

A standing joke: *That makes one always laugh* * A standing joke is always welcome in every society

A stay of some length: *Quite a long stay* * Our soldiers had a stay of some length in trouble-torn countries

A stepping stone: *A source of success* * A failure often proves to be a stepping stone to success in life

A sticky end: *Death; put in prison or get ruined* * He came to a sticky end after meeting with an accident * His habit of stealing brought him to a sticky end as he was given imprisonment

A sticky wicket: *An awkward situation* * He landed himself on a sticky wicket because of his own follies

A stiff-necked person: *Obstinate person* * A stiff-necked person is disliked by everybody

A stitch in time saves nine: *A small piece of work done in time saves from ruin later on* * Better to stop smoking before getting cancer of the throat because a stitch in time saves nine

A stone's throw away: *Quite close* * My brother lives at a stone's throw away from my home

A storm in a tea-cup: *Commotion over a trifle* * The discord between the husband and wife was nothing more than a storm in a teacup

A sweet tooth: *A liking for sweets* * She seems to have a sweet tooth considering the number of chocolates she eats in a day

A tall man of his hands: *A deft worker; a sturdy fighter* * Abraham Lincoln was a tall man of his hands considering the way he wielded the axe

A tall order: *A difficult task* * It is a tall order to restore peace in West Asia

A thankless task: *A work that remains unappreciated* * To be a cricket umpire is a thankless task

A thin time: *A time of little enjoyment* * A thin time during a busy schedule rejuvenates one's energy

A thorn in the flesh: *A feeling of great pain and jealousy* * The all-round progress made by India in the recent past has become a thorn in the flesh for Pakistan

A to Z: *From beginning to end* * The little girl narrated the whole story from A to Z

A toss-up on which one will win: *Difficult to tell as to who will win* * It is a toss-up between two teams as to who will begin to bat first

A tough nut to crack: *A tough person; a difficult problem* * To eradicate corruption in the country is a tough nut to crack

A treat in store: *A special future surprise* * The boy has a treat in store from the parents on his birthday

A turncoat: *A person who changes opinions* * A politician is like a turncoat as he changes his stand often

A turning point: *A significant change* * The war of Kalinga proved a turning point in the life of King Asoka

A useful rule of thumb: *A useful way of calculating; a practical way of approaching a problem* * It is a useful rule of thumb to settle a bargain instantly

A vexed question: *A question that is controversial and hard to explain* * The future of Kashmir continues to be a vexed question

A warm reception: *A display of hospitality; a vigorous resistance or attack* * A warm reception was accorded to the Prime Minister when he visited his constituency

A week from now/A week today: *This day next week* * A week from now, he will come to us to stay for a month

A well begun is half done: *A good beginning* * You are sure to see a fruitful result if you think positively before you act

A wet blanket: *A person whose presence dampens spirit of joy* * The party was in full swing but the entry of my father worked as a wet blanket

A white elephant: *Highly costly* * Maintenance of a large house is like a white elephant for an ordinary Indian

A wild goose chase: *A foolish and useless chase* * The efforts made by the police to capture the dreaded dacoit proved to be a wild goose chase

A will of one's own: *A strong view of his own* * He has a will of his own so nobody can deter him from what he has planned

A windfall: *Unexpected good fortune* * To win a handsome sum in lottery was a windfall for the poor worker

A wishful thinking: *Expect good to happen when not possible** It is a wishful thinking on the part of politicians to talk about removal of poverty

A wolf in sheep's clothing: *A cheat or deceiver; a man who appears friendly but is really an enemy* * Do not place your trust in him as he is a wolf in sheep's clothing

A wool gathering: *A state of absent mindedness* *There is no point in asking him a question at the moment as his mind has gone a wool gathering

A word for word: *To say or write exactly what one has originally said or written* * I have translated his speech word for word in vernacular

A word in the season: *Timely advice* * His was a word in the season that made me give up smoking

A word out of the season: *Ill timed advice* * A word out of the season may not help in getting the desired results

A work of time: *A change; an achievement* * It is a work of Time that from childhood to old age, human beings develop for the better

A.B.C.: *Elementary knowledge* * He does not know even the A.B.C. of the court case

A.I.: *Excellent* * Each and every article displayed in the exhibition was in A.I. order

Abandon oneself: *Give oneself up completely to* * After Krishna's departure Radha abandoned herself to despair

Abide by: *To act in pursuance of; to remain faithful to; to dwell on; act upon* * One must abide by one's promise come what may

Abide the smell: *Like the smell* * I really abide the smell of flowers

Abound with/in: *Exist in great numbers or quantities* * Wild animals abound in forests

Above all: *Something significant* * Rabindranath Tagore was a poet, novelist and above all, a great patriot

Above board: *Honourably open; cannot be questioned* * To achieve popularity, one should be above board in one's dealing with others

Above ground: *Alive; not buried* * Good deeds of great men always remain above ground

Above measure: *To an exceedingly great degree* * Her good qualities are above measure to be explained in a few words

Above one's breath: *Aloud* * The

passenger called for police by shouting above his breath

Above par: *Above normal value* * The vintage car is being sold above par as very few models of the kind are available

Above price: *So valuable that no price can be enough* * The scholar's contribution towards the cause of education is above price

Above the salt: *Among those of high social class* * People above the salt care little about the welfare of the backward classes

Above water: *Out of difficulties* * With grit and determination, the people came above water after an earthquake hit their village

Abraham's bosom: *The abode of the blessed dead* * Those who serve the cause of humanity are sure to reach Abraham's bosom after death

Absence of mind: *Lack of attention to what is going on due to absorption of mind on other things* * He fell in the drain while crossing the road due to his absence of mind * I was so absorbed in my studies that everything happening around me went unnoticed due to absence of mind

Absorbed in: *Completely busy with* * Since the exam are approaching near, most students are deeply absorbed in their studies

Abstain from: *Keep away* * He abstains from non-vegetarian food during auspicious days

Abstract of title: *Summary of facts* * The abstract of title is that where there is a will there is a way

Accede to: *Agree to* * He acceded to my request

Access to: *Approach* * One can have easy access to public servants now-a-days

Accessory after the fact: *One who knowingly helps another who has committed a crime* * Not only the criminal but also his accessory after the fact was sentenced to imprisonment

Accessory before the fact: *Accessory who is not present when the crime is committed* * An accessory before the fact is being interrogated by the police

Accommodate to: *Adapt* * One who is gifted with wisdom knows how to accommodate oneself to changing circumstances

Accommodate with: *Oblige* * He accommodated me with a

loan when I needed the money

Accomplished in: *Perfect* * She is accomplished in her subject

Accord to: *Give* * The Indians accorded a warm welcome to Prince Charles on his maiden visit to this country

Accord with: *Agree with* * What you say is not in accord with what your friend had agreed to do

According as: *In accord with; depending on* * The baby food should be given according as the needs of the baby

According to: *In accordance with; agreeable* * The administrator is supposed to act according to laid down rules * The scholar acted according to the norms set by his teacher

According to one's lights: *As per one's spiritual enlightenment; to enable one to judge* * Gautam Buddha's path to salvation was correct according to one's lights * Mental peace is attained according to one's lights

According to one's power: *As far as one can do* * I shall try to extend all possible help that I can afford according to my power

According to one's sweet will: *As one pleases* * There is no point in saying anything to him as he works according to his sweet will

According to plan: *As has been intended* * Work on the project is going on according to plan

According to rule: *According to established principles* * The department under the ministry has to be run according to rule

Accountable to/for: *Responsible to or for* * Every man is accountable to God ultimately for his deeds.

Account for: *Explain the cause of* * You will have to account for your long absence from the office

Accounts of the firm: *Statement showing the financial position of a firm* * The accounts of the firm should be maintained correctly

Accused of: *Charged with* * The old servant was accused of theft

Accustomed to: *Used to* * I am not accustomed to such improper treatment

Achilles heel: *Vulnerable point* * John's poor serve is his Achilles heel in his game of tennis.

Acid test: *A difficult test; a test to show a true value of some-*

thing * To lead an honest life is an acid test for a bureaucrat

Acids react with metals: *Change their chemical composition* * It has been confirmed through practical experiments that acids react with metals

Acoustic guitar: *Ordinary guitar* * The man is very fond of an acoustic guitar

Acquired character: *A character that is built up over the years and is not inherited* * Pran could be rated as an acquired character in the art of villainy because he was not born a villain

Acquired taste: *A liking that comes after some experience* * Initially he did not like vinegar-cooked food but now, with an acquired taste, he enjoys it

Acquit of: *Declared not guilty* * The accused was acquitted of all the charges

Acquit oneself: *Behave properly* * Suresh has acquitted himself laudably after scoring good marks in the final exams

Across lots: *By short cuts* * The key to success lies not across lots * One will have to spend adequate time to reach a high position in a society which is not possible across lots

Act as: *Do the work as* * One should act as desired by elders.

Act as a tonic: *Make someone more energetic* * The news about a modified taxation policy acted as a tonic for income-tax payees

Act for: *To act as a substitute* * In cricket, a substitute is allowed to act for an injured player

Act of aggression: *Attack* * No act of aggression on any country can be justified on any grounds

Act of God: *A result of natural forces, unexpected, not preventable by human forces* * The destruction by tsunami was an act of God

Act of grace: *Pardon granted by a sovereign authority* * Indian Government released the prisoners of war after 1971 war in an act of grace.

Act of reverence: *Salutations; act of deep respect* * It will be an act of reverence on our part to help the senior citizens

Act on behalf of: *Represent* * The Dean is acting on behalf of the Vice Chancellor, who is away on leave

Act on: *To exert an influence on; to act in accordance with* * Your advice will act on him in changing his wrong decision * To boost our thrust on technology, we should act on the line adopted by the developed countries

Act under: *To act as in subordination* * During training, one has to act under the junior staff also

Act up to: *To put into practice; to fulfil* * We must act up to the expectations of our elders

Actual trust: *A trust in which the trustee's power of management depends upon his having the right of actual possession* * He was given the charge of an actual trust because of his honesty

Acute disease: *Disease being very serious* * A multi-party system becomes an acute disease in the governance of a country

Ad hoc: *Which applies to a particular case* * An ad hoc committee has been appointed to deal with the examination scandal

Ad infinitum: *For ever* * Nothing exists ad infinitum in the world

Adam's wine: *Water* * Life on earth cannot exist without Adam's wine

Adapt for: Make suitable for * This book you can adapt for beginners

Adapted from: *Translated and changed* * The play has been adapted from French to suit our culture

Adapted to: *Be used to; made suitable to* * You must adapt yourself to local traditions quickly * This book is adapted to meet the needs of beginners

Add fuel to flame/fire: *To deteriorate or worsen matters* * The arrest of union leaders added fuel to the flame and the agitation gathered momentum

Addicted to: *Habitual* * The watchman is addicted to smoking

Address oneself to: *Apply oneself to; be busy with* * It is to our benefit to address ourselves to the business on hand

Address something to: *Send complaint, a remark* * Please address your complaint to the manager

Adept in: *Expert in* * My sister is adept in singing

Adequate to: *Enough to* * Unfortunately the supplies are not adequate to meet the demands

Adhere to: *Stick to* * Learn to adhere to your principles

Adjacent to: *Just near* * Our college is adjacent to the police station

Adjourn for/to: *Postpone for* * The meeting was adjourned for a week

Administer an oath: *To make someone commit an oath* * The President administers the oath to a newly appointed Prime Minister

Admit of: *Allow* * You ought to know that this matter admits of no delay at all

Advance by leaps and bounds: *Make good progress* * The new business venture started by him is advancing by leaps and bounds

Advance guard: *Troops sent ahead of the main force* * To take stock of the situation, an advance guard has been sent to find the actual situation

Advanced student: *Student who has studied for several years* * Only an advanced student can become successful in a competitive exam

Adverse to: *Contrary to* * His behaviour is adverse to the interests of the organisation

Advert to: *Refer to* * Please advert to the concerned paragraph of the investigation report

Advertised for: *Put an advertisement in the paper asking people to apply* * The authority concerned has advertised for a new post of the chairman

Afflicted at/by: *Cause mental trouble to* * He feels much afflicted at the sudden demise of his father

Afflicted with: *Cause bodily trouble to* * She is afflicted with rheumatism

After a fashion: *In a way; to a certain extent; somehow or other but not satisfactorily* * Mohan could, after a fashion, manage to get only pass marks in the final exams * This financial help shall definitely help me after a fashion * I can manage to cook after a fashion

After all: *Nevertheless; in spite of; after considering everything* * Health is preferred to wealth after all * The construction project was bound to be delayed after all the negotiations with the striking workers failed * Ultimately the decision was taken by the management after all the pros and cons had been considered

After-effects: *Effects that follow on* * The after-effects of radiation result in side-effects

After lotion: *Lotion for soothing the face after shaving* * An after lotion is applied to save the skin from any infection

After one's own heart: *Exactly to one's own liking* * The new house that Mohan has bought is after his own heart.

After that they never looked back: *Very successful* * West Indies won the first match and after that they never looked back

After the fashion of: *In imitation of* * Mira's articles are published in the newspaper after the fashion of a famous journalist

After you: *To proceed first* * I will follow after you

Aftermath: *What takes place after a catastrophe* * The aftermath of an earthquake is very dangerous

Again and again: *Several times* * The tremors took place again and again within a few minutes

Against lending any more money: *Opposed to lending money* * I am dead against lending any more money to him

Against one's better judgement: *To take action against one's wishes* * It was certainly against my better judgement to punish the innocent boy

Against the grain: *Against the fibre of the wood; against the natural temper* * It goes against the grain to continue with the construction of the house with inferior material * It is against the grain to be cool when someone is being provoked unnecessarily

Against the hair: *Contrary to inclination* * Never act against the hair lest it should prove to be a harmful proposition

Against the word: *Against the texture of the word; the wrong way* * It goes against the word to laugh at the deformity of the old man

Against time: *With utmost speed* * The bus driver was driving rashly as it was running against time

Age gap: *Difference in age* * There should be a proper age gap between a husband and wife

Age of discretion: *Mature years; years of discretion* * A person at an age of discretion is respected in the society by all

Agency for: *Distributors for* * My father has an agency for Suzuki cars

Agree to: *To concur; to consent* * I agreed to my friend's proposal to do social service during the summer vacation

Agree with: *Be in harmony; approve of; to concur; to be in*

harmony with * I do agree with you on this point

Agreeable to: *Pleasing; giving acceptance; readiness to agree* * His arguments were agreeable to all * I am hopeful of my friend being agreeable to my advice and acting accordingly

Aid and abet somebody: *Be an accomplice in a wrong act* * Raman was put behind bars for having aided and abetted Raju in committing a robbery

Air disaster: *Crash of an aircraft leading to death of many people* * An air disaster took place killing all the passengers on flight

Air display: *Exhibition of flying skill by aircraft* * Indian Air Force put up a grandeur display of air drills on Republic Day

Air one's grievances: *To voice one's complaints* * He is airing his grievances on the public platform but to no avail

Air-to-air: *Missiles fired from one aircraft to another* * Our country must have a good stock of air-to-air armaments

Air-to-ground: *Missiles fired from an aircraft to hit a target on the ground* * Air-to-ground missiles prove very destructive in a war

Air traffic: *Aircraft flying* * Air traffic is increasing very fast now-a-days

Aircraft carrier: *Ship which carries aircraft* * The Indian Navy has recently built a modern aircraft carrier

Airs and graces: *Foolish; to act haughtily* * I do not like him for his airs and graces

Akin to: *Like to* * Truth is akin to true love

Alarmed at: *Cause anxiety* * I hope you will not feel alarmed at this sad piece of news

Alfresco meal: *In the open air* * The marriage party was entertained with delicious sweets at an alfresco meal

Alien to: *Foreign to* * Impoliteness is alien to my nature

Alienated from: *Separated from* * His arrogance has alienated him from his relatives

Alight from: *Get off from a train or bus* * I alighted from the train at New Delhi railway station

Alive to: *Conscious of* * I am very much alive to my responsibilities

All modern conveniences: *All modern comforts* * We have got all modern conveniences in our house

All agog: *Very surprised; excited* * The crowd was all agog when the West Indies Cricket team reached the airport

All along: *Everywhere; all the time* * I have been doing physical exercise all along to keep myself fit * All along his life he suffered miserably

All and some: *One and all* * The law of the land must be applied to all and some, irrespective of cast, creed and status

All and sundry: *Everyone* * He invited all and sundry to his birthday

All at once: *Suddenly* * The patient who was well on the path of recovery all at once collapsed and died

All at sea: *Out of one's reckoning; completely at a loss; to be in a state of bewilderment* * I am all at sea in commerce as I don't understand it * The villagers were all at sea when they were taken to the airport to see an aeroplane

All at sixes and sevens: *Very disorganised; not in a regular manner* * The whole team is at sixes and sevens; hence there is no possibility of a win

All but: *Everything short of; almost* * We could understand all but the true meaning of the last speech by the speaker * We reached the destination all but in time before darkness fell

All by themselves: *Without any help from anyone else* * The Japanese have made tremendous economic development all by themselves

All eyewash: *All rubbish* * It is all an eyewash to inform the police when the wrong deed has been done

All in all: *To be everything; the highest in a place* * The principal is all in all in running the day-to-day affairs of the college

All in: *Exhausted* * The players were all in after a gruelling match

All in price: *Including everything* * The cost of food, drinks is all in price of the room rent

All in vain: *Without any success* * I persuaded him not to make fun of old people but my efforts were all in vain

All intents and purposes: *Practically* * To all intents and purposes the production manager is the master of the factory

All is well that ends well: *Everything ends well* * He should not have lost faith due to the initial setbacks though now all is well that ends well

All my eye: *Foolishness* * It was all my eye to tolerate the rascal

All night: *For the whole night* * The patient could not sleep all night because of high temperature

All of a dither: *Very agitated; nervous* * I am all of a dither by the adverse remarks in the press against me

All of a meat: *Anxious or frightened* * We were all of a meat when we heard about our leader's abduction

All of a sudden: *All at once* * All of a sudden I noticed someone following me

All one: *Just the same* * The characters in the drama appeared all one in their similar costumes

All or nothing: *To include all or nothing at all* * The award has to be all or nothing

All out: *At full speed; at full power; completely exhausted* * His all out efforts to win the race proved futile * He made an all out dash to catch the thief but he escaped

All over: *At an end; everywhere; at the most characteristic; thoroughly; entirely* * The game was all over when the whistle blew * Blood was spread all over the area where the dead body lay * The modern means of communication have considerably reduced distance, time and space all over the world

All over the shop: *Dispersed all around* * As the things lay all over the shop, it took time in searching what I wanted

All over with: *Finished; done with; completely at an end* * It was all over with his last subtle move in the game * The champion hit the winning shot and it was all over with the crowd * The crowd sat spellbound at his singing till the show was all over

All right: *A colloquial phrase expressing assent or approbation* * The plan that he placed before the committee was acknowledged to be all right

All right again: *Better* * She is all right again though she was feeling uneasy earlier

All round: *On all sides; completely around* * We were overjoyed to see the greenery all round the hill top

All-round athlete: *Person who is good at all sorts of sports* * There are very few all-round athletes in our country at the international level

All round attack: *Person who is good at all sorts of sports* * The forwards made an all round attack to score the goal

All serene: *Everything is quiet and calm* * It looks all serene at the sea front in the morning hours

All standing: *Everything remaining as it is; fully clad* * The storm uprooted only a tree, leaving the rest all standing in the garden * All standing activities came to an end as declared by the returning officer * The model was all standing in a new style on the ramp

All that glitters is not gold: *Appearance is deceptive* * One should not be deceived by one's appearance because all that glitters is not gold

All the best: *With warmest wishes* * I wished my friend all the best before he left the city on his new posting

All the go: *Very fashionable* * To be all the go is natural for the modern woman

All the rage: *Quite the fashion* * Yoga exercises are all the rage now-a-days

All the same: *No difference; nevertheless* * One may plan on further course of action but all the same it should be finished on time

All the same to me: *It makes no difference* * Whatever views you may have about me, it's all the same to me

All the time: *Continuously* * I do keep my watch in the pocket all the time

All the world: *Everybody; everything* * Death is an inevitable phenomenon for all the world

All the world and his wife: *Everybody; Members of the Indian Parliament resemble all the world and his wife* * All the world and his wife are of different shapes and nature * Members of the Indian parliament resemble all the world and his wife

All the year round: *Throughout the whole year* * I had to travel many countries all the year round on an official trip

All there: *Alert; completely sane* * The sentry was all there throughout the night * The patient was all there in spite of multiple head injuries caused by the accident

All things being equal: *Having considered everything carefully* * All things being equal, the administrative decision proved to be good

All to one: *Altogether* * The sailors all to one had no choice at the time of the jump

All to pieces: *Into a state of disintegration or collapse* * The critical situation tore USSR all to pieces, resulting in creation of many new states * I fear that my dreams are likely to go all to pieces

All told: *Altogether* * All told, he should come up to our expectations

All up with: *At an end with; beyond any hope for* * The doctor could not save the patient as the latter was all up with any further treatment * I think we have lost the battle and now it is all up with

Allege against: *To accuse of* * Malicious things were alleged against my friend

Allegiance to: *Loyalty to* * Mahatma Gandhi owed allegiance to none but the truth

Allergic to jazz: *Dislike jazz intensely* * I am allergic to jazz right from the beginning

Alliance with: *Friendly terms with* * France and Germany are in alliance with each other

Allotted to: *Assigned to* * I shall do only the work that is allotted to me

Allow to breathe: *Give rest* * The dogs were allowed to breathe for a short duration after a long chase * A short period of enjoyment through recreational activities allows us to breathe freely

Allowable expenses: *Expenses which are allowed against tax* * Allowable expenses are exempted from tax

Allude to: *Refer to* * In his speech, the minister alluded to some sinister designs of the enemy

Allude to something: *Refer to something indirectly or briefly* * I have already alluded to the interest that has been shown in the returns filed by me

Ally oneself to: *Join forces with; support* * England allied itself with the USA during the Iraqi war * All the opposition parties have formed an alliance for the coming elections

Along the road: *From one end of the road to the other* * There is always a great rush of traffic along the road in the evening

Aloof from: *Away from* * We must keep ourselves aloof from all evil temptations

Alpha and omega: *Beginning and end* * The alpha and omega of the movie was full of suspense

Amazed at: *Surprised at* * We

were amazed at his shocking speech

Ambling alone: *Walking slowly alone* * I prefer to amble alone every morning in the garden

Amenable to new ideas: *Willing to accept new ideas* * The new generation is very much amenable to new ideas

Amount to: *Be equal to; add up to* * Your bitter remarks amount to insulting me

Amounts to the same thing: *Mean the same* * Whether my son joins a service or starts any business, it amounts to the same thing

Amuse oneself: *To spend time happily* * He amuses himself by listening to music

An absorbing story: *Story that holds one's attention* * It is an absorbing story written by a smart author

An ace in the hole: *Likely to turn a failure into success* * A witty person proved to be an ace in the hole when he defeated his opponent in an argument

An affair with: *Emotional or sexual relationship* * The manager, they say, is having an affair with his stenographer

An all-out effort: *Put in all the effort* * We must make an all-out effort to achieve our goal

An all time high: *The highest point ever reached* * It was an all time high in the temperature last summer

An almighty row: *A very loud argument* * An almighty row among the teachers frightened the children away

An arm of flesh: *Human strength or help* * The reinforcements came as an arm of flesh to rejuvenate the army

An empty vessel sounds much: *A man of little knowledge makes too much noise* * He is like an empty vessel that sounds much when he starts boasting about a subject about which he knows little

An eve to the main chance: *Thought for self-enrichment* * Greed emanates from an eve to the main chance

An even bet: *An equal chance* * Both the teams have an even bet in the coming badminton tournament * Only an intelligent scholar has an even bet to be selected as a professor of English

An extempore speech: *An unprepared speech made at the spur of the moment* * He made an extempore speech which was appreciated by all

An idea at the back of one's mind: *The beginning of an idea* * I have an idea at the back of my mind about the kind of school I would start for poor children

An iron hand: *A severe action* * The army crushed the revolt with an iron hand

An iron will: *Strong determination* * Sardar Patel was a man with an iron will

An oaken towel: *A cudgel* * The policemen now-a-days use oaken towel to disperse the mob

An off the cuff speech: *Impromptu speech* * He delivered an off the cuff speech which was applauded by the gathering

An old hand: *An experienced person* * We do require an old hand to repair this machine

An old master: *A great painter of the past* * The paintings of an old master were auctioned at a very high price

An old sweat: *Person with many years' experience in his job* * The re-employed captain is an old sweat

An unknown quantity: *An unspecified amount* * An unknown quantity of apples was exported out of the country

Anathema to someone: *Dislike intensely* * It is an anathema for him to fill up the complicated income-tax form

And all: *As well as the rest* * The gang leader and all members were hanged * The small box contained love-letters, dirty pictures, small notebooks and all

And all that: *And all the rest* * The teacher asked the students to bring their clothes, bedding and all that which may be needed for the night camp.

And how: *Yes; certainly; to do something howsoever; indeed* * Come what may, the job will be done now and how

And no mistake: *Assuredly* * A right decision should be taken and make no mistake in its implementation

And so forth: *And so on* * The artist displayed his skills by dancing, singing, joking and so forth

And so on: *And in a similar way* * He can talk for hours on any subject like history, economics and so on

And that's that: *And that is the end of that matter; no more of that* * The criminal committed suicide in the jail and that's that

Angle for a rise: *Try to get an*

increase in salary in an disapproving manner * They are obviously trying to angle for a rise by going on a strike

Angry at: *Be irritated at* * We were all angry at his rude behaviour

Angry with: *Annoyed with* * My friend became annoyed with me because of my indifferent attitude

Animal husbandry: *Rearing of animals on a farm* * Animal husbandry is an alternative occupation for farmers

Ankle-deep: *Up to one's ankle* * A short downpour resulted in ankle-deep water on the roads

Annoyed at: *Be irritated* * It was difficult not to be annoyed at her unpleasant behaviour

Annoyed with: *Be rather angry* * The members were annoyed with the chairman for his remarks

Another cup of tea: *A very different thing* * He is adept in carpentry but making boats is another cup of tea

Answer back: *Reply rudely* * I could not resist the temptation to answer back to my boss because of his rude behavior

Answer for: *Be responsible for* * You will have to answer for your wrongdoings one day

Answer of: *Say with confidence* * One should give answer of any query without hesitation

Answer one's purpose: *To serve one's purpose* * This book will answer my purpose as it throws light on the subject in detail

Answer to a description: *Correspond to it or be as described* * He does not answer to the description of the missing person

Answer to: *Be in agreement with* * This exactly answers to the description given by the police

Answerable for: *Account for* * You will have to be answerable for your bad deeds

Answerable to/for: *Responsible to or for* * I am answerable to none except my conscience for my conduct * I am totally answerable for any mishap

Antenatal clinic: *Clinic for pregnant women* * A modernised antenatal clinic is a must in every town

Antidote against: *Sure medicine* * Milk serves as an antidote against the burning feeling in the stomach

Anxious about: *Uneasy about* * There is no need to be anxious about my health

Anxious for: *Really worried for* * I am not anxious for a complete change in my lifestyle

Any more: *Anything additional; further* * I shall not listen your story any more * I was so dead tired that I could not walk any more

Anybody's guess: *No one really knows* * It is anybody's guess where India will be economically after ten years

Anyone else: *Any other person* * We can employ anyone else in his place if he does not join duty immediately

Anything else: *Any other thing* * Do you have anything else to say on this subject?

Anyway: *In any case* * Anyway, I hope you will be successful in the examination

Apart from: *Except; in addition to* * I have no money apart from whatever is in my purse * Apart from sports, I am very fond of reading

Appeal to/against: *To ask for someone to judge; attract; move the feelings; make an earnest request* * He appealed to the judge to have mercy on him * The leader will appeal to the crowd to vote for him in the elections

Appetite for: *A desire for* * I have no appetite for food today

Apple of discord: *Cause of dispute* * A small piece of land was an apple of discord between the two brothers

Apple of the eye: *One who is very dear to someone* * Being the only son, he is the apple of the eye for a widow

Apple-pie order: *Perfect order* * A good housewife likes to keep the household items in an apple-pie order

Application form: *Form to be filled in when applying* * You will have to fill up a prescribed application form for seeking admission in the school

Apply oneself: *Work hard* * You will have to apply yourself if you want to achieve something in your life

Apprised of: *Informed* * The government was well apprised of the likely strike by the workers

Approach road: *Road leading to the main road* * The approach road is very bumpy and unfit to drive

Appropriate to: *Proper for* * He spoke in a manner appropriate to the occasion

Approve of: *Be in agreement with* * The proposal was approved of after due consideration

Approve of something: *To be in agreement with something* * The meeting will end only after the members approve the agenda

Apt test: *Test to see that if you are fit for a job* * An apt test will be conducted to check the suitability of the candidates for the job

Aptitude for: *Natural inclination* * She has an aptitude for singing

Arch-enemy: *Main or chief enemy* * Pakistan continues to be India's arch-enemy

Arc-light: *Very bright light* * The Rashtrapati Bhawan is decorated with arc-lights on Independence Day every year

Argue for: *To argue in favor of* * He has a good lawyer to argue for his case before the judge

Argue into: *To persuade into* * You will have to argue into the problem faced by my friend

Argue the toss: *Argue about someone's final decision* * One should not waste time to argue the toss that does not concern the majority

Argue with: *To discuss with* * The boss is likely to argue with me over the new project

Argument from design: *The argument for existence or God* * The natural calamities occurring frequently are an argument from design

Arm in arm: *With their arms linked* * The young couple walked arm in arm on the main road

Arm of the law: *The authority of the law* * One cannot escape forever from the long arm of the law

Armed to the teeth: *Armed as completely as possible or from top to toe* * The army battalion was armed to the teeth for the encounter

Armour of proof: *Armour that has been tested or can be relied upon* * The army must have an armour of proof regarding the enemy's attack before retaliating

Arrogate to oneself: *Claim without right* * He arrogated to himself the position of a senior engineer without any prior approval of higher authorities

Art festival: *Competition in music, drama, painting, etc.* * The annual art festival has become very popular in the city

Art gallery: *Museum for paintings, sculptures, etc.* * The exhibition held in the art gallery attracted large crowds

Artesian well: *Well drilled in the ground which does not require a pump to make the water rise*

* People have drilled a number of artesian wells in Rajasthan for drinking as well irrigation purposes

Articles of war: *Code of regulations for the government, army or navy in a war* * It is a must to preserve the sovereignty of a country by strictly observing the articles of war

Artist's model: *A person needed to sit while an artist draws the picture of him or her* * It requires lot of patience to be an artist's model

As a last resort: *Compelled to do something when other means failed* * Having lost my job, I took to rickshaw pulling as a last resort to make the both ends meet

As a matter of course: *In the usual way* * Certain things are to be treated as a matter of course

As a matter of fact: *In reality* * As a matter of fact, hard work is the only key to success * As a matter of fact, he is too poor to afford a car

As a precautionary measure: *Avoiding any risk* * The burglar alarm is a safe bet to be installed in the house as a precautionary measure

As a rule: *Generally; usually* * As a rule, I get up early in the morning to go for a walk

As a whole: *Altogether* * As a whole, the college staff is highly disciplined

As accords: *As may be appropriate* * We should adopt a profession as accords our ability to earn a good living

As all that: *To that extent* * It is not as difficult as all that as it may seem

As also: *Likewise* * You will have to follow him as also he is your leader

As black as pitch: *Completely dark* * The colour of my new car is as black as pitch

As concerns/as for/as regards/ as to: *For the matter of* * As concerns my business tours abroad, I shall confirm the dates shortly

As dead as a dodo: *Totally finished* * Latin language is almost as dead as a dodo

As easy as falling off a log: *Very easy* * Do you think that pole vaulting is as easy as falling off a log?

As far as in me lies: *In the best of my power* * I shall help the defendant as far as in me lies

As far as money is concerned: *With reference to money* * He is capable of starting another factory as far as money is concerned

As fast as: *As quick as* * I can

run as fast as a deer

As for: *As concerning; as regards* * As for his talent, he has earned due popularity among his friends and foes

As from: *Starting from* * As from the first chapter, he read the whole book without any break

As good as: *The same as; no less than; virtually* * He is as good as his word * He is as good as I am

As good as gold: *Behaving in an exemplary manner* *An honest person is as good as gold

As good as one's words: *Fulfil one's promises* * Only a few humans are as good as their words

As hard as nails: *Tough and not easy to give in* * He seemed as hard as nails when he began to laugh at the blind man's fall

As if/as though: *As it would be; if* * He looked at me as if I was mad

As if by magic: *Suddenly* * As if by magic, I found a box full of gold coins on the roadside

As is his wont: *As he usually does* * Let him do as is his wont

As it were: *As to speak; in some sort* * I was casually referring to him as it were

As late as: *A particular time considered to be late* * Even as late as the fifties, coal was the main source of energy

As long as: *Immediately; while* * We will have to stay indoors as long as the rain continues

As luck would have it: *As it happened* * I won the first prize in lottery as luck would have it

As many as: *All who* * There are as many as thirty teachers in my school

As much: *Just that; the same* * If you can run in a race for three minutes, I can also run as much

As now: *Just at this time* * I need a large sum of money as now

As plain as the nose on your face: *Very obvious* * The progress made by our country in the economic field is as plain as the nose on your face

As regards: *With regard to* * As regards his conduct, I can say that he is a very reliable person

As right as rain: *To be very well* * I am feeling as right as rain after my recovery from illness

As soon as: *Immediately* * Let me have complete information as soon as possible

As sound as a bell: *In a healthy*

condition * A boxer has to be as sound as a bell before participating in a wrestling match

As such: *Hence; therefore; consequently* * I fell ill and as such I could not attend school

As sure as a gun: *Quite sure; certainly* * Please take my word as sure as a gun that I will never leave you in the lurch

As the crow flies: *In a straight line* * The place we expect to reach before darkness is only about ten miles as the crow flies

As the king, so are the subjects: *Like the king are the subjects* * The morale of the regime depends upon the character of the ruler because as the king, so are the subjects

As then: *Just at that time* * The boy as then was five-years old when his parents died

As though: *As if* * He pretended as though he had not seen me in the market

As to: *For the matter of* * As to his undoubtedly high educational record, none can question his capability

As tough as old boots: *Extremely tough* * The well-trained army personnel are as tough as old boots

As well: *Also; in addition; equally* * He can speak German as well as English

As well as: *In addition to* * Ram as well as Sham are to be punished for being absent from the class

As yet: *Up to the moment* * Raman has not married as yet

As you go along: *Preparation for doing something as you move along* * As you go along you may stop for a breather

As you sow so shall you reap: *A result, good or bad is caused by one's actions* * Why do you complain about his hitting out at you following a fight with her because as you sow, so shall you reap

Ascribe to: *Be the cause of; author of* * He ascribed his failure to bad luck * This play has been ascribed to Shakespeare

Aside from: *Apart from* * Aside from working in the factory, he drives a taxi at night

Ask after: *Enquire about* * I asked after the health of his father

Ask for something: *Asking for something which will cause trouble for you* * Getting drunk before driving your car is like asking for trouble

Ask for/of: *Request for* * I asked for a seat in the train since I was too tired to stand

Ask to: *Invite to; request to* * I have been asked to be the chief guest at the annual college function

Aspiration for: *Ardent desire* * I have an aspiration for contesting the next elections

Aspire after: *Have great desire for* * I am aspiring after to become an officer

Aspire to: *Be filled with high ambition* * I must aspire to be a successful man in life

Assault and battery: *Criminal charge of attacking with violence* * The terrorists are either killed or taken as prisoners for their act of assault and battery

Assault course: *Ground where soldiers practice attack* * Assault course training helps soldiers to achieve perfection in attack

Assembly line: *Continuous moving line in a factory where machines, etc. are put together* * The assembly line has made it possible to turn out beautifully finished products in the shortest possible time

Assent to: *Consent to* * Nobody gave their assent to his suggestion

Assert oneself: *Take a firm position* * The people are asserting themselves when demanding their right to information

Assigned to: *Ordered to do* * This task has been assigned to me by the manager

Astonish at: *Surprise greatly* * I am astonished at your funny behaviour

At best: *On the most favourable condition or situation* * I was at best last evening in the club

At daggers drawn: *In a state of hostility* * Both the brothers were at daggers drawn over their claims to the disputed property

At odds: *At variance* * Both the brothers are very much at odds in their moods

At one: *Of one mind* * My friend and I are at one over this issue

At one's beck and call: *Subject of one's will* * The servant has to be at the beck and call of his master

At press: *In the course of printing* * The new book written by me is at press at the moment

At times: *At distant intervals; occasionally* * I do visit my parents at times since I live far away

At a conservative estimate: *At the lowest; at the most moderate estimate* * He started construction of his house at a conservative estimate

At the crack of dawn: *At daybreak* * The chirping sound of birds at the crack of dawn is very soothing

At a discount: *At less price; not in demand* * Second-hand cars are available at a discount because of the influx of new models

At a good clip: *Quite fast* * The soldiers came marching at a good clip

At a loose end: *Without anything to do* * I am at a loose end at the moment

At a loss: *Uncertain; perplexed* * I am at a loss for words after what you have told me

At a particular time: *On a special moment* * Flowers are in full bloom at a particular time during spring

At a person's heels: *Close behind* * The policeman who was following at the thief's heels soon nabbed him

At a pinch: *In a case of necessity* * My friend did help me when I was at a pinch

At a point: *In readiness; resolved* * The soldiers were at a point of to do or die

At a premium: *Scarce and valuable* * The corner plot in the commercial area has been sold at a premium

At a price: *At a somewhat high price* * He purchased a second-hand car at a price

At a push: *If necessary; when circumstances require* * This small room can accommodate six persons at a push

At a run: *Running* * The thief was at a run when the crowd made noise

At a snail's pace: *Extremely slowly* * The train was running at a snail's pace because of fog

At a stretch: *Continuously* * He is capable of working twenty hours at a stretch

At a tangent: *Change in the direction of a conversation or thought* * It is tough to talk to him because he always goes off at a tangent

At a word: *Without more ado; at once; be brief* * At a word, the story offers a good moral

At all: *The least* * He did not bother at all about his health * We do not like to mix at all with unpleasant characters

At all costs: *No matter what the cost or consequence may be* * The project must be finished by the deadline at all costs

At all events: *In any case* * The show must go on at all events

At all hours: *At irregular or late hours* * The cafeteria near the bus stand remains open at all hours * This hotel provides service at all hours

At all points: *In every point* * I am feeling numbness at all points below the knee of my right leg

At all times: *Always* * I see him busy at all times

At an early date: *Soon* * The troops are likely to be withdrawn from the border at an early date

At an end: *Terminated; discontinued; exhausted* * The tunnel closing at an end looks very scary at night * The play has to be brought at an end as one of the actors has collapsed on the stage * Though I won the long-distance race, I was totally at an end

At an inch: *Ready at hand* * The forces were alert and at an inch of attack

At any hand: *At any rate; in any case* * He is bent on purchasing a music system at any hand * The team had to win their last league match at any hand

At any moment: *Very soon* * The train is likely to arrive at any moment

At any price: *At any cost* * He wants to buy this flat at any price

At any rate: *At least* * At any rate, you deserve to be penalised for traffic violation

At best: *On the most favourable supposition* * The master of ceremonies was at best during the show * I felt that you can at best be a sturdy boxer

At breakneck pace: *Extremely fast* * He could not control the steering while driving at breakneck speed

At close quarters: *In close proximity; hand-to-hand* * The policeman shot the gang-leader at close quarters * Once the ammunition was exhausted, the soldiers had to fight at close quarters with the enemy

At cock crow: *Early morning* * One should develop the habit to get up at cock crow

At command: *Available for use; ready for use at will* * My friend placed his car at my command * My services shall be always at your command at any time

At cross purposes: *In disagreement* * India and Pakistan are at cross purposes over the Kashmir issue

At dead of the night: *In the middle of the night* * The robbers struck at dead of the night

At death's door: *Very near to*

death * The poor man who is suffering from a chronic disease is at death's door

At discretion: *According to one's own judgement* * The higher you go in corporate hierarchy, the more you have the discretion to decide * The committee unanimously authorised the chairman to take a final decision at his own discretion

At fault: *At a loss; unable to find scent (for sniffer dogs)* * Since he was late for the meating he apologised for being at fault * The search made by the sniffer dogs proved to be at fault

At first: *At the beginning; in full detail* * He was very slow at first but later picked up speed in the next round

At first hand: *Directly from the source* * The rich man gifted at first hand the car to his daughter on the occasion of her marriage

At first sight: *Prima facie* * The problem is not so simple as it appears at first sight

At full pelt: *Going fast* * He was penalised for driving the car at full pelt

At full sea: *A full tide; at sea; away from land* * The sailors have to remain at full sea for a longer spell than decided earlier

At full tilt: *At full speed* * The dog rammed at full tilt into me

At gaze: *To keep an eye on* * The suspect's activities are at gaze of the police

At hand: *Conveniently near; within easy reach* * A heart patient must keep his medicines at hand

At heart: *In real character; substantially* * Do not be afraid of his hard face, because at heart he is a thorough gentleman

At his own charge: *At his own expense* * A philanthropist has recently constructed an old home for destitute at his own charge

At home: *In one's own house; familiar; ready to receive a visitor; feel comfortable* * I found him at home when I went to see him * He is at home when speaking in English * He is at home to a person even not known to him * The interviewer told the candidate to feel at home during the interview

At-home: *Reception* * All dignitaries of the city were invited by the Governor for tea at-home

At issue: *In quarrel; controversy* * Kashmir continues to remain at issue between India and Pak * The matter at issue has yet to be reconsidered by the committee

At its best: *In the best condition* * The garden is at its best during the spring season

At large: *At liberty; at random; freely; in full detail* * The murderer is at large (liberty) * Selection was made at liberty at the first instance * People ignore at large matters of no importance * We had a discussion at large on the topic of illiteracy

At last: *In the end* * The team could score the goal at last in the last minute * After hard labour, he breathed a sigh of relief at last

At least: *At the lowest estimate; to emphasise that something is good* * The building will cost at least a few million rupees * He did not come but at least he sent his regrets

At length: *At last; for a long time; in full; in detail; fully extended* * The new subject was discussed at length to adopt a concrete strategy to defeat the enemy * The team was stretched at length * The new subject was discussed at length to help in coming to a decision

At liberty: *Free; not in captivity* * You are now at liberty to leave at any time

At loggerheads: *At issue; quarrelling* * Once they were fast friends but now they are at loggerheads over a piece of land * The matter at loggerheads is so complicated that no settlement is possible easily

At long last: *After a long time; delay* * The promotion came at long last at the fag end of his career

At loose ends: *In disorder* * The facts and figures mentioned in the report are at loose ends

At a loss: *For less price* * I had to sell my property at a loss

At mach one: *At the sound of the speed* * The latest missile can cruise at mach one

At odds: *At variance* * I am at odds with you over this particular issue

At once: *Without delay; alike; at the same time* * Certain decisions are required to be taken at once to clear any misunderstanding * My friend and I jumped at once at the sound of gunshots

At one: *Of one mind* * The workers and the management are at one on the introduction of new technology

At one full swoop: *In a sudden move; all at once* * All our problems cannot be solved at one full swoop

At one's beck and call: *Subject of one's will* * Go and get the card yourself as I am not at your beck and call

At one's best: *In the best spirit* * He was at his best yesterday evening during the party

At one's command: *In pursuance of his bidding* * The troops opened heavy fire at the command of the Captain

At (one's) earliest convenience: *As soon as possible* * Kindly send a reply to my letter at your earliest convenience

At one's elbow: *Close at hand* * In the morning rush hour, the buses are so crowded that one has to stand at one's elbow * I keep my guide-books and dictionary at my elbow so that I can consult them immediately

At one's finger's end: *To know thoroughly* * Unless you have every subject at your finger's end, you cannot be successful in any competitive examination

At one's fingertips: *Know thoroughly* * Our economics teacher had all the statistics on his fingertips

At one's heels: *Behind closely* * Famine often follows on the heels of drought

At one's leisure: *Free from occupation; at one's own ease or convenience* * A good book can be fully enjoyed only at one's leisure

At one's service: *Ready to obey one's order; ready to help* * I am at your service whenever you ask

At one's wit's ends: *Utterly perplexed* * He is at his wit's ends as he does not know whether or not to continue with the job under the circumstances

At par: *At equal value* * I have purchased these bonds at par from the market

At peace: *In a state of peace* * Every human being wants to be at peace

At present: *At the present time; now* * At present he is running a wine shop

At press: *In the course of printing* * The handwritten note of the famous author is now in press

At random: *Recklessly; without aim* * The mad man opened fire at random all of a sudden

At record speed: *Very fast* * Technology has progressed at record speed

At rest: *Free from movement; still* * This piano has since been lying at rest * The wind at the moment is at rest

At rovers: *At a distant mark; at random; conjecturally* * You are at rovers to come to a conclusion * The winner was picked up at rovers as it was not easy to decide the ultimate winner

At short-sight: *Payable soon after being presented* * The King rewarded the brave soldier at short-sight the moment he produced the head of the slain dacoit

At sight: *Without previous view or study; at random; conjecturally; on presentation* * The rioters were ordered to be shot at sight * We rushed to a safe place as the tiger was at sight during the jungle safari * He produced the original document before the inspecting officer at sight

At sixes and sevens: *In disorder* * The thieves left the household items at sixes and sevens after taking away the cash and jewellery

At stake: *In danger; at issue* * There is a great deal of money at stake * His political career is at stake

At street level: *On the same level* * Open courts have initiated a campaign to decide simple cases at street level

At table: *At a meal* * The family members were all at table for dinner

At the back of: *Close behind; just after* * The athlete running at the back of the race sprinted with full vigour and came first

At the beginning: *To start with* * At the beginning of the function, I would like to introduce you to the audience

At the bottom of: *The real origin* * Hatred is at the bottom of all conflicts amongst followers of different faiths * Many secrets of nature lie at the bottom of the sea

At the bottom of my mind: *Deep in my mind* * I have an idea at the bottom of my mind to write a book after my retirement

At the dead off night: *At midnight* * The dacoits attacked at the dead of night

At the double: *At a run* * We had to run at the double to save ourselves from heavy rain

At the drop of a hat: *At once; readily or willingly* * He at the drop of a hat jumped into the river to save the drowning child

At the eleventh hour: *At the last moment* * As the train reached late, he could attend the marriage at the eleventh hour

At the end of one's tether: *Without patience or strength* * I waited for him till 8 o'clock but was at the end of my tether by the time he arrived

At the extreme end: *Right at the end* * He emphasised the role of youth at the extreme end of his speech

At the feet of: *In submission; homage; devotion* * Those who live at the feet of enlightened souls may also achieve salvation * It helps to have mental solace by resting at the feet of saints * The devotees thronged to touch the feet of the Swami after listening to his sermon

At the fore: *Displayed on the forefront* * Artistic paintings pictures were displayed at the fore in the art gallery

At the full: *At the height; as of one's good fortune* * He decided to devote his life for the benefit of poor when he was at the full of his career

At the hand of: *By the act of* * The exact span of our life is at the hands of destiny

At the Hastings: *In an election campaign* * A politician should be very witty at the Hastings

At the head of the poll: *Having the greatest number of votes at the time of elections* * Sanjay Gandhi was at the head of the poll after the first round of counting

At the helm of: *In charge* * The person at the helm of affairs has been booked on charges of corruption

At the instance of: *At the notion or solicitation of* * The invasion was carried out at the instance of the commander-in-chief

At the latest: *Before or not later than* * You must be here by Sunday at the latest

At the mercy of: *Wholly in the power of* * The prisoners are at the mercy of the king

At the moment: *Just now* * I require complete rest at the moment

At the most: *At the utmost computation* * Only this much work can be done at the most within the stipulated time

At the outside: *At the most* * There were fifty persons at the outside in the meeting

At the point of: *On the verge of* * His life was soon at the point of starvation

At the present time: *Now* * At the present time I am too busy

At the quay side: *Next to the quay* * The people at the quay side could have a better view

At the same time: *Simultaneously; notwithstanding* * The story he related to us was not only interesting but at the same time it had a good moral too

At the time: *When it happened* * I was away at the time the result was declared

At the top of one's voice: *At one's loudest* * When the house was on fire, the owner cried at the top of his voice for help

At the very beginning: *Right at the beginning* * The opening batsman hit three successive sixes at the very beginning of the innings

At the very most: *Not more than* * There were only ten people in the meeting at the very most

At the beginning: *To start with* * Let us have a prayer at the beginning of the function

At times: *From time to time; occasionally* * Though a cricketer, yet at times he plays football too * At times, he complained of severe stomach ache

At will: *As you wish; when; as one chooses* * I will teach him a lesson at will

At work: *Busy* * Please do not disturb me when I am at work

At your service: *At your disposal; a mere phrase of civility* * Whenever you need my help, I shall certainly be at your service

Athlete's foot: *Skin infection on the foot* * Athlete's foot is a common disease now-a-days

Atone for: *Make reparation for* * Nothing can atone for your criminal negligence

Attach oneself to: *Join* * He attached himself to a political party last week

Attach to: *Give; consider; fasten* * I attach no value to his work * You will find a sample attached to the letter

Attached to: *Bound by love* * She is deeply attached to her parents

Attain to: *Reach* * He attained greatness through patience and perseverance

Attend to: *Look after; be present at, pay attention to* * I have to attend to my younger brother when my parents are away * You will have to attend to your class regularly

Attend to someone: *Look after someone* * A surrogate mother was engaged to attend to the orphan child

Attend upon: *Wait on* * I was tired of attending upon him for my work

Attribute something to someone: *Say that something belongs to someone* * He attributes his success to hard work

Attribute to: *Be the result of; as coming from; consider as a quality* * She attributed her success to the great help she received from her teacher * He attributes his knowledge to his guides * This comedy has been attributed to Shakespeare

Auction off: *To sell by auction* * He auctioned off his ancestral property at a throw-away price

Auspicious season: *Good opportunity* * We should not let the auspicious season go out of our hands by sitting idle

Avail of: *Take advantage of* * He failed to avail of the golden chance to win the competition

Avail oneself of: *Use* * You must avail yourself of the opportunity that comes your way

Avarice is the root of all evils: *Greed brings all troubles* * After reading this book I realise that avarice is the root of all evils

Averse to: *Disinclined to* * The rich spendthrift was averse to hard work

Averse to hard work: *Dislike it* * He could not make a successful career as he was always averse to hard work

Aware of: *Conscious of* * He was not aware of the conspiracy against him

A ready reply to: *Always has an answer* * He has a ready reply to anything that may be asked of him

Axe to grind: *Selfish interest* * There are a few persons who have no axe of their own to grind except for serving the poor

B

Baby-sitter: *A person who looks after a child when the parents are out* * Working parents take the services of baby-sitters now-a-days

Back and forth: *Backwards and forwards* * For a while, he kept rolling back and forth before falling down

Back benchers: *Ordinary members of Parliament* * The back benchers were hobnobbing with one another before the session started

Back down: *To abandon one's opinion or position* * He backed down from his proposal * They refused to back down on the stand already taken by them

Back in paying bills: *Slow in paying* * The management of this college is rather back in paying bills to the staff

Back out: *To evade an obligation or understanding* * He backed out from his promise to help me financially

Back seat driver: *Passenger in a car; one who offers the driver unwanted advice* * A back seat driver may bring about disaster by diverting the attention of the driver

Back-stairs influences: *Secret and improper influences* * Even undeserved hands can manage jobs through back-stairs influences

Back to front: *The wrong way round* * You have got your jumper on back to front

Back up: *To give support to* * The family stood along with me to back me up in the financial crisis

Backdrop: *The background to any situation* * The steep hills that form the backdrop to the city create a wonderful scene

Back-handed: *Compliment that could be taken also as an insult* * We should refrain from passing back-handed remarks

Bad blood: *Ill-feeling* * Avoid bad blood against close friends

Bad debt: *A debt not likely to be recovered* * You better write off his account as a bad debt as he has been declared bankrupt

Bad language: *Swearing* * The

culprit used bad language to justify himself as being innocent

Bad lot: *A person of bad moral character* * Please do not make friends with him as he is a bad lot

Bad shot: *A wrong guess* * The farmers had a bad shot about the onset of monsoon

Bad temper: *Anger; an inclination to irascibility* * He is a bad-tempered man so it is better to keep him away

Badger one into: *Bother someone* * The inspector badgered me to giving him a handsome sum or otherwise go to prison

Badly off: *Having not enough money; in bad circumstances* * The people in the flood-hit areas are badly off

Badly-behaved child: *Child who is rude* * He is a badly behaved child and that is why other children do not play with him

Bag and baggage: *With complete moveable belongings* * I have shifted to my new residence with bag and baggage

Bag of bones: *An emaciated* * That lanky person looks merely a bag of bones

Bail out: *Scoop water out of a boat; bale out; pay money to let a prisoner out temporarily between hearing* * They began bailing out the water from the boat with their helmets * New technology will bail us out of our production problems * He had to borrow money to bail himself out of the financial crisis

Baker's dozen: *Thirteen* * There was a great rush in the readymade clothes shop as the clothes were sold on the basis of baker's dozen

Balk at something: *Refuse to do something* * He balked at cleaning the toilet

Bandy legs: *When one stands with feet together, the knees do not touch* * He has bandy legs hence cannot run fast

Bane of one's life: *It is what annoys one most* * It is the bane of my life to fall a prey to paralysis

Bank up along the road: *The wind blowing the snow to form banks* * The snow banked up along the road

Bank up the sides of the canal: *Reinforce the canal banks* * They banked up the sides of the canal by heaping sandy bags

Banking on: *Relying on* * I am banking on my friend to lend me some money

Bar none: *With no exception* * They were allowed to enter the hall bar none

Bar to: *Obstacle* * Poverty is not

a bar to scholarly eminence

Barbed comment: *Sharp comment* * The ruling party members had to face barbed comments of the opposition

Barbed wire: *Wire with sharp spikes* * Barbed wire is usually used to protect the boundary

Barbed wire entanglement: *Mass of coiled barbed wire to protect soldiers* * The barbed wire entanglement is very useful for defensive purposes during war

Bare necessities: *Absolutely essential* * To provide bare necessities to every human being is the duty of the government

Bare one's soul: *Tell all one's innermost thoughts* * He bared his soul before a large gathering

Bare something on: *To use something as a base* * The scientist bares his theory on practical experiments

Bargain offer: *Special offer of goods at low prices* *Special bargain offers are made by shopkeepers during the festival season

Barge into: *Intrude* * Please stop barging into our conversation

Bark be worse than one's bite: *One is not as terrifying as he sounds; one is bad-tempered but not dangerous* * His bark is worse than his bite so no harm will be done to you

Bark one's shin on: *Scrape the skin off one's shin* * The deer barked his shin on the rock

Bark up the wrong tree: *Direct one's complaint; accuse wrongly* * If you think that you can borrow money from that miser then you are barking up the wrong tree

Barking dogs seldom bite: *Those who shout are not dangerous* * There is no need for you to fear your teacher because a barking dog seldom bites

Base coin: *Spurious coin* * A person can be arrested for being in possession of a base coin

Basket chair: *Chair made of woven cane* * I have a liking for basket chairs

Batting an eyelid: *Show a sign of surprise* * She did not bat an eyelid over an unexpected misfortune

Battle planes: *Fighter planes* * The battleplanes play a crucial role in a war

Be a bad loser: *Behave badly on losing a game* * He is a bad loser as he always quarrels with the opponents

Be a bit thick: *Be very unrea-*

sonable; stupid * That is a bit thick to have insulted the poor girl * She is a bit thick and also devoid of good manners

Be a catch in it: *Be something wrong with it; a trap* * There must be a catch in it, so one should be cautious

Be a confirmed bachelor: *Will never get married* * He is a confirmed bachelor so the question of getting him married hardly arises

Be a good match: *Be a desirable husband; to match* * It is idealistic to think about becoming a good match * The colour of your coat is not a good match with your trousers

Be a law unto oneself: *Do exactly what one wants, regardless of rules* * It does not behoove a person to be a law unto himself

Be a little annoyed: *Be considerably annoyed* * The boss was a little annoyed at my performance

Be a sheet in the wind's eye: *To be intoxicated* * A drunkard will not stop till he becomes a sheet in the wind's eye

Be a stranger to the town: *Does not know the town very well* * He is a stranger to the town as he has come here for the first time

Be a study: *Amusing to watch* * Her face is a study for all the strangers

Be a weight off my mind: *No longer need to worry about* * That is a weight off my mind and now I can heave a sigh of relief

Be about: *To be astir; to be on the point; to be up and on the go* * We must be up and about after resting at night * It is better to be about immediately without wasting time to sort out the issue * Someone must be about to look after the baby the moment she cries on getting up from her sleep

Be after someone: *Following* * The police will be after the dacoit

Be all alone in the world: *Have no family* * He is all alone in the world

Be all ears: *To give every attention* * Please be all ears to the speaker

Be all of a twitter: *Be very excited* * She was all of a twitter when she got betrothed to a rich boy

Be any the wiser: *Knows no more* * Nobody in the village will be any the wiser because of illiteracy

Be as good as one's words: *To fulfil one's promise* * One should be as good as one's words

Be at a loose end: *Have nothing special to do* * After my retirement from the job, I feel myself to be at a loose end

Be at a loss what to do: *Not to know what to do* * During my vacation, I feel myself to be at a loss at what to do

Be at a loss: *Be puzzled* * He was at a loss for words in the course of his maiden speech

Be at fault: *Puzzled* * One should admit one's mistake when one is at fault

Be at odds with someone: *To quarrel with someone* * The husband and wife are at odds with each other and might divorce

Be at one's discretion: *To surrender unconditionally; to another's discretion* * It should be let to an individual's discretion to choose an appropriate career in life

Be at one's disposal: *Be used as per one's wishes* * My car will always be at your disposal

Be at pains: *Take pains; to put oneself to trouble; be assiduously careful* * One will have to be at pains to achieve something in life

Be at the bottom of: *To be the chief factor* * Terrorism is at the bottom of the conflict in Kashmir

Be at the expense of: *To pay the cost of* * I cannot afford the costly gift at the expense of taking a loan

Be back to the drawing board: *Start the project all over again* * It was decided to be back to the drawing board as the policy has changed

Be behind one completely: *Be in full support of* * I am behind you completely on the point raised by you

Be beneath one's dignity: *Feel too proud* * It is beneath my dignity to ask for any undue favours

Be beside the mark: *To be irrelevant* * What you say is beside the mark in the subject under discussion

Be better than one's word: *To do more than one has promised* * It may not always be possible to be better than one's word

Be beyond a joke: *It is no longer funny* * You are going beyond a joke and that does not look nice for a person of your standing

Be binding on: *Be obliged to do something* * This contract is binding on both the parties

Be bound up in: *To be wholly devoted to* * He has been totally bound up in the new project * Everybody should be bound up in serving the good cause of this country

Be by way of: *To be supposed; alleged to be* * Since no charge has been proved against the accused, he is by way of an innocent person

Be called to the bar: *Be received as a member of the bar* * After completing his education in India, Mahatma Gandhi was called to the bar in England at a young age

Be caught off guard: *Be taken unaware* * The intruders were caught off guard by the vigilant troops

Be construed to mean: *To be in terpreted in a particular manner* * Phrases are capable of being construed differently

Be cut to the quick: *Feel very hurt* * He was cut to the quick when his master dismissed him from the job

Be even with: *Be revenged on; be quite with* * To be even with Pakistan, the West Indies cricket team won the second match

Be excited at/by: *Be very emotional* * He was very excited at the mere thought of going on a holiday abroad

Be expendable: *Can be sacrificed to achieve a purpose* * The armed personnel considered the bunker at the outpost to be expendable

Be familiar with the type of machine: *Know the type of machine* * I am familiar with that type of machine and can handle it easily

Be flat broke: *Have no money* * He is a flat broke to be of any financial help to you

Be fond of: *Like; take pleasure in* * I am very fond of music

Be free from/of something: *Be without something* * He is now free from all ailments

Be free with something: *To give something away generously* * My father was free with me to give me his favourite watch

Be friends with: *To be on good terms with; well disposed towards* * I have to be friends with my schoolmate to be on his good side

Be gathered to one's fathers: *To die and be buried* * I wish to be gathered to my fathers at our family burial ground

Be glutted with: *Have too much* * The market has been glutted with electronic items

Be great fun: *To be very amusing* * The movie was a great fun

Be Greek: *Which cannot be understood* *The speech delivered by the chief guest sounded like Greek as no one was able to un derstand it

Be gunning for someone:

Trying to attack someone * He is gunning for his arch foe who had abducted his son

Be hand in glove: *Be quite intimate* * John and Smith have been hands in glove for long

Be here any minute now: *Any time now* * The director is likely to be here any minute now

Be high time: *Acute times which can brook no further delay* * It is high time that a firm decision is taken to end the strike

Be hoist with one's own petard: *Be caught in a trap which one has set for someone else* * A self-centered and a greedy person can be hoist with his own petard

Be in a blue: *Be depressed* * The accused was in a blue when his punishment was announced

Be in a cold sweat: *Be in a state of fear or anxiety* * When the police raided his house, all the inmates were in a cold sweat

Be in a good state of repairs: *Be in a good condition* * My car is still in a good state of repairs

Be in a mighty hurry: *Be very impatient* * He is in a mighty hurry to go abroad to seek a good job

Be in a mire: *Be in difficulties* * You will be in a mire if you produce a bogus certificate

Be in a tale: *To be in a full accord* * We all must be in a tale to fight against our enemy

Be in abeyance: *Be suspended* * The decision in the matter is kept in abeyance for want of some more information

Be in agreement with: *Agree with* * I am in agreement with you over this issue

Be in arrears: *Be late in paying* * We will have to clear the wages of workers which are in arrears to them

Be in at the kill: *Be there at the end of the affair* * I got the story from Michael who was apparently in at the kill

Be in bad odour: *To become unpopular* * The policies of the government result in bad odour if the poor do not stand to benefit

Be in dock: *Being repaired* * Presently my car is in dock

Be in one's bad book: *To be out of favour* * One cannot get promotion if one is in the bad books of the boss

Be in one's elements: *Be in proper state* * *In one's natural environment* *.Whenever Lata gives a performance, she is always in her elements * He is in his element when taking part in a debate

Be in one's good book: *To be in favour* * One has to be in the good books of the boss to earn a reward

Be in pocket: *To have control or power* * He is in the pocket of his boss and is bound to succeed

Be in the black: *Have money in a bank account* * It is safe to be in the black to avoid any mishap

Be in the red: *Be in debt* * You will soon be in the red if you continue to squander your money

Be in the same boat: *All in equal circumstances* * We are all in the same boat, hence we shall have to swim or sink together

Be in the wrong: *Have made a mistake* * You are in the wrong to show disrespect to the old man

Be in trouble with the police: *Accused by the police for a crime* * My friend is in trouble with the police and is seeking shelter

Be in two minds: *Not to be able to decide* * He is still in two minds whether to join the army or not

Be in vogue: *Be in fashion* * Coloured shirts are in vogue these days

Be jogging: *To move on; to depart* * It is better to be jogging to keep oneself fit

Be led away: *Misguided* * I am afraid you may be led away by bad company

Be little and little: *Little by little; by degrees* * The condition of the patient is improving little and little

Be located: *Be situated* * Where is the new factory likely to be located?

Be lost on someone: *Someone does not understand* * That joke was lost on him else he would have got furious

Be made redundant: *Lose job by not being needed any more* * With the decreasing demand, many coal miners may be made redundant

Be mistaken: *To make a mistake; to be misunderstood* * Nobody dared to point out to him that he is mistaken

Be naught: *Keep out of the way; efface yourself* * If one is careful to be a naught, it will help the matters

Be neglectful of: *Forget about* * We should not be neglectful of our duties towards our parents

Be none the wiser: *No better informed* * Even after having read the article in the newspaper, I am none the wiser

Be nuts on: *To be very fond of* * My son is nuts over his new bike

Be obliged to someone: *Owe gratitude to someone* * I am obliged to you for the timely help you rendered to me

Be off: *To go away quickly* * The boss ordered me to be off immediately and search out the keys

Be off one's head: *Be mad* * After hearing his confusing talk, I thought he was off his head

Be on a committee: *Be a member of it* * He was on a committee soon after being elected

Be on a par with: *Be equal to* * A weak child cannot be on a par with a healthy one

Be on guard: *To keep guards; to act as sentry* * He has to be on guard as he is a watchman on night duty

Be on one's guard: *Be prepared against attack* * Our troops should be on guard always

Be on one's toes: *Be ready; prepared* * Our brave soldiers are always on their toes on the border

Be on one's track: *Follow someone* * The police is on the track of robbers who committed robbery last night

Be on point-duty: *Direct the traffic* * A policeman will be on point-duty during the rush hours

Be on stand by: *Keep waiting if need so arises* * The generator was kept as a stand by during the frequent power breakdowns

Be on the breadline: *Having hardly enough money to live on* * He is on the breadline as he has lost his job

Be on the danger list: *Be dangerously ill* * His name is on the danger list as he has been seriously ill for long

Be on the look out for: *Be in search of* * Since he cannot make both ends meet in the present job, he is on the look out for a new job

Be on the right side of: *Be less than or below* * He married when he was on the right side of thirty

Be on the sick list: *Be reported sick* * John is on the sick list today

Be on the verge of: *About to; on the point of* * Most farmers are on the verge of starvation because of a long drought

Be on the wagon: *Drink only non-alcoholic drinks* * We could get rid of many ailments by being on the wagon

Be on the warpath: *Be angry*

and look for a fight * There are some people who cannot desist from treading on the warpath

Be on the watch: *To be careful* * It is advisable to be on the watch when travelling through dacoit-infested areas

Be on the water-wagon: *To abstain from alcohol* * To preserve a good health, one will have to be on the water-wagon

Be on the wrong side of: *Be more than or above* * Most of our teachers are on the wrong side of forty

Be on watch: *Keep watch* * Our security forces are always on watch to check intruders

Be one's own master: *Be independent* * He is his own master in the choice of a profession since he has finished his education

Be one's treat: *One who will pay* * There will be a treat from me on my promotion

Be oneself: *To be in full possession of one's powers* * To be able to rule like Hitler over the world one has to be oneself

Be out: *Be published* * The new book of my favourite author is likely to be out next week * The result of my exams will be out next week

Be out of a job: *Be unemployed* * So long he is out of job, he will have to depend on his parents

Be out of luck: *Have bad luck* * He was out of luck in not getting the job that went to his friend

Be out of pocket: *Have lost money* * A spendthrift is sure to be out of pocket very soon

Be poles apart: *Very different; never in agreement* * Both the brothers are poles apart as far as their ideology is concerned

Be privy to a secret: *Know the details of a secret* * The police is interrogating him for his being a privy to a secret in the crime

Be put out: *Be annoyed* * I will feel put out if you make noise when I am sleeping

Be quick: *Make haste* * Be quick otherwise we will be too late for the meeting

Be quite a stranger: *Not seen for a long time* * My fast friend has become quite a stranger since the last three months

Be quits: *Be equal* * Since the dispute between us has been squarely settled, we are quits now

Be ruled: *Take advice* * It is better

to be ruled than commit any folly

Be run down: *Feel unwell; tired* * After completing the long distance race, I was run down * The high fever made me feel run down to take bed rest for a week

Be slow on the uptake: *Not to understand quickly* * He is rather slow on the uptake so you will have to repeat your point

Be quick on the uptake: *Quick to understand* * He is so quick on the uptake that you better be careful of saying exactly what you mean without any innuendos

Be something on: *Use something as a base* * One has to base one's arguments on facts and figures

Be spared: *Be saved* * He was spared the embarrassment of making an excuse for not attending the wedding of his friend

Be sparing with: *Be economical* * One should be sparing in consumption of natural resources

Be spotting with rain: *Rain slightly* * It is spotting with rain so you will not get drenched

Be struck down: *Bogged down* * I got struck down with flu and could not attend the office

Be sure: *Do not omit* * Be sure that you complete the assignment within the scheduled time

Be taken aback: *Be startled* * He was taken aback by the surprise visit of the flying squad

Be thank it: *Thank God* * I should be thank the Almighty for His blessings in my life

Be the dead spitting image: *Looks exactly like* * He is the spitting image of his father

Be the end of: *To cause the death of* * Excessive bleeding proved to be the end of the patient's death

Be this late: *Be so late* * I did not expect you to be this late

Be through: *To have done; to be at an end* * One should be through with the assigned task

Be through with: *Break off; finish; be tired of* * I am through with my friend who deceived me at the eleventh hour * When will you be through with your work? * I am through with this job, I must find something more interesting

Be through with someone: *Break off the friendship* * I am now through with my wife forever

Be torn from: *Be snatched away from* * The gold necklace was torn from her by the miscreants

Be two: *To be at variance* * Don't be two if a decision stands in the interest of the whole community

Be unacquainted: *Not to know* * I am unacquainted with the conservative attitude of that person

Be unlike him to be rude: *One who is not usually rude* * It is unlike him to be rude when I have always seen him to be very well mannered

Be up the flume: *To come to grief; to be done for* * Do your duty sincerely else you will be up the flume

Be up to one's neck in work: *Have a lot of work to do* * Since I am up to my neck in work at the moment, I cannot visit you

Be upon the books: *To have one's name in an official list* * His name figures upon the books who have a criminal record * His name is upon the books of the college for having beaten the record of his predecessors

Be vanished without a trace: *Disappear, leaving behind no clue* * The thief escaped and vanished without a trace

Be versed in law: *Be skilled or experienced in law* * He is well- versed in law and bids fair to be a promising pleader

Be washed overboard: *Be swept off the deck of a ship by a wave* * He was washed overboard by the huge oncoming waves

Be well up in: *Knows a lot about* * He is well up in mathematics and is likely to pass his postgraduation with distinction

Be well-versed in: *Be proficient in* * Please consult a lawyer who is well-versed in civil law

Be wide awake: *Watchful* * The sentry has to be wide awake to check the enemy movement on the border

Be wild with excitement: *Be overexcited* * The poor man was wild with excitement when he got the news of having won a prize in the lottery

Be wild with someone: *Be angry with someone* * To have a peaceful life, it would be advisable not to be wild with anyone

Be with it: *Be fashionable; moderate* * We must be with it so that we may keep pace with the latest trends

Be with you: *Agree with you* * I am with you on this point

Be within an ace of: *Almost nearly* * I was within an ace of being killed when a speeding car hit me

Be worthwhile: *Be worth doing* * It will be worthwhile to learn music by joining night classes

Be wound up: *Be nervous* * The accused was wound up on the day of judgement

Be wrapped up in one's work: *Think only of the work and take no notice of other things* * He is too wrapped up in his work to be aware of all that is going around him

Be young for one's years: *Be more sober than expected at his age* * Smith is young for his years as far as his intelligence is concerned

Be-all and end-all: *Sole purpose; the supreme air* * The be-all and end-all of this new scheme is to provide more employment opportunities * Just because he has failed does not mean that it is the be-all and end-all of his world

Bear (to the): *Incline* * When you reach the top of the hill, bear (to the) right for your onward journey

Bear a construction: *To allow of a particular interpretation* * The new proportion set forth by the expert definitely bears a construction

Bear a grudge: *To have bitter feelings* * I am bearing a grudge against my friend for ditching me

Bear a hand: *Take part; to lend aid; to give assistance* * It was proved that he did not bear a hand in the theft hence he was set free * I hope you will bear me a hand in learning English

Bear a person company: *Accompany* * I shall bear your company whenever you visit my place

Bear arms: *Serve as a soldier* * Every young man must bear arms to emerge as a disciplined person

Bear away: *To carry away* * Why must you bear away by his sugar-coated words?

Bear down: *Crush by force* *The government is forced to bear down the revolt

Bear hard: *To press heavily on; afflict; to oppress* * Taxation bears hard now-a-days on every section of the society

Bear in mind: *To remember; to keep in one's memory and attention* * We must bear in mind the noble teachings of great saints

Bear in-hand: *To make cut; maintain one's hopes; to keep expectation; to flatter one's hopes* * It is not easy to bear in-hand with a paltry amount to maintain a good standard of life * One should bear in-hand the spirits high, come what may * The director was trying to bear in-hand the famous actor with the aim to sign him for his new film

Bear it: *To make off hastily or furtively* * One will have to bear the hard realities of life * The man on scooter snatched the golden chain of a woman and bore it.

Bear on: *Aim at* * The opposition is trying to put pressure to bear on the ruling party to change the law

Bear one in mind: *Remember one* * You have to bear in mind that both happiness and sorrow come hand in hand

Bear out: *Confirm* * My professor can bear out my sincerity towards my studies

Bear out: *To corroborate* * The evidence does not bear out with the statement

Bear someone ill will: *Want something bad to happen to someone* * We should take the right decision in the interest of all so that no one bears us any ill will

Bear the brunt of: *To face the shock of* * Hungary had to bear the brunt of the first attack by German troops

Bear the palm: *To be the winner* * John bore the palm in the declamation contest

Bear up: *To keep up one's spirits* * One must bear up even when under severe strain

Bear with: *To make allowance for; tolerate* * Please bear with me and I shall explain in detail later * You will have to bear with me that my remarks against our leader were correct

Bear witness to: *Be evidence of* * The lack of action bears witness to a complacency on the part of the investigator

Beast of burden: *Animal used to carry loads* * Donkeys, camels, yak, etc. are beasts of burden

Beast of prey: *One that devours other animals* * Lion is a beast of prey

Beasts of chase: *Wild beasts that are hunted generally* * Mostly rabbits are beasts of chase for any falcon or eagle

Beat a retreat: *To retreat* * The enemy was forced to beat a retreat when our forces attacked

Beat about the bush: *To go round about anything; to*

evade coming to the point * The advocate kept beating about the bush during the course of debate instead of coming to the point

Beat black and blue: *Bruise* * The thief was beaten black and blue when caught red-handed

Beat down one's price: *Reduce the price by haggling* * I beat down his price but it took me quite some time to persuade him

Beat hollow: *To defeat completely* * The forces beat hollow the invaders

Beat off: *To drive back* * I had to beat off my car because of a traffic block

Beat one down: *Make one to reduce one's price* * He beat me down while selling my wrist-watch

Beat one's brains: *To puzzle one's brains about something* * I could not solve the knotty problem in spite of beating my brain.

Beat out: *To flatten or reduce in thickness by beating* * She beat out her golden ring with a hammer

Beat the air: *To fight to no purpose against an imaginary enemy* * It is useless to beat the air without any purpose

Beat the bounds: *Certain objects in the line of journey being formally struck* * *Sometimes boys are whipped to make them remember* * While beating the bounds, the search party discovered an arms cache * The teacher had to beat the bounds to make the students remember the lesson

Beat the drum: *Indulge in publicity* * All political parties beat the drum of their manifesto on the eve of the elections

Beat the records: *To outdo the highest achievement yet recorded* * His name figures in the *Limca Book of Records* as he has beaten all the records

Beat to sticks: *To defeat and surpass; utterly* * Our hockey team beat the rival team to sticks

Beat up: *To pound or whip into froth, a paste, a mixture, etc.; to put up as by beating the bushes; to be alarmed by a sudden attack; to thrash; to subject to a violent and brutal attack* * *to make way against wind tide* * A good number of vegetables were beaten up to make a different type of mixture * He felt himself beaten up after digging the well * The police beat up the violent mob with a heavy hand * The hunter beat up the track to trace his prey in the forest * Mind your language or I shall beat you up * We did beat the wind up while sailing in the deep sea

Beatific vision: *A glimpse of the glory of heaven* * The priest projected a beatific vision to the audience during his sermon

Because of: *On account of* * He did not attend the school because of his illness

Become a byword: *Become a common saying* * The use of four-letter words has become a byword for the rude man

Bed and board: *Food and lodging* * Poor students are provided with bed and board free of charge here

Bed of down or roses: *An easy or comfortable place* * Life is not a bed of down or roses * One has to go through many ups and downs in life

Bed of thorns: *Full of suffering* * After the death of her husband, the life of the young lady has been a bed of thorns

Before long: *In a short time* * He finished the assigned job before long

Before the wind: *Carried along by the wind* * The masts helped the ship before the wind

Beg for: *Request (thing)* * She begged me for a favour

Beg from: *Request (person)* * She begged a favour from me

Beg off: *To obtain another's release through entreaty; to seek remission of some penalty or liability* * He promised to help me but has since begged off * I have begged off from the Principal the remission of school fee

Beg the question: *To assume the truth of matters in dispute* * Division of property still begs the question

Began to sail before the wind: *To move forward along with the wind* * The ship picked up speed when it began to sail before the wind

Beggar description: *To be incapable of being expressed in words* * Kashmir's scenic beauty beggars description

Beggars cannot be choosers: *A person having limitations has limited choice* * The beggars must take whatever is offered to them

Begrudge one: *Feel resentment* * I do not begrudge his money

Behave yourself: *Be good* * Behave yourself or I will show you the door

Behind one's back: *In one's absence* * It is a bad habit to speak ill of others behind their back

Behind the bar: *Imprisoned* * The troublesome people are now behind bars

Behind the scenes: *Without many people's knowledge* * Certain policy decisions are taken behind the scenes to safeguard the national interest

Behind the times: *Not abreast of changes* * This law is behind the times on a number of important cases

Believe in something: *Believe that something exists* * I do believe in God as he controls the universe

Believe so: *Thinking that is correct* * I believe so since I trust that person

Bell and candle/Book and candle: *A phrase popularly used in reference to a from of excommunication ending* * The clergyman cursed him for committing rape and threatened him to undergo bell and candle punishment

Bell the cat: *To take the leading part in any hazardous venture** Who will bell the cat was the issue before the students who wanted to meet the Principal to explain their problems

Belong to a club: *Be a member* * If you want to belong to a club, you will have to become a member

Belong to someone: *Be someone's property* * This house belongs to that old man

Below one's breath: *In a low voice* * He told me a secret below his breath

Below one's dignity: *Below one' position* * The rich think it below their dignity to serve the cause of the poor

Below par: *Be low normal value* * The shares are selling below par due to a slump in the market

Below stairs: *In the basement; among the servants* * The surplus material is generally stored below stairs * The new servant will use the accommodation below stairs

Below the salt: *Among those of low social class* * The need of the hour is to take good care of the people below the salt

Belt along: *Go very fast* * The tanks belted along the battle-field, firing heavily

Belt out a song: *Sing a song very loudly* * The students were belting out a song while travelling in a bus

Belt up: *Keep quiet* * Belt up boys, we are on the point of danger

Bend the elbow: *To drink too*

much alcohol * John has bent the elbow as he seemed to be staggering quite a bit

Beneath the rose lie the thorns: *Pleasure and pain are inter-mixed* * Complete happiness cannot be found without some bitter experiences because beneath the rose lie the thorns

Beneficial to: *Good for* * Exercise is beneficial to health

Benefit of the doubt: *Favourable judgement when culpability is uncertain* * The jury acquitted the culprit giving him the benefit of doubt

Benefit society: *A friendly society* * Progressive life is possible only in a benefit society

Bent down: *To try to reduce the price of goods* * The new government is bent down in introducing economic reforms

Bent on: *Very keen* * He is bent on becoming a sailor

Bereft of: *Deprived of* * Bereft of all hope, he lived a life of a lonely person

Beset with: *Full of* * The way we propose to follow the rule is beset with many dangers

Beside the mark: *Not properly referring to the matter in hand* * You are just looking at the issue beside the mark, not seriously enough

Bestow on: *Confer as a right* * May God bestow his blessings on us all

Bet one's bottom dollar: *To bet all one has* * He bet his bottom dollar with the hope to recover the lost money

Better off: *In superior circumstances; more fortunate* * One should be helpful to others when one is better off

Better oneself /one's position: *Improve one's status* * Some people better themselves in society by their good deeds

Better wear out your shoes than your bed: *One should prefer working to resting* * One should plan his life with the aim to wear out the shoes than one's bed

Betting shop: *Office where you can bet money on horse race* * You better go to betting shop if you also want to bet money on a horse race

Between the cup and the lip: *Of dashed hopes* * You may plan anything but you must remember that there is many a slip between the cup and the lip

Between sun and sun: *Between sunrise and sunset* * The farmers had to work in the fields between sun and sun

Between the devil and the

deep sea: *In a desperate dilemma; with no escape* * I find myself between the devil and the deep sea because neither can I leave the job nor can I tolerate the scolding from my boss

Between the lights: *In the twilight* * Usually birds gather together and begin to chirp between the lights

Between the whiles: *In the intervals* * Though we have to work throughout the day yet between the whiles, we can enjoy tea

Between times: *In the intervals* * The students skip the classes between times

Between two fires: *Shot at from two directions* * A person caught between two fires is sure to die

Between two lights: *Under the cover of darkness* * The thief ran away between two lights

Between two stools we come to the ground: *Giving attention to two things at the same time will result in a downfall* * Concentration on one job is better than diverting your attention to another job as divided attention between two stools is likely to make us come to the ground

Between wind and water: *That part of a ship's side which is now in will be out of the water owing to the movement of waves in the waters* * The entire body of the ship kept tossing between wind and water

Between you and me: *In confidence* * It is between you and me so please do not leak it out

Beware of: *Take heed of* * Beware of snakes in the grass * Beware of cheap imitations while selecting jewels * Beware of thugs so that you do not get deceived

Beyond all recognition: *So much that one cannot recognise* * My very old friend was beyond all recognition when I saw him after so many years

Beyond compare: *Without any rival or like* * He is man of very high character and beyond compare

Beyond dispute: *Beyond doubt; with certainty* * The claim he made over the ancestral property was beyond dispute

Beyond one's means: *To spend more than one's income* * You will be in trouble if you live beyond your means

Beyond one's reach: *Impossible to attain* * For a poor man it is beyond his reach to think of buying a car

Beyond the mark: *Beyond any doubt* * His description of the issue is beyond the mark

Beyond the pale: *Doing things which are not acceptable in society* * His remarks put him quite beyond the pale

Bias against: *Prejudice against* * I have no bias against you

Bid a welcome: *To say goodbye* * The parents of the bride bid a welcome to the bridegroom

Bid defiance: *Challenge or ignore* * The bold sailor bid defiance to the swirling waters of the sea

Bid fair: *To seem likely* * Tom bids fair to become a lawyer because of his argumentative nature

Bid one's time: *Wait for the right moment* * Lisa is bidding her time till she can take the opportunity to show her worth

Big game: *The large animals hunted* * The kings were very fond of big game in ancient times

Big pot: *Big gun; important person* * Perhaps my friend could help you since he is a big pot of the city

Big shot: *Person of importance* * People usually pay respect to a big shot

Big stick: *Force; coercion* * The police had to use the big stick to make the culprit divulge the motive behind the crime

Big toe: *Largest of the toes* * I cannot chase you so far as I am having a problem with my big toe

Big top: *Large circus tent* * All the spectators were accommodated in a big top laid down by the organisers

Big-wig: *Important person* * A politician becomes a big-wig in the eyes of the people

Bill of rights: *Declaration of rights* * The Bill of Rights is now under consideration of the Parliament

Billion of letters: *A great many letters* * A billion of letters are delivered by postmen throughout the country every day

Bind over: *To subject to legal obligation* * You are bound over to pay the damages as per the judgement given by the court * The magistrate bound him over to keep pace

Biological warfare: *War in which germs are used* * It is inhuman to launch a biological warfare against any country

Bird of passage: *A migratory*

bird; a transient visitor * He comes home during holidays as a bird of passage

Bird's eye-view: *A general view from above; a general view of a subject* * The Commander-in-Chief had a bird's eye-view from the plane of the deployment of forces * He gave a bird's eye-view of the subject

Birds of a feather: *Persons of like taste* * Persons having the same likes are like birds of a feather flocking together

Birds of one wing: *Birds of same kind* * Birds of one wing flock together

Birds of prey: *Birds which eat other birds/animals* * Eagles, owls, vultures, etc. are birds of prey

Bit and sup: *Something to eat and drink* * Can anyone live a healthy life without bit and sup?

Bit by bit: *Piecemeal, Gradually* * He translated the whole chapter written in English bit by bit into Tamil

Bite one's head off: *Speak angrily to* * He bit my head off when I refused to obey him

Bite one's thumb: *To make a sign threatening revenge* * He is a man who is likely to bite his thumb when pressure is exerted on him

Bite the dust: *To fall; to die* * The fallen bodies of the warriors are biting the dust in the battle-field

Bite the hand that feeds one: *To be ungrateful* * Never bite the hand that feeds you

Bite the thumb: *To express defiance by knocking the thumbnail against the teeth* * Smith will bite his thumb and not yield to pressure of any kind from certain quarters

Black and white: *In writing* * The agreement was signed in black and white

Black art: *Magic used for evil purpose* * Some people resort to black art to dupe people * Unscrupulous characters take to black art as a profession

Black box: *Device which stores information about an aircraft's flight* * The installation of a black box in an aircraft helps to locate the cause of any accident that may take place

Black magic: *Evil spells designed to harm people* * The police is after those persons who practice black magic

Black market: *Selling illegally at a high price the products which are not normally available* * One is obliged to purchase onions at black market when it is not available in open market

Black sheep: *A disreputable member of a family or group* * To be a black sheep is a blot on a respectable family

Black spot: *Place where traffic accidents often happen* * This is a black spot and one should be very careful while driving

Blame for the accident: *Hold someone responsible for an accident* * He is to blame for the accident as a result of his rash-driving

Blame on something: *Hold someone responsible for something* * A bad workman often blames his tools for not producing a good product

Blank cartridge: *With no bullet in it* * A blank cartridge will cause no harm to anybody

Blank cheque: *A cheque signed without indicating the amount; giving power without a limit* * My boss gave me a blank cheque since he had faith in me

Blanket order: *Order which covers many items* * I have placed a blanket order with the grocer for supply of miscellaneous domestic items for a month

Blast off: *Take off (rocket)* * The rocket may blast off with a bang towards the sky

Blaze a trail: *Mark a path by cutting the bark on trees; be the first to do something* * They are currently blazing a trail in the bio- technology field

Blind alley: *Very narrow street with no way out* * We had a bitter experience while passing through a blind alley

Blind spot: *Part of the road which a motorist cannot see* * Beware of a blind spot while driving on the hills

Blind to: *Unconscious* * He is blind to his son's evil deeds

Blitz on something: *Sudden campaign to clear something up* * We are going to launch a blitz on construction of the dilapidated house to its original form

Block and tackle: *Arrangement of rocks, pulleys and hooks for lifting heavy weights* * We can use the block and tackle system in loading and unloading cargo from the ship * The block and tackle system could be very useful in harbours

Block letters: *With each letter separate and in capitals* * Please write your name in block letters

Block up: *To stop a hole; to fill* * Do not block up the pipe to let the water run

Block vote: *Group voting together* * The block voting system is not in vogue in our country

Bloom of youth: *Healthy glow of a young person* * She looked very pretty in the bloom of her youth

Blot one's copybook: *Blemish one's record* * Though he was an intelligent student, he has blotted his copybook by committing theft

Blow down: *To make something fall down* * The strong storm blew down many trees on the roadside

Blow great guns: *To blow tempestuously/violently* * The wind blew great guns and uprooted many trees

Blow hot and cold: *To be favourable and unfavourable by turns; to be irresolute* * Nobody takes his words seriously as he blows hot and cold frequently

Blow hot and cold in the same breath: *Appear both favourable and unfavourable at the same time* * He talks against the government but also praises it, thus blowing hot and cold at the same time

Blow in: *To turn up unexpectedly* * To our surprise, the door opened and Avinash blew in the room

Blow one a kiss: *Signal to send one a kiss from a distance* * She blew him a kiss while driving

Blow one's own trumpet: *To sound one's own praise* * It is not graceful to blow one's own trumpet in company

Blow out: *Extinguish* * Do not forget to blow out the candle before going to sleep

Blow something sky-high: *Blow something up with a powerful explosion* * When the bomb exploded, the bridge was blown sky-high

Blow the coals: *To excite passion; foment strife* * The bad elements are likely to create trouble by blowing coals between the rival groups * The lady was adamant to blow the coals with her husband at all costs

Blow up: *To shatter or destroy by explosion* * The building was blown up by a high-powered bomb

Blue blood: *High birth* * Dr. Karan Singh is a blue-blooded person who hails from royal family of the Maharaja of Jammu

Blue book: *Parliamentary report* * The blue book contains all information on the transactions carried out in the Parliament

Blue chips: *Industrial shares considered valuable because of past record* * Persons invest in blue chips to get rich dividends

Blue moon: *A very long but quite indeterminate time* * I was waiting for you like a blue moon in the countyside

Blue-stocking: *Woman having superior literary taste and intellectual interests* * We must hold in esteem the blue-stocking for her knowledge

Blush at: *Become red* * She blushed at the mention of her lover's name

Board and lodging: *Meals and accommodation* * The college authorities provide free board and lodging to poor students

Boil over: *Boil and flow over the side of the vessel* * The milk boiled over as I got engaged in grating carrots

Bolster up: *Support* * We must bolster up the falling morale of the soldiers

Bone idle: *Completely lazy* * You cannot expect anything to be done on time from a bone idle person

Bone of contention: *Cause of quarrel* * Kashmir continues to be a bone of contention between India and Pakistan

Book up: *Reserve* * I will have to book up a seat for him in the train

Booked for speeding: *Charged against speeding* * The police have booked him for speeding

Boon companion: *Great friend* * He is a boon companion of mine

Boost shot: *Injection which provides protection* * The boost shot given to the patient would keep him comfortable for long

Bootlegging: *Transport or sell illicit alcoholic drinks* * Do not get involved in bootlegging if you wish to avoid unnecessary trouble

Border on: *Be next to* * France borders on Germany

Border upon: *Resemble* * This film borders on indecency

Bore down: *Overpower* * We struggled to turn the boat as the waves bore down on us

Bore it: *Ran away* * The man on scooter snatched the gold chain from a lady and bore it

Bored stiff: *Very bored* * I am bored stiff without company * It bored me stiff when I had to cool my heals for a long time

Born in: *Come in to world by birth* * He was born in a rich family

Born in the purples: *Born of exalted birth* * Pandit Jawaharlal Nehru was born in the purples

Born of: *Come in to world by birth* * Indira Gandhi was born of rich parents

Born with a silver spoon: *Born to affluence* * A person born with a silver spoon in his mouth has every luxury at his disposal

Borne in upon: *Forcibly impressed upon* * It was borne upon him to give false evidence in the court

Borrow from: *To take on credit* * I borrowed this money from my fried to pay the bank loan

Bosom friend: *Intimate friend* * I will break the news of my success at first to my bosom friend

Bottle out: *Lose courage at the last moment and give up doing something* * Before making his maiden speech, he bottled out when he saw many other competitors

Bottle up: *To hold back (one's feelings)** All the rage that had been bottled up in me for so long flooded out in a torrent of abuse

Bottomless pit: *Hell* * An evil-doer will, after his death, have no place to stay except the bottomless pit

Bouncing baby: *Healthy looking baby* * Everybody is attracted to a bouncing baby

Bound by: *Compelled by* * I was bound by ill health because of which I could not attend the wedding ceremony of my friend

Bound for: *Leaving for; on the way to* * This train is bound for London

Bound in: *Be in obligation* * I am bound in honour to stand by you

Bound to be late: *Very likely to be late* * They are bound to be late due to a traffic jam

Bounded on: *Be the boundary of* * England is bounded on the north by Scotland

Bounded to: *Limit* * There is not need for him to be bounded to his friend

Bounds of: *Foot of* * We were glad to reach the bounds of the mountain

Box someone's ears: *Pull someone by the ears* * When the child did not stop shouting, the teacher boxed his ears

Box the compass: *To make a complete roundabout* * He just boxed the compass without having come to any authentic conclusion

Boy in buttons: *To fasten by means of buttons; to close up tightly* * Please put the boy in buttons and be dressed properly * Make the boy wear the cap so that the boy is in buttons

Braced oneself for: *Be prepared*

for a showdown * He braced himself for the ordeal he had to face in a week's time

Brag of: *Boast* * Fools always brag of their high birth

Brain drain: *Intelligent persons going abroad to work for higher salaries* * Brain drain is a big loss to the Indian society

Brain trust: *A committee of experts; a number of reputedly well-informed persons chosen to answer questions of general interest in public* * It will be a good thing if a brain trust is constituted to enlighten people on various developments in technology

Branded as a thief: *Called a thief* * The people branded him as a thief when he was caught red-handed while stealing

Brazen hussy: *Wicked girl; woman* * She flirts openly like a brazen hussy

Brazen it out: *Be defiantly unrepentant despite being censured* * He will brazen it out at all costs even though he has been ostracised by the entire community

Brazen-faced: *Impudent; wanting in shame or modesty* * A brazen-faced person is not liked by anybody

Breach of faith: *Going back on what has been promised* * A breach of faith is a moral disgrace

Breach of peace: *Violation of public peace through riots* * The police made firm arrangements to ensure that there was no breach of peace in riot-affected areas

Breach of promise: *Often used for breach of promise in marriage* * The betrothed girl committed suicide for breach of promise by her fiancée

Breach of trust: *A violation of duty by a trustee* * One of the trustees has been expelled from the board for violating breach of trust

Bread and butter miss: *A school girl* * She is still a bread and butter miss though soon she would be going to college

Bread and cheese: *A livelihood* * The poor have to work hard for their bread and cheese

Bread buttered on both sides: *Very fortunate circumstances* * As he has won the world heavy-weight boxing championship his bread seems buttered on both sides

Bread and butter: *Bread sliced and buttered* * People take to different jobs to earn bread and butter for their family

Bread-and-butter letter: *Thanksgiving letter for hospitality* * I have just dispatched a bread-and-butter letter to my friend for having invited me to dinner

Break a jest: *To utter a jest* * He broke a timely jest to ease the tension in the heated discussion

Break a lance with: *Argue against, to enter into a contest with* * It is advisable not to break a lance with a person who is better well versed on the subject

Break an officer: *Dismiss* * Why should the boss break an officer on flimsy ground?

Break away: *As clouds after a storm; to go away; escape abruptly; to sever connection forcibly or abruptly* * After a heavy downpour, the clouds broke away * The United Congress Party broke away to form another party

Break bank: *Exhaust its resources* * I have already broken bank and have nothing left to sustain the business

Break bounds: *Go out of bounds* * If you break bounds in this area, you will be penalised

Break bread with: *Be entertained by; to have a meal (with)* * It will be my pleasure to break bread with you on your birthday tomorrow

Break bulk: *To open the hold and take out a portion of the cargo; to begin to use the goods supplied in bulk* * As soon as the wholesaler broke bulk the traders gathered around him

Break butterfly on wheel: *Waste energy* * You are merely breaking butterfly on wheel by your effort to grow rice in this wasteland

Break cover: *To burst forth from concealment* * The deer broke cover and joined the other deer the moment the lion disappeared

Break down: *Collapse; fail* * My vehicle broke down on the way and I was stranded * They blamed the police for the breakdown in community relations

Break even: *To avoid loss but fail to gain* * I was successful to break even during the collapse of share market

Break forth: *To burst out* * The clouds broke forth instantly and it started pouring heavily

Break ground: *To lead in new work; to take the first step in any project* * Scientists are doing their best to break ground in the mission regarding life on Mars

Break in the weather: *Change in weather* * There is a break in the hot weather and people are leaving for hill resorts

Break in/Break into: *To enter violently* * The robbers broke into the house at midnight

Break into a run: *Start to run* * At times, the soldiers have to break into a run for long distances

Break into a trot: *Start to run well* * I broke into a trot to reach home before day-break

Break jail: *To force one's way out of prison* * The prisoner broke jail and is still absconding

Break journey: *To halt* * He broke his journey while on his way to Calcutta

Break loose: *To escape from confinement; to extricate oneself forcibly; to break through all restraint* * One of the tigers in the zoo has broken loose

Break new ground: *Start something new* * Science and technology are breaking new grounds to make life easy for mankind

Break no squares: *To make no difference; to do no harm; to matter little* * He is so well off that it will break no squares if he resigns from his job

Break of the day: *Dawn* * The enemy attacked at the break of the day

Break of the monsoon: *The first shower of the monsoon* * The weather experts anticipate break of the monsoon early this year

Break off: *Bring to an end; to detach by breaking; to put an abrupt end; to leave off abruptly* * The husband and wife have broken off their marriage through legal divorce * There is a break off in the mill due to the strike * The striking employees suddenly broke off from the meeting

Break one's duck: *To make one's first run* * The athlete is preparing himself to break his duck in the race

Break one's heart: *To die of; be broken down by grief or disappointment* * The sad news broke her heart when she came to know that her son has died in the battle-field

Break one's mind: *To communicate one's thoughts; to make known; confide; divulge one's thoughts* * The orator will break his mind on healthcare tomorrow * I will not break my mind over this issue to you

Break one's neck: *Work extremely hard to achieve some-*

thing * One has to break his neck to be successful in life

Break one's promise: *Not to keep one's words* * My friend assured me of timely help but then broke his promise at the nick of time

Break one's spirit: *To tame* * The police tried to break the spirit of the prisoner but he did not divulge any information

Break one's wing: *To fail to fulfil a promise* * I never believe him as he breaks his wing by lame excuses

Break out: *To come into sudden activity; to appear suddenly ; to break through all restraints* * Cholera has broken out in this village * A fierce fighting broke out between the rebels and the army

Break Priscian's head: *Use bad grammar* * There are many persons who break Priscian's head while writing English

Break promise: *One who habitually does not keep his words* * No one trusts him for he is known to break his promises

Break small: *Become feeble* * Do not break yourself small if you are not wrong

Break step: *To change the sequence of right and left foot; to get out of step* * The soldiers marched through the strike-stricken town without breaking step

Break the back of: *To complete the most difficult or main part of; to overburden; shatter* * We hope they have broken the back of the arduous job by now * The homework given by the teacher has broken my back * The accident has broken the back of my all plans

Break the bank: *Exhaust all resources* * If you give a meagre donation to a needy person, it will not break the bank

Break the heart: *To crush with grief* * The news of assassination of Mahatma Gandhi broke the heart of many Indians * The over-dose of drugs broke his heart

Break the ice: *To get through the initial difficulties* * We sat together for some time without talking as neither of us knew how to break the ice

Break the news: *Make it known* * I was the first to break the news of Mary clearing the entrance test

Break the news to someone: *Tell someone bad; unwelcome news* * He broke the news to me about the death of her husband in the war

Break the record: *Do better than*

anyone had ever done before * Brian Lara has broken the record by scoring the maximum number of runs in Test cricket

Break through: *Make way with force; to force a passage through** The agitators attempted to break through the police cordon but failed * No breakthrough could be achieved in the stalemate over the discussion on increase in pension

Break to pieces: *Go into pieces* * The bone china tea-set fell from my hands and broke to pieces

Break up: *To break in pieces; to break down; to go to pieces; break open* * The cup slipped from my hands and broke up * There was a break up of electricity for two hours at night * He broke down the lock and entered the room * They broke up their journey after a successful campaign

Break upon the wheel: *To punish by stretching on a wheel and breaking the bones* * He rammed his car and broke upon the wheel on the pedestrians

Break wind: *To release gas* * Breaking wind is necessary to ease a full stomach

Break with: *Cease relations with* * He is likely to break his relations with his wife

Break-bone fever: *Dengue* * John is suffering from break-bone fever

Breakdown: *Collapse; stoppage; failure of health or power* * The boundary-wall broke down because of heavy rains * The car suddenly broke down on the road * He suffered severe break-down of his health after he suffered a financial crisis

Breakdown gang: *Wreckage clearers after an accident* * The breakdown gang immediately reached the spot on receiving the information about a major accident

Break-jaw: *Very difficult to pronounce accurately* * Certain words in Latin are like break-jaw to many new learners

Break-up: *Dissolution* * There was a break-up in the mob as soon as the police reached the spot

Break vow: *One who habitually breaks vows* * It is not difficult for some women break vows at the drop of a hat

Breastfeeding: *Feeding a child with milk from the breast* * According to the Health Ministry, breast feeding is ideal for increasing the immunity of the baby

Breast stroke: *A stroke used in swimming* * His style of swimming the breast stroke is somewhat peculiar and not very correct

Breast the tape: *In a race, the runners have to touch the line stretched across the track at the winning post with their breasts* * The runner who first breasts the tape will be awarded a gold medal

Breathe a word about it: *Say anything about it* * Please do not breathe a word about it lest it should spoil her career

Breath of one's nostrils: *Part and parcel* * He has made the motto 'early to bed and early to rise' the breath of his nostrils

Breathe again: *To be relieved from anxiety; to heave a sigh of relief; recover from a shock* * He breathed again the moment he saw him escape death unharmed * I have yet to breathe again after coming out of the tragedy which took place in my life

Breathe deeply: *Take in lots of air* * To breathe deeply early in the morning is a very good exercise

Breathe down someone's neck: *Be close behind someone* * In a tough competition the two top runners were breathing down the necks of each other

Breathe freely: *To be at ease* * We can breathe freely only when the exams get over * He felt completely exhausted, but now he is breathing easily

Breathe one's last: *To die* * He breathed his last in the prime of his life

Breathe upon: *To tarnish the name; taint* * He is liable to breathe upon that gentleman by making false allegations against him

Breathing apparatus: *Mask, etc. which allow one to breathe easily* * In chemical war-fare, the use of a breathing apparatus is a must

Brevity is the soul of wit: *Say or write in brief as it shows intelligence* * Knowing that brevity is the soul of wit, she answered the question to the point

Bridle path/ Bridle road: *A path or way for horsemen* * In hilly areas, one has to make use of the bridle path to enjoy the beauty of nature

Bring a hornet's nest about one's ears: *To create trouble by interfering foolishly* * You will bring a hornet's nest about your ears if you interfere unnecessarily

Bring about: *Cause to happen* * There is a great need to bring about reforms in the education system in our country

Bring back: *Call to mind; remind* * It brings me back to my youthful days when I could run for hours without tiring

Bring credit: *Bring fame and honour* * Your noble deeds will certainly bring credit to your family

Bring down: *To humble; to shoot; to overthrow* * A national strike will bring down the government * The ground-to- air missile brought down enemy aeroplanes * The singer brought down the house by his singing style

Bring down the house: *To call forth a general burst of applause* * He brought down the house by his impressive speech

Bring forth: *Give birth to; produce* * The new health programme will bring forth good results

Bring home to: *Convince; to realise fully; to prove in such a way that there is no way of escaping the conclusion* * The new discoveries will bring home many truths unknown to mankind * I shall bring home the art of jugglery

Bring home: *To prove; impress* * The stupidity of his behaviour was brought home by him

Bring in: *To introduce; to yield* * The government is hoping to bring in a new legislation to curb dowry * The administration has been brought in to accept the demands of the agitating employees

Bring into play: *Bring into exercise, operation, use* * All kinds of forces will be brought into play to defeat the strategic designs of the enemy

Bring into world: *Give birth to* * Who knew that the poor young couple would bring into the world a child destined to be the Prime Minister of India!

Bring off: *Rescue from wreck; conduct to success* * Most brilliant monuments were brought off by Germany after the Second World War

Bring on: *To induce; to cause to advance* * New education reforms will bring on drastic improvements * I shall not advice the use of a new drug as it will bring on some side effects

Bring one to his senses: *To make one recognise the facts* *

Let him bring to his senses that he must mend his behaviour

Bring one to one's knee: *To reduce to subjection* * The Indian army brought the Pakistan forces to their knees during the Bangladesh war in 1971

Bring one's hogs to a fine market: *To make a complete mess of something; bring oneself to believe; persuade* * He tried to bring his hogs to a fine market but failed in the absence of solid arguments

Bring out: *To make clear; to put before the public; to publish* * All the members brought down the house as soon as the Bill was passed * The judgement to be declared will bring out the truth * He has brought out a new book on his own life which is selling like hot cakes

Bring over: *To convert* * During Mughal rule, many Hindus were forcibly brought over to Islam

Bring round: *To restore from illness or unconsciousness; to win over; to change opinion to suit that of someone else* * The doctor gave the patient a pill that brought him round * He brought round the money-lender to give him a loan * We did our best to bring him round to our point of view

Bring to light: *To bring into focus* *An investigation may have to be conducted to bring to light his crime

Bring to: *To restore to consciousness* * The medicine worked wonders to bring the patient to consciousness * The failure of electricity will bring the machines to a standstill

Bring to a pass: *Cause to happen* * Careless driving usually brings to a pass many innocent lives

Bring to bay: *Force somebody to make a stand* * The student was brought to bay by the teacher

Bring to bear: *To bring into operation; apply* * Apply the correct method to bring to bear the machine immediately * The opposition's aim is to bring pressure to bear on the Parliament to get the law changed

Bring to book: *To punish* * Those who indulge in burglary will be brought to book by the police

Bring to justice: *Bring legal proceedings against* * The thief has been arrested and will be soon brought to justice before the magistrate

Bring to life: *To confer life upon* * The appearance of the young man brought all members of his family to life

Bring to light: *To reveal* * The eye-witness brought to light the true facts of the case

Bring to pass: *Cause to happen* * One should be careful to see that nothing evil brings itself to pass at least in one's neighbourhood

Bring to terms: *To compel acceptance of conditions* * The culprit was brought to terms by the police once he admitted his guilt

Bring to the floor/ground: *Knock down* * Mohammad Ali brought many of his opponents to the floor easily

Bring to the hammer: *To sell or cause to sell by auction* * Precious old articles will be brought to the hammer next week

Bring under: *Subdue* * Those involved in the mutiny will be brought under with a heavy hand

Bring up: *To rear or educate; to introduce; to notice; to make prominent; to vomit* * Bringing up livestock is becoming a profitable profession * She is a properly brought up young lady * The manager advised his assistant to bring up the matter at the next meeting * The child is bringing up his breakfast

Bring up on the bottle: *To rear artificially rather than by breast* * The orphan boy was brought up on the bottle rather than the breast

Bringing forth: *The fruits of one's own actions* * Hard work invariably brings forth good results ultimately

Bringing up: *Upbringing; rearing; training* * His parents brought him up with great difficulties due to poverty * The bringing up of kittens is just like brining up one's own children * The good bringing up of a child in early life is very crucial

Bringing up the rear: *To come last** Please push and bring up the rear party also

Bristle with: *Have in large numbers* * The battle-front bristled with spears

Broad daylight: *Fully diffused daylight* * Chain snatching in broad daylight has increased

Broad in the beam: *Rather fat* * He is broad in the beam and must seek advice of some expert to get rid of the same

Broadcast an appeal: *Tell by*

broadcasting (news) * They broadcast an appeal to the public to help the flood victims

Broaden the mind: *Made one's knowledge or interest more extensive* * Travelling broadens the mind in understanding a great deal of issues

Broadly speaking: *In a general way* * Broadly speaking, he is not true to his salt

Broken man: *Reduced to despair* * He is a broken man as he has lost all that he possessed

Broken meats: *Remains; the leavings of a banquet* * The broken meats were thrown before stray dogs after the dinner got over

Broken money: *Small coins* * We must have some broken money to make use of in times of crisis

Broken reed: *Unreliable person or a thing* * John is a broken reed hence nobody trusts him

Broken-hearted: *Crushed with grief* * The broken-hearted woman committed suicide

Bronchial asthma: *Asthma in lungs* * Bronchial asthma is a dreadful disease

Brood on: *Ponder on grievously* * Never brood too much on the past problems

Brood over: *Think over* * She is brooding over her plan to publish a new novel

Brood over something: *Ponder on something* * I am brooding over a plan for building a house

Browbeaten: *Intimidated* * From her long face it appears she has been browbeaten

Brown rice: *Rice which still has its outer covering* *The polished grains of rice did not have even a single grain of brown rice

Brown study: *Reverie; dreaming* * I shouted loudly but the man passing by did not listen as he was in a brown study

Buck up: *To cheer up; to stimulate* * The leader bucked up the morale of the crowd by his speech

Budget for: *Plan how to spend money or something* * We have to budget for the best utilisation of resources at our disposal

Build castles in the air: *Make imaginary schemes* * Mostly people live in dreams and build castles in the air

Build up: *Increase; accumulate; intensify; create* * We must build up the morale of our organisation * The number of vehicles on the road is building up every year *

One day your books will build up into a library * We were in a position to build up our strength

Bulk large: *Appear large or important* * The senate house bulked large on the east

Bulk of sales: *Most of the sales* * The bulk of our sales go to retail dealers

Bull dog: *Powerful and courageous dog* * A bull dog is considered very helpful for maintaining domestic security

Bulldoze one's proposal: *Force to agree upon* * The chairman bulldozed his proposal through the committee

Bulldoze someone: *To force someone* * He bulldozed me through the community to accept his proposal on a new project

Bull-headed: *Obstinate* * A bull-headed person cannot be brought round to one's point

Bully boys: *Thugs* * We must keep some distance from the bully boys

Bump into someone: *Meet someone by chance* * I bumped into an old friend at the railway station

Bunch of fives: *The fist* * He had to face a bunch of fives from the wrestler when he abused him

Bung something in: *Throw something in* * Please bung the waste matter in the wastepaper basket

Bunk beds: *Two beds, one on the top of the other* * Bunk beds for children are the latest fashion

Bur in the throat: *Something sticking in the throat; producing a choking sensation* * I am feeling irritated by the bur in the throat

Burden of proof: *The obligation to prove one's contention* * The burden of proof rests with the accused to prove himself innocent in this case

Burn off someone: *Live at someone's expenses* * He is a chain smoker, yet he burns cigarettes off friends

Burn one's boats: *To decide once for all* * When we decided to leave our village, we had burnt our boats

Burn one's fingers: *To suffer due to one's mistake* * He got his fingers badly burnt dabbling in the stock market

Burn out: *Extinguish* * The fire has burnt itself out as there was nothing left to burn

Burn the candle at both ends: *To waste; to use up resources all at once* * Those who burn the candle at both ends are always in trouble

Burn the midnight oil: *Work*

late; to study late in the night * He had to burn midnight oil to be successful in the competition

Burn up: *To consume completely by fire* * The fire may burn up all the shops in the market if the fire-engine does not reach here

Burning mountain: *A volcano* * Burning mountains play havoc with everything that comes in the path of the lava

Burning question: *A keenly discussed issue* * How to prevent corruption at all levels is a burning question of the day

Burrow into: *Investigate something hidden* * The police is vigorously burrowing into the mystery behind the murder

Burst into: *Rush into* * She burst into the room as she feared getting caught in the hailstorm

Burst into tears: *Start to cry* * The boy burst into tears when the teacher scolded him

Burst of gunfire: *Sudden attack* * At the burst of gunfire, the enemy troops took to their heels

Burst out: *To shout out* * They burst out laughing on my joke

Bury one's head in the sand: *Ignore the facts* * People generally bury their head in sand when they see danger approaching

Bury the hatchet: *To renounce enmity* * India and Pakistan must bury the hatchet over Kashmir if they want to progress

Bus route: *Normal way which a bus follows* * To promote tourism, the government is planning new bus routes to the hilly areas

Bush telegraph: *Passing information through gossip* * The message received through bush telegraph resulted in a silly misunderstanding

Business efficiency: *Ability to work effectively in business* * Everyone does not have the instinct for business efficiency

Busy street: *Street with lots of pedestrians and traffic* * One should be very careful while walking in a busy street

But for: *Had it not been so* * But for the heavy downpour, we would have had a pleasant journey

But for something: *Had it not been* * But for the siren warning, we would have been caught in the gunfire

Butt in: *To interpose; force oneself in* * One should not butt in on someone else's discussion

Butter someone up: *Flatter someone* * He is buttering his boss for getting a promotion

Button up/ Button your lip: *Be quiet* * You are crying for no reason, so button up

Buy off: *To get rid of by paying* * The accused tried to buy off the witness to win the case

Buy on spec: *Buy without being sure of the value or condition* * He bought shares only on spec, knowing little about the trends prevailing in the market

Buy out: *To dispossess entirely by payment* * He borrowed a large sum of money to buy out his partner

Buy shares at par: *At their face value* * Those who bought shares at par have received very good dividends

Buy time: *Delay an event* * The authorities are trying to buy time before declaring the election results

Buy up: *To purchase the whole stock of* * He plans to buy up cotton from the market immediately before the price rise

By all means: *In any way* * He appears to be rough but by all means he is an honest man

By and by: *At some future time; successively* * By and by you will come across a new friend * By and by, one has to pass through odd situations

By and large: *On the whole* * The problem has by and large been sorted out by the management

By any means: *In any way* * By any means his threats are nothing but a bluff

By chance: *Accidentally* * It was by chance that I slipped while crossing the road

By degrees: *By little and little; gradually* * The loan was returned by the farmer to the bank by degrees * He got promotion from a recruit to a Captain by degrees

By dint of: *By force of; by means of* * He could get excellent position in his life by dint of hard work

By far: *In a very great degree* * By far he is feeling better now * He is by far the tallest man in our town

By fits and starts: *At odd moments* * There is no easy way to cope with those orders that come in by fits and starts

By hand: *By use of the hands or*

tools worked by the hand only * The secret letter was delivered to me by hand

By happenstance: *By a coincidence* * It was by happenstance that two accidents occurred due to fog in the early morning hours

By heart: *By rote* * He has learnt the lesson by heart

By hook or by crook: *One way if not another* * You have to get this task done by hook or by crook

By inches: *Inch by inch; by small degrees* * He is growing by inches * There is definitely progress in your work but by inches

By leaps and bounds: *Rapid stages* * He earned name as well as fame by leaps and bounds

By little and little: *By degrees* * I learnt by little and little the history of the culprit and his family

By means: *Because of it* * He was set free by the court by means he was not at fault

By mistake: *To make or have made a mistake; to be misunderstood* * I have not done it intentionally but by mistake * You have taken my book by mistake

By mutual consent: *With the agreement of both parties* * The augmentation of the hydro-electric project is being executed by mutual consents of both the central and state governments

By my will: *Voluntarily* * I am ready to do by my will whatever you desire

By no manner of means: *Under no circumstances* * He vowed that by no manner of means he would give a false statement in the court

By no means: *Certainly not* * I shall by no means help that scoundrel as he has already cheated me

By one's way of it: *According to one's belief* * By his way of it, at least two persons must have committed the theft

By oneself: *Alone* * He is living in a hut by himself for the last so many years

By reason of: *On account of; in consequence of* * I enjoyed a measure of protection by reason of my age

By return of post: *By the next postal service* * I hope to receive your reply in the matter by return of post

By rights: *Justly or correctly* * Honestly speaking, this property is not mine by rights

By-room: *A side or private room* * He used to study in the by-room adjacent to the kitchen

By rule of thumb: *In a rough and ready practical manner; found by experience to be convenient* * There are certain cases which could be settled by rule of thumb

By stealth: *In a secret way* * The thieves entered the office by stealth

By the dozen: *A dozen at a time* * The banana is sold here by the dozen

By the holy poker: *A fictitious oath of unknown meaning* * Be careful and ready to stand by the holy poker

By the same token: *Further in corroboration* * An employee retired from service is considered by the same token as if retired from life

By the skin of one's teeth: *Very narrowly* * I could pass the examination by the skin of my teeth

By the strong hand: *By force* * The rebellion was brought under control by a strong hand

By the sweat of one's brow: *By dint of hard labour* * The farmers have to earn their living by the sweat of their brow

By the time: *When* * By the time I reached the railway station, the train had already gone

By the way: *In passing, incidentally* * By the way, my visit to this place is a secret * By the way, how is he related to you?

By the yard: *In large quantities* * I bought cloth by the yards

By then: *By that time* * If you reach the station by noon, the train would have left by then

By these presents: *By these documents* * We are bound to abide by these presents

By this time: *By now; up to this time* * She must have reached home by this time * He should have been here by this time positively

By time: *Leisure time* * I will read this book by time only

By turns: *One after the another* * The people were allowed to enter the hall by turns

By virtue of: *Because of* * By virtue of his ability, he bids fair to rise in his life

Byway: *A private, secluded or obscure way* * There is no byway to enter this part of garden

By way of: *As if for the purpose of; to show caution in regard to* * By way of his being apologetic, he was granted pardon * By way of doubt he is being held responsible for picking the pocket * He expressed his viewpoint by way of illustration

By weight: *Fully* * I am convinced with your philosophy by weight

By word of mouth: *Orally* * My friend promised to give me loan by word of mouth * People heard about the tragedy by word of mouth

By-and-by: *At some future time; successively* * I will tell you the secret of my success by-and-by * You will get your share by-and-by

By-blow: *A side blow; an illegitimate child* * He suffered a by-blow in a scuffle * The by-blows are taken care of in charity homes

By-corner: *An out of the way place* * The child lying by-corner was saved and admitted to a nursing home

Bypass: *A side track for carrying traffic* * A new bypass has been constructed to ensure smooth traffic * You can reach early if you travel through the new bypass

Bypath: *A secluded or indirect path* * Please don't take that bypath at night as it is not safe

By-speech: *A casual speech* * It was only a by-speech made on his birthday

Bystander: *One who stands by or near one* * The bystander could not explain the reason for the crowd gathering in the market

By-thing: *A thing of minor importance* * Nobody is interested to buy a by-thing

Byword: *Popular short saying** 'An apple a day keeps the doctor away' is a byword in everyday parlance when referring to one's health

C

Call a halt to: *Bring to a stop* * It is time to call a halt to vandalism

Cabbage white: *Common type of white butterfly* * Children are invariably attracted to a cabbage white

Call a halt to: *Bring to a stop* * It is time to call a halt to vandalism

Call bad names: *Abuse* * We should desist from calling others bad names

Call a spade a spade: *To speak out plainly without euphemism* * An honest and truthful person does not hesitate in calling a spade a spade

Call at: *Visit* * I intend to call at your home today

Call attention to: *To point out* * Mass media call our attention to day-to-day events taking place all over the country

Call for: *Demand* * There is no call for his services

Call forth: *Make it exist* * He is not capable of calling forth much emotion in his readers

Call in: *Send for* * I had to call in the doctor when my mother fell seriously ill

Call in question: *To challenge; throw doubt on* * Nobody can call in question the integrity of patriots who sacrificed their life in the freedom movement

Call it a day: *To announce a decision to leave off* * Let us call it a day after having put in more than what we could have done

Call off: *Withdraw; abandon* * Employees called off their strike the moment their demands were met * The meeting had to be called off to condole the death of the chairman

Call names: *Abuse* * He lost his temper and called names to his servant

Call on/upon: *To invoke; to make an appeal; to make a short visit* * The judiciary has called upon strict compliance of law and order against the offenders * I called on him to keep my promise * I called on my friend to seek his advice on some important point

Call over: *To read out* * The teacher called over the students who had not completed their homework

Call out: *To challenge to a fight; to announce a duel; to summon to service; to bring into operation* * He has called out his opponent for a fight * The government called out the army to help the administration during the floods * Students have called out a strike against the fee hike by the management

Call over: *To read aloud* * The teacher called over the names of the students who excelled in the examination

Call someone's bluff: *Claim successfully that someone is tricking or is playing* * It is time to call their bluff out in the open

Call to account: *To summon to render an account; demand an explanation* * He has been called to account for the utilisation of funds earmarked for road construction * He awaits a call to account for his absence from duty

Call to mind: *Remember* * I cannot call to mind the event you are referring to

Call to order: *To call upon (appeal); to observe the rules of debate* * The Speaker called to order the members of the Parliament to maintain the dignity of the house

Call to the bar: *Admit as a barrister* * Pandit Jawaharlal Nehru was called to the bar when he was quite young

Call up: *Telephone to; bring back to the mind; summoned for service; recollect* * I will call you up this evening * When I was alone, I called up scenes of my childhood * If war breaks out, we shall be called up at once to duty * He could not call up where he had seen her.

Call you back: *Phone you again* * I will call you back as early as possible

Camp it up: *Act in an exaggerated manner* * He is camping it up only for amusement of the general public

Can do nothing with him: *Can't change him* * Despite scolding him a number of times over his misbehaviour, I can do nothing with him

Can't have it both ways: *Choose either of the two alternatives* * Either have a party or a gift but you cannot have it both ways

Cannot see the wood for the trees: *Cannot grasp the main point because of the abundance of minor details* * They could not see the wood for the trees as they got to engrossed in the intensive details of planning and forgot the main point

Canon law: *The church's law* * The clergyman attached to a cathedral has to abide by the canon law

Cap in hand: *Submissively; humbly* * It is very embarrassing to go cap in hand to ask for a raise

Cap of maintenance: *A cap of dignity worn by or carried before a noble person of rank* * Cap of high maintenance was awarded in the olden times to a person for his meritorious services

Cap-a-pie: *From head to foot* * In the olden times, the soldiers were armed cap-a-pie before going for the battle

Capital punishment: *Punishment of death* * Many people are of the opinion that capital punishment should be abolished

Capture the market: *Take the possible sales* * They have captured 10 per cent of the market

Car was written off: *Considered a total loss* * The new car was written off as all efforts to locate the same proved futile

Car with a low mileage: *Car which has not traveled much* * He struck a cheap bargain in buying a car with a low mileage

Car engine is misfiring: *Not igniting the petrol at the right time* * I have put off my travel to the city as the car engine is misfiring and requires repair

Cardiac arrest: *Stoppage of the heart* * He died of cardiac arrest

Cardinal numbers: *Numbers expressing the quantity* * Cardinal numbers are different from the ordinary numbers

Cards in one's hands: *Everything under one's control* * The police have the cards in their hands in the disturbed area

Cards on the table: *One's resources and moves freely laid down* * He placed his cards on the table when he found that he was on the verge of losing the game

Card-sharpener: *Person who cheats at cards to win money* * While having a bet at cards, one should be very watchful about the tricks of a card-sharpener

Card tricks: *Clever tricks with cards, hats, handkerchiefs, etc. to amuse the audience* * Many people gathered at a common place to see the card tricks of a conjurer

Care a straw for: *Consider of no value* * A true saint cares a straw for the worldly comforts

Care for: *Look after* * It is our duty to care for the interest of the old people

Carry all before one: *To bear down all obstacles* * A man of strength will carry all before one

Carry along: *Carry something* * He carried along the football till he scored a goal

Carry away: *To carry off; deprived of self-control by exciting the feelings; to transport; to inspire; demolish* * Smith carried away a good number of prizes in the annual sports competition * He was carried away by his enthusiasm to become a good pilot * The goods were carried away from one place to another by trucks * The captain carried away the soldiers with a spirit of high morale * The shipments were carried away during the storm

Carry coals to Newcastle: *Superfluous action; to take a thing where it is already most abundant* * It will be like carrying coals to Newcastle if we were to feed those who are already well-fed * Selling ice to the people in hilly areas is like carrying coals to Newcastle

Carry conviction: *Fit to be believed* * The threat of a general strike by the workers carries little conviction

Carry fire and sword: *Cause destruction* * Pakistan army carried fire and sword in East Pakistan in 1971

Carry it off well: *Make a brave show* * Though he was caught in an awkward situation, he carried it off well

Carry it/Carry it away/Carry the day: *Succeed; win* * He carried the day by winning over the hearts of the audience by his melodious songs

Carry off: *To win; gain; to cause the death of; to cause to bear examination; be well enough* * He carried off most of the prizes in the athletic championship * The murder of a woman carried him off to the gallows * He was successful while carrying off an acid test for a higher post * Even in the face of a troublesome situation, he carried himself and honourably

Carry off one's feet: *Be wild with excitement* * He was carried off his feet when he got the news that he had topped the entrance examination

Carry off the bell: *To have or gain the first place* * In the

Olympic Games, America is normally expected to carry off the bell in the medals tally

Carry off with high hand: *Behave impertinently* * He tends to carry off with high hand when moving in the high society

Carry on: *Manage; proceed; perform* * Rising costs are making it tough to carry on the business smoothly * He is carrying on well with his research work * In spite of disturbances, he hopes to carry on with his studies

Carry one's point: *To gain what one contends for; to defeat one's adversary in debate; to secure one's object* * He insisted on carrying his point even in the teeth of strong opposition * He carried his point on the strength of his skill in argument * By hook or crook he carried his point in defeating his rivals

Carry on regardless: *Carry on despite everything* * He carried on his campaign in spite of many obstacles

Carry out: *To put into practice* * The experiments carried out for application of new medicines have proved quite successful

Carry over: *Induce to join the other party* * Opportunist politicians tend to carry over the opposition party if offered a lucrative position

Carry someone out bodily: *Lift someone up and carry* * We will have to carry him out bodily as he swooned and fell unconscious

Carry the day: *Win* * The West Indies cricket team carried the day by defeating the Australians in the final

Carry the torch: *To suffer unrequited love* * It is useless to carry the torch for a girl who is already engaged to some other person

Carry the war into the enemy's camp: *To take the offensive boldly* * A good commander would prefer carrying the war into the enemy's camp

Carry the world before one: *To pass through every obstacle to success* * A man of determination can carry the world before him

Carry through: *Being safely out of difficulty* * He will manage to carry himself through under unfavourable circumstances

Carry too far: *To continue beyond reasonable limits* * There was no force in his arguments yet he was carrying things too far

Carry weight: *To possess authority; to have force* * Whatever we think of his ability, it does not carry weight * The statement made in support of the accused did not carry weight

Carrying into execution: *Bring into force* * The new laws will be carried into execution from the beginning of the next month

Carve out: *To gain by one's exertions; to hew out* * He carved out for himself a bright future by dint of hard work * The sculptor carved out a very nice statue of Lord Krishna from a piece of marble

Cash flow: *Money coming in and out of business* * There is always a game of cash flow in all business houses

Cash in on: *Make a lot of money; take advantage of* * Unscrupulous persons try to cash in on a person's weak position

Cast a boat adrift: *Let a boat float without control* * They had to cast a boat adrift as it was of no use to them

Cast a chill over: *Depressing influence* * The tragic piece of event cast a chill over the entire gathering

Cast a column of figure: *Add up* * While casting a column of figures, please be careful that no error crops in

Cast a horoscope nativity: *To make an astrological calculation* * Many people approach an astrologer to cast a horoscope nativity they are likely to go through

Cast a spell on: *To put under an enchantment* * The magician cast a spell on the audience by his tricks

Cast a vote: *Make a vote* * In a democracy, citizens have the right to cast a vote in the elections

Cast about: *To contrive; to look about; to search for* * He is casting about for an excuse to prove his innocence * He is casting about for an honest person who would help him in his business * He is casting about for a plan to live on a small income

Cast accounts: *Do sums* * If you find any difficulty in casting accounts, you can take my help

Cast an eye: *Cast a glance* * To cast an eye on the fair sex is improper

Cast anchor: *To anchor a ship* * They cast anchor in the river to prevent the ship from moving

Cast aside: *Laid aside; anything thrown aside; give up using; abandon* * Cast aside all the material that is useless * The authorities have now cast aside all hopes of tracing the missing aircraft

Cast aspersions on: *Make unfavourable remarks on* * The boss has the right to cast aspersions on the conduct of his juniors in their confidential report

Cast away: *Shipwrecked person; to wreck; to waste* * Castaways marooned on a desert island did not know where to find food * A forlorn person finds his life of little account and prefers to cast it away * We should be careful not to cast away anything that could be of value to us

Cast back: *To revert* *Do not cast him back from his present post on flimsy grounds

Cast down: *Depressed in mind* * He need not be harassed as he is already cast down by the responsibilities of a large family

Cast in one's lot with: *Share the fortunes of* * My friend has cast in his lot with his partners in the new venture

Cast in one's teeth: *To fling at one as a taunt or reproach; calculate* * You better resist from casting in your teeth on unimportant matters * He is in the habit of casting in his teeth into the conduct of others

Cast loose: *To set loose or adrift; detach oneself* * The boat was cast loose as it was being driven by high winds * It is not easy to cast loose from the grip of law

Cast lots: *Draw lots in order to reach a decision* * They cast lots to declare the owner of the plots

Cast not a clout till May be out: *Throw off; get rid of* * Do not squander away your savings without waiting for more to come as it has been rightly said that cast not a clout till May be out

Cast of features: *Type (quality of features):* Most of the weddings are settled on the basis of cast of features of both the bride and the bridegroom

Cast of mind: *Quality of mind* * Before offering someone a high post, it is a pre-requisite to ensure one's cast of mind

Cast off: *Laid aside; rejected; anything thrown aside* * I have cast off the old clothes and got new ones to wear * The ideas given by the junior executive were simply cast aside by the commanding officer

Cast oil on troubled waters: *Pacify a bad situation* * Nobody can cast oil on troubled waters when the enmity runs very deep

Cast on: *Make stitches; give a part in play to someone* * Using 4mm needles he cast on only 80 stitches * He will be cast in the play as considered fit for his age and features

Cast oneself adrift: *Separate oneself* * He cast himself adrift from his kith and kin when annoyed at everybody

Cast sheep's eyes: *Glance amorously* * He cast sheep's eyes on her before he took the second step of making advances to woo her

Cast out: To quarrel * Let us not cast out over an issue which does not concern us

Cast pearls before a swine: *Offer something beautiful to those who cannot appreciate it* * To sing a sweet song to a deaf person is like casting pearls before a swine.

Cast to the winds: *To scatter; throw away; to throw off all restraints* * The farmer cast to the winds the seeds behind the plough * The terrorist cast safely to the winds when hurling a grenade on the crowd * I did cast to the winds my patience despite being very angry

Cast up: *Throw up; bring up or mention* * He cast up some new points * He cast up new ideas on the problem not known earlier

Cast water: *To inspect urine in diagnosis* * Athletes are bound to cast water to check if they are free from any kind of drug effects or doping

Castle in the air/Castle in Spain: *Daydream; visionary projects* * He is only building castles in the air to become a king of kings * It would be building castles in the air if we try to wipe out poverty.

Casual labour: *Workers taken on for a very short period* * You can get this minor job done by casual labor

Cat's paw: *Make somebody a fool* * The queen was clever enough to make a cat's paw of the minister

Cat and dog life: *Constantly quarrelsome life* * Due to some misunderstanding, the husband and wife are leading a cat and dog life these days

Cat is a good mouser: *Good at catching mice* * The cat is a good mouser and keeps the house free from rats

Catapult launching gear: *Mechanism on an aircraft*

carrier for sending an aircraft into the air * Experiments on catapult launching gear are in progress

Catch a glimpse: *See* * We can catch a glimpse of the whole city from the clock tower

Catch a Tartar in him: *Find one formidable than one expects* * I am afraid you have caught a Tartar in him as he is not likely to give in easily

Catch at: *Seize* * The young man will catch at her wig and pull it off

Catch at a straw: *Resort to an inadequate remedy in dispersion* * A drowning man catches at a straw to save himself

Catch cold: *To contract a cold* * I caught cold as I got exposed to the chill outside

Catch fire: *To become ignited; take fire; to become aroused about something* * There are many inflammable objects which can catch fire very easily * Guard yourself against catching fire in case the hoodlums play mischief

Catch flame: *Start burning* * Avoid taking the matchstick near the papers as they can catch flame easily

Catch for: *Provide for* * The confectioner has to catch for ice-cream and cold drinks at the wedding of my friend

Catch napping: *To catch someone unawares* * The servant was caught napping by the master and rebuked

Catch on: *Understand* * I could not catch on the reason for the quarrel between two friends

Catch one out: *Detect one making mistake* * The supervisor is likely to catch him out if the clerk is caught napping

Catch out: *Dismissed* * The batsman was caught out at the slip by the fielder

Catch phrase: *Popular phrase* * We can see many catch phrases in advertisements published in newspapers

Catch red-handed: *Catch someone doing something wrong* * The thief was caught red-handed and handed over to the police

Catch sight of: *To get a glimpse of* * I could catch sight of the President escorted by a cavalcade

Catch someone on the hop: *Find someone unexpectedly* * He caught the flying squad on the hop

Catch someone unaware: *By surprise/unexpected* * While he was walking through a rough hilly track, he saw a snake that caught him unaware

Catch the breath: *Stop breathing for a moment; stop breathing out of fear* * We were forced to catch our breath when we saw an explosion occur

Catch the eye: *Be very noticeable* * She puts on fancy dresses that catch the eyes of everybody

Catch up: *To overtake; be in time for* * The accident took place when the truck driver tried to catch up the car running ahead * He was away from school for a month so now he is working hard to catch up with the other students

Catch up/Catch away: *To snatch or seize hastily* * He is liable to catch up and snatch the letter from my hand

Catch up with: *Hold the same level with or go side by side* * John and Smith are both catching up with each other in the class

Catch what one says: *Hear what one says* * I did not catch what he said to me since my attention was elsewhere

Catch-as-catch-can: *A style of wrestling in which any hold is allowed* * Both the wrestlers adopted a catch-as-catch-can trick to win

Catch-phrase: *A phrase repeated by one mouth to another* * An acid test is a catch-phrase used when one has to face a very tough test of any kind

Cattle do not die from crow's cursing: *Wishing ill will or destruction of others gets never materialized* * What is the point of cursing them because cattle do not die from crow's cursing

Cause a flutter: *Create a sensation* * It caused a flutter when a cobra appeared in a street

Cause someone grievous bodily harm: *Attack someone and beat him up* * The robbers caused him grievous bodily harm and ran away

Caution money: *Money paid in advance as security for good behaviour* * He was set free on payment of caution money by the magistrate

Cave in: *To slip; to fall into a hollow; to yield to outside pressure; to give way; to collapse; surrender under pressure* * Due to heavy rains, the highway caved in and blocked the thoroughfare * The road has caved in at many places and it needs to be repaired * The roof of the tunnel caved in and as such traffic has been closed

* The bridge over the river caved in and it is now under repair

Cavil at: *Object to something* * I don't see there is any reasonable cause to cavil at because she has not caused you any bodily harm

Chalk out: *To trace out; to plan* * When in a foreign land, one has to chalk out the route on a map * We have chalked out our programme for the coming vacation

Chance upon: *Find by chance* * I chanced upon an old friend in the street yesterday

Chance-comer: *One who comes by chance* * We extended all possible help to the chance-comer who got stranded on his way

Chanceful: *Full of risk* * As the journey ahead was chanceful we had to retreat

Chanceless: *Without an opportunity* * It is, as a matter of fact, a chanceless job for further promotion

Change colour: *To blush; turn pale* * When found guilty, she changed colour * When the teacher took the student to task for stealing a book, he changed colour

Change hands: *To pass to other ownership* * This car has changed hands recently

Change into: *Become; develop* * The tadpole will gradually change into a frog

Change of venue: *Change of place of trial* * There is a change of venue for the seminar from the conference room

Change one's coat: *Take another instead* * India has not changed its coat as far as India's stand on Kashmir is concerned

Change one's mind: *To form a different opinion* * One should not change one's mind very frequently

Change one's skin: *To undergo impossible change in character* * A committed dacoit would hardly change his skin

Change one's note: *To change from joy to sorrow; to change one's manner of speaking* * He changed his note as soon as he saw trouble brewing * After the death of his only son, he has completely changed his note when talking to his subordinates

Change one's tune: *To alter one's attitude or way of talking* * He is very clever in changing his tune when he sees that his words are not pleasing to the other person

Change-over: *Transition to a new system* * There has been a change-over in the style of governance in Iraq

Change train: *Get off one train to catch another* * While on my way to home town I had to change train twice

Changing-piece: *A fickle person* * Smith is a changing-piece and hence he is not reliable

Chant the praise of: *Constantly praise* * He is always chanting the praise of his own bravery in the battle-field

Chapter and verse: *The exact reference to the passage of the authority of one's statement; full and precise reference* * I do not want chapter and verse of the event as just a rough idea will serve my purpose * He has given chapter and verse for whatever he has stated in his books

Chapter of accidents: *Unforeseen course of events; series of accidents* * We cannot avoid the chapter of accidents we have to meet within our life

Charge against: *Fault against* * What is the charge against him?

Charge on: *Blame* * Theft was charged on the new maid-servant

Charged with: *Accuse of* * The old servant was charged with theft

Charge oneself with: *Entrust with; undertake* * He was charged with a mission to serve the cause of mentally challenged children * The account officer was charged with the task of keeping the accounts

Charge-sheet: *A police list of accused and the charges against him* * The police have produced a charge-sheet against the arrested person before the magistrate

Charity begins at home: *Charity is due first to kith and kin* * Practice virtue at home and then preach it to others because after all charity begins at home

Cheat the gallows: *To deserve but escape hanging* * The murderer is lucky to escape because he could cheat the gallows

Check-in/Check-out: *Record one's arrival, departure from work* * To keep a record of check-in/check-out of the visitors is mandatory for the hotel owners

Check-up: *A testing; scrutiny* * He has gone to see the doctor for a routine check-up * The accounts of the club are under check-up by the auditor

Check over: *Look over something* * I have checked over the accounts maintained by my assistant

Cheek by jowl: *Very close to each other; side by side* * For many years the buildings stood cheek by jowl till they were demolished and rebuilt

Cheer to the echo: *To applaud most heartily* * The speaker of the house was cheered to the echo by all members of Parliament

Cheer up: *Be happy* * I will go to cheer up my friend who is feeling very depressed

Chew the cud: *To masticate food that has already been swallowed and passed into the stomach; to ponder* * Animals living on grass or vegetables chew the cud in order to digest the food * In discussions, we chew the cud over the problems and work out a possible solution

Chew the rag/Chew the fat: *To keep on arguing on the point* * It is useless to chew the rag/fat without coming to a definite conclusion

Chicken-hearted: *With no courage* * A chicken-hearted person should not join the army as he is too weak in heart to face the enemy

Chicken out: *Back out of a fight or argument because one is afraid* * A coward may challenge anybody but he would chicken out when confronted by the opponent

Chicken is off: *Not available* * If chicken is off here, you can give us goat meat

Child's play: *Something very easy to do* * It is not a child's play to succeed in the IAS examination

Chime in: *To join in; in agreement* * He is very much interested to chime in the talks of others * I think your plan will chime in with mine

Chip in: *Contribute* * He will certainly chip in towards the charity fund

Chip of the old block: *One with the characteristics of his father* * The US President George Bush was really a chip of the old block

Chip off: *Break off* * He chipped off a piece from the rim of a cup

Chip on one's shoulders: *A defiant, challenging manner* * He has a chip on his shoulders and would never yield to any kind of pressure

Chipping: *Small bits of stones* * The chippings are used to make roads

Chock-full: *Completely full* * The marketplace was a chock-full with vegetables

Choice peaches: *Peaches which have been specially selected* * I have bought choice peaches which are very tasty

Choke off: *Get rid of; make (person) relinquish an attempt* * I do not know how to get myself choked off the accusations alleged against me * Out of prejudice, my boss has choked me off from the new project

Choke up: *Fill completely; block up* * We felt choked up in the hall as the power was switched off * The drain was choked up with mud

Choose sides: *To pick teams* * The names of players who will choose their sides will be announced by next Monday

Chop and change: *Be inconsistent* * He is always chopping and changing his opinions

Chop down: *Cut down with an axe* * The wood-cutter chopped down a very large tree in the forest

Chop off: *Cut off* * The dacoit chopped off the fingers of the captive

Chop on: *To cut up into tiny bits* * The butcher will have to chop off a piece of meat to give to his customer

Chop out: *Pick up from a greater number* * She took a long time to chop out her hat

Chuck out: *Turn out* * One of the members in the house who began to shout in protest was chucked out by the order of the Speaker

Chuck up: *Give up* * I have chucked up the menial job and will join the military service

Citric fruit: *Fruit such as orange, lemon or grape* * Many of the citric fruits contain healthy vitamins

Civil rights: *Rights of a citizen* * Civil rights are protected by the law of the land

Civil services: *All government departments except for the Armed Forces* * The government runs its administration through the civil services comprising numerous employees

Civil war: *War between two parties of one country* * In America, there was a civil war before it became United States of America

Clamp down on: *To stop petty crimes, etc.* * The authorities clamped down on the agitating workers.

Clap eyes on: *To set sight on* * I have yet to clap my eyes on my old friend since we left school

Clap hold of: *To seize roughly* * The policeman is likely to clap hold of the thief and take him to the police station

Clap on the back: *Slap so in encouragement* * The tutor gave me a clap on my back while appreciating my success in the exam

Clap one's hand: *Applaud by striking palms together loudly* * The audience clapped their hands in appreciation of the melodious song sung by the artist

Claptrap: *Empty words* * The meeting ended in a claptrap without any concrete decision being taken

Clarion call: *Loud clear call* * The clarion call made the regiment alert and ready to attack

Classified information: *Information which is officially secret* * No one is allowed to leak out the classified information

Claw me and I'll claw thee: *Favour me and I shall do you good in return* * It is but natural that you claw me and I claw thee

Clean hands: *Freedom from guilt or corruption* * We must fight for clean hands in every walk of life

Clean slate: *A fresh start* * I vow to start my life on a clean slate

Clear of: *Free from* * Keep clear of bad company

Clear one's throat: *Give a short cough* * Before starting his speech, he cleared his throat

Clear the air: *Simplify the situation and relieve tension* * It would be wise to clear the air by having a healthy discussion

Clear the table: *Remove dirty plates; knives, etc. after a meal* * To set the table for dinner, it is necessary to ask the maid to clear the table

Clear the way: *To make way* * We must bring about a workable education system to clear the way for imparting purposeful and qualitative education

Clear up: *To make clear* * The misunderstanding can be cleared up by a frank discussion

Clinch an argument: *Conclude or settle finally* * Discussion on the bargain was followed with an agreement that clinched the argument for good

Cling to: *Stick to* * True friends tend to cling to each other through thick and thin

Clip the wings: *To deprive of the means of rising* * She is acting big and needs her wings to be clipped before she crosses the limit

Clock in/out: *Record your time of arrival or departure* * Workers in the factory are required to clock in and out

Close a bargain: *To make an agreement* * They have managed to close a bargain to set up a new factory

Close bargain: *Stop speaking* * The quarrel on the property has brought the brothers to a close bargain

Close circuit television: *Private television operating over a small area by cable* * Our shops are linked through close circuit television

Close down: *To come to a standstill; stoppage of work; give up business* * The factory was closed down because of non-availability of raw material * We had to close down our factory for two days on account of holidays * The company has been closed down for its fraudulent dealings

Close-fisted man: *A miser* * You should not expect even a single penny from him as he is a close-fisted man

Close in upon: *To surround and draw near to* * The enemy closed in upon us in the battlefield at night

Close on: *Near* * She is close on turning forty years of age

Close one's days: *Die* * The patient closed his days at the age of eighty

Close season: *Season when hunting is forbidden* * In the close season the animals may breed

Close shave: *Narrow escape* * We had a close shave when our car struck against a tree

Close to: *Just near* * My college is close to the railway station

Close watch on someone: *Watch someone attentively* * Safety staff is appointed in factories to keep a close watch on the visitors

Close with: *To accede to; to grapple with; accept* * Sometimes discretion lies in closing with the enemy * To disperse the agitating crowd, the police had to close with them and fire tear gas * I could not close with his offer

Closed shop: *A place of work where workers have to belong to a single union* * A strike has been declared by the closed shop against fresh taxes

Closing hours: *Last hours* * In the closing hours of the Parliament session, the members of the house extended a vote of thanks to the Speaker

Clothe face in smiles: *Express ideas in words* * He hit upon a new plan and clothed his face in smiles to give it a practical shape

Clothe in words: *To express in words* * He could not clothe his sentiments in words out of emotion

Clothes horse: *Wooden frame used for drying clothes* * We make use of our clothes horse for drying the wet clothes

Cock-a-doodle doo!: *Noise made by a cock* * The children feel amused when they hear the cock say 'cock-a-doodle doo'

Cock a snook at: *Make a rude gesture at someone* * It is very bad manners to cock a snook at another person

Cock-and-bull story: *Imaginary or false story* * He invented a-cock-and-bull story to justify his absence from the office

Cock at the loft: *The head or chief of a set* * The sun can be called the cock at the loft amongst the other planets

Cock of the walk: *A person who thinks he is the most important in a group* * The bridegroom was cock of the walk during the wedding procession

Cock one's eyes: *Glance knowingly* * A vagabond was beaten black and blue for cocking his eyes at a married lady

Cock one's hat: *Set it on a slant; turn up the brim* * He cocked his hat to attract the attention of the man in the chair

Cock up: *Do badly* * We don't want to cock the whole thing up

Cockles of the heart: *The heart itself; one's feeling* * I conveyed my good wishes and blessings to the newly-wed couple from the cockles of my heart * The news of her winning the first prize warmed the cockles of my heart

Cock-sure: *Quite sure* * I am cock-sure about the success of this project

Cock up: *Make a mess of; to upset* * They completely cocked up the arrangement for our holiday

Code word: *Secret agreed word* * The detectives make use of a code word which can be understood only by them

Coincide in: *Be in agreement* * The judge did not coincide in the opinion on the judgement

Coincide with: *Be in harmony; happen at the same time* * His tasks and habits coincide with those of his wife * Both the friends could not go to the theatre as their free time did not coincide with each other's

Coin money: *Earn large sums easily* * He is coining money through his roaring business

Cold as charity: *A proverbial phrase expressing coldness or indifference* * The rich should not be cold as charity towards the poor

Cold war: *An intense or remorseless struggle for gaining the upper hand by all means short of actual fighting* * Before disintegration of USSR, there was a cold war between both the Super Powers

Colour bar: *Objection to persons because of the colour of their skin* * During colonial rule, the British Government brought into force the colour bar while offering prestigious posts to its men

Come a cropper: *To have a fall* * She slipped and came a cropper on her backside

Come about: *Happen in the course of time* * How did it come about that I lost control on the steering wheel?

Come across: *Occur to; find or meet by chance* * The thought came across my mind that I should have helped the poor * I came across my old friend in a street of the town

Come amiss: *Be unwelcome* * It would come amiss if I point out your errors before other people

Come and go: *To fluctuate; to have freedom of action* * Electricity in the town comes and goes very often * Wild animals would come and go of their own accord in natural surroundings

Come apart: *Fall to pieces* * The lid and the pot came apart when they slipped from my hands

Come at: *To reach* * In spite of putting our heads together, we could not come at a unanimous decision

Come away empty: *To come away without having received* * He came away empty from the contest he participated in the hope of winning a prize

Come back: *To return to popularity* * He will come back on winning the general elections

Come by: *To come near; to pass; to obtain; get* * A stranger came by to enquire about the location of the post office * He had a narrow escape when a car came by at a very high speed * Jobs are very hard to come by these days * How did you come by that watch?

Come clean: *Confess to a crime* * At last, the accused came clean on the crime he had committed

Come down: *To descend; to be reduced* * The rain came down in torrents * He has had to make a come down from his original high position

Come down upon: *To be severe with* * The headmaster came down upon the mischievous boy like a ton of bricks

Come down with: *To pay down* * I had to come down with a substantial amount for the charity home

Come forward: *Offer or present oneself; become available* * No witness to the accident has come forward * Due to unemployment a large number of candidates have come forward for the post.

Come high: *To cost much* * Due to inflation in the market, the cost of living has come high

Come home: *To return to one's house; to touch one's feelings* * He came home after completing his studies abroad * The stupidity of his behaviour came home to him rather late

Come home to roost: *Recoil upon oneself* * He wandered from place to place but at last he had to come home to roost

Come in: *To enter; to give in; to yield* * Please come in and see for yourself the new furniture I purchased recently * Rebels were forced to come in unconditionally * He came into temptation and lost his money in a bet

Come in for: *To receive; to receive incidentally* * She has come in for a fortune after her wedding to a rich young man

Come into: *To fall heir to* * Following the death of his father, he came into all the property of the deceased

Come into one's head: *Strike while searching* * While searching in my pockets for the purse, it did come into my head that I could have placed it in my overcoat

Come into one's own: *Receive what rightly belongs to one* * The runner in the last lane was trailing initially, but when he came into his own, he beat all the runners

Come into play: *Come into exercise; come into operation or use* * The task of conducting attack on the enemy will be coming into play shortly * The airbus flight will come into play the moment the sky is clear * The electric power comes into play to run various machines

Come into the world: *Be born* * Whatever comes into this world has to end too

Come low: *To cost little* * The production cost has come low because of the excess of raw material

Come of: *To descend from; become of* * He comes of a noble family * He promised to help but I don't think anything will come of it

Come of age: *To reach full legal age* * Any person who comes of age is eligible for getting a government job

Come off: *To come away; to turn out; to escape* * The wooden handle of the axe came off when I was trying to fell a tree * He really did not deserve to come off as the winner * A button has come off my coat

Come off second best: *Be defeated* * In the declamation contest he came off second best.

Come off with flying colours: *Achieve outstanding distinction* * My friend has come off with flying colours in the admission test

Come on: *Hurry* * Come on you lazy fellow, we are getting late for school

Come on stream: *Start to produce or function* * The mill is likely to come on stream next week

Come one's way: *To come in the same direction; to become attainable* * During the course of my long journey, many new sights came my way * One can learn a lot and make much of the experience from whatever comes into way

Come out: *To result; to be published; to become known or evident* * You have come out well in that photograph * When will his new book come out? * The news about every event comes out in the newspapers

Come out in the wash: *Be made clear in due course* * The matter is under investigation and the true picture will certainly come out in the wash

Come out with: *To utter; to exclaim* * He came out with a most extraordinary story about the time he spent in his exile * The champion has come out with challenge for a bout in boxing

Come over: *Come from a distance; change opinion; start to feel* * When would you come over to Delhi for a holiday? * He will never come over to our side in the debate *

What has come over him?

Come round: *Recover; agree* * I hope he will come round very soon * At last my friend came round to my views

Come short: *To fail; be insufficient* * He came short of expectations on the debate * The box-office receipts came short of the manager's expectations

Come short of: *To fail to attain* * I was surprised to know that he came short of winning a gold medal in the race

Come to: *To obtain to; recover consciousness or sanity* * Lara came to his real form after the first match * Constant care and good treatment by the medical staff help patients to come to their consciousness

Come to a head: *Reach a crisis* * The increase in population has come to a head in India and China

Come to a halt: *Stop* * The train came to a halt at the railway station

Come to a head: *Reach a crisis* * The civil war may come to a head if the people continue to suffer from continuous dictatorship

Come to a standstill: *Come to a complete stop* * Due to a general strike, the office work has come to a standstill

Come to blows: *Start fighting* * Both the brothers came to blows while arguing over a trifle issue

Come to close quarters: *Come in collision with* * The police had to come to close quarters with the violent protestors

Come to fruition: *Bring about good results* * His sincere efforts came to fruition at last

Come to grief: *To meet with disaster* * You may come to grief if you do not follow my piece of advice

Come to hand: *To arrive* * The parcel came to hand through the courier

Come to heel: *Come in behind; to obey or follow like a dog* * I suddenly saw from the corner of my eye a bull coming to my heels * Wherever I may go, my pet dog comes to my heels

Come to life: *To become alive* * The man on the verge of death came to life after he was operated upon

Come to light: *To be revealed* * Through investigation, it came to light that it was not a case of suicide but of murder

Come to naught: *To come to*

nothing * All efforts of the team to score the winning goal came to a naught

Come to nothing: *To have little or no result; to turn out a failure* * All our efforts to save her life came to nothing * His plans to serve his own cause at the cost of others came to nothing

Come to one's hand: *To be found easy; to come to close quarters* * I have kept everything at a proper place so that it comes to my hand when the need arises * Keep these candle sticks in that niche so that these may come to everybody's hand when the power is off

Come to oneself: *Return to normal state of mind* * Due to a sun stroke he swooned but through timely treatment, he soon came to himself

Come to pass: *Happen* * I do not remember how it came to pass that I lost my memory while travelling in a train

Come to quarters: *Begin to fight* * The robbers came to quarters over distribution of booty among them

Come to rest: *Stop moving* * The car came to rest at the bottom of the hill

Come to senses: *Become reasonable* * I hope this severe warning will make him to come to his senses

Come to stay: *Become permanent* * Having established a business in the city, he has left the village to come to stay in the city

Come to terms: *To come to an agreement* * Both the parties have come to terms for starting a new project

Come to the fore: *Become prominent* * Many dark horses have come to the fore in the recent general elections

Come to the point: *Speak on the real questions* * Don't beat about the bush and come to the point in order to reach a conclusion

Come to the fore: *Become prominent* * He has come to the fore recently

Come to the front: *To become noticeable; become conspicuous* * When our car moved through the moors, many kinds of reptiles and wild animals came to the front * Lata Mangeshkar came to the front as a singer of melodious songs

Come true: *To be fulfilled* * His dream to become a millionaire will come true as he is hardworking

Come under: *Be under authority or control* * Maintenance of law and order comes under police jurisdiction

Come unstruck: *Go badly wrong* * Our plan to beat our rivals came unstruck

Come up: *To present itself (in discussion)* * A new point came up before the committee while discussing certain arrangements to be carried out in the town

Come up to scratch: *Satisfy; get ready* * Will your teacher manage you to come up to scratch before you take the examination?

Come up with: *To overtake* * He came up with the necessary answers to my queries

Come upon: *To attack; to affect; to hold answerable* * The disaster that has come upon them has ruined their life * The rough weather has come upon the construction of a new building * A great responsibility would come upon you if you are elected the leader

Comfortably off: *Having plenty of money* * Having earned more than enough, he is now comfortably off so long for the rest of his life

Commend me to: *Remember me kindly to* * Whenever you happen to meet the boss in private do commend me to him about the new plan I had chalked out

Commence on: *Start on* * The annual examinations will commence on 15th April

Commence with: *Start with* * He commenced his speech with an apology for being late

Commit oneself: *Make oneself responsible; admit what one has done* * He has committed himself to support his deceased brother's children * He refused to commit himself by talking about the crime

Commit no nuisance: *Do not defile a place* * We should commit no nuisance around holy places.

Commit to memory: *Learn by heart* * He has committed the whole poem to memory

Comminuted fracture: *The breaking of a bone in several places* * The patient with comminuted fracture has been admitted into the hospital for treatment

Common run of men: *Ordinary people* * Common run of men can easily be wooed by a politician through sugar-coated words

Common sense: *Ordinary good sense* * It is a matter of common sense to give due respect to our elders

Communicating door: *Door which links two rooms* * Our

rooms have a communicating door

Communicating rooms: *Room with a connected door* * My friend and I are staying in a communicating room

Commuter train: *Train for commuters* * Persons who travel in a town or a city every day can make use of a commuter train

Compare notes: *To exchange views* * I have compared notes with my colleagues before undertaking the new scheme

Compatible with: *Consistent with* * Your actions are not compatible with your words

Compensate for: *Make up for* * He is bound to compensate for your loss

Compilation of a contract: *Signing of a contract* * On compilation of a contract the parties deposited the necessary amount for running a new project

Complain of: *Tell about one's pain* * Now-a-days, he often complains of acute pain in the chest

Complain against to: *Statement comprising wrong/suffering* * The head clerk complained to his boss against the rude behaviour of a junior staff

Compliance with: *According to* * In compliance with my wishes, he has withdrawn his resignation

Compliments of the season: *Compliments to suit the time* * There is always an exchange of compliments of the season amongst the near and dear ones

Complimentary ticket: *Free ticket* * Complimentary tickets have been issued to a few eminent guests to a cinema show

Compose oneself: *Be calm* * During the course of an interview one should compose oneself

Concede to: *Grant to* * I cannot concede to your demands at this moment

Conceive of: *Imagine of* * I cannot conceive of such an event taking place

Concentration camp: *Camp where many political prisoners are held in captivity* * I do not know any particular place where a concentration camp has been set up

Concerned at: *Sorry for* * Your father is greatly concerned at your failure

Concerned for: *Anxious for* * I am deeply concerned for you as you are falling ill too frequently

Concerned in: *Implicated in* * Two hundred persons were concerned in the riots that broke out in the small village

Concur with: *Agree with* * I find it very difficult to concur with you on this point

Condensed milk: *Milk reduced by evaporation* * Condensed milk is a great convenience while travelling

Condescend upon: *To specify; to mention* * He is likely to condescend upon the advantages of yoga * Great philosophers have condescended upon the true values of life

Condole with: *Express sympathy to* * I had come here to condole with my friend upon the unfortunate death of his mother

Conducive to: *Helpful* * Reading is conducive to widening one's mental horizon

Conduct oneself: *Behave* * He did not conduct himself well in the debate

Conducted tour: *Tour led by a guide* * Students were taken on a conducted tour to places of historical importance

Confide in: *Trust in* * It is impossible for me to confide in him

Confer on: *Grant to* * An honorary doctorate was conferred on the distinguished scholar

Confer with: *Consult* * The minister did not confer with any of his staff before taking the crucial decision

Confirm to: *Follow to* * You will have to confirm to the rules of the club— This will have to be deleted as there is no sentence like this. Here it should be conform and not confirm

Confirm with: *Agree with* * I will need to confirm with him whether he is coming or not

Conformity with: *Accordance with* * The secretary issued an order in conformity with the rules and regulations

Confront someone with: *Bring someone face to face* * The fact that she had talked ill about me forced me to confront her with what she had said

Confusion compounded: *Make a thing all the more puzzling* * The fact that the twin sisters were dressed in identical clothes compounded the confusion

Congenial to: *Suitable to* * This climate is congenial to my health

Congratulate someone: *Give good wishes* * He congratulated me on my success in getting promotion

Conjuring tricks: *Clever tricks with cards, hats, handkerchiefs, etc. to amuse the audience* * Many people walked away while the conjurer was busy conjuring tricks

Conk out: *Stop working* * If you do not use oil for lubrication, the engine is sure to conk out

Connected to: *Relate to* * My friend is connected to a rich and respectable family

Conscience-smitten: *Filled with remorse* * Do not tease him any further as he is already conscience-smitten

Conscientious objector: *A person who refuses to join the armed forces because he feels war is wrong* * He is a conscientious objector and would never yield to any pressure

Consist in: *Reside in* * True happiness consists in contentment

Consist of: *Contain* * This book consists of fifteen chapters

Consort with: *To spend time in company of; be in harmony* * A criminal will only consort with other criminals * His action does not consort with his exhortation

Content with: *Satisfied with* * Be content with what you have

Contentment is greatest happiness: *Satisfaction and peace of mind keeps one pleased* * It is admitted on all hands that contentment is the greatest happiness

Contend with: *Fight with* * You have to contend with a strong opposition

Contradiction in terms: *A contradicting statement* * If we say 'a generous miser', then it is obviously a contradiction in terms

Contribute to: *To help towards; give to; cause to* * He contributed his ideas with regard to educational reforms * People generously contribute to the Red Cross fund * Drink contributed to his ruin

Convenience food: *Dishes which are easy or quick to prepare* * Whenever we are very hungry, we arrange for convenience food

Conversant with: *Familiar with* * He is not at all conversant with English manners

Convert to: *Turn to* * I am trying to convert him to my way of thinking

Convicted of: *Charged with* * The old servant was convicted of theft

Convince someone of: *Make someone believe* * I will need to convince him to join the navy

Cook the books: *Falsify the entries in the account books* * I reckon they have cooked the books

Cool head: *Calm judgement* * Most of our problems can be solved if we think with a cool head

Cool one's heels: *To be kept waiting* * Let him cool his heels outside the office till he learns to behave

Cope with: *Manage with* * I am unable to cope with such a heavy workload

Coping stone: *Top stone on a wall which protects it from the weather* * A high wall surrounding a jail is protected by coping stone

Cordon bleu: *Top quality (cooking)* * This restaurant has become famous for its cordon bleu

Cordon off: *Separate or keep at a distance from the police or soldiers* * After a bomb explosion, the affected area was cordoned off

Corporate plan: *Overall plan for a whole company* * A corporate plan has to be drawn up for running the big business house

Corn in Egypt: *Abundance* * India has brought about a revolution in food production, like corn in Egypt

Correspond with: *Write to* * I do not want to correspond with him as he writes very long-winded letters

Cost price: *The price the merchant pays* * The workers in the factory are permitted to buy their goods at cost price

Cost-free: *Free of charge* * The enterprises doing roaring business provide their employees cost-free board and lodging

Cotton on: *Understand* * I could not cotton on to his nods as I did not understand what he wanted to convey

Cotton up: *Make friendly advances* * He is trying to cotton up to that girl but she is turning a blind eye to him

Couch a spear: *To fix it in the rest at the side of the armour* * The warriors were getting ready to couch their spear when the enemy suddenly attacked them

Cough mixture: *Liquid medicine to cure a cough* * The doctor has given me this cough mixture to take daily

Count on/upon: *Depend on* * May I count on your help?

Count one's chickens before they are hatched: *Anticipate profit before due time* * A wise and a sober person never count his chickens before they are hatched

Counter-pace: *A contrary measure; a step in opposition to another* * India has been left with no option but to make counter-pace arrangements against a nuclear war

Coup d'etat: *Armed overthrow of a government* * There have been many coup d'etats in Pakistan

Coup the cran: *To upset* * You will coup the cran if you fail to act as per my plan

Courtesy car: *Free car waiting for hotel guests at an airport* * Top-class hotels place a courtesy car at the airport for their guests

Courtesy to someone: *To show respect* * We should show due courtesy to our elders

Cover into: *To transfer into* * The cheating case has been now covered into a case of robbery by the court of law

Cover the buckle: *To execute a certain difficult step in dancing* * It was a bitter experience to cover the buckle while dancing to a jazz

Cover the feet: *To defecate* * All living beings have to cover the feet at least twice a day

Cracking pace: *Very fast pace* * He earned name and fame at a cracking pace

Crack a bottle: *Open or drink a bottle* * He cracked a coke bottle to quench his thirst

Crack a crib: *To break into a building* * The robbers cracked a crib at midnight and looted cash and jewellery

Crack a joke: *To utter a joke with some effect* * He cracked a joke to amuse the audience

Crack credit: *To destroy one's credit* * The drunkard cracked credit that stood against his name in the bank

Crack down on: *Campaign against* * The police cracked down on the gamblers

Crack of doom: *Day of doom; in doomsday; the last trump (judgement)* * All living beings are subject to crack of doom

Crack up: *To fall apart; to fail suddenly; to go to pieces* * The brake of a bus cracked up and it collided into a tree * The overstressed teacher is likely to crack up under the strain of work

Crash barrier: *Strong fence by the side of a road to protect motor cyclists from running off the road* * The crash barrier at dangerous places on the road work as a safety guide

Crash course: *Very rapid course* * A crash course has been arranged for teachers to impart new teaching skills to them

Crash helmet: *Helmet worn by motorcyclists to protect them in case of a crash* * A motorcyclist must use a crash helmet for safety purposes

Crash into: *To hit in an accident* * The bus crashed into a tree

Crave for/after: *Desire for* * Never crave for riches

Crazy paving: *Different shaped paving stones fitted together* * Our house has been linked with the main road by a crazy paving path

Cream of the graduates: *The top few* * The cream of the graduates have been able to get the job they had applied for

Create a diversion: *Do something to distract one's attention from another thing which one does not want one to see* * He ultimately created a diversion to fool you about the real picture

Creature comforts: *Material comforts* * Human beings have been seeking creature comforts throughout their lives

Credit someone with: *To attribute a quality, etc. to someone* * Until now I have always credited you with good sense

Crestfallen: *Dejected or cast down* * My friend was crestfallen for very long on failing in the entrance examination

Crick in the neck: *Sprain; pulled muscle in the neck* * I have been suffering from a crick in the neck

Criminal turned State's evidence: *Give information to court which proves that a person's accomplices were guilty* * The judge gave his verdict on hearing the criminal turned State's evidence

Crocodile tears: *False grief* * Everybody knew that he was shedding crocodile tears at the death of his uncle

Crock up: *Become or cause active to become* * The attack of influenza has crocked me up

Crop up: *Appear or arise* * The subject cropped up in the course of our conversation.

Cross-check: *Verify* * We better do a cross-check on all the statistical information

Cross-country: *A race field or country not on road or track* * He won the first cross-country race of the year easily

Cross-grained: *Bad-tempered* * I don't like to talk to him because he is a cross-grained person

Cross off/out: *Cancel* * I crossed his name off the list * Two of the words in the passage have been crossed out

Cross one's mind: *To flash across the mind* * It had not crossed my mind to tell my friends that I was leaving the town

Cross one's path: *Meet one* * I hope I shall never cross that man's path again

Cross question: *Cross examination* * If he had gone into the witness box, he would have been cross questioned on any evidence he gave

Cross somebody's palm with silver: *Give a coin to him* * I crossed the fortune-teller's palm with silver.

Cross swords: *Fight* * The rival groups crossed swords over a trifle issue

Cross swords with somebody: *Fight* * The two brothers crossed swords with each other on a property dispute.

Cross the Rubicon: *Take a decisive, irrecoverable step* * The principal told the rusticated student to leave as he had crossed the Rubicon

Crow over: *Triumph over* * It does not behove a brave person to crow over a fallen foe

Crow over someone: *Explain happily because one has beaten someone* * Hurrah! I have crowed over my rival in the match

Crown of the causeway: *The middle of the street* * My old school friend met me at the crown of the causeway after a gap of 15 years

Crowning achievement: *Grand accomplishment* * Credit must go to our scientists for their crowning achievement in the field of space technology

Crush a cup: *To empty a cup; to quaff (to drink or drain in large draughts)* * He crushed a cup of tea before he left for the office * He crushed a cup of wine at a reception

Crux of the matter: *Problem that is most difficult to solve* * The crux of the matter is that we have no option but to dissolve the issue

Cry against: *Protest against* * People will cry against the new taxation policy

Cry blue murder: *Shout loudly and in alarm* * He cried blue murder when he was bitten by a stray dog

Cry cupboard: *To cry for food* * Starvation makes everyone to cry cupboard

Cry down: *Condemn* * He was always crying down his son's irresponsible behaviour

Cry for the moon: *Make efforts for something impossible to be attained* * The poor man is thinking of buying a car, but it is like a cry for the moon as he does not have the means for it

Cry halves: *To claim half* * He cried halves on the moveable and the immoveable property of his ancestors

Cry in the wilderness: *A futile attempt which goes unheeded* *T o ask for charity from a miser would be to cry in the wilderness

Cry off: *Withdraw from something that one has undertaken* * I had promised to go but had to cry off at the last moment

Cry on: *To call upon* * If I need your help, I shall certainly cry on you

Cry one's eyes out: *To weep copiously (a lot)* * At the death of his mother, he cried his eyes out

Cry one's eye-tooth: *To cease to be a child* * Better stop crying your eye-tooth since you are a grown up man now

Cry oneself to sleep: *Cry until one falls sleep* * The baby cried himself to sleep

Cry out against: *Protest against* * We must cry out against hooliganism

Cry out: *Shout or explain* * He cried out in pain when the dentist pulled out his tooth

Cry out for: *Expression of alarm for a thing very much needed* * There is a vast surplus of workforce in our country crying out for employment

Cry over split milk: *To waste time in bemoaning what is irreparable* * It is no use crying over split milk because what is lost cannot be recovered

Cry quits: *Declare a thing even* * Both the parties cried it quits when they managed to pay each other in the same coin

Cry roast-meat: *To publish one's good luck foolishly* * We should not cry roast-meat if we are blessed with prosperity

Cry up: *Praise* * The people do cry him up for saving the drowning child

Cry wolf: *To give a false alarm* * The people knew that the shepherd boy was crying wolf so no one turned to his help

Cudgel one's brains: *Think hard* * He had to cudgel his brains to save his son from the clutches of the abductor

Cult hero: *Person worshipped by a group of admirers* * In India, there are many cult heroes belonging to different religions

Cultivate one's friendship: *To seek; to gain or foster one's friendship* * He has the ability to cultivate friendship with people who can be useful in his business

Cup final: *Final match for a football championship* * The Durand Cup final match between Mohammedan Sporting and Mohun Bagan is being played today

Cup tie: *Soccer match as a result of one team is eliminated from the championship* * The soccer match ended in a tie as a result of which the winner team had to be decided by cup tie

Cure for: *Treatment for* * There is no cure for this disease

Cure of: *Relieve of* * Who can cure me of my mental disability?

Curl up: *Be embarrassed; fall to the ground* * The blow curled him up completely * The cricket ball hit him on the head and he curled up with pain

Curious arts: *Magical practices* * He earns his living through a show of curious arts

Currency note: *Paper money* * The circulation of currency notes is facing a threat from plastic money

Current account: *A bank account to meet current expenses* * Businessmen usually keep a current account in the bank to draw money as soon as they want

Current affairs: *Things which are happening at the present moment* * We will have to deal with current affairs rather carefully

Curry favour: *To seek to ingratiate oneself* * He invited his boss to a sumptuous dinner to curry favour for further promotion

Curtain lecture: *Lecture or rebuke given by the wife to her husband in privacy* * Sometimes, he has no voice of his own but to listen to a curtain lecture of his wife and acts as she says

Cut a caper: *Jump about merrily* * The boy who came across a purse full of currency notes was overjoyed and began to cut a caper

Cut a dash: *Cut a figure; to make a conspicuous appearance* * He cut a dash to become the Prime Minister of India

Cut a figure: *To make a conspicuous appearance* * He cut a figure to become a lawyer by dint of his hard work

Cut a poor figure: *Produce a poor*

impression * During the course of cross-examination, the witness cut a poor figure

Cut a sorry figure: *Feel insulted; produce a poor result* * His brother cut a sorry figure in the entrance examination * She cut a sorry figure in the maiden speech and left the hall

Cut and carve: *To refine* * We need a roller and a mower to cut and carve a good playground

Cut and dry: *Cut and dried/ Readymade* * There is no cut and dry formula for success

Cut back: *Reduce expenditure, etc.* * The government has cut back funds under certain unimportant heads

Cut down: *Reduce* * We must economise and cut down on needless expenditure

Cut in one's teeth: *Fling at one as a taunt or reproach* * It would be a rude act if you cut your teeth on an innocent person

Cut it too fat: *To overdo a thing* * He cut it too fat when he took law and order in his hands

Cut no ice: *To count for nothing* * Your statement without evidence will cut no ice

Cut no ice with: *Have no effect or influence* * His lofty ideas could cut no ice with his listeners

Cut off: *To sever; to destroy; put to an untimely death* * He cut off a metre of cloth from the roll * The floods cut off a good deal of crops * The militants cut off the head of the village head

Cut off in bloom: *Destroy in its prime* * It is a pity that the gardener cut off the yellow roses in bloom

Cut off one's nose to spite one's face: *To injure oneself rather than fail to injure another* * You will cut off your nose to spite your face if you take law and order in your hands out of anger

Cut off with a shilling: *Bequeath only a shilling; disinherit* * He cut off his drunkard and loafer son with a shilling

Cut one's coat according to one's cloth: *To adapt oneself to circumstances* * Only those persons lead a pleasant life who cut their coat according to their cloth

Cut one dead: *Deliberately insult one* * He did cut me dead in the presence of my friends.

Cut one's eyes-tooth: *Cease to be a child* * He has since cut his eye-tooth so you can not befool him on any pretext

Cut one's losses: *To have done with an unprofitable matter* * The factory owner has expelled ten employees to cut his losses

Cut one's stick: *Take one's departure; go* * After a day's visit to our place, my friend cut his stick to attend to some urgent business elsewhere

Cut one short: *Interrupt one* * While he was speaking, his father cut him short.

Cut one's throat: *Pursue some course ruinous to one's interest* * You should not cut the throat of the poor boy by dismissing him from service

Cut out for: *Fitted naturally* * I am really not cut out for this type of mechanical job

Cut-price: *Cheap* * I bought cloth at cut-price from the market

Cut short: *Abridge; make shorter; to end something* * Due to paucity of time, the speaker had to cut short his topic of discussion * I did cut a long story short to save time * To answer the call of nature, he cut short the story he was telling to the children

Cut the Gordian knot: *Solve a very difficult problem* * It will certainly cut the Gordian knot if life is found on Mars

Cut the knot: *Overcome difficulty* * He managed to cut the knot by the dint of hard work.

Cut the painter: *To severe ties* * He has cut the painter with his partners with a view to carry out business independently

Cut the teeth: *To have the teeth grow through the gums* * The child is feeling uneasy since he is cutting the teeth

Cut the throat: *To cut the jugular vein* * The butcher himself cuts the throats of many goats every morning to meet the customers' demands

Cut up: *To cut into pieces; cause distress* * He has to have his food cut up for him * His mother's death has cut him up awfully

Cut up rough: *To take something amiss* * He will cut up rough if you do not give him what he asks for

Cycling three abreast: *Three bicycles side by side** I saw persons cycling three abreast on the highway

D

Dabble in politics: *Participate a bit in politics* * He is not a real politician but only dabbles in politics

Daily bread: *Livelihood* * Most of the workers have to earn their daily bread by toiling hard for the whole day.

Daily round: *Ordinary work of day* * Having completed my schedule of taking a daily round, I attend the night classes

Daily routine: *Things which you do daily* * My daily routine is to go for a walk early in the morning

Damocles' sword: *An impending danger* * The spread of terrorism on a global scale is hanging like a Damocles' sword over mankind's head

Damp squib: *Unsuccessful attempt to do something impressive* * The party turned out to be a damp squib

Damp-proof: *Resistant to wet* * Defence contingents are provided with damp-proof uniforms for use when needed

Dance attendance: *To wait assiduously* * The head clerk has to dance attendance to the wishes of his boss.

Dance attendance upon: *Wait on somebody always* * The head clerk dances attendance upon his officer to get a special increment

Dance in a net: *Act in imagined concealments* * He is dancing in a net with the dream to be a perfect match to the princess

Dance to one's tune: *Carry out orders* * The vice-principal always dances to the tune of the principal

Dance upon nothing: *To be hanged* * The murderer had to dance upon nothing in the early morning

Danger to life and limb: *Danger that you may be hurt* * May God save you from any danger to your life and limb

Dark horse: *Competitor of unknown capability* * Many dark horses have been elected in the general election

Darken one's door: *Visit one; to enter one's house* * I had to darken my friend's door for financial help * No one unknown to the owner of the house should darken his house without prior permission or information.

Dash off: *To throw off; leave abruptly; write something quickly and without thinking very much* * Please dash off the contents of the dustbin so that it is empty for rough papers * Seeing the danger ahead, he dashed off for a shelter * His essay seems to have been dashed off within minutes

Dash out: *To knock out by striking against something* * He dashed out his opponent with a strong punch in the seventh round of the boxing match.

Dashed to the ground: *Failed* * His high hopes to get good marks in the examination have been dashed to the ground

Dates from: *Existed since* * This building dates from AD 1500

Dawn on: *Become clear to* * At last the truth that his so-called friend was his foe dawned on him

Dawn on somebody: *Begin to realise* * The truth began to dawn on me about the advantages of good education

Day after the fair: *Too late* * One would have to meet with disappointment by reaching a day after the fair

Day before the fair: *Too early* * One feels rather surprised that he could manage to complete his work a day before the fair

Day before yesterday: *Two days before today* * He met me a day before yesterday in the market

Day-by-day/Day after day: *Every day; daily* * It is a natural process that we grow in age day by day till we breathe our last * I have to do this routine work day-by-day

Day in day out: *For an indefinite succession of days* * Information is coming day in and day out about the killing of innocent people by the terrorist

Day nursery: *Day care centre* * Most of the employed couples leave their babies in the day nursery

Day of reckoning: *Time when you have to pay for your mistake* * Everybody has to face the day of reckoning for one's evil deeds

Day off: *A day's holiday* * The government has declared a day off tomorrow in all offices to celebrate the Diwali festival

Day out: *A servant's free day; a*

day spent away from home for pleasure as a holiday * It is a day out for servants to-day, so we have to manage things for ourselves * We had a day out yesterday to enjoy a picnic

Day trip: *Journey lasting one day* * Even a day trip to the hill station is very enjoyable

Day-break: *Early morning* * I get up at day-break and go for a walk

Days are numbered: *Has not much time to live* * His days are numbered since the treatment is producing no response

Days of grace: *The days allowed for payment of bills, etc. beyond the day fixed* * The government has granted 30 days of grace to renew one's driving licence

Dead (set) against: *Utterly opposed to* * Many people in Pakistan are dead (set) against military rule

Dead alive: *Spiritless* * He is dead alive for appreciating the value of morals

Dead as a herring: *Quite certainly* * It is dead as a herring that this time he would be able to win a gold medal in the Olympic Games

Dead end: *Leading nowhere (street/way)* * The street lane has a dead end * The new project that he took in hand proved to be a dead end

Dead heat: *Race where two competitors stand equal* * The race was finished in a dead heat

Dead language: *A language no longer in use* * Latin has become a dead language in Europe

Dead letter: *Law; regulation that is no longer observed* * Anti-corruption official circular has for a long time remained a dead letter * He is dead to all feelings of shame

Deadline: *Date by which something has to be done* * I have set a deadline to complete this book

Dead loss: *Useless* * It will be a dead loss to sell of a car so cheap

Dead man's shoes: *Succession to one who dies* * After the demise of the principal, the vice-principal stepped into the dead man's shoes

Dead men tell us tales: *Killing of persons whose knowledge of a secret may cause loss or trouble* * We could only repent for the fact that dead men tell us tales

Dead of night: *Quite midnight* * Trekkers reached the camp at dead of night

Dead pan: *Not showing any*

emotion * He maintained a dead pan look on his face though he was deeply hurt

Dead thaw: *The agony of death* * The prisoner has been suffering from death thaw since the day he was awarded capital punishment

Dead to: *Without* * He is dead to all sense of honour so I always keep him at an arm's length

Dead weight: *Heavy and inert* * The ship has left the harbour with its dead weight

Dead-lock: *State where two sides cannot agree* * In many a family, the dowry has been the root cause of throwing a wedlock into a dead-lock

Dead-shot: *An unerring marksman* * He is a dead-shot in shooting the bull's eye with an arrow

Deaf mute: *Person who cannot hear or speak* * He stared at me as a deaf mute

Deaf of: *Disability of hearing* * My old grandfather is deaf of ear

Deaf to: *Not listen to* * He was deaf to my request

Deal by: *Treat* * The master deals by his servant cruelly

Deal in: *To trade in* * That man deals in cars

Deal with: *To take appropriate action in a particular situation* * We should not deal with anybody harshly

Death on: *To be fatal to; fond of; good at* * It may be a death on a person addicted to too much alcoholic drink * The children are death on hearing fairy tales * He has proved himself a death on mathematics

Death toll: *Number of deaths* * The death toll of innocent people in Kashmir runs into hundreds

Death-stroke: *A death blow; shock from which recovery is impossible* * The doctor could not save his life from the death stroke * Depriving him of his due promotion was a death-stroke to his high hopes of a bright future

Death-throe: *The dying agony* * After the bullet injury he was operated but could not be saved and he is now in a state of death-throe

Death-wound: *A wound that causes death* * He suffered a death wound in a serious accident

Debar from: *Prevent from* * The student found guilty of using unfair means in the exam has been debarred from appearing for any other exam

Debar someone from something: *Forbid someone to do something* * The principal has debarred me from appearing in any further examination for three years

Debt of honour: *A debt not recognised by law but binding in nature* * To fulfil one's duty towards parents is a debt of honour

Debt of nature: *Death* * Every living being has to face the debt of nature from which there is no escape

Declare off: *To renounce; to withdraw* * A Hindu declared off his religion to get himself married to a Muslim girl * He declared off his bid to fight a case against one of his relatives

Declare war: *To announce formally that one is about to begin hostilities* * China declared a war against India in 1962 and captured a large Himalayan track which was an integral part of India

Decree of nullity: *A decree that a marriage has never existed* * The couple could not produce a legal marriage certificate since the judge declared a decree of nullity in the case

Dedicate to: *Devote* * I have decided to dedicate my life to social service

Deed of covenant: *An official signed agreement* * According to the deed of covenant, he is bound to complete the contract within four years

Deep rivers move with silent majesty: *A profoundly virtuous man would never boast of his high qualities while a person of low mentality would make a show of his insignificant potentiality* * It is true that deep rivers move with silent majesty and the shallow brooks are noisy

Deep- rooted: *Not easily removed* * Everybody knows his deep-rooted dislike of hard work

Deep water: *Water too deep for safety* * Those who do not have good experience in swimming should not enter deep water as it could be risky

Deep-browed: *Of high intellectual powers* * He is a deep-browed lawyer and all persons in the locality seek his legal advice

Deeply-rooted fear: *Fear which is very strongly felt* * I still cannot escape from the deeply-rooted fear of that ghastly scene

Deep-seated: *Firmly established* * The cause of trouble is deep-seated

Defamation of character:

Saying bad things about someone * He can file a case in court for defamation of his character behind his back

Defer to: *Postpone; give way; yield* * It was decided to defer the discussion on the matter to some other date

Deficient in: *Lacking* * He is deficient in musical taste

Deliver from: *Set free* * It is he who can deliver me from my mental worries

Deliver the goods: *Carry out what is required or promised* * Democracy has delivered the goods to the people of India in many respects

Deliver to: *Give something* * I am instructed to deliver this letter to him

Demand from/of: *Ask for something* * He had no courage to demand an explanation from/of him

Demarcation dispute: *Dispute between workers who should be responsible for certain type of work* * The demarcation dispute in industry, sometimes becomes a serious problem

Demean yourself: *Make yourself appear undignified or contemptible* * Do not give any reason to demean yourself before the society

Demur at: *Object to something* * If it is in public interest so we should not demur at working overtime

Dental floss: *Thin thread for cleaning between the teeth* * To avoid our teeth from trouble we should make use of dental floss after every meal

Dental surgery: *Dentist's office* * Whenever we find our teeth in trouble we visit the dental surgery for advice

Deny oneself: *To refuse to allow oneself gratification; say 'no' to a request or refuse to give (something asked for)* * He denied himself the credit for standing first in his class but attributed the same to his teachers * Anyone who can deny oneself a thing of pleasure is a saint

Depart from: *Leave; go away* * He departed from this place very late in the night

Departed spirit: *Spirit of dead* * They say that departed spirits do come again and again in the form of new beings

Department store: *Large store with many different sections* * We usually purchase our household goods from the department store

Depend upon it: *Be certain* * You can depend on it that it will work

Deposit-receipt: *A receipt for*

money deposited * I have got the deposit-receipt for the telephone bill

Deprive of something: *Take away something from someone* * What can a student do if he was deprived of his books?

Deputise (for somebody): *Act as deputy* * I must find someone to deputise me during my absence

Derive from: *Get; take; have* * He derives great pleasure from reading novels * Many English words are derived from Latin

Descend from someone: *Have someone as an ancestor* * According to Bible, we have all descended from Adam

Descend on/upon: *Attack suddenly* * The bandits descended on/upon the villagers

Descend to: *Lower oneself to* *You would never descend to cheating

Describe as: *Qualify or say* * He describes himself as a doctor * I hesitate to describe him as really clever

Describe to/for: *Say what is like* * Can you describe it to/for me?

Despair of: *Lose all hope of* * Never despair of success even though you may fail initially

Dessert-spoon: Spoon of middle size * Dessert-spoons are generally used in every house.

Destitute of: *Without* * My friend is a destitute as he has no one to support him

Detail someone off: *Give a task to someone* * I have detailed him off to collect all the relevant information on the matter

Detail to: *Appoint for special duty* * The soldiers were detailed to guard the bridge

Detailed: *Giving full particulars* * I have got detailed information on the cause of the accident

Deter from: *Discourage from* * Nothing can deter him from joining the army

Determine somebody to do against something: *Cause to decide against* * The news determined him against further delay

Determine somebody to do something: *Cause to decide* * What determined you to accept the offer?

Detract from: *Remove part of something* * The fact that he succeeded in his third attempt does not detract from his achievement

Detrimental to: *Harmful to* * Drinking is detrimental to health

Deviate from: *Go away from* * Those who deviate from the path of virtue have to suffer

Devil a bit thing: *Not at all* * Though he may be a dreadful rascal, yet give the devil a bit thing

Devil of a mess: *Very bad news* * It was a devil of a mess to hear the death of our popular leader

Devil to pay: *Serious trouble ahead* * You will have the devil to pay if you cheat others

Devil's books: *Playing cards* * Many persons with no particular work in hand take interest in devil's books and waste their valuable time and money

Devil-in-a bush: *A garden flower; love-in-a-mist* * The devil-in-a bush has such a sweet fragrance that I cannot forget it * The sight of the most beautiful girl is still in my memory like a devil-in-a-bush

Devoid of: *Without* * She is devoid of any sense of humour

Devolve upon: *Fall on* * All the responsibility to look after the children of his deceased brother has devolved upon him

Devote oneself to: *Give up to* * I devote my spare time to sports

Devotee of: *Devoted to something* * He is a devotee of music

Devotion for: *Deep/strong love for* * Nobody can under-rate the devotion of a mother for her children

Diabetic food: *Food with a low sugar content* * It would be advisable for a person suffering from diabetes to eat only certain foods

Diametrically opposed to: *Completely against* * The two brothers are diametrically opposed to each other

Diamond cut diamond: *An encounter between two very sharp persons* * Let the diamond cut diamond because both of them are too proud of their riches

Diamond wedding: *60th wedding anniversary* * There are many couples who celebrate their diamond wedding anniversary

Dicker about: *Hesitate* * One is likely to dicker about when making a maiden speech

Dictate terms: *Practice authority* * The General of the triumphant army dictated terms to the defeated enemy

Did win: *Was accomplished* * He did win the marathon and broke the world record

Die a dog's death: *Die miserably* * A professional miscreant tends to die a dog's death

Die away: *To disappear by degrees; become gradually inaudible* * The storm died away after havoc * The protesters raised a great hue and cry in support of their demands but their demands will die away over passage of time

Die back: *To die by degrees from the tip backwards* * There was a time when the British were most powerful but now they have had to die back

Die by: *Die as a result from* * She died by poison

Die down: *To subside; to die above ground leaving only roots* * The wind has died down now * He waited till the laughter died down

Die for: *Die for some cause; have a strong wish/love* * Mahatma Gandhi died for truth and justice * The old man is dying for a cup of tea

Die from: *Die because of* * He died from a contagious disease

Die game: *To keep up one's spirit to the last* * The tennis game between the two top players was applauded by the spectators for it was a do or die game

Die hard: *To struggle hard against death* * Those who fall in the battle-field do die hard

Die in harness: *Die while engaged in duty* * Jawaharlal Nehru died in harness

Die in one's shoes: *To be hanged* * The killer of two boys had to die in his shoes

Die in the last ditch: *Fighting desperately to defend something* * The soldiers preferred to die in the last ditch when surrounded by the enemy

Die of: *Die due to some disease* * My mother died of cancer

Die off: *To die quickly or in large numbers* * The leaves of this tree will die off soon as its roots are termite eaten

Die out: *To become extinct* * The golden eagle is in danger of dying out

Die to: *Eager to* * I am dying to read the new book

Die-hard: *An irreconcilable conservative* * With the exception of a few die-hards, the committee welcomed the proposal for reform

Different from/to: *Not the same* * Your method of thinking is different from/to mine

Different than: *Denoting a substantial difference* * How different life today is than what it was ten years ago

Diffident of: *Doubtful* * I am

rather diffident of getting in that job

Dig in: *To start* * If you tell someone to dig in his meal you want him to start eating

Dig oneself in: *To entrench oneself; to establish oneself* * The troops have dug themselves in to thwart the attack of the enemy * He is determined to dig himself in a new business adventure

Dig somebody in the ribs: *Call attention to something funny* * I will dig him in the ribs to make him take notice of the cock-fight at the corner of the street

Dig something in: *Mix with the soil by digging* * The manure should be well dug in

Dig something into something: *Push; poke; thrust* * The rider dug his spurs into the horse's flank

Dig up: *To remove from the ground by digging* * An old bronze statue has been dug up in this place

Digress from: *Move away* * He has digressed from the main point

Dilly-dally: *Waste one's time (by not making up one's mind)* * He is still dilly-dallying in the matter of applying for the job

Dim recollection of it: *Remember it vaguely* * I have a dim recollection of seeing her face

Dine out: *Have dinner away from home* * Since our cook is on a holiday, we will dine out

Dine with Duke Humphrey: *To go without a meal; loiter about* * As I reached late, the dinner was over and I had to dine with Duke Humphrey * Those who are loafers generally prefer to dine with Duke Humphrey

Dinner party: *Dinner to which guests are invited* * He has arranged a dinner party on the birthday of his only son

Dinner service: *Set of plates for eating a main meal* * No householder can do without dinner service

Dip in/into: *Part or Lower something into a liquid* * He dipped his pen into the ink before writing the letter

Dip into a book: *To read a few lines here and there* * In order to write the book review, he just dipped into a book before he left the place

Dip into one's purse: *Spend money* * Whenever we want to purchase something, we have to dip into our purse

Dip into the future: *Try to imagine what it will be like* * Sometimes, we dip into the future to know how it may affect our life

Dip one's headlights: *Lower the beam of one's headlights when another vehicle is approaching* * While driving a vehicle at night, one should be careful in dipping one's headlights to avoid a head-on collision

Dire necessity: *Urgent necessity* * Food is a dire necessity to stay alive

Directly one gets home: *Soon one gets home* * I will write to you a letter directly on getting home

Dirty trick: *Unpleasant trick* * It is only in politics that dirty tricks are played by politicians

Disagree with: *Make feel ill* * Cabbage disagrees with me

Disassociate from: *Have nothing to do with* * I disassociate myself from what has just been said

Discharge from: *Allow to leave* * The patient has been discharged from the hospital

Discharged bankrupt: *Person who has paid off his debts according to the requirements of the court* * Since he is a discharged bankrupt, he cannot be deprived of his civil rights

Disclaim knowledge of: *Deny the knowledge* * He denies all knowledge of payment being made

Disconnect from: *Detach from* * Before making adjustments inside a television, one should disconnect it from the electric current

Discount store: *Store where the goods are cheaper than elsewhere* * People prefer purchasing goods from this discount store

Discourage somebody from doing something: *Not to encourage one to do something* * We tried to discourage him from climbing the snowy mountains without a guide

Discredited person: *Person who is not believed any more by any one* * He is a discredited person so he cannot be relied upon

Discriminate against: *Make distinction* * We must abide by the laws which do not discriminate against any one

Discriminate between: *Treat two things differently* * Can you discriminate between good and bad books?

Discussions at managerial level: *Discussion among managers* * The discussions at the managerial level have been published

Dish out: *Distribute* * They are dishing out tickets to cricket fans

Dish up the food: *Serve the meal*

* He is dishing up the food for the guests

Disinterested observer: *Impartial observer* * He is a totally disinterested observer

Dismal Jimmi: *Confirmed pessimist* * One of my friends is a dismal Jimmi as he never looks at the bright side of anything

Dispatch rider: *Motorcyclist who carries messages* * I have received the message through the dispatch rider

Dispense with: *Permit the want of; do without* * The new machinery dispenses with hard labour * His knowledge of foreign affairs is too precious to be dispensed with.

Dispensing chemist: *Chemist who has the qualification to prepare medicines* * India does not lack in having well-versed dispensing chemists

Displaced persons: *Refugees who have fled from their homeland* * During India's Partition, the government had an uphill task in rehabilitating displaced persons

Display unit: *Special stand for showing goods for sale* * In the exhibition, there were many display units for the visitors to see

Disposable income: *Amount of income left after the tax has been deducted* * My disposable income for this year stands at a mere two thousand rupees

Dispose of: *To deal with a problem* * Let us dispose of this matter first

Dispossess somebody of something: *Compel somebody to give up something* * The nobles were dispossessed of their property after the revolution

Dispute with/against somebody: *Argue; debate* * Some people are always disputing with each other

Disqualify for: *Make unfit or unable for* * His weak eyesight disqualified him from military service

Disqualify from: *Debar* *As he was a professional, he was disqualified to take part in the Olympic Games

Dissent from: *Differ* * I beg to dissent from you on this matter

Dissipation of energy: *Degradation of energy* * Unwise dissipation of one's energy in wild pursuits can prove very harmful

Dissolving views: *Pictures thrown on a screen and made to pass one into another* * We enjoy looking at dissolved views in the cinema hall.

Dissuade from: *Persuade not to do something; advise against* * I tried my best to dissuade him from cheating but in vain * I dissuaded my friend from marrying till he got a nice job

Distance oneself from: *Put oneself at a distance from* * He is a rogue and you must distance yourself from him

Distant relative: *Related but not closely* * He is a distant relative and comes to see me occasionally

Distaste for: *Dislike* * His distaste for hard work makes him lose one job after another

Distasteful to: *Disagreeable; unpleasant* * It is distasteful for one to be associated with unreliable persons

Distinct from: *Different in kind* * A hare is distinct from a rabbit

Distinguish between: *To make a difference (between)* * It is not easy to distinguish between the twins

Distinguish oneself: *Make oneself noticed* * He distinguished himself in science by scoring very high marks

Ditch one's car: *Leave one's car by the side of the road* * He ditched his car and walked away

Divert from: *Distract attention; turn in another direction* * No one can divert me from my decision * How can we divert his thoughts from the loss he has suffered?

Divert one's attention: *Distract one's attention* * I am trying to divert his attention from the wrong impression he has about me

Divest of: *Deprive of* * The corrupt officer has been divested of all his powers

Dizzy heights: *Great heights that makes one's head turn* * We were determined to cross the dizzy heights of the snow-clad mountains * He is so bright that he is capable of reaching dizzy heights

Do a good turn: *Be kind* * He did me a good turn when I was in trouble

Do a moonlight flit: *Escape quietly at night* * The culprit did a moonlight flit from the custody of the police

Do a ton: *Go at 100 miles per hour* * It is said that a leopard can do a ton while chasing his prey

Do a U-turn: *Change policy completely* * The new government has taken a U-turn in its relations with the neighbouring country

Do all the talking: *Speaking continuously* * He did all the talking on his favourite subject as the others listened quietly

Do away with: *To abolish; murder; get rid of* * The Indian Government has done away with many superfluous laws that existed during the colonial rule * The dacoits did away with the rich man * We would have to do away with unwanted old customs

Do business with: *Trade with* * We are now doing business with many countries by exporting various goods

Do by: *Act towards* * He thinks that he has been badly done by his examiner

Do down: *To subdue; put down; trick someone* * He will do you down as soon as he finds the opportunity to do so * The garrison is capable enough to do down any kind of mob riot in the city * You cannot do him down because he is very smart

Do evil and look for like: *One's unholy acts would always be counter-productive* * Avoid doing harm to others or else be prepared to do evil and look for like

Do for: *To suit; provide for; have serious and harmful effect; wear out* * Sugar will never do for a person suffering from diabetes * What will you do for water while crossing the desert? * If I am unable to finish this report in time, I am done for * These shoes are done for and hence a new pair has to be bought

Do for the best: *Do for good purpose* * I know he needs help and I will do for the best

Do full justice: *Do a thing thoroughly; have one's fill* * I am sorry that for want of time I could not do justice to my examination * He did full justice to his meal at the dinner party

Do good: *Act kindly* * Generous persons always do good to others

Do good and cast it into the river: *Do a kind and noble deed and forget about it* * It is a good thing to do good and cast it into the river without expecting anything in return

Do in: *To kill* * They might do you in while you are sleeping

Do it for toffee: *Do it at all* * He cannot do it for toffee unless you pay him something in cash

Do justice to: *Treat something as it deserves* * Almost all lovers of food do justice to a well-prepared meal

Do naughty: *A lazy person* * Nobody would show any sympathy towards a do naughty

Do not digest one's dinner: *Feeling unwell after one's dinner* * I cannot digest a heavy dinner

Do one proud: *To make one feel flattered; to treat one very well* * Our daughter's performance in the choir did us proud * A member of the committee did me proud by offering floral tributes

Do one reason: *To give one the satisfaction of a duel; to drink without shrinking* * The winner against his rival did him reason. * I would not do one reason if he boasts of drinking half a bottle of wine—I am doubtful about this

Do one right: *To do someone justice; to keep pace with in drinking; drink someone's health* * It will do you right if you serve the cause of the poor * The aggrieved pleaded for doing him right * He is a hard drunkard and can do his right to compete with anybody else without losing his senses

Do oneself wrong: *To be mistaken* * You will be doing yourself wrong if you think you can beat that sturdy man in a wrestling bout

Do one the world of good: *Help one greatly* * My holidays did me a world of good after a hectic period

Do one's best: *Something to one's greatest capacity* * I am doing my best to study hard in order to score good marks in the examination

Do one's bit: *Do one's due share* * It is advisable to do one's bit towards the welfare of one's country

Do one's endeavour: *Do one's utmost* * We must endeavour to work for the welfare of children

Do one's hair: *Comb one's hair* * After changing my dress I do my hair before a mirror

Do one's kind: *To act according to one's nature* * Everybody has to do his kind because it is rather difficult to change what one is born with

Do one's level best: *To do one's very best* * I will do my level best to help you

Do one's part: *Do something allotted to one* * I have already done my part assigned to me

Do one's stuff: *Do what one can do* * After having done his stuff he took rest

Do one's worst: *To do one's utmost in evil or mischief* * He did his worst by getting an innocent person convicted for no fault of his

Do oneself a disservice: *Harm one's reputation* * You are doing yourself a disservice by telling a lie before your employer

Do oneself proud: *Give oneself a large meal* * He did himself proud in the feast

Do out of: *Cheat; swindle* * She was done out of her money

Do over: *To do again* * The essay written by me was not up to the mark, so I had to do it over

Do someone a good turn: *Do something to help someone* * They are blessed who do the poor a good turn

Do somebody: *Cheat* * Please do not think that I am trying to do somebody

Do somebody in: *Kill him* * The terrorists have so far done in thousands of innocent people during the past few years

Do somebody well: *Provide food, comforts, etc.* * They did you well at the luxury hotel

Do something off one's own bat: *Do something on one's own initiative* * He did it off his own free will and became popular

Do something on a shoe string: *Do something on a very small amount of capital* * As he failed to get a suitable job he decided to open a stall to do business on a shoe string budget

Do something out: *Sweep or clean out; put in order* * Tell the servant to do out the stable * You need to do something out with the broken pieces in this room

Do something to salve one's conscience: *Because one's conscience tells one to do it* * We must do something good to salve our conscience as also to please others

Do the handsome thing by: *To treat generously* * He is a praiseworthy host who does a handsome thing by providing every comfort to his guest

Do the handsome thing by him: *Behave towards him in a magnanimous manner* * You have done a handsome thing by him to accept his apology and forgive him for the damages

Do the honours: *To be civil* * The Pathans are known for doing honours to their unknown guests

Do time: *To serve a sentence of imprisonment* * He is doing time in jail and is likely to be released next month

Do to death: *To murder* * In a robbery case at least three persons were done to death by some dacoits

Do up: *To fasten up; make tidy; tie up* * Do up the button of your coat * The kitchen and dining room need to be done up * Please do up these books and post them to the person concerned

Do well: *To be justified; to prosper* * You will do well if you convince them of your honesty and integrity * They are doing well in the business they have started

Do well/badly by somebody: *Treat; deal with well or badly* * The employer is doing well/badly by good/bad workmen

Do with: *To make use of; to meddle wit; quite well* * I can very well do with this pen * I cannot do anything with those stupid women * He is doing well with his classmates.

Do without: *Dispense with* * A chain smoker cannot do without cigarettes

Do you mind: *Please do; would you mind* * Do you mind helping me? * Do you mind if I take your bicycle for a few hours?

Do you think he means business?: *Do you think he is serious* * Do you think he means business? If so, I would like to contact him

Does not mince words: *Tell something unpleasant* * He does not mince words when he finds that something wrong has been done

Dog in the manger: *One who will neither enjoy something himself nor let others do* * Do not behave like a dog in the manger since you could not get what he has got

Dog someone's footsteps: *Follow someone* * All his life he dogged Mahatma Gandhi's footsteps

Dog's chance: *A bare chance* * There is only a dog's chance of her surviving in that strong earthquake.

Do-gooder: *Person who tries to help others ineffectually* * A do-gooder seldom earns blessings for the help he renders

Dog-tired: *Worn out* * Since I am dog-tired, I would like to take complete rest

Dole out: *Hand out* * The children doled out their sandwich crusts to the poor and needy

Doll up: *Dress up smartly* * She was all dolled up for the party

Domestic flights: *Flights inside a country* * It is good to see domestic flights being run in India by international airlines

Domino effect: *When one good or bad event occurs, others inevitably follow* * I hurt my back and soon cut my finger also as though the domino effect was in operation

Don't broadcast the fact: *Keep it a secret* * Please don't broadcast the fact in public interest

Don't hallow till you're out of the wood* *Keep quiet till you are sure you are safe* * The advocate advised the accused not to give any statement to the police or to relations as there was not point in hallowing till he was out of the wood

Don't miss much: *There is not much to see* * We did not miss much in that play

Do-naught: *A lazy person* * Nobody should show any sympathy towards a do-naught

Done in: *Tired out* * I feel done in after hard physical exercise

Done thing: *Accepted thing* * It is a done thing to eat your meal with the hand here in south

Done to a turn: *Well cooked* * The meat is done to a turn

Donkey work: *Hard and dull work* * Do not expect me to do the donkey work

Donkey's years: *A long time* * I have not seen him for donkey's years

Door on the latch: *Door held shut by a latch but not by a lock* * All the doors in this house are on the latch

Dotes on someone: *Be very fond of someone* * The old lady dotes on her grandson

Dotted line: *Line made up of small spots* * The dotted line in the map denotes the bed of a river

Dotted with houses: *Houses built here and there* * The hillside is dotted with houses

Double dealer: *A deceitful person* * Beware of double dealers as they may lead you to unnecessary trouble

Double the distance: *Twice as for* * The road leading to the town is double the distance to the foot path

Double up: *To fold something up; to share with another; be capable of folding up or rolling up* * He doubled up his legs and kicked out * As there wasn't enough space in the car for everyone we had to double up * This carpet is so thick as to double up

Double-dealing: *Duplicity* * Both the partners accused each other of double-dealing.

Double-decker: *The bus with an upper as well as a lower deck* * It is for the first time that a double-decker is being seen on the road in our town

Double Dutch : *Nonsense* * It all sounded a bit like double-Dutch to me

Double-edged: *Something which can hurt or do good both ways* * She made a very double-edged remark about my work * The burglar with a double-edged knife was nabbed by the police

Double-jointed: *With very flexible joints* * Our fingers are double-jointed thus helping us do all kinds of work

Double-quick: *Extremely fast* * Since I was late for office I had to cover the distance by running on a double-quick

Double-talk: *Words which mean something quite different from what is obvious* * Don't fall victim to his double-talk as he never talks straight

Down at heel: *Having the heel of one's shoes trodden down, slovenly; in poor circumstances* *It is for the government to come forward to help those who are down at heel

Downhearted: *Depressed; gloomy* * In spite of a number of failures, there was no need for him to feel downhearted

Down in the dumps: *Depressed; miserable* * We should take pity on those who are down in the dumps

Down in the mouth: *In low spirits* * He was down in the mouth when he learnt of his failure in the examination

Down on one's luck: *In ill luck* * He is down on his luck because he has not secured admission in any college despite scoring good marks in school

Down on the luck: *In bad luck* * When one is down on the luck, even friends become foes

Down the wind: *Moving with the wind* * Our boat was easily floating down the wind

Down tools: *Refuse to work; go on strike* * The labourers have downed their tools in their demand for increase of wages

Down trod: *Trampled; tyrannised over* * In the stampede many men, women and children were down trod * Scheduled Castes and Scheduled Tribes have always been treated as down trods by the upper-class people.

Down with: *Suffering some illness; abolish* * He is down with high fever

Downcast: *Depressed; discouraged* * I tried to make her happy but she continued to look downcast with grief

Downfall: *Fall from fortune or power* * His downfall was caused due to his habit of gambling and heavy drinking

Downpour: *Heavy rainfall* * We were caught in a downpour and were drenched to the skin

Downright: *Forthright; honest; frank* * Everybody likes him because of his downright bold behaviour

Downstairs: *At the lower floor* * He went downstairs to breakfast * Our neighbours on the lower floor are very noisy

Down-to-earth: *Concerned with realities* * He is a down-to-earth sort of man

Downtrodden: *Kept down and treated badly; oppressed* * This country has the most poverty-stricken and downtrodden population in the world

Doze off: *Have a light sleep* * He dozed off during the sermon

Dozens of: *A large number of* * I have been here dozens of time * Dozens of people were standing there

Drag on: *Continue slowly* * Classwork often drags on towards the end of the term

Drag one's feet: *Go forward slowly or unwillingly* * We suspect the government of dragging its feet over getting the roads duly constructed

Drag out: *Make longer (in time); to extract; pulled out* * The meeting had to be dragged out to accommodate more members to speak out their minds * The divers dragged out the river to recover the missing child * I always have to drag out the secret of your beauty from you

Drag somebody into doing something: *Involve someone unwillingly in an undertaking* * He hates picking apples from the tree but we had to drag him into doing it

Dragnet: *Action taken by the police to nab criminals* * The police have widened their dragnet to capture the crooks

Draught horse: *Horse trained to pull heavy load* * We utilise the services of draught horses for pulling the carts

Draw a bead on: *To take aim at* * The correspondent drew a bead on the police for hushing up the case

Draw a blank: *To get a lottery ticket that wins no prize; to*

get no result * Mostly a very large number of people draw a blank when they purchase lottery tickets * The police had to draw a blank when they went to arrest the thief home

Draw a cover: *To send the hounds into a cover to frighten out a fox* * Many farmers rear hounds to draw a cover for saving their pet animals like hares, cock, hens, etc.

Draw a distinction: *Point out the difference* * It is very difficult to draw an exact distinction between all the meanings of any one word

Draw a veil over: *Avoid discussing or calling attention to* * There are many important national issues over which we cannot draw a veil

Draw attention: *Make someone aware of* * The minister drew attention to the rising unemployment problem

Draw back: *To recoil; to withdraw; show unwillingness; weakness; open* * There is a draw back when one fires a gun * He drew back his unpleasant remarks made against one of the members * He drew himself back to accompany me to see a movie * His only drawback is that he is so stupid

Draw blood: *Cut someone so that they bleed* * He gave him a bite in the arm that drew blood

Draw cuts: *To cast lots* * They draw cuts as to who should climb the steep hill first

Draw down: *To handle with severity; to reprimand; to thrash* * He is a person who draws down those found guilty * He was drawn down by his officers for his negligence

Draw flak: *Hit by serious criticism* * He deserves to draw flak for having misappropriated large amounts of public money

Draw in: *To reduce; become shorter* * The new cloth when washed for the first time draws in somewhat * The days begin to draw in after the summer season is over

Draw it fine: *To be too precise* * To draw it fine, you will have to cover a distance of 60 kilometres to reach the town

Draw it mild: *To refrain from exaggeration* * I like that witty person for his straightforward talk as he often tends to draw it mild

Draw lots: *Decide something by taking pieces of paper from a box/throwing dice, etc.* * The recipient of first three positions in the competition had to be decided through draw of lots

Draw near: *To approach* * As a dangerous storm is drawing near, we should run for cover

Draw off: *To withdraw; cause to flow from a barrel, etc;* * When the two-peg glass was filled with wine he drew off the bottle * He drew off some of the beer to see if it was ready for drinking

Draw on: *To pull on; to approach* * The evening is drawing on to an end * The company can draw on their vast reserves to pay for the project

Draw on one's imagination: *To make imaginative or false statements* * In order to save his skin, the accused drew on his imagination and told tall stories

Draw on one's luck: *Unfortunate* * It is not within the reach of a deaf man to live a healthy life

Draw on one's memory: *To try to remember* * I did draw on my memory to recollect my childhood incident

Draw one's first breath: *Be born* * The parents were very happy when the baby drew the first breath

Draw one's last breath: *Die* * He drew his last breath at midnight when he was in his seventies

Draw out: *To leave the place (of an army); to lengthen; to entice into talk and self-expression* * He had to draw out from army on medical grounds * In order to win sympathy, she drew out the story of woes * I could not do justice to my studies as my friend drew me out of my shell

Draw rein: *To slacken speed; to stop* * The labourers had to draw rein after a hard toil when constructing a road * After having enjoyed a hectic race, I had to draw rein of my horse

Draw somebody's teeth: *Make him harmless* * If you want to live a peaceful life, you will have to draw your enemy's teeth

Draw stumps: *End a game of cricket by removing the wickets* * The umpire drew stumps at the end of the day's play

Draw tears/applause, etc.: *Be the cause of; applause* * The death of the nobleman drew tears from many people's eyes * Her singing drew a long applause

Draw the line: *To fix a limit; declare what can not be allowed*

* I have drawn a line to my daily routine of work * I can give you my scooter but draw the line at giving you my car

Draw the long bow: *To exaggerate extravagantly* * He always draws the long bow of his riches and spends very liberally

Draw to a head: *To mature* * He has since drawn to a head and is now able to manage well

Draw up: *Come or cause to a stop; compose* * The taxi drew up in front of the station * He has been asked to draw up a contract for the bidders

Draw upon: *To make a draught upon; to make a demand upon one's credibility and patience; to draw one's sword/pistol* * He could draw upon his sharp knowledge on all subjects of his interest * One had to draw upon some knowledge of human psychology * When he saw his captive angry, the inspector had to draw upon his pistol from the holster

Draw, hang and quarter: *To drag on a hurdle or otherwise to the place of execution before hanging* * Some of the convicts who were awarded capital punishment will be drawn, hanged and quartered

Drawback: *Inconvenient thing; disadvantage* * This machine has a major drawback * Her only drawback is that she is so stupid

Drawbridge: *Bridge which can be raised or lowered to give access across water* * I have yet to see a drawbridge near a fort or a castle

Drawn game: *A game which neither party wins* * It was a drawn game of cricket between India and Pakistan

Dream of: *Think of* * I would not dream of wearing pink socks

Dress down: *Criticise; scold severely* * He was dressed down for his misconduct

Dress somebody down: *To scold severely* * He should not have dressed his servant down for breaking a tea-set

Dressed in rags: *Wearing old, torn clothes* * A person playing the role of a prince was dressed in rags in one of the plays

Dressed up to the nines: *Wearing one's most elaborate clothes* * The bridegroom dressed up to the nines looked very smart and handsome

Dried bread: *Bread with no*

butter or jam * He had only dried bread to eat

Dries out: *If someone dries out, they are cured of alcohol* * They sent him to a special hospital so that he could be dried out

Dries up: *Something stops being productive* * They were worried that the oil-well will dry up before they are able to drill oil

Drift-way: *A road over which cattle are driven* * The drift-way has totally reduced the death toll of the cattle

Drill for: *Make holes for* * He is drilling for oil

Drink in: *Take in* * He is a talented boy and drinks in whatever is taught

Drink in/up: *Take in; absorb* * The thirsty plants drank up the water I sprinkled on them

Drink off: *To quaff wholly and at a gulp* * He drank off a full bottle of wine without a stop

Drink oneself drunk: *To drink until he is drunk* * It is very harmful for health to drink oneself drunk

Drink something in: *Take into the mind eagerly or with pleasure* * The boy drank in every word of the fairy story and fairyland

Drink the others under the table: *To continue drinking and remain (comparatively) sober after others have completely collapsed* * They are more sensible who drink the others under the table

Drink to: *To drink wine with good wishes for one's health* * My friends joined me on my birthday and I expect them to drink to me

Drink to the success of: *Wishing success about something by raising drinking glasses* * Let us drink to the success of the expedition

Drip-dry shirt: *Shirt which does not crease if hung to dry while wet* * He puts on a drip-dry shirt

Drive a hard bargain: *Be a very tough businessman* * He drives a hard bargain when negotiating with his clients

Drive a nail in one's coffin: *To do something to hasten death or ruin* * The Indians did drive a nail in the British government's coffins during the struggle for freedom

Drive at: *Try to say* * What are you driving at?

Drive away: *To turn out* * We smoked constantly in the hope of driving away the mosquitoes

Drive home: *Lay emphasis on* *

I tried to drive home the point that we cannot afford a new car

Drive into a corner: *Difficult position from which there is no escape* * We have driven him into a corner by taking him to court for illegally occupying our house

Drive like a madman: *Drive very furiously* * He drove the car like a madman and this resulted in a serious accident

Drive off: *Stem an attack* * They claimed they had driven off a horde of animals from their farm

Drive on: *Continue one's journey* * They kept on driving till they reached their destination

Drive one to be frantic: *Make one become frantic* * The heavy pressure of work drove him round the bend

Drive out: *Make disappear* * The whole point of exorcism is to drive out evil spirits

Drive somebody into a corner: *Force one into a position from where the escape will be difficult* * The police drove the gang into a corner and arrested them

Drive someone to: *Take someone in one's car* * I will drive you to the airport

Drive something home: *Impress deeply on the mind* * He drove home the necessity of discipline to his audience

Drive something in: *Have a nail, screw, etc. into something* * With one blow, he drove the nail into the plank

Drive to the wall: *To push to extreme* * Our forces have driven the enemy forces to the wall

Driven to: *Forced to* * He was driven to tell a lie in the case

Drop a brick: *To make a horrific blunder in speech or action; do or say something indiscreet* * While referring to a point in the house he dropped a brick by making an unpleasant remark about the minister's wife * A disciplined person would never drop a brick even on his enemies

Drop a courtesy: *To courtesy* * The girls dropped a courtesy to the queen when they saw her coming

Drop a stitch: *Let a stitch slip off a knitting needle* * She dropped a stitch in the process of knitting a sweater

Drop across: *Meet or find by chance* * The two sisters will drop across to their friend's house to meet her

Drop away: *To get further behind* * They will drop away on seeing the other boys come

* The militants hope to drop away in the darkness

Drop back: *Come to a position behind* * The troops dropped back from the border

Drop dead: *Die suddenly* * Our Member of Parliament dropped dead at a public meeting

Drop down: *To move down* * The stage curtains were dropped down the moment the play was over

Drop in: *To come/visit casually* * I thought that I will drop in and enquire about your health

Drop in the bucket: *A quantity infinitesimal in proportion* * Ten rupees is only a drop in the bucket because we need thousands

Drop in the ocean: *Amounting to nothing* * My contribution to the relief fund is nothing but a drop in the ocean

Drop off: *To fall asleep* * He dropped off during the sermon

Drop one a line: *Send one a short letter* * Please drop me a line when you reach home

Drop one at one's door: *Drive one back and leave one at one's door* * Shall I drop you at your door?

Drop round: *Go somewhere casually* * I will drop round when I have finished shopping

Drop serene: *A form of blindness* * This patient has been suffering from drop serene and is being treated for the same

Drop something round: *Take something to a person's home* * He can drop your books round on his way home

Drop the idea: *Give up the idea* * He has dropped the idea of going to live in Canada

Drop through: *Come to nothing* * The big scheme he was busy with seems to have dropped through

Drop-out: *To disappear from one's place; withdraw; person who has stopped studying or living conventionally* * Some naughty boys dropped out of the school to enjoy swimming in the pond * Three of the runners dropped out of the race * There were as many as ten drop-outs in the primary class

Dropping fire: *Supply of small arms* * Some rogue states are dropping fire to be used by the terrorists

Drug addict: *Inability to stop taking a drug* * He is a drug addict and cannot do without it

Drum in/into: *Tell someone many*

times till he understands or listens * The facts were drummed into his mind

Drum out: *Force to leave a club or society* * He was forced to drum out of the club since he was drunk

Drum up support: *To encourage people to give their support* * We were busy canvassing and drumming up support for our cause

Drunk and incapable: *So drunk that you cannot stand up* * He is drunk and incapable of going anywhere

Drunk as a piper: *Very drunk* * Avoid being drunk as a piper or else you will soon be ruined

Dry land: *Solid land* * Dry land is devoid of vegetation, fauna and flora

Dry out/off: *Lose all water or moisture* * You should let that wood dry out before you use it * The clothes soon dried off in the sun

Dry rot: *Disease in wood which makes the wood dry* * Dry rot cannot be used as timber

Dry up: *Make or become completely dry; stop flowing* * The long spell of drought dried up all the wells * He dried up in the middle of his speech

Dual nationality: *Citizen of two countries* * He has a dual nationality

Dud bomb: *Bomb that fails to explode* * Dud bombs do not cause any harm

Due to: *Caused by* * He left school due to high fever

Due west: *Straight in a westerly direction* * The plane flew due west

Dull at: *Not bright; rather stupid* * She is hopelessly dull in English

Dull of: *Slow in understanding* * He is rather dull of understanding

Dumbfounded: *Astonished* * I am dumbfounded at the news

Duplicate one's work: *Doing one's work all over again* * You are just duplicating his work

Dust one's jacket: *To give one a drubbing* * Unless you dust his jacket, he will not give up telling a lie

Dutch comfort: *Thank God it's not worse* * It is Dutch comfort that things are not so bad as they could have been

Dutch courage: *A fictitious courage induced by drinking* * You better give up Dutch courage otherwise you will land in trouble

Dwell under one's vine and fig-free: *To live at peace on one's own land* * A true citizen would like to dwell un der one's vine and fig-free

Dwell upon: *To discuss; to continue* * He dwelt upon the ways and means to be adopted for enhancing the power project * His mind often dwelt upon the fact that there were only a few days left to join the army

Dyed-in-the-wool: *To change the colour of something* * The threads of various suits are differently dyed in the wool at the initial stage * He looks like a gentleman because he is a dyed-in-the-wool crook

E

Eagle-eyed: *Person with sharp eyes; one who notices small details* * An eagle-eyed person can be a good marksman * We need an eagle-eyed personality to read the whole report between the lines

Ear of corn: *Head of corn seeds* * Ear of corn sprouts at the top of the stem of wheat, barley, etc. which, when ripe, is used as food

Early years: *Childhood* * He died in his early years of cancer

Earmark: *Assign to definite purpose* * Sufficient funds will have to be earmarked for the construction of roads

Earn one's keep: *Earn enough money for food and lodging by doing adequate amount of work* * That lady does not earn her keep because she hardly does any work

Earnest money: *Pledge* * You can buy any brand of car by making payment of the desired earnest money in the first instance

Ear-splitting/Piercing: *Too loud* * One could not hear anything in the ear-splitting din caused by the loudspeaker

Earth tremor: *Slight earthquake* * Thanks Almighty that no loss of life took place as a result of the earth tremor

Earth up: *Cover with earth* * We plan to earth up roots of pine plants on the hill sides

Ease nature/Relieve nature: *Relieve nature; to evacuate the bowels* * We cannot do without relieving nature

Ease off: *To slacken gradually; to become less intense* * The pace of our activity eases off as age advances * There was a great turmoil in the city but now the situation will ease off

Ease oneself: *To defecate* * Everybody has to ease oneself once or twice a day

Ease up: *Slow down* * When the train was nearing the railway station, it eased up its speed * The rain has eased up a bit now so we could make a dash for the car

East or West, home is the best: *You may go anywhere but home is the best place* *Only when you experience the discomfort away from home that you realise that

East or West, home is the best

Easy chair: *Large, comfortable arm chair* * When we feel tired, we take rest on an easy chair

Easy-going: *Indolent/Placid* * His father was a gentle easy-going man

Easy money: *Money made without much exertion* * Lucky persons are often blessed with easy money

Easy reach: *Conveniently close* * Our house is within easy reach of the railway station

Easy street: *A situation of comfort or affluence* * He has everything at his command and thus enjoys the life of an easy street

Eat away: *To destroy gradually* * The wooden frame of the portrait has been eaten away by ants

Eat boiled crow: *To be forced to do something very disagreeable; to humiliate oneself* * The countries not following the line of USA are likely to eat boiled crow * He had to eat boiled crow for his misconduct

Eat dirt: *Submissively to acquiesce in humiliation* * A man of guts would never eat dirt under any circumstances

Eat humble pie: *Submit to humiliation* * He was suspended from service, but he tendered an apology and ate humble pie

Eat in: *To corrode; eat at home* * The acid has eaten in the metal * Since we have employed a new cook we eat in our meals without going out

Eat into: *Reduce gradually; destroy as if by eating* * Rust eats into the metal bit by bit * Acids eat into metals

Eating-apple: *Suitable for eating uncooked* * Most of the vegetables in the vegetable kingdom can be used as eating-apple

Eating-house: *Restaurant* * To-night we shall be dining in an eating-house

Eat off: *To clear (a crop) by setting cattle to eat it* * A portion of the crop field has been set aside to be eaten off by the cattle

Eat one's cake and have it: *To have the advantage of both alternatives* * You criticise him and yet want him to do your work amounts to eating one's cake and having it too

Eat one's hat: *An undertaking promised on an improbable condition* * I refused to accept the assignment offered by my friend as it was something like eating one's hat

Eat one's head off: *To cost more for food than one is worth* * Keeping a race horse may eat one's head off

Eat one's heart out: *To pine away: brooding over misfortune* * When the master took the servant to task, the latter ate his heart out * The memory of his lost son is still eating his heart out

Eat one's salt: *Be one's guest* * I had the privilege of eating that gentleman's salt with whom I stayed for a couple of days

Eat one's terms: *To study for the bar* * After having eaten one's terms, one is called to the bar

Eat one's words: *To retract; to recant* * In order to avoid any misunderstanding for what he had said, he had to eat his words forthwith

Eat out: *To finish; to encroach upon* * He ate out his meal before he set out on his journey to Paris * We should not eat out what belongs to others

Eat out of house and home: *To live at the expense of another so as to ruin him* * There are many rouges who eat out of house and home

Eat salt with: *Be guest of* * I was cordially invited by my old friend to eat salt with him

Eat the air: *To be deluded with hopes* * You will have to eat the air if you hope to become a millionaire overnight

Eat the bread of idleness: *To be idle; afflicted* * Due to a dearth of employment opportunities, many people are eating the bread of idleness * Most of the physically handicapped persons have to eat the bread of idleness

Eat to one's fill: *Eat as much as one can* * I ate to my fill at the dinner party arranged by our neighbour

Eat up: *To devour entirely; to consume* * Though he was not hungry yet he greedily ate up the whole plate of rice * The ship ate out a great deal of fuel

Eavesdrop: *Listen to a conversation which one is not supposed to listen* * Some journalists will always try to eavesdrop on the private conversation between politicians

Economise on: *Save on; do not waste* * Do not economise on things which will hardly save you any money

Economy class: *Cheapest class of travel* * I purchased an economy class ticket for my travel to London by air

Economy pack: *Cheaper packet*

of goods * That grocer at the corner supplies all domestic goods in economy packs

Edge in a word: *To get a word in with difficulty* * Due to the din, I could not edge in a word to the chairperson

Efficient cause: *The means by which a thing took its present form* * The present communication system is an efficient cause of technological revolution

E.g.: *For example* * Reasonable work expenses on travel, e.g., will be taken into account

Eggs in moonshine: *An old dish, Fried eggs with onion and various flavorings* * The host provided us with rich food and eggs in moonshine

Egg somebody on: *Urge somebody to do something* * Egged on by him, the robber made up his mind to kill the landlord

Ego trip: *Action which boosts your opinion of yourself; self-centered or self-seeking act* * We always disapprove of his ego trips

Eke out: *Make small supplies of something enough for one's needs by adding something* * He ekes out his livelihood by working overtime

Eligible for: *Qualified* * He is not eligible for such a high post

Elect (to): *Choose* * Two women have been elected to the council * They may elect to opt out of the scheme

Eleventh hour: *The very last moment* * I reached the meeting at the eleventh hour when most of the speakers had delivered their speeches

Elicit something: *Draw out; cause to come out* * In order to elicit the truth the witness was cross-examined in the court of law * He has elicited a reply to the queries on the subject

Else wise: *In a different manner* * I advised him in his own interest but he took it all else wise

Embark at: *Go on board a ship* * The passengers will be expected to embark at Bombay

Embark for: *Go, put or take on board a ship* * The soldiers embarked for Malta

Embark on something: *Start doing something* * He has embarked on a massive reform programme

Emboss with: *Raise the surface of something into a pattern* * I saw a silver vase embossed with a floral design

Embossed letterhead: *Addressed pressed on writing paper so that it stands above*

the surface * Embossed letterhead pads have come into vogue in big business houses

Emerge from: *Come into view; become known* * The moon emerged from behind the clouds * No new ideas emerged from his exhortation

Emigrate to/from: *Go away from one's own country to another to settle* * Many people from India love to emigrate to various countries in the West

Employment agency: *Business establishment which helps persons (for a fee) to find employment* * Employment agencies do help unemployed persons to get employment in keeping with their qualifications

Empty handed: *Bringing nothing* * I went to the moneylender to borrow some money but had to come back empty handed

Empty-headed: *Frivolous; witless; lacking in common sense* * His empty-headed remarks made everybody laugh * We cannot depend on empty-headed persons to make a headway in removing the obstacles that stem our progress

Empty pocket: *Penniless person* * An empty pocket cannot make the labourer work

Enamoured of something: *Love a thing very much* * I am not enamoured by her hairstyle

En block: *Altogether as a group* * They raised slogans en block against the mismanagement of the committee concerned

Encroach on/ upon: *Go beyond what is right or natural; desirable* * The sea is encroaching on/upon the land * I do not like men who encroach on my resting hours

Encourage in: *Give hope or confidence* * Do not encourage him in his idle ways

En route: *On the way* * En route to London you can stop over at Dubai

End and aim: *Sole purpose* * The end and aim of the UN is to maintain peace in the world

End of the world: *Extremely serious* * If I lose the match it will not mean the end of the world *I have replaced the one which was given before with this*

End in smoke: *Show no tangible results* * All his schemes end in smoke

End it all: *Commit suicide* * The girl decided to end it all after failing in the exam

End one's days: *Die* * Every living being has to end its days sooner or later

End to end: *In a line with the ends touching* * We had to arrange the table end to end for the dinner party

End up: *Arrive or find oneself eventually; finish with* * .Many of their friends and neighbours have ended up in prison for terrorist activities * We ended up taking a taxi back home

Endless chain: *A chain whose ends are joined* * My wristwatch has an endless chain

Engage for: *To answer for* * The factory owner has engaged a manager to look after the management of the factory as a whole

Engagement ring: *Ring given by a man to a woman when they agree to marry* * On his betrothal, the man gave an engagement ring to his fiancee

Engrossed in: *Very interested; busy in* * He is engrossed in reading a novel

Engrossing a deed: *Writing it out in full and regular form for signature* * After engrossing a deed, the party concerned was made to sign it for releasing the contract in its favour

Enlarge upon: *Give more details* * I have no time to enlarge upon this serious subject

En masse: *All together and at the same time* * They threatened to resign en masse

Enough is enough: *Stop criticizing* * Listen, enough is enough because if you don't stop, I will thrash you

Enough and to spare: *Adequate* * I have money enough and to spare so I have no reason to worry about my future

Entail upon: *Impose on; cause* * It entails upon you to help your elders

Enter a protest: *Write it in the books; protest* * The authority has entered a protest for consideration of due wages to be given to the labourers * The public at large have entered into a protest against the soaring prices of essential goods

Enter into: *Become a party to; be interested in; understand sympathetically* * He has entered into a partnership with other members in the new business adventure * Many experts took part in the debate to enter into details to make the project a success * The management tried to enter into the feelings of the agitated employees

Enter into a protest: *Protest* * The public at large have entered into a protest against soaring prices of essential commodities

Enter on/upon: *Begin; engage in* * He has entered on/upon a new career * They have entered themselves on/upon augmentation of hydro-electric projects

Enter the lists: *Come forward for contest or to do battle; be a candidate in an election** Many energetic and young persons have entered the lists for wrestling and boxing championships * Many black horses have entered the lists in the forthcoming election

Entitle to: *Get a right* * Every poor scholar is entitled to a free studentship in the college

Entrust with: *Trust to complete; charge* * Can I entrust you with the task? * Do not entrust your dull assistant with any important assignment

Entry money: *The money paid on entering a society, club, etc.* * He has become a member of the Rotary Club by paying the requisite entry money

Epoch-making: *Important enough to be considered as beginning of a new age* * The discovery of America by Columbus was an epoch-making event

Equal opportunity: *Everyone is given the same chances of getting a job; of doing well* * All the candidates will be given equal opportunity for the post applied for

Equal to: *Able to* * This weak man is not equal to such a heavy task

Equal to the occasion: *Fit or able for an emergency* * He stood equal to the occasion and saved the life of a child caught in a house on fire

Ere long: *Before long or soon* * He should have completed the task ere long

Ere now: *Before this time* * Ere now he was working as a clerk but now he has been promoted to the post of assistant

Ere while: *Formerly or sometime before* * Ere while I saw him driving a car on the national highway

Err on the right side: *Make mistake to one's advantage* * He erred on the right side and gained a profit

Err on the safe side: *To choose the safe alternatives* * Sometimes it is better to err on the safe side than to take unwarranted risks

Erratic block: *A huge rock transported by ice and deposited at a distance* * An erratic block is the creation of an avalanche

Esprit de corps: *Regard or loyalty for the honour of the body to which one belongs* * He is a thorough and thorough Arya Samaji and is well known for his esprit de corps towards the Arya Samaj * He is known for his leadership qualities which kept the esprit de corps of the team in a difficult period

Essential to: *Absolutely necessary for* * Open air is essential to good health

Estate agent: *Person who arranges the sale of houses and land* * In order to acquire a suitable house I shall have to consult an estate agent

Estate car: *Long car with room at the back for carrying luggage, etc.* * These days he is driving an estate car as he is working for a businessman

Et al.: *Other people are also involved* * This admirable paper by John et al. has been acknowledged as very interesting

Et cetera (etc.): *And so on* * She had to do cleaning, washing, making beds, etc.

Even a good marksman may miss: *An experienced hand may also fumble* * A situation may arise when a good marksman may miss the target

Even as: *Just at the time when* * Even as I gave the warning signal the car skidded

Even at the best of times: *Even when conditions are good* * He is an irritating fellow even at the best of times

Even chance: *Equal probability for or against* * He has an even chance of winning this match

Even date: *The same date* * I cannot discuss with you this subject as I will be out of station on the even date

Even death cannot be had for the asking: *A prayer for end of our life under the circumstances will not work* * Everything is in the hands of the Almighty that even death cannot be had for the asking

Even-handed: *Impartial or just* * Nobody doubts his integrity for he disperses even-handed justice

Even if/though: *At all cost* * I will get there even if I have to pawn my watch to get the railway fare

Evenly matched: *In competition* * Government soldiers and rebels are evenly matched

Even-minded: *Having an even or calm mind* * We had to think even-mindedly over the execution of the new plan

Even now/then: *A very little while ago; these or those circumstances* * He will wait for you even then * Even now he won't believe me

Even so: *Though that is the case* * It has many omissions, even so it is quite a useful reference book

Even temper: *Never getting excited* * He is a man of even temper

Even things up: *Make things equal* * That will even things up and avoid the chance of mistake

Ever after: *From then; always* * They lived happily ever after

Ever and anon: *From time to time* * My friend who has gone abroad does inform me of his progress ever and anon

Ever and ever: *Always* * I will love you ever and ever

Ever (at): *Always* * You will find me ever at your service

Evergreen: *All the years green* * Pines are evergreen trees

Everlasting: *Endless; perpetual; unceasing* * We must find ways and means for everlasting peace * I am tired of his everlasting complaints * The everlasting war has crippled the economy of the country

Ever more: *For all time to come* * The wedlock bound the couple in love for ever more

Ever see someone: *Almost never see someone* * I hardly ever see that gentleman

Ever since then: *From that time onwards* * Ever since then he has been under the employment of an insurance company

Ever so: *Extremely* * He can talk ever so on any subject

Ever such: *Ever so* * Thank you ever so much

Evermore: *For all time to come* * I shall be always at your service evermore

Every bit: *The whole; quite* * This is every bit as good as that dress * He believes the he is every bit as good as you are

Every dog has its day: *No one is always unlucky* * Every dog has its day and this became clear when he became a millionaire after remaining poor for years

Every here and there: *Dispersed all over* * Rivers, rivulets and streams are found every here and there throughout the globe

Every inch: *Entirely; thoroughly* * He is every inch a gentleman

Every man Jack: *One and all* * He invited every man Jack to the feast

Every man Jack, every mother's son: *Everyone without exception* * Nature has been very kind to provide every man Jack with air to breathe and water to drink

Every now and then: *At intervals* * He visits our place every now and then

Every other day: *Every second or alternative day* * Every other day he is required to report to his new boss

Every potter praises his pot: *All producers praise their products* * It is a natural phenomenon for every potter to praise his pot because he has created it

Every so often: *Every second or alternative* * I do meet my friends every so often

Everything looks yellow to a jaundiced eye: *A suspicious person by nature sees everything as bad because something bad has happened in his past* * I tend to look at the cloth dealer with a jaundiced eye because I have had an unfortunate experience with him in the past

Every time: *Always; whenever* * Our football team wins every time * Every time I meet him, he tries to borrow money from me

Every which way: *In disorder; in all directions* * The whole ceremony went every which way right from the beginning because of improper planning

Evil genius: *Bad spirit; person with a bad influence* * It appears that she has fallen a victim to some evil genius

Evil got evil spent: *Anything obtained through unlawful means is hardly kept under safe hands* * One should not repent on the loss of things not obtained rightfully because after all evil got evil spent

Evil-minded: *Inclined to evil or wicked* * We should be aware of the designs of evil-minded persons

Evil-speaking: *The speaking of evil* * I cannot put up with evil-speaking persons

Evil-starred: *Unfortunate* * The ill-starred person died of starvation after slogging for years

Evil worker: *One who works or does evil* * An evil worker returns evil even for good

Exact sciences: *Mathematical sciences whose results are precise* * Experts in exact sciences win laurels from all quarters

Exact from: *Draw by force* * The police exacted the necessary information from the thief

Exactly: *Quite right* * Exactly, he had no option but to get rid of it

Example is better than precept: *It is better to set a practical example before others rather than to preach morals* * It is better to do good so that children also learn to do good because example is better than precept

Excel at: *Be very good* * He excels at sports but is rather backward in studies

Except: *Not including/But not* * He gets up early every day except on Sunday

Except for: *What is excluded is different from what is included* * Your essay is great except for spelling mistakes

Except from: *Excluding* * A gift can be expected from everybody except from the little girl who is rather poor

Except that: *Apart from the fact that* * She knew nothing about his journey except that he was likely to be away for a long time

Exception to: *Objection* * The student took exception to his teacher's remarks

Excess baggage: *More baggage than is allowed to carry* * He was charged extra by the airline for carrying excess baggage

Exchange address: *Each giving the other his address* * They exchanged their addresses before leaving for their respective places

Exclude from: *Drop* * His name has been excluded from the list of successful candidates

Exclusive of: *Apart from* * The price of this book is a few rupees exclusive of the sales tax

Exclusive right: *Right to do something which no one else is then allowed to do* * This agency has the exclusive right to sell Ford cars in the town

Excuse me: *I am sorry* * Please excuse me for my absence from the meeting

Exempt from: *Exclude* * He was exempted from the fine

Exercise one's right: *Use one's power* * He exercised his right of vote during the general elections

Ex gratia payment: *Payment made as a present with no obligation* * The victims of a railway accident were given ex gratia payment of a few thousand rupees

Expatiate on: *Speak copiously* * The lecturer is likely to expatiate on the present economic condition as this is his pet theme

Expect from/of: *Think or believe that something will take place* * What I expected from/of you was honesty and nothing else

Expose to: *Subject to* * By jumping in front of the train he plans to expose himself to danger

Exposed position: *Not sheltered from the wind* * He was in a very exposed position as to be nabbed easily by the police

Express oneself: *Make clear what one wants to say* * I expressed myself very well in the interview

Expulsion from: *Expelling or being expelled* * His arrogance resulted in his expulsion from the meeting

Extra judicial: *Beyond the jurisdiction* * The cases which are extra judicial are not acceptable for hearing by the court

Extract from: *Taking out by force* * The young boy was not ashamed to extract money from his old parents

Exult at/in: *Rejoice greatly* * He exulted at his success at achieving the desired goal

Exult over: *Triumph* * He exulted over his path-breaking discovery

Eye-glance: *A quick look* * While travelling by air, we could have an eye-glance of the beautiful landscape

Eye-opener: *A startling enlightenment* * The book that I read is really an eye-opener

Eye-popping: *Surprising* * He was standing in an eye-popping state when he first saw the Niagara Falls

Eye-sore: *Anything that is offensive to look at* * The new office building is an architectural eye-sore

Eye up: *Look at a person thinking that he is attractive* * He has been eying her up all evening

Eye-wash: *A lotion for the eye; deception* * Whenever my eyes feel sore, I use a good eye-wash * This report is an eye-wash to please the superiors as it has no substance in it

Eye-witness: *One who sees a thing done* * The lawyer had an eye-witness to give evidence in the murder case

F

Face down: *Browbeat; oppose impudently* * She did not argue with him but she just faced him down

Face out: *Deal with firmly and defiantly* * We will face out the crisis till the last

Face the music: *Face the trouble as a consequence of one's action* * The robber who robbed me is now facing the music in jail

Face to face: *Opposite; in actual presence of a person; in confrontation; facing directly one another* * They were standing face to face while debating the case * In old times the opposite armies used to fight a face-to-face battle * There was a face-to-face argument between the lawyers of the plaintiff and the defendant * The army had to carry out face-to-face battles

Face up to: *Confront a difficult situation* * They had to face up to many setbacks before achieving success

Face-saving: *Action that prevents damage to one's reputation* * He had no option but to come to a face-saving compromise

Face-value: *The value as stated on the face of a coin a note* * I loaned him about a thousand rupees in the form of currency notes each with a face-value of a hundred rupees

Fade away: *Become weaker and die* * He was fading quietly away day by day and might die soon

Fade out: *Process of becoming less great, or intense or strong* * This sort of protest tends to fade out through its foolishness * The sound of the chopper faded out as it flew higher and higher

Fag-end/at the end: *Useless remnant* * The fag-ends of cigarettes have been piled up in the ashtray by a chain-smoker * At the fag-end of the day I was too tired to cook

Fagged out: *Tired out* * After my routine physical exercises, I felt fagged out

Fail of: *Come short of accomplishment* * He will fail of reaching his goals

Faint-hearted: *Cowardly; timid* * This type of arduous and risky enterprise is not recommended for the faint-hearted

Fair and square: *Appropriate; upright* * His reply to the type of questions asked was fair and square * His dealings are fair and square for which he has earned a high reputation

Fair- boarding: *Auspicious* * The Hindus consider it fair-boarding to take a bath in the holy waters of the Ganga.

Fair deal: *A fair and just bargain* * I struck a fair deal with him regarding the sale of his car

Fair weather: *Nice weather or good conditions* * We should make the best of a fair weather

Fair-weather friend: *Selfish friend* * He is not to be trusted to render help as he is only a fair-weather friend

Fair words: *Pleasant; conciliatory words implying flattery or deceit* * It is human nature to get flattered by fair words

Fair-fall: *Good luck to* * We wish a fair fall to our cricket team against its Pakistani rivals in the coming Test match

Fair-field: *Just condition* * The fighter planes took full advantage of the fair-field and destroyed many battle-tanks of the enemy

Fair-minded: *Judging fairly* * Only fair-minded persons are appointed as judges

Fair play: *Impartial treatment; honest dealing* * A person who has a sense of fair play and common justice earns name and fame * He is well known for his fair play * We all believe in fair dealing

Fair-spoken: *Courteous* * He is a fair-spoken person

Fait accompli: *Something done which is irreversible* * The order passed in the lower court on the case has been ratified fait accompli by the high court

Faith healer: *Persons who heals by prayer* * In India there are many people who have faith in faith healers

Faked up: *Invented* *There was not a word of truth in what he said and the whole story seems faked up

Fall about: *Laugh uncontrollably* * They fell about when he slipped on the banana skin

Fall across: *Meet by chance* * An old friend of mine fell across me at the railway station

Fall among: *Find oneself in the midst of* * The drugged person found himself in the midst of hippies when he came to his senses

Fall apart: *Break into pieces* * Fragile material generally falls apart after a short time

Fall away: *Waste away; dwindle; decline gradually; to languish; grow lean; to revolt* * Patches of plaster had fallen away between the windows * During the general strike, the party's membership is likely to fall away * Our energy begins to fall away when we step into old age * That young man is falling away day-by-day on account of certain obstacles in getting married to his beloved

Fall back: *Retreat; give way, no matter what happens* * The armed forces fell back when they could not bear the brunt of the attack from the enemy * At last the rioters fell back * The weak always fall back to the strong * He is determined to take every risk at the cost of any fall back

Fall back upon: *Have recourse to as an expedient or recourse in reverse* * One must save enough in one's life so as to have something to fall back upon in old age

Fall behind: *To lag; be outstripped; get in arrear* * He always falls behind when we go uphill * Do not fall behind with your rent, or you will be evicted * Dull children fall behind the bright children in class * We have fallen back in payment

Fall between two stools: *To lose both possibilities by hesitating between them; succeed in neither of two alternatives* * One is surely to fall between two stools if one fails to make the best of the two courses of action * He hunted two hares and in the process left one and lost the other just as one falls between two stools

Fall down: *Fall to the ground; fail (in task, in expectation)* * He fell down and hurt his arm * He fell down on his promises * He tripped and fell down

Fall flat: *Fail to effect* * My suggestions and advice fell flat on him * The new play has fallen flat * His speech on tariff reform fell flat

Fall for: *Become enamoured of; be taken in* * He falls for every pretty face he sees * The working class was not going to fall for this marginal sop

Fall foul of: *Come against; clash with; get into trouble* * He was found drowned in a river after falling foul of local poachers * This ill-tempered fellow falls foul of everyone * The two friends fell foul of each other over a trifle * He fell foul of the law

Fall from power: *Loss of a powerful position* * The military coup resulted in fall from power of persons in the higher echelons of the toppled government

Fall guy: *Easy victim; scapegoat* * An innocent person generally becomes an easy fall guy for shrewd persons

Fall in: *To stand in line* * On any emergency call the soldiers fall in at once

Fall in love with: *Start to be in love with someone; start to like something very much* * He fell madly in love with that girl at first sight * I have fallen in love with this beautiful valley

Fall in with: *Concur or agree with; comply with; meet by chance* * I have already fallen in with his proposal to start a new business * He fell in with my views at once * A soldier is bound to fall in with the orders of his superiors

Fall into disgrace: *Be out of favour* * The minister fell into disgrace in the eyes of the Prime Minister

Fall into disuse: *Not to be used any more* * Most of the dresses of old styles have fallen into disuse

Fall into steps: *Put left and right foot forward likewise with others* * All three of them fell into step when walking to the garden

Fall into the hands of: *Be caught* * He fell into the hands of his enemies

Fall off: *Become detached and drop; deteriorate; die away* * The admission of new entrants in this college has fallen off * The price of this item has fallen off considerably in the market * The standard of efficiency in public service has fallen off considerably

Fall on: *Begin eagerly; make an attack; to meet* * People were falling on each other with delight * Terrorist groups were falling indiscriminately on men, women and children in the remote village * The falcon's eyes fell on its prey and it pounced upon it to kill it

Fall on one's feet: *Come well out of a difficulty; gain any unexpected good fortune* * Some people always seem to fall on their feet to succeed *

The handsome young man fell on his feet to propose to a lovely daughter of a billionaire

Fall out: *Quarrel; happen; befall* * He has fallen out with the girl he was going to marry * It fell out that I could not get there in time

Fall safe: *Made so that if anything goes wrong it will stop working and not be dangerous* * Fall-safe arrangement is a pre-requisite in the installation of any nuke plant

Fall short: *Turn out to be short or insufficient; get used up; fail to attain or reach what is aimed at* * I could not buy that umbrella because I fell short of money * After having run fast in a long race, I fell short of breadth * The arrow fell short of the bull's eye

Fall through: *Fail; come to nothing; happen to meet* * His scheme fell through for want of money and material * The scheme has fallen through for want of support * The big talk of removing poverty has fallen through

Fall to: *Begin to eat; apply to; begin hastily* * He was so hungry that he fell to eating his meal like a wild beast * I fell to wondering where to go for my holidays * It fell to me to act the part of the host

Fall to the ground: *Come to nothing; fail; be disappointed* * The project plan fell to the ground for paucity of funds * All their efforts to save the drowning woman are likely to fall to the ground

Fall under: *Be classifiable under* * The results regarding the utilisation of funds fall under three heads

Fall upon: *To attack; rush against; developed upon; descend upon* * Our army fell upon the enemy like hawks * The strong storm fell upon us * Whenever the President falls ill, his responsibilities are taken over by the Vice-President * Darkness fell upon the scene * A great stillness had fallen upon everything

Fall wide of the mark: *Long way from being correct* * Your answer fell wide of the mark * His assessment of the situation might fall wide of the mark

Fall wide of the target: *Miss the target* * He hit the football wide of the target and failed to score a goal

Fallen on evil days: *In misfortune* * Many well-educated people have fallen on evil days and are deprived of a square meal

Fallout: *Radioactive dust from a nuclear explosion* * The fall-out of atomic bombardment in Japan caused havoc beyond imagination

False alarm: *A warning without danger* * We have had more trouble with false alarms than actual arson

False bottom: *Secret compartment* * There was a false bottom in my lost bag which contained Indira Vikas Patra worth thousands of rupees

False colours: *A false pretence* * Some of the businessmen sell their goods under false colours

False hearted: *Treacherous; deceitful* * You must beware of the false-hearted people and avoid their company

False shame: *Shame for that which is not shameful* * She took it as a false shame when she was asked to reveal her identity

False-face: *A mask* * He concealed his identity with a false face and plundered the unarmed travellers

False-faced: *Hypocritical* * There are false-faced persons who can swindle others easily

Familiar with: *Acquainted with* * I am quite familiar with his tricks * His name is familiar to me

Fan out: *Spread out like a fan* * The troops stormed the enemy's trenches and fanned out across the fields

Fan the flame: *Aggravate the tension; make a situation more extreme in a way* * He fanned the flame of bitterness between the two parties * Without doubt the rumours fanned the flame of hatred that led to a serious conflict between two parties * Both the films will be big hits and fan the flames of the film director's success

Fancy for: *Liking for* * I have no fancy for this type of work

Fancy oneself: *Have an excessively high opinion of oneself* * He fancies himself as an orator when he cannot speak more than two sentences

Fancy price: *Unreasonable high price* * He is demanding a fancy price for this watch.

Fancy someone: *Attract someone* * I think she fancies you

Fancy-monger: *One who concerns himself with love* * There is no dearth of fancy-mongers in this world

Fancy-sick-love-sick: *One who is sick with love* * A fancy-sick-love-sick man was ready to sacrifice everything that he possessed to win the heart of his beloved

Far and away: *By a great deal; by a large degree, amount* * Rajkumar is far and away the best actor I have ever seen * He is far and away the better of the two players

Far and near: *Everywhere* * People come from far and near to take a holy dip in River Ganges at Prayag * They searched far and near for the missing child

Far and wide: *To a great distance; over a large region* * The bang was heard far and wide * People come from far and wide to take a holy bath in the River Yamuna

Far away: *Distant; abstracted; absent minded; by far* * He is a man who has visited far away places of this globe * She had a far away look in her eyes * A far away student is lost in his stream and does not know what is going on in the class

Far be it: *God forbid* * Far be it that the passengers on the flight to London are not safe and sound

Far Ben: *On terms of great intimacy or favour* * He got quick promotion as a result of far Ben that he has developed with his boss

Far between: *At wide intervals* * We do compare our notes but far between

Far cry: *Long distance* * Ancient India is a far cry from modern India

Far flung: *Thrown far and wide; extensive* * We had a view of far flung areas while travelling by air * We were amazed when he gave a far flung account of his odyssey

Far from: *Not at all* * The newspaper accounts are far from being true

Far most: *Most distant or remote* * This diamond has been brought from a person who lives in a far most place in the lap of a hill

Far off: *In the distance* * You must give up your proposed journey to that far off place which is not free from danger

Far reaching: *Having wide validity, scope or influence* * Our national constitution stands in need of far-reaching changes to adequately meet the new challenges * Our rivers can produce large amounts of hydro-electric power if harnessed properly

Far seeing: *Having foreknowledge*

or foresight * Only far seeing people can think of ways and means to make a bright future for India

Far-fetched: *Fetched or brought from a remote place; forced; unbelievable* * This natural gift has been far-fetched from an unknown area * The ideas he expressed seemed too far-fetched to be believable * It would be a far-fetched scheme to pluck the twinkling stars

Far-framed: *Widely known* * Pandit Jawaharlal Nehru was a far-framed personality

Farm out: *Pass or send (work) to be done by one party to other* * As she has more knitting orders than she can cope with, she farms them out to other ladies

Farm-sighted: *Prudent, having good judgment of future needs, etc.* * His far-sighted plan which was executed long ago is now paying rich dividends in the country

Far-off: *Far away* * The days are not far-off when India will be a Super Power

Fast and furious: *Uproaring; wild* * The fun was fast and furious

Fast bind, fast find: *Make things secure* * If you lock your things you will not lose them and can instantly locate them when needed, thus proving fast bind, fast find

Fast breeder reactor: *Nuclear machine which makes surplus nuclear material* * All the developed countries have got fast breeder reactors to boost their nuclear energy output

Fast by: *Close by* * The five-star hotel is situated fast by the Clock Tower

Fast colours: *Coloured clothes which do not bleed or fade when washed* * We all prefer wearing dresses which are dyed in fast colours

Fast living: *Life given to pleasures* * Rich men indulge in fast living which shortens their life

Fast-and-loose: *A cheating game practiced at fairs* * Never play fast-and-loose with anyone's sentiments

Fasten on: *Direct (one's eyes) on; fix the blame; lay hold of* * He fastened his eyes on me, making me feel embarrassed * We should never fasten on the blame on any person without verifying the facts * Once he had fastened on a schemes he did not let go

Fasten up: *Do up* * Fasten your coat up

Fat fat-head: *Stupid person* * Never depend upon him for he is a fat fat-head

Fat lot: *Very little* * A fat lot you care about your health

Father figure: *Old man respected because of his concern for others welfare* * Mahatma Gandhi was a father figure for the nation where everybody listened to him with reverence

Fathom out: *Find the meaning of (a mystery)* * It took many years to fathom out the immense power of atoms

Fathom upon: *Understand on* * I cannot fathom upon the reason for having written this article on me

Faux pas: *A social blunder* * I committed a serious faux pas by making fun of Tom as I did not know he was her friend

Favours to come: *Favours still expected* * We have submitted a comprehensive plan to the concerned ministry and their favours are yet to come for its execution

Fear for: *Feel anxiety about* * We fear for his safety as he is in a dangerous situation

Fear no colours: *Fear no enemy* * Soldiers who surrender in war have to fear no colours.

Fear of: *Anxiety for the safety of* * He is in fear of his life

Feather in one's cap: *A striking distinction, something one may be proud of* * His promotion to the rank of Brigadier at a very young age is a feather in his cap

Feather in the scale: *Of little importance* * A casual burst of rain in the desert is like a feather in the scale

Feather-brained: *Silly and forgetful* * Our servant is a feather-brained fellow

Feather one's nest: *Accumulate wealth for oneself while serving others; in a position of trust; make things comfortable for oneself; enrich oneself* * There are many instances of persons entrusted with power have tried to feather their own nest at the cost of public money * There was a piece of news that a trustee of a big charity has been booked for feathering his own nest * Only selfish persons think of feathering their own nest in total disregard of the rights of others

Feature film: *A film that is usually one-and-a-half hours long** There are many interesting feature films in Hindi produced by Indian producers

Fed up with: *Bored with; sick of* * Children can never get fed up with listening to stories * I am already fed up with this nonsensical talk

Fed up (with): *Had too much of* * I am fed up with hearing you grumble all the time

Feed on: *Take as food* * Cattle feed chiefly on grass

Feeder school: *Junior school which provides children for a senior school* * Feeder schools play an important role in preparing children for higher education

Feel about: *Search with hand* * He was feeling about in the dark for the electricity switch

Feel as if/though: *Have, give the impression that* * He feels as if his head is about to break into two due to a headache

Feel bound: *Obliged* * We need not feel bound to accept this offer

Feel cheap: *Have a sense of inferiority and humiliation* * As he was not dressed for the occasion he felt cheap in the company of the elite

Feel cold: *Feel by touching; give or produce the impression of being* * The knife felt cold * Your hands feel cold

Feel disinclined to work: *Not feeling like working; unwilling* * She is rather disinclined to go to work today

Feel equal to: *Be capable of* * I don't feel equal to the task

Feel free: *Be at liberty* * I allowed my friend to feel free in using my bicycle as and when he needed it

Feel like: *Be disposed or inclined towards* * I don't feel like (eating) a big meal now * We will go for a walk if you feel like it * It feels as if it is going to rain or snow

Feel one's legs: *Begin to support oneself on one's legs* * It is but natural for a child to feel thrilled when he begins to feel his legs

Feel one's way: *Act cautiously until one has more experience* * He is feeling his way in the cave where he has gone to explore the hidden natural resources * They are feeling their way towards an agreement

Feel rot: *Feel ill* * The stinking pond made me feel rot

Feel small: *Feel insignificant* * I felt small when I could not participate in their intellectual talk

Feel somebody out: *Try cautiously to learn one's opinion* * I will feel out the members of the committee before coming to any decision

Feel the pulse: *Examine the pulse* * The doctor felt my pulse and told me that I had high temperature

Feel up to: *Be well enough to* * He does not feel up to taking a long walk

Feel up to doing something: *Feel strong enough to do something* * Due to weakness he does not feel up to cleaning the cupboard

Feel with: *Feel as; be of same opinion; have sympathy* * I feel with you in your sorrow * I feel with his sentiments that were free and frank * I feel with you in your misery

Feel wretched: *Feel ill* * I feel wretched to hear about the ghastly murder of the young couple

Feet on the ground: *Sensible and practical attitude towards life* * Successful businessmen have their feet firmly on the ground and take things for what they are

Fell: *Cause to fall; strike down; cut down (a tree)* * He felled his enemy with a single blow * He felled a tree with an axe

Felter out: *Speak in a hesitating way or with a broken voice* * He feltered out a few words and then ran away—I think it means falter or stumble upon words and should come four pages above

Fence in: *Surround with a fence* * The cottage stands on a sloping road which is fenced in by iron railings

Fence off: *Build a fence around open space* * The railway line was fenced off

Fend for oneself: *Look after oneself* * Most of the animals let their young ones fend for themselves

Fend off: *Defend oneself from* * He had to fend himself off when attacked with a staff

Ferret about: *Search busily by pushing and pulling things about* * He was ferreting about among old papers for something he had lost

Ferret out: *Discover by searching** Scientists are busy ferreting out secrets of deep seas

Ferry to and fro: *Take back and forth* * The bus ferried people to and fro the railway station

Fertile imagination: *Strong and easy faculty of imagination* * He has a fertile imagination as he can cook up a story in a minute

Fetch and carry: *Perform humble services for another* * Many poor persons earn their living by fetching and carrying loads

Fetch off: *Bring out danger or difficulty* * The young man was rewarded for having fetched off a drowning child from the canal

Fetch out: *Draw forth; develop* * The sale of the old house fetched out more money through auction than was expected * He has to fetch out crockery from the cupboard every day

Fetch up: *Recover; come to a stop; bring up* * This medicine will help him fetch up from his illness * The vehicle fetched up the moment its tyre got punctured * After the death of her mother, the little baby was fetched up by her aunt

Fever pitch: *Great excitement* * Our exhilaration reached fever pitch on the day of the wedding

Few and far between: *Few and rare* * His visits to my house are few and far between these days

Fiddle about: *Useless or wasteful permit; play aimlessly* * I spent about two hours just fiddling about * He was fiddling about with a piece of string

Fiddle about with: *Change position of a thing many times to one's satisfaction* * He has the habit to fiddle about with decorative articles in his room

Fiddle-de-dee: *Nonsense* * Everybody rebuked him for his fiddle-de-dee talk

Fiddle-faddle: *Trifling talk or behaviour; fussy; trifling* * I am already fed up by his fiddle-faddle * An idle person is rather prone to fiddle-faddle action

Fiddle-fiddler: *One who plays music* * You fiddle-fiddler are not playing the right tune

Field day: *Busy and exciting time; a day on which military operations are practiced* * We had a field day while we carried out the work of cleaning dirty gutters and ponds in a nearby village * The local papers had a field day maligning the politician * Our regiment will be observing a field day to get the soldiers acclimatised to the cold environment

Field of view: *What is visible at one moment* * A brown figure dressed in red crept into her field of view

Field of vision: *Range from one side to another over which you can see clearly* * The doctors checked his eyesight and found his field vision quite satisfactory

Fifth column: *Enemy sympathizers inside a country under attack* * Every government of a country should deal with the fifth column mercilessly

Fifty-fifty: *Half-and-half; share and share like* * Profits were to be split fifty-fifty between the two shareholders.

Fight a losing battle: *Try to achieve something but without success* * He fought a losing battle while contesting in the election against his adversary

Fight back: *Exert to avoid possible defeat* * In the first instance he had to suffer many setbacks but he is likely to fight back to win the wrestling match

Fight down: *Try hard to get rid of unavoidable situation* * He had to fight down to escape from the rowdy crowd

Fight fire with fire: *Treat, or pay back in the same coin* * We were left with no option but to fight fire with fire against the enemy

Fight for breath: *Breathe but find it very difficult* * As he suffers from incurable asthma he has to fight for breath during the monsoon season * I had to fight for breath in the suffocative and dingy room

Fight for one's life: *Make great effort to stay alive* * He met with a serious accident and is fighting for his life in the hospital

Fight is on: *Fight is continuing* * The fight against the terrorists is still on in various sectors of the country

Fight it out: *Fight until a dispute is settled; struggle till the end* * He will not give in easily but will fight it out to the last for his rightful claim * The captain and his troops will fight it out till the battle is won

Fight off: *Struggle against* * We had to fight off our cold by taking aspirin and putting on warm clothes

Fight one's way out: *Advance, go forward by fighting* * He fought his way out of the unruly crowd

Fight shy of: *Avoid* * All the children fought shy of remembering their lessons * Do not fight shy of telling the truth * I fight shy of discussions on religious matters

Fight to the finish: *Fight until one side is defeated or exhausted* * He fought the wrestling bout to the finish

Fight windmills: *Struggle with imaginary opposition* * He is really a fool who spends time on fighting windmills

Fighting chance: *Possibility of success if great efforts are made* * It depends on a fighting chance to get elected for the Lok Sabha seat

Figment of imagination: *Thing which has been imagined* * The story he is telling is nothing more than a figment of imagination

Figure of speech: *Colourful expression used to illustrate a meaning* * 'Get up with the lark' is a figure of speech meaning 'get up early in the morning'

File with: *Rank with; be equal to* * A Deputy Inspector General of Police is filed with a Brigadier in the army * During British rule in India the Rajas and Maharajas were filed with the Captain, Major, etc.

Fill in: *Put into* * Fill in the blanks with suitable words

Fill up: *Put into; to complete* * He was busy to fill in the pits with stone and earth * Fill up the blanks with suitable words * All the vacancies will fill up by the month end

Fill up the cup: *Commit offences to the fullest gravity* * The activities of militants and terrorist have filled up the cup of tyranny on a global scale

Final cause: *The end or object for which a thing is done especially the design of the earth* * It is beyond one's comprehension to know the final cause for the creation of this wonderful universe

Find a fig-leaf: *Find conventional device for concealing genital organs in old drawings, statues, etc.* * It was necessary for men and women to find a fig-leaf to cover themselves up for living in a civilised society

Find an indictment: *Of a grand jury to be satisfied that there is a prima facie case and to endorse the Bill* * A judge accepts a case for hearing if he finds an indictment for the same

Find fault: *Censure for some defect* * He always finds fault with my work

Find fault with: *Complain* * Those who find fault with it do so on political grounds * I have no fault to find with your work

Find favour (with): *Win favou*r * It is only for his honesty that he finds favour with everybody

Find in one's heart: *Be able to bring one* * He had to find in his heart a way to bear with a heavy loss that he had suffered.

Find it in one's heart: *Be so unkind or callous as to* * How can you find it in your heart to drown these little kittens?

Find one in: *Supply one with* * I hope this news will find you in happiness

Find one's account: *Derive advantage* * He finds his account by swindling gullible persons

Find one's feet: *Become able to stand; able to cope with new condition* * It will probably be a week or two before he finds his feet after a prolonged illness * It will not take long for him to find his feet as a lawyer

Find one's legs: *Become habituated; attain ease* * When I was transferred to a very cold hilly station, I thought that it would take me a fortnight to find my legs * I shall certainly find my legs under the protection of security guards

Find one's level: *Come to equilibrium in one's natural position or rank* * Everybody feels comfortable when he finds his level

Find oneself: *As regards health; feel; happiness* * When he regained consciousness, he found himself in hospital * How do you find yourself this morning? * He found himself as if he were in a fairy-land.

Find out: *Dig out; discover; try to understand; learn, come to know* * The manager will sack him at once if he finds out that his employee is dishonest * I will find out who is at the bottom of the mischief * We found out that he was wrong

Find somebody out: *Detect somebody in wrongdoing or error* * Do you think the police will find them out?

Fine fettle: *Very good condition* * The very old man is still in fine fettle

Finish (up) with something: *Have at the end* * We had an excellent dinner and finished up with a glass of brandy

Finish neck and neck: *Be equal winners* * The two athletes finished the race neck and neck

Finish off: *Kill; destroy* * The captain finished him off with his revolver

Finish somebody off: *That fever* * The fever nearly finished him off.

Finish something off/up: Eat up completely * We finished up everything on the table

Finish up: *Eat completely* * They have been told to finish up everything that is placed before them

Finish with: *Stop being friendly with someone; stop being*

interested with something * I have not finished with you yet * I had finished with the play for ever

Finish with somebody, something: *No longer is he engaged with somebody or busy with something* * I have not finished with you yet as I still have something to say * Have you finished with that dictionary?

Finishing touches: *Perfect a thing by final polishing* * The portrait is now ready for finishing touches

Fire alarm: *Bell, siren which gives warning that a fire has started* * As soon as there was a fire alarm, the fire engine reached the spot to extinguish the fire

Fire and brimstone: *Hell* * The preacher warned us that fire and brimstone await us if we commit a sin

Fire and sword: *Military devastation* * Pakistan did carry enough fire and sword to crush the rebellion in East Bengal

Fire away: *Go; proceed now without further delay; ask your question* * I will fire away whether he listens to me or not * May I fire a question at you? * Now that you have received your order, fire away

Fire for: *Dismiss* * The employee will be fired for his incompetence

Fire has burnt out: *Fire has gone out because there was nothing left to burn; extinguished* * The fire has burnt itself out in the house that was on flame

Fire is out: *It is not burning* * We cannot prepare tea as the fire is out

Fire off: *Discharge; ask or utter in rapid succession* * The minister fired off his personal assistant for his misconduct * He fired off a bullet from his gun * He was so excited that he fired off his sentiments to the surprise of the people around him

Fire out: *Expel* * Three IAS officers were fired out of service on charges of corruption.

Fire up: *Start a fire; become excited or angry* * At times, they had to fire up to keep themselves warm while on an expedition * She fires up at the least of provocations

Fired with: *Filled with zeal* * Fired with enthusiasm, he proceeded to work without any loss of time

Firing squad: *Group of soldiers who shoot someone who has been condemned to death* * In

China, hard-core criminals are shot by a firing squad

Firm on: *Stable; steady* * The baby is not very firm on his feet yet

Firm up: *Be sure and steady/solid; to finalise* * The exercise will help a person to firm up the loose muscles * Let's firm up this agreement

First and foremost: *Before anyone or anything else* * Rugby is first and foremost a team game * First and foremost remember that fish are live creatures with feelings

First and last: *Altogether; on the whole* * The first and last thing about him is that he is eccentric * The first and last thing of my aunt is that she is crazy about singing

First catch your hare: *Make sure you have a thing before you think what to do with it* * One must first catch one's hare before thinking of what to do with it because it would be like counting your chicks before they have hatched

First cause: *The original cause* * The first cause of his rapid success is his honesty and integrity followed by simplicity

First come, first served: *Those who come first will be served first* * The plots were allotted on the basis of first come, first served * Applications will be dealt with on a first-come-first-served basis

First edition: *Copy of the first printing of a book* * The first edition of this book was published in 1990

First hand: *Obtained directly* * They have first hand experience of managing charitable organisations

First rate: *Of higher rate or excellent; pre-eminent in quality, size or estimation* * We need the services of first rate administrators * He is well known for his first-rate performances

First sight: *Seen or examined for the first time* * He fell in love with Deepa at first sight

First storey: *The first level of a building* * He lives with his family on the first storey of this building

First thing: *As a first action* * For me the first thing in the morning is to remember God and seek blessings from elders at home * The first thing that we have to do is to capture the bandit alive

First things first: *Most important things before the others* * We must deal with first things first before going on to the next

First time: *Immediate* * Our first time concern is to purchase a suitable house.

First water: *The first or higher quality* * He is a scholar of the first water.

First-rate: *Excellent* * We were all praise for his first-rate acting on the stage

Fish in troubled waters: *Take advantage of troubles of others* * During their stay in India, the English fished in troubled waters

Fish out: *Take out* * I fished out a coin from my pocket and gave it to the beggar

Fish out of water: *Be in uncomfortable position* * When the postmaster was transferred to a remote place, he felt like a fish out of water

Fit as a fiddle: *Quite fit* * He takes physical exercises daily to keep himself fit as a fiddle.

Fit for: *Suitable or competent* * It is better for you to make yourself fit for your new duties

Fit in (with): *Be in a suitable or harmonious relation (with)* * I must fit my holidays in with yours * My holiday arrangements must fit in with yours * Your action does not fit in with your work * The colour of your pants does not fit in with your coat

Fit of the face: *A grimace (distortion of the face in jest)* * He made people laugh with the fits of his face

Fit on: *Put into place* * Before he went out, he fitted a new lock on the main entrance door

Fit out: *Furnish; equip* * The ship has been duly fitted out for a long journey * Our military personnel should be fit out with high quality arms

Fit up: *Provide with fittings* * This hotel is fitted up with modern comforts and conveniences

Fits and starts: *Spasmodic and irregular burst of activities* * If you study by fits and starts you cannot succeed in the examination

Five o'clock shadow: *Dark tint on a man's chin as his beard begins to grow* * We can observe the five o'clock shadow on the face of an adult

Five senses: *Sight, hearing, smell, taste and touch* * All living beings are blessed with five senses

Fix on: *Single out; decide for* * The supervisor fixed his attention only on what I was doing * A duty has been fixed on me to collect the monthly charges for boating on the lake * I feel they will fix on staying in a hotel for the night

Fix up: *Arrange; settle* * We have already fixed up a tea party on Sunday * The marriage of my sister has been fixed up to take place on 14th of next month

Fizzle out: *Come to nothing; not to work* * The strike fizzled out after three days * Your tricks will soon fizzle out the moment you are made to lick the dust

Flare up: *Burst into sudden blaze or anger* * The conflict flared up into a civil war

Flash in the pan: *A fitful discharge; a fitful show of beginning without accomplishing anything* * Many of the promises stated in the manifestos of various political parties prove to be a flash in the pan * The teen's good results at the beginning of the season are nothing but a flash in the pan * His enthusiasm to be a good sportsman proved to be a flash in the pan

Flat broke: *With no money at all* * How can he buy this hat when he is flat broke?

Flat out: *At full speed; using every effort* * He was working flat out * He could win the race if he goes for it flat out * Go there flat out and give him this letter

Flat rate: *A fixed uniform rate* * We charge a flat rate of a hundred rupees per magazine that are displayed in the stall

Flat spin: *State of confusion* * He was thrown into a flat spin when he unexpectedly got his transfer orders to a remote area

Flea in one's ear: *A stinging rebuff* * Don't blame me if you get a flea in your ear from your boss for asking such a question

Flesh and blood: *Human nature; one's own kindred* * Flesh and blood cannot tolerate the insult * This is more than flesh and blood can endure * As you are my own flesh and blood, I cannot hurt you

Flesh out: *Add more details and more information* * These are the main points that I have talked about and now I will flesh them out for you

Flex one's muscles: *Preparing to fight* * He is flexing his muscles to participate in the general elections as a candidate for the Lok Sabha seat

Flick off: *Remove with a sudden movement* * She flicked crumbs off the table cloth

Flick through: *Look at quickly by turning over pages* * I only flicked through this book before I purchased it

Flight of stairs: *Series of steps from one floor of the building to the next* * There is a flight of stairs from the ground floor to the topmost floor of the business house

Flimsy excuse, argument: *One that is not convincing* * He was taken to task for his flimsy excuse

Fling dirt: *Talk abusively or slanderously* * It has been noted that politicians fling dirt at one another whenever they can

Fling off: *Take off quickly and carelessly* * He flung his dress and shoes off before going to bed

Fling out: *Discard; go angrily or violently; break out in impetuous plain speaking* * When we moved to our new home, we had to fling out unwanted stuff * He flung out of the room, uttering hot words to his wife * She flung out of the room in anger

Flirt with: *Show affection for without serious intentions; pretend to be interested in but not seriously* * She flirts with every handsome man she meets * He is flirting with the idea of going to London

Float voter: *Person who is uncertain which party to vote for in an election* * Knowing nothing about contesting candidates in the election, there are many float voters who cannot decide who to vote for

Flock together: *Come together or in a group* * Birds of the same feathers flock together

Flog a dead horse: *A wasted effort* * Asking that rich miser for charity is like flogging a dead horse

Flood in: *Come in great quantities or numbers* * Letters of grief came flooding in after his death

Flood of light: *More than sufficient or full information* * The *Gita* throws a flood of light on *karmayoga*

Flood out: *Compel to leave because of flood* * Thousands of people will be flood out from this area during the rainy season

Floodgates: *Making something possible for a large number of people* * This opened the floodgates of revolution in the field of space technology * The new schemes will open floodgates of opportunities to unemployed people

Floodlights: *Artificial lightning thrown in a bright and broad beam* * The stage in the hall was lit up with different shades of floodlights

Flower of speech: *Ornamental phrase* * The formal use of flower of speech is preferred to an informal use in a civilised society

Fluke victory: *Victory resulting from a luck-stroke* * Many a time the victory scored by our cricketers in a Test match is nothing more but a fluke victory

Flunk out: *Fail* * He flunked out in biology * He is likely to flunk out in all his science subjects

Flush out: *Drive out of hiding* * Snipers flushed out foxholes

Flush with: *Level with; having plenty of money to spend* * The doors are flush with the wall * Flushed with funds, they can afford to buy all the luxury items they want

Fly a kite: *Put forward an idea how people react to it* * He is just flying a kite without any serious intent

Fly at a tangent: *To suddenly change from what one is talking or thinking about* *It is difficult to get a firm decision from him because he is always going off at a tangent

Fly at: *Attack suddenly* * He looked angrily at me as though he was going to fly at me * As he could not tolerate abusive language, he did not hesitate to fly at his opponent instantly

Fly high: *Be ambitious* * Almost everybody wants to fly high to have a comfortable life

Fly in the face of: *Set oneself directly against; insult; oppose* * Some new rules and regulations introduced in our Constitution fly in the face of our established old traditions * Morally we should not fly in the face of our elders * You are flying in the face of the law * His version of what happened flied in the face of all the evidence

Fly into a rage: *Become suddenly angry* * She flew into a rage and screamed out with all her might

Fly off the handle: *Lose your temper* * Some people fly off the handle on minor issues

Fly open: *Open suddenly or violently* * The raging storm flew open the doors and windows of every house in the locality

Fly out: *Break out in a rage* * Why

are you flying out when he has paid all your dues?

Fly to arms: *Take up arms eagerly* * Every terrorist flies to arms to create trouble of some kind

Flying saucer: *Object shaped like a saucer which people say they have seen in the sky* * The sight of a flying saucer in the sky has become the talk of the town

Flying squad: *A group of policemen who arrive quickly at the scene of the crime* * A flying squad plays an important role in saving life and property from miscreants

Flying visit: *Very short visit* * The commander of the army paid a flying visit to the border area

Fly-leaf: *Blank leaf of paper at the beginning and end of a book* * Almost all books have a fly-leaf

Flyover: *Road built to pass over another* * In modern cities we see flyovers for smooth running of the traffic

Fob off: *Put off or evade by a trick or a lie* * I asked my friend to accompany me to a cinema show but he fobbed me off by saying that he was not keeping well

Fob off on: *Dispose of something undesirable or inferior dishonestly* * He managed to fob his car off on an unsuspected buyer

Fob someone off with something: *Deceive someone into accepting something which they don't really want* * He may try to fob you with a prescription for pills

Foe-man: *An enemy in war* * They released their foe-men from captivity in peace time

Foist something on someone: *Force someone to accept something which they do not want* * They were not out to foist their ideas and views on the people

Fold up: *Bend something over to make a smaller area than before; finish; cause to finish* * * The bird folded up its wings * The project has since been folded up * The business finally folded up last week

Follow home: *Follow to the end* * It was very difficult for him to follow home the tenets as explained by his mentor

Follow in one's father's foot steps: *Do as he did* * There are persons who follow in their father's foot steps throughout their life

Follow in one's steps: *Follow one's example* * If we want India to be a great country, we should follow in

Gandhiji's steps

Follow in the fashion: *Do what others do in matter of dress* * Most Indian girls are following the fashion prevailing in the West

Follow on: *Continue; endeavour; (in cricket) bat again after failing to get necessary number of runs in the first innings* * He is determined to follow his studies in science and technology * To avoid a follow on, the rival team had to play again in the second innings to level the score and save an innings defeat

Follow one's nose: *Go straight forward* * Be ready to follow your nose when you start a new job

Follow out: *Do something the way directed or indicated* * He promised me to follow out my advice

Follow suit: *Do what another has done* * If you join this club, I will also follow suit

Follow through: *Complete the swing of a stroke after hitting the ball; follow a particular idea to sustain its correctness; complete a task* * You are not following through after playing the stroke * He was asked to follow through a particular line of research * He has followed through the assignment entrusted to him with good grace

Follow up: *Pursue an advantage closely; pursue a question that has been started* * The results of the research were further followed up for the benefit of humanity at large * The question raised in Parliament in connection with corruption is being followed up by the committee set up for the purpose.

Fond hope: *Hope that is held but unlikely to be realised* * Almost every man and woman has a fond hope of becoming a celebrity

Food poisoning: *Illness caused by something eaten* * He died from food poisoning

Food values: *The relevant nourishing power of foods* * Our health depends on the food values that we consume

Fool about, around: *Behave in a silly way* * He was always fooling about * As we do not like to be a laughing stock we refrain from fooling around

Fool away: *Squander to no purpose or profit* * Don't fool away your hard-earned money in wild pursuits

Fool to others, to himself a sage: *Self-praise is no recommendation; one should not*

give airs to oneself * He is a fool to others but to himself a sage because he keeps on saying that he is a great man when he is not * A fool is always a fool in the eyes of others though he may think himself to be wise

Fool with: *Meddle with officiously* * Who was fooling with my papers?

Fool's paradise: *A state of happiness based on fictitious hopes* * The Taliban in Afghanistan is living in fool's paradise if they think that they can survive for long on support from Pakistan

Fool-errand: *Search for what cannot be found; a silly or fruitless enterprise* * He was so far engaged in a fool-errand in his bid to locate the real murderers * It was a fool-errand but he will never accept it

Foolery: *An act of folly; habitual folly* * His foolery has made him a laughing stock in the neighbourhood * He will never refrain from his habit of foolery even when guests are present

Foolhardy: *Foolishly bold; rash* * Do not be foolhardy as to accept a challenge from a person who is stronger than you * It was considered rather foolhardy for him to quit his job * He is a foolhardy driver and tries to overtake other vehicles every time

Foolish witty: *Wise in folly and foolish in wisdom* * It was an interesting experience to be in the company of a foolish witty man for a few hours

Foolproof: *Not liable to sustain or inflict injury by wrong usage; infallible* * The machine is foolproof against theft because it sets off an alarm when a thief draws near * He presented a foolproof scheme before the house which was duly approved

Foot and mouth disease: *An infectious disease of cattle* * Many a time, cattle suffer from foot and mouth disease

Foot it: *Walk; dance* * You will have to foot it for some more distance as the cottage is still some distance away * We decided to foot it rather than wait for the next bus * She did foot it well to the beat of the drum

Foot the bill: *Pay up* * I agreed to foot the bill for the dinner at Marina Hotel * He asked me to dinner, but I had to foot the bill

Foothold: *Grip; A place to fix the foot in* * I tried to gain a foothold in the organisation

Footless: *Having no hold or footing* * In a democracy, a party in minority is footless when confronting a party in majority

Foot-licker: *A fawning; slavish flatterer* * There is no dearth of foot-lickers to our ministers * I do hate a foot-licker

Foot-loose: *Free; unhampered* *A number of foot-loose young men can be found in our country without the burden of any responsibility * He is living a foot-loose life these days

Foot-loose-and-fancy-free: *Independent and without care or responsibility* * A foot-loose-and-fancy-free person has nothing to worry about

Footmark: *Mark or print of foot; a track* * The footmarks of our great men do remind us that we can also make our lives sublime * A big game hunter traces his prey by following the footmarks of the wild animal

Foot-sure: *Not making false steps* * A foot-sure person is bound to succeed in his mission

Foot-work: *Manner of using the feet, e.g. in boxing or dancing* * The foot-work of the dancing couple in the hall was quite in tune with the beat of the drum

For a laugh: *For amusement only or as a joke* * People in the crowd seemed bent on heckling the speakers for a laugh * I have given him the wrong address just for a laugh

For a short: *In the first place* * For a short, we have neither money nor time to undertake the new project

For a song: *For a very little money* * You can buy many items from this store for a song

For a time: *During a time* * While committed to finish a job within a prescribed time we enjoy sipping tea for a time

For a wonder: *By ways of an unexpected but pleasant change* * For a wonder, he paid back the money he had borrowed from me

For account of: *On behalf of* * The Minister spoke in the Parliament for account of the Socialist Party

For ages: *For a very long time* * Good and noble people are remembered for ages

For all: *Notwithstanding* * For all that he put the cards on the table yet nobody believed him

For all it is worth: *To the utmost* * They exploited it for all it is worth

For all that: *In spite of everything*

* He burnt midnight oil on his studies for months together but for all that he could not secure a first class in the B.A. examination

For all the world: *Precisely or exactly* * She took out a paper and began to read for all the world as if she was at home in bed

For all you are worth: *As much as possible* * Please undo this problem for all you are worth

For any sake: *By all means; I beseech you* * He would be helpful to you for any sake * For any sake, please save the life of the child who is in dire need of blood

For better or worse: *For all times be it good or bad* * For better or worse they have fallen in love with each other

For certain: *As being certain* * I cannot say for certain that he would come forward to help

For effect: *So as to make a telling impression* * His appeal before the public was for effect and appreciated by one and all

For eight hours solid: *Without stopping* * He sleeps for eight hours solid

For ever: *All eternity* * He is not here for he has left forever for his heavenly abode

For external application only: *Only to be used on the skin* * This tube contains the medicine for external application only

For fear of: *Because of anxiety about* * She asked us not to be noisy for fear of waking up the baby

For fear (that): *In order that* * I didn't tell you everything about him for fear that he would be angry with me

For free: *Without being paid* * I promised him to give him a wrist-watch for free

For good: *Permanently; irrevocable* * He has left India for good and settled in Canada * When we breathe our last, our departure to another world is for good

For good and all: *Finally* * He had to struggle hard for long but for good and all the case was decided in his favour

For instance: *As an example* * We must know the value of morals, for instance, the principles of right and wrong

For keeps: *As a permanent possession (for goods)* * The farmer rears cattle for keeps

For life: *For the whole period of one's existence; save one's life* * He was destined to suffer the pangs of solitude for life

* He had to run for life when chased by a snake

For love or money: *In any case, whatever* * You cannot find another room at this time for love or money * It is useless to befriend him for love or money

For mercy/For mercy's sake: *An earnest conjunction in the form of an appeal* * For mercy's sake, save the life of that innocent man from the clutches of his abductors

For miles: *Over a distance of* * He can run for miles at a stretch

For my part: *As far as it concerns me* * I do not know who is at fault but for my part, I have nothing to say

For nothing: *Without any reason* * You say that they were fighting for nothing but there cannot be smoke without fire

For old sake's sake: F*or the sake of old times* * History stands for old sake's sake * I do not wish to break our friendship for old sake's sake

For once: *On one occasion only* * Diwali comes for once in a year

For one's own hands: On one's own account * He did all that for his own hand

For one's pains: *As reward or result of trouble taken* * Honest and real freedom fighters got nothing for their troubles

For sale/On sale: *Ready to be sold* * Is this house for sale? * A large variety of clothes are on sale in that shop for ten days

For shame: *You should be ashamed* * For shame, you should not have cheated that poor old man

For short: *As abbreviation* * M.P. for short stands for Member of Parliament and P.M. stands for Prime Minister

For sure: *Certainly* * He will, for sure stand by you in adversity * There was nothing wrong with him for sure

For that matter: *As for that; indeed* * He is shivering with cold and so am I for that matter * He deserves punishment for that matter

For the account: *For settlement* * We shall take this matter for the account in our next meeting

For the best: *With the best intentions or outcome* * Let us hope for the best in what we are doing for our countrymen

For the best part of an hour: *For almost an hour* * He does physical exercises daily for the best part of an hour

For the first time: *Not happened before* * I saw him for the first time at the railway station

For the future: *With future in mind* * A wise person always provides for the future

For the life of him: *Though it were to save his life; try as he might* * His motorcycle skidded off the road in a hilly region, but for the life of him the vehicle stopped near the bushes * For the life of me, I could not recall her name

For the love of: *For the sake of* * Put that gun down for the love of God

For the moment: *For the time being* * I don't want to discuss this at the moment

For the most part: *Chiefly; in the main; commonly; mostly* * .For the most part the Himalayan ranges are covered with heavy snow * Visibly, for the most part, the weather seemed nice in the coastal region * We share our joys and sorrows with one another for the most part * For the most part of the discussion his conduct was free and frank

For the present: *At the present time; now* * For the present he is busy doing something important * He is for the present serving a life sentence * I think this would keep you busy for the present

For the rest: *As regards other matters* * Let's deal with the most important items and for the rest we can tackle them some other day

For the sake of something/For something's sake: *Out of consideration for; in the interest of* * I will help you for your old father's sake * He argues for the sake of arguing * We must be patient for the sake of peace * Do something for the sake of that poor man's family * The company might well decide for the sake of efficiency

For the time being: *At the present time* * You better come after two hours to see him as he is asleep for the time being

For the worst: *To a worse state* * We must be prepared even for the worst

For want of: *As something better is not available* * For want of anything better to do he continued to read * The earthquake victims are suffering for want of food and medical supplies

For what it is worth: *A phrase*

implying that the speaker is doubtful of the truth of what he has reported or unwilling to be responsible for its accuracy; without any guarantee or promise concerning it * I have brought my note-book for what it is worth * Since I heard the news I wanted to pass it on to you for what it is worth

For why: *For what reason* * I do not know for why he was dismissed from service

Forbade: *Prohibition (archaic)* * We did not trespass into the region for it is a forbade

Force and fear: *That amount of constraint which is enough to annual an engagement or obligation entered into under its influence* * Work done under force and fear cannot be fruitful

Force back: *Push back from doing something against a strong emotion* * He forced back the strong urge to speak to her

Force of habit: *Accustomed to doing always something by nature* * Many of them made a fuss in class from force of habit when the teacher left the class-room

Force somebody's hand: *Make him something un-willingly or earlier than he wished to do it* * Untimely snowfall on the hills forced our hands to postpone the expedition to Kanchenjunga

Force the pace: *Bring and keep the speed up to a high pitch by emulation* * To boost our economy we will have to force the pace of our commercial trading with foreign countries like China

Forced labour is better than idleness: *It is a wise thing to compel an idle hand to work* * There can be no two opinions about the saying that forced labour is better than idleness

Forced landing: *Landing of an aircraft under some trouble/emergency* * Because of trouble in the engine, the pilot had to make a forced landing

Forced sale: *A sale compelled by a creditor* * He could square up the loan through forced sale of his cattle

Force-feed: *Feed someone by force* * The persons on hunger strike were force-feed on the tenth day of their strike

Forcible detainee: *Detaining property by violence or intimidation* * The act of forcible detainee to take into custody has legal sanction

Forcible entry: *Taking property into custody or forcing entry into it by violence or intimi-*

dation * Forcible entry to take into custody the property of any person is allowed in many countries

Forcible feeble: *A wealsman; statesman who shows valour* * Forcible feeble persons are tolerable everywhere

Fordo: *Destroy; ruin* * Don't fordo your future career by indulging in idle pursuits

Forefinger: *The finger next to the thumb* * Many people make use of tips of their fingers for calculation purposes

Foreign body: *An object that has come accidentally into something else that should not be in it* * As a foreign body has entered his eyes he is writhing in pain

Foreign to one's nature: *Very strange for him, to do it* * Lying is foreign to his nature

Foreknowledge: *Knowledge in advance* * He had a foreknowledge of his friend's bad intentions

Foremost: *First; chief* * It is our foremost duty to be good citizens * This is the foremost compartment of the ship

Forensic medicine: *Medicine concerned with crime* * With the application of forensic medicine crime experts can dig up a great deal of information about the reason for crime

Forethought: *Thinking ahead* * He already had some forethought on this plot

Forever: *For ever; for all time to come; eternally* * Mahatma Gandhi's deeds will be remembered forever

Forevermore: *For ever here after* * He, being a jail bird, has been ordered to report his presence forevermore to the senior house officer of the police station once everyday

Fore-warm: *Prepare for trouble in advance* * To be forewarned is to forearmed

Forge ahead: *Make steady progress; take the lead (in race)* * He is forging ahead in his career * In the second leg of the race competition, 'B' was forging ahead of all motorists

Forget-me-not: *Small plant with blue flowers* * Forget-me-not is a plant that adds to the beauty of the garden with its tiny blue flowers

Forget oneself: *Lose one's self-control or dignity; resort to words and deeds unworthy of oneself* * 'Oh darling?' cried he, forgetting himself * Nobody likes to talk to him for he tends to forget himself

Forgone conclusion: *Known be-*

forehand * The outcome of both the votes was a forgone conclusion

Fork out: *Hand over (pay)* * I had to fork out a lot of money to pay taxes this year

Forlorn hope: *Desperate plan; enterprise, etc.* * There is a forlorn hope that he may get that job

Formal cause: *The essence or idea of a thing* * The formal cause of music and dance is to entertain the people at large

Foreman of a jury: *Spokesman for the jury* * The press correspondent got this information from the foreman of the jury

Formic acid: *Acid found in the sting of ants* * Formic acid can be exploited to medicinal purposes

Form into: *Move into a particular order* * The company was formed into three ranks

Formulate: *Reduce to or express in a formula; state or express in a clear form* * We have formulated our own strategy * He emphasised the need to formulate a policy that would promote rather than hinder peace * His thoughts were so formulated that they had a telling effect on his followers

Forthcoming event: *Event planned to happen soon* * I wrote to the minister seeking his advice on the forthcoming election

Forthright: *Clear and strong in one's thinking and feeling* * He had a reputation for being a bit forthright

Forthwith: *Immediately* * He will take up his duties forthwith

Fortune favours the brave: *A coward can never become lucky* * It has been said rightly that fortune favours the brave

Fortune hunter: *One who hunts for a wealthy marriage* * The fortune-hunter's main aim is to become wealthy in no time

Forwander: *Wander till wearied; to stray far* * Nomads can be placed in the category of forwanders * Due to heavy fog the tribe of nomads got forwandered * How did they got forwandered? —I think this is some obsolete word because I could not find it anywhere

Forward-looking: *Thinking ahead; dealing with the future optimistically* * It is because of his forward-looking approach that he is now reaping rich dividends

Foster home: *Family and home where a foster child is brought up* * The child is very happy and comfortable at his foster home

Foster-child: *Child brought up by parents who are not his own* * A foster-child has been adopted by the couple because they have not got one of their own

Foul play: *Bad intention; injustice; dishonest dealing* * I suspect foul play in the murder of that innocent girl * Nobody believes him for his foul play * He would be willing to use any ruse, any dirty trick, any amount of foul play to get what he wants

Foul up: *Spoil doing something wrong; make or become foul* * So many good schemes have been fouled up by elementary mistakes in planning * The factory chimneys foul up the air with smoke

Fountain-head: *The beginning; the head or source* * Regions like Africa have proved to be the fountain-head of many new ideas on the causes of cancer * The *Vedas* are fountain-heads of vast knowledge on various aspects of human activities

Fragrant memory: *Pleasant memory* * I cannot forget the fragrant memory of my host who entertained me throughout my stay at his place

Frame house: *Wooden house* * The hermit lives in a frame house near the dense forest

Frame of mind: *Temper; mood* * I am not in the right frame of mind to solve this riddle just now

Frame of reference: *A particular set of beliefs or ideas to base your judgement* * Their frame of reference was totally American

Frame-up: *Conspiracy to make an innocent person appear guilty* * The charges levelled against that poor man were nothing but a false frame up

Frame-work: *The work that forms the frame; the skeleton or outline of anything* * You can't make decisions without an ethical frame-work * They were able to absorb the dangers within the frame-work of traditional institutions and ideas * There are nine large panels set in a richly carved frame-work

Fraternise with: *Become friendly with someone* * One feels a great joy in fraternising with small children * Pakistan has been more successful in fraternising with USA and China than India

Fraught with: *Filled with (unpleasant consequences)* *

Do not venture out any further as the area ahead is fraught with danger

Freak of nature: *Person, animal or plant that is abnormal in form* * It was a freak of Nature that a cow gave birth to a five-legged calf

Freak out: *Get very excited because of the effect of drugs* * He freaked out after taking a doze of LSD that made him violent

Free enterprise: *The conduct of trade and industry with the minimum of state control* * I am a believer in free enterprise as I do not approve of any restrictions from outside

Free fall: *A jump at a great height from an aircraft before the parachute opens* * There was a spectacular show of free fall by dare-devils from an aircraft

Free fight: *A confused or promiscuous fight* * In olden times the soldiers engaged in free a fight on the battlefield

Free from: *Exempt from; without* * He is free from every illness * There are persons who are free from all kinds of care

Free hand: *Complete freedom of action; generous giving; anything done by hand with easy movements without using ruler, compass or other instruments* * He has a free hand in helping the poor generously * It is a free-hand portrait sketched by a well-known painter.

Free holder: *Person who possesses freehold estate* * A freeholder has absolute title to the land

Free in: *Without any influence* * I am free in my decision

Free kick: *Kick allowed for a penalty without opposition from any player* * He scored a goal by a free kick

Free of: *Outside; without hindrance; get away from* * As soon as the ship was free of the harbour, it set sail to its destination * The area here will be reasonably free of pollution by the end of next year * The goods arrived free of duty * We need services of a lady free of encumbrances * At last I am free of his clutches

Freedom of speech: *Ability to say what you like* * In our sacred Constitution there is provision of right to freedom of speech for every citizen

Free-for-all: *A disorganised fight or argument in which everybody joins in* * The fight turned into a free-for-all * This would result in a free-for-all on wage bargaining

Free-handed: *Generous* * A free-handed person becomes popular with poor people

Freehold: *Holding of land in absolute ownership* * The person with freehold has absolute title to the land

Freelance: *To serve anyone for pay* * John used to be a freelance photographer * Are you an employee of that firm? No, I work freelance * He gave up his regular job in order to work freelance

Free-spoken: *Accustomed to speak without reserve* * He, being a free-spoken man, is respected by all

Freeze one's blood: *Fill one with terror* * The appearance of the ghost froze his blood

Freeze out: *Exclude from business, society, etc. by competition or cold behaviour* * The firm has frozen out some of the parasitic employees

Freeze over, up: *Make cold, hard* * This lake freezes up in the winter season * Frozen up food is preserved by being kept very cold * The lock has frozen up

Freight with: *Load with* * The boat has been freighted with fruit

Fresh air: *Open air* * Fresh air is very useful for good health

Frigid zone: *North of Arctic and south of Antarctic Circle* * The frigid zone is not suitable for human habitation

Fringe benefits: *Extra penny on top of salary* * Some well-established business houses give fringe benefits like free car, etc.

Fringe theatre: *Experimental drama often not using a traditional theatre building* * He is working in a fringe theatre that may lead him to become a successful actor

Fritter away: *Waste time, energy or money* * It is very easy to fritter away the best hours of the day in shopping

From a child: *Since the days of childhood* * It is really a usual story of a man growing old from a child

From day to day: *Each day* * He is getting more and more knowledgeable day to day

From first to last: *Throughout* * During the long span of his educational career, he stood at the top from first to last

From force of habit: *Because it is something you ordinarily do* * There are many people who cannot give up smoking from force of habit

From hand to mouth: *Improvidently* * In these days of high prices most people have to live from hand to mouth * Many people in this country live from hand to mouth

From Monday to Friday: *Including both Monday and Friday* * He stayed with us from Monday to Friday

From off: *From a position on* * He cried excitedly from off top of a hill.

From out: *Out from* * How would you identify an Englishman from out of the five Americans?

From pillar to post: *From one state of difficulty to another; hither and thither* * I, being an apprentice, had to rush from pillar to post merely to find out his whereabouts * He wandered from pillar to post to get a suitable job but in vain

From point to point: *From one particular (detail) to another* * He dwelled on his subject from point to point

From stem to stem: *From one end of the vessel to the other; completely; thoroughly* * A ship sets sail only after it is found completely fit for the sail by being checked from stem to stem * Having taken into account all aspects of the new scheme, it has been found free from any fault from stem to stem * I have examined the whole plot from stem to stem and it will certainly deliver the desired results

From that day forward: *From then on* * He is facing many problems from that day forward

From the bottom of my heart: *With heartfelt; sincerely* * I wish you all success from the bottom of my heart

From the bottom of one's own heart: *Most sincerely* * He followed my instructions from the bottom of his heart

From the first: *From the start* * He romped home in the race because he ran fast from the first

From the word go: *From the start* * From the word go, he did not look behind till he reached the goal

From time immemorial: *From remote time* * The dowry system has been in vogue from time immemorial

From time to time: *Now and then* * He promised to remind me from time to time regarding the action to be taken in future

From want of: *In the absence of*

* The plants died from want of water

From within: *From the inside* * We have to fight the enemies not only from without, but also from within

From without: *From the outside* * His friends from within the family are included as also from without

Frontline troops: *Troops facing the opposing enemy's troops* * Our frontline troops are ready to face any attack by the enemy

Front runner: *Person likely to win (in an election)* * Considering the number of votes that have been counted, Subhash is still the front runner

Frost over/up: *Become covered with frost* * The windscreen of my car frosted over/up during the night

Froth at the mouth: *A mass of small bubbles coming from the mouth* * He was rolling on the floor and frothing at the mouth

Frown on: *Disapprove of* * Any sign of priggishness is frowned on/upon by common people * Gambling is very much frowned upon here

Fruit cocktail / prawn cocktail: *Mixture of fruit or prawns in a salad* * The meal for dinner was served with fruit cocktail

Fruition: *Realisation of hopes* * My plan to become rich have come to fruition after a long time * Our aim could be brought to fruition through perseverance and dedication to the job in hand.

Full and by: *Closely hauled to the wind* * We found it difficult to move easily under the pressure of full and by

Full boarding: *Bed and all meals* * It will cost only a few hundred rupees a day for full boarding in this hotel

Full brother, sister: *Son, daughter of the same parents* * We are full brothers and full sisters

Full fling: *At the utmost speed; recklessly* * The vehicle was at full fling when it collided against an electric pole * Refrain from driving at full fling to avoid serious accidents

Full of: *Completely filled* * The room was full of people * She was full of news (could not refrain from talking about it)

Full of beans: *In high spirits* * The brave and the courageous are always full of beans

Full of fire and fury: *Full of haughty temper* * A person full of fire and fury would not yield to any pressure

Full of years: *At a good old age* * We are now full of years and thus losing agility and energy day by day

Full pelt: *At full speed* * He ran at full pelt to win the race

Full sail: *With sails filled with the wind* * The ship covered the voyage in full sail from London to Bombay

Full speed: *Highest possible speed* * While competing in a race I did try to run at full speed to be a runner-up at least

Full speed ahead: *Go forward as fast as possible* * They reached their destination with full speed ahead

Full steam ahead: *Forward at the greatest speed possible; with maximum effort* * They chased the enemy with full speed ahead of the stipulated time * The commander ordered his platoons to pounce on the enemy with full steam ahead * The power project was completed at full steam ahead of the given time

Full tilt: *At full speed in a headlong course* * He was running at full tilt

Full up: *Full to the limit* * The car parks are all full up

Full well: *Very well* * We know full well that he would leave us in the lurch

Full-blooded: *Vigorous, hearty* * There is a great demand for full-blooded young people in the army

Full-blown: *Completely open* * The roses in the garden are full-blown

Full-blown doctor: *Thoroughly qualified* * He is a full-blown doctor

Full-fledged: *Having complete training* * He is a full-fledged colonel in the army

Full-scale: *Fullest extent* * We are prepared for any crisis including a full-scale warfare

Full-throated: *Singing; laughing, etc. with the whole power of the voice* * She sang a full-throated song

Full-time: *All the time* * The needy man has been able to get a full-time job

Fulminate against: *Protest loudly and bitterly* * It is but natural to fulminate against the apparent idleness of the younger generation

Fumble in/at: *Feel about uncertainly with hands* * He fumbled in his pockets for the key * He being drunk fumbled at the lock for a long time

Fun and games: *Lively merry-making* * I was sick of their fun and games

Fun fair: *Amusement park* * Children usually go to the fun fair to pass some pleasant time

Fur and feather: *Furred animals and birds* * In the West, people hunt for fur and feather which should be banned

Furnish with: *Supply or provide with* * The library was furnished with books and periodicals

Furnished rooms, flat: *Rented place where the furniture is provided by the owner* * He has rented a furnished flat at the hill station

Further to: *In addition to* * Further to your second query, the payment of the goods will be sent to you immediately on receipt of your bill

G

Gain from: *Benefit from* * We always gain from somebody's experience

Gain ground: *Advance; obtain advantage; become more general; make progress; win a success or advantage* * Our forces are gaining ground in the pursuit of the enemy * One cannot gain ground without proper planning * The belief in efficiency of vaccination is gaining ground * Literacy is gaining ground in the backward areas of our country * You cannot gain ground unless you become regular or serious in your job.

Gain on: *To overtake by degrees; to encroach on* * I was gaining on him towards the end of the race * We should desist from gaining on the rights and privileges of others

Gain one's point: *Persuade somebody to agree to one's objectives* * He was able to gain a point in the discussion with his persuasive powers

Gain time: *Improve one's chances by delaying on some pretext; obtain extra time by making excuses* * It was a ruse to gain time for fighting a wrestling match * The job which could have easily be done in a day was prolonged for two days by gaining time

Gain upper hand: *Gain control over* * At last he was able to gain the upper hand over his adversary

Gall and wormwood: *Too bitter or very annoying; hateful* * He is hated by one and all for his gall and wormwood remarks * Prohibition is gall and wormwood to distillers

Game was washed out: *Could not be played because of rain* * The cricket match was washed out today

Garden of remembrance: *Garden dedicated to the memory of the dead* * He has gone to the garden of remembrance to pay homage to his dear mother

Garden syringe: *Instrument for spraying tree with insecticides, etc.* * To keep your plants and trees healthy it is advisable to make use of a garden syringe

Gasp for breath: *Have difficulty in breathing* * While climbing the summit of the mountain at high altitude, we had to gasp for breath due to insufficient oxygen

Gasp out: *Utter in a breathless way* * He was so breathless that he could hardly gasp out a few words

Gates of death: *The point of death* * It is surprising that all of us are oblivious of gates of death from which there is no escape

Gather breath: *To recover wind* * We found it difficult to gather breath in the gale

Gather ground: *To gain ground* * Their ideas are gathering ground to come to a meaningful conclusion

Gather one's way: *Gain speed* * He gathered his way to reach home before sunset

Gather oneself together: *To collect all one's powers; like one about to leap* * The army had to gather itself together to repulse the heavy enemy attack * The fox gathered herself together and made a sharp attack on its enemy

Gather thistles and expect pickles: *True enjoyment never comes out of evil deeds* * To expect a reward for his evil deeds would be like gathering thistles and expecting pickles

Gather to a head: *To come into a state of preparation for action or effect; reopen* * The mutiny had to be crushed when it gathered to a head * The boy has mentally gathered himself to a head for undergoing an operation

Gather way: *To get headway by sail or steam so as to answer the helm** The sailors managed to gather way in the high sea against the tempest

Gathering dust: *Not being used regularly* * My old briefcase has since long been gathering dust

Gay science: *The provincial name for the art of poetry** The gay science is a subject which is very academic but interesting

Gazump someone: *Accept a higher price for a house which someone has already agreed to buy* * You should not have cheated that gentleman by gazumping him

Gear something to: *To fit; to match* * They were not geared up to participate in an armed combat * A new policy is being geared towards rehabilitation

Gear to: *Adjust one thing to the working of another; make dependent on; to match* * The country's economy must be geared to wartime requirements * A new policy is being geared towards rehabilitation

General rules: *Established rules* * There would be lawlessness everywhere if we do not abide by the general rules of life

Generation gap: *Difference in years between one generation and another* * The generation gap creates tension between parents and children

Gentleman at large: *One who has no occupation* * As a result of unemployment we find many gentlemen at large these days

Gentleman of the robes: *Pleaders; barristers* * The gentleman of the robes has been helpful in enabling the judge to understand the true facts of the case

Gentleman's agreement: *Agreement which is not written down* * He borrowed some money from me on a gentleman's agreement

German Shepherd: *Alsatian dog* * Have you had a German Shepherd to look after the flock of your sheep?

Get a blow in: *Succeed in placing a blow* * The boxer defeated his opponent by getting a blow in the cheek of the latter

Get a ducking: *Fall into the water* * It was raining heavily and we all got a ducking

Get a glance of: *Have a quick view* * We got a glimpse of odd objects from the window of the running train

Get a line on: *Get information* * The police have got a line on the hideout of the criminal

Get a look-in: *Get a chance (of winning)* * You will not get a look-in with such strong competition

Get a lot of bounce: *Be full of energy* * He has got a lot of bounce and has made a mark in boxing

Get a lot of mileage out of: *Gain benefit to a large extent* * We can get a lot of mileage out of the new economic policy

Get a move on: *Make progress; hurry up* * He is getting a move on his first adventure * We are a bit late for the party so we had better get a move on to

Get a nerve: *Be cheeky; rude* * He has got a nerve to break the promise he made to her

Get a rap over the knuckles: *Be criticised for* * We got a rap over the knuckles for being late

Get about: *Be no longer confined to bed or to the house; spread from person to person quietly; travel* * He is getting about again after the accident * The news of defeat was censored but it will soon get about

Get above oneself: *Have too high an opinion of oneself* * Rich persons generally get above themselves

Get across: *To take effect; make understand successfully* * Make sure that the message gets across immediately regarding the need to start the machine * I spoke slowly but my meaning did not get across to him * We managed to get our message across

Get ahead: *To make progress; attain* * John has got ahead of all the boys in the class * To get ahead to the topmost rank in the merit list is my aim this year

Get along: *Manage; make progress* * We can't get along without money * How are you getting along with your new job?

Get an eyeful of something: *Have a good long look at something* * I got an eyeful panoramic view of the lush green valley

Get another thing coming: *Change plan, opinion or idea* * You will have to get another thing coming as the proposal put forth by you won't work at all

Get at: *Reach; attain; bribe; corrupt; discover; criticise; taunt; attack* * I must get at his secret plan * One of the witnesses had been got at * He has been able to get at the facts of the case * He got at me bitterly * He is always getting at his wife * The stray dog tried to get at me

Get away: *Manage to leave or escape* * Two of the prisoners got away from jail * There is no get away from the arms of law

Get away with: *Execute something successfully; pull it off* * The thieves got away with the contents of the safe * If I cheat in the examination, do you think I can get away with it?

Get back: *Return to power or prominence after losing it for a time; be in the same state, condition or situation as before; revert to talking something again that was discontinued; start work again after you have stopped doing it* * The Congress party hopes to get back in the general elections * Things would soon get back to normal * Let us get back to the argument for a proper conclusion * Do get back to your seats without wasting any more time

Get bogged down: *Get struck* * The discussion got bogged down in details

Get by: *Pass or be accepted without comments, criticism; manage; survive* * I am happy that I could get by my extempore speech in the conference * How can he get by on such low wages?

Get by heart: *Commit to memory* * That scholar has got by heart all the scriptures

Get cold feet: *To get nervous enough to continue* * He got cold feet in the wrestling bout and had to give a walk over

Get down: *Lower one's body for sitting or lying on the ground; depress; swallow; write down; deal seriously with; make one unhappy* * They got down on their knees for the prayer * Do not let this cold weather get you down * The medicine was bitter and I could not get it down * Did you get that telephone message down? * After sipping his cup of tea, he got down to his work * Don't let them get down with your ugly remarks

Get down to: *Start to* * The poor man got down to hard work for earning his living

Get down to brass tacks: *Begin to discuss in straightforward terms* * It was considered necessary to get down to brass tacks before signing the agreement

Get down to business: *Start the work that must be done* * It was incumbent on him to get down to business assigned to him

Get even with: *Take revenge on* * He did not let his foe go till he got even with him * On the bases of give and take, they got even with each other

Get hitched: *Get married* * My friend got hitched at the age of twenty-six

Get (hold of) the wrong end of the stick: *Misapprehend a matter fundamentally* * You got hold of the wrong end of the stick by making false allegations against the innocent boy

Get home: *Be fully understood* * That remark of yours about the merits of punctuality has got home to him

Get in: *Arrive; be elected* * The train got in five minutes late

* He got in the Parliament as a member

Get in a latter: *Get upset; flustered* * The witness got in a latter when he turned up hostile before the judge * He got in a latter when he heard the sad news of his failure in the examination— I find this rather unusual

Get in the neck: *Be severely dealt with* * If you break discipline in the army, you are sure to get in the neck

Get into: *Get inside* * He got into his car and drove off * He got into my room without my permission

Get into a groove: *Become set in one's ways, one's style of living* * After completing his education, he got himself into a groove as a manager in some factory

Get into a mess: *Get into muddle* * His accounts seem to have got into a mess

Get into a temper: *Become angry* * When he got into a temper, he began to punch me hard * He got into a temper over a trifling matter

Get into bad habits: *Acquire them* * Do not let yourself get into bad habits

Get into difficulties: *Be in danger* * He got into difficulties when swimming

Get into hot water: *Involve in difficulties* * The professor got into hot water with the principal for taking part in politics

Get into mischief: *Do something naughty* * This boy is always getting into mischief

Get into a scrape: *Get into trouble* * Avoid mixing up with undesirable elements or you might get into scrape

Get into touch with: *Contact with* * For further information, you can get into touch with me on phone

Get into trouble: *Be in a difficult situation; do something that will bring in happiness, punishment, etc.* * If you break the law, you will get yourself into trouble * He got into trouble with the police

Get it /Something together: *Organise or manage it; put it in order* * We got it together by building trenches as a safety measure against the air-raid

Get it all taped: *Everything is under control; know how to do it perfectly* * You have got it all taped and therefore need not worry

Get loose: *Escape* * One of the tigers in the zoo has got loose

Get lost: *Go away* * The speeding aircraft got lost in the sky * He got lost in his own dream

Get lost your way: *Be unable to find way to where you were going* * In the pitch dark he got lost his way in the thick jungle

Get more than one bargained for: *Be unpleasantly surprised at the consequences* * People criticised him for getting more than he bargained for in the deal with his tenant

Get no change out of: *Fail to get the better of him* * He tried all kinds of tactics to defeat his opponent but could get no change out of the latter

Get nowhere: *Totally unsuccessful* * I got nowhere despite trying to persuade him to agree with me

Get off: *Escape; start; alight* * He got off by paying a small fine instead of a possible imprisonment * We got off immediately after breakfast * I got off immediately when the train stopped

Get off lightly: *Escape severe punishment or suffering* * The juvenile got off lightly with a small amount of fine

Get off scot-free: *Escape punishment* * The accused got off scot-free for want of solid evidence

Get off the ground: *Rise into the air; pass from the planning stage and make its start* * The helicopter got off the ground and then took flight to its destination * There was a hurry to get the new film off the ground

Get off the hook: *No longer in a difficult situation* * He got off the hook by paying a fine

Get off with somebody: *Have a romantic encounter with someone* * The nurse got off with a young doctor at the dance

Get on: *Proceed; make progress; advance; board; agree; pass* * How are you getting on with your new business? * He is sure to get on in life very well * Either get on in your mission fearlessly or get out * When the train arrived, he got on it

Get on (with somebody): *Work or live in a sociable way* * The new manager is easy to get on with * They do not get on at all together

Get on like a house on fire: *Quickly become friendly and jolly together* * They get on like a house on fire

Get on one's feet: *Recover after a setback* * The industry needs some time to get on its feet again

Get on one's high horse: *To act high and mighty; show off;*

boast * One must always be polite and should not get on one's high horse with poor persons

Get on to somebody: *Get in touch with* * If you are not satisfied with the firm's services, get on to the manager

Get one taped: *Understand one completely* * I have been in his association since childhood so I have got him taped

Get one's breath: *Get back to normal state* * After having run a marathon race, I felt the necessity of getting my breath

Get one's cards: *Be told to leave* * On getting one's cards one must leave immediately rather than hanging around

Get one's eye in: *Follow with one's eyes in the movement of the ball* * A good player always gets his eyes in the ball to get control over it

Get one's fairings: *Get one's rewards* * A suitable award must be given to him so that he gets his fairings for his sacrifice

Get one's fingers burnt: *Be in trouble* * If you fall out with your boss in office you will surely get your fingers burnt

Get one's goat: *Enrage; irritate; annoy* * Do not let them get your goat

Get one's hand in: *Get control of the play so as to turn one's cards to good use; get into the way or knack* * Once he gets his hand in the affair, he will certainly make the most of it * He has got his hand in driving the car smoothly

Get one's hand on: *Find or obtain* * That is what happened when the poor get their hands on money

Get one's knickers in a twist: *Become harassed or confused* * He got his knickers in a twist when severely grilled by the police

Get one's monkey up: *Become or make angry* * His interference in my affairs got my monkey up

Get one's own back: *Retaliate; be even; have one's revenge* * He is committed to get his own back for the harm you have done to him * In order to get his own back he has already compensated you for your loss * He tricked me this time but I will get my own back one day on him

Get one's sea legs: *Be used to travelling by sea* * He has got his sea legs and never feels sea-sick

Get one's second wind: *Breathe again easily after having lost*

one's health; get new energy for a task; cover the ability to breathe regularly after the first period of breathlessness * He was lucky enough to get his second wind after a very severe heart attack * Having recouped his health, he was able to get his second wind * It is good that he got his second wind after a major heart-attack

Get one's teeth into something: *Attack (a job) vigorously* * The labourers got their teeth into completing the construction of the road within the given time

Get out: *Produce; extricate oneself; take oneself off; become known; remove* * Will we be able to get out the new book by the end of this year? * He could get himself out of the trouble involved * You better get out of the room or I will kick you * The secret got out * If the news gets out, there will be trouble * I cannot expect to get out of this stain

Get out of hand: *Be out of control* * The children have been pampered so much that they have got out of hand of the parents

Get out of somebody: *Extract* * The police have got a confession out of him for the theft committed by him

Get out of something: *Avoid doing something* * I have got out of the habit of eating chocolates

Get out of the bed on the wrong side: *Arise in the morning in an ill temper* * He got out of the bed on the wrong side and began to make fuss over trifles

Get out of the habit of: *Abandon the habit of* * The sooner you get out of the habit of taking alcohol the better for you

Get over: *Recover from; forget; surmount* * I could not get over the heavy loss in the business * He cannot get over his beloved wife who left for her heavenly abode last year * He could not get over his rage

Get over to: *Cause to make something understand* * He got his meaning over to me at the fourth time of trying

Get over with: *Reach the end of something troublesome* * I could not get over with severe pain after getting my tooth removed

Get people or things together: *Collect them* * The rebel leaders could not get an army together

Get rid of: *Be free* * Those who

have strong will power can get rid of smoking

Get round: *Circumvent; persuade; evade; become well known* * I could not get him round to my view * At last I could get him round to follow my instructions * A clever lawyer can find ways of getting round that penal clause * The news is getting round that weapons of mass destruction are reaching the wrong hands

Get sight of: *Succeed in seeing* * Whoever can get sight of the murderer will be awarded handsomely

Get somebody by the short hairs: *To get complete control over someone* * The money-lender has got the poor farmer by the short hairs for exacting a loan taken by the latter

Get somebody in: *Call somebody to one's house to perform a service* * We must get somebody in to repair the computer

Get somebody into the habit of: *Cause one to have the habit of* * Don't let him get you into the habit of taking drugs

Get somebody off: *Save from punishment or a penalty* * A clever barrister may get you off from this accusation * His youth and inexperience got him off

Get somebody off to sleep: *Help him to fall sleep* * She got the baby off to sleep by singing a hymn

Get somebody or something off: *Send* * They got their children off to school in time * Get this parcel off so as to reach him tomorrow before noon

Get somebody under one's skin: *Annoy somebody* * She is foolishly getting under his skin by rankling him with her foolish talk

Get somebody up: *Cause to rise* * Get the children up and dressed for the school

Get someone into trouble: *Make someone accused of doing something* * He got me into trouble by giving false witness against me in the court

Get someone off the hook: *Release someone from a difficult situation* * He cannot be let off the hook as he has admitted his guilt * He felt he had got off the hook too easily

Get something/Get it together: *Cause something to be organized; bring under control* * We have to get everything together before we launch an attack on our enemy

Get something down: *Complete it* * The farmer hopes to get down to planting of new saplings before the rain comes

Get something for nothing: *Get something free* * I have got this pocket-watch for nothing

Get something in: *Collect or gather; obtain a supply of something* * We had been able to get the crops in before it began to rain * You had better get coal in for the winter

Get something of: *Receive (have)* * I have got the possession of the bungalow allotted to me by the housing board

Get something off: *Remove; learn it until the words can be repeated mechanically* * The bridegroom got the ring removed off his finger and put the same in the finger of his bride * He has got many poems off without understanding the meaning

Get something off one's chest: *Say something one is anxious to say; taken from one's responsibility* * I have got the truth off my chest from which I would never budge an inch * My sharp words had been troubling me and now that I have got it off my chest my apologising to her, I am feeling greatly relieved

Get something off the ground: *Start something successfully* * If you want to get the project off the ground, you must have a well-disciplined staff

Get something on one's mind: Be *worried about something* * He has got something on his mind that has made him shaky

Get something out: *Utter; bring out* * He managed to get out a few words of thanks * We will get the new dictionary out by the end of the year

Get something out of the way: *Settle it; dispose of it* * He got the long-standing issue out of the way

Get something up: *Organise* * We are getting up a party for his birthday

Get something wrong: *Miscalculate or misunderstand it* * They got their plan wrong as a result of which the project failed

Get somewhere/Get anywhere/Get nowhere: *Obtain result or no result; make some, any or no progress* * If you are not regular in your work, it will get you nowhere

Get spliced: *Get married* * They got spliced when they

reached the age for marriage

Get square with: *Settle accounts; have one's revenge* * I have got square with him and therefore nothing stands due to him * He is determined to get square with you for the harm done by you to him

Get steamed up: *Become excited and violent* * Now don't get all steamed up over nothing

Get the better of: *Defeat; outwit; be overcome* * He got the better of his opponent in the wrestling bout * He got the better of his adversary in the argument * His shyness got the better of him

Get the blame for: *Said to be responsible for* * One of the employees of the firm got the blame for withdrawing a huge amount from the bank under forged signature

Get the boot: *Be dismissed; be kicked out* * He got the boot from his job for dishonesty

Get the day: *Get or gain the victory* * In the battle with the enemy, we got the day

Get the general drift: *Understand the general sense* * I got the general drift of his argument

Get the hang of something: *To learn how something works* * He is so sharp that he can get the hang of everything that he comes across

Get the laugh off somebody: *Score a point (against somebody)* * I got the laugh off my adversary in the argument

Get the measure of somebody: *Form an estimate of character, ability, etc.* * The interviewer had the acumen to get the measure of the candidates to be selected for a particular post

Get the message: *Understand* * I think now you must have got the message on how to tackle the issue

Get the needle: *Be irritated* * He got the needle when he was informed of his blunder

Get the point of: *Understand or comprehend* * He got the point of what she wanted him to do

Get the push: *Be dismissed* * He got the push from his job for his rude behaviour

Get the rise out of somebody: *Cause one to show petulance or weakness* * I got the rise out of him when I began to tease him on his stupidity

Get the run of something: *The permission to use it* * I have got the run of his library

Get the sack: *Get dismissed* * Do not break the rules or you will get sacked from your position in the job

Get the upper hand: *Have or get the advantage or control* * India is getting the upper hand over other advanced countries in the development of software

Get the wind of: *Get on the windward side of* * The sailor got the wind of sailing his vessel smoothly

Get the wind up: *Become nervous or apprehensive; be frightened* * He got the wind up when he saw the non-bailable warrant for his arrest * They got the wind up for having committed a great blunder

Get the worst of it: *Be defeated in a contest* * She got the worst of it in the declamation contest

Get the wrong end of the stick: *Misunderstand the meaning* * You seem to get the wrong end of the stick regarding his honesty and integrity

Get there: *Succeed; accomplish something* * To become an athlete of repute, he spared no effort to get there

Get this or it into one's head: *Become convinced; to understand* * The Iraq war broke out when the US administration got this into their head that Iraq had nuclear weapons of mass destruction

Get through: *Finish; put in telephonic communication; pass; spend; ensure that something is done; communicate* * I have got through a lot of correspondence today * As soon as I get through (with) my work, I will give you a call * As soon as your message got through to me, I rang you up * Though I worked very hard, yet I could not get through the test * I failed but my friend got through the examination * He has got through all his money * Please get the proposal through the committee * Try to get through to him that he is ruining his life

Get to: *Reach a particular state; safe custody; allow (somebody or something) in to the care or custody of/entrust to* * The vice-principal got to the post of principal ultimately * Get your money to the hotel manager to be looked after

Get to grips with something: *Begin to fight in a close combat* * It was not very long before they got to grips for distribution of booty

Get to sleep: *Manage to fall asleep or succeed in passing into the condition of sleep* * I could not get to sleep last night as I was having fever

Get to the point: *Give the facts that are essential (ignoring what is irrelevant)* * He got to the point when discussing the illicit connection between the two

Get to windward of: *Secure an advantage over* * He got to the windward of his adversary after a good deal of tussle

Get to work: *Start doing it* * The officials get to work on their allotted duties right from the morning

Get together: *Come or meet together* * Let us get together one evening to discuss some social issues

Get told of: *Be abandoned* * I dare not be late home or I will be told off

Get tough with someone: *Deal harshly; roughly with someone* * To extract the necessary information, the police had to get tough with the dreaded criminal

Get under: *Subdue; control* * The rebel of the tribal chiefs has been got under * They soon got the fire under (control)

Get underway: *Start to move forward* * He is underway to reach his destination

Get up one's nose: *To annoy someone* * His selfishness really gets up my nose

Get up to monkey business: *To make mischief* * An idle hand is generally prone to get up to monkey business

Get up to somebody: *Catch up with them* * We caught up to the others who were running ahead of us

Get up to something: *Reach* * We have get up to our eighth lesson of this holy book

Get value for money: *Get a good bargain* * It no longer gets value for money

Get weaving: *Get busy; get on the way* * He got weaving with his daily routine work * Come let us get weaving as we have to be there by 10 o'clock

Get wind: *Be rumoured; get a hint or intimation of* * I got wind of the fact that a bomb had been planted in the aeroplane * The police got wind of the criminal and arrested him red-handed

Get with it: *Become aware of what is popular and up to date* * In order to get with it, it is necessary to go through the leading newspapers

Get your bearings: *Find out where you are* * After a week at the job, he got his bearings

Get your own back: *Have your revenge* * I think the tussle is now over as you have got your own back on him

Get-a table: *Easy to reach* * Important documents must be kept at some get-a table place

Getaway: *An escape* * The prisoner was successful in making a getaway under the darkness

Get hold of: *Catch or seize; learn or understand well; obtain; have an idea; find out someone in order to contact* * The police got hold of the underground proclaimed offender * Once one has got hold of certain basic facts the rest is comparatively easy * How did you got hold of this car? * It is easy to see how they have got hold of this impression * This friend of mine got hold of me in Paris

Get on one's nerves: *Become oppressively irritating* * That noise gets on my nerves * Too much smoking is getting on my nerves

Get it in the neck: *Be punished or criticised* * You will get it in the neck if you are not careful

Getting for: *Becoming for* * He is getting too old for this job

Getting on for: *Approaching (of age or time)* * He is getting on for old age but he looks quite healthy and strong * It is getting on for midnight

Getting on in years: *Quite old* * We must give our due respect to all those who are getting on in years

Get-together: *A social reunion of old friends* * There was a get-together of retired employees of the university last night

Get up: *General appearance; rise up* * The general get-up of this magazine is rather elegant * I get up early in the morning and go out for a walk * The sun is getting up (ascending) * He has got himself up with his lesson (committed to memory)

Get up with the lark: *Get out of the bed early in the morning* * He gets up with the lark and goes to bed early to keep hale and hearty

Gift of the gab: *A talent (or propensity) for speaking* * There are rare persons who are naturally endowed with a gift of gab

Gild the lily: *Spoil the beauty of something by unnecessary embellishment* * It is an act of foolishness to gild the lily by adding to its natural beauty

Gild the pill: *To make a disagreeable thing seem less so* * It will be something like trying to gild the pill if we say that doping boosts energy

Gilded youth: *Rich young people of fashion* * The modern gilded youth enjoy life without a purposeful aim

Gilt spurs: *A mark of knighthood* * He was honoured with gilt spurs by the queen for his bravery

Gird oneself: *To brace up for any trial or effort* * We girded ourselves up for the fray

Gird up one's loins: *Prepare for action* * We must gird up our loins to fight against colonialism

Girdle stead: *The waist* * He always places hands at his girdle stead whenever he stands to sing a song

Give a bad name: *Give a bad reputation* * Ill deeds invariably give one a bad name

Give a cold shoulder: *Entertain poorly* – The treasury bench gave a cold shoulder to the purposeful proposal

Give a false colouring: *Misrepresent* * The police gave a false colouring to the case to save their own skin

Give a good account of oneself: *Do well, act in a way that brings credit* * He gave a good account of himself by topping the list of successful candidates in the final examination

Give a good run for one's money: *Obtain something in return for one's expenditure* * We must give him a good run for his money invested in the business

Give a hand with: *Help with* * My friend gave me a hand in climbing up the steps

Give a handle to: *Furnish an occasion for* * By your strange conduct, you will give a handle to suspicion and scandal

Give a horse his head: *Let him go as he chooses* * He is deeply interested in joining the army, so why not give a horse his head?

Give a lift: *Offer a ride in a vehicle; boost one's spirits* * Can you give me a lift to the railway station? * The big increase in my salary gave me a tremendous lift

Give a loose to: *Give rein or free vent to* * He gave a loose to his feelings in his impassioned speech

Give a new lease of life: *Give a better chance of living longer* * That service has given my car a new lease of life

Give a new look: *A new and more up-to-date appearance*

* The highway here has been given a new look

Give a piece of one's mind/ Give a bit of one's mind: *Rebuke; scold* * The boss gave a piece of his mind to the employee for coming late to office * I had to give him a piece of my mind for his negligence

Give a stone for bread: *Offer a mocking help* * It does not behove a good person to give anybody a stone for a bread

Give a wide berth to: *Avoid* * We should always give a wide berth to selfish persons

Give airs: *Boast* * He can't help giving airs to himself for his exceptional proficiency in sports

Give an eye to: *To attend to* * It would be a rational thing to give an eye to our shortcomings

Give and take: *Reciprocity in concession; mutually compensatory variations* * There must be a policy of give and take if some disputes are to be settled amicably * Is marriage a give-and-take affair?

Give arms: *To show armorial bearings* * The army gave arms with a lot of destructive power

Give away: *Distribute; give for nothing; reveal* * The governor gave away the prizes on the occasion of annual college function * He gave away a large amount in charity * Do not give away my secret to anyone

Give birth to: *Bring forth; originate* * She gave birth to a male child * Hunger for money have throughout given birth to many gory disputes

Give chapter and verse: *Give proof* * The judge set the alleged accused free when he gave a chapter and verse of his innocence

Give chase: *Go in pursuit* * The police gave chase to the pick-pocket and caught hold of him

Give colour: *To give plausibility (applause); give appearance or probability* * His timely help to needy people gave colour to his generosity * His torn clothings gave colour to his story about being attacked and robbed

Give countenance to: *Lend support* * He is always eager to give countenance to those who really stand in need

Give credence to: *Trust* * He did not give much credence to the concocted story

Give currency to: *Circulate* * Avoid giving currency to gossip

Give ear: *To attend; to listen* * The government must give ear to the plea of senior citizens for their safety * He gave ear to my request for help

Give effect to: *To carry out* * The new scheme will give effect to many social reforms

Give false colour to: *Give a wrong tone to* * Newspapers often give false colours to news reports

Give for something/Give to do something: *Exchange for something else with payment as compensation* * How much will you give for my old car?

Give forth: *Emit; publish* * The false news gives forth wrong signals amongst the people * Sensational news items are a common feature of some newspapers

Give ground: *Fall back; give way; yield; lose advantage* * The heavy gun fire made the enemy troops give ground * We should not give ground to enemy forces at any cost * They did not give ground to any person from outside * They did not give ground even in an adverse situation

Give grounds for: *Give a cause or reason for* * They do not give me much grounds for complaint

Give him an inch and he'll take an ell: *A concession will encourage the taking of liberties* * We may reduce the price of our goods but he is a person to whom even if we give an inch, he'll take an ell

Give hostages to fortune: *Take the risk of being harmed in future or take unwise step* * A wise person would never give hostages to fortune as he would avoid every risk

Give in (to): *Accept; surrender; yield to* * He has given in to my views * She usually has to give in to her brother's plan * The rebels were forced to give in * He would never give in to your warnings

Give in charge: *To hand over to the police* * The thief who was caught red-handed by the owner of the house was given in charge to the police to take necessary action against him

Give it to one: *Scold or beat one severely* * He gave it to the scoundrel

Give line/head/rein: *To give more liberty or scope* * The commander gave his army rein to crush the rebels

Give name: *The name bestowed upon the individual* * At the time of baptism a new-born child is formally given name by which he is called throughout his life

Give notice: *Warn beforehand; inform; intimate especially the termination of an agreement* * The court has given him notice to be present in the court by next week * The authority concerned has given him notice about the cancellation of his contract

Give offence: *Cause displeasure* * The play is liable to give offence to a particular community

Give on to: *Look out on; overlook* * The bedroom windows gave on to a courtyard * I can give one to my neighbour's room from my balcony easily

Give one a big hand: *Applaud one with enthusiasm* * People gave him a big hand for his melodious songs

Give one a prod: *Nudge one; try to get one to act* * He gave me a prod to retort to the bitter remarks of the speaker * My mother prodded me to get into the swimming pool

Give one beans: *To treat one severely* * You better give beans to the students if they do not obey the instructions

Give one rope: *To allow a person full scope to defeat; to hang himself* * The Spanish hockey team was given a long rope before our players tricked them and won * He gave himself rope as a result of long frustration because of poverty

Give one rope to hang oneself: *Allow a person full scope to defeat his or her own ends* * Give a fool a rope and he will hang himself.

Give one self away: *Betray one's secret unawares* * He was very particular not to give himself away while facing cross-examination in the court

Give one the creeps: *Make a person feel terrified or make one tremble with fear* * The live scene of the murder of the young man gave me the creeps

Give one the go by: *Let one pass; ignore* * He always drives fast so that every vehicle driver gives him the go by * He is a barking dog so people give him the go by

Give one the lie: *Charge one to one's face of lying* * I gave him the lie for spreading false news against me

Give one the lie in his throat: *Accuse one to his face of a lie* * In spite of giving him the lie in his face, he never fell ashamed of it

Give one the life: *To charge one to one's face of lying* * He was given the life as the evidence was against him

Give one the sack: *Dismiss him* * As soon as he was found to be guilty of taking bribe, the authority concerned gave him the sack from service

Give one the slip: *Escape stealthily* * The police ran after the robber but the latter gave them the slip

Give one the willies: *Make one scared* * This old house gives me the willies because of its dark, dingy rooms

Give one the works: *Inflict punishment on one or severe pain* * It would be fair to give devil the works

Give one's hand on a bargain: *Take somebody's hand and clasp it to seal the bargain* * He gave his hand on a bargain that he clinched after a good deal of haggling

Give one's love: *Give an affectionate greeting* * They give you their love on the auspicious occasion of your birthday

Give one's mind to: *Direct one's attention* * He passed his exam creditably by giving his mind to his studies

Give one's name in: *Make known one's willingness for something* * There are many persons ready to give their names in for serving the cause of the country

Give oneself airs: *Behaving arrogantly; have a sense of superiority* * Recently he has been giving himself airs as a result of his good results * The rich often give themselves airs in front of the poor

Give or take: *Plus or minus* * He is 6 feet tall, give or take an inch or two

Give out: *Declare out; distribute; emit; exhausted; run short; report* * The empire did not give the batsman out on the appeal of the bowler * He is out to give out handbills to certain concerned persons * The messenger be asked to give out these books to the library * His patience gave out when abused repeatedly * Our food supplies began to give out as a result of decline in food production * It was given out that the dacoit was killed in an encounter with the police

Give over: *Cease; hand over; set aside* * Please give over crying * He asked me to give over humming * The thief was caught red-handed and given to the police * The response was so great that the whole material has to be given to the readers

Give pause: *Blink seriously before doing something* * Popular resistance to the measures should give the government a pause

Give place: *Make room; be superseded* * Retired persons give place to young ones in government service * Motorways have given place to ordinary roads for long-distance travel

Give points to: *Give odds to; give an advantageous hint on any subject* * He can give me points at golf to be able to be a good striker * I have asked him to give me points on how to deal with a tough rival in wrestling

Give quarter: *Mercy to an enemy; have sympathy with* * When soldiers of the enemy's forces surrendered, they were given quarter * We must give quarters to the poor and needy

Give reins to: *Allow free play; apply no check* * Why not to give reins to his imagination? * The general gave reins to his army to crush the enemy forces * You need not give reins to his bad behaviour

Give rise to: *To cause; bring about* * The conflict gave rise to a war between the two nations * The scientific inventions have given rise to progressive developments in every walk of life

Give shape to: *Express clearly* * He has some difficulty in giving shape to his ideas

Give somebody a black eye: *Give one a blow so that there is a discolored bruise round the eye* * Each of the contestants in the boxing bout tries to give the opponent a black eye

Give somebody a broad hint: *A strong unmistakable hint* * He gave us a broad hint of the imminent danger

Give somebody a fit: *Do something that greatly shocks or outrages him* * His rude remarks gave the young lady a fit

Give somebody a good hand: *A lot of applause* * Having won a tough match, the audience gave him a good hand

Give somebody a hand: *Help with* * Would you please give me a hand with washing-up?

Give somebody a leg up: *Help him to climb to a higher position or to mount a horse* * He gave me a leg up to reach the top of wall

Give somebody a piece of one's mind: *Punish or scold* * He came to office late so the boss gave him a piece of his mind

Give somebody an advantage: *Give a better position or advantage* * His university education gave him an advantage over other boys * His strength gives him an advantage over those who are physically weak

Give somebody away: *Hand over (the bride) to the bridegroom at the wedding* * The bride was given away by the father at the wedding

Give somebody back: *Restore or return* * The captured man was given back his liberty

Give somebody best: *Admit the superiority* * He outdid everybody in the contest so we must give him best

Give somebody enough rope: *Allow freedom in the hope that he will make mistake or look silly* * The question was vague and this gave the interviewee enough rope to hang himself

Give somebody his head: *Allow him to act freely; unchecked* * There would be no harm if we give him his head in the pursuit of higher studies

Give somebody one's word: *To promise* * I give you my word the goods will reach you in time

Give somebody out to be/Give it out that somebody is: *Announce* * It was given out that Brian will be the new speaker of the house

Give somebody something to cry for: *Punish him for crying without a good or obvious cause* * He had to give that insolent child a sound thrashing for crying for nothing

Give somebody the boot: *Dismiss from the job* * The employer gave him the boot for misappropriation of funds

Give somebody the creeps: *Cause a feeling of scare* * This old house gives me the creeps

Give somebody the glad eye: *Give an inviting look* * He gave her the glad eye as a gesture for seeking friendship with her

Give somebody the glad hand: *Offer the hand of welcome* *

Everybody gave her the glad hand for her exquisite athletic performance

Give somebody the hump: *Bend in a hump* * The heavy weight that he carries daily has given him the hump

Give somebody the lie: *Accuse him of lying* * The judge on the basis of evidence gave the criminal the lie and sentenced him to undergo imprisonment

Give somebody to someone: *Deliver him to someone* * Shall we let the cheat go or give him up to the police?

Give somebody to understand that: *Inform or assure* * I was given to understand that you might help me to find employment

Give somebody up for lost: *No longer expect him to be found or saved* * The divers have given the child up for lost in the canal

Give somebody or something up as a bad job: *Decide that somebody is no good or something would happen* * I had to give it up as a bad job in the end

Give someone a big leg: *Help one to climb to a higher position or mount a horse* * He gave me a leg up to reach the top of the well * The girl was given a leg to ride the horse

Give someone a buzz: *Make a telephone call* * You give me a buzz tomorrow morning after reaching there safely

Give someone a rocket: *Reprimand someone; criticise* * He was given a rocket for not obeying the instructions

Give someone a rough time: *Treat someone badly* * A good employer would never give his employee a rough time for minor lapses

Give someone his due: *Be just to someone* * I feel you should give him his due as he works very hard

Give someone the push: *Dismiss someone from a job* * The manager gave him the push when found sleeping during the course of his duty

Give someone the works: *Give someone everything* * I will give you the works for competing that long overdue task

Give someone two metre's start: *Place them at the beginning of a race two metres in front of you* * The participants in a race are usually given two metre's start before the beginning of a race

Give something a miss: *Omit it or leave it alone* * I will give the management course a miss

Give something back: *Restore or return* * He gave the missing purse to the right owner

Give something in: *Handover* * Give in your answer book to the examiner

Give something off: *Emit or send out, e.g. smell, smoke* * Some rotten fruit is giving off a pungent smell

Give something up: *Part with; stop* * After some time we gave up our food so as to devote time to the Taj Mahal * I wish I could give up smoking

Give something up for lost: *Have no hope of ever having it again* * He has given the wrist-watch up for lost

Give teeth: *Give effective free* * When will the new legislation be given teeth?

Give the alert: *Give a warning signal* * The constable in plain clothes gave the alert

Give the bucket: *To dismiss* * The authority concerned gave bucket to the false plea

Give the cold shoulder: *To show studied indifference; to give a rebuff* * I requested him for help but he gave me the cold shoulder * The people gave him the cold shoulder for his mischief

Give the devil his due: *To give a fair hearing or fair play to one whom you disapprove of* * There is a provision in our Constitution to give the devil his due * Justice demands that we must give the devil his due

Give the game away: *Reveal the secret or trick* * The key words have been omitted because they would give the game away

Give the lie to: *Charge openly with falsehood; show that something is not true; to charge with lying; prove something is wrong* * He gave the lie to my credentials * These new statistics give lie to the belief that unemployment is going down * He was given the lie to in the statement recorded by the judge * Through the cross-examination, it became obvious that the accused gave the lie to the real facts

Give the particulars: *Give the detailed description* * I gave him all the particulars for his information and necessary action

Give the show away: *Let out a secret* * One of the accused in the theft case gave the show away to the police in the course of interrogation

Give tongue: *Give utterance; voice a feeling* * He kept silent for a while but later gave tongue to his feelings * He had to give tongue when he was insulted for nothing * All that he gave tongue to was nothing more than nonsense

Give up: *Abandon; regard as hopeless; stop keeping company; surrender* * He has given up smoking * Even the teachers have given him up as he cannot be reformed * He did not keep his word, so I have given up his company * The murderer gave himself up to the police

Give up the ghost: *To die* * We are destined to give up the ghost sooner or later

Give up to somebody: *Surrender* * I gave up my seat in the bus to an old man

Give vent to: *Allow to escape or break out* * He gave vent to his complaints through a newspaper

Give way: *Fall back; yield; withdraw; break; collapse under strain; be replaced by; abandon; make concession; lose firmness; row hard* * Our attack was so vigorous that the enemy had to give way * The poor have no option but to give way to the rich * I gave way to my friend to contest in the forthcoming election * The rope gave way to the heavy weight * The bridge gave way due to floods * Tears gave way to smiles * Don't give way to despair * We must not give way to unreasonable demands * The branch gave way to heavy snowfall but did not break * The oarsmen had to give away when chased by some pirates

Given to: *Yield to* * She is given to crying in sensitive matters

Glad neck: *A neck exposed in front* * She has a glad neck

Glad of: *Glad to have* * I am glad of your achievement

Glad rags: *Best clothes* * People are seen dressed in glad rags on festive occasions

Glare at: *Stare angrily or fiercely* * They stood glaring at each other * They glared defiantly at me

Glint and sheen: *Flash and bright; glaze* * The girl's hair has a glint and sheen like gold

Gloat: *Look at with selfish delight; look at something greedily* * A miser gloats over his gold * Don't gloat at the woes of another person

Gloss over: *Cover up; explain away* * We should be

accommodative to gloss over the small faults

Go (to somebody) for: *Be sold (to somebody) for* * I shall not let my watch go (sell) for less than millions of rupees

Go (very) far: *Last; succeed* * A rupee does not go (very) far nowadays (does not buy much) * He will go far in the diplomatic service (will earn promotion)

Go a long way: *Be successful; last; be helpful in achieving something** The bright young manager bids fair to go a long way in earning a distinguished position * The savings made by you will go a long way during adversity * A little of this paint will go a long way * A little of his company goes a long way (be as much as one can bear) * His goodwill and cooperation can go a long way in making him reach the top

Go about: *Preparing to do; move from place to place; deal with; spend time; to set oneself about* * He wanted to know how to go about the new job * I do not go about much any more * I find it very difficult to go about my own household affairs * You are not yet fit to go about that kind of work

Go about one's business: *Attend to one's own affairs; to be off* * You go about your business and I go about mine * You better go about your own business without interfering in my personal matters

Go abroad: *To go to a foreign country; to circulate* * My elder brother has gone abroad to pursue higher studies * To go abroad you need a huge amount of money

Go after: *Try to win or obtain* * He is going after that pretty girl * He has gone after a job in the town

Go against: *Oppose; have an unsatisfactory outcome; be contrary to; be lost* * Do not go against your father * The war is going against them * It goes against my principles to abuse anybody * The case in the court went against him

Go against the grain: *Go against the natural temper or inclination* *It goes against the grain to mix with undesirable elements

Go all out: *Spare no efforts* * We should go all out for making our country second to none

Go along: *Proceed with; agree with* * You may have some difficulty first but you will find it easier as you go along * I will go along with you up to the railway station * I can't go along with you on that point

Go as low/high as: *Reach a certain level* * The price of potatoes this season has gone as low as five rupees * I will be going for this plot as high as one crore rupees

Go aside: *To err; to withdraw* * You have gone aside the real point of view * He thought it proper to go aside the contest against his strong adversary

Go astern: *Go backward* * The steamer is capable of going astern some forty knots

Go astray: *Depart from what is correct* * My letter did not reach the destination and it appears it has gone astray

Go at: *To attack* * They went at each other furiously over a minor matter

Go at it hammer and tongs: *Fight or argue with great energy and noise* * The people are going hammer and tongs at the new taxation policy

Go away: *Go beyond a certain point; leave* * I will give you a few thousands but cannot go further * He has gone away to the town this morning

Go away with somebody: *Abscond with* * He has gone away with a young girl and is likely to be arrested soon

Go away with something: *Take with* * He has gone away with my cycle

Go back: *Return* * When will you go back to your native town?

Go back on: *To betray; to draw back from* * He went back from his word at the eleventh hour * He has preferred to go back on the contentious issue as he does not want to take unnecessary tension

Go back to the land: *Go back to being a farmer again* * He left the job in a factory and went back to the land

Go bad: *To decay* * The offensive smell indicates that something has gone bad somewhere near this spot

Go badly: *Proceed unsatisfactorily* * The project has gone badly right from the beginning

Go bail: *To give security for* * The alleged accused had to go bail for his release from police custody

Go before: *Precede* * Pride goes before a fall

Go begging: *Be in want of a purchaser* * The disposal of the estate by sale is still going begging

Go behind somebody's back: *Do or say something without one's knowledge* * He went behind his father's back to start smoking again

Go behind something: *Search for something* * He is going behind that rumour and its fabricator

Go berserk: *Become violently angry* * He suddenly went berserk with rage

Go beyond: *To surpass; exceed; to circumvent* * You have gone beyond your limits * That is going beyond a joke

Go boating: *Go out for pleasure (in a rowing-boat)* * It is a holiday today so we would like to go boating in the lake

Go broke: *Become penniless* * Don't squander your money in gambling lest you go broke

Go by: *Pass* * We waited for the procession to go by

Go by something: *Be guided or directed by; form an opinion or judgement* * I shall go entirely by what my solicitor says * It is not always wise to go by appearances

Go by the board: *Fail completely and give up* * Our plan to undertake an expedition to the North Pole has to go by the board for paucity of necessary funds

Go by the book: *Follow the rules closely* * A policeman must go by the book while dealing with any criminal

Go by the head: *Sink head foremost* * While diving into the swimming pool, one should avoid going by the head

Go by the worse: *Lose; be defeated* * Without a good coach, the team is likely to go by the worse in any game * The enemy's force went by the worse for lack of proper manoeuvering

Go by/under the name of: *Use the name of* * That wrestler goes by the name of King

Go down: *To sink; decline; to be swallowed; to fail to fulfill one's contract; be defeated; become lower; become calm; be remembered; be accepted; approved; be appreciated* * We reached home before the sun went down * The ship went down when it struck against a rock * The speed of the storm went down after an hour * The pill will not go down without water * He was black-listed for going down in the written agreement * William is likely to go down by three sets to one in the final tennis match * The price of the mangoes will go down now that there has been a surplus crop * The heat has gone down after a light rain * His name will go down in history for his achievements in the field of science * The new movie has gone down well with the audience * Her melodious songs will go down in the hearts of the people

Go down before somebody: *Be defeated or overthrown* * Rome went down before the barbarians

Go down in something: *Be written in or be recorded in; remembered in* * It all goes down in his notebook * He will go down in history as a great statesman

Go down to: *Be extended as far as; be continued* * This tennis match will go down to five sets before one can say who will be the winner

Go down to the sea/country: *Pay a visit to the sea-side/ country* * During the coming summer vacation, our class will go down to the sea to enjoy

Go down with: *Be acceptable to; fall ill* * That explanation cannot go down well with me * That old man has gone down with fever

Go dry: *To enforce liquor prohibition* * No government in the world would like its country to go dry for the sake of earning revenue

Go Dutch (with somebody): *Share expenses* * I went Dutch with my friend in hiring a room for our stay in the hotel

Go easy on: *Be careful; handle gently* * Go easy with her as she is too young to realise her mistake * Go easy on brandy as it is the last bottle!

Go far: *To last long; to go a long way; to come to importance; be successful; do much (of money) by goods/services, etc.; go beyond the limits; help greatly* * Without accommodative spirit the war of ideology among the different sects will certainly go far * The new act passed by the Parliament will go far in removing illiteracy * His name has gone far for discovering new methods of bringing about prosperity in life * He is clever and intelligent and as such he will go far * A rupee does not go so far as it did some years ago * Do not go too far in cutting the jokes * The loan taken by me will go far towards running my business

Go far afield: *Cover a long distance* * The police had to go far afield in pursuit of the culprit

Go for a walk/swim: *Go out in order to walk or swim* * We must go out for a walk in the morning and breathe fresh air

Go far towards doing something/Go a long way: *Make a considerable contribution towards* * The Prime Minister's statement went far towards reassuring the nation of all round development in the country

Go fishing: *Spend time fishing for pleasure* * Let us go fishing this weekend

Go flat (of liquid): *Lose its gas content* * The beer has gone flat

Go flat out: *As fast as you can go* * In order to catch the train in time, I had to drive flat out

Go for: *To assail; to set out to secure; be applicable; go to fetch; ability to do something easily* * The dog went for the postman as he opened the gate * He has gone for seeking his friendship * What I have said about him goes for you too * Shall I go for a doctor? * Depend on him as he can go for solving the problem in no time

Go for a run: *Take some exercise by running* * Let us go for a run in the open air

Go for a song: *Buy something for a small amount* * That residential plot has gone for a song

Go for nothing: *To have no value; be without reward* * All his work went for nothing * My hard work for bringing the project on the track has gone for nothing

Go forth: *Be published or issued* * The order went forth that no leave would be granted as a matter of right

Go forward: *Advance; make progress* * A patrol went forward to look into the case * The work is going forward very well

Go from bad to worse: *Become seriously worse* * In spite of good treatment, his health is going from bad to worse

Go from/to: *Reach** This road goes to Mumbai * I want a rope that will go from the top window to the ground

Go further and fare worse: *Lose an opportunity in the hope of a better one* * We should not allow ourselves to go further and fare worse but make best of the chance in hand

Go great lengths: *Go to extremities* * He is willing to go great lengths to win her favour

Go halves: *To share equally* * I had to go halves with my partner in distributing the profit from our business

Go hand in hand: *To go together* * Rights and duties go hand in hand

Go hard with: *Turn out unfavourable* * It will go hard with you if you lose your temper

Go haywire: *Become badly disorganised; go mad* * The water plant has gone haywire and the people have been deprived of water in various cities * He has gone haywire under the influence of evil spirits

Go ill with: *Result in danger or misfortune* * It will go ill with you if you try to backbite behind my back

Go in: *To assemble; to admit the audience or congregation; enter; be obscured by clouds; begin an innings (in cricket); be spent in* * They have gone in to discuss some intricate problems * Let them go to enjoy fun and frolic * This key won't go in the lock * The sun went in and it grew rather cold * Who will go in next? * Go in and win! (used as a form of encouragement)

Go in and out: *To come and go freely* * The people can go in and out at public places as a matter of right

Go in at one ear and out at the other: *Leave no impression* * Whatever you tell him goes in at one ear and out at the other

Go in for: *To make a practice of; devote oneself to; have an interest in* * She regularly goes in for dancing * If you want to achieve distinction in any trade, you will have to go in for hard work * He would like to go in for stamp collecting

Go in off the deep end: *To express strong feelings with abandonment* * He went in off the deep end when he gave up all worldly pleasures

Go into a coma/trance: *Pass into such a sleep* * As a result of a serious accident, he has gone into a coma * The passenger who went into a trance was cheated of his purse and bag

Go into a dead faint: *Be in complete unconsciousness* * By consuming some poisonous food he has gone into a dead faint

Go into a huddle: *Meet together to discuss something in secret* * They are going into a huddle to plan the overthrow of the Junta government

Go into abeyance: *Be suspended; be no longer observed* * I have told her to keep the matter in abeyance and not take any action

Go into details: *Give the facts item by item* * He had to go into details about the immediate defence requirements

Go into exile: *Be banished* * He went into exile for a period of 14 years to repent for his bad behaviour

Go into hiding: *Be hidden; hide oneself* * The rioters to be booked have gone into hiding

Go into liquidation: *Become bankrupt* * On account of a complete setback in the business, he has gone into liquidation

Go into mourning: *Wear black clothes as a symbol of mourning* * A great crowd of people will go into mourning as soon as they hear the news of the assassination of their President

Go into particulars: *Give details* * He went into the particulars of the case to apprise his boss of the true picture

Go into retirement: *Retire* * Many persons have got into retirement this year from our department

Go into retreat: *Be on temporary retirement for religious exercises* * He was allowed to go into retreat for a month before rejoining

Go into the lead: *Have first position; take first action* * As he is very good in the relay race he will go into the lead * Who will go into the lead to emerge the winner

Go it: *To act in a striking or dashing manner* * Go it if you want to catch the train in time

Go like hot cakes: *Sell off or disappear promptly* * The new book published by my friend has gone like hot cakes

Go like the wind: *Run quickly* * The sturdy man went like the wind and returned like the whirlwind after finishing the assigned task

Go nap: *Take a short nap* * As he was continuously yawning, I told him to go nap rather than put others to sleep too

Go native: *Associate oneself with and adopt the ways of the natives* * An immigrant must go native for furthering the cause of his own interest

Go off: *To leave; to die; to explode; be fired; to fade; deteriorate; turn sour; fall asleep; become unconscious; be got rid off; proceed well* * He has gone off to work * Many of the creatures like reptiles and frogs go off after the rainy season is over * I could hear the bomb going off on the other side of the city * The colour of my coat has gone off * The cooking in the hotel has started to go off * Has not the baby gone off? * The goods went off quickly * The performance concert went off well * How did the sports go off?

Go off a score: *Make a spirited start* * He will go off a score in the 100-metre sprint

Go off at a tangent: *Change direction or follow another line of thought* * While dwelling on the subject of poverty, he all at once went off at a tangent to speak highly of rich persons

Go off at half-cock: *Have a bad start; too soon and fail* * Those who take a leap in the dark are sure to go off at half-cock

Go off one's head: *Become crazy* * He has gone off his head to learn dancing at this age

Go off somebody/something: *Lose interest in or one's taste* * He seems to have gone off his best friend * I have gone off beer

Go off the air: *Stop broadcasting* * Due to heavy air raids, the broadcasting station went off the air for about two hours

Go off the beaten track: *Do something different* * The present generation is going off the beaten track which their forefathers had trodded

Go off the deep end: *Express strong feeling without trying to control it* * He should not have gone off the deep end if he was rebuked by an elderly man

Go off the rails: *Deviate from the right course or path* * He used to be a steady and reliable person but he has gone off the rails recently

Go off with somebody/something: *Go away with especially abscond with or steal* * The maid-servant went off with some of the jewellery belonging to her mistress * He has gone off with his neighbour's wife

Go on: *To proceed; pass; conduct oneself in a shameful way; take place; happen; be in progress; take one's turn at doing something (e.g. cricket); continue to do; do something after one*

has finished something else; continue to walk or drive in a particular direction; be spent on * Let us go on further to discuss the next item on the agenda * As the matter went on, he became impatient * If you go on like this, you will be thrown out * What is going on over here? * There is nothing interesting going on here at present * The captain told me to go on next * I went on writing till late at night * He went on to get his degree * I intend to go on up the hill * How much of your money goes on food and clothes?

Go on a journey: *Trip; outing* * He has gone on a journey for a month

Go on a spending spree: *Have a happy time spending money* * On the eve of his marriage, he went on a spending spree

Go on about something: *Talk persistently and often irritatingly* * I wish you would stop going on about my smoking habit

Go on at somebody: *Nag; scold* * She goes on at her husband continuously for reasons best known to her

Go on board: *Go on to a ship or into an aircraft* * He has gone on board to reach London by tomorrow night

Go on something: *Take or accept an evidence* * What evidence have we got to go on to getting him convicted

Go on strike: *To stop work* * The workers have decided to go on strike if their demands are not met

Go on the dole: *Obtain payments under various government schemes* * Many of needy and helpless persons are going on the dole in our country

Go on the pill: *Start using contraceptive pills* * To go on the pill is one of the safe methods to avoid pregnancy

Go on the rampage: *Go about breaking things* * The prisoners may go on a rampage destroying everything if their demands are not met

Go on the stage: *Be an actor* * Those who go on the stage are likely to earn wealth and popularity

Go on the street: *Earn one's living by prostituting* * The government must do something to come to the rescue of helpless women so that they do not go on the street

Go on to something/To do something: *Do or say;*

proceed to it * Let us now go on to the next item in the agenda * He went on to say that there could be no progress without observing strict discipline

Go on wheels: *Move swiftly* * If it gets too late, you will have to go on wheels to catch the train

Go one better: *To take a bet and add another more; to excel* * After having won the first bet, he was lured to go one better * I hit the target ten times but my friend went one better

Go one's ways: *To depart* * He camped for the night and went his ways the next morning

Go out: *Be extinguished; attend social functions, etc.; be announced; be broadcast; leave the room or building; strike; become unfashionable* * The fire will soon go out * He still goes out a great deal, even at the age of 85 * The news went out from Washington that the President has declared a war against terrorism * The series on a new episode will go out on television from Monday onwards * He often goes out riding * Are we likely to gain anything by going out? * The fashion of wearing well-bottom pants has gone out

Go out for a breather: *Go out to get some fresh air* * When we feel tired after hard work, we should go out for a breather

Go out of one's mind: *Be forgotten* * It went out of mind to bring the book you needed for some reference purpose

Go out of one's way: *Make a special effort; give oneself trouble; make a special point* * He went out of his way to help me * It will mean going out of the way if your take me there * He really did not go out of his way to help me

Go out of use: *Be no longer used* * Old customs have almost gone out of use

Go out on a limb: *Put in a vulnerable position, because separated from supporters* * I never heard him go out on a limb like that before * If you speak ill of that big gun, you will go out on a limb

Go out on a spree: *Go out to enjoy* * They have gone out on a drinking spree

Go out on the town: *Go out to enjoy the entertainment facilities of a town* * It was a thrilling experience to go out on the town

Go out to: *Leave one's country* * He could not get work in India, so he went out to Canada

Go out to somebody: *Be extended to, and go to* * Our heartiest sympathies go out to those poor orphans

Go out with somebody: *Be regularly in somebody's company* * For how long have John and Smith been going out together?

Go over: *To pass in review; revise; make an impression* * The Bill has been gone over by the Parliament * Please go over this manuscript for publication * I wonder if this play will go over

Go over something: *Examine the details of; inspect; rehearse study or review carefully* * We must go over the accounts carefully before we settle them * We would like to go over the house before deciding whether to buy it or not * Let us go over this chapter

Go over to: *Change one's political party; side a preference* * He has gone over to the Communist Party * I am going over to a milder brand of cigarette

Go overboard for: *Be enthusiastic about* * Refrain from going overboard on your physical exercises as it may cause you harm in furture

Go pear-shape: *Go wrong* * Things started to go pear-shaped when he got addicted to drugs

Go phut: *Collapse* * The old car went phut half way up the hill * His plan has gone phut

Go pit-a-pat: *Have irregular beating caused through fear* * Her heart went pit-a-pat at the sight of a lion

Go places: *Have increasing success* * His talent would certainly go places in the time to come when his article which is in press comes out

Go round: *Supply everybody; be sufficient in number; amount to have a share; reach one's destination by using a route other than the usual or nearest way* * Have we enough food to go round? * There are not enough apples to go round * The main road to the town was flooded and we have to go round

Go round the bend: *Become hysterical; irritated* * I would have gone round the bend if I had stayed there any longer

Go round to a place: *Visit* * I am going round to my friend's house in the town to attend his marriage

Go Scot free: *Escape unpunished* * He went Scot free for want of evidence

Go scrum ping: *Steal apples from an orchard* * You will be caught and punished by the gardener if you go scrum ping

Go shares: *Divide* * We decided to go shares when travelling together in the same taxi

Go short: *Deprive oneself* * I do not want you to go short of money in order to lend me what I need

Go skiing: *Travel on skies as a sport* * Many sportsmen go skiing in Switzerland and move over snow on skies

Go sledging: *Play at sliding on the snow on a sledge* * It is really enjoyable to go sledging

Go slow: *Move forward slowly; work slowly; be less active* * The traffic on the main road was going slow * In order to get their wages raised, the labourers have decided to go slow in the factory * You ought to go slow unless you recoup your health fully

Go slow policy: *Deliberately restricting output or effort so as to force the hands of opponents* * Let us adopt a go slow policy to frustrate the designs of the enemy

Go so far as to do something: *Do or say something to a certain limit* * I would go so far as to suggest that the superfluous laws should be abolished

Go something too far: *Go beyond the limit of what is considered reasonable* * Do not allow your modesty to go too far

Go stale: *Become bored; tired so that one can not work well* * You need a break because you are going stale here

Go straight: *Lead an honest life after having been a criminal* * After having had the taste of imprisonment, he has decided to go straight in earning his living

Go the pace: *Go at a great speed; live a fast life* * You will have to go the pace if you want to catch the train in time * Only the rich could go the pace to their own liking

Go the round of: *Make one's usual visits; be passed on* * The night watchman goes on the round of every street every hour * The news of her marriage is likely to take a round of the village in no time

Go the way of all flesh: *Die* * Every human being has been destined to go all the way of all flesh

Go the way of all the earth: *Die* * All the beings have to go the way of all earth

Go the whole hog: *Go to the fullest extent* * We will have to go whole hog to strengthen our defence

Go the world: *Get married* * A responsible and mature person deserves to go the world

Go through: *Perform to the end; remain in order; be passed; approved; conclude; discuss something in detail; search; perform; take part in; complete; reach the end of; spend* * I have gone through your newly published book and find it very interesting * The proceedings of the air show went through as per the plan * The Bill in the Parliament did not go through * The deal did not go through for one reason or the other * Let us go through all the items on the agenda again * The police went through the pockets of a suspected thief * She made him go through both a civil and religious wedding * How long will it take to go through the programme? * He has gone through the fortune * Don't go through all your money

Go through fire and water: *Undertake any trouble or risks* * Our national leaders went through fire and water to achieve freedom

Go through something with a fine-tooth comb: *Examine it closely and thoroughly* * The examiner had to go through all the answer sheets with a fine-tooth comb so that no injustice got done to any candidate

Go through the mill: *Undergo or Subject to probationary hardships* * He reached the topmost position but not before going through the mill

Go through with something: *Continue until it is finished* * He has gone through with seminars and tutorials

Go to/towards something: *Continue to/Be contributed to* * What qualities go to the making of a statesman?

Go to any length: *Do anything necessary to get what one wants* * He can go to any length to achieve his goal

Go to Davy Jones's locker: *Be drowned at sea* * The enemy's warship went to Davy Jones's locker

Go to extremes: *Use extreme measure* * We had to go to extremes to extract full information from the traitors

Go to grass: *Be turned out to pasture especially of a horse too*

old to work; go into retirement; rusticate * The owner has decided to let his old horse go to grass * After having completed his tenure in service, the employers decided to allow him to go to grass * The student found guilty of using unfair means in the exam had to go to grass for three years

Go to great lengths/troubles/pains: *Take care to do something well* * He went to great lengths to make his guest comfortable

Go to ground: *Hide oneself where one cannot be easily found* * All the persons involved in the conspiracy have gone to ground

Go to law: *Appeal to the law court* * The victim in the dowry case has gone to law

Go to one's account: *Go to the last judgement* * Our good or bad deeds go to our account

Go to one's head: *Disturb one's sobriety; intoxicate; excite* * The whisky went to his head * His success has gone to his head

Go to one's heart: *Touch one deeply* * It goes to his heart to see so much misery

Go to pieces: *Break up entirely; lose completely; break down physically, mentally or morally; decline in power* * The China tea-pot went into pieces when it fell down * You will go to pieces if you challenge him to a bout * He has gone to pieces after having met with a serious accident * The empire went to pieces once the king was dead

Go to pot/Go to ruin: *Be ruined; destroyed; go to pieces* * He was so spendthrift that all his money got exhausted and he had to go to pot in the long run * He did not go to pot as I feared he might

Go to press: *Begin to print* * The new edition of this book has gone to press * The sensational news will go to press as soon it is received there

Go to rack and ruin: *Be destroyed* * Everything went to rack and ruin at the place where the bomb exploded

Go to roost: *Take rest at night* * With the fall of dusk, all the birds go to roost

Go to sea: *Become sailor; fall asleep* * Many persons are very fond of going to the sea * The child has gone to sea in the course of his cradle being rocked

Go to seed: *Stop flowering as seed is produced; become less physically fit or less mentally effi-*

cient; become careless of one's appearance and clothes * The lettuce grown in my garden has gone to seed * A person above 90 years of age generally goes to seed * We should not go to seed on festive occasions

Go to sleep: *Become numb* * Sometimes it happens that my hands and legs go to sleep for if kept in one position for long

Go to somebody: *Pass with somebody's possession; be allowed to* * Who did the property go to when the old man died? * Honours do not always go to those who merit them

Go to stake: *Be burned at the stake* * In earlier times a number of English Catholics went to the stake as a punishment

Go to the bad: *To go to moral ruin* * The society does condemn those who go to the bad

Go to the block: *Be sent to death* * In olden times, people who committed heinous crimes had to go to the block

Go to the bottom of: *Go exhaustively* * The police is going to the bottom of the whole tragedy

Go to the country: *To appeal to the community by a general Election* * The candidates for the presidential election in America go to the country with their respective manifestoes to woo the voters

Go to the devil: *Go away!** He has gone to the devil with a full bottle of wine!

Go to the dogs: *Be ruined* * The country will go to the dogs if we do not plan properly for its overall development

Go to the wall: *To be hard pressed; to be forced to give way; to fail; to give precedence to something else; be ruined; be pushed aside* * He has been forced to go to the wall because of the rising costs and lower income * I was forced to go to the wall since I had limited choice * The whole plan has gone to the wall * This scheme will have to go to the wall immediately * The scheme has gone to the wall for want of funds * In these days of tough competition inefficient people are bound to go to the wall

Go to the wars: *Go to fight in a foreign country* * The British and the American forces went to the war in Iraq

Go to war: *Resort to armed conflict* * The people went to war against the tyrannical rule of the dictator

Go to waste: *Be wasted* * What a pity to see all that water go waste

Go together: *Be a normal accompaniment; match* * Crime and poverty often go together * Do my green shirt and blue jeans go together?

Go too far: *Go beyond acceptable limits* * It is going too far to say that we have reached the limit in our development

Go under: *Be called by some title or character; be submerged; die; overwhelmed; become bankrupt; fail* * His name goes under the title Lion after having won the heavyweight boxing championship * The alligator showed its snout before he went under * Many people went under the bomb attack * The whole country went under grief on hearing the sad news of the death of Mahatma Gandhi * The firm will go under unless business improves * Many small-scale industries have gone under for want of supply of raw material

Go up: *Rise, be erected; be destroyed in fire or explosion* * The temperature is going up * New office blocks are going up everywhere * The bridge went up with a roar when the mine exploded

Go up in the world: *Be successful in rising to a higher social or financial position* * He got married to the daughter of an industrialist and has thus gone up in the world

Go up something: *Climb* * We plan to go up the hill to get a better view of the town below

Go up the wall: *Become furious* * Everyone tends to go up the wall when abused for no reason at all

Go well: *Proceed satisfactorily* * All has gone well with our plan.

Go with: *Accompany; agree with; do as others do; be a normal accompaniment of; be equal to; grief-stricken* * I will go to see a movie along with my friends tomorrow night * I can't go with you on this point * He always goes with his partner's decisions * Ten acres of land will go with the house (becomes the property of the buyers) * The credit for his achievement must go with his parents * Do not get into mischief or else you will go with grief

Go with a swing: *Proceed smoothly without delay; have a good rhythm; go very well*

* The sports events are going with a swing * The music programme went with a swing * So far as the entertainment of the audience is concerned, the concert is going with a swing

Go without: *Suffer the want of* * The poor boy often has to go without supper

Go without saying: *Understand without actually being stated; be plainly self-evident* * It goes without saying that honesty is the best policy * It goes without saying that he is a good coach

Go wrong: *Make a mistake; stray from virtue; stop progressing; stop working; fail to work properly* * At last he realised that he had gone wrong while solving the sum * He has gone wrong in observing self-restraint * Their relations went wrong after the birth of their child * Something has gone wrong with the car and it needs to be shown to the mechanic * You can see where you are going wrong

Go (any) further: *Go beyond a certain point* * I will give you a few rupees but I cannot go any further.

Go/Report sick: *Report to the doctor for medical treatment* * Four of the soldiers may go sick as they have eaten wrong food

Goad somebody into doing something: *Drive forward* * He was goaded by hunger into stealing * His hateful remarks goaded us into taking action against him

Goad somebody on: *Urge* * The cowherd goaded the cattle on with his pointed stick

Go ahead: *Make progress; progressive people; proceed without hesitation; permission to proceed* * He is going ahead with his higher education * The Jews are very go-ahead people and it is difficult to keep up with them * May I go ahead now? * The participants in the car rally were given the go-ahead at 10 o'clock in the morning

Go-between: *An intermediary* * Rather than being hasty on serious matters it is better to adopt a go-between approach * In some countries the marriages are arranged by go-betweens

God bless/Save the mark: *A phrase or expression; ironical astonishment; scorn* * God bless/save the mark for all the evil things you have done!

God helps those who help themselves * *The Creator*

helps those who make efforts to do things themselves * Believe it or not, but God helps those who help themselves

God's will be done: *We cannot defy the will of the Almighty* * There is no escape from death and God's will be done

Going concern: *A business in actual activity* * It is only through a going concern that one can build up one's assets

Going forth: *An outlet* * There is no going forth from this trap

Going full blast: *Working at full power* * The factory is going full blast in its output

Going on: *Reprehensible behaviour; noisy behaviour* * What is going on here that you are making so much hullabaloo?

Going out: *Expenditure* * We should not be lavish when going out to eat

Going rate: *Usual or current rate* * The going rate of onion today is the same as it was during last season

Going strong: *In full activity; flourishing* * Though he is above 90, yet he is going strong * The new industry is going strong day by day

Going to do something: *Determined to do something* * We are going to spend our holidays in Goa

Going-over: *Process of examining or putting in good working order; beating* * The document requires a thorough going-over before we can make a decision * The thieves gave him a thorough going-over

Goings-on: *Happenings; behaviour* * I have never seen such queer goings-on

Go-kart: *A small low racing car with open framework* * The go-kart is becoming very popular among the children

Golden handshake: *Sum of money presented when one leaves work* * He was very happy to have received a golden handshake

Golden key opens all the doors save that of heaven: *Money can do and undo many problems but it cannot overcome the destiny* * He had everything but he died before enjoying all the pleasures of wealth thus proving that a golden key opens all the doors save that of heaven

Golden mean: *The middle way between extremes; moderation* * In order to avoid mass destruction of life and property between two warring parties, it is better to adopt a policy of golden mean

Golden opportunity: *A favourable chance* * He did not miss the golden opportunity that came his way to boost the business

Golden rule: *Very important rule* * The golden rule he follows is always tell the truth

Golden wedding: *Fiftieth anniversary of the marriage* * The old couple is celebrating their golden wedding anniversary

Gone to Kingdom come: *Dead and gone to the next world* * That old millionaire has since gone to Kingdom come

Gone under: *Ruined beyond recovery* * The car that met with an accident has completely gone under

Good and chattels: *Belongings* * They have shifted to their new house with goods and chattels

Good at: *Able* * He is good at French

Good fellowship: *Companionship* * I am fortunate to have a good fellowship

Good for: *Safely to be trusted for; having the necessary energy, inclination, etc.; valid* * His credit is good for a few thousands of rupees * He is good for several years of service * This insurance policy is good for one year

Good for anything: *Ready for any kind of work* * He, being an all-rounder, is always ready for anything

Good form: *According to good or recognised social usage* * He is in a good form, hence expect positive contribution from him to our cause * Society needs every man and woman to be in good form

Good hand: *A trustworthy source; good keeping; care of those who may be trusted to treat one well* * She has a good hand at embroidery * Things are progressing well under good hands * The abandoned child is now in good hands

Good health is above wealth: *Wealth has no meaning without a sound mind and healthy body* * It is a perfect saying that 'good health is above wealth'

Good innings: *Long and happy life* * That gentleman breathed his last after having had a good innings

Good job: *Fortunate state of affairs* * He lost his seat in Parliament and a good job too!

Good judge of character: *Person with good judgement* * He is a good judge of character

Good looks: *Beauty; pleasing personal appearance* * Everybody stared at the good looks of the young lady

Good mind good find: *Kind person would get kind response* * I am lucky to have the services of that man and I consider him to be a good mind good find

Good offices: *Mediation* * You can use your good offices to help me resolve this knotty problem

Good riddance: *Welcome clearing away* * He was happy at good riddance of all the charges levelled against him

Good sort: *Pleasant type of person* * He is liked by everybody for his being a good sort

Good spirits: *Happy mind* * I found all the boys in good spirits when at play

Good sport: *Pleasant person always willing to help* * A good citizen should also be a good sport

Good standby: *Thing which is good to have at hand in case of need* * A diary is a good standby for jotting down anything of importance

Good taste: *Intuitive feeling for what is aesthetically right* * He has a good taste for dancing

Good temper: *Unruffled humour* * He possesses a good temper for which he is acclaimed by all

Good timekeeper: *Person who is always on time; watch which always shows the correct time* * He is a good timekeeper and is never late * The wall-clock purchased by my grandfather has always served as a good timekeeper

Good to look at: *Of good appearance* * This hotel is not much good to look at

Good/Bad company: *Having or lacking companionable qualities* * His is good company and you will really enjoy it

Good odour: *In favours* * He is in good odour with his boss

Gorge oneself on something: *Eat greedily* * He gorged himself on chocolates

Grain elevator: *Large building for storing grain* * The grain elevators have been useful in protecting grain from all kinds of damage

Grand Prix: *Motor or motorcycle race* * Grand Prix has become an important sports event in many countries

Grand slam: *Winning all major championships in a season* * He had a grand slam to his credit in tennis this season

Grant something difficult: *Admit something difficult* * I grant you it is a difficult job

Grasp at: *Try to seize, asset eagerly* * A man who grasps at too much may lose everything

Grass growing under feet: *Not become stale but remain active* * It is nice to see him working in the garden and it obviously shows that he is not the one let grass grow under his feet even at the age of 90

Grass widower: *Man whose wife is away from home on business* * The grass widower has to look after the children when his wife is away

Grateful to: *Feeling or showing thanks* * I am ever grateful to you for your invaluable help

Grease one's palms: *Bribe* * The gate-keeper won't let you in unless you grease his palm

Great a hand at: *Expert at* * He is great a hand at organising public meetings

Great at: *Clever or skilled at* * He is great at carpentry

Great command of language: *Skill in speech* * Winston had a great command over English language

Great cry and little wool: *Much ado about nothing* * Politicians came out with great cry and little wool as their much publicised programme failed to take off

Great go: *A degree examination* * I have made up my mind to have a great go in the next academic session

Great gun: *A cannon; a person of great importance* * In olden times, the great gun was considered to be a very powerful weapon * Pandit Jawaharlal Nehru was considered to be a great gun

Great on: *Having a good knowledge of* * You will, no doubt, find him great on historical events

Great shakes: *Of great account* * The whole issue has been in great shakes and very clean * He is not great shakes at his job even though he keeps on boasting about his abilities

Great thinker: *Philosopher* * Socrates was a great thinker of his time

Greed for: *Always wanting (power etc.)* * Many people generally have greed for power and money

Greek gift: *A treacherous gift* * Don't accept his Greek gift, otherwise you will have to repay it through your nose

Greek nose: *Straight nose* * A man having a Greek nose looks really smart and attractive

Grey matter: *Active part of the brain* * Some of the terminally-ill patients were found without grey matter in the course of a medical test

Grief-stricken: *Very sad* * The grief-stricken people were standing at the spot, mourning the death of their near and dear ones

Grin and bear it: *Endure pain, disappointment etc; to accept things bravely* * When there is no escape from a trouble, one should learn to grin and bear it

Grind away: *Work or study hard and long* * One has to grind away at one's studies to score good marks

Grind one's teeth: *Rub together the upper and lower teeth; to be angry* * Some people grind their teeth when asleep * When his daughter did not obey him all he could do was to grind his teeth in anger

Grind to a halt: *Stop slowly* * All the industries will grind to a halt due to repeated strikes

Grist to the mill: *Particular situation to make use of* * You might as well take another examination if you have time as it is all grist to the mill in getting a good job

Grit one's teeth: *Show courage and endurance* * We must grit our teeth when faced with an adverse situation

Groan under a weight: *Be heavily laden* * The poor clerk was groaning under the weight of extra work

Groaning board: *A table laid with very generous supplies of food* * Their mouth watered at the sight of the groaning board

Grope (about) (for/after): *Feel or search about as one does in the dark* * I groped about in the dark room for my gun to shoot the intruder

Gross income: *Total income before the income tax is deducted* * His annual gross income is falling every year

Gross injustice: *Great; excessive injustice* * A gross injustice was done to him by punishing him for no fault of his

Gross weight: *Combined weight of container and contents* * The gross weight of the trunk was 100 kg

Ground rule: *Basic rule of procedure* * All members of the Parliament have to follow the ground rules to maintain decorum of the house

Ground under: *To sink* * The large crane will soon ground under if made to lift still heavier loads

Groundwork: *Basic work* * We need to think of some solid groundwork to enhance our economic progress

Grow apart: *Start to have different interest or opinion for each other* * As we travelled together, we started to grow apart

Grow on: *Gain a greater hold on; gain in estimation of* * The frightful appearance of the ghost has grown on him * His plain thinking and plain speaking have positively grown on his admirers

Grow out of: *Issue from; result from; pass beyond; abandon or stop a type behaviour; become too big for; have as a source* * The smoke grows out of chimneys * The quarrel grew out of property dispute * The bitterness between the rival parties has grown out of bounds * I have rather grown out of my taste for the bizarre * He has grown out of his clothes * His trouble grew out of his bad temper

Grow rich: *Be wealthy* * He grew rich by dint of hard labour within a short spell of time

Grow to be: *Reach to the point or stage* * My friendship with them will grow to be very close

Grow to like: *Reach to the point or stage one likes* * One grows to like what one gets accustomed to over the years

Grow to waste: *Come near an end* * His life span has now grown to waste

Grow together: *Become united by growth* * In a family, we grew together that binds us in true love and unity

Grow up: *Advance in growth; become full grown; mature; develop* * From childhood stage, we grow up to be an adult * He has a grown up son * When a boy grows up he becomes more and more sensible * A warm friendship grew up between the two strangers * The big cities are growing up with the increase in population

Growing pains: *Problems arising while a new enterprise is developing* * Our business is still suffering from growing pains

Grown up: *An adult* * Every grown up person has the right to vote

Grub up: *Dig or turnover soil to get something up or out* * The pigs were grubbing up something in the bushes

Grudge a thought: *Thank someone resentfully or grudgingly* * I did grudge a thought in response to his kind behaviour

Guard against: *Use care and caution to prevent* * We must guard ourselves against contagious diseases

Guard from: *Protect from* * Before he left, the master instructed his servant to guard the house from thieves

Guard of honour: *Group of soldiers acting as ceremonial escort to an important person* * The distinguished state guest inspected a guard of honour soon after he landed at the airport

Guide dog: *Dog which is specially trained to lead a blind person* * A guide dog is very helpful for a blind person

Guided missiles: *Rockets which can be guided to its destination while in flight by electronic devices* * Guided missiles can hit any desired spot to destroy everything there

Guided tour: *Tour where the tourists are led by a guide* * Guided tours are required to attract foreign tourists

Gulp down: *To swallow hastily* * He gulped down a cup of tea and then got down to his work

Gum up the works: *Prevent an event from happening* * You all go along and gum up the works if anything crops up on the way

Gun runner: *Person who brings guns into a country illegally* * Some traitors do gun running to supply the same to the traitors

Gun-boat diplomacy: *Diplomacy backed by the threat of force* * Super powers do believe in gun-boat diplomacy to frighten the weaker nations

Gunning for: *Out to compass the downfall of* * The American army has now been gunning for the leaders of terrorist organisations

Gun-shy: *Frightened by guns* * The gun-shy rich man was looted of his money by the brigands

Gut reaction: *Instinctive or natural reaction* * As a result of gut reaction people do rise against tyrannical rule of the dictator

Gutted by fire: *Destroyed by fire* * The house was gutted by fire

Gutter press: *Newspaper which specialises in scandals** A gutter paper generally draws a large number of readers

H

Habeas corpus: *Order to bring a prisoner to answer a charge in court* * It is of little consolation to a poor peasant that the habeas corpus exists * Two days later he was released at the habeas corpus

Habit and repute: *Notoriety that affords strong and generally conclusive evidence of fact* * In Scotland, the judges give their judgement on the basis of habit and repute

Hackles up: *Be angry; ready to fight* * That rude man gets his hackles up even on the least bit of provocation

Had a bilious attack: *Was sick* * He had a bilious attack

Had as good: *Might as well* * He had as good as killed the innocent man in the firing spree against the militants

Had as life: *Should like as well to* * Apart from being a good dancer, he had as life be a good singer

Had better: *Would do best to* * You had better give due respect to that old gentleman

Had like: *Was likely; came near* * It had like a storm that frightened everyone * As soon as the sea tides had like the shore, we took to our heels for shelter

Had like to: *Was likely to* * I think that he had like to give a good performance on stage

Had rather: *Would progress* * I had rather join the army than be a civil servant

Haggle with: *Argue; dispute* * He haggled with the shopkeeper over the price of an umbrella

Hail from: *Come from* * They hail from all parts of the country to witness the Republic Day parade

Hail something down: *Come or send down* * Blows hailed down on his head and back * They hailed curses on us

Hair breadth escape: A *narrow escape* * Yesterday our car struck against a tree but we had a hair-breadth escape

Hair restorer: *Liquid which is supposed to make hair grow again* * A bald man stands in need of some hair restorer to look handsome

Hair stand on end: *Sign of fear*

and surprise * At the sight of the lion, my hair stood on end

Hair-raising: *Frightening* * The long ride was bumpy and at times hair-raising * It was a hair-raising experience to see the dead body of a young man in a pool of blood

Hale and hearty: *Strong and healthy* * Daily physical exercise keeps one hale and hearty

Half a loaf is better than no bread: *It is better to take what one can get than to run the risk of having nothing* * Half a loaf is better than no bread for a hungry man

Half- bred: *Poorly bred or trained* * A half-bred mare is not as sprightly as a pure bred

Half the time: *Half of the time available; for long periods of time; (loosely) very often; nearly always* * He did the work in four hours though I could have done it in half the time * He says he works hard but he is day-dreaming half the time

Half way house: *Half the distance* * Our car got out of order when we had covered half way house of our journey

Half-and half: *In two equal quantities* * The robbers shared the booty half-and-half between themselves * Their ancestral property was divided half-and-half among the brothers

Half-face: *Profile* * In the first instance he came up with a half-face outline of his portrait

Half-hardy: *Able to grow in thee open air except in winter* * There are many half-hardy plants that need protection from frost

Half-hearted: *Lacking in zeal* * Half-hearted attempts to do good are of no use

Half-length: *A portrait showing the upper part of the body* * The sculptor has made a half-length stone sculpture of a very beautiful lady

Half-mast: *Position of the flag near the middle of a mast to indicate mourning* * Flags flew at half-mast everywhere on the day of the President's funeral

Half-sword: *Fighting with a half-sword's length or close fight* * In olden times soldiers had to face the enemy in a half-sword fight

Ham-fisted/handed: *Clumsy* * I dislike that ham-fisted man

Hammer out: *Make something flat with a hammer; come to an agreement after long and difficult discussions* * He hammered out that metal into a sheet * Let us sit down together and hammer out an agreement

Hand and foot: *With assiduous attention* * The patient came home from the hospital where he had been waited upon hand and foot

Hand and glove or hand in glove: *On very intimate terms; in close cooperation* * These two friends are hand and glove/hand in glove with each other * Many countries are hand and glove with one another in fighting terrorism

Hand back: *Return something borrowed* * He handed back his room key to the receptionist

Hand brake: *Brake operated by a hand lever* * My motorcycle has a hand brake also

Hand down: *Transmit in succession or by tradition* * Certain customs which are still in vogue have been handed down from generation to generation

Hand in: *Tender* * On being sure of getting a more lucrative offer, the man handed in his resignation from his present post

Hand it out to somebody: *Give one the credit that is one's due* * You have got to hand it to him that he has done well in life

Hand it to one: *Admit one's superiority as shown in a difficult matter* * People hand it to him for having rendered yeoman's service to uplift the downtrodden

Hand of God: *Unforeseen and unavoidable accident* * We can easily see the hand of God in natural calamities

Hand on: *Pass on* * Property is something handed on from generation to generation * Kindly hand on this book to the man sitting next to you

Hand out: *A portion handed out; a prepared statement issued to the press; an issue; distribute* * He has handed out a sum of five thousand rupees towards charity * A critical hand out with regard to the corrupt officials has appeared in today's newspapers * A hand out about the winter clothes for the troops will be coming up soon for the discussion * Birth-control pills are being handed out free of charge to the public by the government

Hand over: *Give something to someone; transfer* * The new manager has handed over charge to his successor * The thief was handed over to the police by the people * You cannot play with my gun, so hand it over at once

Hand over hand or hand over fist: *By passing the hands alternately one before above another as in climbing a rope or swimming with a certain stroke with a steady and rapid gain* * We were amazed to see his feat of hand over hand while climbing a steep hill with the help of a rope

Hand over head: *Headlong* * He dived into the river hand over head from the bridge over it

Hand play: *Dealing off blows* * After a great deal of quarrelling, there was a hand play between the two rivals

Hand round: *Pass round by hand* * He handed round the sweets to the children standing in a row

Hand to hand: *At close quarters* * There was a hand to hand fight between the two unruly groups

Hand-in-hand: *Holding hand together* * The lovers walked away hand- in-hand

Handle someone with kid gloves: *Deal gently with someone* * If you are able to handle him with kid gloves, he can be of great help to you

Hand-pick: *Pick by hand; select very carefully* * The hand-picked mangoes that I bought yesterday are very delicious * These are hand-picked bananas and apples

Hands down: *With utter ease* * He won the race hands down

Hands off: *Keep off* * This is my area of responsibility so you better keep your hands off

Hands up: *Hold the hands above the head in surrender* * Our commander ordered the defeated enemy to surrender with their hands up

Hand-to-hand: *At close quarters* * From hot words they descended to hand-to-hand fighting

Hand–to-mouth: *With provision for immediate needs only* * The poor generally have to live hand-to-mouth

Handwriting on the wall: *A foreshadowing of disaster* * The appearance of dark clouds in the sky is a clear handwriting on the wall that a heavy downpour will follow soon

Hang about: *To loiter* * We will hang about as idlers since our interview has been delayed

Hang back: *Show reluctance* * She hung back at his amorous glance

Hang by a hair: *Be in delicate*

state * Though he has been operated upon, his life is still hanging by a hair

Hang by a thread: *Depend upon very precarious condition* * The survival of the coalition government is now hanging by a thread

Hang by the wall: *Remain unused* * That heavy woollen overcoat has been hanging by the wall for quite a long time

Hang fire: *Be long in exploding or discharging; be slow in taking effect; hesitate* * The launching of long- range missiles has been hanging fire for a long time due to some technical problems * Due to the long process of law, execution of punishment hangs fire in a democratic set-up * The decision on the problem of Jammu & Kashmir has been hanging fire as a result of some misunderstanding on the part of the government

Hang heavy on one's hands: *Time passing holidays* * I have been out of job since the last one week as a result of which time is hanging heavy on my hands

Hang in the balance: *Be in doubt or suspense; undecided* * The fate of Kashmir is still hanging in the balance * The fate of the accused still hangs in balance

Hang off: *To let go; hold off* * He was given a hang off by the police when nothing objectionable was found in his car * His cold manner holds people off * Our Jawans were strong enough to hang off a much superior attacking force

Hang on: *To cling; persist; wait about; persevere; depend on; rely on* * He hung on until the rope broke * He hung on his statement even in the teeth of strong opposition * He hung on for a little time to think of a proper reply * It is hard work, but if you hang on long enough, you will succeed * Everything hangs on money at the moment * He hung on until the rope broke

Hang on one's lips: *Listen eagerly to one's words* * While he spoke, the audience hung on his lips

Hang on one's sleeve: *Depend or rely entirely upon others* * The young man has fallen a victim to paralysis and his life now hangs on his sleeve

Hang one's head: *Look ashamed* * He will hang his head low as he is feeling ashamed at his stupidity

Hang out: *Display as a sign; lodge or reside; hang wet clothes to dry* * Flags will be hanged out for the visit of the Prime Minister * Where are you hanging out these days? * She is hanging out wet clothes in the yard

Hang out for: *Insist on* * The child kept hanging out for the chocolate of his choice

Hang out the red flag: *Give a signal for batter* * He hung out the red flag for a tough fight in a boxing bout —The red flag signifies danger but here it does not mean anything like that. Moreover the use of batter does not mean beaten up or flattened or to mix flour, milk, etc. to make cake

Hang over: *Project over or lean out from* * He hung his head over the balcony to see the visitor who had rung the bell

Hang together: *Keep united; be consistent* * Reformists and hardliners are likely to hang together at the same party * If we all hang together, our plan will certainly succeed * The statements made by the two witnesses do not hang together

Hang up: *Suspend; delay; replace the telephone receiver; break of communication* * The discussion in the house had to be hung up when the opposition party made a din * The chairman had no option but to hang up the proceedings for an hour for want of quorum * I hung up the phone after having talked with my friend * He did not answer my call but just hung up on me

Hang up one's hat: *Take up one's abode; to give up* * You better hang up your hat before this arduous job kills you

Hang, draw and quarter: *Hang, cut down while still alive* * To hang, draw and quarter was a barbarous punishment given in old times in some countries

Hangover: *After effects of drinking* * He got a severe hangover since he was drinking till late last night

Hanker after: *Have a strong desire* * There are very few who do not hanker after wealth

Hanky-panky: *Jugglery; under hand trickery* * We should be honest in our dealings and avoid any kind of hanky-panky business

Hapless: *Unlucky or unhappy* * Very few people came forward to help the hapless

Happy event: *Birth of a child* * It was a happy event for the married couple to be blessed with a baby boy

Happy medium: *Compromise* * He struck a happy medium during his negotiations with the other party

Happy-go-lucky: *Easy going; take things as they come* * Tension cannot subdue her as she is a happy-go-lucky child * Avoid taking life so seriously because it is better to be happy-go-lucky and face life as it comes

Hara-kiri: *A Japanese method of committing suicide by cutting one's stomach open* * Hara-kiri was traditionally regarded in Japan as an honourable way to avoid disgrace

Harbour of refuge: *A harbour constructed to give shelter to ships* * In an emergency, ships can be accommodated in a harbour of refuge

Hard and fast: *Rigidly laid down and adhered to; definitely true and correct; strict* * We are bound to abide by the hard and fast rules of the company * There are no hard and fast rules regarding admission to the school * It is mandatory for players to observe hard and fast rules in almost all games

Hard by: *Very near* * We spent the night in a house hard by the river.

Hard case: *A person difficult to deal with* * The jail-bird is a hard case to stop from committing any further crime

Hard cash: *Ready money; special coined money* * You can purchase this item only on payment of hard cash * I have hard cash in my bank

Hard core: *Broken bricks, rubble etc.; solid or basic part* * We do make use of hard core in making roads or foundations of building * The proposed council will constitute the hard core of the future regime

Hard currency: *One which does not lose its value compared to other currency* * Pounds and dollars are considered as hard currency

Hard done by: *Badly treated* * The poor servant was hard done by his master

Hard drinker: *One who drinks excessively and persistently* * A hard drinker squanders his money at the cost of his health

Hard facts: *Undesirable and stubborn facts* * We have no escape from the hard facts of life

Hard-headed: *Shrewd* * You

cannot tackle that hard-headed person easily

Hard hit: *Gravely affected by some trouble or by love; with great force* * Hard hit by separation from his beloved, he committed suicide * Small businesses have been hard hit by recession

Hard- hitting: *Vigorous; direct* * The orator made a hard-hitting speech to direct his attack on strikers

Hard labour: *Punishment involving difficult manual work* * The culprit has been given rigorous imprisonment that includes hard labour

Hard lines: *A hard lot; hard luck; bad luck* * The astrologer foretold him about his hard lines and advised him to be very careful while driving * Though he is highly qualified yet his hard lines do not allow him a good living * He is under the influence of hard lines these days.

Hard money: *Metallic money* * Paper money has taken the place of hard money in almost all the countries of the world

Hard nut to crack: *A problem difficult to solve* * This problem has become a hard nut to crack for many a talented person * The question of removing unemployment is a hard nut to crack for our government

Hard of hearing: *Pretty deaf; one who is quite deaf* * That old man is hard of hearing and needs a hearing aid * He is hard of hearing and so makes use of the hearing aid

Hard pressed to do: *Find it difficult* * I would be hard pressed to do the job if you were to offer it to me

Hard pressed/pushed: *In difficulties* * We should be sympathetic and helpful towards the hard-pressed people * Things are changing so quickly these days that we are hard pressed to keep up to date

Hard put to it: *Find it difficult; in great strains; in difficult position* * He was hard put to explain what had happened * He, being hard put to it, went from bad to worse while struggling for the betterment of his career * He was hard put to it to explain what had happened.

Hard shoulder: *Reinforced side part of a road* * As our car broke down, we had to pull it over to the hard shoulder

Hard swearing: *Persistent and reckless swearing* * Taking into account his hard swearing, let us give him a chance to prove his stance in the court

Hard up for: *At a loss for; in want of or at a loss for* * He was hard up for ideas on how to explain the knotty problem * He is hard up for ideas and cannot suggest anything that is worthwhile

Hard visage: *Of hard, coarse or forbidding look* * We were frightened to look at the hard visage of that sturdy man

Hard words: *Words that give difficulty to a half-educated reader; harsh words* * That book is full of hard words and hence beyond the grasp of my understanding * Everybody dislikes him for his hard words

Hard-bitten: *Stubborn or tough because of a difficult life* * He is a hard-bitten warrior who has been decorated for his heroic deeds in many battles

Hard-earned: *Earned with difficulty* * We should be rather economic in spending our hard-earned money

Harden the neck: *Grow more obstinate* * Ego is one of the factors that hardens the neck of an individual

Hardened criminal: *Regular; permanent criminal* * Due to repeated crimes, the hardened criminal made prison his permanent home

Hard-favoured: *Hard-featured; coarse-featured; forbidding-featured* * You will find it difficult to please that hard-favoured person * I cannot put up with your hard-favoured commands * She looked rather hard-favoured in the official photographs

Hard-fisted: *Having hard or strong fists; close fisted* * A hard-fisted punch made him fall flat on the ground * A hard-fisted person would never be helpful to anyone

Hard-got: *Obtained with difficulty* * He is very careful in preserving his hard-got medals and bravery awards

Hard-handed: *Having hard hand; severe* * He is a hard-handed employer and would never tolerate any kind of indiscipline * His hard-handed approach to quell the strike proved futile

Hard-hearted: *Unfeeling or cruel* * That hard-hearted man killed his wife mercilessly

Hard-hit: *Seriously hurt* * He was found hard-hit by a sunstroke * The hard-hit person who fell victim to the accident was admitted to the hospital

Hardish approach: *Somewhat hard approach* * We should avoid a hardish approach while dealing with children

Hardly anything: *Almost nothing* * I have hardly anything to say on this topic

Hard-mouthed: *Of a horse with mouth insensible to the bit; not easily managed* * To domesticate a young hard-mouthed horse, one needs to use harsh tactics * It is really a hard-mouthed task to tame the wild animals for the circus organisers

Hard-ruled: *Ruled with difficulty* * Hard-ruled tribes still exist in many parts of the globe

Hard-run: *Greatly pressed* * The hard-run troops had no option but to surrender

Hard-set: *Beset with difficulty; rigid* * The hard-set people of the South Asia region are being helped by all the countries of the world * People are protesting against the hard-set rules of bank

Hard up: *Short of money or of anything else* * I am hard up these days and cannot afford any luxury

Hard-wearing: *Which does not wear out easily* * Some garments are made of hard-wearing material

Hard-won: *Won with toil and difficulty* * It is up to the coming generation to preserve the hard-won freedom of this country

Hardy: *Which can survive in difficult conditions* * Nomads are accustomed to leading a hardy life * The hardy bark of the tree can be used for manufacturing furniture

Hare-brained: *Mad or senseless; giddy; headless; headlong* * The hare-brained plan was rejected outright * He all at once felt hare-brained and began vomiting * A hare-brained person is not serious about his duty * The hare-brained decision was beset with danger

Hare-foot: *Swift of foot* * A hare-foot postman distributes the mail rather quickly

Hark at: *Listen to* * Just hark at him!

Hark away: *Cries to urge hounds and hunters* * Some persons interested in big game are expert in harking away to lure a particular wild animal

Hark back: *Revert; to go back in the past* * He is always harking back to his childhood days and saying how things were better then

Harp on: *Talk repeatedly about something that may bore others* * He continues to harp on the theme of his being a brilliant sportsman this year

Harp on about: *Keep talking about* * She always harps on about her misfortune

Harp on one string: *Dwell constantly on one topic* * He always harps on his string about his heydays

Harp on the same string: *Talk continuously* * He has nothing to say except to harp on the same string

Has a nose for: *Have an instinctive ability to find or recognise something* * She has a good nose for finding rare classical music discs

Has been dropped: *Has been stopped* * The whole project has been dropped

Has had a taste of prisons: *Has been in prison once* * He has had a taste of prison as he was convicted in a rape case

Has not an earth: *Has no chance at all* * He has not an earth to show his worth here

Hats off to: *All honour to* * Hats off to our brave soldiers who laid down their lives for our country

Hat trick: *Taking three wickets by consecutive balls in cricket* * Marshall took three wickets and achieved a hat trick

Hatched-faced: *With a grim pointed face* * He is a hatched-faced person to look at

Haul down one's flag: *Surrender* * The enemy forces had to haul down their flag when we mounted heavy pressure in the battle-field

Haul over the coals: *Reprimand for having done something wrong or foolish* * The boss hauled me over the coals for not attending the office on time * His editor hauled him over coals for missing the story

Haul round: *Turn a ship's course away from an object* * The warship hauled round when it detected the enemy's submarine in deep water

Haul up: *Come or bring to rest after hauling; call to account* * The elephants hauled up timbers to the saw-mill * He got hauled up in court for assaulting a girl student

Haunted house: *In which ghosts or spirits are supposed to live* * I will not sleep here at night as this is a haunted house

Have a bee in one's bonnet: *Take a remark seriously; be*

obsessed by an idea * It is better not to discuss the subject with him as he has a bee in his bonnet regarding it * That eccentric man has a bee in his bonnet abut gardening and will do anything to devote his time to it

Have a bye: *Pass to the next round of a sporting tournament without having to play; get a walkover* * He has had a bye to the next round without having had to lay a single match

Have a change of heart: *Experience a change of opinion* * He was such a miser earlier but the way he is gifting things today it seems he has had a change of heart

Have a charmed life: *Be very lucky* * He has led a charmed life as he has faced no accident till today despite rash driving

Have a crow to pluck with: *Have something to settle* * He has come here to have a crow to pluck with me about the sale of his old car

Have a face as long as a fiddle: *Look dismal* * Something wrong seems to have gone with him because he had a face as long as a fiddle

Have a feather in one's cap: *To add another achievement* * He has added another feather in his cap by breaking the world record in swimming

Have a finger in the pie: *Take part in a matter; have a share in the doing of something* * He loves to a finger in the pie in all that happens in the neighborhood * He is keen to have a finger in the pie regarding the opening of an educational institution in the town

Have a free hand: *Permission to do what seems best without consulting others* * When he is well-versed in this trade, why not to let him have a free hand in it

Have a friend at court: *Have a friend in a position where his influence is likely to prove useful* * It is an advantageous affair to have a friend at court

Have a good head on one's shoulders: *Have the ability and balance** This post needs the services of a person who has a good head on his shoulders * The manager of this firm has a good head on his shoulders and runs the business affairs very smoothly

Have a good mind: *Inclined strongly; strong desire* * He has a good mind to become a lawyer * I have a good mind to report you to the police

Have a good night: *Sleep well* * After a day's toil, I had a good night of sleep

Have a good opinion of: *Think well of* * The boss has a good opinion of his personal assistant

Have a good time: *Enjoy oneself* * Did you have a good time? * We had a good time during our summer vacation at Shimla * We had a good time in visiting the places of historical importance

Have a half mind: *Be somewhat inclined* * I have a half mind to give up the job and start an independent business

Have a hand in: *Have a share; share in action* * The investigation has amply revealed that he had no hand in that conspiracy * In the course of interrogation, it was found that he had no hand in the crime

Have a hard job to do something: *Have a difficult task* * It is a hard job for a poor man to keep his family clothed and fed

Have a heart: *Show sympathy; understanding* * She has a heart for the poor who find difficulty in making the two ends meet

Have a hunch that: *Think it likely* * I have a hunch that she will go to Kanpur tomorrow to see her mother

Have a joke with somebody: *Share one with someone* * In order to avoid boredom, I thought it proper to have a joke with my friend

Have a level head: *Be steady and well-balanced* * A good teacher must have a level head

Have a long arm: *Be able to make one's power felt far* * The law has a long arm and can catch any culprit

Have a loose tongue: *Be in the habit of talking too freely* * We should be careful when speaking to him as he has a loose tongue and can say anything to upset us

Have a lump in the throat: *Feeling of pressure* * He had a lump in his throat and could not express his feelings out of emotion

Have a maggot in one's head: *Have a strange fancy or whim* * There is not point in discussing the scheme with him as he has a maggot in his head and may not be agreeable to our views

Have a monkey on one's back: *Be drug addict; bear a grudge* * A man having a monkey on his back is like a live corpse * He will not help the man as he has a monkey on his back which will prevent him from being kind

Have a nerve: *Self-assured; bold* * He had a nerve to accept the challenge to a duel

Have a niche in the temple of fame: *Have achievement that will not be forgotten* * He already has a niche in the temple of fame as a dramatist

Have a night out: *Spend an evening and might in pleasure* * Yesterday I had a night out by having dinner in a posh hotel followed by a visit to the cinema

Have a nodding acquaintance: *Have some acquaintance* * One should at least have a nodding acquaintance with the subject of sanitation

Have a part in: *Be connected with* * The judge ordered the court to set the man free when it was found that he did not have a part in the crime

Have a person's ear: *Be secure of his favourable attention* * It is a good thing to have your boss's ear when working in an office

Have a ready tongue: *Be fluent, quick to answer questions* * He is known to have a ready tongue for every question that is asked of him

Have a ready wit: *Be quick to make clever and amusing remarks* * He is well known for having a ready wit for any questions asked

Have a right: *Be entitled; be under a moral obligation* * Everybody has a right to earn his living through fair measures * One has the right to live but not at the cost of others

Have a rod in pickle: *Have a punishment ready* * This organisation has a rod in pickle for anyone who breaks the established rules

Have a screw loose: *Be a little stupid; be unsound in one's mind* * He has a screw loose so the people tend to ignore his folly * He seems he have a screw loose as he tends to make very unpleasant remarks for no rhyme or reason

Have a short temper: *Lacking self control so as to get angry* * One who has a short temper is never respected in high society

Have a shot at: *Try to do something* * Let us have a shot at solving this problem * This striker had a shot at goal

Have a split personality: *Have*

two ways of behaviour which are quite different in varying circumstances * A man having a split personality can be quite a strain on the family

Have a stab at: *Try to do* * Though he found the test difficult, he had a stab at it

Have a stake in the company: *Have invested some money in the company hoping to make a profit* * Our government has a stake in the oil industry to improve its financial position * Those who have a stake in any large company have a strong hope of earning good profit

Have a sweet tooth: *Be fond of sweet food* * There is a general feeling that children have a sweet tooth

Have a thick skin: *Be insensitive* * A person having a thick skin will not react to any criticism

Have a thing about: *Be obsessed with* * She has a thing about the girl reporter working in the newspaper

Have a way with one: *Have a fascinating personality* * He has a way with him for which he is held in high esteem

Have a whack at: *Try to do* * Let us have a whack at it!

Have a whale of a time: *Enjoying very much* * We had a whale of a time when rowing our boat in the lake

Have a whip-round: *Ask everyone to give some money* * People working at the same place have a whip-round and money so collected is used to buy something for all

Have a windfall: *Unexpected good fortune* * The death of his childless aunt proved a windfall for him as he has received all her moveable and immovable property

Have a wolf by the ears: *Be in a very difficult situation* * How can he be helpful to you when he himself has a wolf by the ears?

Have a wolf in the stomach: *Be ravenously hungry* * One can involve oneself in any theft when one has a wolf in the stomach

Have a word with: *Have s short talk; have some conversation with him* * I had a word with him about his future career * I hope you can spare some time to enable me to have a word with you on a very important point

Have an eye: *Watch out for* * For the time being he is having an eye to the main chance in the tournament

Have an eye for: *Be a good judge of* * He has a good eye for beauty in any form

Have an eye to: *Contemplate; have regard to; incline towards; regard one's own interest* * He has an eye to become rich by hook or by crook * You certainly have an eye for all that you have done so as to emerge a winner * The boss has an eye to give his flatterer a further promotion * In everything he does he has an eye to the main chance

Have an eye to the main chance: *Be aware of opportunity for self-enrichment* * It is but natural for everyone to have an eye to the main chance for promotion

Have an oar in another's boat: *Meddle with the affairs* * Some people are so meddlesome that they have an oar in another's boat

Have an old head on young shoulders: *Ripe in wisdom but young in years* * He appears to have an old head on young shoulders considering the wise steps he has taken to promote his factory

Have at heart: *Cherish as a matter of deep interest* * I have the welfare of my employees at heart when looking after their interests

Have at one's finger ends: *Be perfect master of a subject* * That barrister has many important law points at his finger ends

Have been in sunshine: *Be drunk* * It is reported that he killed his wife when he had been in sunshine * Having been in sunshine, they began to sing and dance in the rain

Have been in the wars: *Signs of having been knocked about* * From your looks it appears as if you have been in the wars

Have cause: *Have to give reason for a certain line of action* * He has been served with a notice to have cause with regard to contempt of court

Have connections: *Have friends; relations* * He has connections in the higher echelons of the local government

Have done: *Desist; stop it; have no more dealing* * I have done with telling lies * He has done to attending a cinema hall * I have since done with him for his rude behaviour

Have eyes like a hawk: *Have sharp eyesight* * She has eyes like a hawk and can thread the needle within no time

Have got a nerve: *Be cheeky;*

rude * He has got a nerve to abuse his elders

Have got to do something: *Be obliged to* * You have got to do something in return for his kindness * You have got to go something about your yellow teeth

Have got to hand it to someone: *Admire or praise someone's skills or achievements* * You have to hand it to them for they are wonderful entertainers

Have had it: *Be punished; have missed an opportunity* * He have had enough of him and do not want anything more to do with him

Have hand in something: *Help to make something happen* * He was found to have a hand in the conspiracy

Have heard of it: *Know about it* * He has never heard of it

Have in common: *Share (with)* * They have nothing in common with one another regarding sports

Have in stock: *Have in store* * We have in stock sufficient wheat grains to meet the demands from all quarters

Have it: *Prevail; get punishment; unpleasant consequences; exceed in any way* * Rumour has it that the minister is going to resign * He is sure to have it for slapping the child * We could not escape from having it as a result of our ill designs

Have it out: *Discuss or express explicitly and exhaustively* * The complicated issue has been referred to a standing committee to have it out for proper guidance

Have it out with somebody: *Reach an understanding about something by frank discussion* * I need to have it out with him over the controversial issue once and for all

Have itching ears: *Desirous of hearing novelties* * He has itching ears to get new information on any subject

Have lost one's tongue: *Be too shy to speak* * A shy person is bound to lose his tongue if asked to make a public speech

Have nerves of steel: *Be or remain calm in different situation* * A person having nerves of steel can overcome crises without any difficulty

Have no bearing on: *Have no connection with* * Your statement has no bearing at all on this case

Have no leg to stand: *Have no case at all* * A liar has no leg to stand despite making all kinds of excuses

Have no mean opinion of oneself: *Think a lot of oneself* * He, as a scholar, has no mean opinion of himself

Have no patience with: *Be irritated* * He will have no patience with a stupid child

Have no right: *Not entitled; without obligation* * A killer of innocent human beings has no right to live under law * We have no right to harm others for our selfish ends

Have no truck with: *Not to have anything to do with; have no dealing with* * We shall have no truck with any political party that favours the nepotism

Have no use for: *Have no liking for* * We have no use for people who waste their time

Have nothing to do with: *Avoid or have no dealing with; not to be concern of* * I advise you to have nothing to do with that man * That has nothing to do with you

Have on: *Wear; take in; hoax* * He had a woollen suit on to protect himself from the cold * He had the scene on at a glance * He may have something on his mind that day

Have on the hip: *Get an advantage over someone* * On the strength of wit and wealth, it is quite possible to have your rivals on the hip

Have one foot in the grave: *Be not far from the death* * My friend who is suffering from asthma has now one foot in the grave

Have one's cake and eat it: *Benefit from both two quite opposite things* * He wants to go to the movies without spending money little knowing that you cannot have your cake and eat it too

Have one's fingers all thumbs: *Be awkward in handling* * I tried my hand at knitting but with my fingers all thumbs I gave up the effort

Have one's gorge rises: *Be filled with loathing* * The man's gorge rises the moment he sees the crook

Have one's hands full: *Be over busy; be very busy and have no time to do anything extra; have all the work one can do or fully occupied* * He has his hands full these days and has no spare time to coach you * I have got my hands full, so you have to do it yourself * Presently I have my hands full and cannot think of taking up any other job in hand

Have one's heart in one's

boots: *Feel a sinking of the heart* * He had his heart in his boots when he staggered to render his maiden speech

Have one's heart in one's mouth: *Be in trepidation* * She had her heart in her mouth when someone knocked on the door at the dead of the night

Have one's heart in something: *Be interested and fond of it* * He has his heart in dancing and music

Have one's heart in the right place: *Be faithful and true-hearted* * He is blunt to her but he has his heart in the right place

Have one's heart set on something: *Desire greatly* * As a matter of fact, I have my heart set on political science and not on pure science

Have one's knife in: *Be persistently hostile or vindictive towards* * Pakistan has all along been having its knife in regarding the issue of Kashmir

Have one's monkey up: *Be angry* * He had his monkey up at your harsh attitude

Have one's nose in a book: *Engrossed in reading (noticing nothing going around one)* * He had his nose in a book and so did not notice the cat that licked up his glass of milk

Have one's number: *Size him up* * He had his number to consider his suitability for the post concerned

Have one's sleep out: *Continuous sleeping until one wakes naturally* * Let her have her sleep out

Have one's way: *Carry one's point; get what one wants; do according to one's own will* * He has his way that brings him credit * If John has his way, the money will be forthcoming in abundance * He is fed up with the unfaithful attitude of his son who has his own way in everything

Have one's will: *Obtain what one desires* * He, being a dare-devil, always gets his will fulfilled

Have one's wits about one: *Be a quick to see what is happening; alert and ready to act; be alert and resourceful* * Those who have their wit about them cannot be betrayed by a cheat * You have to keep your wits about you when moving in a crowd

Have one's work cut out: *Have one's work prescribed; be faced with a difficult task* * He has his work cut out for him for the whole week * We will have our work cut out to finish on time

Have other fish to fry: *Have something else to do or attend to* * Apart from doing teaching, he has other fish to fry like going to work in a shop

Have out: *Be removed; sort out a quarrel* * He was suffering from a severe toothache so he plans to have it out * Let us have it out with him

Have place: *Have existence* * You cannot find place in high society unless you fulfil some pre-requisites

Have recourse to: *Turn to for help; seek help from* * Your only recourse is legal action against them * I don't advise you to have recourse to the moneylender

Have seen one's best days: *Be now on the decline* * The poor old man had seen his best days and is now submissive to the existing state of affairs

Have seen services: *Have fought in war; have been put to long or hard use* * He has seen services and lost his right arm in the battle-field * In the whole course of his active life he has seen services while taking part in one adventure or another

Have shot one's bolt: *Be unable to do more than one has done* * He has already shot his bolt by giving you adequate help

Have somebody do something: *Want him to do it* * I would not have you do that * What would you have me do?

Have somebody down: *Entertain somebody as a visitor or guest* * We are having the cricket team down to our place for dinner

Have somebody eating out of one's hand: *Make somebody do everything one tells him to do* * I had him eating out of my hand and thus he obliged me

Have somebody in: *Receive him in the house, etc.* * We shall have the tribal chief in our house with full respect

Have somebody round: *Be visited at home by one* * We had John and his wife round for dinner last night

Have someone on: *Tell someone a lie as a joke* * We must have someone on to drive away the boredom in our free hours

Have someone on the carpet: *Criticise someone* * The minister had the officer on the carpet for neglect of duty

Have something back: *Be returned* * You shall have your money back by tomorrow

Have something done: *Experience or suffer it* * He had his pocket picked

Have something in: *Possess something in the house; etc.* * Do we have enough sugar in the jar?

Have something in prospect: *Expect something to happen* * Everybody has something in prospect for a bright future * He is out of job and has nothing in prospect at present

Have something off pat: *Know something perfectly* * He had all the answers off pat

Have something on: *Be wearing; have an engagement* * He had nothing on when he came out form the bathroom * I have nothing on tomorrow evening

Have something on the tip of one's tongue: *Just going to say it* * I had some words to say on the tip of my tongue but I kept quiet

Have something out: *Cause something to be taken out* * Due to unbearable pain, Sunil will have his two teeth out by the dentist * I will have it out with him for abusing me in public

Have something up one's sleeves: *Have an idea, plan, etc which one keeps secret for the future use* * He thought the old man had some clever tricks up his sleeves as he was not willing to show his papers

Have taken: *Have sprouted roots* * The rose cuttings have taken root

Have the advantage of: *Benefit of* * India and China have the advantage of manpower

Have the agency for: *Be the distributors for* * We have the agency for Ford cars

Have the ball at one's feet: *Have a good chance of attaining success* * He has the ball at his feet because he is leading by a good margin in the match

Have the best of it: *Gain the advantage in a contest* * Since he can speak well he has the best of it in winning in any declamation contest

Have the black ox tread on one's foot: *Experience sorrow or misfortune* * It appears that he has the black ox tread on his foot as nobody is showing any sympathy with him

Have the courage of one's convictions: *Stick fearlessly to one's true words or true act* * He is a man who has the courage of his convictions in all that he says and does

Have the gorge: *Strain as if to*

vomit; to eat ravenously * The smell of the rotting fish made his gorge rise * the way he was gorging on food it seemed as though he had not eaten for days

Have the heart to: *Be hard-hearted or unsympathetic enough to* * How can you have the heart to drown the kitten?

Have the honour of: *Giving of honour* * May I have the honour of your company to dinner tonight?

Have the hump: *Fit of depression or irritation* * The poor farmer who had the hump for not being able to bear the debt committed suicide

Have the last laugh: *Get one's satisfaction* * I had the last laugh after making him feel ashamed at his boastful attitude

Have the last word: *Make the final remark in an argument* * He did not miss to have the last word by warning his opponent of serious consequences

Have the makings of: *May develop into* * He has in him the makings of a great man

Have the mercy on: *Forgive; not to want to punish or harm someone* * We must show mercy to those who do not commit crime intentionally

Have the nerve to: *Have the necessary courage or self-reliance; be imprudent enough* * He has the nerve to outdo his rivals in any declamation contest * He has the nerve to drive a racing car on any track * He had the nerve to suggest that I was cheating

Have the pas of one: *Take precedence over* * You must have the pas of that prudent man in order to lead a purposeful life

Have the sight of: *See or succeed in seeing* * Please inform the police the moment you have the sight of that dreaded murderer

Have the time of one's life: *Experience a period of happiness or enjoyment* * I had the time of my life when I made a double century in my maiden debut

Have the upper hand: *Have the advantage or control* * Neither of them is concerned with having the upper hand in the argument * So far as his talent is concerned, he is quite capable of having the upper hand in the competition

Have the whip-hand of someone: *Be in a position to control* * The policeman, having disarmed the bandit, had the whip-hand of him

Have the wind of: *Be on the trail of* * The detective is very alert in getting the wind of the missing child

Have the worse: *Be at a disadvantage; be defeated* * You will have the worse if you give in to his demands * He accepted the challenge for boxing but had the worse at the actual scene

Have the wrong: *Suffer injustice or injury* * He has the wrong as he has been made a scapegoat

Have to do with: *Be connected with, result from; have any sort of connection with* * I know he behaved badly but it has to do with the way he has been brought up * He is quite a stranger to me so the question of having to do anything with him does not arise

Have to eat one's words: *Take back what one has said* * He had to eat his words when he realised his mistake

Have to go the way of all flesh: *Die* * Every human being has to go the way of all flesh sooner or later

Have too many irons in the fire: *Have too many responsibilities to cope with at once* * A Prime Minister in a democratic set-up has too many irons in the fire to cope with * I have too many irons in the fire and that is my trouble * If you have too many irons in the fire, then you cannot concentrate on anything

Have two faces: *Be two-faced* * He has two faces because he plays with his hares and hunts with the hounds

Have two strings to one's bow: *Have an alternative in reserve* * The recession won't hit him because he has two strings to his bow

Have up: *Call to account before a court of justice* * The police will have him up for over speeding

Have vision of: *Looking ahead of* * Have you ever had a vision of possessing great wealth and success?

Have water laid on to a house: *Have pipes put from the main water supply to the house* * The plumber will have water laid on to my house by tomorrow evening

Have way: *Be in motion* * The fishing vessel will have way towards its destination

Have way on: *Be moving through water* * The cargo ship is having its way on to London

Have with you: *I am ready to go with you* * It would be my pleasure to have dinner with you

Have words: *Quarrels* * The two brothers were having words over some disputed property

Have words with: *Quarrel with* * They were having words with each other over money matters

Have you any money on you?: *Have you any money with you?* * Have you any money on you as a provision for your old age?

Have-not: *One who lacks possession* * There has always been a conflict between the haves and have-nots

Have-on: *A deception; a hoax* * A credulous person easily falls a victim to any kind of have-on coined by cheats

Haw and haw: *Hesitate* * We should never haw and haw in doing right things

Haw-haw: *Loud vulgar laughter; affected by superior in enunciation; boisterous laugh* * People thrashed some drunkards who were making haw-haw * A sensible person would never haw-haw in a public place * He felt disgusted at the haw-haw of some rude persons

Hayseed: *Silly country person* * We had some very happy moments with that hayseed

Hazard a guess: *Make a rough guess* * I can hazard a guess about the expenditure to be incurred in the new project

He breaks his wife's head and then buys a plaster: *Think of some remedy when a thing becomes irreparable* * It is really ridiculous if a person breaks his wife's head and then buys a plaster as a remedial course

He has had it: *There is nothing for him* * There was no cure for his disease and so he has had it

He jets at sears who never felt a wound: *No one knows the weight of another's burden* * It is all very well for him to laugh at the poor man's plight as he jets at sears who never felt a wound

He who laughs last laughs longest: *To tell somebody not to be proud of their present success* * It is well said that he who laughs last laughs longest

He that is warm, thinks all are so: *Person having convenient lifestyle is practically ignorant of ordinary people's problems* * A person who is warm thinks all are so are also living a convenient life

He who would catch fish must not mind getting wet: *Those who want to reap the rich divi-*

dends should also be prepared to face risks if any * If you enjoy playing out on the road, you should be prepared to get hurt as has been rightly said that he who would catch fish must not mind getting wet

He who would sow well must reap well: *Do good to others if you wish to be done by; good deeds bring good returns* * If you do good to others, you would enjoy the benefits of your good deed because he who would sow well must reap well

Head and shoulder: *Very much standing above other things; far superior* * The clock-tower of this town is head and shoulders above other buildings * As a diplomat, he was head and shoulder above his contemporaries

Head first/Head foremost: *With head in front* * She projected her head first while performing the long jump

Head I win, tails you lose: *Gain no advantage* * You will never get the better of that rascal because he believes in the philosophy 'head I win, tails you lose'

Head lugged: *Dragged by head* * They head lugged the killed deer down to the road and then carried it away in a vehicle

Head mark: *A peculiar characteristic* * To show mercy towards the poor is one of the head marks of that gentleman

Head off: *Get ahead of so as to turn back; deflect from path or intention* * We started running and shouting in our effort to head off the goats * They gave wrong information to the police to head off their attention from the target and divert their attention elsewhere

Head on: *With head pointing directly forward* * The rocket took its head on flight in the sky

Head or tails: *An invitation to guess how a coin will fall* * The tossing of coin decides the fortune of the bidders of a bet on the basis of heads or tails

Head over ears: *Entirely* * He is head and ears in debt and is likely to be declared bankrupt

Head over the heels: *In a somersault or upside down; completely* * Jumping head over the heels by a small girl was a thrilling item at the circus show * He is head over the heels in love with that girl

Headway: *Progress; motion ahead* * He is making a satisfactory headway in his career as a researcher * He maintained his headway on the road lying ahead

Head wind: *The wind blowing towards the face* * We had to face head wind while climbing up the snow-capped mountain

Head-first: *With the head in front* * He had fallen head first into the ditch

Headlines: *Main points of news; piece of writing with titles* * The news headlines are broadcast every half hour * The headline on today's paper talks about kidnapping only

Head-on: *Head to head; direct conflict; disagreement* * There was a head-on collision between the two vehicles * The government did not want to risk a head-on confrontation with the workers

Heads and thaws: *Side by side* * We have worked heads and thaws together for many days * The soldiers marched heads and thaws in the parade ground

Heads of sheep: *Number of sheep* * That farmer has many heads of sheep

Headstrong: *Self-willed* * A headstrong person will never yield to pressures from other persons

Heels over head: *Upside down* * Running on the slippery path, he fell heels over head and got injured

Hear about something: *Be given information about or learn about* * I have just heard about his dismissal

Hear from somebody: *Receive a letter* * How often do you hear from your brother who has gone abroad?

Hear of it: *Allow it* * He will not hear of it no matter how convincing you sound

Hear of somebody/something: *Have knowledge of* * I have never heard of her or the place you refer to

Hear tell of: *Hear people talking about* * I have often heard people telling of such unusual happenings

Heard it from second hand: *Not from the original source of news* * I heard it from second hand about the death of my dear friend

Heart and hand/soul: *With complete heartiness or devotion to a cause; with full energy* * He decided to throw himself heart and hand/soul into a great cause * Unless you throw yourself heart and soul in your studies, you cannot get through the competitive exam

Heart bleeding for: *Feeling sorry for* * My heart is bleeding for the loss of your only son in a fatal accident

Heart leaps: *Feel excited about something* * His heart leapt when he came to know that he had won the first prize in the lottery

Heart of grease: *A fat heart* * Despite his heart of grease he does not keep a watch on his diet

Heart of hearts: *The inmost feelings; deepest affections* * In his heart of hearts, he does not trust the authority concerned * I do love you from my heart of hearts

Heart of oak: *A resolute heart; brave* * A soldier must have a heart of oak when in action

Heart searching: *Deep thought about how to deal with a problem* * After a good deal of heart searching the problem was solved satisfactorily

Heart warming: *Pleasing; encouraging* * It was a heart-warning spectacle for us to watch him perform the air exercise

Heart's content: *As much as you like* * He enjoyed the concert to his heart's content

Heart's desire: *Wanted very much indeed* * The hungry man ate the food to his heart's desire

Heart-ache: *Deep sorrow* * He experienced a severe heart-ache when he received the news of his failure in the annual exams

Heart-breaking: *Causing overwhelming grief; which makes one very sad or upset* * The death of his family members in an accident was a piece of heart-breaking news * It was heart-breaking news for her when she heard about the fatal accident of her mother

Heartfelt: *Sincere* * He expressed his heartfelt congratulations on the birthday of his friend

Heartland: *Central part of a country* * Delhi province lies in the heartland of India

Heart-quake: *Trembling; fear* * With the jolt given by the earthquake, I also suffered a serious heart-quake

Heart-rending: *Agonising; pitiful* * People got shocked on hearing the heart-rending news about the disaster caused by the tsunami * It was heart-rending news to hear about the havoc caused by the recent tsunami

Heart-searching: *Examination of one's feelings* * After doing a thorough heart-searching of the causes for his failure, he turned a new leaf to study more seriously

Heart-stirring: *Rousing; accelerating* * The poor boy did not know that heart-stirring moments are in store for him in future

Heart-throb: *Popular film star* * Geeta Bali was the heart-throb of the people when she was alive

Heart-to-heart: *Candid; intimate; unreserved* * The newly engaged couple was engrossed in a heart-to-heart talk with each other * Unless we have a heart-to-heart talk, things cannot be clear

Heart-whole: *Whole at heart or sincere; out-and-out* * A heart-whole person can earn respect everywhere

Hearty: *Vigorous; strong; loud; cheerful and hearty* * We had a hearty meal to satiate our hunger * We spent our evening singing hearty songs

Heated discussion: *Discussion where people become quite angry* * There was a heated discussion in the meeting for quite a long time

Heave a sigh: *Give a big sigh* * They heaved a sigh of relief on completion of the project

Heave in sight: *Come into view* * Many attractive places heaved in sight during the course of our expedition to North Pole

Heaven of heavens: *The abode of God; the highest of* * The sole aim of the hermit was to seek heaven of heavens in next life

Heaven-sent: *Providential or lucky* * While travelling through an isolated hilly track, he came across a diamond which he thought to be a heaven-sent gift

Heavy-hearted: *Profoundly aggrieved and sad* * We went to offer our condolences to the heavy-hearted woman who had lost her only son in the war

Hedge one's bets: *Arrange things so that one will be protected against losing* * He is very shrewd in hedging his bets while investing his surplus money in shares

Heel and toe: *With strict walking pace as opposed to running** It was a treat to watch the heel-and-toe march of the troops on the parade ground

Heel-tap: *A layer of material in a shoe-heel; a small quantity of liquor left in the glass after drinking* * He got the heel-tap of his shoes mended by a cobbler * He gulped down the full glass of whisky save the heel-tap

Heir to: *Legal right to* * She is the only heir to property of her father * He is heir to a large fortune

Hell for leather: *At a furious pace* * In order to save his life from his killers, he ran hell for leather

Hell of a noise: *Very loud noise* * Some miscreants created a hell of a noise in the cinema hall

Hell of a party: *Very good party* * It was really one hell of a party on the occasion of his marriage

Hell-bent on: *Determined to do something* * The two sides seem hell-bent on spoiling the interests of each other

Help lame dog over stile: *Be friend in need* * A soft-hearted person is always ready to help a lame dog over the stile

Help off with: *Aid in taking of; aid in disposing or getting rid of* * He helped him off with his overcoat * He helped me off with the heavy load of work

Help on with: *Help to put on* * The servant helped him on with his boots and coat

Help oneself to: *Take for oneself without waiting for offer or anything* * He helped himself to the curry since no one was around to pass it on to him * May I help you to some more drinks?

Help out: *Supplement* * I was asked to come in for a few days to help them out

Help yourself too: *To steal* * He helped himself to the contents of the drawer when no one was looking

Helter-skelter: *In a confused hurry; disorderly motion* * When there was a bomb explosion in the market, people began to run helter-skelter for safety * People were seen running helter-skelter to push their way through the entrance doors leading to the hall

Hem in: *Surround* * The Prime Minister was hemmed in by his bodyguards

Hempen widow: *The widow of a man who has been hanged* * The hempen widow had to earn her living doing menial jobs

Hen party: *Party for women only* * About a hundred women took part in the hen party in the club

Henceforth: *From now on; from this time forth* * Henceforth his life would never be same again * This rule will remain in force henceforth

Henceforward: *From this time forward; from this time on* * Henceforward, I shall be happy to abide by your instructions in totality * Henceforward you will hold charge of this company also

Henchman: *Accomplice; helper* * The criminal has been arrested along with his henchman

Hen-hussy: *A man who meddles with women's affairs* * It is ridiculous to be a hen-hussy

Henpecked: *A person whose wife nags him continuously and tells him what to do* * He is a henpecked husband and can not go against the wishes of his wife

Herculean task: *A very difficult task* * The government and the people performed a Herculean task by rehabilitating the victims of the floods

Here and there: *In various places* * Here and there we could see stray dogs and cattle in the town * Tourism is being promoted in India almost here and there

Here goes: *An explanation indicating that the speaker is about to do something* * Here she goes telling a tall story * I have never driven a truck before, so here goes!

Here you are: *This is what you want; this is something for you* * Here you are, my boy, have the pears to your heart-fill * Here you are in the open place to enjoy fresh air and to play about

Here, there and everywhere: *In all parts* * One can see the sky here, there and everywhere

Here's to: *To drink the health of* * Cheers! Here's to the health of the bride and the bridegroom

Hereabouts: *Near or about* * Is there any village hereabouts?

Hereafter: *The life to come; in the future* * Hereafter she will live in a perpetual state of boredom * The vast garden made of different kinds of models will hereafter be known as rock-garden

Hereby: *By means of this* * Since you were found guilty of corruption, you are hereby dismissed from service * Some allegations have been made against you so you are hereby informed to be present in the court tomorrow as a defendant

Herein: *In this* * Herein lies the truth when you say that honesty is the best policy

Hereof: *Of this* * We have told the truth in the matter and swear hereof about the same

Hereon: *On or upon this* * As for your query, I have no comments hereon at present

Hereto: *To this* * I agree hereto without any reservation with the comments made by you in his praise

Heretofore: *Before this time; formerly* * You must stick to the points referred to heretofore

Hereunder: *Under this* * The names of the firms mentioned hereunder have been blacklisted

Hereunto: *To this point or time* * His work has been found satisfactory hereunto so we should give him due incentive by way of an increase in the salary

Hereupon: *On this; immediately after this* * This problem is so tough that nobody can dwell hereupon properly * As soon as the quorum is full, the item of the agenda would be taken for consideration hereupon

Herewith: *With this* * Attached herewith please find a leaflet that would give you the desired information

Hermetically sealed: *Closed completely; made air-tight by melting glass* * They found themselves in a hermetically sealed small room, making them gasp for breath * Here it solidified and hermetically sealed before putting on the counter for sale

Het up: *Excited; anxious* * There is no need to get so het up over a trifle

Hue and cry: *An outcry calling upon all to pursue one who is to be made prisoner* * The old lady raised a hue and cry against her chain-snatchers who sped away on their motorcycle

Heyday: *Memorable days* * He was missing very much his heydays when everything was under his command

Hey-go-mad: *Expressing a high degree of excitement* * When I met him there, I found him in a hey-go-mad mood

Hide one's light under a bush: *Keep secret; conceal one's talent* * Scientists hide their light under the bush until their discovery has been successfully tested * Before completing his masterpiece, he hid his light under a bush

Hidebound: *Unwilling to change ideas; narrow-minded* * A conservative person has a hidebound attitude even on small matters

Hideout: *A retreat or hiding place*

* Terrorists attacked the troops from their hideout

High and dry: *Up out of the water; stranded* * The lotus flower that grows high and dry has its own charm * The shipwrecked travellers were left high and dry over the beach for a long time

High and low: *Rich and poor; people of all conditions; wherever possible* * The laws of the land are equally applicable to high and low * I have searched high and low for the keys but am unable to find them

High and mighty: *Arrogant or exalted* * Generally the high and mighty are able to rule the roost * I do not understand the reason for his acting so high and mighty about

High colour: *Redness of complexion* * Her face was beaming with high colour

High density of population: *Many people per unit of area* * This city has a high density of population which is putting a strain on civic amenities

High fidelity: *Radio equipment which gives excellent reproduction of sound* * You can have this tape which has been recorded at high fidelity

High-flyer: *Very intelligent or ambitious person* * Credit must go to high-flyers who make new discoveries every now and then * He is a high-flyer who is constantly on the move in connection with his business

High life: *Fashionable society or its manner of living* * Only wealth makes it possible for one to lead a high life

High road: *Main road* * There is a web of high roads in all parts of our country * There was a great rush of traffic on the high road

High seas: *The oceans* * The globe is surrounded by five high seas

High society: *Top class of people* * Generally the most wealthy and influential people are referred to as part of the high society

High spirits: *Be very happy* * After having passed his annual examination he seems to be in high spirits

High spot: *An outstanding feature; most enjoyable part of an entertainment* * We felt exhilarated on hearing about the high spots of his adventure story * The Taj Mahal was the high spot of our tour

High tea: *Tea with eggs, meat fish or the like* * I have been invited to high tea by my friend

High time: *Quite time* * It is high time that we did something about improving the situation * It is high time you started studying hard as the examinations are approaching near

High winds blow on high hills: *High views are embraced only by persons of high moral character; only top class characters embrace higher values of life* * Mahatma Gandhi could have such a large number of followers because high winds blow on high hills

High words: *Angry altercation* * What began as a discussion soon ended in exchange of high words between the two parties

High-brow: *Intelligent person* * The new magazine should appeal to high-brows

High-flying: *Very ambitious* * They were all very high-flying people but I think I managed to impress them

High-handed: *Done without considering the feelings of other people* * There is really no need for such high-handed behaviour

Highlight: *Most important event* * The highlights of the last week's events have been listed in today's newspapers

Highly strung: *Very nervous; excitable* * As highly-strung persons get easily provoked one should be careful when saying anything to them

High-minded: *Having lofty principles and thoughts* * This book seems to be a product of some high-minded scholar

High-pitched: *Sharp and shrill sound* * The dog hit by a stone whined in a high-pitched voice

High-sounding: *Impressively pretentious; pompous* * There is no doubt that love, sympathy and other high-sounding principles have lost their value * The speech made by the politician was full of rather high-sounding words

High-spirited: *Lively; difficult to control* * A high-spirited person always wants to have fun and adventure * Generally a high-spirited person is very lively and active

High-up: *Person of high rank or great importance* * Only those who are high-ups take their meals in this hotel

Highwayman: *Person who attacks travellers and robs them* * Most travellers from Bihar fall victim to highwaymen on the road

Hindrance to: *Obstacle to* * His marriage proved to be a great hindrance to his studies

Hinge upon: *Depend on* * The whole thing hinges upon our shoulder

Hint at: *Indicate or refer indirectly* * He hinted at my inability to take up the challenge

Hint to somebody: *Suggest indirectly; give a hint* * I hinted to him to work harder

Hip-hip-hurray: *An exclamation to invoke a united cheer* * The supporters of the match-winners exclaimed enthusiastically, "Hip-hip-hurray!"

Hire off: *Split off* * A proposal is in the offing for some public organisations to hire off their services to the private sector

Hire-purchase: *System where you buy something by paying in instalments* * I have purchased this new car on hire-purchase basis

His blood ran cold: *Horrified* * His blood ran cold when he heard that his friend was murdered * His blood ran cold when he saw the police at his doorsteps

His cake is dough: *His hope has failed* * Since his cake is dough, he looks dejected these days

His fingers are all thumbs: *He is clumsy* * You will have to handle this job at your own end without depending on him because his fingers are all thumbs

His nibs: *Himself; his mightiness* * Let the truth be revealed by his nibs * They had to submit to his nibs

His number is up: *He is doomed; has not long to live* * Taking into account his heart trouble and old age, his number seems to be up * As the mercy appeal of the prisoner stands rejected, his number is definitely up

His tongue runs: *He talks incessantly* * Everybody in the college knows that his tongue runs even on useless issues

His wits have gone a wool-gathering: *Be absent-minded* * You cannot make him understand your point because his wits have gone a wool-gathering

Hit a blot: *Find a weak place or point* * If you could hit a blot in their working system, it would be easier to set the same right

Hit a boundary: *Hit the ball beyond the edge of the field* * In the international cricket match, he hit many a boundary that pleased the cricket fans

Hit-and-run: *Lasting only a very short time* * The death of a motorist was reported to be a hit-and-run accident

Hit at: *Aim a blow* * The fighter plane got ready to hit at the target

Hit back: *Defend oneself from/ against attack* * Our army had been able to hit back the sudden assault of enemy forces

Hit below the belt: *Deal a blow disallowable in the rules of the ring; do an injury to another unfairly* * Neither of the two contestants was allowed to hit below the belt * A sportsman would never hit anyone below the belt *

Hit him one: *Hit him a blow* * She hit him one for his rudeness

Hit it off: *Agree* * My friend and I can never hit it off on this particular issue

Hit off: *Intimate or describe felicitously* * He hit off well with his new friend

Hit out: *Strike out especially with the fist; criticise strongly* * He, being in a rage, hit his wife out who got hurt seriously * The minister hit out against the trade union leaders

Hit parade: *List of top selling popular records* * Enclosed herewith is the list of hit parade records available with us for your information

Hit somebody hard: *Cause him to suffer* * The slump hit his business hard * He was hard hit by a financial crisis

Hit the headlines: *Be printed prominently in the headlines* * The havoc played by the tsunami hit the headlines in almost all the newspapers of the world

Hit the high spots: *Go to excess; reach high level* * Don't hit the high spot while drinking strong alcohol * It was due to his sense of duty and honesty that he hit the high spots from one high rank to another

Hit the jackpot: *Have great success or good fortune; win a large prize in a lottery* * He hit the jackpot by winning the highest prize in the lottery * The poor farmer was lucky enough to hit the jackpot and become a millionaire overnight

Hit the nail on the head: *Touch the exact point* * When the Prime Minister referred to the involvement of government officials in corruption, he hit the nail on the head * You have hit the nail on the head by stating the right point

Hit the road: *Set out on the road* * The trucks loaded with consumer items have already hit the road

Hit upon: *Devise* * He hit upon a plan to disrupt the supply line to the enemy troops in the battle-field * The shrewd businessman hit upon an idea to make quick money

Hit-and-miss: *Hitting or missing; doing one thing or another according to circumstances* * Getting a good job in any institution could be a hit-and-miss affair these days * Development of new cancer drugs is a hit-and-miss affair, subject to chance

Hitch up: *Pull up with a quick movement* * He hitched up his trousers before climbing into the car

Hitch-hike: *Get a free lift in someone's car* * I went off with a friend for a hitch-hike to Delhi

Hither and thither: *All over* * The crowd dispersed hither and thither on noticing a wild bull run amuck

Hive-off: *Split off* * The Syndicate Congress is a hive-off part of the major Congress Party * A proposal is in the offing that some public organisations will be hived off

Hobbyhorse: *Subject which someone always talks about* * Film censorship is a personal hobbyhorse of mine

Hobnob: *Be on friendly terms* * The Democrats are now hobnobbing with the opposition party for the forthcoming election

Hobson's choice: *Take it or leave it* * Our national leaders had but a Hobson's choice in the matter of India's Partition

Hodge-podge: *Confused or disorderly mixture of different types of things* * The old towns in India have a hodge-podge building structures

Hoist with one's own petard: *Be caught in one's own trap; be beaten with one's own weapon* * We should never think of harming others for we can get hoisted with our own petard due to some mistake * The dacoits were hoisted with their own petard by the persons who waylaid them

Hoity-toity: *Snobbish; superior (air)* * I dislike talking to that person who is always acting so hoity-toity

Hold a man to ransom: *Keep him as a captive and ask for ransom* * The son of a landlord was abducted and held to ransom by some miscreants

Hold against: *Allow to influence one's opinion adversely* * Do not hold his criminal convictions against him * His refusal to cooperate will be held against him

Hold back: *Keep back; hesitate; show unwillingness; keep secret or to oneself; keep back* * The police held back the crowd * Buyers are holding back from the market due to shortage of funds * His poor education is holding him back from sitting in any competitive examination * He held back the information for fear of being harassed * The court verdict has held him back from going abroad

Hold by: *To believe in; act in accordance with* * He held by the holy tenets of the *Gita* throughout his life * He holds by the instructions given to him by his mentor

Hold down: *Keep under control; keep something down; use force to keep someone in a particular place and not allow him to move* * These measures would still not be enough to hold down the rioters * Some policy has to be adopted to hold down inflation * The prisoners of war have been held down in a camp surrounded by a strong barbed wire

Hold fast: *Adhere strictly* * He held fast to his moral principles

Hold forth: *Talk at great length* * He is a good speaker and can hold forth on any issue that comes up for discussion

Hold good: *Prove valid* * The new factory rules will hold good from next month onwards

Hold hard: *Stop* * The driver applied the brakes to hold hard the momentum of the speeding bus

Hold in: *Refrain; check* * Women are expected to hold in their anger

Hold (one) in hand: *Amuse in order to gain some advantage* * One must hold a true friend in hand

Hold in play: *Keep occupied especially to gain time* * He is ostensibly holding himself in play in order to wait for the opportune moment to arise

Hold it: *Stop doing something for a moment* * Hey, just hold it, we have to shoot the scene again!

Hold no brief for: *Be not retained as counsel for; argue in favour* * As he holds no brief for the issue it is not possible for him to argue over the case * I have already engaged a pleader to hold a brief for me in the court

Hold: *Regard* * Everyone holds him in high esteem

Hold off: *Keep at a distance; delay action; remain at a distance* * They managed to hold off a much superior attacking force * Hold off beating the culprit for a moment * The storm held off till we reached home

Hold office: *Have a post (in government)* * He is now holding office of the Director General of Police in the state

Hold on: *Persist in something; continue; cling; stop; wait a bit; keep in position* * We should not hold on to false excuses * How long could we hold on fighting against the enemy? * The boy held on to the bush till someone climbed down the cliff to rescue him * Please hold on a minute with your argument * I hope you won't mind to hold on till I close the door * These bolts and nuts hold the wheels on

Hold one's peace: *Keep silence* * It is better to hold one's peace when confronted with some awkward situation

Hold one's horses: *Hesitate or show restraint* * He held his horses even though he was provoked beyond endurance

Hold one's breath: *Cease breathing temporarily in suspense; stop breathing for a moment* * The watchers held their breath as the acrobat crossed the tight-rope * She held her breath at the sight of a cobra

Hold one's ground: *Stand firm; not retreat* * He held his ground on the statement that he made in public * Our soldiers held their ground bravely

Hold one's head high: *Be proud* * We should lead a life in which we can hold our head high

Hold one's jaw: *Cease from talking and scolding* * When I found that he is a habitual liar, I decided to hold my jaw

Hold one's own: *Maintain one's position; not give way* * He is able to hold his own even in front of his superiors * The patient is still holding his own in maintaining his strength

Hold one's peace: *Remain silent* * He managed to hold his peace even in the teeth of opposition

Hold one's sides with laughter: *Laugh heartily* * He held his sides with laughter when the clown cracked a joke in a circus show

Hold one's tongue: *Remain silent; be silent or say nothing* * He thought it proper to hold his tongue in the company of talkative persons * In the face of opposition, he preferred to hold his tongue.

Hold oneself in readiness: *Be prepared* * He held himself in readiness for any challenge or any emergency

Hold out: *Endure; continue resistance; offer; to last* * How long can we hold out against these attacks? * The rebels would hold out for at least two years * He holds out no promise of future prospects * Science may hold out some prospect for feeding the hungry * One cannot tell how long our food supplies will hold out

Hold out on: *Refuse to deal with* * He is still holding out on me

Hold over: *Postpone; no influence; keep possession of land or a house beyond the terms of the agreement* * It has been decided to hold over the case till the summer vacation * How can I persuade her to go as I have no hold over her * He has filed a case against the tenant for holding over his house

Hold somebody in high esteem: *Have a high regard for one* * The principal of our college is held in high esteem by everyone

Hold somebody to something: *Make somebody keep e.g. a promise* * We must hold the contractors to their estimates

Hold someone to ransom: *Demand payment before someone is set free* * Some miscreants have held the son of the landlord to ransom of rupees ten lac

Hold someone to ridicule: *To laugh at someone* * Don't hold him to ridicule when he has apologized for his folly.

Hold something dear: *Place a high value on it* * He holds his reputation dear

Hold something in one's head: *Retain* * I still hold the memory of my school days in my head

Hold something in readiness: *Keep something ready for use* * We must hold everything in readiness before we set out for the long journey

Hold the key of the street: *Be locked out; be homeless* * A black sheep has to hold the key of the street. Many victims of the earthquake have been compelled to hold the key of the street

Hold the line: *Keep a telephone connection* * Please hold the line, I am just calling the man whom you would like to talk to

Hold the purse-strings: *Have control over expenses* * The ministry of finance holds the purse-strings over the allocated funds

Hold the scale even: *Be impartial* * The judiciary has to be very careful in holding the scales even in all the cases which come for their judgment

Hold to: *Stick or cling* * He kept holding to the rope when climbing down to steep hill

Hold to account: *Hold responsible* * The accountant has been held to account for misappropriation of funds

Hold to something: *Remain loyal; keep to* * He held to his convictions of action; the ship held to a soothing sail

Hold together: *Remain united; cohere* * We have always held together whenever we had to face a national crisis * This plastic tape will hold together the torn parts of the map

Hold up: *Raise; keep back; endure; bring to a standstill; stop and rob; rob by threatening assault* * The audience held up their hands in support of the slogans raised by the speaker * The air flight was held up due to dense fog * How did your boots hold up? * The work in the factory has been held up as a result of a strike by its employees * The travellers were held up by bandits who robbed them * The dacoit held me up at the point of a gun and looted the valuables

Hold up one's head: *Face the world with self-respect* * He lives a true life who holds up his head through thick and thin

Hold water: *Be correct or well grounded; bear examination* * His argument on this topic holds water * That argument will not hold water * The theory no longer holds water

Hold with: *Take sides with; approve of* * I hope you would never hold with the rumour-mongers * Do you hold with nudity on the stage?

Hold with the hare and run with the hounds: *Play a*

double game or be with both sides at once * The diplomatic policy of America towards India and Pakistan looks like holding with the hare and running with the hounds

Hole-and-corner: *Secret; in obscure places; underhand* * Some people play hole-and-corner policy to damage interests of the others * The militants are in look out for hole-and-corner sites to hide arms and ammunition * I do not like these hole-and-corner method at all

Hole and corner transaction: *Underhand dealings* * A straightforward person would never involve himself in a hole and corner transaction

Hole up: *Hide away* * Two terrorists managed to hole up in the bushes in the darkness

Hollow out: *Make hollow* * The river banks were hollowed out by rushing water

Hollow-hearted: *Having hollow or untrue heart; faithless; treacherous* * Don't make friendship with that hollow-hearted person * A hollow-hearted person can never rise in his life * He is a notorious hollow-hearted rogue

Holocaust: *Large-scale destruction* * The atom bomb attack on Japan resulted in a holocaust during World War II

Home in on: *Go to a target* * The missile is homing in on with pinpoint accuracy

Home thrust: *A pointing remark that goes home* * The warning worked as a home thrust to the perpetrator of crime

Home trade: *Trade inside the country* * The home trade in our country is progressing by leaps and bounds

Home-croft: *A cottage with a small piece of land for an industrial worker to grow his own food* * Home-croft had its own importance in old times

Home-keeping: *Staying at home* * Many people prefer home-keeping to wandering about aimlessly like a vagabond

Home-made: *Make at home; not bought* * I put on home-made woollen sweater only

Homesick: *Pinning for home* * He felt homesick when he had to stay abroad for quite a long time

Homestead: *Farmhouse and field around it* * At this time you can find him at his homestead

Homing device: *Device which*

guides it to the target * All the missiles used in a war are guided by homing device * Even small misslies have built-in homing devices

Honey-mouthed: *Having a honeyed mouth or speech; soft or smooth in speech* * We have no complaint against that honey-mouthed gentleman * The honey-mouthed discourse by the speaker was applauded by one and all

Honey-sweet: *Sweet as honey* * The children are very fond of honey-sweet chocolates

Honey-tongued: *Soft, easy persuasive in speech; eloquent* * That honey-tongued woman has earned respect in the neighborhood * The old lady told a honey-tongued story to the kids surrounding her

Hook and eye: *A contrivance for fastening dress by means of a hook that catches in a loop or eye* * Some dresses have hook and eye contrivance depending upon the choice of the users

Hook it: *Make off; decamp* * The scooter rider snatched her necklace and hooked it

Hooked on: *Very interested in; addicted to; completely committed to* * They are all hooked on the melodious tune sounds of the music * Don't get yourself hooked on the drugs * My uncle is hooked on bring about revolutionary changes in our education set up.

Hook-up: *Network of broadcasting stations connected to transmit the same programme* * The President of the U.S.A. spoke over an international hook-up.

Hooley and fairly: *Fair and soft* * I found him Hooley and fairly in his dealings

Hoot with laughter: *Laugh hilariously* * The drunkards were hooting with laughter at the nasty fall of one of them

Hop it: *Go away; take oneself off* * Don't make noise here, hop it you kids! * You had better hop it before the police arrives here

Hop off: *Go away* * Don't disturb me, you better hop off or I will punish you hard

Hop the twig/perch: *Escape one's creditors; die* * Once you have hopped the twig, you do get rid of all kinds of botherations

Hope against hope: *Continue to hope when all ground is gone* * The doctor has declared the case to be serious even the family is hoping against hope that the patient may survive * Poor fellow! He is hoping against hope.

Hopping mad: *Very angry* * He was hopping mad when he was insulted

Horn in: *Butt in; interpose* * It does not behove a person to horn to someone else's discussion

Horn in (on): *Join in without being invited/Intrude* * Don't let him horn in my party at all

Horn of a dilemma: *A state of being in a fix* * I was on the horn of a dilemma when the manager asked me either to quit the service or to tender an apology in writing

Horn of plenty: *Abundant supply* * They discovered a small island which was found to be a horn of plenty for its medicinal herbs

Hornet's nest: *Source of trouble* * By becoming rude with the new manager, you will only invite a hornet's nest

Horn-handed: *With hands hardened by toil* * The horn-handed labourers have to work hard to earn their living

Horse around/about: *Play roughly* * Children were horsing around during recess hours in the school compound

Horse laugh: *Loud unpleasant laugh* * When he cracked a vile joke, some loafers began to have a horse laugh

Horse sense: *Commonsense* * Even many of the rustic people are endowed with a horse sense

Horse trading: *Arguing between parties before coming to an agreement* * The bargain was struck after a good deal of horse trading

Hose down: *Spray with water* * I hose down the plants in my garden to keep them healthy

Hostages to fortune: *Wife, children, etc.* * All the members in a family are hostages to fortune and the loss of any one of them would be particularly painful

Hostile to: *Opposed to* * He is hostile to every plan that I suggest

Hot air: *Meaningless talk or promise, etc.; empty talk* * The speech made by him was just hot air * The speech that he made before the audience was nothing promises in hot air

Hotline: *Direct telephone line between heads of state* * Our Prime Minister got through on the hotline to the President of USA

Hot news: *Recent sensational*

news * Today's newspaper carries many hot news

Hot potato: *A dangerous, highly controversial or embarrassing issue to deal with* * Spread of terrorism has become a hot potato problem for many states of the world

Hot seat: *An important position in which one is open to criticism, etc.* * As managing director of a big company, he is continuously in the hot seat

Hot spot: *Area of political unrest or danger* * I don't think I would like to be a journalist, being sent around the globe to all the political hot spots

Hot stuff: *Any person, thing or performance that is outstandingly remarkable or of first rate quality* * A hot stuff in the form of person, thing or performance is always appreciable on all hands

Hot under the collar: *Annoyed and irritated* * The editor has just been told to cut his budget so he is rather hot under the collar

Hot up: *Become hotter or more exciting* * The things are hotting up due to misunderstanding between the two rival groups

Hot water: *A state of trouble* * You will involve yourself in hot water if you dare to be rude with your boss

Hot-blooded: *With a violent temper* * It is very difficult to reconcile with that hot-blooded person

Hotchpotch: *Things mixed together without order* * His essay was a hotchpotch of other people's ideas.

Hour of cause: *Hour or time of trial* * Let us see how does he fare under hour of cause

Hour's that for high?: *Beat that if you can* * How's that for high? Go, and get the better of him if you have a stamina to do that

House agent: *Person who sells or lets houses for others* * Those who stand in need of residential accommodation utilise the services of a house agent

House arrest: *Not allowed to leave one's home which is being guarded by the police* * By the orders of the court, he is under house arrest

House of correction: *A jail* * Having committed theft, he has been sent to house of correction by the judge

House of ill-fame: *A brothel* * He earns his living by running a house of ill-fame

Housebound: *Confined to the house; not able to leave the home* * Should wives with children be housebound? * As a result of severe illness, he is housebound till he recovers fully

Housebreaker: *Burglar who breaks into a house to steal* * The housebreaker was caught red-handed and handed over to the police

Household God: *One's favourite saying or name* * At different places, people may be having different household God

Household words: *A familiar saying or name* * Tsunami-killer has become household words these days

Hover about: *Loiter* * Do not hover about here

How goes the enemy: *What o'clock is it?* * By the way, how goes the enemy? I don't think I am late to attend the office

How is that: *Appeal of the fielding side to the empire to give the batsman out in the game of cricket* * The umpire rejected the loud "how's that" of fielders

How now: *What is this; why is this so?* * How now that you are going to eat your words?

How squares go: *How things are going* * We don't know how squares go with him in his project in the absence of requisite funds

How the wind blows: *Matter stands; the state of the wind; position of the affairs* * While taking stock of the working in a large factory, we got an idea of how the wind blows there * This devise shows how the wind blows * Let's see how the wind blows in the market

How's that for high: *Beat that if you can* * How's that for high? Go, and get the better of him if you have a stamina to do that

How-dy–do: *A troublesome state of matter* * Take my advice in good spirit and do not get yourself involved in how-dy-do * Well, here's a pretty how-dy-do!

However: *In whatever way or degree* * He will never succeed however hard he tries

Hubble-bubble: *Hookah* * Many people in India use hubble-bubble for smoking tobacco

Hubbub: *Confuse sound of voices* * There was an increasing hubbub from the reception hall below

Huddle up: *Curl; coil up against* * Tom was feeling cold, so he huddled up against his brother in bed

Hug oneself over something: *To hug with delight* * I hugged myself with delight when I heard the news that I have topped the list of all successful candidates

Hug the shore: *Keep close to the shore** During the voyage from India to England our ship mostly hugged the shore

Hum and haw: *Make inarticulate sounds when at a loss; to shilly-shally unable to make up one's mind* * The poor fellow had to hum and haw when his glass full of milk fell down * He hummed and hawed knowing nothing how to extricate himself from the mess

Human nature: *Attitude and behaviour which are typical of human beings* * To err is a human nature

Humdrum: *Dull or monotonous* * He is living a humdrum life * He is engaged in humdrum tasks

Hump up: *Make hump-shaped; gather the soldiers into a hump* * The cat humped up her back when she saw the dog * The commander ordered the Adjutant to hump up the soldiers immediately and be ready for the next order

Hunch up: *Arch to form a hump* * The old man was sitting at the table with his shoulders hunched up

Hundred per cent: *Out and out* * You need not doubt his integrity, he is hundred per cent a gentleman

Hung jury: *Jury which can not reach a majority decision* * When the jury is unable to come to a majority decision, it is called a hung jury

Hung over: *Falling ill after drinking too much alcohol* * He, being in hung over condition, has not been able to get up at his usual time

Hung parliament: *One where no party has an absolute majority* * In the last general election, no party has been able to get absolute majority, so we have had a hung parliament

Hunt after: *Seek for* * He is hunting after getting rich through fair or foul means

Hunt counter: *Follow the scent backwards* * The detective had to hunt counter to get at the real culprit

Hunt down: *Pursue to extremities; persecute out of existence* * The police ultimately succeeded in hunting down the escaped prisoner * The sleuth hunted the criminal down for heinous crime

Hunt the letter: *Affect alliterations* * It is only for an idle person to hunt the letter to amuse himself or others

Hunt up: *Seek out* * Need may arise to hunt up old records for a particular reference

Hunt with the hounds and play with the hares: *Remain in good terms with both sides* * There are many persons who hunt with the hounds and play with the hares

Hunting ground: *Place where one may search for something with hopes of success* * This street has always been a happy hunting ground for antique collections

Hurdle off: *Fence with hurdles* * The rose garden has been properly hurdled off so that stray animals may not enter into it

Hurl at: *Throw at* * He hurled a shoe at the rival in the open court

Hurly-burly: *Rough activity* * He was annoyed with the hurly-burly of the excited children

Hurry up: *Go fast; make someone go faster; make haste* * The furious storm is approaching fast so all of us must hurry up to a safe place * Hurry up! We may not miss the bus

Hurry-scurry: *Confusion and bustle* * People ran in hurry-scurry when there was a sudden explosion of bomb in the market

Hush money: *Money paid to someone to stop them revealing a secret; bribe for hiding crime** He was given a huge hush money to give shelter to some notorious characters * Hush money is one of the factors to delay the justice

Hush up: *Stifle; suppress; be silent* * The police had hushed up the matter for fear of public disturbances * Hush up about this damage done so carelessly to avoid wrath of our father

Hush-hush: *Secret* * The working in this office involves a hush-hush job to maintain hush-hush affairs

Hustle and bustle: *Quick and energetic activity* * The railway station was a scene of hustle and bustle when the train arrived there

Hydra-headed: *Difficult to root out; spring up vigorously again and again* * In spite of exemplary capital punishment to the wrong-doers, the crime-rate has, since time immemorial been taking hydra-headed form

I

I dare or will be bound: *I will be responsible for the statement* * I dare or will be bound to all that has been published in today's newspaper

I dare say: *Perhaps; probably* * I dare say he will come later

I don't think: *I disbelieve* * I don't think what he said would prove to be true

I had best: *It were best for me* * I had best join the college after having completed the secondary education

I pray you: *I ask you* * I pray you to show me the way that I should follow

I see: *I think or understand* * I see your point vividly

I shouldn't think of: *I would not under any conditions* * I shouldn't think of allowing him a free hand in the matter

I will see you far first: *I will not do it by any means* * If you bribe me for doing that sordid deed, I'll see you far first

I will trouble you to: *Please* * I will trouble you to provide me room to have rest in the crowded bus

Ice over/up: *Become covered with a coating of ice* * The pond was iced over * The wings of the aircraft had iced up

Identical parade: *Line of people in a police station from whom a witness is asked to identify the criminal* * The real culprit was recognised by the witness in an identity parade

Identical to/with: *The same as* * Your solution is identical to mine

Identical twins: *Two children born at the same time who look similar* * The newly married couple has been blessed with identical twins

Identify with: *Treat as identical; be associated with* * His views on this subject identify with those of mine * He refused to identify himself with the new political party

Idle talk: *Gossip* *I am very particular not to indulge in idle talk

If anything should happen: *In case of death* * If anything should happen to anybody, one must report the matter to the police

If he's a day: *(of age) at least* * He's eight if he is a day

If it comes to the pinch: *If there is need and if there is no other way* * You may rest assured of our timely help if it comes to the pinch

If it kills you: *Be determined to do even an extremely difficult or painful task* * I was determined to finish the job even if it killed me

If need be: *If necessary* * If need be, we can send more forces to crush the mutiny

If needs must: *If it has to be done* * If needs must, you will have to pay the full amount

If the cap fits: *If the allusion is felt to apply* * We will try the formula in case if the cap fits

If you don't like it you may lump it: *Take it as you like, but there is no remedy* * You are advised to compensate him for his loss and if you don't like it you may lump it

If you don't mind: *If you have an objection* * If you don't mind I would like to use your bike for two hours at the most

If you please: *If you like* * The Superintendent of Police stopped me at the door and asked, "Smith, If you please, can I have a word with you?"

Ill at ease: *Uncomfortable* * He was ill at ease with people whom he did not understood

Ill blood: *Enmity* * The dispute over ancestral property has created ill blood between the two brothers

Ill of: *Suffering from* * He is reported to be ill of fever

Ill weeds grow space: *Harmful things grow or spread rapidly* * We all agree that ill weeds grow space

Ill-advised: *Imprudent* * It was an ill-advised action on your part to have him insulted in the open

Ill-assorted: *Not matching each other* * My friend has an ill-assorted collection of works

Ill-boding: *Inauspicious* * Any bad event that takes place is considered to bear ill-boding

Ill-bred: *Badly bred or educated* * Most of the people in the Third World countries are considered ill-bred by the West

Ill-deadly: *Mischievous* * It is a mere speculation that ill-deadly children become more sober in their youth

Ill-disposed: *Unfriendly or inclined to evil* * Some people are always ill-disposed towards others by nature

Ill-equipped: *Be wanting in equipment* * The police were plainly ill-equipped to deal with the rioters

Ill-faced: *Ugly faced* * Though he is ill-faced yet he is good at heart

Ill-fated: *Unlucky* * Who knew that the ill-fated bus will meet with an accident? * He told us the story of his ill-fated boating expedition

Ill-founded: *Baseless* * His observation on that case was ill-founded

Ill-humoured: *Bad tempered* * An ill-humoured man gets irritated unreasonably

Ill-mannered: *Rude or ill-bred* * He is ill-mannered by birth

Ill-natured: *Of a bad temper; cross, peevish* * An ill-natured person cannot be friendly * His ill-natured habits have made him notorious in the area * He sounded ill-natured and his hands made pointless nervous movements

Ill-off: *Poor* * An ill-off person cannot afford to rise high

Ill-omened: *Ill starred* * An ill-omened person is destined to suffer troubles throughout his life

Ill-spent: *Spent amiss* * The rich don't bother about their ill-spent money on carnal desires

Ill-starred: *Born under the influence of an unlucky star* * He thought himself to be an ill-starred individual for having lost the opportunity

Ill-tempered: *Having bad temper* * An ill-tempered person may kick up a row on any flimsy excuse

Ill-timed: *Done at the wrong time* * His comments were ill-timed

Ill-treat: *To treat ill or abuse* * He is a drunkard and ill-treats his wife

Ill-treatment: *An act of unkindness* * Brave men never yield to threat of ill-treatment from any quarter

Ill-usage: *Cruelty* * Many wild creatures have become victims of man's ill-usage

Ill-will: *Enmity; unkind feeling* * We should not bear ill-will towards anybody

Ill-wresting: *Misinterpreting disadvantage* * His statement stinks of ill-wresting

I am of opinion: *I think* * I am of the opinion that we should not trouble him over the issue

Imbibe from: *Received from* * He has imbibed his passion for knowledge from his father

Immerse in: *Put under the surface of water or liquid; involve*

deeply * The dead body's ashes were immersed in the Ganges * The rich merchant is immersed in debt

Immune from: *Free or secure* * He is now immune from infection

Impart to: *Give* * I have no important information to impart to you today

Impatient of: *Intolerant of; not patient* * The candidates were impatient of the delay in the declaration of their results * The children were impatient for the film to start

Impediment to: *Obstacle* * Indolence is a serious impediment to success in life

Implicated in: *Involved; concerned* * This is the man who was implicated in that scandal

Impose upon: *Deceive; lay or place a tax, duty, etc.; force on; take advantage of* * All his efforts to impose upon me sadly failed * New taxes were imposed upon wine * Do not impose yourself on people who don't want you * It would be in your interest to impose upon your teacher's good nature

Improve on: *Produce something better than* * Our techniques are already far advanced and being improved on still further

Impute to: *Consider as the act or outcome of* * They imputed the accident to the driver's carelessness

In a bad way: *In a serious condition; much upset* * He is in a bad way due to injuries he suffered in the accident * I am in a bad way at his rude behaviour

In a big way: *On a large or grand scale* * The firm is now running in a big way

In a brown study: *Be absent-minded* * We found him in a brown study as he did not notice our cries

In a cleft-stick: *In an awkward situation* * He found himself in a cleft-stick situation with no escape at all

In a dither: *Indecisive state* * He was in a dither at taking part in the contest

In a family way: *In or familiar informal manner; pregnant* * He is so close to us that we treat him in a family way * She is unable to come as she is in a family way

In a flash: *At once* * I was out of the room in a flash

In a good hour: *Under fortunate impulse* * He was in a good hour to have received happy news

In a good light: *So as to be seen well; so as to make a good impression* * The portrait has been placed in a good light * He took my advice in a good light

In a huff: *In a bad temper* * The people walked out of the room in a huff when their complaint was not heard

In a jam: *In a difficult situation* * The debtor found himself in a jam for not being able to clear his debts in due time

In a jiffy: *In a minute* * I will be back in a jiffy

In a kind: *In a way; to some extent* * We should deal with him in a kind that he may not feel offended * In a kind, we find some truth in his statement

In a manner: *In a sense* * What you say is true in a manner

In a measure: *Partly* * We know in a measure how to keep ourselves immune from disease

In a nutshell: *In brief* * In a nutshell it could be said that he was a nice person * He told me the story of his escape in a nutshell

In a Pickwick in sense: *In an imaginary sense* * We did not welcome his remarks that he made in a Pickwick sense

In a quandary: *Puzzled; not knowing what to do* * I found him in a quandary when I saw him there

In a sense: *In a sense other than the obvious one; in a way; after a fashion* * What you say is true in a sense * In a sense, it was right to take him to task instead of beating him black and blue * He can write and speak English in a sense after all

In a small way: *On a petty scale; with little capital or stock* * He started his business in a small way * He continued with his scientific experiments in a small way

In a sorry plight: *In miserable condition* * Everyone extended me a helping hand when they saw me in a sorry plight * Don't wager more money lest you should find yourself in a sorry plight

In a sort: *In a manner* * In a sort, he resembles his father

In a split second: *Very fast* * Under the circumstances, the decision had to be taken in a split second

In a state of nature: *Naked* * The murdered man was found in a state of nature

In a state of nerves: *In a tense or anxious state* * I was in a state of nerves when expecting to be arrested at any moment

In a stew: *In an awkward situation* * The farmer was in a stew as he did not know where to go in a crowded city.

In a tizzy: *In a nervous state* * I was in a tizzy when I entered the examination hall

In a trice: *Very rapidly or in an instant* * He seized the situation up in a trice * I will be back in a trice

In a way: *In state of agitation or distress; to some extent; from one point of view* * There was a public cry in a way when the police failed to catch the murderers * In a way, he is on the recovery path of his health * People did admire him in a way that he never yielded to any pressure whatsoever

In a word: *In short; to sum up* * In a word, I must warn you to be on your toes * In a word, he apprised the judges of the case with his evidence

In abeyance: *In a state of suspense* * The decision on the new project has been kept in abeyance for the time being

In account with: *In business relations requiring the keeping of an account* * The traders are in account with one another to carry out their transactions in a fair and square manner

In actual fact: *Really* * He looks honest but in actual fact he is a rogue

In advance: *Early; beforehand* * It is unwise to spend your income in advance

In all: *In total* * He has in all, ten heads of cattle

In all conscience: *Certainly by all that is right and fair* * I cannot, in all conscience, agree that he is a cheat

In all good faith: *Honestly believing* * We must work in all good faith to serve mankind

In all probability: *Most likely* * In all probability, they would fight the case in court

In all weathers: *In every sort of weather* * The higher reaches of the Himalayas remain snowbound in all kinds of weather

In an accusing tone: *As if accusing* * He uttered a few words in an accusing tone which was objected by me

In an evil hour: *Under an unfortunate impulse* * He was in an evil hour to have received the bad news

In an interesting condition: *A vulgar euphemism for*

pregnant * In place of using the phrase 'in an interesting condition', an educated man would prefer the use of expression' in the family way' for a pregnant woman

In any case: *At all events; at any rate* * You may take it for granted that I will stand by you in any case * I cannot take shelter behind you all the time and in any case you are not always with me

In any event: *Whatever is so* * In any event, he was required to prove his worth

In any shape: *At all* * I am strongly opposed to violence in any shape or form

In any wise: *In any way* * In any wise, he had to finish the job within a fixed time

In appearance: *So far as appearance is concerned* * In appearance it is a strong building * In appearance he looks to be a well-to-do man

In arms: *Armed* * The people rose in arms to revolt against the cruel regime

In as much as: *Considering that* * His duty is to assist the aggrieved person in as much as he is able to do

In at the death: *Climax of anything* * This scandal proved to be in at the death of his political career

In bad odour: *In bad repute* * His statement has been held in bad odour by many critics

In bad part: *Unfavourably* * The way he conducted himself has been taken in bad part

In between: *In the middle of* * We visited the museum in the morning and the art gallery later, with a hurried lunch in between

In black and white: *In writing* * I want to see that agreement on paper in black and white

In brief: *In a few words* * What is today's news in brief?

In broad daylight: *During daytime* * The scooter riders snatched the purse of the lady in broad daylight in the bus

In brown study: *Absorbed or intent in thought or unaware of people or happenings* * He, being in a brown study, did not even know what was happening under his nose

In buff: *Naked* * The criminal was whipped in buff

In bulk: *Wholesale* * He bought household goods in bulk

In case: *In the event that; lest; if* * In case of a fire, ring the alarm bell * We were afraid in case he should get here too late * In case you have finished with that book, take it back to the library

In character: *In keeping with the person's usual conduct* * Such a gesture would be in character with his behaviour

In character with: *In keeping with* * The screen is in character with the rest of the furniture

In charge: *In control or authority; responsible; care; duty; custody; commission* * Who is in charge here of this office? * The nurses are in charge of the children in this orphanage * The parents left the baby in charge of a maid in their absence * A housewife is in charge of household affairs in the family * The alleged accused was remanded in charge of the police * A tribunal has been put in charge to investigate the cases of corrupt officials

In charity with: *Christian love of fellowmen* * All religions preach us to live in charity with all the people at large

In chase of: *Pursuing* * I saw the leopard in hot chase of a deer

In clover: *In ease and luxury* * A poor farmer cannot think of living in clover throughout his life

In cold blood: *Not in the heat of passion but deliberately* * He was murdered in cold blood

In command of: *Authority of commanding* * In a democracy, the constitutional head is in command of the three wings of the armed forces

In common: *Together; equally with others* * In common with many people, he prefers meat to fish * We do enjoy in common the beauty of Nature in many forms * We had a dip in the holy water in common with other devotees

In company: *Not alone* * He came in company with a group of boys

In concert with: *Together with* * He is working in concert with his colleagues

In conclusion: *Finally* * In conclusion, it was decided to dwell on the knotty problem in the next meeting

In conformity with: *In accordance with* * The concerned officer issued the final notice in conformity with the rules

In conjunction with: *Together with* * We have either to work separately or in conjunction with our colleagues

In connection with: *With reference to* * They are discussing the proposal in connection with the construction of a new swimming pool

In consequence of: *As a result of* * Huge loss of life and property occurred as a consequence of floods

In course of: *In regular order; in process of* * River water makes a gurgling sound in its course to the sea * The railway is in course of construction

In days of yore: *In the past* * In the days of yore I shared all my secrets with my friend

In dead earnest: *Very serious* * That young man is in dead earnest to become an astronaut

In deep water: *In difficulty; undergoing difficulty or misfortune* * The embezzlement case has landed him in deep water * As he has broken the law, he is now in deep water

In default of: *If or since such a thing is wanting; in case of failure* * In default of convincing economic arrangements, the proposals are likely to be rejected * In default of his capability to handle the job properly, he was dismissed from his post

In defiance of: *Contrary; against* * The houses in the colony were erected in defiance of all building regulations * People raise their voice in defiance of stipulations imposing heavy duty on many essential commodities

In demand: *Popular; wanted* * The new book released on sports is very much in demand

In detail: *Circumstantially point by point; piecemeal* * We need hard evidence in detail to come to a fair conclusion * You will have to collect the information about the daily progress of production in the factory in detail

In disguise: *Change in appearance to deceive* * He went among the enemy in disguise

In disrepair: *Needing to be repaired* * This old house is in disrepair

In due course: *In ordinary way when the time comes* * There is no doubt that every home will have a computer in due course

In ease to: *In a fit condition for* * Only those persons who were found in ease to the higher ranks in the army were promoted

In effect: *In truth; really; substantially* * In effect he has no choice in the matter * What in effect I am saying is that he could not write that novel * The rule is still in effect

In either event: *Whichever is so* * Whether you go or not, in either event you will miss the rally

In embryo: *In an early stage* * The electron microscope has been in embryo for a long time

In every way: *By all means* * He was ready to help me in every way

In evidence: *Visible* * There was nothing in evidence except for the blue water when we entered the deep sea * Lawlessness was in evidence in the heart of the town

In excuse of: *On the pretext of* * Where the law is concerned, you cannot plead ignorance as an excuse for your conduct

In eye: *In sight* * The automatic camera snapped the movements of wild animals that came in its eye

In fact: *Indeed* * I was, in fact, very glad to hear the news

In fault: *To blame* * Who is in fault for committing this blunder?

In favour of: *For; on the side of; for the advantage of* * We are in favour of quick justice * Both of them claimed to have a majority in favour of their candidate * The cheque should be drawn in favour of the society and not the chairman

In fine: *In short; to sum up* * In fine, he has no alternative but to accept the new appointment * We could say it in fine that ultimately he landed himself in jail

In flesh: *In good condition; fat* * Daily exercise will keep you in flesh * You are getting in flesh too much, hence you should control your diet

In focus: *Adjust to get a clear vision* * As soon as the images came in focus, I clicked the camera

In for: *Doomed to receive, especially unpleasant consequences; committed to* * You are all in for an unpleasant surprise * I am in for the competition

In front of: *Before* * There are some trees in front of the temple

In full: *Completely; entirely* * One must be in full control of oneself to behave properly

In full bloom: *Flowering* * The apple trees are in full bloom

In full cry: *In full pursuit; eagerly attacking* * The hounds were in full cry while hunting for two ferocious bears * They were in full cry against their tormentors

In full swing: *At the height of activity* * The sale of the mobile phone in the market is in full swing

In full view: *Fully seen by* * The speaker stood in full view of the crowd

In fun: *In joke; not seriously* * He made those remarks in fun only

Infuse into: *Put* * The captain infused a new enthusiasm into the soldiers

In future: *Now on* * What lies in store for us in future we cannot tell

In gears: *With the gears connected* * The car was in gears when it began to slide down the road

In general: *As a rule* * The workers want shorter working hours in general

In good faith: *With sincerity* * We should do our duty in good faith

In good form: *In a good mood* * He was in good form to hit a century in the one-day cricket match

In good hands: *Being well cared for* * The adopted child is now in good hands

In good heart: *In sound or fertile condition; in good spirits* * The doctor found him in good heart * The children at play were in good heart

In good order: *Without any confusion* * The troops retired in good order

In good part: *To a great extent; with good humour* * The contents of his thesis have been appreciated in good part * He took my advice in good part

In good running order: *Working well or smoothly* * The engine has been tuned and is now in good running order

In good spirits: *In happy mood* * You tell him about your problem when he is in good spirits

In good time: *Quite early; with some time to spare* * The commuters are usually in good time for the train * He is in the good books of his boss for clearing work in good time

In grain: *In substance* * What he is saying in grain is that the present system can not continue indefinitely

In great demand: *Much sought after* * Mobile phones are in great demand these days

In great price: *In high estimation* * His suggestion stands in great price with regard to investment in trade

In hand: *As present payment; in preparation; under control; in*

reserve; receiving attention * I have enough money in hand to buy a new car * We are getting things together in hand for the journey * Initially there was public disorder but now the situation is well in hand * We should have some money in hand to meet the emergency * The work is in hand and will be completed as per schedule

In harness: *In routine of daily work; to work* * I was ultimately able to get the work finished in harness with my colleagues * I would like to back in harness after a long absence

In high dudgeon: *Offended and feeling indignation* * He went off in high dudgeon

In high feather: *Greatly elated* * After winning the first prize in the lottery, the poor man is in high feather

In high leg: *In great excitement* * Scientists were in high legs when the long-range missile successfully hit the target

In high spirits: *Cheerful* * He was in high spirits on getting a lucrative job

In high winds: *In very strong winds* * Technology has made it possible to fly easily in high winds

In his cups: *Under influence of liquor* * His tongue staggered when he was in his cups

In hole out: *To play the ball into the hole in golf* * More and more people are becoming fond of in hole out

In hot blood: *In excitement or sudden passion* * In hot blood he slapped the innocent child

In hot water: *In trouble* * The bribe-taking official is now in hot water

In isolation: *Separately from the other similar things* * These varied questions cannot be answered in isolation

In its entirety: *In its completeness* * We must examine the issue in its entirety

In itself: *In its own nature* * Card playing is not harmful in itself

In jeopardy: *In dangerous situation* * She has placed herself in jeopardy in order to save the life of her child from the engulfing flames

In jest: *As a joke, not in earnest* * I know she will not mind what all has been said in jest

In keeping with: *Suitable to* * His actions are in keeping with his promises

In league with: *Allied with* * They pointed out that he was really in league with the police

In lieu of: *Instead of* * I paid him a substantial amount in lieu of his watch

In line/for: *In a straight line; in agreement; in the running; in harmony* * People stood in line to cast their votes * I was in line for promotion * He is in line for reaching his destination * His conduct is in line with the desired standard

In line with: *In agreement with* * The supply of the material is in line with the demands of the people

In little: *On small scale* * We are waiting for complete information and whatever we have in little with us will be made available to you

In love: *Enamoured* * They are in love with each other and wish to marry

In low water: *Short of money* * We, being in low water, had to drop the idea of taking that enterprise in hand

In many ways: *In lots of aspects/points* * We can achieve our goal in many ways

In memory of: *Serving to remember* * Rajghat has been set up in memory of Mahatma Gandhi

In mothballs: *Stored for further use* * During summer, we put our warm clothes in mothballs

In motion: *Moving* * The engine which has been in motion for a long time now needs refuelling

In my voice: *In my name* * He has composed music in my voice

In name: *Fictitiously; as an empty title* * The account given by him about his movements is only in name * He is a tiger in name only but lacks the spirit of the animal (meaning, he is a timid fellow)

In need: *In trouble; in very poor condition* * A good friend is one who helps the one in need

In need of: *Requiring* * My old vehicle is in need of repair

In neutral: *Not in gear; that which does not disturb or clash with anything else* * The car is in neutral * Grey is a neutral colour

In no case: *In no circumstances* * It is crystal clear from the evidence that in no case is he involved in the conspiracy

In no time: *Quickly* * He was so hungry that he finished his meal in no time

In no way: *Not at all* * In no way should he poke his nose into my affairs

In no wise: *In no way* * In no wise I am a politically effective person

In one's bad books: *Out of favour with* * I am afraid I am in the bad books of my boss

In one's black book: *Having incurred one's displeasure* * I am in his black book at the moment

In one's debt: *Under pecuniary obligation to one* * So long as we are in your debt we are bound to obey your instructions

In one's element: *In a congenial state* * I am very happy to see him in his element

In one's face: *Straight against; with no attempt at concealment* * The sun was shining on our face * Death stared him in the face

In one's heart of hearts: *From the depth of one's heart* * In my heart of hearts, I wish you every success in life

In one's mind's eyes: *In imagination* * He was dreaming in his mind's eye to be the richest person

In one's own right: *By absolute and personal right, not through another* * He emerged as a leader in his own right

In one's own words: *In one's own way* * He was asked to tell the story in his own words

In one's power: *At one's mercy; within the limits of what one can do* * Our fate is not in our power * It is not in my power to revoke the punishment imposed upon you

In one's right mind: *Quite sane* * He is suffering from neurosis and will be in his right mind after necessary treatment

In one's senses: *In one's right wits; normal and rational condition* * When he is in his senses, he can be very interesting with his wonderful ideas * He is always in his senses and thus always acts properly

In one's shirt: *Wearing nothing but a shirt, nothing over the shirt* * I attended the meeting in my shirt and a matching pair of trousers to my friend's house

In one's shirtsleeves: *With coat or jacket or jersey off* * It being a very hot day, I was in my shirtsleeves only

In one's sleeves: *Not wearing a jacket* * He was in his sleeves when I met him

In one's stocking feet: *With stocking but no shoes* * It was really a very funny thing to have trudged through a rough track in our stocking feet

In one's teens: *Minor* * In some parts of the country, the girls are still married in their teens

In one's teeth: *To one's face; indirect affront* * I will tell him so in his teeth * He was dismissed in his teeth and made to suffer helplessness and agony

In one's tracks: *Just where one stands* * We were eager to see him in his tracks

In one's true colours: *As one really is* * We can see a friend in his true colours in need

In one's twenties: *Age above twenty and below thirty* * She is still in her twenties

In or out of pocket: *With or without money; the rich or the poor* * The poor fellow is totally out of pocket these days * Those who have the money in their pocket must come out to help those who are out of pocket

In order: *Correct or valid* * Is your passport in order? * He put his accounts in order for necessary audit checking

In order to: *For the purpose of; so that* * He is studying hard in order to secure an 'A' grade * He is doing physical exercises regularly in order to become a world-renowned wrestler

In ordinary way: *Usually* * In the ordinary way, he gets up early in the morning

In other words: *Explaining something in a different way* * She is coming, in other words, she will be going to the movie

In our midst: *Among us* * We have in our midst two Nobel Prize winners

In place of: *Instead of* * In place of the balcony, let us have tea in the garden * Shall we have fish in place of meat today?

In part: *Partly; so far as part is concerned* * The book is good in part and not so good on the whole * The work has been finished in part only

In part exchange: *As a part payment for something new* * He took my old car in part exchange for a new car

In particular: *Especially; in detail; severally* * I remember one of them in particular * He has already informed me about everything in particular * He was criticised in particular for pursuing a policy of conciliation and reform

In parts: *In proportion* * You have to select the subjects in parts which you can digest easily

In peace: *In enjoyment of peace* * We must live in peace with everyone

In person: *Personally or physically present* * I shall be present at the meeting in person

In phase: *In the same phase together* * The light came on in phases

In pieces: *In a broken up state* * I found the vase in pieces

In place: *In position; opportune* * I like to have everything to be in place * The proposal is not quite in place

In play: *In such a position that it may be played* * We were amused to see the kittens in play

In point: *Opposite* * Your views appear to be in point to mine

In point of: *In the matter of* * There will be no delay in point of his promotion to a higher rank

In point of fact: *As a matter of fact* * In point of fact they arrived an hour late due to a traffic jam

In principle: *As a policy* * In principle, we are willing to simplify the complicated procedure with regard to direct income tax

In private: *Secretly* * He met me in private to tell me about his secret plans

In proportion to: *Relative to* * The appointment of teachers in the school is in proportion to the number of children in each class

In public: *Openly* * The rapist and the murderers of children must be hanged in public

In pursuance of: *According to* * It was all done in pursuance of his duties

In pursuit of: *Act of pursuing* * The hounds were in hot pursuit of a herd of deer * He is actively engaged in pursuit of higher studies

In question: *Under consideration* * The point in question is to choose either of the two prospective offers

In reality: *In actual fact* * The heavy downpour has in reality destroyed crops in this whole region

In regard of: *In view of; with respect to; in comparison with* * In regard of his excellent performance, he has been offered further promotion * I have nothing more to say in regard of his integrity and honesty * Their possessions were few in regard of those of older men

In retrospect: *When you look back* * In retrospect, we may deplore the methods used to enslave innocent people * It was, in retrospect, one of the worst blunders I ever made

In rotation: *In turn or in regular succession* * The class monitors are appointed in rotation

In safe keeping: *Being kept carefully* * My valuables are in safe keeping by her

In season and out of season: *At all times* * Commercial business activities continue in season and out of season

In secret: *Without anyone knowing* * I have a special thing in my mind that I will tell you in secret

Insensible to: *Unconscious of; unaware of* * He is insensible to all sense of honour * He seems to be insensible to dangers to his life

In serried ranks: *In rank close together* * The soldiers marched in serried ranks towards the parade ground

In session: *In the process of meeting* * The Parliament is in session these days

In short: *In a few words* * He narrated the cause of the accident in short

In sight: *Visible* * We kept looking for the train till it came in sight * We kept observing her till she was in sight

In sight of: *Where something can be seen* * We are now in sight of the end of this arduous task

In single file: *One behind other* * We crossed the old wooden bridge in single file

In small: *On a small scale; in miniature* * Today the earthen pots are being made in small * The painter has tried to depict the scenery of the beautiful valley through a portrait in small

In so far as: *In as much as; to the extent that* * He is a tyrant in so far as his behaviour towards children is concerned * In a democratic set-up, strikes are allowed in so far as the peace is not disturbed

In so many words: *Explicitly; bluntly* * He explained to us in so many words the exact position of the case * He told them in so many words what was acceptable and what was not

In some sort: *In a way* * In some sort, he could provide a helping hand to the needy

In sort: *In a body; in as much* * The staff resigned in sort * They enjoyed fun and games in sort they liked

In spirits: *Cheerfully vivacious* * Early to bed and early to rise keeps a man in spirits throughout the day

In spite of: *Without bothering about* * In spite of all his efforts, he failed in the examination * He went out of the house in spite of the rain

In spite of one's teeth: *In direct opposition* * He managed to complete the job in spite of the teeth of serious opposition

In state: *With ceremonial formality* * The President of India was driven in state through Rajpath on Republic Day

In stays: *Head to windward in tacking* * The ship kept moving in stays because of the wind coming from the wrong direction

In step: *With simultaneous putting forward of the right or left foot in the marching* * A contingent of soldiers marched in step at the parade ground

In stitches: *In pained helplessness with laughter* * We were in stitches after hearing her humorous stories

In store: *In hoard for future use; ready for supply; in reserve; awaiting* * We have enough foodstuff in store to last for three months more * They have material in store to be dispatched immediately * The store-owner has large quantities of essential commodities in store to meet any emergency * Who knows what the future has in store for us?

In succession: *One after the other* * He won the European Cup three years in succession

In sum: *In short; to sum up briefly* * In sum, he has been witness to many ups and downs in his life * I find it difficult to make you understand his whole philosophy in sum

In tears: *Crying* * Everybody was in tears when they heard the sad news of passing away of the great leader

In terms: *In so many words; explicitly* * I have already advised you in terms of what they expect of you in the matter * This in terms was admitted by the Prime Minister

In terms of: *Having or using as unit in a language peculiar to* * It has been a terrible year in terms of business

In terms of health: *Regarding health* * In terms of health, the wrestler seems fit as a fiddle

In terms of weekly payments: *Payments to be made every week* * I am thinking in terms of weekly payments to be made to the labourer

In that: *For that reason; since or because* * I am confused in that I have been offered three jobs and they all sound pretty good * A higher income is harmful as in that it may discourage people from trying to earn more

In that event: *If that is so* * Should you like to be successful, in that event you need an earnest application of your mind on the matter

In the affirmative: *Yes* * The response of the people for him was in the affirmative

In the air: *Prevalent in an indefinite form; spreading about; unprotected* * My plans are still quite in the air * There are rumours in the air that weapons of mass destruction can be used by a rogue country * The border of the country was left in the air.

In the article of death: *At the point of death* * They did not surrender to the enemy even in the article of death

In the ascendant: *Becoming powerful; powerful* * His party is no longer in the ascendant

In the back of beyond: *In an inaccessible place* * We found ourselves in the back of beyond

In the background: *Not in prominence* * He does keep himself very much in the background

In the bag: *Secured* * The victory of our army is in the bag

In the balance: *Undecided* * It is still in the balance whether or not to launch the expedition this summer

In the bowel of the earth: *Deep underground* * The roots of all big trees spread in the bowl of the earth

In the care of: *Being looked after by* * The married couple will need to leave their baby in the care of a maid- servant

In the case of: *As regards* * In the case of his appointment to this post, he will prove an asset

In the chair: *In charge of a meeting* * Who will be in the chair for the next meeting of the committee?

In the circumstances: *Such being the state of affairs* * There was no way out to save his skin in the circumstances

In the cotton line: *Follow the trade in cotton* * He is in cotton line

In the course of events: *As things turned out* * In the course of events, they have to struggle hard to save their lives

In the dark: *In ignorance* * For a long time he kept me in the dark about his true state of affairs

In the dark of: *Not to know* * I am in the dark of his real intentions behind helping the poor man

In the day: *During the day* * It is said that the owls do not fly in the day

In the days of steam: *When the railways used steam locomotives* * There was also a time when we lived in the days of steam

In the distance: *Quite a long way away* * London is quite in the distance from Delhi

In the doghouse: *In disgrace* * The poor man is in the doghouse for no fault of his!

In the doldrums: *Not making any progress; in low spirits* * The stock market seems to be in doldrums

In the end: *After all; at last* * He tried many ways of earning a living and in the end chose to work on the farm * He kept on raising the price and in the end received a handsome amount for his crop

In the event: *As it in fact happens; in one of the competition in the sports* * In the event there were no formalities * He won the first prize in the event of discus throw

In the event of his refusing: *If he should refuse* * In the event of his refusing to come to terms, we would sever our dealings with him

In the extreme: *In the last; highest degree; extremely* * In the extreme of bad weather we may be forced to abandon the match

In the eyes of: *In the estimation; opinion* * In the eyes of most people, he is held in high esteem * He lowered himself in the eyes of everybody by his foolish conduct

In the face of: *In defiance of; despite* * What could he do in the face of strong opposition against him? * He succeeded in the face of all odds

In the face of the day: *Openly* * In a democratic regime, everything is done in the face of the day

In the fashion: *In accordance with the prevailing style of dress* * Wearing Western clothes is now the fashion amongst men and women in our country

In the first flight: *In the highest class* * Passengers in the first flight were provided special security arrangements by the government

In the first place: *First of all* * In the first place the happy news is that all of you have been declared successful candidates

In the flesh: *Alive or in bodily life** We were happy to see the victims of tornado in flesh

In the fullness of time: *At the due time* * This tree will bear fruit in the fullness of time

In the good books of: *In favour with* * I am in the good books of my boss

In the guise of: *Appearing like* * A lot of nonsense is talked about under the guise of philosophy

In the hands of: *Being looked after or managed by* * The management of this factory is in the hands of a highly experienced director

In the heat of action: *In a state of excitement* * The whole audience was in the heat of action during the pop music programme

In the interim: *Meanwhile* * Little seems to have happened in the interim

In the know: *Having information not shared by all or not available at* * Only a few administrators are in the know of the outcome of the new research

In the lap of luxury: *In fortunate circumstances* * Only rich persons can afford to live in the lap of luxury

In the lap of the gods: *Uncertain* * Our good or bad fortune is in the lap of the gods

In the last resort: *When everything fails* * When we were hotly pursued by our enemies, we had no alternative but to fight tooth and nail in the last resort

In the least: *In the smallest degree* * It does not matter in the least whether you go or not * I don't understand in the least what this author is trying to say

In the light of: *Keeping in view* * In the light of your poor class-work, you cannot get through the examination * In the light of the new evidence it was decided to take the matter to the court * The development is significant in the light of what happened there earlier

In the limelight: *Receiving publicity* * That new actress is very much in the limelight these days

In the long run: *In the end; eventually; ultimately* * It pays in the long run to buy goods of high quality * Steady work is sure to be rewarded in the long run

In the long term: *For a long period from now* * Some projects that have been planned could be of great advantage in the long term

In the lump: *In gross* * He has stored good stuff in the lump

In the main: *For the most part; on the whole* * The story told by him is true in the main * In the main, he is a very difficult character

In the mass: *In the aggregate; as a whole; indiscriminately* * The panel in the mass passed the order unanimously * The nation in the mass is not interested in elections at this time * The statement in the mass favours the interest of one and all

In the matter of: *As regards* * In the matter of knowledge, none can doubt his ability * He is very strict in the matter of discipline

In the mean: *In the meantime* * Please go and prepare tea for me and in the mean I will finish writing this letter

In the meantime: *In the mean* * I will come here in double-quick while in the meantime you can keep yourself busy

In the name of: *On behalf of; by the authority of* * The group claims to speak in the name of simple people of the country * People have to obey certain rules in the name of law

In the neighbourhood: *Around or near to* * He is conscientious about providing good amenities in the neighbourhood

In the nick of time: *Just at the right time* * The police came on the scene in the nick of time

In the nude: *Unclothed* * He posed in the nude for an artist

In the picture: *Having a share of attention; adequately briefed* * He was not in the picture about all what happened there * I have already been in the picture on the recent developments

In the pink: *In perfect health* * You certainly look in the pink of health

In the pipeline: *Being worked on or on the way* * A new taxation policy is in the pipeline

In the presence of: *In front of* * He was calm in the presence of danger * He was insulted in the presence of his friends

In the present case: *In the matter now in hand* * No argument seems plausible in the present case

In the prime of life: *In youth* * He met with a fatal accident in the prime of his youth

In the process: *While doing something* * Many important questions were raised in the process of discussions in the meeting

In the red: *In debt* * I am in the red as I have overdrawn money form my bank * He is in the red to the tune of a million rupees which has to be paid back within one year with interest

In the region of: *About* * You will have to spend a large sum of money, say in the region of one lakh rupees for the repair of the tank

In the right: *Right; maintaining a justifiable position* * From his explanation, he seems to be in the right * He has put himself in the right by his generous apology

In the road: *In the way* * An elephant caused a blockade in the road for a short period

In the round: *Capable of being viewed from all sides, not merely in relief* * From the top of the hill we could see the whole town in the round

In the round number: *Roughly; approximately* * The casualty in the stampede in the round number runs to a hundred persons

In the running: *Competing with a fair chance of success* * He was able to fight the duel in the running

In the saddle: *In control* * The chairman is determined to stay in the saddle at all costs

In the same boat: *In the same circumstances* * We are all in the same boat, so we will sink or swim together

In the same breath: *At the same moment* * They are not to be mentioned in the same breath

In the same way: *Similar condition* * Just as every baby's face is different from another, in the same way, every baby's pattern of development is different from other's

In the secret: *Among those who are allowed to know* * Is your brother in the secret with the crime branch?

In the seventh heaven: *In a state of the most exalted happiness* * If you want to be in the seventh heaven, live in peace and content

In the shape of: *In the guise of; of the nature of* * Ravana, who came in the shape of a hermit, abducted Sita * There was entertainment too in the shape of a couple of songs and mimicry

In the short term: *For a short period from now* * The projects to be completed in the short term would bear fruit in the very near future

In the smallest: *In the least* * I don't mind his displeasure even in the smallest * It does not matter in the smallest whether he goes or not

In the soup: *In trouble* * We will really be in the soup if the car fails to start

In the swim: *Up-to-date or aware of current affairs* * The media is always in the swim about all important events that take place here, there and everywhere

In the teeth of: *In spite of* * He took his test even in the teeth of high fever

In the teeth of wind: *Against the wind* * We found it very difficult to row in the teeth of wind

In the thick of time: *Just in time* * The police invariably fail to reach the site of crime in the thick of time

In the throes: *In travail; in the thick; in the struggle* * He has been transferred with immediate effect and as such is in the throes of packing his luggage * I am in the throes of my competitive exam for which I have to study many subjects * Madam is in the throes of becoming a famous writer

In the throne: *Become king or queen* * It is not yet decided when the young prince will be in the throne

In the twinkling of an eye: *In a short time* * The table was laid in the twinkling of an eye

In the wake of: *Close behind; immediately after* * Traders came in the wake of explorers * Famine came in the wake of disastrous floods

In the way: *On the way; in the path; obstructing progress* * A stranger accosted her in the way * We have to meet with many ups and downs in the way to success * Only a coward gives in to difficulties that come in the way

In the way of: *In a good position for attaining; in the habit of; in respect of* * Our cricket team is well in the way of winning the match against the South African team * He is always in the way of making excuses even for small lapses * He received very little in the way of wages

In the wild: *Animals living free in natural surroundings* * We have yet to catch a glimpse of rare animals in the wild

In the wind: *Afoot* * It is now in the wind to launch a new scheme for women

In the wind's eye: *Right against the wind* * We had to strive hard to row our boat in the wind's eye

In the wrong: *Holding an erroneous view or unjust position; guilty of error* * He admitted that he was in the wrong * He was punished when found in the wrong

In the wrong box: *In a false position or scrape* * Keep yourself at an arm's length from those who are in the wrong box

In theory: *In general principle* * In theory it should work without any flaw

In this day and age: *In this present period* * In this day and age, machines are doing wonderful jobs at a very fast rate

In this neck of the woods: *In this part of the world* * In this neck of the woods, you will find no trace of wild animals

In this regard: *In this respect* * As for the reason for his failure, it is very difficult for me to say anything in this regard

In time: *After lapse of time; quite early enough; keeping rhythm* * You will learn how to do it in time * He finished his work in time and went to relax * The dancers were all dancing in time to the beats of the drum

In token of: *As a sign of* * Accept this wrist-watch in token of my love for you

In torment: *In great pains* * I was in torment due to the fracture of my knee-bone * I was in torment when I lost my best friend in an accident

In toto: *Totally; altogether* * The scheme placed for consideration of the Parliament has been approved in toto

In touch: *In communication* * We do keep in touch with old friends

In tow: *Behind or together with* * He usually has his family in tow * He visited us with his family in tow

In triplicate: *In three identical copies* * I have filled in the form in triplicate

In trust: *As a charge; for safe keeping; for management as a trustee* * The business of the factory is being carried out in trust of a Board of Directors * People deposit their money in trust with the banks * His mother's money was left in trust for him to acquire on becoming an adult

In two: *Be at variance* * The believers in autocracy and democracy are in two as far as their ideology is concerned

In two minds: *Wavering* * I was very much in two minds whether or not to apply for that job

In two ticks: *In a moment* * I will come to that in two ticks

In two twos: *In a moment* * You think of a ghost and there you find him in two twos!

In unison: *Singing the same note all together; in total agreement; in one voice* * They sang the morning prayer in unison * They were all in unison in their condemnation of the murderer * The people raised their protest in unison against the highhandedness of the authorities

In use: *In employment; practice* * In case of war, only conventional weapons are in use these days

In very deed: *Of a truth; certainly* * He could taste good results in the very deed * Those who are credulous are sufferers in very deed

In view: *In sight; in mind; as an aim* * For a long time there was no oasis in view while travelling through the desert * I have many important ideas in view to write in my story * What end he has in view?

In view of: *In a position to see or to be seen by; having regard to* * In view of his high status in society, he commands great respect and admiration * In view of the facts, it seems useless to continue with the monotonous work

In violation of an agreement: *Against the terms of an agreement* * They blockaded the Suez Canal in violation of the international agreement

In virtue of: *Because of* * He claimed compensation in virtue of his long military service

In vogue: *Popular* * In olden times, such beauty lotions were not in vogue

In voice: *In good condition for singing or speaking* * Lata, the Indian nightingale, is still in voice, even at an old age

In waste: *To no effect; in vain* * We should not let our money lie in waste * All his efforts went in waste

In weal and woe: *In prosperity and adversity* * He stood by me in weal and woe

In word: *In speech only; in profession only* * He could be called a good orator in word * He is well known as a cook in word for preparing tasty meals

Incense breathing: *Exhaling fragrance* * His incense breathing attracted attention of many who were seated near him

Incentive bonus: *Extra money paid when the production is increased* * Each employee of the company was paid an incentive bonus for the first time in the history of the company

Incentive to: *Encouragement* * This reward will act as a great incentive to further studies

Include in: *To be a part of the whole* * Your suggestions will be included in the report

Inclusive of: *Including* * He paid the shopkeeper the total amount, inclusive of the sales tax

Indebted to: *Owing money or gratitude* * I am greatly indebted to you for your help

Independent means: *Private means* * She was a woman of independent means

Indifference to: *Absence of interest or feeling* * His indifference to his future needs is unfortunate

Indifferent to: *Having no interest in; neither for nor against; not caring for* * How can you be so indifferent to the sufferings of poor children? * He has a very indifferent approach to the task on hand * The explorers were indifferent to discomforts and dangers in the course of the expedition

Indispensable to: *Absolutely necessary* * This book is indispensable to students engaged in higher studies

Induce to: *Persuade; influence* * We could not induce the old lady to travel by air

Induct into: *Admit as a member* * He was willing to be inducted into the army

Induction course: *Training course for somebody in a new job* * An induction course helps a new employee to become familiar with the job

Indulge in: *Allow oneself the pleasure of* * He occasionally indulges in the luxury of a good cigar

Indulgent to: *Sympathetic; fond of* * The old teacher is indulgent to his pupils

Industrial action: *Action or protest by workers* * The number of days lost through industrial action is at the maximum during a strike

Ineligible for: *Unqualified for* * I am ineligible for employment benefits

Infer from: *Conclude* * Am I to infer from your remarks that you think I am a liar?

Inferiority complex: *Feeling that one is inferior* * He suffers from an inferiority complex for his poor status

Infested with: *Full of* * The storehouse is infested with rats

Inflict on: *Give* * The judge inflicted a death penalty on the murderer

Inform against: *Bring evidence; an accusation against* * He has promised to inform against the proclaimed offender

Inform of: *Give knowledge* * Have you informed them of your intended departure?

Infra dig: *Beneath one's dignity* * He thinks it an infra dig to do a menial job

Ingratiate oneself with someone: *Bring oneself into favour* * Many persons dislike and resent his knack for ingratiating with officers

Inherent in: *Natural to* * Honesty is inherent in an upright man

Inimical to: *Unfriendly* * His actions are inimical to his own interest

Injurious to: *Harmful* * Smoking is injurious to health

Inland navigation: *Travel by boat along rivers or canals* * Inland navigation is one of the means to ferry persons or goods from one place to another

Innocent of: *Ignorant of* * She is innocent of English

Inoculate someone against: *Prevent someone from catching a disease by injecting him with a vaccine* * The doctor inoculated him against cholera

Inoculate with: *Fill the mind with opinions, etc.* * He has been inoculated with evil doctrines

Inquire about: *Ask for information about* * He inquired about the train timings bound for Bombay from Delhi

Inquire after: *Ask for (health, welfare)* * I went to inquire after his health

Inquire for: *Ask for* * The father inquired for the son where he was

Inquire into: *Investigate* * I wish to inquire into the cause of the accident

Inquire of: *Ask to be told* * I inquired of my mother about the painful event

Ins and outs: *Turning this way and that; nooks and corners; the details and complexities* * You must have learnt from the map the ins and outs of that road leading to your destination * The detectives discovered the ins and outs of the hideouts * We had to discuss all the ins and outs of the problem

Inside out: *With the inner side turned out* * He put his socks on inside out

Insist on/upon: *Urge with emphasis* * She insisted on my going to the college

Inspire with: *Put uplifting thoughts* * The example set by the patriot inspired us with a sense of respect for our country

Instalment plan: *Hire purchase* * I have purchased this new car under the instalment plan

Intellectual snob: *Person who looks down on those not so well-educated as he himself* * He is an intellectual snob and boasts of his own intelligence

Intensive care unit: *Section of a hospital dealing with seriously ill patient who need a lot of attention* * The patient was kept nearly for three weeks in the intensive care unit

Intent on/upon: *Committed to* * She is intent on getting to the office on time

Interfere in: *Break in upon* * Please don't interfere in my business

Interfere with: *Meddle; temper; come into opposition* * Don't interfere with this machine * Do you ever allow pleasure to interfere with duty?

Internal evidence: *Evidence as afforded by the thing itself* * The blood-stained knife found in the possession of the murderer was clear evidence to frame charges against him

Into one's clutches: *Into one's tremendous influence/power/control* * He fell into the clutches of the abductors

Into the bargain: *In addition; over and above* * He spent over it much time and energy and lost a large sum into the bargain * He bought a horse and got a saddle in the bargain

Intolerant of: *Not tolerant* * He is a man intolerant to any opposition

Introduce into: *Bring into use or operation for the first time* * Tobacco was introduced into Europe from America

* He introduced new ideas into his business

Introduce somebody to: *Make known by name* * He introduced me to his parents * The chairman introduced the lecturer to the audience

Intrusion on/upon: *Intruding to* * He felt offended at the numerous intrusions on his privacy by the rude journalists

Inundated with: *Flooded with water; overwhelmed with* * A large area of cultivated land has been inundated with heavy rain * The advertiser's office was inundated with applications

Inure oneself to: *Accustom* * Living in the far north had inured him to cold

Invalid carriage: *Small vehicle for one disabled person* * The disabled person has been provided an invalid carriage

Invest in: *Put money in* * He invested his savings in a business enterprise

Invest with: *Endow* * The president has been invested with full authority

Ipso facto: *By that very fact* * An elected prime minister can wield unlimited executive power ipso facto

Iron curtain: *Impenetrable barrier to observation or communication* * There was an iron curtain rule in the Soviet Union under the dictatorship of Stalin

Iron hand: *Severe hand* * Akbar put down the revolt with an iron hand

Iron out: *Remove* * I thought we have yet to iron out most of our problems

Iron will: *Strong determination* * Sardar Patel was a man of iron will

Is expendable: *Can be left behind or killed* * He is expendable in any case

Is no more: *Not alive* * Nothing can hurt him any further as he is no more

Is not very much mobile: *Cannot walk easily* * He is not very mobile and is still confined to bed

Isolated attack: *Single attack, not repeated* * He got an isolated attack of hysteria

Issue something to somebody/ Issue somebody to something: *Distribute for use* * New warm clothing is required to be issued to the troops

It all boils down: *The main question is* * It all boils down to whether he will resign willingly or not

It costs the earth: *A great deal of money* * It will cost the earth to link Sri Lanka with

India through a bridge over the sea

It is a good thing: *It is lucky* * It is a good thing you came with us to get the problem solved smoothly

It is an ill wind that blows nobody any good: *An affair must be very bad if it does not benefit somebody* * No one can deny the fact that it is an ill wind that blows nobody any good

It is as broad as it is long: *It is all the same however you view the problem* * Whether you take up this way or that, it is as broad as it is long to face the apparent trouble.

It is common knowledge: *Everyone knows it* * It is common knowledge that there is no escape from death

It is in the news: *It is of topical interest* * It is in the news that a man has bitten a dog

It is incumbent on you: *It is your responsibility* * It is incumbent on you to warn the boy of the dangers of smoking

It is said: *Commonly reputed* * It is said that Rana Pratap preferred death to dishonour

It never rains but it pours: *Things never happen singly* * His condition went from bad to worse all of a sudden proving that it never rains but it pours

It seems: *It appears; it would seem* * It seems that no one knew what had happened

It stands to reason: *It is obvious to sensible people* * It stands to reason to apologise at once for your transgressions

It will serve: *It will suffice* * It will serve my needs if you give me a loan * Thanks for the timely help as it will serve my purpose

It would seem: *It turns out; I have been told* * It would seem to be alright if he goes away at this time * It would seem that he would go to London on a short trip

It's all up: *No use making further efforts* * It's all up with the patient now

It's no joke: *It is a serious matter* * It's no joke to break the record set by the heavyweight champion

Ivory tower: *Place of seclusion or retreat from the realities of life* * He urged his friend to get out of his ivory tower and tour the country during summer vacations

J

Jab at: *Poke or push with force; aim a quick blow at* * He jabbed at me with a knife * He jabbed at his opponent many a time (boxing)

Jab something into: *Force something into* * He jabbed his elbows into my side.

Jab something out: *Force or push out by jabbing* * Be careful as not to jab my eye out with your umbrella

Jack in: *Abandon or stop doing an activity or a job* * One of these days I am going to jack this job in and sail round the world

Jack-in-the-box: *Box from which a toy figure springs up when the lid is opened* * The child's joy knew no bounds to see Jack-in-the-box

Jack of all trades: *One who can turn his hand to anything* * He is a Jack of all trades but master of none

Jack is so good as his master: *Workman is the equal of his employer* * Nobody denies the fact that Jack is so good as his master in the factory

Jack up: *Use a jack to raise something heavy* * Make sure you have got the tools ready before you jack up the truck * Jack up the car and change the wheel with the punctured tyre

Jactitation of marriage: *Pretence of being married to another* * The expression 'jactitation of marriage' is an indirect way of not agreeing for an engagement

Jail bird: *A person who has been to jail so many times* * Kalu, a jail-bird, was again sentenced to five years of rigorous imprisonment

Jam-packed: *Packed full* * The drawers were jam-packed with old notes and letters

Janissary music: *Military music with much percussion* * The triumphant army was marching on the tune of Janissary music

Janus-faced: *Two faced* * A Janus-faced person is always kept at bay by people

Jar on: *Have an unpleasant effect; strike with a harsh unpleasant sound* * His laughter is a jar on my ears

Jar on someone's nerves: *Annoy* * His ugly face and

biting tongue are a jar on my nerves

Jar with: *Be out of harmony* * His opinions jar with mine

Jay-walker: *Who walks erratically across or along/streets without paying attention to traffic* * A jay-walker can be knocked down by a speeding truck

Jazz something up: *Liven up or put more energy into* * They have certainly jazzed their cricket team up for future Test matches

Jeer at: *Mock at* * A sensible person would never jeer at others for any reason whatsoever

Jene's eyes: *Proverbially of very high value* * Kohinoor diamond was a Jene's eyes with many of its possessors from time to time

Jerk out: *Say in an abrupt and nervous way* * He jerked out an apology when taken to task

Jest with: *Make jests* * I advise you not to jest with that man as he does not have a sense of humour

Jesting stock: *A buff for jests* * He is a jesting stock of the whole school

Jet-black: *Dark black in colour* * His hair was jet-black and well combed

Jet set: *Wealthy people who frequently travel for pleasure world over; successful people living in a luxurious way* * The Olympic Games bring the jet set from the world over * This was once a popular place for jet-set travellers

Jib at: *Show unwillingness or dislike* * He jibbed at working overtime every time every day * My car sometimes jibs at a steep hill

Jiggery-pockery: *Tricks* * The joker amused us all with his jiggery-pockery

Job's comforter: *One who aggravates distress of the unfortunate man he has come to comfort* * A job's comforter must be kept at an arm's length

Job's for the boys: *Positions for one's supporters or friends, etc.* * The whole project is unnecessary as it is just jobs for the boys

Job lot: *A collection of odds and ends especially for sale as one lot; any collection of inferior quality* * He is well known for his job lot * There are rare persons who are interested in job lot

Job's news: *Bad news* * He felt alarmed at the Job's news

Job of work: *A task or bit of work* * Let me finish the job of work in hand before I have a talk with you

Job's post: *The bearer of bad news* * He hesitated to carry a job's post

Jog on/along: *Make slow or patient progress* * We jogged along the bad roads * We must jog on somehow until business conditions improve

Jog someone's memory: *Make him remember or recall something* * He jogs my memory on what to do on a particular occasion if I forget

Join battle: *Begin a fight or contest* * Many persons joined battle to speak for or against the new ideology of running a government

Join forces: *Unite in action* * We must join forces with our colleagues in order to achieve a common goal

Join hands up: *To associate with* * The people have joined hands up with the government to support the earthquake-stricken victims

Join in: *Associate with or come into the company of* * I will join you in a few minutes * May I join in the game?

Join issue: *Take an opposite position in dispute; enter into dispute; take up a point as basis of argument* * The Leftists will join issue on the subject of reforms that comes up for discussion in Parliament * The two brothers joined issue with each other over distribution of property * I was bold enough to join issue with the manager of the firm in the matter of running the administrative machinery

Join the colours: *To enlist* * He is determined to join in the colours when he comes of age to serve his country

Join the majority: *Die* * All off us have to join the majority sooner or later

Join the palms: *Fold hands* * He bade me goodbye by joining his palms

Join up: *Enlist especially in participation in a general movement* * A large number of people joined up Mahatma Gandhi's movement called the Dandi March

Joke Smith: *A maker of jokes* * I think he is born as Joke Smith to amuse others

Jolly: *Very good natured* * Jolly well, he will return the money to me on time

Jolly good time: *A very good time* * During the last summer vacation we had a jolly good time at Shimla

Jolly someone along: *Keep in a good humour* * They jollied me along until I agreed to help them

Jot something down: *Make a quick written note of* * The policeman jotted down his name and address before letting him go

Judas-kiss: *Any act of treachery under the guise of kindness* * Some persons are betrayed by the Judas- kiss and the result is to suffer

Judas hole: *A spy hole* * Be alert about Judas hole so that you do not get entangled in serious trouble

Judgement by default: *Judgement given against a person because he fails to plead or make an appearance in the court* * It was a judgement by default on the failure of the complaint to plead his case

Judgement reserved: *Decision delayed after the close of a trial* * We cannot offer any comments on the outcome of the fate of the defendant so long the judgement remains reserved * Since the court has announced judgement reserved, we cannot guess anything about the fate of the defendant

Judgement respite: *Execution of the sentence delayed* * The accused is relieved as he is getting some judgement respite till the decision is taken on his mercy appeal

Judicial separation: *The separation of two married couple by order of the divorce court* * The married couple is bound to remain under judicial separation for two years

Juggle with: *Do tricks to amuse people* * The audience was amused to see him juggle with balls and later with plates

Jumble sale: *A sale of miscellaneous articles often for charity* * The items acquired from the jumble sale serve to raise money for charity besides helping a person to purchase the same at a very small price * He has gathered these (goods) from the jumble sale

Jump a page: *Miss out a page* * In a hurry I jumped a page of my book which could have given me necessary information that I needed

Jump at: *To accept with eagerness* * I suggested to him to jump at the idea * He jumped at the offer of a lucrative job

Jump down one's throat: *Assail one with violence* * There was no need to jump down his throat for his silly statement

Jump off: *The start; starting place* * The jump off of the athlete in the long jump was exceptional * The runners taking part in the race are readying themselves for their respective jump off

Jump on: *Jump so as to come down heavily upon; censure promptly and vigorously* * He jumped on his servant for his rude behaviour * The boss jumped on his secretary for his lapses

Jump one's bail: *Forfeiting one's bail; abscond* * By jumping his bail, he forfeited the amount of bail surrendered to the court * The police has arrested the accused who had jumped his bail

Jump out of one's skin: *Be surprised* * He nearly jumped out of his skin when he saw her face at the window

Jump over: *Leap over* * The cat suddenly jumped over the table

Jump over the bail: *Disregard it* * He is now in trouble for jumping over the bail

Jump the gun: *Begin before the correct time* * Some newspapers at home or aboard jump the gun by giving premature news

Jump the queue: *Obtain something without waiting for one's proper turns* * He jumped the queue to get the cinema ticket from the booking window

Jump to conclusion: *Form inferences permanently* * We should never jump to a hasty conclusion * On the basis of evidence, the judge jumped to the conclusion that the culprit deserved punishment

Jump upon: *To bounce upon* * The cat jumped upon the mouse and killed it in no time

Jump on the bandwagon: *To join a popular movement* * A politician is keen to jump on the environmental bandwagon

Jump to it: *Hurry; be quick!* * You are already late to pack your bag, so jump to it now or you will miss the train

Jump with joy: *Feel overjoyed* * He jumped with joy to see his long lost son

Junior sophomore: *An undergraduate of the second year at Cambridge* * He has now been promoted to junior sophomore for his excellent performance

Junk food: *Bad commercially prepared food with little nutritional value* * Persons dealing in junk food have been booked by the police

Just a minute: *For a short time* * Wait for just a minute so that I may see him off

Just about: *Something close to* * He was just about my age when he joined the school

Just about ready: *Almost ready* * He is just about ready to leave for his office

Just as: *Exactly as* * Leave everything just as (tidy as) you find it * Come just as you are (without any special preparation)

Just in case: *Guard against a possible emergency* * Be careful just in case snakes are hidden in the grass

Just now: *At this moment; a short time ago* * I am busy just now * He left this place just now

Just on: *To specify an exact number or amount* * It was just on seven when he reached the farmhouse

Just on a year ago: *Approximately a year ago* * We met each other just on a year ago

Just one of those things: *Something that is unavoidable and must be accepted* * Leaving school and not being able to get a job is unfortunately just one of those things that happen

Just talked round the subject: *Never discussed the main problem* * We just talked round the subject while exchanging our views

Just the job: *It is exactly what is wanted or needed* * That is just the job I want you to do

Just the same: *However; still* * There was no news but just the same he kept on hoping

Just the thing: *Exactly the thing that is needed* * It is just the thing that I would like to buy today * A nice cup of hot tea would be just the thing that I need

Just then: *A particular time in the past* * He informed me just then of all that he had seen his own eyes

Justice of the peace: *Magistrate* * He has been summoned to appear before the 'justice of the peace'

Justifiable homicide: *The killing of a person in self defense or prevent an atrocious crime* * They claimed that killing of the robber with a lethal weapon by him was justifiable homicide.

K

Kangaroo court: *Illegal court set up by the terrorists or mafia* * The captives held by the terrorists were tried and executed by the kangaroo court

Keel over: *Upset; fall sideways; capsize* * The pillar was likely to keel over any moment * When the boat keeled over, its occupants got drowned

Keen on: *Devoted to; fond of; much interested in; very desirous of* * He is very keen on his studies * She is rather keen on music * He is keen on shipping * I am very keen on getting this post

Keen prices: *Very low prices* * He is very particular in purchasing articles that are available at keen prices

Keep a (bad) quarter: *Make a disturbance* * Tell the children not to keep a (bad) quarter here when I am engrossed in my studies

Keep a civil tongue in one's head: *Not be rude* * He is loved by his friends for keeping a civil tongue in his head

Keep a diary: *Write notes every day about what you have done* * It is a good habit to keep your diary

Keep a firm/tight hold: *Not let go* * Keep a firm/tight hold on the horse's reins

Keep a good house: *Keep up a plentifully supplied table* * Those who keep a good house never fall short of anything at any time

Keep a good table: *Provide with good food* * He is very hospitable and keeps a good table

Keep a place warm: *Occupy or hold it for someone until he is ready to fill it himself* * The chief minister has kept a place warm for the portfolio of a Law Minister till a suitable person is found

Keep a secret: *Not tell anyone else* * It is very difficult for a talkative person to keep a secret

Keep a straight face: *Refrain from smiling; stop yourself from smiling* * He kept a straight face when he saw me falling flat on the slippery road * The brave soldier kept a straight face while receiving the gallantry award from the president

Keep a term: *Give the regular attendance during a period of study* * Students who keep a term are sure to pass in their terminal examinations

Keep an act: *Hold an academic disputation* * The curriculum for higher studies would be referred to an academic council for keeping an act

Keep an eye on: *Watch* * Please keep an eye on the baby while I am in the garden

Keep an open mind: *Be willing to listen to or accept new idea or suggestions* * We should keep an open mind on every fresh news of high value

Keep at arm's length: *Be in unfriendly term* * Keep him at arm's length since he is a well-known gambler

Keep at bay: *Keep in check; keep away* * Keep at bay that black sheep * Our security personnel kept the attackers at bay

Keep at it: *Persist on anything* * The students will keep at it all afternoon till they learn all the important points by heart

Keep at something: *Work at it* * Keep at it till you finish the job! * Keep them at it or they will get lazy

Keep away: *Prevent from; avoid* * Keep the child away from the fireplace * Try to keep away from the building site as accidents are likely to happen

Keep abreast (of): *Keep up, not behind* * He could not keep abreast of all day-to-day events by reading the newspaper only

Keep abreast (with): *Keep up with progress or thought* * The dull boy could not keep abreast with the class

Keep aloof: *Avoid or remain distant from* * She is a very snooty person and keeps aloof from all the other girls

Keep back: *Withhold; keep down; repress* * She cannot keep back anything from her friends * He is very keen to keep back from superfluous expenditure * For centuries men have been trying to keep back women from working away from home

Keep body and soul together: *Maintain life* * The poor have to work hard to keep their body and soul together

Keep books: *Keep accounts* * We need the services of an efficient man who can keep books

Keep company: *Associate with* * He keeps company with eminent scholars * He kept his father company in the late afternoon

Keep cool: *Don't get excited* * It is a good thing to keep cool even in the teeth of hostile opposition

Keep dark: *Be silent or keep secret* * He kept dark on/about his misdeeds

Keep down: *Restrain; repress; remain low* * He could not keep down his anger * The dominating rulers used to keep their subjects subjugated * We must keep down our expenses

Keep early hours: *Rise and go to bed betimes* * Those who keep early hours become healthy and wise

Keep fair with: *Keep on amicable terms with* * It is advisable to keep fair with the doctors and the cook

Keep fit: *Remain in good health* * It is very necessary to keep fit to lead a long life

Keep from: *Refrain* * I could not keep from laughing at his queer behaviour

Keep from doing something: *Prevent; hold back; refrain* * What kept you from joining me? * We must keep them from getting to know our plans * We must do something to keep the roof from falling in

Keep going: *Not stop; not give up; continue to function* * The work was very tiring but I managed to keep going * I am not sure that the enterprise can keep going

Keep going in: *Keep one supplied with* * Pakistan keeps the terrorists going in arms and ammunition to continue with their evil designs

Keep good/bad times: *Show the hour correctly/incorrectly* * My watch always keep good times * I had to get my watch repaired by the watchmaker because it was keeping bad time

Keep good hours: *Go to bed and to rise early; lead a quiet and regular life* * You must keep good hours to stay fit * He keeps good hours and that is the secret of his progress

Keep good quarter: *Keep good order or keep good watch* * We should keep good quarter in our dealings with others

Keep house: *Maintain or manage an establishment* * We need the services of honest and responsible persons to keep house at the new factory

Keep hold of: *Not let go* * He

kept hold of the reins even when the horse started galloping

Keep in: *Prevent from escaping; confine in school after school hours; conceal; restrain; continue* * They were kept in as hostages for many days * I was kept in at school for not doing my homework * He tried to keep in the secret to the last * I could not keep in my anger when he called me names * Shall we keep the fire in or let it out?

Keep in step: *Move at the same pace as everyone else* * It was a wonderful treat to see the soldiers keep in step while marching in the parade ground

Keep in the dark: *Be in ignorance* * We were completely in the dark about his movements.

Keep in with: *Maintain confidence or friendship of someone* * You must keep in with your customers * If you keep in with him, he would never harm you

Keep in the dark: *Conceal it* * Why keep your relatives in the dark about your affair with that girl?

Keep late bows: *Keep awake late at night* * The examiner is keeping late bows as he has to examine the answer books

Keep mum: *Not to say a word* * He kept mum on my query

Keep off: *Hinder from approaching or making an attack; remain at a distance; not come; refrain from** You must keep off that sulky bull * Keep yourself off drugs * If the rain keeps off, we will play the football * Do keep off from him as he has a volatile temper

Keep on: *Continue; persist* * Despite the torrential rain we will need to keep on our course all morning * Keep straight on until you reach the turning that leads to the church * He kept on working although he was tired

Keep on a tight rein: *Be firm with; allow little freedom to; keep under strict control* * It is a discipline alone that keeps our security forces and police on a tight rein * The new boss has kept his employees on a tight rein * A new horse-rider must learn to keep on a tight rein on the horse even when it is not galloping

Keep on at: *Criticise without stopping* * It is his nature to keep on at any person who offends him

Keep on doing something: *Do something frequently or repeatedly* * My shoe lace keeps on getting undone

Keep one at a distance: *Treat with aloofness* * It would be wise to keep him at a distance to be on the safe side

Keep one to oneself: *Avoid meeting people* * Since the examination is approaching near, he is so engrossed in his studies that he keeps to himself

Keep one's balance: *Keep steady; keep calm* * Every person tries to keep one's balance * A small child has to learn to keep its balance before it can walk * Keep your balance even if he tries to annoy you

Keep one's countenance: *Avoid showing one's emotions* * I could hardly keep my countenance when I saw the young widow receiving the posthumous award given in memory of her dead husband

Keep one's day: *Be punctual* * It is a good habit to keep one's day

Keep one's distance: *Abstain from familiarity with; keep aloof from* * They were careful to keep their distance from the police officials * It would be in your own interest to keep distance from bad company

Keep one's end up: *Maintain one's part; be content to keep one's wicket standing without trying to score; continue to be in good spirits* * He was dead sure of keeping his end up against any odds * It was thought proper by the two cricketers to keep their end up during the last half an hour of play * He kept his end up even in difficult times

Keep one's eye on: *Observe closely* * The policeman has been told to keep his eye on miscreants and vagabonds

Keep one's eye skinned: *Be keenly watchful* * Invigilators had to keep their eyes skinned in the examination hall to ensure that all students submitted their answer sheets

Keep one's hair on: *Keep cool* * He kept his hair on even in the face of provocations

Keep one's hand: *Retain one's skill by practice* * He still keeps his hand in typewriting even at the age of 65

Keep one's head: *Keep one's self possession* * I managed to keep my head in spite of the panic all around

Keep one's head above water: *Stay out of debt, difficulty,* *etc.** The poor man had to work hard for long hours to keep his head above water

Keep one's incognito: *Be concealed under a disguise* * The policeman kept himself incognito by putting on a simple civil dress and sporting a false beard

Keep one's own mind: *Know what one wants, have no doubts* * He never knows his own mind (often doubts)

Keep one's mind on: *Continue to pay attention to; not to be diverted from* * Keep your mind on what you are doing * It was too hot to keep my mind on my studies

Keep one's nose to the grindstone: *Subject one to severe continued toil or punishment* * In the olden days the white made every effort to keep the nose of the black slave to the grindstone

Keep one's nose out: *Do not interfere* * Keep your nose out of my business

Keep one's own counsel: *Keep a secret or remain silent* * He kept his own counsel in order to avoid getting embroiled in any controversy

Keep one posted: *Keep one informed* * He promised to keep them posted with every piece of news he received

Keep one's powder dry: *Keep one's energies ready for action; observe all practical precaution* * We should keep our powder dry to meet any emergency * In order to save our skins from any unexpected danger we must keep our powder dry * If you want to succeed in your project, keep your powder dry

Keep one's shirt on: *Keep calm; keep one's temper in control* * In spite of his provocation I managed to keep my shirt on * He kept his shirt on when confronted with strong opposition

Keep one's temper: *Keep one's temper under control* * He kept his temper and did not get angry even when the man pushed him to one side

Keep one's thumb on: *Keep a secret* * He is still keeping his thumb on his misdeeds

Keep one's weather eye open: *Be alert or keep a sharp lookout* * It would be in our own interest to keep our weather eye open against any calamity

Keep one's wits around: *Keep calm in difficult situation and think hard what to do next* *

You should keep your wits about you when confronted with an awkward situation

Keep one's word: *Do what one has promised to do* * He is a trustworthy gentleman and would always keep his word

Keep open house: *Give entertainment to all comers* * He is well known in the neighbourhood for keeping an open house

Keep out: *Remain outride; prevent from entering* * As there lies danger ahead, it is better to keep away from the road under construction * We should keep out of their quarrels * Shut the window and keep the cold out * Keep the dog out of my study

Keep pace with: *Go as fast as* * He is doing his best to keep pace with the intelligent boys of his class * We must keep pace with the advances in science and technology

Keep somebody going: *Help him to continue in some way* * Will a hundred bucks keep you going until payday? * The doctors managed to keep me going and remain active

Keep running: *Continue running* * He kept running from pillar to post to seek redressal of his grievances

Keep somebody something off: *Hold or cause to remain away* * They lighted a big fire to keep the wild animals off

Keep somebody under observation: *Watch him carefully* * The police is keeping all the suspects under observation

Keep somebody up: *Delay somebody from going to bed* * It is wrong to keep children up so late * I don't want to keep you up because you look sleepy

Keep something down: *Control; limit; retain* * He could not keep down his anger * This chemical will keep the weeds down * We must keep the expenses down * He could not keep his food down (had to vomit)

Keep something in mind: *Remember something* * Keep my words in mind when you go to strike a bargain with him

Keep something on ice: *Not do anything about it for the moment* * He has chosen to keep his decision about our demands on ice for the time being

Keep something to oneself: *Not express one's comments,* *views, etc.* * Keep your remarks to yourself as I don't want to hear them * He kept the good news to himself (refuse to share)

Keep something up one's sleeves: *Have an idea to be kept secret for future use* * He has kept some plans up his sleeves which he does not want to reveal

Keep step: *Continue in step* * The soldiers kept their steps with one another when marching in a parade

Keep tabs on: *Keep a check on; keep account of* * We must keep tabs on our expenses * A businessman is very particular to keep tabs on each aspect of his enterprise

Keep time: *Run accurately as a clock; move or perform in the same rhythm; record times of workmen* * My watch keeps good time * All the trains are supposed to keep time * The factory management keeps time of the employees working in different shifts

Keep the ball rolling: *Keep things going* * The banks are still keeping the ball rolling in providing house loans on low rates of interest

Keep the balance of power: *Maintain; to be equal in power* * The atomic weapons have made it possible to keep the balance of power in the world

Keep the door open: *Be hospitable* * Very few persons keep the door open to all

Keep the field: *Keep the campaign open; maintain one's ground* * He kept the field so long as he was able to achieve his goal * He was determined to keep the field at all costs

Keep the pot boiling: *Earn enough money to meet one's requirements* * We have to keep the pot boiling so long we are able to do so

Keep the weather of: *Be to the wind-ward of or have the advantage of* * A wise man would keep the weather of every opportunity that comes his way

Keep the wolf from the door: *Keep away poverty or hunger* * A poor man has to work hard to keep the wolf from the door

Keep to: *Stick closely to; confine oneself to; continue; retain* * It is a good thing to keep to one's promise * We must keep to the deadline * Keep to the letter of law * While that big truck keeps to the middle of the road, we cannot overtake it * He was ill and had to keep to his bed

Keep track of: *Keep oneself informed about* * We read newspapers to keep track of current events

Keep under: *Hold down in restraint* * The firemen were able to keep the fire under control * The patient crying with pain was kept under pain-killers

Keep under wraps: *Conceal* * He is very good at keeping his emotions under wraps

Keep up: *Retain one's strength or spirits; support; prevent; continue; prevent from ceasing; maintain in good condition; continue to be in touch with; keep pace; carry on; keep abreast* * He could not keep up with his competitors in the race * Wages of the workers are increased to keep up with the rising prices * One must keep up courage even in adversity * They kept up with the attack all day * It kept on raining for hours * They are still keeping up the old customs * How much does it cost you to keep up your large house and garden? * The headquarter staff keep up their link with field workers day in and day out * He finds it hard to keep up with the developments in nuclear physics

Keep up appearances: *Maintain outward appearance* * He is a bankrupt but he puts on fine clothes to keep up appearances

Keep up with: *Keep yourself informed about* * We have kept up with each other ever since we left school.

Keep up with the Joneses: *Compete with a neighbour or anybody else to show that one is not inferior to them* * In order to maintain his status he always keeps up with the Joneses by purchasing whatever they buy

Keep watch: *Be on guard* * It is the duty of the police to keep a watch on bad elements

Keep wicket: *Act as wicketkeeper* * Who do you think would keep wicket in the forthcoming cricket Test match?

Kept woman: *A mistress* * Many rich persons in the past tended to maintain a kept woman to satiate their lust

Keep your breath to cool your porridge: *Keep your advice to your own use* * I know all about it so please keep your breath to cool your porridge

Keeping-room: *A sitting room or*

parlour * As I was out for a while, the guest kept waiting for me in the keeping-room

Kennel-maid/man: *An attendant upon dog* * He needs the services of a kennel-maid/man

Key-hole: *Hole in a lock into which a key fits* * He slid the key into the key-hole to open the lock

Key in: *Have instruction on a key-board of the computer; bring into harmony* * To extract information, key in the word you require * He succeeded in getting the two erring friends keyed in

Key-man: *An indispensable worker* * The manager in the factory is a key-man who looks after its working in a proper way

Key-note: *Fundamental note or topic; any central principle or controlling thought* * The key-note to success lies in hard work * The key-note of the minister's speech laid stress on higher productivity

Key something into something: *Make connection between* * He keyed the plug into the socket to switch on his radio

Key speech: *Main speech* * The crux of his key speech was that work is worship

Key-stone: *Central principle on which everything depends* * The first national insurance was the key-stone of the future welfare state

Key to: *Something that provides an answer* * Hard work is the only key to success

Keyed to: *Made to harmonise* * The system of education has to be keyed to the demands of different trades

Keyed up: *Raised in pitch or standard; stimulated; be in a state of nervous tension; be excited or nervous* * The thought of the coming trip to the hills keyed him up in a state of excitement * The crowd was keyed up for the football match * The siren alarm about an impending air-raid keyed up the people who began running helter-skelter * He should not feel keyed up but different in some ways * The crowd was keyed up for the hockey match

Kick a goal: *Score a penalty* * The football match was won by kicking a goal at the end of the game

Kick against: *Show annoyance, protest* * He kicked against the treatment he was receiving

Kick at: *Show dislike of* * I kicked at his proposal

Kick-back: *Part of a sum received or paid to another by confidential agreement* * The kick-back involving the Bofors deal is still hanging fire in the court

Kick in the pants: *Criticism that shocks one into positive action* * A reprimand from my teacher for failing in the class tests proved a kick in the pants and I started taking my studies seriously

Kick-off: *The first kick in a game of football; start some event; remove by kicking* * The game started with a kick-off of the football * They kicked off a two-month tour to England * He kicked off his slippers in a hurry

Kick one's heel: *Be idle* * After the examinations get over, I plan to kick my heels for a month or so

Kick over the traces: *Throw off control* * Those who try to kick over the traces will be severely punished

Kick somebody out: *To expel* * The drunken man was kicked out of the bar

Kick somebody upstairs: *Get somebody out of the way by giving him higher position* * The cabinet has decided to kick one of the Members of Parliament upstairs as Governor

Kick-start: *The starting of an engine by a treadle* * The engine of the motorcycle started when I gave a kick-start

Kick the beam: *Be of little weight or importance* * His progress due to hard work has kicked the beam for his parents

Kick the bucket: *To die* * Immediately after he kicked the bucket, people from all parts of the country came pouring in to pay their last respects

Kick-up: *A disturbance; a dance; a depression in the bottom of a bottle* * I could not concentrate on my studies due to a kick-up in the neighbouring house * The kick-up performance given by the women was very amusing * That whisky bottle has a kick up

Kick-up a dust: *Create a disturbance* * Some miscreants kicked up a dust by throwing a missile towards the playground

Kick-up a fuss: *Cause a disturbance* * The opposition members kicked up a fuss in the house and brought the proceedings to a halt

Kick-up a row: *Create a disturbance or a great noise* * They kicked up a row when the lights went off in the cinema hall

Kick-up one's heels: *Enjoy oneself* * In the wedding procession of the bridegroom, his friends and relatives kicked up their heels in tune with the band * After having broken the back of the project, they started to kick up their heel

Kid's stuff: *Very easy task that requires no effort* * It is, of course, a kid's job to preach but very difficult to practice

Kill by inches: *Kill by gradual means, as by torture* * It is alleged that the police killed the arrested man by inches

Kill off: *Exterminate* * The bacteria will need to be killed off to prevent the spread of bacterial infection

Kill oneself with laughter: *Laugh very heartily* * He will kill himself with laughter if he continues laughing like this

Kill somebody with kindness: *Harm him by being excessively or mistakenly kind* * He killed his friend with kindness by offering him too many pegs of liquor

Kill the goose that lays the golden eggs: *Sacrifice future gains to satisfy present needs* * People who kill the goose that lays the golden eggs have to feel sorry later in life

Kill time: *Consume spare time as with amusement* * Reading novels is a good means to kill time

Kill two birds with one stone: *To achieve the aims at the same time* * Getting himself married to a pretty girl from a rich family, he killed two birds with one stone * Not only do I take my meals but also read the newspapers at the same time thereby killing two birds with one stone

Kind-hearted: *Thoughtful about other people* * A kind-hearted person is loved by all

Kindred spirit: *Person with whom you have something in common* * There are many kindred spirits in the Congress Party

Kinless: *Without relation* * They adopted a kinless child abandoned at a deserted place

Kinetic energy: *Energy possessed by a body in virtue of its motion* * The potential energy can be turned into kinetic energy

Kingpin: *Central person in an*

organisation * The kingpin of the mafia has been arrested

King's English: *Correct standard speech* * Our professor of English is well versed in King's English

King mob: *The vulgar multitude* * That particular place is a rendezvous for the king mob

King of beasts: *The lion* * The king of beasts has a fine appearance and is known for its courage

King of birds: *The eagle* * The king of birds pounces on food if it is eaten out in the open

King of kings: *God* * Most of the people are forgetful of king of kings when they are happy

King-size: *Very large* * He would very much like to smoke king-sized cigarettes

Kinship: *Family relationship* * It is kinship that keeps them bound together

Kiss of death: *It is certain to make something fail or be a disaster* * It is the kiss of death whenever he says he would extend me a helping hand in cooking

Kiss of life: *Something which gives life or energy to something else which is failing; put one's mouth onto mouth of a drowned person and breathe into his lungs to make him start breathing* * The investment made by the government proved to be a kiss of life to the coal industry * He pulled the child out of that deep tank and gave him the kiss of life

King of metals: *Gold* * Gold is called the king of metals for it is used for making coins, ornaments, jewellery, etc.

King of terrors: *Death* * The king of terrors is always there in wait for us

King of the forest: *Oak* * An oak tree is called king of the forest for its large size and hard wood

Kiss-curl: *A small curl at the side of the forehead* * She looks beautiful in her kiss-curl

Kiss the book: *Kiss a holy book on taking an oath* * The witness kissed the book in the court before he was cross-examined

Kiss the dust: *Give abject submission to a conqueror; be killed* * The defeated general had to kiss the dust before his conqueror * In the battle-field many soldiers on both the sides kissed the dust as a result of fierce firing

Kiss the gunner's daughter: *Be tied to a gun for a flogging* *

In old times, a traitor had to kiss the gunner's daughter

Kiss the rod: *Submit to punishment* * He kissed the rod for his wrong doings

Kit out: *Supply with clothes and equipment* * The soldiers were well kitted out with arms and ammunition for action in the field

Kitchen physics: *Substantial fare or feeding up* * There are many poor people who need kitchen physics

Kite-flying: *Testing public opinion by circulating rumours* * A shrewd person fulfils his aim of gauging his popularity through kite-flying

Kith and kin: *Friends and relatives* * He invited his kith and kin to a grand feast on his birthday

Klieg eyes: *The effect of strain on the eyes caused by the brilliance of floodlights in film production* * The actors are accustomed to tolerating the klieg eyes

Knee-deep: *So deep as to reach the knees* * Children waded through the knee-deep water

Knee-high: *So high as to reach the knees* * There was knee-high snowfall in the hilly areas * The grass was knee high

Kneel down: *Go down on your kneel* * He knelt down to pray

Knight of St. Crispin: *Shoemaker* * The knight of St. Crispin is an indispensable member for protecting the feet against injury

Knight of the pestle: *An apothecary* * In order to protect ourselves from various diseases, we do stand in need of a knight of the pestle

Knight of the post: *A professional witness who offers bail* * He earns his living by acting as a knight of the post

Knight of the road: *A highway; a commercial traveller; a tramp* * Various kinds of vehicles almost keep the knight of the road humming with vibrations continuously * In the interest of spreading the business, a knight of the road has to visit his customers living at far and wide places * There is a knight of the road at the door begging for food

Knight of the shears: *A tailor* * A knight of the shears is one of the most important persons responsible for making us keep warm and look good

Knight of the spigot: *A tapster, a publican* * A knight of the spigot owned a pub in the olden times when the common people used to come to enjoy their drinks

Knight of the stick: *A compositor* * A knight of the stick is busy in setting up the text and illustration for a book before it is printed

Knight of the whip: *A coachman* * In the past a knight of the whip used to drive a horse-drawn coach

Knit one's brows: *Frown* * An angry man instantly knits his brow

Knit-wear: *Knitted clothing* * There is good sale of knitwears in the market, especially in the winter

Knock about: *Saunter or loaf about, travel about; roughing it and having varied experience; hit repeatedly* * He has knocked about all over Asia * She is knocking about with a married man * There is a loafer knocking about from place to place * I knocked about the country area for few months to apprise myself of the lifestyle of the people there * The ship had been knocked about by storms

Knock all of a heap: *To confound* * He got knocked all of a heap when he found himself between the devil and the deep sea

Knocked against: *Collide with* * The two vehicles knocked against each other head on

Knock at the door: *Strike* * Go and see who is knocking at the door!

Knock back: *Drink; to cost* * He knocked back a pint of whisky and went to sleep * How much did that car knock you back?

Knock down: *Fell down with a blow; assign to bidder with a tap of the auctioneer's hammer; demolish; take to pieces to save cost and space; compel to lower a price; very low (price)* * The hailstorm knocked down the ripe crop * He was strong enough to knock me down with a single punch * The painting was knocked down to the highest bidder for five million rupees * The old houses are to be knocked down * The heavy machine will be knocked down before being packed for shipment to Singapore * He wanted to sell his car for a higher price but I managed to knock him down to a lower amount * I had to pay a knock-down price for this vintage car

Knock into a cocked hat: *Give a profound beating* * The heavyweight wrestler knocked his opponent into a cocked hat

Knock-kneed: *Having knees that touch other when walking* * He is knock-kneed by birth and cannot run at all

Knock off: *Leave off; accomplish hastily; strike off; deduct; steal* * It is time to knock off the work for tea * I thought I would knock off the essay in no time * He was smart enough to knock off six runs needed to win the match * I will knock off the price of this article by a few rupees only * He was planning to knock off a few videos from my room

Knock one off the perch: *Stop one from being confident and superior* * We knocked that fastidious person off his perch by exploiting his weak points in public

Knock on the head: *Suppress, put an end to* * America knocked on the head of Japanese military strategy by using atom bombs

Knockout: *The act of knocking out; a blow that knocks out; a combination of dealers at an auction; any person or thing surpasses eliminating losers at each end; overwhelm, stun; empty by knocking; extremely attractive* * The boxer won the bout by a knockout of his opponent * He succeeded by a knockout victory * The sale of a commercial plot would be decided through a knock out * Last year we won the knockout cup * She was knocked out by sad news * He knocked out his pipe for a fresh smoking * She looked a knock-out in her new dress

Knockout competition: *Contest where several teams compete against each other and are eliminated in turn* * Several hockey teams have gathered here for a knockout competition

Knock spots off somebody: *Easily surpass* * There is one student who knocks spots of all the others

Knock together: *Get together or construct hastily* * As the book-shelves had obviously been knocked together, they look rather out of place in the beautifully furnished room

Knock the bottom out of: *Make invalid or make ineffectual; bring to naught* * Please let us know the justification for knocking the bottom out of this suggestion * He knocked the bottom out of the draft agreement with his arguments

Knock up: *Practice immediately before a match; wake or rouse somebody by knocking at the door; make tired or exhausted; arrange or put together quickly; score* * Let us do some knocking before we start the football game or tennis game * Please could you knock me up at seven o' clock * He will knock up after the steep climb * Knock up a meal from whatever there is in the kitchen * He knocked up a century in the cricket match

Knock under: *Give in or yield* * He had to knock under pressure and remain silent over the matter

Knotty problem: *Very difficult problem to be solved* * Sometimes we have to face knotty problems for which we find no easy answers

Knowing card: *One who is wide awake* * You cannot throw dust into his eyes for he is a knowing card

Knowing to: *Informed; aware* * It is a good thing to keep oneself knowing to important events happening over the globe

Know a hawk from a hand saw: *Be able to judge between things very well* * A scrupulous person can know a hawk from a hand saw and does not need anybody's guidance

Know a man by his company: *Determine his character by the quality of his friend* * If you want to be known as a good person, then be friendly with good persons because it has been rightly said that it is easy to know a man by his company

Know a move or two: *Be sharp or knowing* * He knows a move or two to be able to respond to your tricky question

Know a thing or two: *Be shrewd* * He knows a thing or two on how to tackle a given situation

Know about: *Have information concerning; be aware of* * I know that * I did not know about that * I know of an excellent little restaurant near here

Know all: *Person who claims he knows everything* * He always boasts of his being a know-all

Know better: *Be too wise or well instructed* * We must depend on him for our safety because he knows better than us

Know better than to do something: *One should have better knowledge of the work* * You ought to know better than to go swimming on such a cold day

Know by repute: *Not seen but know from the people who know* * I know the person you are talking about by repute only

Know by sight: *Be familiar with appearance only* * Though I do not know his name and native place, yet I do know him by sight

Know-how: *Knowledge about how something is made* * India is now second to none in the know-how of advanced information technology

Know-nothing: *One who is quite ignorant; totally ignorant person* * Know-nothing persons still can be found in remote hilly tracks * He is know-nothing on this subject, so it is useless to seek his advice

Know no bounds: *Be beyond control* * His joy knew no bounds when he hit the jackpot

Know of: *Be aware of* * I know of him very well

Know one's business: *Have common sense, good judgments, practical experience* * You need not guide him as he knows his business very well

Know one from Adam: *Have no idea who one is* * I don't know him from Adam

Know one's onion: *Be clever (be experienced)* * He knows his onions and can easily surmount the mechanical difficulties

Know one's own mind: *Be clear and firm in one's views* * As he knows his own mind you need not guide him on this point

Know somebody from somebody: *Distinguish from* * They are twins and it is almost impossible to know one from the other

Know the ropes: *Understand details of procedure; know all about something* * A lawyer knows the ropes on how to defend his clients in court under different circumstances * The moment he got to know the ropes of his profession, his happiness knew no bounds

Know the time of the day: *Be wide awake* * Those who know the time of day cannot be befooled by anyone

Know what it is like to: *Have personal experience of* * He knows what it is like to be a statesman

Know what o'clock it is: *Be wide awake or know things are* * You need not advise him on the issue as he already knows what o'clock it is

Know which side one's bread is buttered on: *Know how to act from self interest or where one's interest lies* * *Know where one may have advantage* * Almost everyone knows which side his bread is buttered on * Let him do his own business because he knows on which side his bread is buttered

Know where the shoe pinches: *Know by direct experience what the trouble or difficulty is* * Only the wearer knows where the shoe pinches * He has already been through many difficulties and knows where the shoe pinches

Know who's who: *Know the position and influence of everyone* * It would help you to know who's who as it may help you in your profession as a public relations officer

Known as: *Going by name of* * Bombay is now known as Mumbai

Knuckle down: *Apply oneself earnestly to work* * It is high time for you to knuckle down to some hard study

Knuckle under: *Submit; yield* * He refused to knuckle under any threat from any quarter

L

Labour of love: *Work undertaken without hope of emolument* * I will certainly do that for you as a labour of love

Labour the point – *Place too much stress on an argument* * I had to labour the point repeatedly to bring home the necessity of observing punctuality in every walk of life

Labour under delusion: *Be affected by a false notion; have a persistently wrong impression* * I still laboured under the delusion that policeman never told lies * He is still labouring under a delusion that he would get a handsome prize for his achievements

Labour with: *Take pains to convince* * He had to labour with solid examples to drive home his point to the audience

Lace up: *Fasten with laces* * Put on your shoes and lace them up properly

Laced mutton: *A prostitute* * He thought she was a laced mutton

Lack for: *Need* * They lacked for nothing as they had everything they wanted

Lack in: *Not have enough of; be without* * He is lacking in courage * What I lack in experience I make up with my knowledge

Lack of: *Want of* * There is no lack of fair-weather friends

Lack of restraint: *Excessive freedom* * Lack of restraint led him to lose his temper at the drop of a hat

Lack-love: *One who is deficient in love* * A lack-love person cannot be a good husband

Lack-lustre: *Dull* * Everybody felt disappointment at her lack-lustre performance

Laden with: *Carrying a heavy load* * The ship laden with cargo will reach the port tomorrow

Ladle out: *Give freely and in large quantities; serve with a ladle* * Our educational institutions ladle out knowledge on all aspects of our life * He ladled out the curry to the guests sitting in a row

Lady's man: *A person who makes*

*efforts to charm women** A lady's man would like to be in the society of women

Lag in quality: *Not keep up with quality** It has been found that in comparison to Japanese products, Chinese goods lag in quality

Laid to rest: *Buried** The dead body of the great hero has been laid to rest in the churchyard

Laid up with: *Suffer from* * My uncle is laid up with high fever

Laid work: *In embroidery, couching of the simplest kind* * She is deeply interested in learning laid work

Laid-back: *Unhurried; relaxed* * A laid-back man loves to work at his own sweet will

Lame duck: *A defaulter; bankrupt; anything disables; disabled person or business organization in financial difficulties* * Don't be a lame duck in your official duty * The company has become a lame duck as it is not able to clear its debts * He is a lame duck and stands in need of an artificial leg * He was yet another of my mother's lame ducks

Lame excuse: *Unsatisfactory cause* * Offering a lame excuse will not help you in getting pardoned by your boss

Land on one's feet: *Be lucky; escape injury* * We were lucky to land on our feet after our successful expedition to Mount Everest * It was a miracle that all the passengers landed on their feet when the plane caught fire while landing the airport

Land somebody in: *Get into trouble, difficulties* * What a mess you have landed us all in!

Land up: *Arrive or find oneself* * If you go on behaving in this manner, you will land in prison one day

Landed property: *Immovable property* * He is the owner of a great deal of landed property

Landmark: *Outstanding /Important event* * The history of mankind is replete with many landmarks

Landslide: *Slipping of large amount of earth* * A landslide is a common phenomenon on the hills in the rainy season

Lap of luxury: *Great luxury* * It is said that Motilal Nehru was brought up in the lap of luxury.

Lap up: *Drink by taking up with*

the tongue * The cat quickly lapped up all the milk

Lapse from something into something: *Fail to keep one's position (from good ways into bad ways)* * It was disgraceful on his part to lapse from virtue into vice

Lapse of time: *Gliding away of time* * Many changes have occurred with lapse of time

Lard with: *(often derogatory) Enrich* * The speech that he made was larded with boring quotations

Large paper edition: *A special edition with wider margin* * The large paper edition of *India Today* is out of print

Lark about: *Fool around* * Juveniles were larking about on the festive day

Lash into: *Rouse into* * The speaker lashed at his listeners for interrupting him

Lash out: *Hit violently; kick out; fling out; hit out without restraint* * The hijacker of the plane was cornered but he savagely lashed out at the police * The landlord lashed out at the defaulting tenant * She lashed out of the room fearing some danger * Our security force lashed out at the hostile militants

Lash out on: *Become very extravagant and spend a large sum of money* * The rich anthropologist plans to lash out on the needy and poor people on the auspicious occasion

Lash something down: *Make it secure with rope* * You had better lash the car with the trunk of this strong tree to avoid any damage to it against the fury of the tornado

Lash things together: *Fasten tightly together (with rope, etc)* * They lashed the boats together on the bank of river at the fall of night

Lashed out against: *Attack violently (with woods)* * He lashed out against the government for its diplomatic lapses

Last but not the least: *Used when mentioning the last person or thing of a group in order to say that they are not less important than the others* * I am grateful to you all and last but not the least to my parents who have always stood by me through thick and thin

Last but one: *The one before the end one* * For answer to the question you can refer to the paragraph last but one on Page 18 of your history book

Last castes: *Extremities* * To get rid of the biting cold I had to warm my last castes by sitting before the fire

Last honours: *Funeral rites* * The corpse of the brave soldier is being readied for the last honours

Last out: *Last as long as; last to the end* * The food stored in the house is enough to last out for a month * Will Smith last out on his new job?

Last straw: *That beyond which there can be no possible endurance* * He kept on annoying me and if he does it any more it will turn out to be the last straw in my patience

Last thing at night: *At the very end of the day* * The last thing at night to do is to say your prayers

Last rites * *Communion for someone who is dying* * He died after receiving the last rites of the Church

Latch on: *Cling to; understand; get possession of* * We see the young ones of the monkeys latching on to the chest of their mother * I could latch on the riddle all at once * He latched on to the secret documents which revealed his role in the conspiracy

Later on: *At a later time* * He was arrested as a suspect but released later on

Latter end: *The final part; the end of life* * The latter end of the story will be told tomorrow * After all we have to kiss the latter end

Laugh at: *Ridicule* * It is unkind to laugh at a person who is in trouble

Laugh away: *Dismiss* * He laughed away his fears that had troubled him without real cause

Laugh down: *Silence by laughing scornfully* * They laughed the proposal down as it was not found free from flaws

Laugh in somebody's face: *Defy openly or show contempt for* * Everybody laughed in the face of the thief for his ill-deeds

Laugh off: *Escape from or get rid of by laughing; make light of* * They laughed off an embarrassing situation they landed in * We should laugh off the insults heaped on us by those trouble-makers

Laugh on the other side of one's face: *Change from joy or triumph to sorrow or regret* * The people had to laugh on the other side of their faces in the cinema hall when they heard a fire-alarm

Laugh on the wrong side of the mouth: *Be made to feel*

disappointment or sorrow especially after boasting* He had to laugh on the wrong side of the mouth when his friends rebuked him

Laugh one's head off: *Laugh heartily* * We laughed our heads off at the pranks played (or cracked) by one of our friends

Laugh over: *Discuss with laughter; laugh while discussing or examining, etc;* * There arose many occasions in the meeting when the members could not help laughing over them * He laughed over the contents of the letter he was reading

Laugh to scorn: *Deride or jeer at* * I had laughed him to scorn for his sense of superiority

Laugh up one's sleeves: *Be secretly amused* * They laughed up their sleeves when the speaker fumbled when making his maiden speech

Laughing stock: *An object of ridicule* * Clowns in the circus are expected to make themselves a laughing stock * The unruly race-horse became a laughing stock for the spectators * Do not make yourself a laughing stock by wearing that ugly dress

Launch into: *Make or start (on); send* * He launched into a long speech about the dangers of taking drugs * Many countries have been launching missiles in the orbit

Launch out: *Start doing something expensive or ambitious* * They have launched out a plan to explore outer space phenomenon

Launch something against: *To push something against* * It has become necessary to launch an attack against the damage caused to crops by locusts

Launch something at: *To start a campaign* * I have decided to launch a party at the release of my book

Lavish favour upon: *Show generous or profuse favour* * The king lavished his favour upon the loyal soldier

Lavish in: *Unrestrained* * That landlady is rather lavish in her expenditure

Law and order: *Peace and cooperation* * It is necessary for the government to maintain law and order in the state

Law of Nature: *Invariable order of Nature; Nature's law* * Birth and death just like day and night or change in seasons is the law of Nature

Law of succession: *Law relating to succession* * In England the law of succession is still in force for the successor to the throne * The case was decided under law of succession in his favour

Law of the land: *The established law of the country* * Every citizen has an obligation to abide by the law of the land

Law-abiding: *Having respect for and obedient to law; obeying the law* * The first duty of the state is to ensure that law-abiding people are protected from law-breakers * Peace and prosperity are the primary needs of law-abiding citizens

Law-breaker: *Person who disobeys the law* * A law-breaker is a curse on any society

Laws of honour: *Rules prevailing in fashionable societies* * It is a good thing to abide by laws of honour

Lax in: *Loose in* * He is lax in his morals

Lay a burden on somebody: *Cause him to be responsible for something* * Our educational system lays a heavy burden on our school-going youngsters

Lay a carpet: *Place in the right position* * The servant was asked to lay a carpet in the drawing room

Lay a ghost/spirit: *Causing it to stop appearing to people* * They had to call in an exorcist to lay a ghost from the affected person

Lay a great store on something: *Value very much* * He lays a great store on leading a disciplined life

Lay a siege to: *Surrounded and blockade it* * The English forces laid a siege to the Red Fort at Delhi during Mughal rule

Lay a snare: *Prepare one* * He is thinking of laying a snare to bring the cheat to book

Lay a strict injunction on somebody: *Give one strict orders* * The magistrate has laid a strict injunction on his movement

Lay a tax on something: *Impose on* * The municipal committee is thinking of laying a tax on all residential premises

Lay a wager: *To bet* * Do not compel me to lay a wager on this particular business

Lay about one: *Deal blows vigorously on all sides* * The policeman sprang forward and began to lay about the unruly mob with his baton

Lay aside: *Discard; put apart for future use* * He laid his book aside to listen to me * Should they lay aside the present system entirely? * We must lay aside some money for our rainy days

Lay at: *Endeavour to strike* * A lay at the mill is possible if the employees' demands are not acceded to

Lay at the door of: *Impute; be imputed* * The responsibility for the strike was laid at the door of the employers * A great many faults may be laid at his door but he is certainly not dishonest

Lay bare: *Disclose; expose; make bare* * The commission will soon lay bare its report in the rioting case * The Queen's Rose Garden was laid bare to the common public * The police party grilled the spy to lay bare his hidden activities

Lay before: *Submit (as of plans)* * He will lay his plans before the committee for necessary consideration

Lay by: *Keep for future use; dismiss; put off* * A wise person would lay by some money for his old age * He laid by his ideas that did not work * Never lay by anything for tomorrow as it never gets done then

Lay by the heels: *To fetter or put into confinement* * He was laid by the heels for having committed a crime

Lay claim to: *Assert a right; demand as one's due* * He is likely to lay claim to further promotion on the basis of his seniority * If the land really belongs to you, why don't you lay claim to it?

Lay down: *Give up; deposit as a pledge; delineate; assert; plant; place in a lying or recumbent position; begin to build; sacrifice; convert (land to pasture); place or ground; store* * He laid down the title given to him * How much are you ready to lay down in this hire-purchase bargain? * These prices have been laid down by the manufacturers * You cannot lay down hard and fast rules in this connection * The area where mines have been laid down is a danger zone * Lay the baby down gently on the bed * He laid down his life for the country * This land has been laid down to make a playing field * He laid down his clothes before he began to swim in the pool * He has been accused of laying down unauthorised wine in the cellar

Lay down one's arms: *Surrender; submit* * The terrorists had no option but to lay down their arms before the security forces

Lay down the law: *Authoritatively or dictatorially in place of authority* * Nobody can lay down the law against the Constitution of the country

Lay flat: *Damage* * The crops were laid flat by the heavy rains and hailstorm

Lay hands on: *Seize; obtain; subject physically to rough treatment; bless or ordain by touching with the hand; try to commit suicide; find; assault* * The police failed to lay their hands on the most wanted criminal * He keeps everything he can lay his hands on * How dare you lay hands on me? * I considered myself lucky when the Bishop laid his hands on me * I have the book somewhere but am unable to lay hands on it just now * It is reported that some ruffians laid hands on him while he was returning home

Lay heads together: *Confer and cooperate* * The jury laid heads together for a few minutes before announcing the verdict * They laid their heads together and expressed their opinion

Lay hold of: *Seize* * The policeman laid hold of him by the collar

Lay in: *Get in a supply of* * The government has laid in a sufficient supply of foodgrains to meet any emergency

Lay in ambush: *Lie in wait* * The police laid an ambush to arrest the smugglers

Lay into: *Beat thoroughly* * He hopes to lay into the intruders before handing them over to the police

Lay it on: *Charge exorbitantly; do anything as to exaggerate* * We would advise you not to lay it on the already large structure of the existing building

Lay it on thick: *Flatter or praise extravagantly* * To win his sympathy, he laid it on thick with his master

Lay low: *Overthrow; fell; kill* * A heavy storm laid the crops low * Either of the two wrestlers will be laid low at the end of the bout * We don't know how to lay low the stinking smell

Lay of the land: *Nature or foundation of an area of land* * The lay of the land at the foot of the hill is quite plain

Lay off: *Discontinue work; mark off; dismiss temporarily* * The doctor told me to lay off for a week * He has laid off the area with lengths of string * The director made plans to lay off 500 workers * He laid off his hat and coat before he went to bed

Lay on: *Instal a supply of; provide; deal blows vigorously* * We cannot occupy the new house until gas and water pipes are laid on * Bus service is likely to be laid on to distinguished visitors for sight-seeing * Both of the boxers laid on punches on each other during the match

Lay on load: *Belabour* * The robbers laid him on load soundly

Lay on the table: *Lay aside for further discussion* * This important item may be laid on the table for discussion at the forthcoming meeting

Lay one self out to: *Take great pains; make it one's professed object* * The host laid himself out to make his guests comfortable * That man has laid himself out to be an eminent musician

Lay one's fingers on: *Point out precisely* * At last I could lay my fingers on the real culprit during the course of investigation

Lay one's hopes on: *Pin one's hopes on* * He lays his hopes on his only son to look after him in his old age

Lay oneself open to ridicule: *Behave so that people are likely to make fun of one* * A foolish person does not mind laying himself open to ridicule

Lay oneself open to something: *Behave so that one is vulnerable to something; render oneself liable to criticism* * Don't lay yourself open to ridicule * He laid himself open to strictures for filing an incomplete report

Lay open: *Cut open; make bare; expose; show* * He had a nasty fall and laid open his head * Do not lay yourself open to ridicule * He jumped down and his shoelaces lay open * He had to lay open his passport at the check-post

Lay out: *Prepare for burial; expend; display; plan; fell; take measure; seek* * We laid him out in his old military uniform * We have to lay out our money carefully * Clothes, jewels, etc. were laid out on the counter of the shop * An informal lay out of the streets and avenues is being prepared by town planners * He laid out his enemy with a single blow * The commander laid out the enemy's strength before making an attack * He is going to Canada to lay out his fortune

Lay over: *Stop at a place during a journey because of a requirement in schedule* * I had to lay over at Delhi in connection with some business dealings

Lay salt on one's tail: *Find or catch one from the recommended method of catching a bird* * The best way to bluff that cunning man is to lay salt on his tail

Lay seize to: *Besiege; importune* * The Muslim soldiers laid siege to the fort for two months * He began to lay siege to her with offers of marriage

Lay somebody under contribution: *Compel one to contribute money* * Many societies have laid their members under contribution to help the victims of the tsunami tragedy

Lay somebody's doubts: *Get rid of them* * He laid his doubts on seeing the concrete proofs

Lay something to somebody's charge: *Hold one responsible* * The university has laid evaluation of answer books to the charge of a highly qualified person

Lay stress on something: *Treat it as importance* * We must lay stress on discipline in every walk of our life

Lay the blame on somebody: *Say that he is responsible for what is wrong* * The people laid blame on him for neglect of his duties

Lay the cloth: *Prepare table for meal* * The maid knew the timings to lay the cloth for lunch or dinner

Lay the table: *Place dishes, etc.* * Do lay the table for three persons only

Lay the venue: *Specify the place where the trial is to be held* * Just lay the venue where we can meet and have a heart-to-heart talk

Lay to: *Apply with vigour; bring a ship to rest* * He laid himself to studies * The overused ship has been laid to rest

Lay to heart: *Store in the mind for future guidance; be deeply moved by something* * I have laid to heart the good piece of advice that my teacher gave me * He laid to heart his failure in the examination

Lay to rest: *Bury* * He was laid to rest in the churchyard

Lay under: *Subject to* * He was laid under an obligation to support the wife he had deserted

Lay up: *Store up; preserve; confine to bed or one's room; put in dock after dismantling* * Do all the squirrels lay up food for the winter? * He has been laid up with a broken leg * The bout of flu has laid him up for a few days * The old warship was laid up for repairs

Lay up with: *Unwell* * He could not attend office because he was laid up with high fever

Lay upon: *Wager upon* * He laid five dollars upon that black, sturdy race horse

Lay wait: *Lay in wait or in ambush* * The highwayman lay in wait to loot the passengers

Lay waste: *Devastate* * The crops were laid waste by hailstorm

Laying on of hands: *Confirmation; ordination; consecration* * Laying on of hands admits persons to full membership of the church

Lay-man: *Person having no expert knowledge* * So far as the law is concerned, I am a layman

Layout: *Design* * The layout of this garden is rather attractive

Lazy painter: *A small painter for use in fine weather only* * A lazy painter can be employed for painting the boat for immediate use

Lead a cat and dog life: *Lead a life of constant quarrelling* * The old husband and young wife are living a cat and dog life these days

Lead a woman to altar: *Marry her* * One who leads a woman to the altar becomes her husband socially and also in the eyes of the law

Lead apes in hell: *Thought to be the lot of old maids in afterlife* * It would like leading apes in hell if we employ aged persons for delivering the goods

Lead astray: *Draw into a wrong course; reduce from right conduct* * The boy was laid astray by his bad companions * Don't be laid astray in making use of narcotics

Lead by the nose: *Make one follow submissively* * She leads her husband by the nose in almost every matter * He refused to be led by the nose

Lead in: *House the harvest* * The farmers are doing their best to lead in the crops in time before the advent of bad weather

Lead me to think: *Make me think* * The servant's tall stories led me to think that he was lying

Lead off: *Begin or take the start in anything* * The chairman will lead off the proceedings of the meeting

Lead on: *Go ahead so that other will follow; persuade to go on; draw on* * He led them all to take part in the strike * The proper way to lead him on towards the progressive path is to boost his morale * The company can lead on their vast resources to pay for the project

Lead one a dance: *Keep one involved unnecessarily in a series of wearying perplexities and vexations* * I left the job because he wanted to lead me a dance

Lead one up the garden: *Mislead one* * Do not lead me up the garden by enticing me into gambling

Lead out: *Conduct to execution; a dance* * The hangman led out the condemned person to be hanged

Lead somebody on: *Entice somebody to do more than he intended* * Do not lead him on to earn more money at the cost of his health

Lead somebody to a dog's life: *Make his life wretched* * His habit of gambling made him lead a dog's life

Lead the way: *Act as a guide in any movement; go first; show the way; go first and guide others* * Abraham Lincoln led the way successfully in the movement to set his countrymen free * Who will lead the way in the climbing expedition? * He will lead the way on how to lay an ambush to hold the smugglers * Who is going to lead the way in this risky expedition?

Lead to: *Carry* * This road leads to the general post office * Your habit of stealing would certainly lead you to jail one day

Lead up to: *Bring about by degrees; prepare for steps or stages; prepare the way for* * The hostility between the two nations led them up to the war * That is just what I was leading up to * Your efforts would certainly lead you up to some positive results

Lead with: *Have as a main article or news story* * We will lead with the story of dock strike in our today's newspapers

Leading business: *The acting of principal parts or roles in plays* * Who do you think will be entrusted with the job of leading business in the next film of Karan Johar?

Leading light: *A very influential member* * Lala Lajpat Rai was a leading light in the Congress Party in days of yore

Leading man or lady: *Actor or actress taking the main role* * Who is the leading man or lady in this movie?

Leading question: *A question so put as to suggest the desired answer* * The leading question on how to bring about harmony and peace in the country depends on the politicians

Leaf mould: *Compost made of rotten leaves* * Farmers make use of leaf mould in enriching the soil for their crops

Leaf through the pages of a book: *Turn them rapidly without reading* * Why are you leafing through the pages of your book?

Leak out: *Find vent; get to the public ears* * The floods leaked out through the dykes * It has been leaked out that Pakistan provided nuclear know-how to North Korea, Libya, etc. * The corruption racket has been leaked out by the subordinate

Lean a hand (with): *Help with* * Please lean me a hand with the washing-up

Lean on / upon: *Depend* * Sometimes I have to lean on/upon my friend's advice for proper guidance

Lean on a reed: *Trust in something weak* * Everybody is prudent enough not to lean on a reed

Lean over: *To bend* * He leaned over the window to get a better view

Lean over backwards: *Be accommodative; make every effort* * He leaned over backwards to please his old friend at the cost of his own comforts * He leant over backwards to help the poor boy

Lean towards: *Have a tendency* * Why do most oriental philosophies lean towards fatalism?

Leap at: *Seize or accept eagerly* * A wise man would certainly leap at the opportunity

Leap in the dark: *Action where you are unsure of the consequences; an act of which we cannot foresee the consequences* * He took a leap in the dark by sitting in the competitive exams without preparation * His hasty marriage to an actress was a leap in the dark

Leap year: *Year with 366 days* * Any year in which February has 29 days instead of the usual 28 is called a leap year

Learn by heart: *Commit to memory* * That scholar has learnt by heart all the hymns written in Sanskrit

Learn by rote: *Cram* * Most of the students learn a few questions by rote and sit in the examination hall

Learn the hard way: *Learn with perseverance and hardship* * We have to learn everything the hard way if we want to attain a prominent place in life

Leave a margin for error: *Allow extra space or time in case you have made a mistake in your calculation* * Make sure not to leave any margin for error in the completion of this crucial project

Leave alone: *Let remain undisturbed* * You had better leave that dog alone if you do not want to get bitten by it

Leave behind: *Forget to take* * The luggage has been left behind * Do not leave me behind

Leave for: *Go away to* * We are leaving for London next Monday

Leave go (of something): *Cease holding* * Leave go of my hair, you brute!

Leave in the dark: *Conceal* * It would be in your own interest to leave this matter in the dark

Leave in the lurch: *Leave in a difficult situation without help; leave in difficulties* * When he fell prey to adversity, even his best friends left him in the lurch * Selfish persons tend to leave their friends in the lurch

Leave it at that: *Be wild about someone (with worry/grief)* * Let us leave it at that as there is nothing we can do in it

Leave it to one's discretion: *Leave it to one's decision* * I leave it to your discretion to either join government service or do some private business

Leave no effects: *Die without property to bequeath* * He died peacefully and left no effects behind

Leave no stone unturned: *Do everything that can be done in order to secure the effect desired* * They left no stone unturned in search of the missing girl

Leave nothing to be desired: *Be satisfactory* * His behaviour leaves nothing to be desired

Leave of absence: *Permission to be absent* * The soldier asked for leave of absence for four hours

Leave off: *Desist; terminate; give up using* * They have been warned to leave off such foolish activities * It is time to leave off your work * Do leave off biting your nails

Leave one cold: *Fail to impress* * We expected a good performance from him in the declamation contest but he left us cold

Leave out: *Omit* * I have left out attempting two difficult questions in the mathematics paper

Leave out in the cold: *Neglect; ignore* * A progressive nation cannot afford to leave out in the cold the deprived section of the society

Leave somebody out on a limb: *Put one in a vulnerable position* * Help your brother instead of leaving him out on a limb at the time of adversity

Leave somebody to himself: *Not try to control or direct his activities* * The children were left very much to themselves during the holidays

Leave something or somebody alone: *Not touch; spoil or interfere with* * Let him leave alone so that he may pay full attention towards his studies * Do not leave that beautiful oil painting out in the open for exposure to the sun's rays

Leave something over: *Postpone* * After you have eaten all that you want leave something over for her to eat

Leave something to: *Bequeath by will* * She left all her money to charity * He left me a large sum of money before leaving the country

Leave something unsaid: *Not say it* * Some things are better left unsaid

Leave to one's own resources: *Leave to look after oneself* * He was left to his own resources by his parents soon after his employment

Left-luggage office: *Place where suitcases, etc. can be left and collected later on for a fee* * Before leaving the hotel for sightseeing, we handed over our clothing kits and attaché cases to the left-luggage office

Left to one's devices: *Left to do whatever one wanted* * He has been left to his devices in the matter of choosing his career

Left-handed: *Using the left hand more than the right* * He is a left-handed man

Left-handed compliment: *A saying intended to seem a com-*

pliment but in reality the reverse * He extended a left-handed compliment to his wife when she was going out in a dirty dress

Left-over: *Remaining over from a previous occasion; survival* * The left-over agenda is likely to be taken up for consideration by the committee tomorrow * The stone tool is a left-over from the pre-machine age

Leftovers: *What is not used especially food which has not been eaten* * Having done full justice to our bellies, we distributed the leftovers to the beggars

Legal tender: *That which a creditor can not refuse in payment of a debt* * A legal tender is a binding and must be accepted under all circumstances

Lend a hand: *Give assistance; help* * I was expecting you to lend me a hand on that occasion * When he was in trouble, I lent him a helping hand

Lend a hand (on): *To settle* * It is the need of the hour to lend a hand on the bargain

Lend an ear: *Listen* * He did not lend an ear to my genuine request

Lend credit to: *Strengthen belief in* * The latest news lends credit to the earlier reports

Lend oneself to something: *Give or accommodate* * Do not lend yourself to such dishonest schemes

Lend to the ground: *Destroy completely* * The dilapidated building was lend to the ground

Lend wings to: *Cause to go fast* * The fear of getting reprimanded lent him wings

Lending-library: *One from which books may be borrowed* * The college management has opened a lending-library for the benefit of its students

Length of days: *Prolonged life* * Advanced medicinal therapy has enhanced our length of days to a great extent

Let alone: *Absence of restraint; refrain from interference; leaving things to themselves; to say nothing of; not to mention; not to interfere with* * He cannot find money to buy the basic necessities, let alone buy luxury goods * Let the sleeping dog lie alone * Let him alone carry out his work independently * There were five people in the car, let alone a pile of luggage and two dogs * It would be advisable to let this critical matter alone

Let by-gone be by-gones: *Let*

past quarrels be ignored * Let the by-gone be by-gones and forget the enmity of the past few years

Let down: *Allow to fall; to lower; leave in the lurch; fail to back up at need* * She let down her hair on reaching her favourite city * This skirt needs letting down * You can depend on his help for he is not the one to let you down * A true friend would never let you down under difficult situations

Let drive: *Aim a blow* * He let drive at me with his left fist * He let drive at me with a stone

Let fall: *To drop* * Let the curtain fall as the play has come to an end

Let fly: *Attack; throw or send fired* * He lost his temper and let fly at my face * He aimed carefully and then let fly off at the duck

Let go: *Cease holding; slacken; release; or; quit hold of* * He let himself go on the subject * Why don't you let go your tough attitude? * Don't let the rope go * The police let him go after some interrogation

Let in: *Allow to enter; take in or swindle;get fooled by a false claim or promise; insert; leak inwards; make narrower* * The windows let in light and air * Who let you into the building? * Do not let yourself in by his false promises * By voting for the dark horse in the election, they did not know what they were letting themselves in for * He let in the wooden peg into the hole * The boat was letting in badly * This skirt needs letting in at the waist

Let into: *Admit to the knowledge of; allow to share* * They agreed to let him into their secret * He has been let into their plan by an informer

Let it pass now: *Let it take place* * I do not like it but I will let it pass now

Let it to me: *Let me deal with it* * This matter is beyond your comprehension, so let it to me

Let loose: *Allow to be free; set at liberty; allow to be free from control; set free what was bound* * Do not let that dog loose * The accused was let loose for want of solid proof on his misconduct * He let out his indignation after hearing the whole story * Violence was let loose by the Americans in North Vietnam

Let me alone: *Don't pester me* * Let me alone as I am

trying to complete my homework

Let me see: *A phrase employed to express reflection* * Well, let me see if I can complete my work in time

Let off: *Allow to go free* * *Without exacting all; fire off; discharge* * He was let off with a fine instead of being sent to prison * The boys were letting off fireworks * He was let off from the hospital last week

Let off steam: *Release steam into atmosphere; work off energy; give vent to anger* * Remove the lid of the kettle to let off steam * She let off her steam by weeping * He let off his feelings in an impassioned speech

Let on: *Allow to be believed; pretend; reveal; divulge; betray awareness* * I was furious when he let on to everyone about my being involved in taking drugs * The beggar let on himself by acting as a blind and dumb * He knew where the boy was hiding but he did not let on * To save his skin, he let on his ignorance of the antecedents of the accused

Let one know: *Inform one* * Let him know that his request has been turned down

Let one stew in one's own juice: *Let one alone and await development* * He let her stew in her own juice for a day or two to make her realise her blunder

Let oneself in for: *Allow oneself to get in* * Be careful and do not let yourself in for any difficult situation

Let oneself lose: *Let go of restraint; indulge in extravagant talk or conduct* * Do not let yourself lose on his provocative remarks * He let himself lose in self-praise which he hardly deserved

Let out: *Allow to get free; strike out; kick out; enlarge; widen; slacken; put to hire; leak outwards; allow to go out (flow); put out to hire; way of avoiding something which you ought to do* * He has been let out by the judge on bail * Avoid getting hurt by a mule that has a habit of letting out at people * He is getting so fat that his trousers need to be let out round the waist * In order to let out the horizon, they are being given training in dancing * He did not let out his grip on my right wrist for a long time * The vacant accommodation in this building is to be let out * This tap is letting the water out and needs due repair * He let the air out of the tyres * He used to let out house by the day * There is no let out for this stinking stagnant water

Let sleeping dogs lie: *Let well alone, not look for trouble; avoid discussing problems that are likely to cause trouble* * It is better not to rake up the issue as it is advisable to let the sleeping dogs lie * Since he has forgotten the issue, let us allow the sleeping dogs to lie

Let something pass: *Overlook; disregard* * Let us allow it to pass since it is not a serious error

Let something pass unchallenged: *Let something be said or written without questioning it* * The Speaker let the discussion pass unchallenged in the House

Let something slip: *Miss an opportunity* * Do not let this last chance slip by at this stage

Let the cat out of the bag: *Disclose the secret* * We tried our best to guard our secret but John let the cat out of the bag

Let the grass grow under one's feet: *Linger* * We should remain active and not let the grass grow under our feet

Let the matter rest: *Not to deal with the problem any more* * Let this matter rest since the authority concerned is not interested in it

Let the past bury its dead: *Forget all about the past lost opportunities or lapses* * Instead of weeping for the past, let the past bury its dead

Let things go hang: *Take no interest in or care of them* * We should let things go hang which are beyond our grasp

Let things slide: *Allow things to become worse or not to take care if things get worse* * I have just let things slide which may now turn to be detrimental to my own interest

Let up: *Become less; abate* * Will the rain never let up? * The ship will sail when the storm lets up

Let up on: *Cease to do with; treat more leniently* * He let up on his neighbour after some quarrel * I cannot let up on him for his insolence

Let well alone: *Don't try to improve something that is already satisfactory; let things remain as they are from fear of making them worse* * There is trouble brewing in the house, so it is advisable to let well alone the issue * It is better to let well alone rather than to stir up a hornet's nest

Let your hair down: *Relax; become less formal* * You had better let your hair down rather than stand on formalities

Let's adjourn to the bar: *Let's stop talking here and leave for the bar* * Instead of wasting time over here, let's adjourn to the bar

Let-down: *Disappointment* * I felt let-down at his disparaging remarks

Let-off: *Laid aside; discarded* * They let-off their woollen garments when the weather got warm * The censor has let off two of the scenes from the film

Letters: *Literary learning* * He is very fond of letters and bids fair to be a good author one day

Level best: *One's utmost* * He promised that he would do his level best to help me

Level down: *Lower in the same level or status* * He has levelled down his high standard of living

Level off: *Cause an aircraft to fly parallel to the earth's surface; reach a point in one's career, etc.* * On reaching the 1,000 metre height, the pilot levelled off the flight * You are unlikely to get further promotion since you have levelled off the topmost rung of hierarchy

Level to the ground: *Destroy completely* * They will level the building to the ground to make way for a new structure

Level up: *Raise to the same level* * The mason will level up the ground before laying the bricks

Levy in mass: *A levy of all able-bodied men for military service* * It is proposed that all levy in mass be limited to a maximum of six months

Liable for: *Responsible according to law* * Is a man liable for his wife's debts in your country?

Liable to: *Be likely to; subject to; likely to get* * We are all liable to make mistakes * If you drive a car to the danger zone you are likely to get hurt * He is liable to punishment for negligence of duty

Liaise with: *Act as a link* * We have to liaise with them very closely to derive mutual benefits

Liaison officer: *An officer forming a link with another unit or force* * Many organisations appoint a liaison officers to work as the mediator with the government

Liberty hall: *A place where everyone may do as one pleases* * This is not a liberty hall for doing anything you may like!

Liberty of conscience: *Freedom to have one's own belief* * Everybody enjoys liberty of conscience in our country

Liberty of the press: *Freedom to write and print in periodicals, books, etc. whatsoever one wishes without interference; the right of publishing books, etc. without submitting them to a government authority for permission* * Liberty of the press is playing an important role in enlightening the people on various aspects of political and social life * The publication of all types of novels, stories, news, etc. means that there is liberty of the press

Liberty of speech: *Freedom to say openly* * We allow liberty of speech to one and all so long as it is not based on falsehood

Licenced victualler: *Public housekeeper who is licensed to sell food, spirits, beer, etc. to be consumed on the premises of housekeeper* * A licenced victualler generally satiates the needs of the people of lower and middle income groups by allowing them to eat, drink and make merry

Lick one's lips: *Slow eagerness or satisfaction* * He is licking his lips before partaking in a sumptuous meal

Lick into shape: *Mould into satisfactory form* * The house was in a complete mess but we soon licked it into shape

Lick off: *Remove by licking* * The boy licked the jam off his lips

Lick one's boots: *To toady* * He is always licking the boots of his boss to get promotion

Lick one's wounds: *Try to recover after a defeat* * It would be better to leave him alone to lick his wounds in solitude

Lick the dust: *Be slain* * In the battle-field many soldiers on both sides had to lick the dust

Lick up: *Take up by licking* * The cat licked up the milk

Lie along: *Be extended at full length* * He loves to lie along on the grassy ground to enjoy the sunshine

Lie at host: *Be lodged* * You will lie at host so long as you pay the fixed amount of rent for this room regularly

Lie at one's door: *Be directly imputable to one* * The responsibility for this heavy loss clearly lies at your door

Lie at one's heart: *Be an object of interest or affection to one* * It lies at her heart to become a star actress

Lie back: *Be in a resting position* * Now lie back and relax

Lie by: *Be inactive; keep out of the way* * We cannot afford to lie by for long periods * It would be in your own interest to lie by a murderer

Lie by the heels: *Be in prison* * You will have to lie by the heels if you involve yourself in a crime

Lie doggo: *Lie without making a moment or sound* * We were lying doggo in wait for the bootleggers to arrive so that we can nab them

Lie down: *Take rest or sleep* * I helped him to lie down again

Lie down under (an insult): *Fail to protect or resist, etc.* * He found himself helpless to lie down under the pressure

Lie hard upon: *Oppress; burden; distress* * The theft lay hard upon his conscience * The lobster lay heavy on his stomach

Lie in: *Be in childbed* * She is still lying in and is under labour

Lie in one: *Be in one's power* * Legally it lies in him to sentence a criminal up to three years of imprisonment

Lie in one's throat: *Lie shamelessly* * He was found guilty of committing a heinous crime yet he lies in his throat about it

Lie in the bed one has made: *Have to accept the consequences of one's own acts* * The murderer had to lie in the bed he had made for killing an innocent woman in cold blood * You must lie in the bed you have made

Lie in the way: *Be ready; at hand; be an obstacle* * The party is lying in the way for its next move * The photographer snapped all the beautiful spots that lay in the way * We had to overcome all the difficulties lying in the way

Lie in wait: *Lie in ambush* * The soldiers on patrol lay in wait for the arrival of the militants

Lie low: *Keep quiet or hidden; conceal one's actions or intentions* * The escaped prisoner had to lie low for months * The perpetrators of crime lay low their plan for looting the passengers till the train passed through a deserted place

Lie on: *Be incumbent on* * It lies on you to warn the boy of the dangers of smoking

Lie on one's hands: *Remain unwanted or unclaimed* * The suitcase which I found in the train compartment still lies on my hands

Lie on one's oars: *Abstain from rowing without removing the oars from the locks; rest; take things easily; cease working* * They prepared to lie on their oars until the tornado came to a halt * After the examination was over, he went to Paris to lie on his oar * There is now no danger ahead, so we can lie on our oars free from any tension * Since you have succeeded in your mission you richly deserve to lie on your oars

Lie out of: *Remain without the good of or without payment* * Since we were out of pocket, we had to lie out of food for two days

Lie over: *Be deferred to a future occasion* * The meeting had to lie over for want of the necessary quorum

Lie to: *Become almost satisfactory with head to wind* * The ship lay to as a result of the turbulent waves

Lie under: *Be subject to or oppressed by* * The case to be decided lies under the law of the land * His conscience is lying under his own sins

Lie up: *Abstain from work; take to or remain in bed; go into or be in dock* * The doctor has advised him to lie up at least for a fortnight * He has been told to lie up on account of a bad cold * The ship is lying up for loading and unloading the goods

Lie with: *Lodge or sleep with; rest with as a duty, choice, etc.* * A married man should not lie with another woman * The onus of proof of his innocence lies with the accused

Life and soul: *Main figure; a lively and amusing person* * Our principal is the life and soul of our college * He has become the life and soul of every party that he attends * The bridegroom looked to be the life and soul of the marriage party

Life insurance: *Insurance paid if you die* * He is paying his life insurance policy in half yearly instalments

Life like: *Looking like the real person or thing* * Television gives us a life-like view of living beings and other objects

Life's roses: *Delights of life* * He is blessed with life's roses

Lift off: *Rise from the launching site* * We saw the lift off of the long-range rocket as depicted in the television

Lift one's hand: *Raise it in hostility* * I would be forced to lift my hand at you if you are rude to me

Lift shaft: *Hole down the centre of a building or a coal mine in which a lift moves up and down* * All the sky-scrapers have been provided with lift shafts for smooth and comfortable movement

Lift tariff barriers: *Reduce import taxes* * The authorities have lifted tariff barriers on some luxury goods

Lift the face: *Perform an operation for smoothening and firming* * It is up to the surgeon to see how to lift the face of his patient

Lift up one's voice: *Cry out; raise it* * The people will lift up their voice against the price hike of essential commodities * They lifted up their voice against the highhandedness of the police

Light as a feather: *Very light* * This silken dress is as light as a feather

Light at the end of the tunnel: *Promise of better success after a long spell of difficult time* * After months of hard work and no income I saw some light at the end of the dark tunnel when he gave me a job

Light dressed: *Wearing thin clothes* * In summer, people like to be light dressed

Light literature: *Such literature as calls for little mental effort* * He is interested in reading only light literature

Light music: *Such music as calls for little mental effort* * She used to sing light music earlier but is taking pains at learning classical music now

Light of one's eyes: *Person whom one loves* * Their only son is the light of his parents' eyes

Light on/upon: *Come upon a find by chance* * I lighted on/upon a rare book in a secondhand bookshop

Light out: *Make off* * They did not let the thief light out with the stolen purse

Light purse: *Poverty* * We should not ignore the interests of those people who hold a light purse

Light up: *Give light to; become bright; start to smoke; switch car light on as it gets dark* * The burning building lit up the surrounding area * The night sky lit up with fireworks * He lit up the cigarette as soon as he came out of the conference hall * According to traffic rules, all vehicles must light up as soon as it gets dark

Light up with: *Become bright* * Her face lit up with pleasure

Light year: *The distance travelled by light during one year* * It is said that the nearest star to earth is four light years away (a light year is about six million miles)

Light come, light go: *What is easily gained is soon lost* * It is usually said that money earned through irregular means is light come, light go

Lightning strike: *Strike taking place without warning* * The factory workers went on a lightning strike

Light-fingered: *A person who is likely to steal* * A light-fingered person is very clever in picking pockets

Light-footed: *Nimble; active* * The eel is an attractive and light-footed animal

Light-handed: *With light and delicate touch; having little in hand; empty-handed* * I was surprised to see his light-handed movements while playing the piano * I found him light-handed when he was asked to raise his hands * The hunters came back light-handed

Light-head: *Giddy in the head; delirious; thoughtless; unsteady* * I stopped reading when I felt myself feeling light-headed * She was in a light-head state due to high fever * Light-headed persons are often careless about their future * She looked light-headed on her feet

Light-hearted: *Unburdened or merry at heart; cheerful; inconsiderate* * A light-hearted person is almost free from care and anxiety * The light-hearted boy was dancing on his way to home from school * Most children are light-hearted about the feelings of others

Light-heeled: *Swift of foot* * She is a light-heeled dancer

Light-minded: *Frivolous; unstable; inconsiderate* * His light-minded remarks will not carry any weight * Don't be light-minded in the matter which means serious business

Light-o'-love: *Fickle woman; unwanted* * Do not place your trust in that light-o'-love

Light-spirited: *Having cheerful spirit* * It is a good thing to be in the company of light-spirited persons

Light-winged: *Having light wings; volatile* * A light-winged aeroplane can be inducted for multipurposes

* He is a man of light-winged tastes

Like a bird: *With alacrity; cheerfully* * He accepted my humble gift like a bird

Like a dying duck: *Languishing* * He looked at her like a dying duck

Like a house on fire: *With astonishing rapidity* * The bomber that was shot down was burning like a house on fire

Like a lamb: *Without resistance or protest* *A domestic or pet animal generally behave like a lamb

Like a log: *Unconscious; immovable* * The drunkard lay like a log on the roadside

Like a millpond: *Perfectly calm* * It is rather difficult to stay like a millpond under all circumstances

Like a red rag to a bull: *A great annoyance* * Communism to a capitalist is like a red rag to a bull

Like a shot: *Very rapidly* * If I had the chance to go there, I would go like a shot

Like a ton of bricks: *Heavily and promptly* * The judges came down on the police like a ton of bricks

Like anything: *Very strongly* * It was raining like anything * The sun was blazing like anything

Like cures like: *Poison could be an effective remedy against the poison affected* * Since he has been bitten by a snake, venom may be introduced in his body since it is said that like cures like

Like draws like: *Like-minded persons soon come close to one another* * The way both the robbers are enjoying each other's company it seems true that like draws like

Like father like son: *As the king so are the subjects* * The father likes flying kites and so does the son, thus proving that like father like son

Like hay-go-mad: *Helter-skelter* * The people were running like hay-go-mad in the stampede

Like hell: *Furiously; energetically* * He moans like hell when he loses a bet

Like it or lump it: *Whether you like a situation or not* * You will have to go through this acid test whether you like it or lump it

Like lightning: *Very fast* * The lion pounced on its prey like lightning

Like mad: *With great energy* * I don't know why he was smoking like mad

Like smoke: *Very quickly* * The ghost disappeared like smoke when I tried to catch hold of him

Like the back of one's hand: *Very well indeed* * He knows London like the back of his hand

Like water: *Copiously; extravagantly; recklessly* * At this old age he is still producing paintings like water * Some rich persons in India spend money like water to live a life of ease and luxury * In America, nominated persons for the presidency squander money like water to win in the election campaign

Like water off a duck's back: *Without producing any effect* * All my efforts to persuade him to desist from bad company have proved like water off a duck's back

Likely as not: *Most probably* * He has as likely as not forgotten his promise

Likely that: *Be expected* * It is highly likely that he will succeed

Like-minded: *Having a similar disposition or purpose* * Like-minded persons generally group together

Likes and dislikes: *Preferences and aversions* * He has so many likes and dislikes that it is difficult to please him * Everybody has his/her likes and dislikes

Likewise: *In the same manner; also; moreover* * The teacher sang the song and then asked the pupil to sing the same likewise * If you don't stop weeping then I will start doing likewise * He is a great poet and likewise a good novelist

Limb of the devil: *Mischievous child* * That limb of the devil got on my nerves and I found it difficult to get rid of him

Limber up: *Do exercise to warm up the body* * Both the players were limbering up before the start of the match

Limelight: *The glare of publicity* * As Sania is a good tennis player, she is constantly in the limelight

Limit to: *Put a limit to* * We must limit the expenses to what we can afford

Line of life: *A crease in the palm in which palmists see a promise of longevity* * A long line of life on his palm means that he has a long life

Line one's pockets: *Make money (usually dishonestly)* * He is lining his pockets by running a prostitutes' den

Line up: *Be in a line* * The general lined up his troops

Line up for: *Queue for* * The people were lining up for purchasing tickets at the railway booking window

Lion-hearted: *Very brave* * The lion-hearted soldier was richly awarded for fighting the terrorists

Lion in the way: *Danger to be overcome* * Though we have done well so far, yet we have to face the lion in the way to complete our adventurous expedition

Lion's mouth: *Perilous state* * He found himself in lion's mouth when the brakes of his motorcycle failed all of sudden

Lion's share: *Whole or greater part* * The lion's share of investment has gone to a few favoured companies

Lip-service: *Insincere profession or worship* * An ideal leader never pays lip-service to his followers

Listen in: *Listen to a wireless broadcast; overhear intentionally; a message intended for others* * Did you listen in the broadcast made by the prime minister yesterday? * Do you really think they bother to listen in to us by tapping our telephone lines?

Little by little: *Gradually* * Infants learn to speak little by little as they grow older

Little horror: *Very naughty child* * That little horror should have been named Dennis the Menace

Little or nothing: *Hardly anything* * I could make out little or nothing from his gestures

Little squirt: *Small insignificant person* * They are all cheeky little squirts

Little toe: *Smallest of the toes* * His little toe seems to have been frost-bitten

Live a lie: *Express a lie by one's manner of living* * For years I have been living a lie by wearing costly dresses to show myself as a rich person

Live and let live: *Give and expect toleration; forbearance* * Instead of criticising her for her lavish lifestyle despite not having enough money, we should live and let live

Live by: *Earn one's livelihood by* * It is a good thing to learn to live by honest means

Live by one's wits: *Gain a livelihood by ingenious expedients rather than by honest labour* * I know a fellow who lived for years by his wits

Live down: *Live so as to allow to be forgotten* * He hopes to live down the scandal caused by the divorce proceedings

Live for: *Attach great importance*

to * India's freedom fighters were known to live for fulfilling their ideals

Live in: *One's place of employment; reside* * He will go to live in Canada to earn his living there * One of my friends lives in London and the other in Delhi

Live in a glass house: *Be open to attack* * Those who live in a glass house should not throw stones at others

Live in sin: *Live together without being married* * A cultured society would never tolerate any person living in sin

Live in style: *Had a certain type of life* * He lives in style just to attract the attention of his neighbours

Live it up: *Lead a life of hectic enjoyment; pursue pleasure* * We have been living it up for a long time in wild pursuit of eat, drink and be merry * During our summer vacation, we will do nothing but live it up just as we desire

Live off the land: *Use its agricultural products for one's food needs* * Farmers generally live off the land except perhaps for some other necessities

Live on: *Have it as food or diet* * She is advised by the doctor to live on milk only

Live out: *Dwell away from one's place of employment; to survive; be in a domestic service* * He left his village at the age of 16 to live out in a town * Each of us has to live out our destiny * He is living out as a housekeeper

Live tally: *Cohabit without marriage* * Why don't you marry her instead of living tally?

Live through: *Experience and survive* * He has lived through two wars and three revolutions

Live to oneself: *In isolation, without trying to make friends* * He is living to himself for reasons best known to him

Live together: *Live in the same house* * While in service of the university, my colleague and I lived together for a long time

Live under: *Be tenant to* * He lives under his landlord in a hired accommodation

Live up to: *Rule one's life in a manner worthy of; spend up to the scale of* * We must live up to our reputation * It is difficult to live up to the principles of Jainism

Live with something: *Accept and endure it* * I don't like the noise this aircraft makes but I have learnt to live with it

Live-shell: *A shell still capable of exploding* * Live-shells were used in a mock battle

Livestock: *Domestic animals* * Most of the farmers here are rich in livestock

Live-wire: *One carrying electric current; a person of intense energy or alertness* * He lost his life on touching a live-wire * He runs as a live-wire constantly for hours without getting tired

Living memory: *The memory of anybody or somebody still alive* * Hitler is a living memory to many as a devil of destruction

Living rock: *Rock still in its natural position* * There are still a countless number of living rocks of giant sizes in different parts of the globe

Living room: *Room in a house for general use* * Whenever any guest comes to stay with us, he is accommodated in the living room

Living wage: *A wage on which it is possible for a workman and his family to live fairly* * It is impossible to employ so many people and go on paying them a living wage

Load on: *To load* * Load the sacks on to the cart

Load someone with: *To overburden* * The poor clerk has been loaded with a heavy schedule of work

Load the dice against someone: *Deprive someone of a fair chance of success* * He shrewdly loaded the dice against his rival to make him lose the game

Load up: *Fill up with goods or material* * Have you finished loading up the van with goods for delivering to the customers?

Loaded question: *A question that is intended to trap a person into making an admission which may be harmful* * A loaded question spoiled the career of the poor innocent man

Loaded with: *Burdened with; very full and unable to hold any more* * It is only at the tree loaded with fruit that the people threw stones * The car was loaded with people

Loads of: *Plenty* * In prosperity, all kinds of friends crowd around you

Loaves and fishes: *Material possessions* * Most of our leaders run after their own loaves and fishes with scant love for the country

Local anaesthetic: *Substance which numbs part of the body* * Before being operated on, he was administered a local anaesthesia

Lock in: *Confine by locking doors*

* They captured the big wild cat, locked it in and then informed the authority concerned

Lock on to: *Find and automatically follow by radar* * The launching of a missile has been locked on to hit the target

Lock out: *Keep out by locking doors* * If you don't return before midnight, you will be locked out

Lock the stable door after the horse has bolted: *Take precautions when it is too late* * He closed the door after his pet escaped from the house so why lock the stable door after the horse has bolted?

Lock up: *Confine; keep in prison cell; lock securely; lock whatever is to be locked* * The thief was locked up so that he may not escape * Don't forget to lock up the whole building when you are away for a few days * It is advisable to lock up the jewels in some safe place

Lockout: *Industrial dispute in which employees are kept out of the factory until they agree to certain terms* * There is a lockout in the factory for an indefinite period

Lock, stock and barrel: *The whole or altogether* * I purchased this building lock, stock and barrel for a very reasonable amount

Lock-up: *Place for locking up prisoners* * He landed himself in a lock-up for his criminal acts

Lodge at: *Live as a paying guest* * Where are you lodging now?

Lodge in: *Enter and become fixed* * The bullet lodged in his jaw

Lodge something with: *Place a complaint with the proper authorities* * He has lodged a complaint against his neighbour with the police

Lodge with: *Live as a paying guest* * They are lodging these days with my sister

Lofted house: *A house of more than one storey* * They all live in the lofted house

Lone wolf: *Person who prefers to be alone or who does not associate with other people* * A hermit could be called a lone wolf

Long and short: *Substance* * The long and short of it is that they are bankrupt now

Long dozen: *Thirteen* * This shopkeeper sells bananas by a long dozen

Long drawn out: *Taking too much time* * The long drawn out speech of the Prime Minister on the Republic

Day was not appreciated by the public

Long for: *Desire earnestly* * The children are longing for holidays

Long haul: *A long distance to travel* * We began a long haul up the cobbled street

Long-headed: *Shrewd* * You can't cheat that long-headed man

Long home: *The grave* * It is said that life is real and earnest and long home is not its goal * No one knows as to when one is destined to go to long home

Long in the tooth: *Elderly* * He is getting a bit long in the tooth for this sort of thing

Long purse: *Abundance of money* * There is no harm if a woman with a long purse goes on a shopping spree

Long shot: *An attempt which has little chance of being successful; hopeful guess* * It is a long shot but I think he must have known the murderer * For present, it is a long shot to say which new countries are likely to be included in the UN Security Council

Long-drawn: *Prolonged; unduly protracted* * They had to fight a long-drawn battle * There was a long-drawn debate with no conclusion

Long-faced: *Dismal looking* * All sympathised with that long-faced girl

Long-lived: *Who lives for a long time* * That long-lived senior citizen is given due respect by one and all

Long-nine: *A cheap cigar* * He prefers smoking a long-nine to other costly cigars

Long-range: *That covers long distance* * Indian scientists have successfully tested the long-range missiles

Long-sighted: *Able to see far but not alone at hand; having foresight; sagacious* * Some long-sighted persons have predicted that by 2021 India would become a Super Power * Had you been a long-sighted individual, you would have saved yourself from a lot of trouble * We should be rather long-sighted when planning for the future

Longstanding: *Of long existence* * The long standing payment of our bill is still awaited

Long-suffering: *Enduring long and patiently* * He has become a victim to long-suffering for the last three years when his young son died suddenly

Long-tongued: *Babbling* * I could not understand

anything in the long-tongued discussion they were holding

Long-winded: *Tedious and talking too much in a boring way* * We are fed up with his long-winded lectures

Look a gift horse in the mouth: *Criticise a gift* * It is not right for a wise person to look a gift horse in the mouth

Look about: *Be on search, be in search of* * What are you looking about in this deserted place? * Are you still looking about for a job?

Look about one: *Examine one's surroundings* * We hardly had time to look about us before we had to continue our journey

Look after: *Take care of* * The old lady needs someone to look after her

Look after number one: *Look after yourself first* * It is necessary to look after number one because only then you can be of some help to others

Look ahead: *Make plans for the future; think of and prepare for future needs* * A prudent person looks ahead on how to make a bright future * A wise person would always look ahead on how to deal with the coming happenings

Look alive: *Bestir oneself* * Why doesn't he look alive and get down to completing his work?

Look at: *Consider; examine; use one's sight* * They have decided not to look at my proposal * We must look at this question from all angles * Look at this beautiful picture which would give you a view of the hilly resort

Look away: *Turn the eyes away* * Don't look away if someone comes to seek your help

Look back to: *Turn one's thought to something in the past* * It gives me great joy whenever I look back to my childhood

Look before you leap: *Avoid acting hastily, without considering the possible consequences* * We should live cautiously and carefully looking before leaping into trouble

Look black: *Have angry look* * She looked back at me when my bag fell near her foot in the crowded bus

Look blank: *Seem puzzled* * He looked blank as he could find no way out to get rid of the troubles looming large

Look blue: *Be nervous; depressed;* He looked blue when he entered the examination hall * He looked blue when he heard that he had failed in the examination

Look daggers: *Look in a hostile manner* * He looked daggers at me when I refused to dance to his tune

Look down one's nose: *Regard with displeasure or contempt* * The minister's daughter always looks down her nose at her classmates, considering herself to be superior to others

Look for: *Search for* * Presently I am looking for a job

Look for a needle in a haystack: *Engage in a hopeless search* * You will not find your book in this cupboard full of rubbish as it would be like looking for a needle in a haystack

Look forward to: *Regard a future event with pleasure* * We are looking forward to seeing you again

Look here: *I say; Attend to this* * Look here, I have decided to sue you in the court

Look in: *Make a short call* * Why don't you look in next time when you are in town?

Look into: *Inspect closely; investigate* * They wanted an independent financial controller to look into the city's accounts * The police has to look into the murder case

Look like: *Show a likelihood of; appear similar* * It looks like it is going to rain * She looks like her mother

Look likely: *Seem possible* * It looks likely that she will get married to him

Look on: *Regard; view; think; be a spectator* * Do you look on him as an authority on the subject? * Different people take a different look on the cause of his death * I don't look on him to deliver the goods * Why don't you play instead of just looking on?

Look at the bright side: *Be optimistic* * A hopeful person would always look on the bright side of things

Look on to: *Overlook or give a view of* * My bedroom looks on to the garden

Look one's age: *Have an appearance that confirm to one's age* * She looks her age no matter how hard she tries to hide it

Look one's best: *Appear to the greatest advantage* * She looks her best in jeans

Look oneself: *Have one's normal appearance* * You are not looking yourself today

Look out: *Be watchful; be on one's guard; look for and select; show; appearance; see something* * Look out that nobody enters the room until the meeting is over * The security guard is always on the look out against any trouble * The director of the company is on the look out for a highly qualified person for the post of a manager * The disordered placement of articles does not give a nice look out * Everybody was impressed by his first look out on the stage * He stood at the window and looked out at the outside view

Look out on: *Supply an outlook or view* * Our hotel room looks out on the sea front

Look over: *Examine cursorily; overlook* * We must look over the house before we decide to rent it * His resume has been looked over by his employers

Look round: *Examine possibilities before deciding; turn the head (to see); go sight-seeing, etc.* * Look round before coming to a hasty decision * When I looked round for her, she was leaving the hall * Have we time to go look round the town before lunch?

Look sharp: *Be quick about it* * Look sharp before the teacher enters the class and finds you sleeping

Look small: *Feel ashamed; look mean or insignificant* * When the money lender was produced in the court, he looked small * We made him look small by exposing his conduct

Look something in the eye: *Confront calmly and bravely* * While fighting in the battle-field, he looked at death in the eyes

Look through: *Examine thoroughly* * He looked through the proposals before approving them * I must look through these bills and check them before I clear them

Look to: *Take care of; depend on; expect* * Look to it that you leave no question without attempting it * I don't look to anybody's help in the work I have taken in hand * He looks to a good piece of advice from you on this matter

Look to one's laurels: *Beware of losing one's reputation; be on the lookout for possible success among rivals* * You will have to look to your laurels before you accept the new challenges * The genius looks to his laurels in the next competitive examination

Look up: *Search for; refer to; take courage; improve; have taken*

a chance for the better; seek out and call upon; visit; raise the eyes; respect * You may consult the dictionary to look up the meaning of this particular word * For understanding the basic principle of 'civil liberty', you better look up the same in our Constitution * The footprints left by great men help us to look up to brighter prospects * The physical exercise has given you a very healthy look up * The business in garments is looking up day by day as a result of greater demand * I am looking up for an opportunity to discuss all matters of importance * Do look me up next time you are here in town * Don't look up towards the blazing sun

Look up to: *Respect* * They all look up to him as their leader

Look you: *Observe or take notice of this* * Look you better not get late for the show!

Loom large: *Be seen in vague and after magnified or threatening shape* * The fear of H-bomb loomed large in their mind

Loop back: *Tie back with a cord* * Loop back the curtain

Loophole: *Way of escape from control especially one provided by careless and inexact wording of a rule* * The House of Commons intends to tighten the loopholes found in some of the Acts

Loose change: *Money in coins only* * I have no loose change with me to give to the beggar

Loose-bodied: *Flowing; loose fitting; loose in behaviour* * She looked like a fairy in her loose-bodied dress whenever she walked about * I prefer putting on loose-bodied clothes to the tight ones * A loose-bodied person would never stand straight

Loosen the purse-strings: *Increase expenditure* * In war times America invariably is the first one to loosen the purse-strings

Loosen up: *Make or become loose* * I must take some exercise and loosen up my muscles

Lopsided: *Ill-balanced; heavier; bigger on one side than the other* * You should know that lopsided views would never carry weight * The picture was looking lopsided as it was not hung in the centre

Lord it over: *Behave arrogantly* * Those who try to lord it over in all matters are despised for their conduct

Lord of seats: *Lord of session* * The judgement has been announced after taking the jury into confidence

Lose by: *Be or become worse* * You will lose nothing by waiting

Lose caste: *Lose prestige or social status* * A criminal has to lose his caste in a society

Lose colour: *Lose one's good looks* * You would lose colour if you put on shabby and torn clothes

Lose face: *Lose prestige* * He had to lose face for being unable to pay his debts

Lose ground: *Decreasing; become less powerful or acceptable* * The *purdah* system is losing ground day by day * The belief in witchcraft is losing ground

Lose hair: *Become bald* * Those who have lost hair should be careful while scratching their head

Lose head: *Lose balance of mind; be proud* * Sir John never lost his head even when he was face to face with serious problems * He seems to have lost his head on account of his sudden prosperity

Lose heart: *Be discouraged* * We should not lose heart when beset with difficulties

Lose interest: *Cease to be interested; cease to be attracted by* * An over-aged person loses interest in almost everything * After having lost a great deal of money, he has lost interest in gambling

Lose one's balance: *Become unsteady; be upset mentally* * Under the influence of liquor, he was losing his balance at every step * He was surrounded by so many dangers that he lost his balance

Lose one's bearings: *Become uncertain of one's position or orientation* * It is but natural to lose one's bearings when faced with unbearable troubles

Lose one's cool: *Lose one's composure* * I was on the brink of losing my cool to hear his taunting remarks * We should not lose our cool in difficult times

Lose oneself: *Loose one's way; become bewildered* * He is so absent-minded that he is liable to lose himself in the middle of a jungle * He loves music so much that he is likely to lose himself in it

Lose one's hair: *Grow angry* * A sober person would never lose his hair under any circumstances

Lose one's head: *Lose one's self-*

possession * He lost his head at his rude and crude behaviour

Lose one's heart to: *Become very fond of or fall in love with* * She lost her heart to a handsome soldier

Lose one's nerve: *Lose courage* * We should not lose our nerves when beset with difficulties

Lose one's rag: *Lose one's temper* * Why do you lose your rag over this trifling matter?

Lose one's senses: *Become insane or wildly excited* * He looked too much furious when he lost his senses

Lose one's tongue: *Become speechless from emotions* * I tend to lose my tongue whenever I see my teacher

Lose one's way: *Get lost or be unable to find the right way, road, etc.* * We lost our way in the dark

Lose oneself: *Get lost* * Don't lose yourself in empty dreams

Lose sight of: *Overlook; fail to take account of; no longer be able to see* * The employee has lost sight of his valuable services * We must not lose sight of the fact that to err is human * We lost sight of him in the crowd

Lose temper: *Become angry* * A sober person does not lose his temper unnecessarily

Lose the day: *Be defeated* * With the arrival of reinforcement, they became firm in not losing the day

Lose the lead: *Fall behind in a race* * I wish to bet on a horse that would not lose the lead

Lose the thread of a conversation: *Miss what the conversation is about* * We lost the thread of our conversation all of a sudden when one of the participants fell down

Lose time: *Fall behind hand; let time pass without full advantage of lost time* * He did not want to lose time in generosity * Those who lose time in idle gossip cannot make most of their time

Lose touch with: *Be out of touch (with)* * If we correspond regularly, we shall not lose touch with each other

Lose track of: *Lose touch with or fail to follow the course or development* * We lost track of the advancing patrol party when our radio system went out of order

Losing game: *A game that is going against one* * *One in which defeat is likely or certain* * To challenge that robust and sturdy wrestler to a fight would be a losing game for you * It would be a losing game for you to get the better of him in the deal

Lost cause: *One that has already been defeated or is sure to be defeated* * It is useless to repent over a lost cause

Lost in: *Absorbed* * When I went to see him, I found him lost in deep thought

Lost in admiration: *Admire greatly* * We were lost in admiration of the beautiful scenery

Lost in thought: *Get engrossed in thinking* * He was found lost in thought in his study room

Lost one's touch: *Be not as successful as one was* * He has lost his touch in cracking jokes

Lost to: *Have nothing of; insensible to* * I wonder how he is lost to all sense of shame * He is lost to all norms of good behaviour

Lot of (or lots of): *Great amount or number of* * What a lot of time you take to dress!

Lots to blanks: *Any odds* * A man indulging in bets should not mind lots to blanks

Lotus-eater: *An eater of lotus; one given up to indolence* * Would you please let me know the particular species that is called lotus-eater? * A lotus-eater is always lost to the woes of others

Loudly dressed: *In bright colours* * The young lady was loudly dressed

Loud-mouthed: *Talking in a way, which is too easily heard* * Don't be loud-mouthed while conveying the secrets to somebody

Lounge suit: *Informal suit* * When I went to see him at his home, he was wearing a lounge suit

Love light: *Lustre in the eye* * Love light between the girl and her boyfriend may bind them in wedlock

Love me, love my dog: *Accept my friend as yours* * If you love that girl, be prepared to love everything about her because it is well known that she believes in the adage 'love me, love my dog'

Love-child: *Illegitimate child* * The love-child found at a lonely place has been sent to an orphanage

Love-letter: *A letter of courtship* * The exchange of love-letters resulted in their marriage in a church

Lovelorn: *Forsaken by one's love* * The poor lovelorn youth has reduced himself to a skeleton

Love one to distract: *Be wild (with worry/grief) about someone* * He loves her to distract and so is pinning for her

Love-seat: *An armchair for two* * The married couple, seated on a love-seat, were eagerly watching the television programme

Love-shaft: *A dart of love from Cupid's bow* * There is a general feeling that every young person (man or woman) falls victim to the love-shaft

Lovesick: *Languishing with amorous desire* * That lovesick person seems to have been deserted by his beloved

Low life: *Humble life* * Some persons are destined to live a low life

Low oneself: *Do something of which one should be ashamed* * You will low yourself if you tell a lie

Low season: *Season when there are few tourists* * Going to Venice in the low season is bound to be a lot cheaper

Low voice: *Not easily heard* * I could not make out what he said in a low voice

Low-bred: *Of vulgar manners* * A low-bred person has no sense of civility

Low-down: *Mean or despicable* * I hate your low-down tricks

Low-pitched: *(Of sound) low in pitch* * She sang a song in a lovely, low-pitched voice

Lowlihead: *Humility* * He has the virtue of lowlihead

Lukewarm: *Moderately warm; half-hearted* * I drink only lukewarm coffee * A lukewarm pursuit of studies will not bring you credit

Lumber room: *A room for storing things not in use* * The things that are not needed presently may be placed in the lumber room

Lumber-mill: *A sawmill* * Have you ever been to a lumber-mill?

Lumberyard: *A timber yard* * The tree trunks, logs, etc. are sold at a lumberyard

Lump it: *Endure or put up with something unpleasant; unwanted* * If you don't like it, you can lump it * Well, you will just have to lump it

Lump sum: *In single installment* * You will need to pay a smaller amount if you pay in lump sum towards the cost of this car

Lump together: *Put together in one lump; put together in one place or in one group* * Can we lump all these items together under the heading

'Incidental Expenses'? * During the harvest season, farmers lump together the sheaves at a particular spot

Lurk in: *Linger around furtively* * Some suspicion is still lurking in my mind about his strange movements

Lurking-place: *Hiding-place* * The police party could not locate the lurking-place of the outlaw

Lying-in hospital: *Maternity hospital* * As she is in family way, she has been admitted to a lying-in hospital

M

Macadamised road: *Road covered with several layers of crushed rock or stone* * We had made a mark in making a close net of macadamised roads in our country

Mad as a hatter: *Quite mad* * He was as mad as a hatter and kept abusing all those who came near

Mad one's ways: *Reform one's behaviour* * If you do not mend your ways, you will ruin yourself

Mad with: *Angry with* * Why he is mad with you today?

Madcap: *Person acting recklessly or on impulse* * This is a job not to be entrusted to a madcap

Made man: *One whose success has been assured* * Get the minister's help and you will be a made man

Made to measure: *Made to individual requirements* * I always put on clothes that are made to measure

Made to order: *Made according to the customer's special requirements or instructions* * I have got this new dress made to order to be used only during special functions

Magnetic tape: *Sensitive plastic tape for recording* * We can use magnetic tape for recording a speech or a music piece

Magnum opus: *A work of art, music or literature that people think is the best that artist, etc. has ever produced* * Shakespeare's magnum opus in English literature will always be considered a masterpiece for ages to come

Maid of all work: *A maid who does general housework* * We need a maid of all works to attend to all the chores at home

Maid of honour: *A lady in the service of a queen or princess; a bridesmaid; a kind of cheesecake* * A maid of honour waits upon the queen * Usually a maid of honour attends a bride at her wedding * Have you ever had the taste of the maid of honour?

Maid-servant: *A female servant* * The maid-servant left the house in a fit of anger

Maiden assize: *An assize at which there are no criminal cases* * A maiden assize has yet to deal with a criminal case if it comes for a hearing

Maiden battle: *First contest* * She has yet to fight a maiden battle in the game of tennis

Maiden castle: *A castle never taken* * That pre-historic castle has the record of being a maiden castle

Maiden fortress: *A fortress that has never been captured* * I have not heard the name of any maiden fortress in Rajasthan

Maiden name: *The family name of a married woman before her marriage* * People still call her by her maiden name in the family

Maiden over: *An over in which no runs are scored* * The spin bowler has to his credit nine maiden overs bowled in the first innings

Maiden speech: *One's first speech especially in Parliament* * The newly elected member's maiden speech was appreciated in the house by all

Maiden tongue: *Gentle in voice* * A maiden tongue soothes even hardened hearts

Maiden voyage: A first voyage * It was my maiden voyage in a ship from London to Paris

Maiden widowed: *Widowed while still a virgin* * It is really a matter of fate that she had to see herself as a maiden widowed

Mailed fist: *Physical or military force* * It is said that China ranks first in so far its mailed fist is concerned

Main chance: *Best opportunity; the chief object* * We must have an eye on the main chance to win the game

Mainstay: *Chief support* * A balanced diet is the mainstay of maintaining good health

Maintain a low profile: *To keep oneself unnoticed* * He maintains a low profile as he is very shy

Maintain an open mind on: *Be ready to listen to and consider the views of others* * A sober person maintains an open mind on all matters of importance

Maintenance order: *Order made by a court of law obliging somebody to support someone* * Legally there is no escape from the maintenance order to support an abandoned wife

Major term: *The term which is the predicate of the conclusion* * We had to abide by the major terms of the agreement

Make a bed: *Put a bed in order* * It is necessary to make a bed to have a sound sleep

Make a bee-line for: *Go forward by the shortest way; go quickly forward* * He made a bee-line for drinks at the bar

Make a bid: *Make an offer* * Will anybody make a bid f for this antique piece?

Make a bolt for: *Rush towards* * I made a bolt for a nearest safe place when a bomb exploded nearby

Make a clean breast of: *Make a full confession* * He made a clear breast of his sins in the church

Make a clean sweep of: *Complete change by winning or gaining something; get rid of* * He made a clean sweep of votes in the house in his favour * They made a clean sweep of their old furniture and replaced it with brand new pieces

Make a common cause with: *Cast in one's lots with or have the same interest and aims with* * It is a good thing to make common cause with others to lead a purposeful life

Make a concession: *To concede to* * It has become mandatory for all colleges to make a concession to Scheduled Caste students when granting admission

Make a dash for: *Go quickly* * We made a dash for the parade ground to watch the ceremony

Make a face: *Make grimaces; show disgust or defiance* * We should never make a face at disabled persons * The children made faces as soon as he entered the classroom

Make a fast buck: *Earn a lot of money quickly through dishonest manner* * They made a fast buck through various means

Make a fuss about: *Be seriously agitated; be ostentatiously active; complain vigorously* * He always makes a fuss about food * She often makes a fuss about her appearance * He made a great fuss and swore to end our friendship

Make a fuss of: *Pay ostentatious attention to* * Don't make so much fuss of the children

Make a gesture: *Movement of hand or head to indicate ideal feeling* * He made a friendly gesture when I went to bat in the field

Make a good dinner: *Dine heartily* * We made a good dinner at a hotel

Make a good haul: *Stole a lot of valuable property* * The burglars made a good haul when the landlord and his family were away

Make a good job of: *Do well* * He will make a very good job of repairing my bathroom

Make a good thing of it: *Reap a good advantage from* * Now that you have succeeded in your efforts, you can make a good thing of it

Make a grab for: *Try to seize* * He made a savage grab for the knife from the robber's hand

Make a guess: *Guess* * He asked me to make a guess about his age

Make a hash of it: *Make a mess of it* * What a hash that man has made of things! * I am afraid I may make a hash of it as I am not good at painting

Make a hit: *Make a very favourable impression* * She is trying to make a hit with my brother but his interest lies elsewhere

Make a hole in: *Use up a large amount of money* * The purchase of a new car made a hole in my savings

Make a hole in the water: *Drown oneself* * The depressed farmer made a hole in the water by jumping into a canal

Make a killing: *Be extraordinarily successful* * He made a killing by buying up all the prime shares

Make a Kirk or mill of it: *Do what you please or can with it* * You are blessed with all round prosperity and it is now up to you to make Kirk or mill of it

Make a lip: *Pout in sullenness or derision* * Generally sexy women tend to make a lip to look more sexier

Make a long arm: *Help oneself freely at table* * At the dinner party all the guests had to make a long arm while taking their meals

Make a long nose: *Put a thumb to the nose as a vulgar gesture* * The person who was making a long nose at the girl was badly thrashed by the public

Make a man of: *Cause to behave like an adult* * The mother asked her young son to read the biographies of brave men so as to make a man out of him

Make a matter of conscience: *To have scruples about* * Don't make it a matter of conscience to tell a lie if it has not harmed anybody

Make a merit of something: *Represent it as deserving reward or praise* * We need to make a merit of the plan drafted by him as it is worthy of our attention

Make a mess of: *Make matters worse or spoil something* * I thought my servant would make a nice cake but he made a mess of it

Make a mockery of: *Ridicule* * If he succeeds in disturbing the proceedings, it will make a mockery of parliamentary democracy

Make a mountain of a molehill: *Magnify a trifling matter* * Some people unnecessarily make a mountain of a molehill over insignificant issues

Make a move: *Leave; begin to act* * It is getting dark so we must make a move to reach home in time * Unless we make a move, we shall be in a hopelessly weak position

Make a muck of: *Make a mess of* * He is prone to making a muck of any dish that he prepares

Make a name for oneself: *Become well known* * Mahatma Gandhi made a name for himself by winning freedom through peaceful means

Make a night of it: *Keep it up for the night* * Let us make a night of it by attending a night club

Make a noise: *Talk or complain in order to get attention* * Traders are making a great noise against the levy of new taxes

Make a noise in the world: *Achieve great notoriety; be widely talked of* * Rogues make a noise in the world after achieving success through underhand means * The first successful test of atomic bomb by America made a noise in the world

Make a parade of: *Make a show* * Don't make a parade of your virtues

Make a pass at: *Aim a short blow at, especially ineffectively; make an unwelcome amorous advance to* * He felt annoyed when I made a pass at him * You will invite trouble if you do not refrain from making a pass at that young girl

Make a person open his eye: *Cause astonishment* * It is hoped that a major loss in the share market will make him open his eyes

Make a pile: *Acquire a great deal*

of money * My friend made a pile by selling videos

Make a point of: *Treat as essential; make a special object of; regard or treat as important or necessary* * I hope you will make point of observing discipline in class * It would be in your own interest to make a point of learning good manners in society * One should make a point of observing civilised behaviour

Make a poor mouth: *Profess poverty* * Why do you make a poor mouth when the country is developing on all fronts by leaps and bounds?

Make a practice: *Do it habitually* * If you make a practice of cheating at examinations you will get rusticated from school

Make a request: *Request* * They have made a request for opening a dispensary in the locality

Make a shaft or a bolt of it: *Venture and take what comes of it; the shaft and the bold being arrows of longbow and the crossbow respectively* * We could not make a shaft or bolt of it without necessary guidance

Make a song and dance about: *Make unnecessary fuss about; make over much of* * Her father made a song and dance about her returning late from office

Make a spoon or spoil a horn: *Attempt something at the risk of failure* * In the absence of necessary expertise in trade, I am afraid you may make a spoon or spoil a horn

Make a stand: *Offer resistance* * We had no option but to make a stand against the enemy charging us from behind

Make a study of: *Make a thorough investigation of* * The economists in our country are making a keen study of how to increase the inflow of funds

Make a success of something: *Succeed in doing something* * He has been able to make a success of his approach solving the problem

Make a virtue of necessity: *Do as if from sense of duty* * The girl knew that she would be dismissed, so very smartly she made a virtue of necessity by submitting her resignation before she was thrown out

Make a vow: *Promise solemnly* * He made a vow that he would avenge the insult

Make account of: *Set value upon* * Can you please make an account of this property before I decide to purchase it?

Make advances: *Try to start friendly or sexual relationship* * He was taken to task for making advances at that young girl

Make after: *Follow or pursue* * My mother made after me like a mad woman when I broke the glass pane

Make against: *Disapproval; tell against; militate* * We have collected all the necessary material to make our point against the proposal put forth by him * If you make a charge against him he may not like it

Make all by oneself: *Cope; can do a work by oneself* * Can she make this task all by herself?

Make allowance for: *To consider something* * We must make allowance for this youth

Make amends: *Render compensation* * Unless you make amends for the loss, nobody will be willing to excuse you * He touched his mother's feet to make amends for his bad behaviour

Make an application: *Apply* * I need to make an application before submitting to the university

Make an ass of oneself: *Behave like a fool* * Don't make an ass of yourself at the party

Make an effort: *Make an attempt* * In order to win a scholarship, he has to make an effort

Make an end of something: *Finish it or get rid of it* * The need of the hour is to make an end of discrimination between man and woman

Make an errand: *Invent a reason for going* * On the pretext of making an errand to buy medicines to his ailing wife, he made for the cinema show

Make an example of somebody: *Punish him as a warning to others* * It was decided to make an example of some of the top conspirators

Make an exhibition of oneself: *Behave foolishly; exciting ridicule; behave in public so that one receives contempt* * He made an exhibition of himself in public by taking an overdose of drugs * The people disapproved and resented him for making an exhibition of himself * We should not make an exhibition of ourselves by boasting our achievements

Make an honest woman of: *Marry her after seducing her*

* It was a right step taken by him to make an honest woman of her by marrying her

Make an impression: *Impress* * He has been able to make an impression on the public with his gift of the gab

Make an issue of: *Have a big discussion about* * As life is full of weal and woe, we should not make an issue of it

Make approaches: *Make contacts* * He made approaches to her to join his firm

Make arrangements for: *Arrange for* * We have to make arrangements for the stay of all the guests at our house

Make as if: *Act as if* * He was making as if he were a hero on the stage * She made as if to speak but then kept quiet

Make as though: *Pretend that* * As he did not want to listen to her he made himself as though he was deaf

Make at: *Make a hostile movement against* * The scooter rider made at the old lady to snatch her golden chain

Make away with: *Kill; destroy or steal; get rid of; put out of the way* * Why did he make away with himself? * He made away with all the evidence * The snatcher made away with her purse in broad daylight * He thought it proper to make away with the bad company * We must make away with this hurdle for free movement

Make bad blood between persons: *Cause them to feel ill will towards one another* * It is good that all his efforts to make bad blood between the two fast friends have come to a naught

Make bad weather of it: *Behave badly in a storm* * Don't make bad weather of it in case you meet with a storm

Make bold: *Take the liberty (of using); make free* * He made bold with my torch in my absence * He seems to have made bold with my whisky bottle while I was away

Make both ends meet: *Try to live within one's income* * It is always difficult for poor people to make both ends meet in these days of rising prices

Make bricks without straw: *Try to make things without necessary material* * You must have some solid proof to get him legally punished because one cannot make bricks without straw

Make capital out of: *Turn to*

one's advantage * He always makes capital out of the weakness of his rivals * Pakistan has all along been trying to make capital out of the border infiltrations

Make choice of: *Select* * One should be very careful in making a choice of subjects for study at the high school

Make common cause with: *Take side with and support* * During the Khilafat agitation, the Hindus made a common cause with the Mohammedans

Make demands: *Make a firm request for* * Rise in the prices of essential commodities has made extra demands on the state exchequer

Make do: *Put up with even if it is not suitable* * We had to make do with his childish behaviour * I have to make do with a cleaner who is useless at his work

Make down: *Refashion so as to fit for a smaller person* * Make down this coat of mine to the size of my younger brother

Make ducks and drakes: *Use recklessly; squander; waste* * Don't make ducks and drakes when driving your vehicle * It is an act of foolishness to make ducks and drakes of our hard-earned money * We should not make ducks and drakes with our valuable time

Make exit: *Go out* * He made his exit by the window

Make eyes at: *Look at in an amorous way* * The boy was taken to task by the public for making eyes at young girls

Make fair weather: *Be conciliatory; flatter* * When in trouble, he had to make fair weather with his opponent * Those who make fair weather with their boss are likely to get promotion out of turn

Make figure: *Be conspicuous* * He has made a figure of himself by putting on that fancy dress

Make fish of one and flesh of another: *Make invidious distinction* * It would be injustice on our part to make fish of one and flesh of another in a similar case

Make fool of: *Bring a person into ridicule* * We should not make a fool of elderly persons

Make for: *Set out for; seek to reach; conducive to* * We made for our further journey after having our breakfast * To avoid delay, he swiftly made for his office

* Contentment makes for happiness

Make for somebody: *Charge at or rush at* * The bull made for me and I had to run

Make for something: *Contribute to; tend towards* * Does early rising make for good health? * The improved lid of this jar makes for easier opening

Make free with: *Be familiar with; take liberty with* * He makes rather free with the waitress * He seems to have made free with my drink while I was away

Make friends: *Become friendly; equal friends* * During my goodwill tour of London I made friends with a number of persons

Make fun at: *Laugh nastily at* * He giggled and made fun at the poor fellow's helplessness

Make fun of: *Ridicule* * It is cruel to make fun of a crippled

Make game of: *Make sport of or ridicule* * They make game of bureaucrats who adopt a dogmatic approach

Make good: *Compensate; fulfil promise; prosper* * He had to make good the loss by paying in cash for damaging my motorcycle * He made good his words by helping me financially * He went to Canada where he soon made good

Make good one's escape: *Effect* * On the pretext of answering the call of Nature, the accused made good his escape

Make good the loss: *Compensate for the loss* * You will have to make good the loss suffered by me

Make good weather of it: *Behave well in a storm* * The dauntless sailors made good weather of it despite the stormy sea

Make great play about: *Give great emphasis about* * I made great play about the fact that computers do the job in a fraction of the time taken by man

Make haste: *Hurry* * Make haste as we are getting too late to catch the bus

Make hay: *Toss and turn cut grass for exposure to the sun* * Farmers make hay to be stored in the form of stacks for use by their cattle

Make hay of: *Throw into confusion* * You have made hay of your books and papers in the reading room

Make hay while the sun shines: *Seize an opportunity while it lasts* * It is wise to play when the teacher is away for it has been rightly said that make hay while the sun shines

Make head or tail of: *Find any sense in* * I could not make any head or tail of his story * He spoke so rapidly that I could make no head or tail of his speech

Make headway: *Progress* * He is making satisfactory headway in his studies * India has been able to make headway in the field of science and technology

Make heavy weather of a job: *Find to be troublesome; have unnecessary difficulty in doing the job* * He made heavy weather of the task assigned to him * Those who shirk work generally make heavy weather of the job given to them

Make in free as to: *Be daring* * Don't make yourself so free as to let others feel irritated and annoyed

Make inroads into: *Encroach* * Corruption has made inroads into various government departments

Make it one's business: *To undertake to accomplish something or see it done* * He has made it his business to complete the project within this month

Make it snappy: *Do it quickly* * Keep the pamphlets in a pile and make it snappy

Make it strange: *Make difficulties; show reluctance* * You will make it strange for yourself by being careless * Don't make it strange on the pleas that you have guts to do anything without due preparation

Make it up: *End a quarrel or dispute or misunderstanding* * They quarrel every morning and end up making it up every evening * Why don't you make it up with him?

Make it up to someone: *Compensate someone* * He has been directed to make it up to him for the damaged car

Make it worth somebody's while: *Pay or reward someone* * If you will help me with this job, I will make it worth your while

Make light of: *Treat as of little consequence* * One should not make light of one's illness * He made light of my warning and had to suffer in the long run

Make light work of something: *Do it without much effort* * He is so dexterous that he can make light work of any job assigned to him

Make little difference: *Be of no importance* * Your advice will make little difference to them

Make love to: *Try to gain the affection of* * The best way to make love to anyone is to be humble and helpful

Make merry: *Have a good time* * In order to make merry, we went to see a film

Make mincemeat of: *Defeat a person; an argument* * The man made mincemeat of his rival in the debate

Make mischief: *Cause discord or ill feeling* * He was at the root of making mischief between the two fast friends

Make money: *Earn it* * Many people go abroad in the hope of making money

Make much ado: *Make much excitement or fuss* * He has the habit of making much ado about nothing

Make much of: *Treat with fondness; cherish; foster; turn to great account; find much sense in; succeed in understanding* * They made much of their guests by providing all kinds of comforts * We really make much of the affection we receive from them * We continued to make much of our friendship * He was able to make much of his business at home and abroad * The audience made much of the speech made by the speaker * He made much of the guidance received for pursuing a bright career

Make no bones of: *Have no scruples about* * They dismissed him and made no bones of it

Make no doubt: *Have no doubt* * I make no doubt of his honesty

Make no matter: *Be of no importance* * It makes no matter whether you arrive early or late

Make no odds: *Make no difference* * It makes no odds for me whether he loses or wins the game

Make noises: *Talk in an indirect way; about which one thinks he might do* * The company has been making noises about closing several factories

Make nonsense of: *Cause to become ridiculous* * Most of his policies made nonsense of his call for moderation

Make not much sense: *See to have little sense* * His arguments have never made much sense

Make nothing of: *Think it in no great matter; have no hesitation; be totally unable to understand; not to understand; treat as trifle* * Generally we make nothing of the trivial events * He made nothing of exposing the true state of affairs * I could make nothing of the reason that made him run amok * I could make nothing of his nonsensical remarks * I could make nothing of his lengthy lecture

Make of: *Constructed from; understand by; consider* * This big building seems to have been made of concrete material * I wondered what they made of my nod to that girl * Why do you make of it as a probable alternative?

Make off with: *Run away with* * The thief dodged the police and made off with the stolen items

Make on: *Make much of* * The cheat is still at large and is making on his treacherous tactics

Make one his ape: *Make a fool of* * You will make your own ape if you betray your principles

Make one's adieu: *Say goodbye* * On his retirement day, he made his adieu to all the members of the staff

Make one's blood boil: *Anger one; make one very angry* * His unbearable rudeness made his blood boil * His wild allegations against me made my blood boil

Make one's blood creep: *Fill with horror* * The broad daylight murder of my friend made my blood creep

Make one's bow: *Retire ceremoniously* * He made his bow to the company

Make one's bread: *Earn one's living* * The labourers leave home for town to make their bread

Make one's day: *Make one feel very happy* * His smile however makes my day

Make one's flesh creep: *Frighten or horrify* * At the dead of night he saw something that made his flesh creep

Make one's hackles rise: *Make one very angry* * His impudence makes my hackles rise

Make one's hair stand on end: *Fill one with fright or horror; give the greatest astonishment or fright to another; shock or frighten one* * The very sight of the ghost made my hair stand on end * The sight of the lion made my hair stand on the end * His ghost story made our hair stand on end

Make one's living: *Have as one's work or livelihood* * He makes his living by working as a newsreader

Make one's manners: *Salute a person on meeting by a bow;*

to courtesy * They made their manners before their leader

Make one's mark: *Distinguish oneself; make a notable impression or great influence* * He has already made his mark as an orator * He has made his mark in the subject of Sanskrit

Make one's peace with: *Reconcile or be reconciled with* * It would be advisable for you to make your peace with him and avoid unnecessary wrangling * He was obliged to make his peace with the salesman

Make one's point: *Win acceptance for an argument* * He made his point by saying that united we stand and divided we fall

Make one's points: *Establish what one is proposing* * He was applauded when he made his points in improper handling of financial matters

Make one's way: *Go; progress; proceed; succeed; push oneself forward* * He has since made his way to the railway station * What is your plan for making your way in the world? * He made his way home soon after the school closed * He made his way by throwing dust in our eyes * He made his way in life through hard work and perseverance

Make oneself at home: *Be as free and unrestrained as in one's own house* * I stayed with my friend at his house and made myself at home there

Make oneself useful: *Do something to help* * Instead of standing there and doing nothing, why don't you make yourself useful?

Make or break/mar: *Either be successful or be ruined* * God has blessed us with a sense of understanding so that we do not take decisions which break or mar our life

Make out: *Decry; discern; decipher; seek to make it appear; draw up; prove; write out; manage to see; understand somebody's nature; discover* * He made out that he had been badly treated * It is often difficult to make out the truth of an event from a newspaper report * I could not make out all that he scribbled in his notebook * His guilt was clearly made out * He is not such a good lawyer as some make him out to be * His guilt was clearly made out * I have asked the bank to make out a demand draft * We made out a figure in the darkness * What a queer fellow he is that I can't make him out at all * I could not make out the meaning of this verse

Make out a case for: *Argue for* * He has made out a strong case for prison reforms * A case could be made out for his release from imprisonment

Make out one's case: *Give good reasons for one's statement or position* * They made out their case in support of improving the lot of the poor

Make out with: *Progress; get on* * How are things making out with you? * How are you making out with your girl friend?

Make over: *Remake; transform; transfer; present or give in charity* * You can't make over a personality in one day * The basement has been made over into a workshop * He has made over the whole of his property to the national trust * He made over his bungalow to the orphanage

Make overture to: *Try to begin a conversation with* * He began making overtures to a number of merchant banks

Make peace: *End war* * The two warring nations agreed to make peace

Make place too hot for one: *Make impossible for him to stay there* * I think the bitter temperament of the boss will make the office too hot for me to survive

Make play: *Keep things going or push the game on* * They made play of tennis to make the game last for a long time

Make provisions against: *Guard against* * It is a wise thing to make provision against rainy days

Make provisions for: *See that something is for in the future* * We must make provision for old age by way of saving money

Make question: *Demure* * The boys are so inquisitive that they are likely to make question at my suggestion

Make rapid strides: *Make quick progress* * Our country is making rapid strides socially and economically

Make room: *Accommodate* * We must make room for elderly people while travelling in a crowded bus

Make sail: *Increase the quantity of sail; set sail* * The ship made sail before undertaking a long sea journey * The ship made sail down the east coast of South Africa

Make sense: *Have a meaning** What you say does not make any sense

Make sense of: *Understand something difficult* * I cannot make sense of that painting

Makeshift: *Get along as best as could be; a temporary expedient or substitute* * One of our best workers was ill so we had to shift without him * The police have erected makeshift barricades at the crowded places to control the heavy traffic

Make short work of: *Deal with quickly; settle or dispose of promptly* * In the tennis match, Chris made short work of her opponent and won the match easily * We made short work of left-over food to keep the wolf from the door

Make so free as: *Be daring to abrupt* * Do not make yourself so free as to let others feel irritated and annoyed

Make somebody's acquaintance: *To meet somebody for the first time* * I am delighted to make your acquaintance

Make somebody into something: *Change* * He was not always a bully but you made him into one

Make somebody of something: *To follow someone* * We must make an example of him

Make somebody open his eyes: *Make him take notice* * I have been able to make him open his eyes about the consequences of his involvement in the misadventure

Make someone's life a burden: *Life having no liveliness* * The loneliness has made my life a burden

Make something into something: *Converted to* * The huts can be made into temporary houses

Make something of somebody: *Cause to be or become something; understand; interpret* * His parents want to make a doctor of him * What do you make of it all? * What are we to make of his behaviour?

Make something out of nothing: *Exaggerate something** I do not like that person who makes something out of nothing

Make sport of: *Ridicule* * It is inhuman to make sport of physically challenged persons

Make sure of: *Ascertain; put beyond doubt; secure; feel certain* * He made sure of the time of the arrival of the train before leaving home

* The eyewitness story made the judge sure of the involvement of the culprit in the murder case * Don't go higher up the cliff unless you are sure of the footholds * He made sure of the fact that no harm would get done to him under any circumstances

Make the acquaintance of: *Gets to know* * That evening he made the acquaintance of a young actress

Make the best of: *Turn to the best advantage; take in the best spirit; obtain the best result* * We have only a few hours, so we must make the best of our time * In sports, a sportsman makes the best of his defeat without any grief * We should make the best of our poor resources

Make the best of a bad bargain: *Get maximum advantage out of bad circumstances* * Agreed our system of education is not good but why not make the best of a bad bargain

Make the best of one's way: *Go as far as one can* * The traveller made the best of his way to cover up a distance of 50 miles a day

Make the feathers fly: *Cause a quarrel; throw into confusion by a sudden attack* * Persons of mean mentality make their feathers fly over trifle matters * When the bomb exploded in the heart of the city, people made the feather fly to save their lives

Make the grade: *Succeed in climbing steep hill; overcome obstacles; stand a test; be up to standard* * Hillary was the first dauntless person to make the grade by scaling the Mount Everest * Many athletes have made the grade in running the obstacle races * He made the grade in the matriculation examination by standing first in the class * Those who made the grade would be admitted to the next higher class

Make the money fly: *Spend it recklessly* * A frugal person would never make the money fly

Make the most of: *Get as much profit as from something as possible* * We should make the most of the time at our disposal

Make the mouth water: *Arouse a delightful feeling of anticipation or desire* * The very sight of sweets at the confectioner's shop made my mouth water

Make the pace: *Regulate the speed for others by example* *

He made the pace for me on how to dispose of urgent matters

Make the running: *Take the lead; set the pace* * He was ready to make the running of the expedition to the North Pole * The guide has already made the running for him on how to reach his goal smoothly

Make things hot for someone: *Make life unbearable* * A quarrelsome wife makes things hot for her husband

Make things hum: *Set things going briskly* * The beginning of the new admission session in the university has once again made the campus to hum with activity

Make time: *Regain the advantage of lost time; find an opportunity* * I remained in bed for two days, so I had to work hard to make time by covering the loss of school days * I would try to make time for playing cricket

Make tracks: *Make off; go quickly* * It is time we made tracks for home * The snatchers of the purse made tracks towards a dark lane

Make tracks for home: *Set off for home* * After a day's work; they make tracks for home

Make up: *Fabricate; feign; collect; put together; to parcel; put into shape; compose; constitute; repair; complete; supplement; adjust to one's appearance; paint and powder the face; put type into columns and pages; compensate; settle an argument; become friends again; apply cosmetics to the face; decide* * He was very good at making up convincing excuses * He made up to be ill with fever as an excuse for his absence from duty * Have you made up Smith's order yet? * He asked me to make up a bundle of old clothes for distribution to the poor * The grocer was making up the almonds into packages * He was finding it difficult to make up his mind clear as a crystal * Are all animal bodies made up of cells? * An ad hoc committee has been made up to deal with this particular problem * No one knew how to make up for the damaged vehicle * They need eight more men to make their bus full * They would sometimes eat fish to make up for their natural diet * The actor is taking his time to make up for his role * A lady with natural beauty needs no make-up * Who is in charge of making up for the financial page? * He has been ordered to make up for the loss caused due to damage to the scooter * Do the employers in this factory make up for the injuries suffered by the workers at work? * I had hoped to get only a small amount for selling my car but the money I have received makes up for more than expected * The two friends who were at loggerhead with each other have since made up * Most of the people are fond of make-up to attract the attention of others * Have you made it up to go to Canada?

Make up leeway: *Make up for lost time; get back into position* * He will make up leeway towards recovery of his health

Make up one's mind: *Come to a decision* * He has made up his mind to join air force

Make up to: *Make friendly; compensate; to win favours* * He is always making up to influential people * I will make it up to you later * How can we make it up to them for what they have suffered?

Make use of: *Use; employ* * We should make best use of every opportunity that comes our way * How do you make use of your spare time?

Make void: *Make useless* * All his efforts to overtake the top runner in the race were made void

Make war: *Carry on hostilities* * The terrorists are still making war in fulfilment of their ill-designs * They made war on the enemies of mankind

Make water: *Urinate* * If you have any difficulty in making water, you must consult the doctor

Make way: *Give place; advance* * All traffic has to make way for a fire-engine * Our forces are making way against the enemy

Make whoopee: *Take part in noisy rejoicing* * We made a hearty whoopee in the dance club yesterday

Make wing: *Begin flight; depart* * The passenger air bus has already made wing for New York * Suddenly the crows made wings * We made wing to London by air bus in the early morning

Make with: *Have to do with* * I have nothing to make with your personal affairs

Make-believe: *Pretend; pretending; feigning* * The children made believe that they were shipwrecked on a desert island * His whole life these days is a game of make-believe

Make-shift: *A temporary expedient; substitute* * The police have erected make-shift barricades at the crowded places * You can use an empty crate as a make-shift for a table

Making: *Formation* * It took three years in the making of this group

Man about town: *A fashionable idler, dangling about clubs, theatres, etc.* * The man about town has been well known for his modus operandi

Man and boy: *From boyhood onwards* * He has worked for the firm, man and boy, for 30 years

Manhunt: *Search* * The police has been carrying out a manhunt for the proclaimed offender

Man in the street: *The ordinary man* * How will these changes affect the man in the street?

Mankind: *The human race* * Mankind has been in existence since time immemorial

Man of business: *An agent or a lawyer* * You had better consult the man of business in your case

Man of God: *A holy or clergy man* * Religious–minded people were gathered to hear the sermons by the man of God

Man of his hands: *A man of powers* * He is a man of his hands in the art of painting

Man of his word: *Trustworthy man* * He is a man of his word, so you can trust him * He is a man of his word and you can depend upon his help without an iota of doubt

Man of ideals: *Person who has standards of perfection* * A man of ideals is respected everywhere

Man of law: *A lawyer* * He bids fair to be a man of law

Man of letters: *A scholar; a writer* * Winston Churchill was not only a great politician but also a man of letters

Man of parts: *Man of uncommon ability* * The president of our college is a man of parts and therefore everyone respects him

Man of sin: *The devil; anti-Christ* * A man of sin has no eye for right or wrong

Man of straw: *A person of no substance especially financially; imaginary person,* *easily overcome* * A man of straw cannot be a good husband * The husband is only a man of straw in comparison to his wife who controls all household affairs

Man of substance: *Rich man* * A man of substance has a bigger role to play in the society

Man of the world: *One accustomed to the ways and dealings of man* * A man of the world is held in high esteem by the society

Man proposes, God disposes: *We can not escape the fate* * You can make all kinds of plans but they may not materialise because man proposes, God disposes

Man stealer: *One who steals human beings, especially to make slaves of them* * It was also a time when a man stealer used to capture Negroes to serve vested interests

Man to man: *One man to another as individuals in fight or talk; frank and confidential* * Many soldiers fell as a result of a man-to-man fight in the battle-field * Their dealings rest at man-to-man level

Man's estate: *The state of manhood* * When he reached the man's estate, he became rather mature and responsible

Manage to: *Succeed* * In spite of these insults, she managed to keep her temper in control

Manage with: *Contrive* * If I cannot borrow the money, I shall have to manage without it * If only I could manage with whatever I have at present

Man-at-arms: *A soldier especially mounted and heavily armed* * The man-at-arms has been decorated with many medals and awards for his valiant feats in the battlefield

Manhood suffrage: *Right to vote accorded to male citizens in general* * Manhood suffrage is still practiced in various countries

Man-jack: *Individual man* * Every man-jack has his own likes and dislikes

Man-milliner: *Man engaged in millinery (often in contempt)* * A man-milliner is looked down upon by many people for his silly deeds

Mannerly: *Well behaved* * His mannerly style of speaking has been much praised by the people

Man-queller: *A man-killer; murderer* * That man-queller has been sentenced to death * A tiger is also said to be a man-queller

Man-slayer: *One who kills a man* * The convicted man-slayer was hanged to death

Mantrap: *Any insidious danger to passengers; a trap for catching trespassers* * Many travellers have fallen prey to mantraps and lost their lives in the past * The setting up of a mantrap is a good device for safety

Many a: *Many* * Many a boy was there to see the feats of the juggler

Many a little makes a mickle: *Every little helps* * It is to be admitted that many a little makes a mickle, particularly when a small child is working all by herself with no help

Many a time: *Often* * Many a time one has to face odd situations in life

Many, many happy returns of the day: *Best wishes for a happy birthday* * On the eve of my friend's birthday, I wished him many, many happy returns of the day

Many men, many minds: *The more the men the more wider is the pool of wisdom* * All the staff was invited to the brainstorming session to present their views because many men meant many minds

Many-headed: *Having many heads; consisting of many* * Many-headed creatures have been found in the sea * Efforts are afoot in solving the many-headed problems

Many-headed beast: *The people* * It was very difficult to control the many-headed beast gathered to block the road traffic

Many-sided: *Having many aspects* * The company is taking into consideration the many-sided possibilities available for increasing trade with that foreign country

March past: *The march of a body in front of one who reviews it* * It was really a treat to watch the march-past ceremony at the parade-ground

Mare's nest: *Something which does not exist* * The police followed up the clues but it proved to be a mare's nest

Mark down: *Set down in writing; lower the price of* * If you witness an accident, mark down the licence of the car * Increase in supply and decrease in demand naturally marks down the prices of essential articles

Mark my words: *Note what I say* * You better mark my words about your future progress

Mark off: *Lay down the boundary lines of; graduate; mark(on a list as attended to or disposed of; show a difference* * The plot purchased for building a house has been marked off with a fence * This measuring tape has been marked off in both inches and centimetres * We have marked off today's sale figures on the list * This very characteristic marks her off from her mother

Mark out: *Lay out the plan or outline of; to destine* * The boundary lines on the tennis court has been marked out with white paint * He has been marked out for a special management course

Mark something on: *Put or leave a mark on* * My friend has got his name marked on his jacket.

Mark time: *Move the feet alternatively in the same manner as in marching but without changing ground; keep things going without progress* * The soldiers were marking time on the parade ground * I am marking time in wait for an opportunity * He is adopting strange methods just to mark time

Mark up: *Put higher prices* * The new tax has made it mandatory to mark up all the goods in the shop * All the items have been marked up for sale in our shop

Mark with: *Have natural marks or visible signs; have the scars* * A zebra is marked with strips * His face is marked with smallpox * Her face was marked with grief

Mark with a white stone: *Mark as particularly fortunate* * It appears as if he was marked with a white stone to become a millionaire overnight!

Marked with a T: *Branded as a thief* * He is a habitual thief marked with a T on his chest

Market overt: *Open or public market* * You will never get a picture as good as this one on the market overt

Marksman: *Person who shoots well; a man good at hitting a mark or one who shoots well* * He has bagged many prizes as a marksman * My brother was an expert marksman

Markswoman: *A woman good at hitting a mark or one who shoots well* * That markswoman has won many medals in rifle-shooting competitions

Mark-white: *The centre of target* * He is a well-trained rifleman to strike the mark-white

Marry money: *Marry a rich person* * Her sole aim is to marry money

Mar-sport: *A spoilsport* * We should not mar-sport and ruin the people's pleasure

Mar-text: *An ignorant preacher* * The mar-text did not know that his good words were falling in deaf ears

Martial arts: *Oriental fighting techniques using swords/ sticks, etc.* * Countries in the east have interest in the martial arts

Martial law: *Maintenance of law by the army instead of police* * Cases pertaining to the army personnel are dealt with under martial law

Mass media: *Means of communication (TV, radio, newspapers)* * Mass media has been playing a significant role in conveying information on various events to a large number of people

Mass murderer: *Killer of a large number of people* * Taimur Lang was a mass murderer as also an invader

Mass production: *Production in large scale by a standard process* * A rat race for mass production of weapons all over the world is a matter of worry

Mass-meeting: *A large meeting for a public protest; assertion* * In the mass-meeting of political parties it was decided not to accept the membership of the UN Security Council

Mastermind: *A piece of work worthy of a master* * The mastermind behind this project has already been adequately given credit for his work

Master of situation: *One who has a situation under control* * We should strive to be the master of every situation that calls for solution of unforeseen problems

Master of the Rolls: *Head of the record office* * He had to approach the Master of the Rolls for getting necessary information

Masterpiece: *One's greatest achievement* * *Macbeth* is one of the masterpieces by Shakespeare

Masterwork: *The best example of the artist's work* * The museum houses several of the masterworks of Vinci

Match for: *Equal* of * He is no match for me in tennis

Material distinction: *The distinction between individuals of the same species* * The material distinction should be given less importance between man and man

Material evidence: *Evidence tending to prove or to disprove the matter under judgement* * An individual has a legal duty not to withhold material evidence from a grand jury

Material fallacy: *A fallacy in the matter or thought rather than in the logical form* * A material fallacy can never provide a strong foothold to serve your cause

Matter in question: *Which is being discussed or under consideration* * The matter in question before the house is how to bring about educational reforms

Matter of course: *A thing occurring in natural time and order, as to be expected; usual affair* * It is a matter of course that we are ultimately bound to go to dust * You need not ask him to come as he will come as a matter of course

Matter of fact: *Truth of facts* * *practical; said or done without showing emotion or keeping to the fact* * The cycle of birth and death is an obvious matter of fact * They are facing matter-of-fact difficulties of organisation and finance * He told us the news of her death in a very matter-of-fact way

Matter of life and death: *Matter of great importance* * To root out terrorism from our soil has become a matter of life and death for all of us

Matter of opinion: *Something about which opinions may differ* * What kind of a political order is best for our country is a matter of opinion

Matter of time: *Certain to happen and will probably happen quite soon* * It appeared to be only a matter of time before they would be apprehended

Matters of moment: *Matter of importance* * This magazine publishes the matters of moment in great detail

May it please you: *Deferential or polite formula to address or request* * May it please you to keep quiet while the speaker is making his speech

Mean business: *Be in earnest* * I mean business when I say that I will teach him a lesson for his rudeness

Mean nothing to: *Have no meaning for; have no concern of / interest in* * These technical words mean nothing to me * He used to like her but she means nothing to him now

Mean-spirited: *Sly; unpleasant* * We should avoid

mean-spirited remarks about any person

Means well: *Has good intention* * He means well when he warns you of the danger

Meant to: *Supposed to* * You are meant to be regular in your studies

Measure for measure: *Equal retaliation* * Justice always demands measure for measure

Measure length: *Engage in a contest* * He is preparing himself to measure length in a declamation contest

Measure one's length: *Fall or be thrown down at full length* * He had to measure his length in the wrestling bout

Measure one's strength: *Try or test* * America with its allies has been carrying out military exercises from time to time

Measure others' corn by one's own bushel: *Judge others by oneself* * He would be a blind person who measures others' corn by his own bushel

Measure swords: *To fight* * He has made up his mind to measure swords against his adversary

Measure up to: *Be able to do (a different job)* * The state of repair failed to measure up to their exacting standards

Meddle in: *Interfere in* * Do not meddle in the affairs of others * Do not meddle in politics

Meddle with: *Interfere with* * Who has been meddling with my papers?

Media gaze: *Fixed, long and steady look of mass communication* * In modern times nothing remains hidden from the media gaze

Medicine chest: *Cupboard for keeping medicines in* * That doctor had a medicine-chest full of various kinds of medicines

Meet all expenses: *Pay them* * The rich man met all expenses incurred in the marriage ceremony of the poor girl

Meet half-way: *Make concessions in compromise; meet something half-way; worry about it before it comes* * At last they agreed to meet half-way to settle the deal * It is silly to meet worries half-way

Meet in with: *Meet with; come across* * We never thought that we would be destined to meet in with this kind of chaos * Your stars foretell that you will meet a strange person who may influence your future

Meet one's fate: *Be killed* * The

bus fell into the river and all its occupants met their fate

Meet one's Waterloo: *Have a disaster* * That contestant had to meet his Waterloo in the inter-college elocution contest

Meet the eye: *See with eyes* * She was afraid to meet my eye

Meet with: *Come to one especially unexpectedly; undergo; chance to experience* * He met with an old friend at a dinner party * The new aircraft met with its first accident * One will have to meet with many ups and downs in life

Mega bucks: *Good deal of money* * The rare antiques when put to auction brought him mega bucks

Melt something down: *Melt a metal in order to use it as a raw material* * Railings were melted down for cannon production

Melted at: *Became softened* * My heart melted at the sight of the puppies

Melted away: *Disappeared* * The rioters melted away when the police appeared * The snow melted away when the sun came out

Melted into: *Fade slowly away* * One colour melted into another in the sky at sunset

Melted with: *Became sympathetic* * Her heart melted with pity

Melting-point: *Temperature at which a solid melts* * Lead has a lower melting-point than iron * Gold has a low melting-point

Melting pot: *Undecided; place where people of different origins come to live together* * The fate of Kashmir is still in a melting pot * India can be called melting pot of diverse cultures and customs

Men in the minority: *More women than men* * In some states the men are in the minority

Men of mark: *Distinguished persons* * As a matter of fact men of mark are always held in great esteem everywhere

Men of the day: *Persons of importance at any time* * Men of the day find greater place in the news

Menace to: *Danger* * A gambler like him is a menace to the society

Mend fire: *Make fire* * We had to mend fire to get rid of the biting cold

Mend one's pace: Go quicker * We had to mend our pace to reach the railway station on time

Mend one's ways: *Reform one's*

behaviour * If you do not mend your ways, you will ruin yourself

Mere: *Not more than; nothing of any value or importance* * She is merely a child * It is a mere trifle

Mere words: *Words without acts* * Mere words do not help in grief

Merely: *Simply* * I said it merely as a joke

Merry-go-round: *A revolving machine with horses, cars, etc. .on which the children ride at fun fairs* * The boys and girls liked to sit on the merry-go-round

Merrymaking: *Celebrations; festivity* * The merrymaking continued late into the night

Mesh-work: *A network; web* * An intelligence mesh-work is a must for every state to guard against any attack by the enemy * There is a mesh-work of electric lines that provides light and power throughout the region

Mess about: *Spend spare time doing something; waste time with; disrupt or interfere; treat badly* * Some of the lads had been messing about when they should have been working * He was messing about, doing nothing * He didn't want you come and mess about with things * You have been messing about all the summer and I am fed up with it

Mess of pottage: *A material advantage accepted in exchange for something of higher worth* * In case you abide by his instructions, you will certainly get a mess of pottage that would stand you in good stead

Mess up: *Spoil or ruin; make untidy or dirty* * That will mess up the whole analysis * I am used to him messing up the kitchen

Mete out: *Give (reward or punishment)* * Justice was meted out to them * The magistrate meted out fines as high as a thousand rupees

Middle-of-the-road: *Moderate in politics)* * It has been observed that political parties try to stick to the middle-of-the road policies

Midsummer madness: *Temporary madness or erratic behaviour attributed to the sun of mid-summer* * People perspire profusely and gasp for breath as a result of midsummer madness when the sun blazes with all its fury

Might and main: *Utmost strength; utmost struggle* * He had to fight with all his might and main to defeat the opponent in the boxing bout * We will have to fight with might and main to eradicate terrorism once and for all

Might as well: *It would be better if* * You might as well take your dog with you

Miles too good: *Much too big* * It's miles too good to be in your sweet company

Milk and water: *Weak* * The sentiments he expressed in the public comprised only milk and water

Milk of human kindness: *Real and natural kindness* * The milk of human kindness resides in those noble souls who help all human beings in trouble

Milk teeth: *First set of teeth produced by a child* * Every child cuts milk teeth at the initial stage

Mill around/about: *Move in various directions* * There were many boys and girls milling around on the lawn

Mince (one's words): *Not speak freely and directly* * Stop mincing your words and just tell me in short what you think of my idea

Mince along: *Walk along in an effected manner, taking small steps* * He minced along the road just to attract the attention of others

Mince matters: *Speak of things with affected delicacy or to soften an account unduly* * He is mincing matters just to delay action from being taken

Mind field: *The scope of the mind* * Our mind field can soar limitlessly

Mind one's own business: *Confine oneself to one's own efforts* * Please mind your own business and do not interfere in my work

Mind one's p's and q's: *Be watchfully accurate and punctilious* * You mind your p's and q's or I will hit you * He who minds his p's and q's makes for a good citizen

Mind your eye: *Look out; take care* * Mind your eye that no scamp hangs about here! * I have already alerted him to mind his eye against the dangers looming large

Mind your own business: *That is none of your affair* * I ask you to mind your own business and not poke your nose in my work

Mind's eye: *Visual imagination; mental view; contemplation; imagination* * Mind's eye can soar limitlessly with matchless speed * He pictured the scene in his mind's eye * According to my mind's eye, he has an aptitude for sports * I have to set my mind's eye on this very knotty problem * Nothing would be far from our mind's eye over this issue

Minded to do something: *Disposed or inclined* * He could do it if he were so minded to do

Mind-reading: *Thought reading* * Some astrologers are very quick at mind-reading

Mine of information: *Full of information; plenty of information* * He is really a mine of information and always keeps abreast of the times * Newspapers do bring to our doors a mine of information about day-to-day happenings

Mineral pitch: *Asphalt* * People make use of mineral pitch to get rid of cold or weakness

Mineral rights: *Permission to dig out minerals* * Many private agencies have been given mineral rights by the government on agreement

Mingle tears: *Weep together* * The aggrieved people mingled their tears on the passing away of their popular leader

Mini and maxi: *Small and large size* * This emporium has mini and maxi dresses for sale at cheaper rates

Ministry of the Interior: *Ministry dealing with the affairs inside a country* * My uncle is an official working in the Ministry of Interior

Mint condition: *Perfect; exactly as when made initially* * This car, though manufactured five years ago, looks in mint condition

Minus somebody/something: *Without somebody* * He attended the function minus his wife * He came back from the war minus a leg

Mirror image: *Exact copy but reverse as in a mirror* * That room beyond proved to be the image of the first room * West Indian communities in London are a mirror image of the black community of North America

Miscarriage of justice: *Failure of the course to do justice; wrong decision by a court* * He was reasonably convinced that there was a miscarriage of justice * The decision taken by the lower court has been declared as miscarriage of justice by the higher court

Mischief in brewing: *Mischief is gathering force* * Some positive steps have to be taken to nip the mischief in brewing

Mischief-maker: *One who makes mischief* * The worst mischief-maker has since been transferred elsewhere

Mischief-making: *Causing mischief* * The naughty boy was taken to task for mischief-making

Mischievous prank: *Playful trick* * We should avoid playing mischievous pranks on any person

Misconduct oneself: *Behave badly* * Those who misconduct their business affairs are sure to suffer sooner or later

Misfortune never comes alone: *Unwelcome events or happening taking place all at once* * It has been rightly said that misfortune never comes alone

Misprision of heresy: *Knowledge of and failure to give information about treason* * He has been held for misprision of heresy by the authority

Miss a trick: *Be not attentive* * He does not miss a trick

Misfire: *Fail to go off or explode* * It was a bad news for the army that the maiden test-firing of the missile misfired

Miss Nancy: *A very effeminate person* * People call him Miss Nancy in jest for his womanlike voice and behaviour

Miss one's tip: *Fail in one's plan or attempt* * Don's miss your tip of securing first grade in the test

Miss one's vocation: *Should be in another job for which one is better suited* * She missed her vocation

Miss something out: *Omit; fail to put in; say* * The printers have missed out a line * I shall miss out the sweet course

Miss stay: *Fail in going about from one task to another* * The sailor miss stayed in taking advantage of the wind blowing from the side when sailing windward

Miss the buss/boat: *Lose one's opportunity* * If you miss the bus/boat now, you will have to repent later on **Miss the point of:** *Fail to see* * He missed the point of the story

Missing link: *Any point of fact need to complete a series or a chain of argument* * The police is striving hard to find the missing links in the evidence provided by him

Mission in life: *Calling or chosen task* * His mission in life is to help orphans

Mist over: *Cover or covered with mist* * Her eyes misted over as she listened to the speech of Mahatma Gandhi * The mirror misted over as a result of stormy weather / rough weather

Mistake one's man: *Think too lightly of the man one has to deal with* * It would be unwise to mistake your man about his potentiality

Mistake one's way: *Take the wrong road* * You seem to have mistaken your way to the taxi-stand

Misthought: *A wrong notion* * Your head is full of misthoughts about his prospective ability

Mistress of the sea: *Chief naval power* * The United States of America is now reckoned to be the mistress of the sea

Mix up: *To confuse; to involve; assume someone is someone else* * I think you must be mixing up with someone else * Those who got mixed up in the conspiracy have since been arrested * I mixed him up with his brother

Mixed blessings: *In some way it is a good thing but in others it is not* * Our discovery campaign proved to be a mixed blessing

Mixed doubles: *Doubles match where a man and a woman play against another man and woman* * The mixed doubles players were having a field day on the tennis court

Mixed feelings: *Feelings for and against* * I have mixed feelings about the project

Mixed marriage: *Marriage between two people of different races* * Time is not afar when mixed marriages would become a common affair

Mixed school: *School with boys and girls* * Mixed schools are increasing progressively in our country

Mocks the pauses: *Throws away the opportunities given by the pauses* * He who mocks the pauses is a silly man

Mole out: *Seek or elicit* * We will have to mole out information through all the sources to make out a strong case

Money begets money: *Money generates more money* * It is acknowledged on all heads that money begets money

Money for jam: *Money very easily earned* * The purchase of a lottery ticket brought him money for jam

Money is no object: *No obstacle; problems* * Since money is no object, the cabinet will unanimously approve the new project

Money makes the mare go:

Money is a good servant always at our command * We shall not be forgetful of the fact that money makes the mare go

Money to burn: *Money in great abundance* * Those who have money to burn can go to any extent in spending it

Money-grubber: *A person whose chief or only interest in life is to make money* * Some persons are only born as money-grubbers

Money-spinner: *Book, play, etc. that make a lot of money* * The book titled *God's Own Country* has proved to be a money-spinner for its author

Monkey-nut: *Ground nut* * Monkey-nuts taste like almonds

Monkey about: *Play mischievously* * Stop monkeying about with those tools!

Monopolise the conversation: *Do all the talking and not let anyone speak* * Some people take pride in monopolising the conversation while others hate it

Month's mind: *Commemoration by masses one month after death or burial; strong desire or inclination* * The Reverend Father along with the masses in the church said prayers as a mark of month's mind for seeking peace for the departed souls * He showed me his month's mind to be a doctor and serve the poor

Monumental mason: *Person who makes gravestones* * A monumental mason has a conspicuous standing in the society

Moonlight flitting: *A hasty removal by night with rent unpaid* * They dodged the landlord through moonlit flitting

Moonshine: *Something which is unreal or foolish* * People in common are tired and sick of war because they know that its glory is all moonshine

Moot point: *Question which is open to discussion* * How serious is the government to provide free education to the weaker section of the society is still a moot point

Mop of hair: *Long and untidy hair* * In the play, the actor sported a mop of hair which made him look handsome

Moral fibre: *Strength of moral feelings* * In our present-day educational system, the moral fibre has been ignored to a great extent

Moral support: *Encouragement; without active help* * We should offer our moral support to those who abide by truth and honesty

More and more: *Continuously increasing* * The cost of living is rising because of the soaring prices of essential commodities

More by token: *In proof of this; besides* * What would you like to say more by token that he had no hand in the mischief-making * He is quite vulgar more by token

More and yet more: *In addition* * Having had enough money at his disposal, he needs more and yet more of it

More hurry, less speed: *The more you hurry, the less real progress you will make* * There is no point in rushing to meet the deadline because the more you hurry, the less speed you will acquire

More in sorrow than in anger: *With more regret than anger for what was done* * The miscarriage of justice by the court of law was taken more in sorrow than in anger by the general public

More often than not: *Usually* * More often than not, he is late for lunch

More or less: *About or in round numbers; approximately; practically* * It is an hour's journey more or less * There were, more or less, a hundred persons at the party * There were more or less eight candidates who applied for the job

More praise than pudding: *Material reward* * The poor people need more praise than pudding

More than bargain for: *More than expected* * I got more than I bargained for

More than enough: *Too much* * Despite having more than enough to live on they still find themselves to be rather poor

More to the point: *More important than something else* * I ignored the idea of accepting a job in Paris because apart from other problems like food, etc., I don't speak French to be more to the point

Morganatic marriage: *Marriage of a king or queen to someone of lower rank who does not take their title* * There was only a rare case of morganatic marriage in England in the past

Mort ice lock: *Lock which is fitted into a door* * A mort ice lock is found safer than ordinary locks

Mortal rate: *Number of deaths* *

Due to medical facilities, the mortal rate has decreased to a very large extent

Most favoured nation: *A nation that has been accorded the lowest scale of import duties* * Pakistan is still reluctant to grant India a most-favoured nation status in commercial matters

Motor mover: *Lawn mover powered by a motor* * Our lawn is kept trim by a motor mover

Mount guard at: *Act as a guard or sentinel* * Household troops mount guard at Buckingham Palace

Mount up: *Become greater in amount* * Our family expenses are mounting up day by day

Mounted police: *Police on horseback* * The mounted police play an important role in maintaining law and order

Move heaven and earth: *Make every possible effort; do one's utmost* * Indian citizens should move heaven and earth in reviving its past glory of the golden age * He had to move heaven and earth to win the case

Move in: *Settle with furniture in a new house* * We have moved into our new house only yesterday

Move off: *Go away* * The train has moved off from this station for Ludhiana

Move to: *Arouse the feeling* * We were moved to tears at the pitiable sight of the poor widow

Move with: *Cause to be* * I was moved with pity for him

Moving staircase: *Escalator* * The multistoreyed building has been provided with moving staircases to be run by electric power

Much cry, little wool: *Much show and little substance* * It is better to do work and complete it rather than to much cry, little wool without putting in any effort

Much less: *Often used by confusion for much more* * I did not speak to him, much less to discuss your problems with him

Much maligned: *Much criticised* * He has been much maligned for his neglect of duty

Much of a muchness: *Very similar or almost the same* * The two candidates are much of a muchness and it is hard to choose between them

Much the most expensive: *By far the most expensive* * We have since disposed off our old automobile which was proving much the most expensive

Much the same: *About the same* * The patient's condition is much the same

Much to: *Greatly to* * Much to her surprise, she came across a snake while strolling in the lawn

Much to my amazement: *To my great surprise* * I had a nasty fall though I did not suffer any serious injury

Much to my regret: *I am very sorry* * Though all religions preach non-violence, yet, much to my regret, much blood has been shed by the followers

Muck about: *Do useless or unnecessary things* * I saw him mucking about with a jug of flowers on the table

Muck in together: *Cooperate in the work* * If we muck in together, we will have the job done in no time

Muck out a stable: *Clean a stable* * He mucks out the stable every morning

Muck sweat: *Profuse sweat* * The exercise of body-building brought him out into a muck sweat

Muck up: *Fail badly* * I have taken the driving test twice and both the times I have mucked it up

Muck-raker: *Person who is always looking for scandal* * A muck-raker is despised by everyone

Muck-raking: *Anything disgusting or dirty* * Those who involve themselves in muck-raking cannot save their skin from the long arm of the law * The act of muck-raking landed them behind the bars

Mud slinging: *Malicious slander intended to discredit another* * There is a good deal of mud slinging going on amongst various political parties these days

Muddle along: *Get on in a foolish or helpless way with no clear purpose or plan* * He is still muddling along aimlessly

Muddle away: *Squander or Fritter away confusedly* * We should not muddle away the public money that is allocated for a specific purpose

Muddle through: *Get through difficulties blunderingly* * How did they muddle through the undertaking is a long story

Muddle-headed: *Confused in mind* * He was dismissed as a muddle-headed mischief-maker

Mull over: *Think about; ponder* * I sat there and tried to mull things over in my head

Multiples of five: *In quantities of five, ten, fifteen, etc.* * All the articles available in this shop are sold in multiples of five

Multiples store: *Company with many shops in several towns* * All items of essential commodities can be easily had from the multiples store

Multiply words: *Say much or be wordy* * It is useless to multiply words on bogus matters

Murder will out: *Murder can not remain hidden; the truth will come to light* * Surely the murder will out and the culprit will have to face the music * Everybody knows the fact that murder will out one day

Murmur at: *Complain in a low tone* * The child murmured something when scolded by his teacher

Muscle dystrophy: *Disease causing gradual weakening of the muscles* * He is a patient of muscle dystrophy and is receiving the necessary treatment

Muscle in on: *Use force to get a share of something considered advantageous* * I don't like the way he has muscled the way in here

Muse on: *Meditate upon* * The old professor mused long on his past

Mute of malice: *Refusing to plead* * It is up to the judge to apply his discretion against a person's mute of malice

Mutter under one's breath: *Say quietly* * He muttered something under his breath to her

Mutton dressed as lamb: *Use of an elderly person dressed in a style suitable for a young person* * The people standing there burst out laughing when they saw that old man mutton dressed as lamb

Mutual consent: *With the agreement of both parties* * This project is being executed by the mutual consent of both the partners

Mutual friend: *Friend of the both* * He is our mutual friend

Muzzle the press: *Stop newspapers from printing what they want; gagging news* * In a democratic system, there is no undue muzzling of the press

My fingers itch: *Impatient to do* * My fingers are itching to give him a sound beating for his misdeeds

My folks: *My family* * My folk comprise five male and three female members

My hands are full: *I am very busy* * Just now my hands are full

My hat!: *An exclamation of surprise or disbelief* * My hat! How could he have defeated his opponent who was far superior to him?

Myrmidons of the law: *Policeman; bailiff* * It is the duty of myrmidons of the law to maintain law and order at any cost

N

Nail a lie to the counter: *Expose it and put it out of currency* * The base coins were nailed a lie to the counter

Nail in someone's coffin: *Destruction or downfall of someone* * Debit cards are the first nails in the coffin of traditional financial methods * Addiction of drugs proved a nail in his coffin

Nail one's colours to the mast: *Commit oneself to some party or plan of action; refuse to climb down or surrender* * He is ready to nail his colours to the mast to promote the interests of his party * You can do what you want but I will nail my colours to the mast

Nail something down: *To reach an agreement or a decision* * All parties seemed anxious to nail down a ceasefire

Naked eye: *The eye unassisted by glasses of any kind* * The planet should be visible with the naked eye.

Naked flame: *Flame with no protective shield* * The gas cylinder burst into naked flame.

Name after a person: *Give the name to in honour of a person* * Tasmania was named after its discoverer, A.J. Tasman

Name the day: *Fix a day* * Soon after their engagement, the priest was asked to name the day for the marriage

Name worthy: *Worth naming; distinguished* * There are many names-worthy celebrities who sacrificed their lives to serve the cause of humanity

Namesake: *Person or thing with the same name as another* * I remember that my namesake friend was abducted by some miscreants

Naming or call names: *Bestow abuse upon* * A gentleman would always desist from naming or calling names to anyone.

Narrow circumstances: *Poverty* * He managed to pull on even in the narrow circumstances.

Narrow escape: *Saved with a difficulty; close shave* * Thank

God you had a narrow escape yesterday in a motor accident

Narrow majority: *Very small margin of votes* * The Bill was passed in the lower house with a narrow majority

Narrow squeak: *Near miss or narrow escape* * They had a narrow squeak from being hurt by the bomb blast

Narrow-minded: *Not easily seeing or sympathetic zing with the ideas of others* * He is narrow-minded nationalist * He has a narrow-minded attitude towards others

Nasal twang: *Accent made by speaking through the nose* * Some people, by nature, have a nasal twang

Nasty piece of work: *Unpleasant, unkind and dishonest person* * He, being a nasty piece of work, has since been ostracised by the whole village

National service: *Temporary conscription into the armed forces* * Young people must join in the national service

Nationwide: *All over the country* * There was a nationwide protest against the suicidal attacks launched by the terrorists

Native bear: *The Koala* * The native bear named Koala is an Australian animal with thick grey fur, large ears and no tail.

Native to: *Plant or animal which originally comes from a certain country* * Tobacco plant, it is said, was native to America only

Natural gas: *Gas which is found in the earth* * The Oil and Natural Gas commission has been leaving no stone unturned to exploit natural gas in the country

Natural wastage: *Reducing the number of workers by not replacing those who leave* * Half of the posts will be lost through natural wastage

Naughty pack: *A person, especially a woman of loose life* * There will be no end to crimes unless we are able to control the naughty pack

Naval engagement: *Battle at sea* * Our naval forces are always on the alert to tackle any naval engagement

Ne'er do well: *Person who is good for nothing* * I have nothing to do with that ne'er do well

Near-legged: *Walking so that the legs interfere* * A near-legged persons cannot have a brisk walk

Near-sighted: *Short-sighted* * He is near-sighted and wears glasses * A near- sighted person has a very short vision of things

Near at hand: *Within easy reach; not far distant in the future* * Your reference book should always been kept near at hand * The examinations are near at hand

Near by: *Not far off* * The bathing pool is just near by the rose garden

Near miss: *A miss that is almost a hit; a fortunate escape from danger* * He hit the ball to score a goal but it was a near miss * I had a near miss when a time bomb exploded at a very close distance

Near on/upon: *Not far in tie from or almost* * It was near upon midnight when the police raided the den of the dacoits

Near point: *The nearest point the eye can focus* * The group photograph of the team was taken from the near point

Near side: *On the side of the road, i.e. nearest the edge of the road* * The driver lost control of the steering wheel and veered to the near side

Near the knuckle: *Verging on the indecent* * His last remark to her was a bit near the knuckle.

Near touch: *Close shave* * Yesterday I had a near touch in a major motor accident

Nearer the church farther from God: *Darkness prevails beneath the lamp* * It seems that nearer the church farther from God because despite his being a priest, God is making him suffer from a severe illness

Nearly related: *Closely related* * He invited to the feast all his nearly related family members

Necessary evil: *Evil which can not be avoided; something bad but which can not be done with reasonably* * Examination is a necessary evil

Neck and crop: *Completely; bodily; summarily; unceremoniously* * He was neck and crop under debt * The man who resisted the robbers in the train was thrown out of compartment neck and crop * They rejected our problems neck and crop as being unimportant * He walked off neck and crop, giving her friendly smile

Neck and neck: *Side by side; exactly equal* * The two athletes kept running the race neck and neck throughout the entire course * The bout between the wrestlers was a neck and neck fight

Neck of the woods: *A particular place or area* * He is from your neck of the woods (area where you live)

Neck or nothing: *Risking everything* * One should not go to the extent of neck or nothing while gambling

Necking party: *Petting party (a gathering for the purpose of amorous caressing at an organised sport)* * He is very much interested to be present at every necking party held in the surrounding area

Need (to have) one's head examined: *Be crazy* * You need to have your head examined because how can you cry for the moon

Needful: *Necessary* * Do what is needful

Needle in a haystack: *A thing almost impossible to find* * Searching for one man in this crowded city is like looking for a needle in a haystack

Needless to say: *Unnecessary to say* * It is needless to say, he kept his promise * The problem, needless to say, is the cost involved

Neither chick nor child: *No issue* * The young married couple has neither a chick nor a child

Neither fish nor flesh/Neither fish nor good red herring/ Neither fish nor fowl: *Be neither one thing nor another* * The irrelevant points that cropped up in the course of discussion made it difficult to make neither fish nor flesh of the subject

Neither here nor there: *Of no special importance; irrelevant* * The idea expressed by him could stand neither here nor there * What you say is neither here nor there * This may be neither here nor there but I have to say it

Neither hup nor wind: *Neither do one thing nor another* * He could make neither hup nor wind of the assignment offered to him

Nerve-racking: *Distressfully straining nerves* * It was a nerve-racking drive up the mountain

Nerve centre: *Place from which an activity or organisation is controlled and instructions are sent out* * Mumbai is considered to be the commercial nerve centre of India

Nerve oneself for: *Summon up one's strength* * He nerved himself to save that woman from the clutches of a ruffian

Nerveless: *Having no strength or feeling; having no fear* * The knife fell from her nerveless fingers * He is a nerveless rider

Nervous breakdown: *Physical*

and mental collapse caused by worry; state where one becomes surely depressed * He has been admitted to hospital for his nervous breakdown * He had a nervous breakdown when he heard the sad news of his failure in the intermediate examination

Nervous system: *Brain, spinal cord and nervous collectively; pattern of fibres in the body* * Our body is made up of a very complicated nervous system * The nervous system has been damaged as he received a stroke

Nest egg: *A sum of money set aside or saved for the future* * They don't worry for rainy days who are prudent enough to arrange the nest egg

Net a big profit: *Make a lot of money* * The bumper crop has helped the farmer to net a big profit this season

Net profit: *Actual gain after expenses have been paid* * He earned a net profit of a few lakh of rupees out of his business this year

Nether regions: *Bottom part* * He is feeling a great pain in nether regions of his body

Nethermost: *Lowest* * The nethermost depth of the ocean is perhaps yet to be discovered by the explorers

Network: *Interconnecting system* * Our great country has set up an advanced television network through various satellites to bring the people very close

Never hear the end of it: *Hear a talked about again and again* * My brother was so angry when I lost his wrist-watch that I will never hear the end of it

Never mind: *Don't worry about it; it does not matter* * Never mind, if you have broken the watch because we can buy a new one * Never mind if you have forgotten to bring your exercise book

Never mind about something: *Should not think because it is not as important as something else* * Never mind your car but what about the damage to my fence? * Never mind washing the dishes as I would do them later on

Never more: *At no future time* * God may forbid that such an earthquake should occur never more

Never say die: *Never give up hope of success* * In spite of repeated failures one should never say die

Never set the Thames on fire: *Never do anything remarkable*

* He is a mediocre person and can never set the Thames on fire

Never so: *Ever so* * He never so much as smiled when he saw her

Never the wiser or none the wiser: *Still in ignorance* * I have read the instructions but I am still never the wiser on how to operate the machine * He came away none the wiser after attending his language class

Never was: *Someone who never was of any account* * Do you think him to be a never-was to his near and dear ones?

Never you mind: *Not to ask about something because you are not going to tell them* * Never you mind, how I found it out?

Never-ending: *Seeming to last for ever* * House work is a never-ending task

Never-never land: *An imaginary place which is nice and pleasant* * Who would not have liked to go to a never-never land had it really been there?

Never-never: *Higher-purchase system* * It is now very easy to have a car of your choice on never-never

Nevertheless: *Notwithstanding* * There has been no news, nevertheless I cannot give up on hoping * Our defeat was expected, but it was disappointing nevertheless

Neverthemore: *None the more* * He has neverthemore skill to give this job a fine touch

Never-to-be-forgotten: *Memorable* * The beautiful scenery of Kashmir leaves an impact of never-to-be-forgotten on those who have a chance to be there

New departure: *Change of purpose or method or a new course of procedure* * We were surprised at his new departure from the profession of a doctor to that of a businessman

New-laid: *Fresh; just laid* * The new-laid eggs by the hens will be available in the market tomorrow only

New look: *A new and more up-to-date appearance* * The high street has been given a new look

New to: *Existing but not seen; experienced before or not familiar; not yet familiar with something* * Our system of handling the job is probably new to you * I should tell you I am completely new to this kind of work

New twist to the story: *Unexpected change* * Police investigation has given a new twist to the story dealing with the 'stamp scam'

News ran: *News spread* * The news ran like a wild fire that three most wanted dacoits were killed in an encounter with the police

News-stand: *Place where you can buy newspapers and magazines* * The first issue of the magazine hit the news-stands today

Newspaper round: *Number of houses where a boy regularly delivers newspapers* * He has to cover a large area during his newspaper round every morning

News value: *Value as news from the journalist's point of view* * This newspaper publishes the events of news value only

News-vendor: *A seller of newspaper* * We get our daily newspapers from the news-vendor

Next but: *Merely* * Next but doubts can prevent you from succeeding

Next door: *The next house/room* * The manager's office is just next door * Our next-door neighbour is a principal of the government college.

Next door to: *Nearly; near to* * He is our neighbour and lives just next door to our residence

Next of kin: *The relatives of a deceased person among whom his personal property may be distributed if he dies intestate;* * The personal property of the deceased person was equally distributed amongst his next of kin

Next to: *Up to; thoroughly acquainted with; adjacent to; almost* * The temperature went next to 35°C * Which are the towns next to Chandigarh in size? * It is next to impossible to be friends with him * Next to our relatives are friends, teachers and neighbours

Next to nothing: *Almost nothing at all* * He knew next to nothing about horticulture

Ni distance: *Not at all far; very short distance* * There is ni distance left to get at the desired spot

Nice-looking: *Attractive* * That nice-looking young girl has been crowned as Miss World.

Nick stick: *A tally* * He hopes to improve on his nick stick of three goals in the next game

Nid-nod: *Keep nodding* * He answered all my queries in nid-nod without uttering a single word

Nigger in the wood-pile: *A hidden motive* * We must be watchful of the people having nigger in the wood-pile

Nigh-hand: *Near hand* * The robbers kept their weapons nigh-hand so that they could easily make use of them in self-defence

Night after night: *For many nights in succession* * It is strange that snowfall is taking place this winter night after night

Night and day: *All the time; continuously* * The machines kept running night and day * He had to travel night and day for a week to search for his son

Night-out: *A festive night away from home, work and responsibility* * They enjoy a night-out occasionally

Night owl: *Person who enjoys staying up late at night* * A night owl prefers to be more active at night than in the day to fulfil his tasks

Nightmare: *Vivid frightening dream* * He still has nightmares about the ghastly accident

Nimble-footed: *Swift of foot* * This company needs the services of a nimble-footed young man

Nimble-witted: *Quick-witted* * He is a nimble-witted man who can resolve any knotty dispute * Our college has a nimble-witted group of students

Nimble-fingered: *Skilled with the fingers* * Our country does not lack in nimble-fingered persons to work as masons and as carpenters

Nine day's wonder: *Something that astonishes everybody for the moment* * A married life is a nine day's wonder

Nine times out of ten: *In most cases or very often* * We have to discuss nine times out of ten all matters of mutual interests

Nineteen to the dozen: *With great volubility* * She was chatting away, nineteen to the dozen

Ninety-nine times out of hundred: *Almost always* * He is as busy as a bee and you will find him ninety-nine times out of hundred doing one thing or another

Nip and tuck: *Full speed; neck and neck* * It was a treat to watch the nip-and-tuck flight of missiles towards the outer space * The two competitors finished the race nip and tuck

Nip in: *Cut in* * He nipped his fingers in the door (between the door and the door-port)

Nip in the bud: *Destroy at its*

very beginning * We should nip our bad habits in the bud

Nip the evil in the bud: *Do away with the evil in the very beginning* * It would be wise to nip the evil in the bud, otherwise you will find it very difficult to get rid of it

Nitty-gritty: *The basic or essential detail* * Time ran out before we could get down to the real nitty-gritty

No admission: *Entrance not allowed* * No admission is allowed in the danger zone

No buts: *Admit no reason for compromise* * Let us have no buts; instead go ahead and finish the work

No call for: *No need* * There is no call for alarm

No concern of one's: *None of one's business* * Why are you worrying about it when it is no concern of yours?

No doubt: *Surely* * There is no doubt about his bidding fair as a pleader

No end: *Very much* * It upset me no end to know that they are at dagger's drawn

No end of: *Very many or much* * *Very great* * He has no end of books on football * We met no end of interesting people * We had no end of a good time

No fewer than: *As many as go* * No fewer than nine workers were absent due to illness

No flies on: *No want of alertness in or no flaw in* * We could see no flies on the security arrangements

No go: *Not possible; futile* * There is no go to climb the steeply mountain in a stormy weather * It is no go to waste time and energy in this dubious enterprise

No good: *Useless; worthless; unavailing* * It is no good to make any further attempts on this account * He proved himself to be no good for this responsible job * Their efforts were no good

No great shakes: *Of no great account* * She certainly is no great shakes as a mother

No joke: *A serious or difficult matter; not a trifling matter* * It is no joke trying to find a job these days * It's no joke to face an acid test successfully * It's no joke to get through all the hurdles successfully

No laughing matter: *Something serious or something not to be joked about* * It is no laughing matter to be ready to meet any challenge

No longer: *Not now as formerly* * He no longer stands in need of any financial help * He no longer lives in this house

No love lost between: *Hate each other* * There is no love lost between them

No matter: *It does not matter; it makes no difference* * Call me when you get there, no matter what time it is * You may do this at your own convenience, no matter if it remains incomplete today

No matter what, who, where, etc.: *Whoever (it is), whatever (happens) etc.* * Don't trust him no matter what he says * Do not believe the rumour, no matter who says it

No more than: *Nothing in addition to [than]* * There is room for no more than three cars

No more: *Dead* * He is no more now

No news is good news: *If there were bad news we would hear it* * I have not heard from my friend since long, but I am not worried because I know that no news is good news * For us no news is good news

No object: *Of no importance* * He had the appearance of a man for whom time was no object * For a spendthrift, money is no object

No one: *Nobody* * There was no one to save the child from the clutches of the kidnapper

No one knows the weight of another's burden: *The wearer knows where the shoe pinches* * It seems that my problems are greater than yours but no one knows the weight of another's burden

No pains, no gains: *One must strive hard to achieve worthwhile* * Many people have risen to great heights in their career knowing that no pains, no gains

No question of: *Impossible* * There is no question of his coming late

No reason but: *No possible alternative* * Since you have failed in the examination, there is no reason but to join the very same class again

No right to be here: *Should not be here* * He has no right to be here in our secret meeting

No sooner said than done: *It will be done immediately* * She asked for a glass of water from him because she knew that he is a man who believes in no sooner said than done

No thanks to: *Not owing to, implying that gratitude is far from being due* * We managed to get it finished in the end no thanks to him

No, thanks: *No, thank you* * I am thirsty but no, thanks, I do not want to drink in that dirty cup

No time: *A very short time* * He finished his job in no time

No time to be lost: *Must hurry* * There is no time to be lost, otherwise we would miss the train

No way/No ways/No wise: *Certainly not; in no way, manner or degree* * It is no way justifiable to be impolite to an elderly gentleman * The murderer should no wise get rid of capital punishment

No wonder: *It is not surprising* * No wonder you are tired as you have been working for hours

Nod and a wink/Nod is a good as wink: *You mean that a hint given by someone has been understood without an oral talk* * Many things can be done by a nod and a wink

Nod off: *Fall asleep for a short time* * I saw some members in Parliament nodding off to sleep

Nodding acquaintance: *Person you know only slightly; slight knowledge* * I have a nodding acquaintance with the man you are mentioning * I cannot throw light on this particular subject about which I have only a nodding acquaintance

No-go area: *Area barricaded to prevent police or security force from entering* * No-go areas are strictly prohibited for police as well as for soldiers

Noise something abroad: *Make something public or spread the news* * It has become a general practice with the tycoons to noise their products abroad to boost their business

No-man's land: *Land between two armies which belongs to neither side* * Nobody can enter the no-man's land for fear of being fired from either side

Nominal fee: *Very small amount* * This teaching institute charges a nominal fee from the students

Nonce-word: *A word coined for one occasion* * He is a man who can coin a nonce-word to be printed on the invitation cards of your marriage

None but: *Only* * None but he knew the truth * They chose none but the best

None of one's business: *Nothing to do with one* * Please don't interfere as it is none of your business

None of your cheek: *Don't be rude* * Avoid being rude because he will tolerate none of your cheek here

None other than: *Only and not anybody else* * The next new VIP arrival was none other than the president

None-sparing: *All destroying* * Unless we get rid of none-sparing weapons, there can be no end to the rat-race between the countries manufacturing weapons of mass destruction

Nonetheless: *Nevertheless* * Though he was seriously struck by chickenpox, nonetheless he took the examination * The problems are not serious, nonetheless we should tackle them

Nonplus: *Surprise or puzzle so much that he does not know what to do or say* * I was completely nonplussed when my bosom friend turned hostile towards me

Nose about/around: *Search; pry* * We found a man noising around in our backyard

Nose into: *Pry into* * He is a man who is always nosing into people's affairs

Nose running: *Fluid running from nose* * His nose is running due to a bad cold

Nose something out: *Discover by smelling* * The dog nosed out the real culprit

Nose up: *A good meal; eat* * My nose is up to the kitchen smelling so good * I nosed up to the delicious meal at the party

Nosy parker: *Prying person; very inquisitive person* * A nosy parker is interested in keeping himself abreast of other people's affairs * That journalist is a nosy parker as he wants to go to the root cause of the event

Not a few: *Many* * Not a few people gathered round the juggler * The entire serial had not a few errors

Not a hundred miles from: *At; very near* * We are now not a hundred miles from our destination

Not a leg to stand: *No use at all* * We have not a leg to stand on in exercising our claim without solid evidence/proof

Not a patch on: *Not fit to be compared with; not nearly as good as* * I am not a patch on him in swimming * He is not a patch on his friend at horse riding

Not a penny the worse: *None the worse* * We do have harsh conditions, but we are not a penny the worse for that

Not any more: *No longer* * Not any more will he be able to walk due to a paralysis attack

Not anywhere near: *Not at all* * The job does not pay anywhere near enough for me to live well

Not as black as painted: *Not as bad as people say* * He is not very friendly, but he is not as black as he is painted

Not at all: *Certainly not; do not mention it; or it is a pleasure; used as a polite response to thanks or enquiries* * He is an honest officer and would not at all accept any bribe under any circumstances * He should bother not at all about reaching on time because his boss is never pleased

Not at home: *Out of one's house; not receiving a visitor* * I went to see him but he was not at home * He will not be at home to anybody on this Sunday

Not be on speaking terms with somebody: *Not know him well enough to speak; no longer speak to him because one has quarrelled with him* * I, not being on speaking terms with him, cannot make him understand your difficulty * Since the day I fell foul of him, I am not on speaking terms with that arrogant man

Not but what: *Nevertheless or although* * I cannot do it as it is not but what a younger man can do

Not dissimilar: *Quite alike* * The twin brothers are not dissimilar in shape and stature

Not do a hands turn: *Do no work* * That idle man has not done a hands turn all week

Not fit to hold a candle to: *Not to be compared with* * He is not fit to hold a candle to me in running fast

Not for Joseph: *Not on any account* * Not for Joseph must strangers be let into the house * Do not for Joseph leave the baby alone in the house

Not for nothing: *For a very good reason* * Not for nothing was Sardar Patel called the Iron Man

Not for nuts: *Not on any account* * Do not for nuts leave the dog with the rude man

Not for the world: *Under no circumstances* * I would not leave you on your own for the world, so don't be afraid

Not give a toss: *Not to care all* * You need not give a toss to false rumours

Not half: *Extremely* * Not half was she annoyed at me

Not half bad: *Not bad at all* * It really isn't half bad as it looks

Not half such a: *Not nearly* * He is not half such a fool as they think

Not have a penny to one's name: *Be without money* * A person not having a penny to his name cannot fight an election these says

Not hide candle under bushel: *Set example* * Great men do not hide their light under the bushel as they become icons for other to follow

Not in his right mind: *Mad* * He is not in his right mind since he had a stroke and is in need of medical attention

Not in one's line: *Out of one's province* * Printing is not in my line

Not in so many words: *Express in an indirect way* * For a member to say not in so many words that she has lied is not acceptable in Parliament

Not know chalk from cheese: *Know nothing about the matter* * How can I expect you to deliver the goods when you do not know chalk from cheese?

Not known which way to turn: *Be in a hopeless situation* * On the one end he has lost his job and on the other, his wife has left him because of which he simply doesn't know which way to turn

Not lift a finger: *Do nothing to help* * They did not lift a finger to help the child in need

Not much of a: *Not a good* * He is not much of a linguistic scholar * It was not much of a dinner * I am not so much of a cinema lover

Not near: *Far from* * The auditorium was not near half occupied by the audience

Not near big enough: *Far too small* * A rat is not near big enough to an elephant

Not nearly: *Not much thaw, Not at all* * There is not nearly enough time to get there now

Not-negotiable: *Not exchangeable for cash* * He issued a not-negotiable cheque which had to be credited to the payee's account

Not on your life: *Not under any circumstances* * Not on your life would I give a lift to a crook in my car

Not on your Nelly: *Certainly not* * I will not on your Nelly go to see that despicable man

Not only, but also: *Emphasising that something else is also true* * He not only wrote the text but also selected the illustrations

Not out of the wood yet: *Problems or not yet free from difficulties* * He has opened his eyes but he is not out of the wood yet as he is still in the intensive care unit

Not quite proper: *Rather improper* * Whatever you have said or done is not quite proper

Not somebody's scene: *Not the type of thing that somebody likes or enjoys doing* * It is not my scene to indulge in back talk

Not stand even a dog's chance: *Not even the least chance* * He did not stand even a dog's chance to clear the preliminary test for the post applied for

Not take no for an answer: *Refuse to accept one's denial* * Your presence is necessary in the meeting and I will not take no for an answer

Not that: *It is not suggested that* * If he ever said so, not that I ever heard him say so, he told a lie

Not the word for it: *Not a strong word nor enough word to express or describe* * Warm is not the word for it

Not to be sneezed at: *Not to be despised at* * A handsome prize in the lottery is not to be sneezed at

Not to be sniffed at: *Good enough to be accepted* * Gone are the days when a sum of 10,000 rupees towards the cost of 10 grammes of gold was not to be sniffed at

Not to do with you: *Not your concern* * It's not to do with you to guide him in his personal affairs

Not to lead the life of a dog: *Lead a life so wretched that even a dog would not be content with it* * We impressed upon him not to lead the life of a dog when he is so young hale and hearty

Not to mention: *Not forgetting; as well as* * He has two big houses in this country, not to mention his villa in Paris

Not to mince words: *Be frank* * I am not one to mince words wherever I find someone doing wrong

Not to say: *Indeed one might go further and say* * He has a big farm in the country, not to say his invaluable immovable property in the town

Not to see the wood for the trees: *Concentrate on the details and not appreciate the main problem* * I do not think your efforts might bear fruit if you do not care to see the wood for the trees

Not to turn a hair: *Be quite undisturbed or unaffected; show no emotion; trouble* * I was surprised to see that the ghastly accident that happened caused him not to turn a hair * We should be calm and not turn a hair when confronted with an awkward situation

Not too well: *Badly* * He has finished painting the wall not too well

Not U: *Not polite in upper class style* * This sort of word is not U? * This way of speaking the vulgar words is not U

Not without reason: *With good reason* * They were suitably rewarded not without reason

Not worry to leave: *Glad to leave* * I do not worry to leave you in the hands of those good friends who will take care of you

Not worth one's salt: *Quite worthless; not deserving one's pay* * He is not worth his salt if he fails at this juncture * When found not worth his salt, he was dismissed from the service by his employers

Not yours but mine: *Used to show opposition* * The fault for this is not yours but mine

Not-being: *The state of fact of not existing* * Who knows how this universe came into being from the state of not-being!

Notch up: *Achieve; score* * Our team notched up 10 goals more than scored by the rival team * The team has notched up 20 goals already this season

Nothing but: *Only; no more less than* * I want nothing but the best career for my children * Nothing but a miracle can save him now

Nothing could be further from truth: *Used to say that a fact or comment is completely false* * I told him to his face that nothing could be further from truth when he spoke about fidelity

Nothing for it but: *Nothing else to be done in the case* * There was nothing for it now but to go straight with the plan

Nothing if not: *Extremely, very* * The trip was nothing if not varied

Nothing in it: *No truth; no importance; no difficulty in the matter; no important difference* * There is nothing in it to believe * There was a rumour he was going to resign, but there was nothing in it * I found nothing in the new technique that he spoke about * There is nothing in it when we weigh the pros and cons between the two prospects * They saw nothing in it that could hinder their progress

Nothing less than: *Quite as much; used to emphasise how great or extreme something is* * This was nothing less than tragic * It was nothing less than a disaster

Nothing like: *Not at all like; not nearly; not at all* * It looks nothing like a horse * I had nothing like enough time to answer all the questions

Nothing much: *Nothing of great value or importance; not a great amount of something* * There was nothing much in his speech he made yesterday * You will find nothing much in the fridge

Nothing short of: *Nothing less than* * Our escape from captivity of the dacoits was nothing short of a miracle

Nothing to choose between them: *Of things merely equal* * Of the two, there is nothing to choose between them as far as their capability and ability is concerned

Nothing to do with: *Not to be involved in or not to associate* * I have nothing to do with him as he is not clean in his dealings

Nothing to it: *No difficulty in doing it; very easy* * There is nothing to it * You will learn soon that there is nothing to it really

Nothing to say for oneself: *No defence* * The culprit had nothing to say for himself

Nothing to say to: *No dealings or conversation with* * Since the day he cheated me, I have nothing to say to him

Nothing to speak of: *Nothing worth mentioning; not much* * There is nothing to speak of his regarding his health * I have nothing to speak of considering the existing situation

Nothing to write home about: *It is nothing special* * Everybody knows the advantages brought about by electricity and so there is nothing to write home about it

Nothing untoward: *Nothing unpleasant and unusual* * Nothing untoward took place in our risky expedition to the snow-capped mountains

Nothing venture, nothing have: *One has to take risk if one wants to achieve success* * There can be no two opinions on the fact that nothing venture, nothing have

Not-I: *That which is not the conscious ego* * Those induced with not-I are nearer to God

Notice to quit: *Legal documents to telling someone to leave premises* * A notice has been officially served on him to quit the house with immediate effect

Nowadays: *At the present time* * Nowadays most kids prefer watching television to reading

Now and again: *Occasionally* * He has to run errands for his master now and again

Now and then: *Sometimes; from time to time* * My friend visits our place now and then to discuss with me matters of mutual interest * We go to the opera now and then

Now then: *Used at the beginning of a sentence often as a protest or warning or simply to call attention* * Now then, what is troubling you * Now then, that's enough noise

Nowhere in sight or nowhere to be found, seen: *Impossible to find or see* * A peace settlement is nowhere in sight

Nowhere near: *Not nearly* * Lions are nowhere near as fast as the *cheetah*

Nowhere near completion: *Far from being finished* * The project still stands nowhere near completion

Nowhere/Not near: *Far from* * The concert hall was nowhere near full

Nuclear deterrent: *Nuclear weapon which it is hoped will discourage the enemy from attacking* * The need of the hour is large-scale production of nuclear deterrents to save humanity from mass destruction

Nuclear fission: *Breaking up of an atom in an explosion* * Nuclear fission leads to production of large amounts of energy

Nugget of information: *Piece of useful information* * He has given us a nugget of information about the hide-out of the terrorists

Null and void: *Useless or non-effective* * The contract was declared null and void due to breach of its clause

Number is up: *Dying* * The old man's number is up

Number off: *Call out one's number in a rank of soldiers* * The company numbered off from the right

Number somebody among: *Include* * I wish to number him also among my friends.

Nurse a constituency: *Look after the needs of the electors with a hope for getting their*

votes in the next election * Any elected member is very particular to nurse a constituency for getting votes in the next election

Nursing mother: *Mother who breastfeeds her baby* * A nursing mother gives growth to a healthy baby

Nuts about: *Very keen on, enthusiastic about; in love with; infatuated with* * He is absolutely nuts about making his own mark as a promising cricket player * He is madly nuts about her

Nuts and bolts: *Essential, practical details* * Do not go into the other details because all I need are the nuts and bolts of the conversion plans for the house

O

Oath-breaking: *Not abiding by one's promise* * The defence witnesses were found guilty of oath-breaking

Ob-and-soller: *A disputant* * There is no room for an ob-and-soller in our club

Object against: *Give as a reason against* * I object against him as he is too young for the position

Object to: *Say that one is not in favour of something; be opposed to; make a protest against* * He objected to his poor choice of a cheap gift * They objected to the new proposal placed by him * I object to all this noise

Obliged to: *Required or bound to* * I am obliged to you for your kind help

Oblivious of: *Forgetful of* * He is dancing away oblivious of the crowd that has gathered at his strange behaviour

Obstacle race: *A race in which obstacles have to be passed* * Only five athletes took part in the obstacle race in the athletics championship

Obtrude on/upon: *Push forward especially when unwanted* * He did not want to obtrude on her privacy

Occasioned by: *Owing to* *A special commission will enquire into the death caused by police activity during the riot

Odd and even: *A short remnant* * A gambler knows the odd and even he has to wager on

Odd jobs: *Occasional piece of work* * He is still living on odd jobs

Odd lots: *Group of different items for sale* * That shopkeeper has odd lots for sale

Odd man out: *A person who is different from others* *At school he was always odd man out

Odd-come-short: *A short remnant; odds and ends* * An odd-come-short of the temple is still visible on the top of the hill * He is very much interested in the collection of odd-come-short

Odd-come-shortly: *An early day or any time* * It would be my pleasure to see you on odd-come-shortly to sort out things amicably

Odd-even: *Apparently neither one thing nor another* * The matter seems to be odd-even and confusing too

Odds and ends: *Small miscellaneous objects; small jobs* * Valuable odds and ends are on exhibition at that shop * I have got a few odds and ends to do before leaving

Odds-on: *Of a chance; better than even* * He is on the look out for an odds-on to eke out his livelihood

Of a kind: *Not as good as it could be* * You are making progress of a kind

Of a large nature: *Of charitable disposition* * We should be of a large nature to help the disabled persons

Of a night: *In the course of a night* * It was an event of a night that his house was burgled

Of a piece: *The same in nature; as if of the same piece; homogenous; in keeping consistent* * Houses in that village are all of a piece * I saw a large number of fragrant flowers of a piece in the backyard of our house * The working class is not quite so of a piece in its political preference * All the players of our cricket team are of a piece as far as their performance is concerned

Of a sort or a sorts: *Inferior* * They served coffee of a sort

Of age: *Old enough to be legally deemed mature* * Only persons of certain age are eligible to apply for the said post

Of all arms: *Of every kind of troops* * We enjoyed the march past of all arms on the Republic Day

Of an opposite kind: *Of contrary sex* * I can't reveal all the facts of an opposite kind in the open

Of broad shoulders: *Strong* * When he fell down, he received help from a person of broad shoulders

Of course: *By natural consequences; indisputably* * We are, of course, slated to die sooner or later * Of course, everybody has the right to live

Of great article: *Of great importance* * The unsolicited gift that he gave me was of a great article to me

Of high stamp: *Of high character* * Only a man of high stamp is adored everywhere

Of kin: *Related* * One of my kins is presently serving in the army as a commanding officer

Of my own: *Belonging to myself* * I need a room of my own

Of necessity: *Necessarily* * This is, of necessity, a brief and incomplete account * Herdsmen must, of necessity, move with their herds

Of new: *Anew; of late* * They started life of new thousands of miles away * I have met him of new and discussed some urgent matters

Of no avail: *No use; of no use* * Your ability to argue is of no avail if the facts are wrong * I advised him to work hard but of no avail as he ignored my advice

Of no use: *Useless* * This tight jacket is of no use to me, so I gave it to my younger brother

Of old: *Long ago; in or of ancient times; formerly* * These were the events of old but are still fresh in my mind * Many folks of old are still alive in various tribes and aborigines * The legendary wrestler of old has now fallen prey to cancer

Of one mind: *Of a mind or agreed; having same opinion* * We were of one mind in wanting to teach him a good lesson for his impudent behaviour * We are all of one mind to make necessary reforms in our existing educational set-up

Of one's own accord: *Without being asked or forced; of one's own spontaneous action; willingly* * The scratches on your body would soon disappear of their own accord * He came forward to help the victims of the storm of his own accord * He joined the army of his own accord

Of one's own choice: *Of one's own liking* * I wish to buy a new car of my own choice

Of one's own free will: *Not forced* * I did it of my own free will

Of price: *Of great value* * This old pocket-watch is certainly of price to me

Of purpose: *Intentionally* * I am convinced that he has been doing all these wrongly of purpose

Of strong mind: *Capable of strong reasoning* * That lawyer is a man of strong mind

Of strong smell: *Of stinking smell* * The passer-by complained of a strong smell emerging from the garbage-heap on the roadside

Of the common stamp: *Of ordinary type* * We can find men of the common stamp almost everywhere

Of the first water: *Of the finest quality* * The diamond necklace round her neck is really of the first water

Of the same age: *Identical in age* * They are fast friends and are almost of the same age

Of the same stamp: *Of similar nature* * Persons of the same stamp tend to group together

Of two minds: *Uncertain what to think of* * He was of two minds whether or not to leave the present job

Of unsound mind: *Mad* * The doctor has declared him a person of unsound mind

Of use: *Useful* * He retained all that was of use to him and did away with all the rest

Of warrant: *Allowed or warranted* * The genuine remarks he made were of warrant for public information

Off and on: *With occasional break* * The rainy weather remained off and on all day * I have been coming here off and on for years

Off colour: *Faded; indisposed; part one's best* * The old man was putting on an off colour blue shirt * Her face looks off colour as a result of illness * He is off colour these days due to depression

Off day: *A day when you do not do things as well as usual* * Even the best of players sometimes have an off day.

Off his onion: *Mentally unbalanced* * He seems me to be off his onion, so do not depend on his advice

Off one's feed: *Without appetite; disinclined to eat* *A child would not cry when he is off his feed * Due to stomach ache, I am off my feed

Off one's guard: *Not on the watch* * The night watchman was found off his guard by the manager of the factory * The lawyer's innocent question was designed to catch the witness off his guard

Off one's hands: *No longer under one's responsible charge* * I would be glad to get it off my hands

Off one's head: *Crazy* * Do not be off your head to lend him so much money without a bond written in black and white * On hearing his foolish talk, I thought he had gone off his head

Off one's nut: *Mad* * He is off his nut and goes on talking something to himself

Off one's rocker: *Out of one's right mind* * The statement of a person off his rocker cannot be held valid in any court of law

Off season: *Less busy season* * During the off season, there is no hustle and bustle in the market and commercial activities remain dull

Offspring: *Child; children* * He is the offspring of a scientific genius and a ballet dancer * Their offsprings are slightly mad

Off the beaten track: *Far away from other people, houses, etc.* * They live miles off the beaten track

Off the hinges: *Disorganised; out of gear* * The whole show was off the hinges except one or two scenes * He retorted something in rage thinking that by doing so things may go off the hinges

Off the hook: *Ready-made; out of difficulty; not on the rest or cradle* * I would advise you to purchase a house that is off the hook * He had to strive hard to be off the hook * The telephone receiver is kept off the hook so that nobody can call you

Off the mark: *Well away from the start in the race; off target* * As the race is now off the mark, we have yet to see who will be the winner * Your plan seems to be off the mark for any purposeful end

Off the peg: *Readymade* * He buys his clothes off the peg

Off the rail: *Disorganised* * The company has gone off the rail in recent years due to mismanagement

Off the record: *Not for publication in the press* * The remarks made by the honourable member in the house were treated to be off the record * All that he said was only a matter off the record

Off the reel: *Without pause; in uninterrupted course of succession; without stop or hesitation* * One finds him off the reel when he starts chatting on any topic * He immediately stated off the reel all the events of his life to his listeners * He was attentive enough to recite off the reel the verses from a very long poem

Off the shelf: *Buy something immediately irrespective of its design or any special order* * I bought this package off the shelf

Off with: *Take off at once* * I wanted to be off with my wet boots and sit by the fire to warm my cold feet

Offend against: *Do wrong or commit an offence* * She made a remark which is bound to offend the people against her

Offended with: *Give offence to* * She was offended with her husband * He is offended with you at your bad manners

Offensive to: *Disagreeable* * The smell of the cheese is offensive to me

Offer battle: *Give the enemy an opportunity of fighting* * Strategically we offered battle to our enemy

Offer one's hand: *Hold it out to shake hands* * He offered his hand towards me in a goodwill gesture

Offer one's hand in marriage: *Make a proposal of marriage to a woman* * He offered his hand in marriage to his girl friend

Offer something: *Present something* * We must offer prayers to God for our well-being

Offer something up: *To give something willingly* * He offered up a precious diamond to save the life of his only son from his abductors

Off-hand: *Without preparation; careless without forethought* * His off-hand speech on a tough subject was well appreciated by his audience * I cannot answer your queries off-hand * His off-hand views were not helpful to us

Off-peak: *Away from busiest used times* * It was an off-peak period for demand of this product.

Oftentimes: *Many times; frequently* * Oftentimes we have to face disappointments too * Buses do run oftentimes between the city and the airport

Oil on troubled waters: *Anything that allays or assuages, from the effect of pouring oil on rough water* * The man's efforts at pacifying the two hostile nations had the effect of pouring oil on troubled waters

Oil one's palm: *To bribe him* * Unless you oil his palm, you won't be able to get that job

Oily tongue: *Flattering tongue* * Beware of his oily tongue as he does not normally mean what he says * His aunt wins over every heart with her oily tongue

Okay: *Alright* * Okay, I will see you tomorrow in office

Old as the hills: *Very old* * This boulder is as old as the hills

Old hand: *One experienced; very experienced person* * There is no harm in consulting an old hand over this problem * He is an oid hand in repairing damaged motor-cars

Old head on young shoulders: *Wise young person* * That young man has an old head on young shoulders

Old maid: *A woman left unmarried; a card game* * The old maid still commands respect from all who know her * They are interested in playing the old maid

Old soldier: *An empty bottle; an experienced person who knows how to make himself comfortable or how to turn things to his or her advantage* * Do not throw away this old soldier because we may stand in need of it any time * We can learn a lot of things in the company of an old soldier

Old thing: *A familiar disrespectful kindly mode of address, irrespective of age* * Hey! You old thing is still having an amorous instinct!

Old Tom: *Gin (a drink)* * They prefer old Tom to any new brand of whisky

Old wives' tale: *A marvellous story for the credulous* * It is an old wives tale that make-up ruins the skin * People have to be educated so as not to believe in old wives' tale

Olive branch: *A symbol of peace; a child* * The management is holding out an olive branch to the strikers

Omnibus train: *One that stops at every station* * There are many omnibus trains running in every part of the country

On a large scale: *In a great way* * America is in a position to supply all kinds of weapons to its friends * There is corruption in this department on a large scale

On a lay: *On shares instead of wages* * The project contracted on a lay was completed quite before the stipulated period

On a small scale: *In a small way* * He has started his business on a small scale

On a string: *Under complete control; kept in suspense* * India has always rejected aid from any country on a string * The decision to give veto power to the newly developed states in the Security Council is still on a string

On a time: *Once; at a time in the past* * On a time there was a great famine and the people had nothing to live on * It happened upon a time that a magician transformed a lion into a lamb

On a wild-goose chase: *A foolish and fruitless search* * I suspect that fellow has sent us on a wild-goose chase *

Some scientists are still on a wild-goose chase trying to find an immortal man

On account: *As an installment or interim payment* * The loan taken by him was returned to the lender on account only * He was ordered to pay the company some money on account pending a final assessment of his liability

On account of: *Because of* * He could not attend his office on account of high fever

On all fours: *On four feet or hands and feet, hands and knees* * He crawled on all fours to the window * We were crawling around on all fours

On all hands: *On all sides; by everybody; universally* * The whole area was soon covered with snow on all hands * His efficient performance was appreciated on all hands * The USA is presently acknowledged to be a Super Power on all hands

On all sides: *In all directions* *On the high sea we could see only water on all sides

On an even keel: *Stable; steady* * His business is running on an even keel

On and on: *Without stopping* * We went on and on in search of the hidden treasure in an isolated place

On application: *When you apply* * More information on the subject would be made available on application

On approval: *On trail* * On receiving approval from the concerned authority, she will be sent abroad

On at someone: *Scolding; criticising* * He was on at me again for lending him money

On bail: *Being free on security* * The accused was released on a bail of 10,000 rupees

On behalf of: *For, as a representative of* * I thank you on behalf of the association for extending your kind cooperation

On board: *Abroad* * The airline took off soon after the passengers were on board

On brink of grave: *Soon to die* * The occupants of the ill-fated airbus that crashed did not know that they were on the brink of grave

On call: *Available for duty* * In theory I am on call day and night

On condition that: *Provided that* * You can go for a swim on the condition that you will not venture out far from the river bank

On credit: *Without paying*

immediately * I have sold my old car on credit * I have purchased this second-hand car on credit

On edge: *Nervous; jumpy* * Due to high blood pressure, I was constantly on edge

On end: *Continuously; erect; at a stretch* * We talked on end with the stranger about his new discoveries * The smart soldier stood on end before the president to receive the prestigious medal for his meritorious services * The patient remained under a coma for eight hours on end

On fire: *A state of fiery combustion* * The fire brigade soon reached the spot where the shops were on fire

On foot: *Walking or running; in activity* * To keep fit and healthy, one should have a long walk on foot early in the morning every day * After a long span of illness he is now on his foot

On friendly terms: *In mutual friendship* * They have started a new business on friendly terms

On good terms: *Having a friendly relationship* * It is a good thing to be on good terms with your colleagues

On hand: *Ready; available; in one's possession* * Everything is now on hand to set out on a long journey * I have not enough money on hand to strike a bargain * The legal documents are no longer on hand

On heat: *Sexually excited a female mammal* * There is a particular season when the female mammals go on heat

On high aloft: *In heaven* * May the soul of that noble man rest in peace on high aloft

On hire: *For hiring* * The costumes are on hire from the local theatre

On liking: *On approval* * We hope to receive your final order on your liking of the samples

On my return home: *When I got back home* * He came to see me on my return home

On no account: *Not for any reason or consideration* * On no account should the house be left unlocked

On no condition: *Not in any situation* * You must on no condition tell them what has happened

On oath: *Sworn to speak the truth* * Are you prepared to give evidence on oath?

On occasion: *In case of need; as opportunity offers; from time to time* * He promised to extend his help to me on occasion * On occasions we have to adapt ourselves to the changing circumstances * Some laws and bye-laws have to be reviewed on occasions in the interest of the people

On offer: *For sale at certain price; something available to be used or bought* * This antique painting is on offer for a pretty reasonable price * The high ratio of interest on offer does involve penalties

On one's day: *When one is at his best* * He still takes pride on his day as a top-class race winner

On one's guard: *On the watch* * He is constantly on his guard against any threat of humiliation * We must be on our guard against pick-pockets

On one's hands: *Under one's care and responsibility; encumbrance; remaining as a burden* * You need not worry as everything is running smoothly on his hands * I have an empty house on my hands * Apart from doing house chores, taking care of the baby is also on her hands

On one's high horse: *In an attitude of one's fancied superiority* * He is always on his high horse whenever we ask him about his past

On one's last legs: *On the verge of utter failure or exhaustion* * In that old city we saw some buildings on their last legs * The over-aged man is said to be on his last legs and may breathe his last any time

On one's legs: *Standing especially to speak* * As soon as the president was on his legs to address the house, there was a loud applause from the audience

On one's mind: *Weighing upon one's spirit* * Her loss is weighing heavy on my mind and I am not able to do anything about it

On one's own: *On one's own account; on one's own initiative; independently; set up in independence; by one's own effort* * He did all the work on his own for reasons best known to him * They have accepted the challenge on their own to fight against illiteracy * Let him solve the problem on his own * He has since been thinking of a plan on his own to open a charity home without any help from outside * He overcame all the difficulties on his own

On one's own hook: *On one's own responsibility, initiative or account* * They fought the war on their own hook

On one's uppers: *Very short of money* * The poor man on his uppers was pulling a rickshaw in scorching heat * He, being on his uppers, could not afford to buy a cycle

On pains of death: *At the risk of being sentenced to death* * He committed this cold-blooded crime on pains of death

On principle: *Because of what you believe* * He refused on principle to understate his income for taxation purposes

On sale: *Available to be bought; products available in shops for the purchase; products which can be bought in a shop for less than their normal price* * Tickets are on sale from the booking office * English textbooks and dictionaries are on sale everywhere * He bought a sports jacket on sale from that store house

On sale or return: *Sale where the wholesaler will take the product back if the retailers can not sell it* * We have enough items on sale or return in the fair taking place next week

On second thought: *Having considered everything a second time; on reconsideration* * On second thoughts we decided not to continue with our campaign against globalisation * The impracticable project was rejected on second thoughts by the upper house

On Shank's mare/nag/pony: *On foot* * To have a close view of the vast natural beauty of the area, they preferred to travel on Shank's mare/ nag/pony

On shore: *On the land* * After alighting from the ship, we walked on the shore for quite a long time

On short commons: *Not having enough food* * The government is making all efforts to help those people in the backward areas who are on short commons

On sleep: *Asleep* * I was fast on sleep when someone knocked on the door at midnight

On speaking terms: *Friendly enough to speak to each other; well enough acquainted to speak* * Both of them are on speaking terms now after a violent fight * He has not been on speaking terms with his uncle for years as a result of some dispute * After having buried the hatchet, the two friends are now on speaking terms

On strike: *Taking part in a strike*

* More than half of the factory workers are on strike

On tap: *Kept in cask; ready to be drawn upon; readily available* * We have plenty of beer on tap to serve all the members at the party * They have many sources on tap to deal with any emergency * We have this sort of information on tap

On tenterhooks: *In a state of suspense; in a state of suspense and anxiety* * I have been on tenterhooks all the week in anticipation of my results * I should like to settle the matter immediately instead of making the other party remain on tenterhooks

On terms: *In friendly relations; on an equal footing* * He is still on excellent terms with his ex-wife * The two partners are on terms in running their business on a fifty-fifty basis

On that score: *As far as that is concerned* * You do not have to worry on that score

On the air: *Broadcast by wireless; in the act of broadcasting* * We will be back on the air tomorrow morning at 7 o'clock * The news bulletin will be on the air three times a day in English

On the alert: *In state of caution* * More than 10,000 troops have been placed on the high alert to deal with any untoward situation * A watchman has to be on the alert, especially at night

On the ball: *Having awareness and understanding of what is happening and ability to react quickly* * The new publicity manager is really on the ball

On the bow hand: *Wide of the mark* * Their prediction about a timely monsoon proved to be on the bow hand

On the brain: *Think constantly* * He has politics on the brain

On the brink of: *Very close to* * Scientists are on the brink of making a major new discovery

On the cards: *Probable* * A treaty on the commercial front between India and Pakistan now seems to be on the cards

On the carpet: *Under discussion; being reprimanded* * A new protocol treaty between the two countries is on the carpet * It is on the carpet that the USA may support India's claim for being a permanent member of the Security Council * He got called on the carpet for being late * You will certainly be on the carpet for your egoistic approach

On the chance: *In view of the possibility or in the hope* * I will call at his office on the chance that I will see him before he leaves

On the cheap: *Cheaply or cheap* * We know well enough that a quality product cannot be had on the cheap

On the contrary: *Against; for; otherwise* * It is unprincipled to ignore moral values but, on the contrary, there are many who ridicule this idea * All that he said was contrary to the expectations of the general public * He is a very unruly youngster but today he behaved quite well on the contrary

On the credit side: *Used to introduce the good points after the bad points have been mentioned* * He may be quarrelsome with other members of the family but on the credit side he has always been wonderful with his mother

On the debit side: *Against a proposal* * An amount of 5,000 rupees withdrawn from the bank has been recorded on the debit side of my saving bank account

On the defensive: *Feeling one has to justify oneself* * Warnings of an enemy's attack forced the troops to go on the defensive

On the dole: *Unemployed and Receiving money from the government or other recognised institution* * It is not easy living on the dole * He has been on the dole since he lost his job

On the dot of three: *At 3 o'clock* * He arrived here on the dot of three

On the edge of one's seat: *Very excited and giving one's full attention to something* * The exciting hockey game had the crowd on the edge of their seats

On the eve of: *Immediately before* * We met him at the airport on the eve of his departure to London * A farewell party was given to the manager on the eve of his transfer to Jalandhar

On the face of it: *On its own showing; palpably plain; at first glance* * On the face of it, it seems like a great deal of amount * The earthquake played havoc with the life and property of the people and on the face of it, rescue operation had to be carried out on a war-footing * On the face of it, it seems to make sense, but the figures betray this fact

On the go: *Moving about* * I am always on the go in search of some job

On the grounds of: *By reasons of* * He was dismissed from service on the grounds of undisciplined behaviour * The court overturned its decision on the ground of withholding crucial evidence in the case of prosecution

On the heels of: *Immediately behind* * Famine often follows on the heels of war

On the high ropes: *Elated; arrogant; in an elated or highly excited mood* * I was on the high ropes for having topped the list of successful candidates in the written test * People who are on the high ropes are seldom held in esteem anywhere * He was on the high ropes for having found a privileged place in the higher echelons of the civil service

On the hoof: *Alive* * Most of the animals are sold on the hoof to the butchers

On the hop: *In the act; unawares; at the very moment* * He was caught on the hop for selling stolen valuables * The holder of the fake currency notes was nabbed by the police on the hop * The police arrested the most wanted criminal on the hop while he alighted from the train

On the horns of a dilemma: *Equally disfavourable situation in either way; position that leaves only a choice between equal evils* * I was on the horns of a dilemma when the manager asked me either to leave the office or to apologise * He was on the horns of a dilemma on what to do when trapped between the unwanted troubles

On the house (of drinks): *Free, with no charge* * Drinks by this restaurant are on the house today

On the instant: *Forthwith* * The agreement between us has been terminated on the instant

On the job: *At work; in activity* * You can meet him after some time as he is still on the job, * The police is on the job of controlling the unruly crowd

On the knees of gods: *Awaiting the decision of fate* * The ailing old man is on the knees of gods and may collapse any time

On the last legs: *On the verge of ruin* * People say that the banker is on his last legs

On the latch: *Not locked but to*

be opened by a latch * The door is on the latch only and you can enter inside for a short nap

On the level: *Fair; honestly speaking* * I don't think the deal is on the level * I am convinced he was not treated on the level he deserved

On the look out for: *In search of* * He is on the look out for a new job elsewhere

On the long side: *Rather too long* * These shoes are a little on the long side to me

On the loose: *Indulging in a bout of unrestraint; free* * It was not fair on his part to let his tongue loose on his tough opponent * The prisoners are still on the loose in spite of a high alert all around

On the make: *Bent on self-promotion or advancement of* * The morality of the decision was of no concern to businessmen on the make

On the market: *Available for buying* * There are plenty of new brands in cars in the market

On the mend: *Getting better; improving; recovering* * His progress is on the mend now * His economic condition is now on the mend * My fractured arm is definitely on the mend

On the move: *Changing or about to change one's place; travelling from place to place* * Our intelligence agency has reported that large enemy forces are on the move * The absconder is still on the move to avoid getting caught

On the nail: *On the spot* * They are good customers and make the payment of goods on the nail

On the nod: *On tick* * Some of the important issues were accepted by both the parties on the nod

On the other hand: *Used to introduce something in contrast to an earlier statement, etc.* * It is cheap but on the other hand, the quality is poor

On the other side: *An opposite side or bank* * There was a large window on the other side of the front door

On the part of: *Proceeding from or done by or on the side of* * There was no objection on the part of the owner regarding the sale of his land

On the pill: *Taking contraceptive tablets* * She is on the contraceptive pill

On the point of: *Ready to; very near* * He was on the point of saying something when the phone rang * The seriously injured man was close on the point of death but for the timely operation

On the prowl: *Hunting for something* * There was a fox on the prowl near the chickens

On the question of: *In secret* * On the question of his private life, I have nothing to comment on * We have to do something on the question of distribution of funds

On the quiet: *Clandestinely; unobtrusively* * He had a drink on the quiet * She slipped in on the quiet through the backdoor

On the rack: *Feeling extreme pressure, anxiety or pain* * I find myself on the rack on how to save the life of my mother lying on the verge of death

On the rampage: *Breaking things and creating disorder* * Gangs of youths went on a rampage in the city yesterday

On the rebound: *Being sad and confused after a relationship has ended* * He took heroin for the first time when recovering from a broken relationship

On the right side of: *Less than or below* * He married when he was on the right side of thirty

On the right side of forty: *Less than forty* * He appears to be on the right side of forty

On the right tack: *Doing right thing* * He is one the right tack in his teaching profession

On the rise: *In process of rising especially in prices* * The prices of essential commodities are on the rise as a result of lack of rain

On the road: *Travelling especially as a commercial traveller of a tramp; travelling from place to place; on the way to some place* * How long have you been on the road for promoting the cause of your business? * The salesman is on the road for propagating his goods * A convoy of trucks loaded with medicines is on the road, moving towards the border

On the rope: *Very close towards defeat* * He gave all hopes of winning the race when he found himself on the rope

On the run: *Fleeing or trying to avoid being captured* * He is still on the run from the police

On the scale of: *In the ratio of* * The length and breadth of the floor of this hall is on the scale of 50 by 100 metres

On the scent of: *Following a trail*

* We are on the scent of something big

On the score of: *On the ground of* * He left his studies on the score of ill health

On the shelf: *Buy something immediately irrespective of its design or any special order* * I bought this package on the shelf

On the short side: *Rather too short than contrary* * These boots are a little on the short side of her feet

On the side: *In addition to ordinary occupation; secretly or illegally* * Apart from doing a government job he does cleaning of cars on the side * He is married but has a girlfriend on the side

On the skew: *Not straight* * There was no shutter on the window and the door of the room was on the skew

On the sly: *Surreptitiously* * He is carrying out many unlawful activities on the sly

On the spot: *At the very place; there and then; straight way; alert; equal to the occasion; in difficulty or danger* * The criminal was nabbed on the spot of the crime * The opposition parties came to a compromise on the spot * The arbitrator decided the dispute on the spot * He was ordered to be on the spot so that nothing went wrong at the party * A well-armed cop was on the spot to deal with any emergency * He was very careful and vigilant on the spot rescue operation

On the spur of the moment: *Without premeditation** I informed the police about a minor accident on the spur of the moment* He changed the programme on the spur of the moment

On the square: *Honestly* * Can we expect them to act on the square?

On the stocks: *Being built; being worked on** Our new model is already on the stocks and will be available shortly

On the street: *Not in a house or other building; living by prostitution** The problems of the people living on the streets is on the increase * It is a slur on society not to be able to solve the problems of people on the streets

On the strength: *On the muster roll* * The road-work was finished by the bonded labour on the strength

On the strength of: *In reliance upon; founding upon* * I employed the boy on the strength of your recommendation * He has been able to earn a name on the strength of devotion to work

On the stroke: *At right time* * He reached his office on the stroke of nine (at 9 o'clock exactly)

On the stroke of five: *At 5 o' clock exactly* * Do wake me up on the stroke of five in the morning

On the tapis: *On the table; under consideration* * The management has put several new proposals on the tapis * Some important matters are currently on the tapis

On the tight side: *Rather too tight than contrary* * In autocracy, the media is generally kept on the tight side so as not to divulge any news against the government

On the tip of one's tongue: *On very point of being spoken* * It was on the tip of my tongue to reveal the truth but I hesitated to do so

On the turn: *At the turning-point; changing the point of turning sour* * His career seems to be on the turn as a result of his promotion to a higher rank * His luck is on the turn for the better

On the verge of: *On the point of; on the brink of* * This old building is on the verge of collapsing * They are on the verge of signing a new contract for a further two years * This country is on the verge of disaster

On the wane: *Decrease in power* * The chill of the winter is on the wane with the advent of spring season

On the warpath: *Engaged in conflict; in a mood for battle* * The terrorists are on a warpath in some of the countries * The two main opposition parties are on the warpath for winning votes in the general elections

On the wave: *In a deceiving state* * Rescue operations are necessary when floods or storms are on the wave

On the way: *Moving towards a destination or event* * A warning has been sounded as a fierce storm is on the way

On the whole: *For the most part* * His performance, on the whole, was satisfactory

On the windy side: *On the windward side from which one cannot be attacked, hence safe; at an advantage* * The ship was sailing smoothly on the windy side * By supporting the party in majority, he is certainly now on the windy side

On the wing/ upon the wing: *Flying; in motion; departing* * He shot the bird on the wing * The eagle was on the wing hovering in the air in search of its prey * The airbus is ready to be on the wing for London

On the wings of the wind: *With the highest speed* * The factory is running on the wings of the wind to boost its quality products

On the wrong side of: *More than or above* * Most of our professors in the college are on the wrong side of 40

On the wrong track: *Working wrongly; making a wrong assumption* * We would be on the wrong track if we hide the truth

On this side of the grave: *In world; in life* * We all have a transitory stay on this side of the world

On this wise: *On this way* * If you go on working on this wise, you will certainly reap rich dividends without fail

On tick: *On credit* * We buy household goods on tick every month

On time: *Up to time; punctually; at the right time* * The train reached the station on time * He has earned a reputation for attending and leaving office on time * The train arrived on time

On tiptoe: *In a state of excitement; walk quietly on tiptoe* * He was on tiptoe on being given the charge of escorting the foreigners on a sight-seeing trip * She moved on her tiptoes beside the cradle of the sleeping child

On to (on a position): *Forward to* * The security officer was on to launching an attack when the bootlegger did not stop his vehicle

On toast: *Served as a slice of toast; swindled* * I liked baked beans on toast at my friend's house * Be careful so that you may not be on toast of those rogues

On top of everything else: *In addition to everything else* * On top of everything else, my car has been stolen

On top of the world: *In a very happy mood because of success* * He is naturally on top of the world for having won a jackpot of two million dollars

On trust: *Without proof; on credit* * You will have to take my statement on trust * He has been assigned this responsibility on trust only

On your marks: *Get ready on your places* * On your marks, get-set-go!

On your own: *Alone; by yourself* * He did all this on his own

Once and for all: *Once only and not again* * I have decided to give up smoking once and for all

Once and again: *More than once; now and then* * You were adviced once and again to avoid bad company but all in vain * That foolish man has to do his hair once and again

Once errand: *For the express purpose and nothing else* * She was here on once errand to dupe me of my jewellery by taking it on a loan basis

Once in a blue moon: *Very seldom* * His visits our place are only once in a blue moon

Once in a way: *Occasionally* * Large fairs are organised once in a way

Once in a while: *Now and then; occasionally; rarely* * It would be very nice of you to pay us a visit once in a while * Due to stress and strain, one may feel disgusted once in a while * Once in a while we go to a movie in a cinema hall

Once or twice: *A few times* * I went to enquire about his health only once or twice

Once upon a time: *At a certain time in the past* * Once upon a time there lived a king in Ujjain who was known for his peaceful nature

One after the other: *In succession, not together* * They trooped in one after the other to enter the hall * They do seldom attend the functions but usually come one after the other

One and all: *Everyone* * The Royal Gardens are open to one and all for two weeks

One another: *Each other* * The old friends met one another by chance in a market place

One by one: *Singly in order* * They were allowed to enter the hall one by one

One day: *On a certain day; at an indefinite time* * You will have to repent one day for your foolish actions * We have all to depart from this world one day

One flesh: *United in marriage* * Young couples are joyously leading a life of one flesh nowadays

One foot in the grave: *Extremely old or diseased; about to die* * It is a matter of prolonging life by treating him as his one foot is in the grave now * The operation did not work and the patient is said to have one foot in the grave

One for his head: *A blow on the head* * I gave him one for his head for deceiving me

One for his nob: *A point scored for holding the nob in cribbage* * He had one for his nob in the card game through pilfering

One in a thousand: *Anything exceedingly rare or excellent* * There is hardly one in a thousand who sticks to honesty and integrity

One of their number: *One of them* * This person is one of their number

One of these days: *Some indefinite time in the near future* * He is likely to be promoted one of these days

One or two: *A few* * I shall be away for one or two days

One swallow does not make a summer: *Isolated example does not prove rule* * Receiving one child in school will not help to run the school because one swallow does not make a summer

One's cup of tea: *What is to one's taste as appeals to one* * An evening at the opera was my cup of tea * To witness a cricket match is my cup of tea

One's fingers all thumbs: *Awkward and fumbling* * Can you button my coat as my fingers are all thumbs out of nervousness? * My fingers are all thumbs when I sit to play on the piano

One's opposite number: *Person accompanying the same or similar position in another group* * The British Foreign Minister is in Washington to discuss problems with his opposite number

One's own flesh and blood: *Near relations* * He invited all his own flesh and blood on his birthday

One-horse town: *Small town where very little happens* * Life is almost peaceful in one-horse town

One-sided: *Treating; giving justice to one side* * The press has been accused of presenting a one-sided picture of the issue

One-time: *Former* * I was pleased to see my one-time friend at the village fair

One-track mind: *Mind which concentrates on one thing at a time* * He is interested in his recovery only as he has a one-track mind and cannot think of anything else

One-upmanship: *Art of putting yourself at an advantage* * It was the expression of a man who had won a trifling game of one-upmanship

One-way: *For traffic in one direction only* * We have to observe one-way traffic on narrow lanes

Onion-eyed: *Having the eyes full of tears* * I got onion-eyed when he chopped some onions near me

Only joking: *Not meaning it seriously* * I was only joking for the sake of fun

Only pretty Fanny's way: *Only what must be expected and accepted of a person* * He offered due regards to the old gentleman only pretty Fanny's way as a graceful gesture

Only skin and bone: *Skeleton; very thin* * The old man walking on the road was only skin and bone

Only too: *Very* * I was only too pleased to help the needy persons

Onside: *Not offside* * The attacking game on the onside helped him in winning the match

Onslaught: *An attack or onset; assault* * The opposition members criticised the recommendations of the minister regarding the functioning of the Panchayat system * They responded with onslaught against the enemy bases

Open a door to: *Make possible* * A golden key opens a door to one's entry into heaven * Only hard work and good intention can help one open a door to success

Open a person's eyes: *Make him see; show him something of which he is ignorant* * The whipping of the criminal in public opened my eyes to resist from indulging in wrongful activities * Travelling to different countries opens your eyes to other cultures * The book containing various facts of life opened my eyes to the realities

Open one's mind: *Make known one's ideas or feelings* * He opened his mind about the new scheme which he wanted to be executed in public interest

Open out: *Open fully or spread out widely* * The street opened out into a small square

Open question: *A matter undecided* * As to which form of government is better is still an open question

Open secret: *A matter known to many but not explicitly divulged* * It is an open secret that some politicians are prone to nepotism

Open the ball: *Begin operation* * The religious missionaries must come forward to open the ball for preaching people on the value of humanity

Open to dispute: *Debatable* * There are many problems open to dispute for settling at the international level

Open up: *Talk about what you feel and think; begin shooting; open a door, container; make possible; open to bring into use* * It helps to discuss your problems provided you are willing to open up first * Anti-aircraft guns will open up their attack at noontime * Open up or we will break the door down! * The new arrangements between the two countries will open up doors for settling other disputes also * This new job could open up whole new vistas for him

Open up the throttle: *Make the engine go faster* * We had to open up the throttle of the car engine to reach well in time

Open verdict: *A verdict that a crime has been committed without specifying the criminal* * An open verdict will be given before revealing the name of the criminal

Open weather: *Clear weather* * The Sunday cricket match was played in an open weather

Open-eyed: *Watchful; astonished; fully aware of what is involved* * An open-eyed youth caught the pickpocket on the spot * He stood open-eyed when he saw the magician swallow many pieces of handkerchief one by one * The open-eyed view of the murder is still haunting him

Open-handed: *Generous; using the flat part of the hand* * The open-handed host provided us with all possible comforts * I gave that rogue an open-handed blow

Open-hearted: *With an open heart; frank; generous* * He is an open-hearted man and does his best to help anybody who might need his care * This problem could be solved through an open-hearted discussion * You go to that open-hearted person who will certainly be of help to you

Open-minded: *Without prejudice* * An open-minded person would never mislead anyone

Open-mouthed: *With your mouth open because you are surprised or shocked* * He stood open-mouthed on hearing the sad demise of his brother in a ghastly accident

Operate on: *Perform a surgical operation* * The doctors decided to operate on him to save his life

Oppose to: *Against; in contrast* * I am very much opposed to your going abroad * The company has earned less profit this year as opposed to last year

Opt for something: *Choose or decide on* * Fewer students are opting for science courses nowadays

Opt out of: *To decide not to take part* * The employees may opt out of the company's pension plan

Optic lobe: *Part of the midbrain with sight* * In case you need more information about optic lobe, you better go to some eye-specialist

Optical illusion: *Thing which appears different from what it really is because the eye is being deceived* * The lines were circular but he thought they were arcs and this could be due to optical illusion

Or else: *Otherwise; if not* * Hurry up or else you will be late * Pay up or else I will beat you up

Or so: *Or thereabout; vagueness; uncertainty about quantity* * He has reached the age of 40 or so * There were nearly 50 or so boys attending the class

Order of merit: *Arrangement in which the best is placed first, next best second and so on* * To be fair and square, promotions must be given in order of merit in every institution

Order of the day: *Something in common/general* * Corruption in every department is the order of the day these days

Ordinal numeral: *First, second, third, etc. or numerals indicating order of sequence* * The chapters of this book have been shown in ordinal numerals

Organic farming: *Using only natural fertilisers* * Organic farming is expanding everywhere for healthy growth of crops

Originate in: *Have a cause or beginning* * The quarrel originated due to rivalry in childhood between the two brothers

Other fish to fry: *Other business to do* * I can't devote more time to this particular job as I have other fish to fry

Other ranks: *Ordinary soldiers* * Officers and other ranks were seen in the parade ground

Other things being equal: *If conditions are/were the same or alike except for the point in question* * Other things being equal, she would marry John and not Smith

Otherwise: *In another or different way; in other or different respect or different conditions; if not or else* * He should have been working but he was otherwise engaged * The rent is high, but otherwise the house is satisfactory * Do what you have been told to do, otherwise you will be punished

Out and about: *Able to go out; convalescent* * We have been out and about talking to people of the surrounding villages * I treated him as an out and about; not as a sick man

Out and away: *By far* * I was out and away the handsomest man in the group

Out and outer: *Anything or person that is complete or extreme type; a thorough-going partisan; a great lie* * It is not an easy affair to acquire an out and outer high personality * Most newspapers are out and outer supporters of some political party or other * He wove a tissue of out and outer that landed him behind the bars

Out at elbow: *With coat ragged at the elbow; showing or threatening to show the elbow* * He was putting an old sweater that was out at the elbow * He had to discard his old coat when he found it out at elbow

Out at heels: *Having one's heels showing through holes in the socks or stockings* * It is ridiculous to wear socks/stockings out of heels

Out at knees: *Showing or threatening to show through the knees of trousers; pyjamas, pants, etc.* * The poor beggar was wearing a pair of trousers which was out at knees

Out for: *Abroad in quest of; expressly aiming at* * He was out for England to learn about the political system of that country * The Indian people are now out for accelerating the economy of the country

Out for the court: *Unconscious or completely exhausted* * One of the boxers was out for the court and hence the bout had to be stopped

Out loud: *So that it can be heard* * They played the music out loud

Out of: *From within; from among; not in/within; excluded from; beyond the bounds; in*

disagreement with; from; away or distant from; without; outside of or away from * He blessed me out of his heart * Out of the many employees only five attended duty today * He is out of town on some business * This old book is now out of study-course * Those who spend out of their limit are sure to suffer in the long run * The two friends are now out of the terms of the contract on the project * He jumped out of the bed * He is out of the country and gone abroad to see his relatives * I wish to remain out of his reach * It was an awful job and I am glad to be out of it

Out of all nick: *Out of all reckoning; exceedingly* * The interviewers found him to be out of all nick for a higher post * He is out of all nick despite being an amiable fellow

Out of bounds: *Place where people are not allowed to go; people not allowed to know or use or see something* * For the last few days the area has been out of bounds for foreign journalists * American parents may soon declare show of violence on TV as out of bounds

Out of breathe: *Having difficulty in breathing* * There he was standing out of breath after running home

Out of cash: *Without money* * A life out of cash is nothing short of a curse

Out of character: *Not in keeping with character* * The way he treated the old gentleman was out of character for which he was reprimanded

Out of commission: *Not in working order* * Some of the aeroplanes are temporarily out of commission and undergoing safety checks

Out of context: *Without the surrounding text* * Don't quote my words out of context, so as to give a false impression of what I mean

Out of course: *Out of order* * It was out of course that you called him names at the meeting place

Out of court: *Without claim to be considered* * The madman was kept out of court

Out of cry: *Beyond measure; beyond dispute* * Mankind's knowledge of the universe has been increasing out of cry * The nature of case was out of cry to be settled by the law of court

Out of curiosity: *For sake of knowing* * The letter was not addressed to me but I opened it out of curiosity

Out of danger or off the danger: *No longer likely to die* * Though he was seriously injured in the accident yet he is reported to be out of danger after surgery

Out of date: *No longer in fashion; no longer valid; antiquated* * Many of the old customs are becoming out of date * The old map of India that existed during English regime has since become out of date * It is observed that wide-bottomed trousers are slowly going out of the date

Out of doors: *In or into the open air; in the open air* * We should spend more time out of doors in the fresh air * The weather in the open air was fine enough for working out of doors

Out of drawing: *Inaccurately drawn or drawn in violation of principles of drawing* * All the pictures or models executed by him were considered to be out of drawing for the public exhibition

Out of earshot: *Beyond hearing distance* * The bomb exploded out of earshot

Out of favour: *Disliked; lacking approval* * It became clear that we were out of favour when our proposal was rejected * The decision taken by the judge is out of favour under the spirit of law

Out of focus: *Blurred; not clear; something which is not discussed or its purpose or nature is not clear* * In some of the pictures the subjects are out of focus while the background is sharp * The movement towards democracy in Latin America has gone out of focus * The camera was a bit out of focus when I took that picture

Out of gear: *Out of order* * The Indo-Pak conflict has all along been out of gear

Out of hand: *At once; immediately; without premeditation; out of control; instantly; beyond control* * The matter needs to be settled out of hand * The simple cases were disposed of out of hand by the open court * This kind of crime could not have been done out of hand * Positive steps were taken beforehand not to let the situation go out of hand * The ugly scene of beheading him took place out of hand * It was quite out of hand to extinguish the house on fire without damage

Out of humour: *Out of temper; displeased* * A sober person would never be out of humour as the foolish people are * He was not out of humour at the way the members expressed their anguish in the meeting over some lapses

Out of it: *Excluded from participation; without a chance* * It is a dishonest scheme and I am glad to be out of it

Out of joint: *Dislocated; disordered; not in proper connection* * The bone of my right knee is out of joint through a fall from the stairs * He fell and put his knee out of joint * There was something out of joint in the situation * The whole institutional machinery seems to be out of joint and hence the need for taking corrective measures

Out of measure: *To an exceedingly great degree* * Man's knowledge of universe has increased out of measure

Out of mind: *Forgotten; out of one's thoughts* * Once a friend goes far away she is likely to go out of your mind * I am out of mind as not to have fulfilled the promise of giving her a suitable gift on her birthday * I was completely out of mind to have given her that much money

Out of money: *Having no money* * We ran out of money at the shop

Out of one's element: *Out of one's spirits; unhappy or uncomfortable* * He felt out of his element when he was posted to a lonely remote place * I was out of my element when I saw the large crowd enter the place

Out of one's head: *Spontaneously; of one's own invention* * A new workable suggestion came out of his head and was accepted unanimously * He made the story up out of his own head * We should be grateful to all those persons who invented various machines out of their heads to make life more comfortable

Out of one's mind: *Mad* * He seems to have gone out of his mind due to depression

Out of one's senses: *Mad; senseless* * He drank too much and went out of his senses

Out of order: *Not in proper order* * Our telephone is out of order * My stomach is out of order

Out of patience with: *No longer able to endure* * I tend to run out of patience on seeing these rowdy children

Out of phase: *Not working in the right way* * The traffic lights were out of phase

Out of place: *Out of due position; inappropriate; unreasonable* * Some of these files are out of place * I felt completely out of place among all these successful candidates * Your bitter remarks were out of place on the occasion

Out of play: *Temporarily removed from play* * He had to remain out of play for some time as a result of his injury

Out of pocket: *Short of money* * I am running out of pocket as a result of some unexpected expenses

Out of position: *Not in proper place* * Our troops were out of position to carry out the assault on the enemy at that occasion

Out of practice: *Not having done enough practice* * I am out of practice for participating in a tournament * He remained out of practice which prevented him from giving a good performance in the cricket match

Out of print: *No longer to be had from the publisher* * His first novel is now out of print

Out of question: *Doubtless; impossible* * Honest dealings with that man is simply out of question * His integrity is out of question * He is so weak that his success in the examination is out of question

Out of season: *In bad time; period of the year when few people go on vacation* * Mangoes are rather expensive as they are out of season now * Hotels are cheaper out of season

Out of sight: *Not in a position to be seen or see; out of range of vision; beyond comparison* * We kept gazing at the flight of the aeroplane till it disappeared out of sight * We are yet not out of sight of land * She is out of sight in the winning spree of the race against her contestant

Out of sorts: *Out of order; slightly unwell* * He was so irritated that he felt out of sorts in doing the things in a proper way * He was tired and out of sorts by the time he finished the arduous job

Out of spirits: *Depressed* * Whenever one feels out of spirits, it is wise to give him some brandy

Out of step: *Not in step* * He was out of step with the rest of the marchers

Out of temper: *Annoyed; cross* * Don't be out of temper with anybody over minor issues * He is never out of temper even when provoked beyond measure

Out of the blue: *Entirely unexpected* * His resignation came right out of the blue * He came across a diamond out of the blue in a deserted place

Out of the common: *Unusual* * It was something out of the common for him to have won three gold medals in three different events

Out of the frying-pan into the fire: *Out of one evil into a greater one or from a bad situation to one that is worse* * He tried to swim away from the fish but ran into a whale which was like jumping out of the frying-pan into the fire * Occasionally Destiny may compel us to pass out of the frying-pan into the fire-like situation

Out of the order: *Extraordinary* * The task needed out of the order patience and endurance

Out of the ordinary: *Unusual* * I am looking for something more out of the ordinary * The boy's knowledge was out of the ordinary on the subject

Out of the question: *Not to be thought of* * Another trip to the USA this year is out of the question

Out of the road or out of one's road: *Out of the way* * Our region is poised for growth once the election is out of the road or out of our road

Out of the running: *Competing without a fair chance of success* * He is hopeful of winning a prestigious position even though it may be out of the running for him

Out of the top drawer: *Of top grade especially socially* * He is considered to be out of the top drawer for his social activities

Out of the way: *So as not to hinder or abstract; away from main routes or remote; no longer stopping* * The plan has to remain confidential at least till the local elections are out of the way * The farmhouse lies out of the way from any other building * I didn't say anything until he was out of the way

Out of the woods: *Out of difficulty or danger* * We are not yet out of the woods unless we destroy the enemy's training camps completely * Even after so many years, our government is not out of the woods economically

Out of thin air: *From nowhere* * The story I told you about him has not come out of thin air, you know

Out of this world: *Wonderful; magnificent* * He is a brilliant designer and his designs are really out of this world * The meal prepared for all the guests was out of this world

Out of time: *Too soon or too late; not keeping time in music* * Sorry, you are out of time for the lunch * The new dancers were dancing out of time in the programme

Out of touch: *Out of communication or direct relations* * Due to my prolonged illness, I remained out of touch with the political situation

Out of true: *Not quite straight* * The beam on the roof here is out of true

Out of tune: *Not true in pitch; not in harmony* * The piano and the violin were being played out of tune * We should not be out of tune with our companion

Out of use: *Not used or employed* * This defective radio set has been out of use for a long time for want of repair

Out of warrant: *Not allowed* * Trespassing of this private land is out of warrant

Out of work: *Without employment* * Many educated persons are out of work these days

Out on a limb: *In a different exposed situation* * Are you prepared to go out on a limb and make your suspicions public?

Out of one's depth: *In water where one cannot touch bottom or too deep for one's safety; beyond one's understanding* * Don't try to wade into the water here because it is out of your depth to reach across safely * I can't solve this riddle as it is out of my depth

Outspeak: *Say aloud; speak more; speak louder* * The media is open to outspeak against deficiencies prevalent in the administrative set-up * The quality of work at all levels outspeaks itself

Out to: *Trying or hoping to; trying to or aiming for* * I am not out to reform the world * The firm is out to increase its sales in the market * The company is out to capture the Chinese market

Out to out: *In measurement from inside to outside; overall* * He has taken stock of the position out to out and reported the same to his superiors * The general manager has been made the out to out incharge of the factory

Out upon: *Shame on* * He felt that his failure would bring out upon his family

Out with: *Away with; not friendly with; to utter; ejaculate; divulge; bring out; whip out* * He is out with his family for a few days * As a result of some dispute, he is out with his friend * She was out with a bitter salvo against the offensive remarks made by him * The volcano was out with a stream of fire burning everything that came its way * Police is not yet out with the identity of the suspect * The robber was out with a knife, threatening his victim to hand over all the cash and valuables

Out with him: *Turn him out* * It would be wise to be out with him so that he does not create a fuss in the meeting

Out-and-out: *Thoroughgoing; thorough-paced; utter; absolute; finally and completely; definitely; undeservedly; complete; unqualified* * He wants an out-and-out investigation in the whole case * The mill is working day and night at an out- and-out speed * He was in an out-and-out dilemma on how to deal with the controversial situation * He is out-and-out a thorough gentleman * There was out-and-out no solution to the natural calamity * You are out-and-out treading a right path * He out-and-out deserved to be elected as the president of the college management committee * What he said before the police was an out-and-out lie * He was academically out-and-out for the post of the manager * I gave him my out-and-out support in election time

Outbalance: *Outweigh* * The advantages far outbalance the disadvantages of this plan

Out-bargain: *Get the better of in a bargain* * The shrewd merchant out-bargained me through a higher bidding for the rough diamonds

Outbid: *Bid a higher sum than someone; make a higher bid than* * The museum has antagonised rivals by outbidding them for the world's greatest art treasures * He outbid all the bidders and bought the unique picture

Out-bounds: *Boundaries* * Human knowledge has no outbounds

Outbrag: *Surpass in bragging or boasting; surpass in beauty or splendour* * None can outbrag him on any subject even though it is beyond his knowledge * Miss Sushmita ran outbragged other world beauties in a pageant held in America

Outbrave: *Excel in boldness; to outface* * They were all praise for him for outbraving all the other pilots in shooting down three jet fighters of the enemy * That dauntless soldier was ready to outbrave the repeated air attacks of the enemy in the battle-field

Outbreak: *Breaking out; sudden occurrence of an illness or unrest* * The outbreak of cholera took a heavy toll of men, women and children in the town

Outburst: *To burst out* * There was an outburst of laughter in the hall at his funny remarks

Outcast: *One who is cast out of society or home; anything rejected; eliminated* * The outcast was not allowed to stay at the village for a year even * The perpetrators of the heinous crime are treated as social outcasts * He was outcast from taking part in the games as he had taken drugs

Outcaste: *One who is of no caste or has lost caste* * An enlightened movement is afoot everywhere for uplift of the outcastes

Outclass: *To surpass so far as to be seen in a different class* * Some countries are in a rat race to outclass one another in the use of high-tech weaponry

Outcome: *The issue; result; consequence* * Four possible outcomes have been identified for consideration * We are waiting to hear the final outcome of the negotiations * The costs are payable, no matter what the outcome of the case is

Outcrop: *The cropping out of a crop;* to crop out * The age of outcrop of these boulders is yet to be confirmed by the geologists * Many kinds of rock surfaces, gases, trees and other objects outcropped with the emergence of human life on the earth

Outdated: *Old-fashioned* * In order to get acquainted with outdated objects, we have decided to visit the museum tomorrow

Outdo: *Do better than* * Sometimes small firms can outdo big business when it comes to customer care

Outer space: *Space beyond the earth's atmosphere* * In 1957, the Soviets launched Sputnik I into outer space

Outfit: *Set of equipment needed for a particular purpose; set of clothing; organisation* * The soldiers are ready with their outfits for action in the battle-field * The campaigners have left for their expedition with necessary outfits * She was wearing on outfit she had bought the previous day * The school boy looked smart in his new outfit * He works for a private security outfit

Outgrow: *To grow too big for clothes; leave behind as one grows up; last longer than* * He has already outgrown his school uniform * He has outgrown his elder brother in a very short span of time

Outlast: *Last longer than* * He can outlast anyone on the dance floor

Outlaw: *Person punished by being placed outside the protection of the law or criminal; declared something or someone, to be beyond (the protection of law)* * An outlaw must be kept at an arm's length * He has been outlawed for being a dacoit * Gambling and flesh-trading have been outlawed in our society

Outlay on: *Spending or laying out money* * The business house repaid the initial outlay on advertising * The outlay on this big project would run into millions of dollars

Outlet for: *Way out for water/steam, etc.; means of or occasion for expressing feelings, ideas or energy* * Streams and rivers are natural outlets for flowing water caused by rain or melting of snow * A machine working through steam or gas or liquid must have an outlet for release of the same * Children need an outlet for their energy * We need to find an outlet for our many talents and interests

Outline: *Lines/drawings showing shape or boundary* * The outlines of the maps of various countries in the world have been defined very clearly * Following is an outline of the survey findings * He could see only the hazy outline of the post

Outlive: *Live longer than* * The machine had outlived its usefulness

Outlook: *A view; prospect; mental point of view* * Everybody has his own outlook about the mode of living * My outlook for a better career is rather bleak * It is my own outlook about life that as we sow, so shall we reap

Outmoded: *Old-fashioned* * This organisational structure is now outmoded

Outnumber: *Be greater in number than* * In this educational institute, girls outnumber the boys

Out-of-date: *Not abreast of the times; absolute* * Many writers now do not make general use of out-of-date words or ideas * So much equipment becomes out-of-date almost as soon it is made

Out-of-doors: *Open-air or outdoor* * We must take part in some out-of-door games

Out-of-the-way: *Uncommon or unusual; singular; secluded; lost or hidden; out of the ordinary; remote* * It is not out-of-the-way for college students to live at home * It is not out-of-the-way for young doctors to work a 70-hour week * He shows an out-of –the-way lack of concern for other people's feelings * Hermits lead an out-of-the-way life * My cheque seems to have gone out-of-the-way in postal transit * There are fears of an out-of-the-way agenda behind this new proposal * I am looking to a little more out-of-the-way happening * I have noticed nothing out-of-the-way * Landslides have cut off many villages in out-of-the-way areas

Output: *Quantity produced* * The manufacturing output of the cars is on the increase these days

Outrage: *Vigorous attack; offence; make somebody very shocked and angry* * The judge's remarks caused public outrage * He was outraged at the way he was treated

Outrank: *Be of higher quality or rank, etc.* * A brigadier outranks a colonel in the Indian army

Outright: *Out-and-out; unqualified; unmitigated; downright; direct* * Much of what has been written about us is an outright pack of lies * He asked for an outright apology for his friend's misconduct * He is leading a life of outright misery * You had outright been a menace to society * He had an outright approach even when dealing with the president

Outrun the constable: *Go too fast; get into debt* * He was able to outrun the constable to his hiding place * A spendthrift is obliged to outrun the constable

Outset: *Beginning* * From the outset, he loved the art of music and dance * Decide at the outset what kind of learning programme you want to follow

Outshine: *Do much better than* * He far outshone the rest of the class in the final examination

Outside chance: *A remote chance* * There is an outside chance of his getting through the acid test for a higher post

Outskirts: *Outer edge of a town, city* * They live on the outskirts of a small town

Outspent: *Thoroughly tired out* * When he got outspent, he stopped working at once

Outspoken: *Frank or bold of speech; uttered with boldness* * He was outspoken in his criticism of the plan * His outspoken remarks against the prime minister on the floor of the house were rejected by the Treasury Bench

Outstanding: *Prominent; unsettled; unpaid; sill to be attended to or done* * They praised him for his outstanding achievement in the field of science * The firm has asked its client to make payment of the outstanding bills at the earliest possible * They deposited the outstanding amount of tax immediately on receipt of the notice * All the outstanding items have been included in the agenda to be discussed in the next meeting of the committee

Outstand: *Withstand; to stand or endure through or beyond; to remain* * Nobody can outstand taunts * This old wooden bridge cannot outstand the weight of only a single man walking over it * It outstands true that sport is not only about winning but competing also

Outstay one's welcome: *Stay too long, until one is no longer a welcome guest* * One who outstays his welcome proves to be an unwanted and unnecessary burden on the host

Outstrip: *Run past; ignore or to do better than* * In one of the old tales, there is a mention of a tortoise that outstripped the hare to reach the post

Out-therod: *Outdo, especially in*

what is bad * He will outherod his accomplice in many cheating cases

Outweigh: *Be more important than* * Do the disadvantages outweigh the advantages?

Outwit: *Trick someone by being cleverer* * Somehow he always manages to outwit his opponents * The thief outwitted the police and got away with his loot

Over again: *Afresh; anew* * He left his job to start life over again * They started life all over again thousands of miles away * It was like war over again

Over against: *Opposite to; in contrast with* * Everything he does is over against what is considered normal behaviour * Democratic system is preferred over against other types of political systems

Over and above: *In addition to; besides* * There are other factors over and above those we have discussed * I think she has many good qualities over and above being beautiful

Over and over again: *Many times; repeatedly* * I have told you over and over again not to do that kind of mischief * Over and over again he puts me the same question about which I have no answer

Overflow with: *Be more than filled* * My heart overflowed with gratitude for all the facilities he provided to me

Over God's forbade: *God forbid* * May over God's forbade that natural calamities like earthquakes, floods, storms, etc. do not come to trouble us

Over head and ears: *Completely submerged; deeply engrossed* * He was over head and ears in debt for the reason best known to him * The young man was over head and ears in deep love with that beautiful young girl

Overnight: *In a short time* * He became a millionaire overnight

Over our/one's head: *Beyond one's conception; to a higher position of authority than somebody* * A lot of jokes went right over my head * I could not help feeling jealous when a junior person was promoted over my head

Overreact: *React very violently* * The financial markets overreacted to the news about the lower interest rates

Overseas: *To foreign lands* * He had been overseas many a time on business trips

Over the heads of: *Above the comprehension of* * For some days the new professor lectured over the heads of his pupils

Over-age: *Too old or beyond the age limit specified for* * A government servant having acquired an over-age is retired from his service under specified rules

Overall: *Everywhere; altogether; above all; over the whole* * It is an overall problem on how to get rid of unemployment in every state * The different reports overall testify the same result * Overall you have to stick to your gun * We must have to think overall on the reasons for our lack of progress

Over-anxious: *Too anxious* * The relatives of the passengers travelling in the ill-fated bus were naturally over-anxious to know about the accident

Over-arm: *With the arm raised above the shoulder* * The player threw the ball over-arm right into the net-basket

Overawe: *Frighten* * The younger players were over-awed by the occasion and played badly

Overbalance: *Cause to lose balance; outweigh* * He overbalanced and fell into the river * The gains overbalance the losses

Overbear: *Overcome* * My objections were overborne in the argument

Overbearing: *Trying to dominate others* * We should avoid an overbearing attitude * My husband can be quite overbearing with my son

Overcast: *Heavy or cloudy; dull* * The sky is overcast and it looks like it will rain

Overcharge: *Charge too much for something; fill or load too heavily* * We were overcharged for the breakfast in the hotel * It may be dangerous to overcharge an electric circuit

Overcome: *Succeed in dealing with or controlling a problem that has been preventing one from achieving something; to defeat somebody; be extremely affected by something* * He overcame injury to win the medal in the athletics championship * In the final game, Sweden easily overcame France * Her parents were overcome with grief at the funeral

Overcompensate: *Do too much when trying to correct a problem and so cause a different problem* * She overcompensated for her shyness by talking too much and laughing too loud

Overdo: *Exaggerate something; to use too much of something; cook something for too long* * He overdid the sympathy bit at the death of his friend's wife * Don't overdo the salt in the food * The fish was overdone and very dry

Overdo it/things: *To work, study, etc. too hard or for too long* * He has been overdoing things recently * I overdid the physical exercise and hurt my back

Overdue: *Not paid, done, returned, etc. by the required or expected time; that should have happened* * The employees are on strike to protest for not releasing their overdue salaries * Her baby is two weeks overdue * The new reforms are still overdue

Overestimate: *To estimate too much; think something in larger than it is* * They overestimated his ability when they promoted him * The importance of these findings cannot be overestimated

Overflow with: *Be more than filled* * My heart overflowed with gratitude for all the facilities he provided to me

Overhead expenses: *General expenses incurred by a business as a whole* * Almost all big business houses make a provision for overhead expenses to be utilised for paying salaries, rents, etc.

Overhear: *Hear accidentally a conversation in which one is not involved* * I overheard two doctors discussing my case

Overland: *By land* * We had to travel overland by hiring a taxi

Overlap: *Involve duplication; mount by which something overlaps* * His duties and mine overlapped * There is considerable overlap between the two subjects

Overleaf: *On the other side of a page* * The changes are explained in detail overleaf

Overlook: *Have a view from above; fail to see or notice; see something wrong or bad but decide to ignore it* * Our garden is overlooked from the neighbour's windows * He seems to have overlooked an important point * We could not afford to overlook such a serious offence

Overpass: *Fly over or road which crosses the top of another road* * Many overpasses have been structured on the highway leading from Chandigarh to Delhi

Overplay one's hand: *Attempt to gain too much in negotiations* * The United States has to be careful in overplaying its hand

Overpower: *Gain control by force* * The police finally overpowered the criminal

Overpowering: *Very strong* * I am glad to have met an overpowering personality the other day

Overreach yourself: *Go too far and fail in what you are trying to do* * He overreached himself and lost much of his fortune * The company had overreached itself and made unwise investments

Override: *Pay no attention to; be more important than other things* * The chairman overrode the committee's objections and signed the agreement * Consideration of safety overrides all other concerns

Overrule: *To rule or order against* * The verdict of the High Court was overruled by the Supreme Court

Overrun: *Be not within limit; succeed in occupying a place or area very quickly; spread over; take more time than was intended* * He was found guilty of overrunning his authority * The centre of this city was overrun by an armed mob which attacked government buildings * The house was overrun with rats * His lectures never overrun

Oversee: *To supervise; to superintendent* * United Nations observers oversee the elections

Overshadow: *Make less conspicuous; throw a shadow over something; make an event less enjoyable than it should be* * He had always been overshadowed by his elder sister * The garden is overshadowed by tall trees * Fears for the president's safety could overshadow his peace-making efforts

Overshoot the mark: *To go too far* * He was successful in overshooting the mark in discus throw * You have overshot the mark in making false allegations against him

Oversight: *Not doing something because of forgetfulness; not noticing* * The committee did not carry out the suggestions due to an oversight

Overstep: *Go further than you ought to* * He tends to overstep the boundaries of good taste

Overstep to mark line: *Behave*

in a way that people think is not acceptable * He overstepped the mark/line and we had no option but to suspend him

Overt act: *Something actually done publicly or open* * The killing of a man in cold blood is broad daylight was an overt act

Overtax one's strength: *Do more than one is physically capable of* * Instead of overtaxing your strength by too much physical exercise, it is better to relax

Overthrow: *Removal of a government dictator from power* * The democratic regime in Pakistan has been overthrown through military coups from time to time.

Overturn: *Fall over or turn upside down; subvert* * The car skidded and overturned * His sentence was overturned by the appeal court

Overview: *General view of a subject* * The central section of the book is a historical overview of drug use

Overwhelmed with: *Weighed down; submerged* * The old woman was overwhelmed with grief at her son's death

Overwhelmed with work: *Having more work than one can do* * He has been overwhelmed with work which is telling upon his health

Overwrought: *Very agitated; under a lot of stress* * One overwrought member had to be restrained by friends

Owe something: *Have something because of* * He owes his success to hard work

Owing to: *Because of* * Owing to his bad health he could not attend office * The game was cancelled owing to torrential rain

Own up to: *Confess fully and frankly* * I am still waiting for someone to own up to the damage caused to the windowpane

P

Pace out/ off: *Measure distance by walking one end to other* * I marked the ground and then paced it out to be sure

Pace up and down: *Walk hither and thither* * It is good for health to pace up and down after having had your meals

Pace-maker: *A device placed inside the body to set the heart beat in the right way; a competitor starting a race quickly so that other runners will try to copy the speed to achieve a very fast time* * She was fitted with a pace-maker after suffering serious heart trouble * Pace-makers usually stop before the race is finished

Pace-setter: *A person or a company considered to be the leader in a particular field; activity; a person or team that is winning in a sports competition* * The big banks have been the pace-setters in developing the financial system * The local club is now only one point off the pace-setter

Pack a jury: *Fill up with persons of particular kind for one's own purpose* * The king had to pack a jury to serve him on secret plans

Pack a punch: *Hit very hard; have a powerful effect on* * Both the boxers packed powerful punches at each other in the first round of the wrestling bout * The advertising campaign packs quite a good punch

Pack and peal: *To have any dealing* * I do not know if they would like to pack and peal in this particular drive

Pack away: *Be capable of being folded in small when not being used; put something in a box, etc. when you have finished using it* * The tent can be folded to pack away in a small bag * We packed away the summer clothes when the winter set in

Pack in: *Stop doing something in a limited period of time; do a lot of things; put a lot of things or people in a limited space* * He decided to pack in his job * You seem to have packed a lot in your life * They have managed to pack a lot of information in a very small book

Pack into something: *Go somewhere in large numbers so that available space is filled* * Over 8,000 fans packed into the stadium to watch the final match

Pack of lies: *Completely untrue* * All that he told you against me was nothing but a pack of lies

Pack of wolves: *Group of wolves* * A pack of wolves chased a deer from all sides

Pack off: *Send someone away when you do not want him with you* * My parents always pack me off to bed early

Pack out: *Attract enough people to completely fill a theatre* * Opera houses are packed out whenever she sings * The band can still pack out concert hills

Pack up: *Stop working; stop doing something, especially a job* * The fax machine is packed up again * What made you pack up a good job like that?

Package deal: *Deal where several items are agreed* * A package deal is likely to be signed between the two countries to strengthen their alliance

Package tour: *Tour which is organised and paid for in advance* * Representatives of various companies are allowed package tours to go abroad for boosting their trade

Packed like sardines: *Crowded close together* * The travellers were packed like sardines in the bus

Pad out: *Add things that are unnecessary* * The report was padded out with extracts from previous documents

Pad the hoof: *Walk or trudge* * He will have to pad the hoof wearily along the tough hilly path

Paddle one's own canoe: *To depend on oneself* * It is better to paddle our own canoes than to be a burden on others

Paint the lily: *Attempt to beautify that which is already beautiful* * You are a fool if you are going to paint the lily by way of improving the face of this girl in the photograph

Paint the town red: *Break out in a boisterous spree* * While celebrating a function in the club, the youngsters painted the town red after having drunk too much whisky

Pair of colours: *Two flags carried by a regiment, one the*

national flag and the other the flag of the regiment * The regiment observed its Raising Day with a pair of colours during the course of march-past

Pair of scales: *Weighing machine* * The grocers make use of a pair of scales while selling their goods to their customers

Pair off: *Arrange or set against each other; set aside in pairs; become associated in pairs* * He knew that she would resist pairing him off with someone * The squad members paired off to find places for each other * He is always trying to pair me off with his cousin

Pale in comparison: *Seem less important when compared with* * Last year's riots pale in comparison with this latest outburst of violence

Palm of victory: *Sign of victory* * The regiment returned to the barracks with their palm of victory after giving a crushing defeat to the enemy

Palm off: *Persuade to believe an excuse or explanation that is not true; tell that something is better than it is in order to sell it* * He made sure that he was never palmed off with such inferior stuff * They were trying to palm the table off as a genuine antique

Palm-grease/oil: *Bribe* * He was being questioned for receiving palm-grease

Palmy days: *Time of prosperity* * The old fellow loves telling the story of his palmy days * India enjoyed palmy days during the Golden Age of the Guptas

Pan for gold: *Sift mind in a stream hoping to find gold* * Many people earn their living by panning for gold

Pan out: *Develop in a particular way* * I am happy with the way the things have panned out

Pander to: *Try to please others for something that is not acceptable or reasonable* * The speech was just pandering to his professor's ego

Panel saw: *A saw for cutting very thin wood* * The carpenter does make use of the panel saw wherever needed

Panic-stricken: *Wild with fright* * Many people were killed in the stampede caused due to the panic created

Paper tiger: *A person or organisation that appears to be powerful but in fact not so* * Some persons or countries are adept in playing the role of a paper tiger

Paraffin wax: *Solid white substance used for making candles* * Paraffin wax is used for making candles to be lit on certain occasions

Parcel out: *Divide into parts* * They will have to parcel out the land into small lots to divide it equally

Parley into: *Use money or skill to make it more successful* * She wants to parley her success as a model into an acting career

Part and parcel: *Essentially a part* * Games are a part and parcel of education

Part company: *Separate; end relationship; disagree* * The two friends parted company at the railway station * This is where we part company * He parted company with me on a number of important issues

Part of speech: *One of the various classes of words* * We can acquire clear knowledge of the part of speech from our grammar book

Part the hair: *Separate hair of head with comb* * He parts his hair in the middle

Part with: *Give to someone else that you would prefer to keep* * Make sure you read the contract before parting with any money

Partake of: *Take some, especially of food and drink* * Would you like to partake of some refreshment?

Parthian shot: *Parting remark which is generally sarcastic* * I could not tolerate the Parthian shot, so I chased him to take revenge on him

Participate with: *Take part with* * I will not participate with them in the general merry-making

Parting cup: *A two-handled drinking cup* * He uses a parting cup for drinking milk or soup

Parting of the ways: *A point at which a fateful decision must be taken* * The two colleagues were on parting of the ways after they stopped working together

Parting shot: *Unpleasant or forceful remarks at the end of a conversation* * She made a very nasty remark as a parting shot before embarking on her journey

Parting word: *Said or done when leaving each other* * His parting words were really very touchy * He gave her a parting kiss at the end of their journey

Party line: *Particular official views of a political party supported by its members* * He was turned out for ignoring the doctrines of the party line

Party to something: *Involvement in an agreement or action* * He refused to be a party to any violence

Party whip: *Member of Parliament whose job is to keep order among members of his party* * Party whip plays an important role when a party in power has to face a motion of no confidence

Pass a vote of thanks to someone: *Thank someone officially in the minutes of a meeting* * The members passed a vote of thanks to the vice-chancellor at the close of the meeting

Pass away: *Come to an end; go off; die; elapse* * The happy days of our life passed away in a short period * The man passed away leaving behind a large amount of cash * He passed away peacefully * Many years passed away before they met again

Pass by: *To disregard; go past; overlook* * I cannot let the matter pass by without a protest * The procession passed right by my front door * He generally passed by the faults of his subordinates

Pass current: *Be received as genuine* * I doubt if your story would pass current before anybody

Pass for: *Be accepted as; be regarded as; be thought as somebody or something* * Your remuneration bill has been passed for payment by the auditor * With his knowledge of more than two languages he can pass for a multilinguist * He is so fair in complexion that he could easily pass for a foreigner

Pass key: *Main key which opens several doors* * The thief was caught red-handed when opening the main door with a pass key

Pass muster: *Be regarded as up to the mark* * I could not pass muster in his language * With fashionable clothes and good make-up, she could pass muster

Pass off: *Impose fraudulently; palm off; take it course satisfactorily; pretend to be* * He escaped by passing himself off as a guard * Make sure that he does not try to pass you off with spurious goods * When her tears had passed off their course, she felt calmer and more in control * With minor ailments, the best thing is often to let Nature pass off its course * He passed himself off a nobleman

Pass on: *Go forward; proceed; to die; transmit; practice artfully; impose upon* * The project will pass on as planned * Work is passing on slowly * He passed on with a heart attack at the age of 72 * The ceremony was passed on live by satellite to many countries * Don't try to pass on false blame on others * The court of law has passed on him a penalty of 50,000 rupees for jumping the bail

Pass one's comprehension: *Be more than one can understand* * The practical solution to this knotty problem has really passed my comprehension

Pass one's word: *Make a promise* * A politician passes word before the election that he would bring about many reforms but forgets it on coming to power

Pass oneself off as: *Pretend to be* * The dacoit put on a *burkha* (robe) and passed himself off as a Muslim woman

Pass out: *To distribute; to die; to faint, become unconscious or dead drunk; go off; leave college, etc. having passed one's examination** The organisation passed out food and blankets to the earthquake victims * The old customs are passing out * He felt sick and dizzy and then passed out * His students will pass out next year from the class * That cadet passed out in the street

Pass out of mind: *Be forgotten* * It passed out of mind to send my friend New Year's greetings

Pass over: *Overlook; ignore* * He seems to have passed over one important fact * He was passed over for that post while he had all the necessary qualifications * He was passed over in favour of a younger man

Pass remarks about: *Make rude comments* * It does not behove a person to pass remarks about anybody's character

Pass sentence upon: *Order of sentence* * The judge passed sentence upon the culprit who fainted on hearing it

Pass the bottle of smoke: *Acquiesce (assent) in some falsehood* * He had no option but to pass the bottle of smoke with others

Pass the buck: *Shift the responsibility to someone else* * You are passing the buck by putting the blame for your mistake on others

Pass the mark: *Pass on the badge of demerit to the next offender* * We plan to pass the mark to others to make them a scapegoat in our effort to cover up for our mistake

Pass the time of day: *Exchange ordinary greetings of civility* * It is a good thing to pass the time of day in a good society

Pass through: *Enter; to undergo; experience* * Our train bound for Shimla had to pass through many tunnels * He had to pass through many ups and downs in life * The country has yet to pass through many obstacles to find acceptance amongst the world communities

Pass up: *Renounce or having nothing to do with* * We have passed up the use of force to settle our disputes

Pass water: *Urinate* * A sensitive bladder can make you feel the need of passing water frequently * The student sought permission from the teacher to leave class for passing water

Passage beds: *Transitional strata* * Our life passes through many passage beds

Passage money: *Fare* * What is the passage money to travel by air from Delhi to London?

Passage of arms: *Any feat of arms; an encounter, especially in words* * There was a passage of arms in the Sam battle exercise * We witnessed a passage of arms between the two rival groups

Passageway: *A way of access* * A dark narrow passageway led to the main hall * There is an underground passageway that connects the five buildings

Passer-by: *Person who is walking past* * The policeman asked the passer-by if they had seen any accident on the road

Passive obedience: *Absolute submission to the ruling power* * It is expected of every employee to perform his duty in passive obedience

Passive resistance: *Deliberately refused to do what law or regulation orders and submission to consequent penalties* * Mahatma Gandhi enunciated his vision about passive resistance

Password: *Secret word which you say to go past a guard* * An officer on his checking round has to utter the password when going past a guard

Past it: *Too old to do what you*

used to be able; too old to be used for its normal function * In some sports you are past it by the age of 35 * That coat is looking decidedly past it

Past master: *One who is an expert in his field; a thorough proficient* * He was a past master at manipulating the media for his own ends * He is an adept rock-climber and a past master in climbing hills * Your cousin is really a past master in telling lies

Past one's bedtime: *Later than you usually go to bed* * It is past your bedtime

Past the garden: *By and beyond the garden* * While jogging in the morning, we run past the garden daily

Pastime: *Amusement; sports* * My favourite pastime is to play cards

Pasty-faced: *Pale and dull of complexion* * Feeling dejected at my failure, I remained pasty-faced the whole day

Pat on the back: *A mark of encouragement* * The player who was in form deserved a pat on his back * If you do something remarkable, give yourself a pat on the back

Patch through: *Connect telephone or electronic equipment temporarily** He was patched through to London on the satellite link

Patch together: *Form from a number of parts* * They hope to be able to patch together various differences for a temporary settlement

Patch up: *Provisional repair of something; treat injuries; stop quarrelling and be friends again; come to an agreement after long discussions* * Just to patch up the boat will cost a substantial amount * The doctor will soon patch you up * They have patched up their differences * In the long run they will try to patch up the deal

Patrol wagon: *A prison van* * Police have to make use of a patrol wagon to transport the prisoners to and from the jail

Pattern something on/after: *A new pattern* * A new approach patterned on the Japanese concept is likely to be adopted in this project

Pave the way for: *Prepare the way for; make easier; help to bring on* * The new Bill, if passed, will pave the way for greater women's representation in Parliament * Your passing the examination creditably have paved the way for the next higher promotion * The discussions are aimed at paving the way for formal negotiations

Pave the way to: *Lead to* * It is only the hard work that paves the way to success

Pay attention to: *Listen carefully to* * Please pay attention to what I am saying

Pay back: *Pay in return; give tit for tat* * I have paid back the money that I borrowed from him * I will pay him back for making me look like a fool in front of the gathering

Pay down: *Pay in cash on the spot* * I need to pay down the shopkeeper one thousand rupees for the articles I purchased from him

Pay for: *Make amends for; suffer for; bear the expenses of* * He wanted to pay for causing their marriage fail * He will have to pay for his foolish behaviour * He promised to pay for the dinner at a grand hotel.

Pay heed to: *Pay attention to* * We must pay heed to our studies to succeed in life

Pay home: *Strike to the quick; retaliate* * We will need to pay home five successive goals to level the scores * Our troops were already on the alert to pay home against any attack by the enemy

Pay in: *Contribute to a fund* * Pay this sum in the account of my wife * I have already paid in a large sum of money towards the national emergency fund

Pay lip-service: *Give a false respect or obedience* * Political parties pay lip-service to environmental issues without taking any action

Pay money on advance: *Pay part of the total bill in advance* * I paid half the money towards the total cost of the car on advance

Pay off: *Pay in full and discharge; take revenge upon; to requite; fell away to leeward* * The crew were paid off as soon as the ship docked * He swore to pay off his political enemies * Will she ever be able to pay off my love? * Luckily for us the wind did pay off as we steered the ship safely towards the destination * The gamble at last paid him off.

Pay off old scores: *Repay old grudges* * I paid off old scores by giving him a sound thrashing

Pay one back in the same coin: *To give tit for tat or treat a person in the same manner as he treats* * If he does not return the money you lent to him, when he comes to borrow from you next, you should also pay him back in the same coin

Pay one's compliments: *Give one's respects* * It is a good thing to pay our compliments to our elders

Pay one's respects: *Salute* * We must pay our respect to the elders

Pay one's score: *Settle; reckon* * We are now in friendly terms after paying our score between us

Pay one's way: *Have or bring enough to pay expenses* * I went to college as a part-time student, paying my own way

Pay out: *Cause to run out; disburse; punish deservedly* * Many policies pay out after a period of months * The bank has paid out a large sum of money for the project * He needs to be paid out for his lewd behaviour

Pay round: *Turn the ship's head* * The navigator was obliged to pay round the ship against high tides

Pay the Cain: *Pay the penalty* * He had to pay the Cain for driving without a licence

Pay the piper: *Bear the expenses; have to pay heavily* * He who pays the piper calls the tune * They had to pay the piper in completing the new film

Pay through the nose: *Pay dearly* * The country has to pay through the nose to fight against terrorism * This is a nice hotel but you will have to pay through the nose here

Pay tribute to: *Praise; admit one's gratitude* * Citizens of the country must pay tribute to the sacrifices of martyrs

Pay up: *Pay in full; pay arrears; accept the security and pay* * If you don't pay up the amount loaned, I will take you to court * The government willingly agreed to pay up the arrears accumulated in the form of dearness allowance * The victims of the accident have been paid up by the authority concerned

Paying guest: *A boarder in a private house* * John stayed as a paying guest in London to study law

Payload: *Load carried by an aircraft or rocket; quantity of explosives a missile or rocket could carry to hit at a particular range* * The payload of an aircraft is determined according to its capacity as well as safety * India has been able to build heavy payload missiles which can accurately strike at a long range

Payment in kind: *Payment in goods, not in money* * The labourer working here is being given payment in kind

Pay-off: *Reward; final success* * You deserve a pay-off for being so honest and helpful * His sincere efforts resulted in a rich pay-off to him

Peaceful coexistence: *Where countries of different types of government exist side by side in peace* * China and India have agreed to follow the path of peaceful co-existence

Peach on someone: *Inform about someone* * The people peach on the suspect to the police for further interrogation of his bona fides

Peak and pine: *Sharp-featured* * He would like to marry a girl who is peak and pine to look at

Peak load: *Load in a power station; maximum demand of electricity* * This power house can meet a peak load of 500 MW * The whole town needs a peak load of 50 MW

Peal of thunder: *Loud sound of thunder* * There was a peal of thunder in the sky before it began to pour

Pearl barley: *Grains barley used in working* * Many countries make use of pearl barley as food or for making beer and whisky

Pearl of wisdom: *Wise remark* * Your pearls of wisdom have prompted me to become more cautious

Peck at: *Strike with peak* * The hens are pecking at the corns

Peculiar to: *Belong especially to* * Such a violent outbreak of temper is peculiar to him

Pecuniary loss: *Loss of money* * He had to bear a heavy pecuniary loss in the new enterprise

Pedal bin: *Container for putting rubbish or waste matter; rubbish container which opens with a pedal* * We make use of a pedal bin for disposal of rubbish or waste matter * Many people make use of a pedal bin for putting in waste or rubbish

Pedestrian precinct: *Streets or shopping areas closed for vehicular traffic* * There is no chance of a serious accident occurring within the pedestrian precinct

Peek at: *Look at* * She peeked at the audience from behind the curtain

Peek out: *Pierce hole in* * The woodpecker peeked out at the middle of the tree-trunk to be used as a nest for laying eggs

Peeking order: *Order of importance or prevalence* * He does not like to be rated at the bottom of the peeking order

Peel off: *Leave a group of vehicles, like aircraft, etc. and turn to one side; remove clothes* * The leading car in motorcade peeled off to the right * He peeled off his clothes under the scorching heat of the sun

Peeping Tom: *A trying fellow especially one who peeps in through the window* * Don't be a Peeping Tom by peeping though the hole in the wall

Peep-of-day: *The first appearance of light in the morning* * He rises with the peep-of-day as a matter of routine

Peer group: *Group of people of equal (social) status* * They are getting along very well with their peer group

Peg at: *Keep or fix it* * The bank wants to peg interest at 8 per cent per year

Peg away: *Work on assiduously* * He would rather keep on pegging away at a beginner's book

Peg down: *Restrict by rule* * They have pegged down their daily routine work

Peg out: *In croquet; finish by driving the ball against the peg; the mark off with pegs; become exhausted; be ruined or die* * You might see him pegging out at that grass lawn this time * He pegged out the game successfully * The grassy lawn has been pegged out for the croquet game * I did try to run in a marathon once, but I pegged out half way through * I nipped round the corner for a quick beer and nearly pegged out on the spot * He looked as if he was going to peg out any moment * I thought the old members were going to peg out

Pelican in her piety: *A pelican, with wings indorsed, feeding her young with her blood* * Some poor people are forced to feed their offsprings like pelican in her piety

Pell-mell: *In confusion* * All three of us rushed pell-mell into the kitchen

Pelting down: *Pouring down* * By now the rain was pelting down on the roof

Penal code: *Law of crimes* * All the criminal cases are disposed of under a particular section of the penal code

Penal law: *Law pertaining to crimes and punishment* * The police have arrested him under penal law

Penal servitude: *Imprisonment with hard labour* * Hard-core criminals have to undergo penal servitude

Penalty goal: *One scored by a penalty kick* * Finally our team won the match through a penalty goal

Penalty kick: *A free kick or the privilege granted to a player to kick the ball as he pleases because of some breach of the rules by the opposing side* * In a football match, he could score a goal through a penalty kick

Penalty line: *The boundary of the penalty area* * A penalty kick is generally allowed when a player of the defending side infringes rules of the game within the penalty line

Pen-and-ink: *Writing material; a pen drawing; writing; written; executed in pen-and-ink* * Pen-and-ink is necessary to write down anything we think or say * This bridge sketch on the paper is a handwork of pen-and-ink * He put it all in a pen-and-ink drawing * You can see pen-and-ink drawings of the proposed buildings to be constructed * There is no way out but to carry out correction work in pen-and-ink

Pencil in: *Write down name or details of arrangements for a probable purpose* * We will need to pencil in the details of the meeting on Monday afternoon * Shall I pencil in your name for a meeting on Friday?

Penny wisdom: *Prudence in petty matters* * This type of work can be easily handled by a person with penny wisdom

Pennywise and pound foolish: *Careful in small matters and wasteful in large matters* * He has become a laughing stock for being pennywise and pound foolish.

Penny-a-line: *Cheap writing* * Media should be alive not to publish any matter worth penny-a-line

Penny-fee: *A small wage* * There are still many poor people who live on a penny-fee

Pension off: *Dismiss or allow to retire with pension; to place something at rest* * He was pensioned off and his job was given to a younger person * That car of yours should have been pensioned off years ago

People at large: *Ordinary people* * There is great awareness among the people at large

Pep pill: *Medicine taken to make you more lively and active* * When he gets tired, he takes pep pills to finish his daily work as a matter of routine

Pep up: *Make somebody full of energy* * A walk in the fresh air will pep you up

Pepper something with: *Include large number of something* * He peppered his speech with jokes

Pepper with: *Hit with a lot of small objects* * Suddenly the garden was peppered with pellets

Per annum: *In each year* * For getting a car loan from the bank, the per annum interest is quite high

Per capita: *For each person* * In India the per capita income is now on the increase

Per se: *In itself* * The drug is not harmful per se, but is dangerous when taken with alcohol

Percussion instruments: *Musical instruments which are hit with stick or band like drums, guitar, etc.* * We can enjoy hearing different percussion instruments in an opera house

Perk up: *Be cheerful or lively after feeling tired or bored or depressed; increase in value; show interest* * He soon perked up when his friends arrived * Share prices have perked up slightly at close of trading * I tried to think of some ways to perk up his spirits when playing in a tournament

Persona non grata: *Person who is not accepted to a foreign government* * The government has declared the French ambassador persona non grata

Persons of name: *Famous men* * Only persons of name have been invited to attend the seminar

Pervading all space: *Omnipresent* * Fresh air is pervading the entire space for all living beings

Pervert the course of justice: *Influence a court so that justice is not done; tell a lie or do something to prevent from finding out the truth about a crime* * He was charged with conspiring to pervert the course of justice

Pest of the people: *Troublesome to people* * All the criminals should be ostracised as they are pests of the people

Pet name: *A name used in familiar affection* * Smith's pet name is Sim

Peter out: *Gradually become smaller, quieter, etc. and then*

end * The campaign petered out for lack of support

Petroleum products: *Substances which are made from petroleum* * Today petroleum products flood the markets in a big way

Petticoat government: *Domination by women* * In some countries, the administration is run by petticoat government

Phase in: *Introduce gradually in stages over a period of time* * New taxes will be phased in over two years

Phase out: *Stop gradually in stages over a period of time* * Subsidies to farmers will be phased out by the year 2010

Photo-finish: *Very close end of a race when a photograph is used to decide the winner* * He was beaten in the race in a photo-finish

Photographic memory: *Ability to remember things in exact detail, as if seen* * He at once recognised the real culprit on the force of his photographic memory

Phrase book: *Book of translation of common expressions* * We bought a Danish phrase book

Pick a hole in one's coat: *Find fault with one* * Some people have an inborn habit of picking a hole in other's coat on some ground or other

Pick a lock: *Open a lock without a key* * He lost the key to the main door of the house, so he had to pick the lock with a piece of strong wire

Pick a person's pocket: *Steal from his pocket* * While travelling in a train some pickpocket picked my pocket, taking away my purse containing cash and important documents

Pick a quarrel: *Intentionally begin a quarrel* * This naughty boy picks a quarrel with everyone

Pick a winner: *Choose a horse, etc. that one thinks is more likely to win a race* * He was prudent enough to pick a winner that fetched him a handsome amount

Pick and choose: *Select carefully* * You have to take whatever job if available as you cannot pick and choose

Pick at: *Find fault with; to pull or touch something several times; eat food slowly when you are not hungry* * Why are you always picking at the poor child? * He tried to undo the knot by picking at it with his fingers * He picked at a plate of cheese for supper as he was not really hungry

Pick brains: *Ask a lot of questions to know more about the subject that one is conversant with* * Why should you pick his brains when he is not capable of answering your queries?

Pick holes in: *Find weak points in* * It was easy to pick holes in his argument

Pick of the bunch: *The best out of the group* * I watched many cricket matches of the World Cup and Kapil Dev was the pick of the bunch

Pick off: *Shoot persons, etc. deliberately one by one; select from a number and shoot; detach and remove* * Snipers were picking off innocent civilians * Pick off all the dead leaves from these plants

Pick on: *Single out especially anything unpleasant; nag at; carp at* * He picked on two of my statements which he said were provocative * Why should you always pick on me to do the chores? * Stop picking on me or I will not do it * He cannot understand why she is constantly picking on him

Pick one's way: *Choose carefully where to put one's foot* * They were afraid of snakes in the forest and picked their way along with extreme caution

Pick out: *Make out; pluck out; select from a number; discover or recognise after careful study; mark out with a colour* * I heard the voices but I could not pick out what they were saying * He suddenly picked out a new idea of bringing her round to our point of view * He could pick out a good cook in a crowd * The name is picked out in gold letters over the shop * Read the play again and pick out the major themes

Pick over: *Go over and select* * I have picked over the facts of the case

Pick purse: *One who steals purse* * My purse containing a handsome amount has been taken by some pick purse

Pick to pieces: *Pull asunder* * In the violent scuffle, my clothes were picked to pieces

Pick up: *Lift from the ground, floor, etc.; improve gradually; gain strength bit by bit; take into a vehicle or into one's company; scrape acquaintance informally with; acquire as occasion offers; gain; come upon; make out; distinguish* * Please pick up this table to take to the dining room * I am happy to see you picking up your health day by day * Economically our country is picking up * The bus picks up the passengers outside the airport * While travelling by rail, I picked up a stranger to talk with * Young people are picking up ideas about drugs * Where did you pick up this kind of civility? * I would like to pick up that question later * I could hear voices but I could not pick up what they were saying * At what age are children to pick up between right and wrong?

Pick up speed: *Go faster* * Soon after leaving the station, the train picked up speed

Pick up the momentum: *Gain force of movement* * As soon as the car left the city, it began to pick up the momentum

Pick up the pieces: *To help somebody return to a normal situation particularly after a shock or disaster* * You can only be there to pick up the pieces when things are wrong

Pick up the tab: *Pay for something* * The company picked up the tab for his hotel room * The government will continue to pick up the tab to clear the college fees for some students

Pick up the threads: *To return to an earlier situation or way of life after an interruption* * Having suffered disasters many a time, he managed to pick up the threads

Pick your way over: *Walk very carefully* * The old man picked his way delicately over the slippery path

Pick-and-mix: *Choosing things from a large variety of different items* * She possesses a keen eye for a pick-and-mix selection of fabrics and wallpapers * It was a pick-and-mix programme which the students enjoyed

Pick-me-up: *A stimulation drink* * Let us have a pick-me-up before we start dancing * This deal could offer the best possible pick-me-up to the town's ailing economy

Pick-pocket: *One who picks or steals from other people's pockets* * Three of the pick-pockets have been arrested at the railway station

Pick-up: *An act of picking-up; reception; a recovery; accelerating power; a thing or person picked up* * You have had a nice pick-up of sweet mangoes * My radio set has a poor pick-up * Wish you a speedy pick-up after a long ailment * There is nothing wrong in the pick-up of my car * The company had many pick-up points in most cities

Picnic apple: *Pomegranate* * Everybody cherish the taste of picnic apple

Pictures: *Cinema* * We are now going to see the pictures

Pie in the sky: *An event unlikely to happen* * My wish to go to London is all just a pie in the sky * Everyone knows that it is only a pie in the sky to eradicate unemployment

Piece of goods: *A woman* * What do you know about that piece of goods?

Piece of one's mind: *Frank, outspoken words* * I had to give him my piece of mind for his unwanted attention

Piece of work: *A task; a fuss; ado* * I have an urgent piece of work to do today * It was all a piece of work about nothing * He signed the document without making it a piece of work

Piece out: *Eke out* * He managed to piece out his living within the small amount of salary he received

Piece together: *Join separate parts together; understand a story or situation, etc.; put together bit by bit* * He could easily piece together a jigsaw * The police are trying to piece together the clues found at the site of the crime * I found out the truth by piecing together hints and rumours that I heard at school * Doctors painstakingly pieced together the broken bones

Piece up: *Patch up; incorporate in one's own share* * It is time you started piecing up the differences with him * He has obliged me by piecing up in his own venture/enterprise

Piece-meal: *Happening gradually* * The reforms were implemented piece-meal

Piecework: *Work for which you are paid by the amount of work done and not by the hours* * All my men are on piecework

Pied-a-terra: *A small flat/ apartment in a town to be used when necessary* * He lives permanently in a village but he has a pied-a-terra in the town as well

Pie-eyed: *Drunk* * They got pie-eyed on vodka

Piercing to the quick: *Wounding feeling* * His rude and disgusting remarks kept me piercing to the quick

Pig out: *Eat too much food* * They pigged out on pizza

Pig-headed: *Insist on one's opinion which other people think*

unreasonable; obstinate * He is always in his pig-headed way insisting that he is right and that everyone else is wrong * A pig-headed person would always insist that he is right * He is a pig-headed man and would never give up

Pile on: *Increase quickly (especially a person's weight); make something increase rapidly; give a lot of something to do; express a feeling more strongly than is necessary* * The weight just piled on while I was abroad * The team piled on the points in the first half of the match itself * He felt his boss was piling too much work on him * Don't pile on the drama!

Pile on the agony: *Overdo painful effects by accumulation* * Bosses piled on the agony with threats of more job cuts

Pile up: *Become large in quantity or amount; heap up; give somebody more or too much of something; to run ashore; crash; accumulate; form a disorderly mass or heap* * Work always piles up at the end of the year * Snow was piled up against the door * The German team piled on the pressure in the last five minutes of the match * Under the cover of a thick fog, many vehicles piled up on the road * The aeroplane caught fire suddenly and piled up while landing * My work keeps piling up * Bulldozers piled up huge plies of dirt * Mail was still piling up at the office * Many dead bodies of the soldiers piled up in the battle-field during the course of action

Pile-it-on-thick: *Exaggerate when praising or criticising* * He gave a good talk at the conference but his colleague was piling-it-on-thick when he spoke of an unforgettable experience

Pillar of faith: *Supporter of belief* * My father was a pillar of faith in keeping high character and living a simple life

Pillow slip: *Cloth bag to cover a pillow* * A pillow slip keeps the pillow neat and clean

Pin down: *Explain or understand something exactly* * The cause of his disease is difficult to pin down precisely

Pin on: *Be blamed for something especially for something they did not do* * No one would admit responsibility and everyone is trying to pin on the blame on someone else

Pin on one's sleeves: *Make entirely dependent* * The poor farmer found it rather difficult to pin on his sleeves due to a drought

Pin one (down) to: *Keep one strictly to* * It is difficult to pin her down to fix a date for a meeting * You cannot pin him down to give you a helping hand in making dresses.

Pin one's faith on: *Put either trust on* * The company is pinning its faith on the manager for progressive function of the firm

Pinch pennies: *Try to spend as little money as possible* * Don't be a spendthrift; you must pinch pennies on wasteful material

Pine for: *Longing earnest for* * She is pining for her lost son

Pink gin: *Gin with angostura bitters* * He gulped down a full glass of pink gin and fell fast asleep

Pink of perfection: *The acme* * The spring season is now in the pink of perfection * The artist has been able to make this portrait which is considered to be a work in pink of perfection

Pinnacle of something: *Most important or successful of something* * It represents the pinnacle of intellectual capability

Pins and needles: *A tingling feeling as numbness passes off* * I felt pins and needles in the tips of my fingers.

Pipe down: *Dismiss from muster, as ships' company; subside into silence* * One of the sailors was piped down for his impudence * Just pipe down and I will tell you what I want

Pipe hot: *Extremely hot* * We should avoid to eat piping hot food

Pipe off: *Watch a house or person for purpose of theft* * The robbers piped off the locked house and its surroundings before committing theft

Pipe one's eye: *Weep* * The way she tuned her song in praise of martyrs could not help me pipe my eyes

Pipe up: *Begin to speak* * The man next to me piped up with a silly comment

Pique somebody's interest: *Make somebody very interested in something* * Playing upon a flute piqued his interest when he was a child

Pirate radio: *Illegal radio station* * Some rogues make use of pirated radio for spreading false propaganda

Piss about/around: *Waste a lot of time by behaving in a silly way* * Don't piss about by saying that you have many important things to be done within a stipulated time

Piss down: *Rain very hard* * It was pissing down out there

Piss off: *Go away* * Why don't you just piss off and leave me alone?

Piss somebody off: *Make annoyed or bored* * I will piss him off if he does not treat me properly

Piss yourself (laughing): *Laugh very hard* * The witty jokes pissed them (laughing) during the recess period

Pit against: *Test strength, intelligence, etc.* * Lawyers and accountants felt they were being pitted against each other * It is now a chance for you to pit your wits against the world champion

Pit-a-pat: *Light steps or beats* * I could hear the pit-a-pat of running feet in the corridor * His heart went pit-a-pat on seeing the girl

Pitch a tent: *Put up a tent* * During our expedition to Mount Everest, we had to pitch our tents at various places day by day

Pitch at: *Set at particular level; aim or direct a product or service at a particular group of people* * They have pitched their prices too high * The new software is being pitched at banks * Orange juice is to be pitched as an athlete's drink

Pitch dark: *Very dark* * The room was pitch dark and I could not see anybody present

Pitch for: *Persuade for; persuade to make a deal* * It was the middle-class voters they were pitching for * We were pitching against a much larger company for the contract

Pitch in: *Set to work briskly* * The firemen pitched in extinguishing flames that engulfed the cloth store

Pitch into: *Assail vigorously* * This could pitch the government into confrontation with the labour force * I rolled up my sleeves and pitched into cleaning the kitchen

Pitch up /Pitch on: *Let one choice fall upon* * Since the children were pitched up/on having sandwiches, I had to satisfy their desire accordingly

Pitched battle: *Fight that involves a large number of people; battle fought on a selected piece of ground* * The demonstration escalated into a pitched battle with the police * Pandavas and Kauravas fought a pitched battle at Kurukshetra

Pivot on: *Depend completely on* * How can a developing country progress if it pivots entirely on overseas trade?

Place of business: *The ordinary place for the practice of one's vocation* * Almost everybody has to manage a place of business to earn his living

Plaidman: *A highlander* * The plaidman of Scotland are very fond of playing bagpipes

Plain as a pikestaff: *Perfectly plain or clear; obvious* * The statement he made was plain as a pikestaff * The fact that he will challenge him to a duel is not plain as a pikestaff.

Plain sailing/Clear sailing: *Simple and free from trouble* * The new job is not going to be a plain sailing for him * Now that he has overcome the hurdle in his career, it should be plain sailing from now on

Plain speaking: *Straightforwardness or bluntness of speech* * Nobody grudged his plain speaking in the meeting

Plain spoken: *Plain, rough and sincere* * A plain-spoken person would always call a spade a spade

Plain-dealer: *One who is candid and outspoken* * A few people place their faith on a plain-dealer

Plain-hearted: *Having a plain or honest heart* * Everyone respects a plain-hearted leader

Plainwork: *Plain needle work as distinguished from embroidery* * She is quite an expert in the plain work of weaving designs on sweaters

Plan for/Plan to: *Something you plan to do or achieve; things considered in detail in advance to be achieved; plan arrangements to be done in future* * Do you have any plan for the summer? * There are no plans to build new offices * The government has announced plans to create new jobs for the unemployed * Both sides agreed to a detailed plan for keeping the peace * A meeting has been planned for early next year

Plan on: *Intend or expect to do* * We hadn't planned on going anywhere this evening

Plan out: *Plan carefully something in detail* * He has yet to plan out his career

Plan upon: *Practice upon; work upon* * He is playing upon a piano * He used to play upon their prejudice and their fears

Plaster over: *Cover cracks or old wall with plaster* * The original brickwork has been plastered over

Plastic art: *The art of ceramics, sculpture, modeling* * He is well-versed in plastic art

Play a good knife and fork: *To eat one's fill* * The invitees played a good knife and fork in the wedding feast

Play A off against B/play A off B: *Put two people or groups in competition for taking advantage in your favour* * He played his two rivals off against each other and got the job for himself

Play a trick on: *Deceive* * Your oily tongue cannot play a trick on him

Play a waiting game: *Avoid action as far as possible in the hope of having as opportunity later to use one's energies with maximum effect* * It is not a good policy to play a waiting game as it has been wisely said that never put off till tomorrow what you can do today

Play along: *Pretend to agree* * He decided to play along with the idea

Play around: *Behave in a silly way; illicit love affair; try different ways of organising an arrangement of objects* * Has he taken the keys to play around with my car? * He has been arrested for playing around with another woman * I can play around with the pictures in all sorts of ways to make them more eye-catching

Play at: *Engage in the game of; make a pretence of; practice without seriousness* * They are now playing at cards * Let us play at being pirates * We are still playing at war-dropping leaflets instead of bombs

Play at cross-purposes: *Try to thwart one another* * You all will be harming your own interests if you play at cross-purposes

Play back: *Tape or film you listen to; watch the pictures after recording them* * He might benefit from hearing his own voice recorded and played back * Geeta Dutt was an exceptional playback singer

Play by Shakespeare: *Which Shakespeare wrote* * The plays written by Shakespeare are considered to be masterpieces

Play down: *Make or seem less important than it is* * He is playing down the rumour that he would be fighting in the election campaign

Play ducks and drake: *Spend*

lavishly * Most of our ministers play ducks and drakes with public money

Play fast and loose: *Be unreliable; act in a shift, inconsistent and reckless fashion* * Don't play fast and loose by deceiving others * We should not play fast and loose with our relatives * They are the people who play fast and loose with rules and regulations

Play for love: *Play without stakes* * Every evening we play volleyball for love

Play havoc with: *Do a lot of damage* * Continuing strikes are beginning to play havoc with the national economy

Play hooky: *Avoid going to school* * A devoted student would never play hooky to deceive his parents

Play into one's hands: *Act for the benefit of another person* * His activities have been unearthed for playing into enemy's hands

Play on: *Continue to play; take advantage of someone's feelings* * The home team claimed a penalty but the referee told them to play on * Advertisements often play on people's fears

Play one false: *Act falsely or treacherously to a person* * He played me false by duping me of 10,000 rupees on the pretext of paying my son's fee

Play one's cards badly: *Not to make best of one's chance* * He played his cards badly during the course of interviews and lost the opportunity of being selected for the prestigious post

Play one's cards well: *Make the best of one chance* * Had he been able to play his cards well, he would have been appointed manager of the cricket team

Play out [written]: *When an event is played out, it happens* * Their love affair was played out against the backdrop of war

Play possum: *Feign dead or pretend to be asleep to trick* * He caught hold of the intruder by playing possum

Play second fiddle: *Be in a subordinate position* * A modern girl refuses to play second fiddle to her husband * The head clerk plays second fiddle to the principal

Play the devil: *Make havoc* * He played the devil with the looted money

Play the double game: *Have double dealings* * He is a past master in playing the double game with anyone to serve his own interest

Play the fool: *Behave as a fool* * Quit playing the fool and get some work done!

Play the game: *Act in a fair, sportsman-like and straight forward manner* * We must play the game with all those with whom we deal * It is expected of all people to play the game well to the best of their capacity

Play the role: *Take part* * He is playing the role of a villain in the new film

Play the wanton: *To trifle; behave lewdly* * Do not waste your precious time in playing the wanton * He is facing music for playing the wanton with that lady

Play the woman: *Give way to weakness* * A courageous man would never play the woman in adversity

Play to the gallery: *Play for applause of the least cultures* * If anyone was playing to the gallery, it was the prime minister

Play truant: *Not to go to the school; stay away from school without permission* * Students who pay truant cannot earn a good grade * Students, who play truant, cannot give good performance in the examination

Play up: *Strike up; begin the music; redouble one's effort, play more vigorously; show up well in crisis; cause somebody problems or pain; make something seem more important than it is* * The media played up the prospects of a settlement * The orchestra is playing up the national anthem * In the driving competition, he had to play up to surpass his rival in the motor-race * Both the teams played up at the hockey match to a draw * Our troops played up by defeating the heavily-armed enemy in the battle-field * My shoulder is playing me up today * He is befooling himself by playing up his mediocre knowledge of dance

Play up to: *Act so as to afford opportunities to* * He is playing up to her to win her favours

Play upon words: *A pun or other manipulation or words depending on their sounds; clever and amusing use of word or phrase; utter a phrase or words of different meanings* * We play upon word 'bank' when we say we are banking on them to help us open our account in the bank * He has an amazing skill in playing upon words that makes the people laugh *

He is constantly plays upon words to amuse his companions * He played upon the words that his dog was a champion boxer

Play with: *Play in company of; deal with* * The children love to play with one another the game of hide and seek * That shopkeeper is honest in playing with his customers

Play with edge-tools: *Deal carelessly with dangerous matters* * Don't let the children play with edge-tools like knives or anything very sharp

Play with fire: *Do something dangerous; trifling ignorantly with matters liable to cause trouble or suffering* * You do not know that you are playing with fire when you criticise your boss * The recent riots should warn the agitators that they are playing with fire

Play-day: *Holiday* * We are enjoying a play-day today with no studies involved

Play-debt: *A debt incurred in gambling* * Those involved in a play-debt are, in a sense, ruining their life

Playful: *Sportive; playmate or a companion in play* * A man with playful spirits is liked by all * The playful disposition of kids causes great amusement * He was just being playful when he hit her on the nose

Play-house: *Theatre* * I was once a worker in that play-house

Play-out: *Exhausted; used up; no longer good for anything* * When he got play-out, he gave in to his opponent in the duel * Long and continuous physical exercise made him feel play-out * I have discarded my old pair of shoes as they are now play-out

Play-spell: *A time allowed for play* * Children are now enjoying a play-spell of half an hour

Play-time: *A time for play* * Our play-time is between 4 and 5 p.m daily

Play-way: *The educational use of play* * The pictorial demonstration is a good play-way

Play-world: *An imaginary world feigned in play* * We enjoy a play-world by watching a drama or cinema show

Playwright; play-writer: *A dramatist* * He is a play-writer who writes plays for theatre, television or radio

Plead guilty: *Admit guilt* * He pleaded guilty to murder * He pleaded guilty of passing on our secret papers to a foreign power

Plead not guilty: *Refuse to admit guilt* * The accused has not yet pleaded guilty before the judge for having committed a theft

Pleasant surprise: *Surprise as well as pleasure* * When the parents found their missing daughter, it was a pleasant surprise for them

Please to: *A polite formula equivalent to if you please** Take a seat, please to!

Please you: *May it please you* * I stand in need of your kind help, please you!

Please yourself: *Do as you like* * There were no children to cook for, so we could just please ourselves * There is no compulsion of doing this job today, so you can please yourself

Pleased with: *Be happy* * I felt pleased with his sweet remarks * He was looking very pleased with himself

Pleasure of senses: *Pleasure depending on sensation* * Extreme pleasure of senses may lead us to unwanted trouble

Pleasure trip: *An excursion for pleasure* * It was a pleasure trip to the Kashmir valley

Pleasure-giving: *Affording pleasure* * It was a pleasure-giving experience to watch the tussle between the two players of tennis

Pleasure-pain principle: *Principle in which activities are directed towards pleasure and avoiding pain* * Those who adopt the pleasure-pain principle in life would never mind facing disturbing events

Plough a lonely furrow: *Be separated from one's former friends and go one's own way* * A time may come in life when we shall be obliged to plough a lonely furrow

Plough back: *Increase the size of business or improve it* * About 80 per cent of the profits are being ploughed back in investment

Plough in: *To cover with earth by plough* * The stalks are left to be ploughed in for the next planting

Plough into: *Go out of control and crash violently* * A young girl and her little brothers were seriously hurt when their car ploughed into a crossing * A truck ploughed into the back of the bus

Plough on: *Continue something difficult or boring* * No one was listening to him but he ploughed on happily

Plough the sand: *Work in vain or to no purpose* * It would be something like ploughing the sand if you waste your time in growing some useless crop

Plough through: *Force one's way through; turn violent and out of control; progress slowly doing something difficult and boring* * The ship ploughed through the waves * The truck ploughed through the gardens and flattened a tree * The plane ploughed through the trees * I had to plough through dozens of legal documents to strengthen the case of my client

Plough up: *Turn a vacant land with a plough for growing crops; break up some surface by walking or driving across it again and again* * It would help farmers to plough up the scrub and grow wheat * The paths get all ploughed up by motorbikes

Plow write: *One who makes and mends ploughs* * A plow right is there to meet the needs of the farers concerning the plough—I am not able to find such a word

Pluck at: *Take with fingers to pull gently and sharply* * The child plucked at my sleeves * The wind plucked at my jacket

Pluck off: *To abate; come down the scale* * The industry should use the best method to pluck off pollution * Luckily for us, the flood waters are now plucking off

Pluck out: *Pull out hair* * She plucked out her grey hair

Pluck out of the air: *Answer a question or say without thinking* * I just plucked a figure out of the air and showed my willingness to give the amount to her

Pluck up: *To pull out by roots; summon up as courage; gather strength* * He plucked up the weeds that were harming the crop * I could not pluck up energy to cope with the fight against my opponent * I was so tired with the long walk that I sat down for a moment to pluck up my strength to complete the tough journey

Pluck up courage: *Nerve oneself; gather boldness* * He plucked up the courage to ask his employer for a pay rise * There was no other alternative left for him but to pluck up the courage to meet the challenge

Plucky: *Having courageous spirit and pertinacity* * The plucky patient suffering from cancer hung on to life for nearly six months

Plug away: *Continue to work hard at something* * My confidence is still there and I will just keep plugging away

Plug in/Plug into: *Push a plug into an electric socket; become involved with a particular activity* * They plugged their guitar into amplifiers * I plugged in my tape-recorder * The company has doubled its profits since it plugged into hardware business

Plug up: *Fill a hole with a substance or piece of material* * He plugged up the hole in the pipe with an old rag

Plum job: *Easy, well paid job* * Teaching used to be regarded as a plum job in the long past

Plumb in: *Connect some apparatus to the water supply in a building* * He has a washing machine plumbed in

Plumb the depths: *Experience extreme unpleasant state of affairs* * His latest novel plumbs the depths of horror and violence * The team's poor performance will plumb new depths if it loses the last match

Plump down: *Sit down suddenly and clumsily; put down something carelessly* * He plumped down in one of the chairs * I plumped down my shopping bag on the floor

Plump for: *Choose someone of something suddenly after a lot of hesitation; vote for or choose with confidence* * The judge eventually plumped for Smith's novel * The man eventually plumped for Shakespeare being an excellent playwright

Plump up: *Squeeze or share something back into its proper shape* * She plumped up her pillow

Plunge in/out: *Jump into; thrust into; put into a state of chaos; make or experience something unpleasant; act of becoming involved in a situation or activity* * It was a wonderful experience to plunge into the pool from a great height * The soldier plunged his bayonet into the man's body * The government's political and economic reforms threaten to plunge the country into confusion * The news plunged them into deep depression * The company is planning a deeper plunge into the commercial market

Plunk down: *Sit down heavily and clumsily* * He plunked down in an armchair and lit a cigarette * He plunked the package down on the desk

Plus or minus: *Approximately/ More or less* * The poll has a margin of error of plus and minus 5 per cent

Ply for hire: *Look for customers/ passengers in order to do business* * It is illegal for unmarked taxis to ply for hire

Ply one's trade: *Do one's work or business* * This is the restaurant where he may ply his trade as a cook

Ply somebody with something: *Keep giving somebody large amount especially for food; keep asking somebody question* * He plied on us tea and cake * He plied me with questions since the moment he arrived

Pneumatic tyre: *Tyre filled with air* * Use a bicycle pump to keep the pneumatic tyres full of air

Pocket an insult: *Submit to or put up with it without protest* * A self-respecting person would never pocket an insult from any quarter

Poet laureate: *Leading poet who is asked to write commemorative verse for special occasions* * A poet laureate has a reputable position in a civilised society

Poetic justice: *Ideal administration of reward and punishment* * Poetic justice still remains a daydream in any form of government * Administering of poetic justice still remains a pious hope

Poetic licence: *A departing from strict fact or rule by a poet for the sake of effect* * He used a little poetic licence to embroider a good story

Point a finger at: *Accuse of doing something* * The article points an accusing finger at the authority

Point at: *Aim at* * He pointed his gun at her head

Point at issue: *The point in dispute; subject of discussion* * What is the point at issue? * The point at issue is who would bell the cat

Point for point: *Exactly in all particulars* * He dwelled upon the problem point by point

Point of contact: *A place of enquiry* * The receptionist is the first point of contact to seek necessary information in any enterprise

Point of honour: *Any scruple caused by a sense of duty; obligation to demand and to receive satisfaction for an insult, especially in the duel* * He preferred death to the point of honour * Both the contestants had to be fair and square in the matter of point of honour

Point of no return: *Not possible to get back to earlier situation* * We had already burnt our boats behind, so there was point of no return to us but to do or die

Point of order: *A question raised in a deliberative society whether the proceedings are according to the rules* * A point of order was raised in Parliament by one of the members * The postponement was demanded and won on a point of order

Point of view: *The position from which one looks at anything liberally* * My point of view was only to apprise the member with the true facts

Point out: *To indicate or to show* * I will point him out to you next time he enters the room * He tried in vain to point out to me that he was not involved in the crime

Point something up: *Emphasise something so that it become more noticeable* * The conference merely pointed up the decision in the party

Point taken: *Accept that somebody is right to disagree or criticise one* * Since your point has been taken, let us drop the discussion

Point to: *Make mention of some reason behind something; suggest something is true or likely to be true* * The board of directors pointed to falling productivity in justification of their decision * All the signs point to a successful year ahead

Point-blank: *Directly* * He shot dead the officer at point-blank range * He gave me a point-blank reply to my simple query

Pointing stock: *Laughing stock* * I would not wear that kind of dress to become a pointing stock

Point-to-point: *From one fixed point to another; across country* * The horse rider completed the various hurdles successfully point-to-point * His family is scattered point-to-point in various areas of rural localities

Poison one's ears: *To prejudice* * The stepmother poisoned the ears of her husband against her stepson

Poke about: *Be inquisitive* * The police spent the day poking about in his office but found nothing * He poked [around] about in the cupboard for a bottle of whisky

Poke fun at: *To banter* * His novels poke fun at the upper class

Poke one's head: *To stop or hold*

the head forward * People who lead a busy life have no time to poke their heads and ponder

Poke one's nose into another's affair: *Interfere in another's business* * You have no right to poke your nose into another's affair

Poker face: *Expression which shows no emotion* * He maintained a poker face

Police state: *Country which is terrorised by the police* * India remained a police state for a very long period under foreign rule

Polish off: *Finish something; dispose of finally* * He polished off the remains of the apple pie * He polished off his opponent easily in the tennis match

Polish up: *Improve* * The company needs to polish up its performance to earn more

Political asylum: *Permission to stay in a country when one is politically undesirable in one's own* * He has been given political asylum in Pakistan after he failed in carrying out a coup in his own country

Pomp and circumstance: *Formal and impressive ceremony* * The royal wedding was a pomp and circumstance to watch

Ponce about/around: *Fool about/around* * I spent my working life pouncing about on a beach instead of doing a proper job

Ponder over: *Give much thought to* * Do not ponder over the past incident

Pooh-pooh: *Treat with contempt* * They are pooh-poohing the suggestion of a split in the party

Poor hand: *An unskilled one* * We need the services of some poor hands to collect a few loads of goods at the railway station

Poor in: *With very little (of something)* * The soil in this area is poor in nutrients * Our country is not poor in natural resources

Poor-spirited: *Lacking in spirit* * Persons who are poor-spirited cannot make a mark in their life

Pop off: *Make off; to die; fall asleep* * He popped off with her gold necklace under the cover of darkness * None of his relations seem likely to pop off soon * He kept dozing off for a while and then popped off to sleep

Pop on: *Put on a piece of clothing* * I will just pop on a sweater and meet you outside

Pop one's clogs: *To die* * If he

does not want to play with us, let him pop his clogs

Pop the question: *Make an offer for marriage* * He popped up the question subject to fulfilment of certain conditions

Pop up: *Appear unexpectedly* * You solve one problem and another immediately pops up

Pop-shop: *A pawnshop* * He took some money from a pop-shop to clear his bills by depositing his gold chain in exchange

Popular language: *Language of people* * Hindi is a popular language in India

Popular scandal: *General bad rumour* * No popular scandal has taken place in the city throughout this month

Pop-visit: *A visit at an odd time or casual visit* * It was only a pop-visit to him to find out about his health

Pore over: *To look at very closely* * We will have to spend hours poring over travel brochures before we undertake a trip

Porous plot: *Leaky plot* * Some mischievous persons have been arrested by the police for their porous plot

Port of entry: *A port where merchandise is allowed by law to enter* * They have got a permit of port of entry to sell or buy goods here

Portion out: *Share out* * The money collected in charity fund was duly portioned out among the famine-stricken people

Pose for: *To stand or sit still while someone photographs you* * They posed briefly for photographs before driving off

Positive laws: *Enacted laws* * Some new positive laws are likely to come into effect from next month

Possession is nine-tenths of the law: *It is easy to claim ownership of something which is already in your possession* * It is rather prudent to say that possession is nine-tenths of the law

Poste restante: *Service where letters can be addressed to someone at the post office from where the addressee can collect them* * A poste restante service is also available in various post offices in our country

Post-haste: *Very fast* * The pilot wisely decided to return to the air base post-haste

Pot (s) of money: *A large amount of money* * As he is running a roaring business, he must be having pots of money * He must have pot(s) of money to live a luxurious life

Pot boiler: *Any literary or artistic work produced to make money* * Many renowned playwrights live richly on pot boilers

Potential energy: *The power of doing work possessed by a body in virtue of its position* * That sturdy man has the potential energy to cope with extra heavy loads

Potshot: *A shot fired without aiming carefully; criticise* * Somebody took a potshot at him as he drove past * The newspaper took constant potshots at the remarks of the minister

Potter about: *Not do anything in particular* * At weekends he would potter about (or around) the garden

Pounced on/upon: *Jump on something; notice quickly something said in order to criticise* * The cat pounced on the pigeon and took it away * His biting comments were pounced on/upon by the press

Pound of flesh: *Invitation to trouble and sufferings for not being able to pay back full amount of borrowed money within a fixed period of time* * One should think twice about his pound of flesh before borrowing money from a person like Shylock

Pound out: *Play music loudly on a musical instrument* * Nobody pounds out a tune on the piano quite like her

Pour cold water on: *Discourage* * Her parents poured cold water on her trying to become an actress.

Pour down: *Rain hard* * The floods caused havoc in the city with trees getting washed away

Pour forth arrows: *Shoot continuous arrows* * It was a time when warriors from both sides used to pour forth arrows in the battlefield

Pour into: *Provide a large amount of money for something* * The government has poured millions of pounds into the education system

Pour money down the drain: *Waste the money* * Most of the countries are pouring money down the drain for acquiring weapons of mass destruction

Pour oil on troubled waters: *Pacify troubled matters* * Your kind and soft words poured oil on troubled waters

Pour out: *Put a drink in a cup or glass; express hidden thoughts, feelings, etc.* * He was pouring out four glasses of champagne for his guests * He poured out his heart, expressing his hopes and fears about the present situation

Pouring wet: *Raining hard* * It has been pouring wet for the last two days

Pouring with rain: *Raining hard* * It kept pouring with rain for quite long hours

Poverty breeds strife: *Poverty is the root cause of violent disagreement* * It is an accepted fact that poverty breeds strife

Poverty-stricken: *Suffering from poverty* * The prime minister is visiting the most poverty-stricken areas in the eastern state

Pow-wow: *Meeting to discuss some problem* * The labourers have called a pow-wow to discuss some difficult problems

Practical purpose: *Reality of a situation* * There are five minutes to go before though for practical purposes it is all over

Practice penance: *To carry on amends for a sin* * A man of conscience will practice penance for any wrong or sin committed knowingly

Practice what you preach: *Do things yourself that you tell other people* * Morally a person must practice what he preaches

Prairie value: *The value of land in its natural state before it has been improved by man* * The prairie value of a large area of flat grassy land is not much

Praise to the skies: *Praise a lot* * In order to win her heart, he praises her to the skies

Pray a tales: *To plead that the number of jurymen be completed in this way* * An answer to pray a tales is still awaited

Pray be seated: *Please sit down* * He came panting and stood before me to complain about something when I told him, "Pray be seated"

Pray in aid (law): *To call in or call for help* * He just prays in aid (law) occasionally

Preach down/up: *Decry; extol* * The measures were preached down as useless * Doctors often preach up with the virtues of eating less fat

Preaching with a view: *Preaching as a candidate in a vacant pastoral charge* * He is preaching with a view to win some favour from the priest

Precede with: *Do or say to introduce something else* * He preceded his speech with a vote of thanks to the committee

Preen yourself: *Smarten yourself up* * Most young persons spend some time over preening themselves every morning

Preen yourself on something: *Congratulate yourself* * He was boastful in preening himself on his success before his friends

Prefer something to something: *One's preference for a particular thing* * I prefer reading to writing

Preferential tariff: *One by which lower custom duties are on goods from certain countries than from others* * Indian government has allowed preferential tariff to a few countries for boosting the economy

Pregnant pause: *An occasion when nobody speaks* * There was a pregnant pause before she replied

Prejudiced against: *Bias against* * I am not prejudiced against this writer.

Prejudicial to: *Sue* * Evil thoughts are prejudicial to the purity of mind

Premium offer: *Especially attractive price* * My brand new car was disposed of on a premium offer

Preparatory school: *One which prepares pupils for a public or other higher school* * A preparatory school generally runs in the evening to help children prepare for higher education

Prepare against: *Make ready* * Every citizen was instructed to prepare himself against the air-raid

Prepare the ground: *Make possible or easier to achieve* * The committee will prepare the ground for next month's meeting

Presence of mind: *A state of calmness in which all the powers of mind are on the alert and ready for action* * He had the presence of mind to turn off the gas

Present arms: *Hold a rifle upright in front of the body as a mark of respect* * The battalion presented arms as a mark of respect to their commander

Present oneself: *Arrive or come* * You will be asked to present yourself for the interview * He has been ordered to present himself in court in May

Press against: *Exert force against* * He pressed against the steam by putting the lid on the kettle of boiled water in vain

Press ahead: *Hurry toward* * The

company is pressing ahead with its plans for a new warehouse

Press for: *Keep asking for* * They continued to press for a change in the law

Press money: *Earnest money* * It is now easy to buy a new car on payment of prescribed press money with the remaining amount to be paid in instalments

Press of sail: *As much sail as can be carried* * The requirement of press of sail of a vessel perhaps depends upon its size and capacity

Press on: *Try to make somebody to accept something* * The people kept pressing delicious dishes out of love on soldiers going to the warfront

Press upon: *Urge, exert strong influence* * Don't try to press your false ideas upon others

Pressed for time: *Have not much time* * He is pressed for time to do anything else

Pressure cooker: *An autoclave especially for domestic use* * A pressure cooker has made it easy to cook food quickly

Pressure of business: *Urgency and over burden of business* * I am sorry I could not see you as promised earlier

Pressurise someone into: *Try to force someone into* * He was pressurised into accepting the job

Presume on/upon: *Make use of somebody's friendship by asking more than one should* * I felt it would be presuming on our personal relationship to keep asking for his help

Pretend to: *Lay claim* * A modest man never pretends to be great when he is not so

Pretty clear: *Almost clear* * It was pretty clear from his face that he had been under severe stress

Pretty kettle of fish: *An awkward state of affairs* * I felt worried at getting rid of a pretty kettle of fish honourably

Pretty much: *Almost; very nearly* * One dog looks pretty much like another to me * He looks pretty much like his father

Pretty spoken: *Speaking prettily* * The pretty spoken words of the preacher are still ringing in my ears

Pretty warm: *Lukewarm* * He was taking a bath with pretty warm water

Pretty well all the family: *Almost all the family* * You know pretty well all the family is good natured

Prevail against: *Overcome* * He

was successful in prevailing against all opposition

Prevail upon: *Persuade* * He tried to prevail upon me to accept a bribe * I am sure he could be prevailed upon to give a talk

Prevail with: *Prove effective* * The teacher's advice did not prevail with them

Prevent someone from: *Stop someone from* * Nothing would prevent him from speaking out against injustice

Prevention is better than cure: *It is better to nip the evil in the bud to get rid of its bad consequences* * It has been nicely said that prevention is better than cure

Previous question: *In Parliament, motion that the question be now put* * Parliament is now engaged in dealing with previous questions

Previous to: *Before* * Previous to this he had always been keeping well

Pre-war: *Happening before a war* * The pre-war leaders of both the countries failed to come to a truce

Prey to: *Victim to* * Any person can fall a prey to the cruelty of a king

Prey upon/on: *Exert baneful influence upon; hunt and kill animal for food; worry about too much* * Grief at the death of her sister preyed upon her mind * Hawks prey on rodents and small birds * The thought that he could have helped her preyed upon/on his mind

Price of money: *The rate of discount in lending or borrowing capital* * In days of yore, a moneylender used to reap a rich harvest on money lent to a borrower

Price on one's head: *A reward offered for one's capture or slaughter* * He still remains at large despite the high price put on his head by the authorities

Price up: *Lift up with the help of a lever* * Heavy loads of goods are priced up while loading in a cargo boat

Price yourself out of the market: *Try to sell goods or services at a higher price than other people with the result that no one buys them from you* * At 1,000 rupees a ticket, he really is pricing the show out of the market

Prices have touched rock bottom: *They are at their lowest* * There is a great rush of customers in the market as prices of various goods have touched rock bottom

Prick up one's ears: *Begin to listen intently; become alert all*

of a sudden * They pricked up their ears at the shocking news of a blast killing many people on the spot * The very mention of the dreaded terrorist made me prick up my ears

Prick your conscience: *Make you feel guilty* * His harmful deeds did not prick his conscience at all

Prickly heat: *Skin rash caused by hot climate* * Many kinds of powder are available in the market to save you from prickly heat

Prick-me-dainty: *An affected person; over-precise* * He is not licked for his prick-me-dainty show by his neighbours * He can be unreasonably prick-me-dainty

Prick-song: *Written music* * He is adept in setting tunes to any prick-song * An elderly woman, arms crossed, sang a prick-song.

Prick-the-garter: *Fast-and-loose* * At the fair many people were befooled at the prick-the-garter game

Prick-the-louse: *A tailor* * We cannot do without the services of the prick-the-louse

Pride of one's birth: *Pride of one's family* * She feels pride of her birth that produced such a statesman

Pride of place: *Culmination of an eagle's or hawk's flight; distinction of holding the highest position* * Some birds of prey have a keen sight in spotting their preys even from the pride of place * The manifesto gives pride of place to employment * That man has been able to achieve pride of place by dint of hard work and honesty

Pride oneself on: *Be extremely proud of* * He prides himself on having won many gold medals in sports events

Prime cost: *The price of production, without regard to profit of overhead expense* * The prime cost of the new model car has been estimated to be very high

Prime of life: *The most fully developed period of life* * The poor man died in the prime of his life

Prime the pump: *Encourage growth of a new or weak business or industry by putting more money into it* * At the initial stage they had to prime the pump for proper establishment of the new enterprise

Prince consort: *Husband of reigning queen* * The prince consort of Queen Elizabeth is also held in high esteem in England

Prince of darkness: *Satan* * A prince of darkness is a constant terror to a civilised society

Prince of Wales: *Title of eldest son of English sovereign* * Prince of Wales is the next heir to the throne of England

Principle of contradiction: *The logical principle that a thing cannot both be and not be* * A principle of contradiction never stands for any ambiguity

Principle of excluded middle: *The principle that a thing must be either one thing or its contradictory* * It needs to be realised that he can be either good or bad as revealed by the principle of excluded middle

Principle of sufficient reason: *That nothing happens without sufficient reason why it should be as it is and not otherwise* * The principle of sufficient reason enables us to reach towards a right conclusion

Prior to: *Before* * Prior to taking up the new job, he was working in some ordinary firm * I went to see him prior to his departure for London

Prise something from: *Force to separate something from something else* * He prised her fingers from the bag and took it from her

Prise something out: *Force somebody to give you information about somebody or something* * The sleuth prised some important information out of the hard-core criminal to file a case against him

Prisoner on the run: *An accused running away from prison* * The police is hunting for a prisoner on the run

Private apartment: *Rooms allotted to women* * All these women are staying in a private apartment

Private enterprise: *Business firms which are not state-owned* * Private enterprises are playing an important role in boosting the economy of the country

Private eye: *A private detective* * In order to know the true facts of the case against his son, he has engaged a private eye

Private war: *Warfare between persons in their individual capacity, as by dwelling, family feud, etc.* * The two neighbours are fighting a private war over some old disputes best known to them

Private wrong: *A violation of civil or personal rights of an*

individual; an injury done to an individual in his or her private capacity * It is, of course, a private wrong to tease anybody for nothing * It is also a sin to do any private wrong

Privy purse: *An allowance for a sovereign's private expenses* * The amount that the government gives to the king or queen for their own private use is referred to as privy purse

Prize fight: *Boxing match for prize* * Many countries are encouraging boxing for prize fighting

Prize money: *Share of the money from any prizes taken from enemy* * The days have gone when the war was fought only for the sake of prize money

Problem child: *One whose character presents as exceptionally difficult problems to parents* * It is better to be issueless than have a problem child

Problem novel/Problem play: *One presenting or expounding a problem, social, moral, etc.* * He is a well known problem novel to dwell on any problem at great length

Proceed against: *Sue* * I do not wish to proceed against him in a court of law

Proceed with: *Go on* * Now proceed with your work * We are not sure whether we still want to proceed with the sale

Procurator fiscal: *Public prosecutor* * It is the duty of a procurator fiscal to bring a criminal to trial

Proficient in: *Well up* * She is proficient in French

Profit by: *Gain by* * I profited by his good piece of advice

Profound sigh: *Deep sigh* * She heaved a profound sigh at the sad news

Profound sleep: *Sound sleep* * He fell into a profound sleep after a hard day's work

Progress in learning: *Advancement of learning* * Ignorance can be overcome by progress in learning

Progress to something: *Move on from doing one thing to doing something else* * He started off playing the records and then progressed to the clarinet

Project oneself: *Present oneself to other people in a particular way* * He projected himself as a man worth listening to

Promissory note: *A written promise to pay a sum of money on some future day or on demand* * A document containing a promised date is regarded as promissory note * All notes of different denominations not circulated by the Government of India are also treated as a promissory note

Prompt at: *Done without delay* * He is prompt at doing his work

Prompted by: *Inspired by* * His act was prompted by good intentions

Prone to: *Disposed of* * The new servant is prone to idleness

Pronounce for/ against: *Give a judgement in a court of law for or against; deliberate; declare* * The judge pronounced for the defendant * The minister will pronounce against special security measures later today

Pronounce on/ upon: *State your opinion on* * He feels able to pronounce on all kinds of subjects

Proof-charge: *A charge used to test the strength of a gun* * What proof-charge is this gun? * The proof-charge of this gun is nine metres

Proof-correct: *To correct in proof* * This printed document is now under the process of proof-correct

Prop up: *To give support to survive from falling) (often disapproving); help something that is having difficulties* * They had to prop up the young tree with poles and wires to save it from the stray animals * The government was accused of propping up the declining industries

Proper noun: *A name given to a particular person, place or thing* * Mohan, Delhi and India are said to be under the category of proper noun

Propose a toast to: *Ask people to wish somebody health, happiness and success by raising their glasses and drinking* * I would like to propose a toast to the bride and groom

Propose to: *Ask someone to marry* * He is likely to propose to a nice beautiful girl of a well-to-do family

Proprietary right: *Relating to an owner* * The company has a proprietary right to the property

Pros and cons: *Advantages and disadvantages of something; reasons or arguments for and against* * We weighed up the pros and cons about setting up a new firm * He cannot give you his opinion till he has considered carefully the pros and cons of the case

Prosecute studies: *Pursue studies* * He has gone abroad for prosecuting higher studies abroad

Prostrate yourself before someone: *Lie downwards as a mark of respect/worship* * Many devotees prostrate themselves before the idol of Lord Krishna

Prostrated with: *Shocked or upset* * She was prostrated with grief at the death of her son

Proud-hearted: *Having a proud spirit* * He is a proud-hearted man as his son received the Param Vir Chakra as a gallant soldier

Proud-minded: *Proud in mind* * He is a proud-minded scholar for his scientific research work

Proud-pied: *Gorgeously variegated* * The peacock is considered to be a proud-pied bird for its strikingly colourful feathers

Proud-stomached: *Of haughty spirit; arrogant* * I dislike to be associated with proud-stomached people * He was petulant, selfish, proud-stomached and occasionally callous

Provide against: *Make preparation to deal with tough times in future* * A prudent person provides for himself against rainy days

Provide for: *Support* * His father always ensured that he was well provided for in order to enable him to make a bright future

Provide with: *Supply with* * The government was not in a position to provide them with food

Provided that/providing: *On condition that* * You would be offered that lucrative post provided that/ providing you get through the test creditably

Proximate cause: *A cause which immediately precedes the effects* * The sudden drop of temperature was proximate cause of a thunderstorm

Proximate object: *Immediate object* * They were very happy to be successful in their proximate object

Pry out: *Investigate or find out by prying* * The detective kept prying out the activities of the suspected traitor

Public good: *Good of people* * Many new projects are being planned for public good

Public house: *Towers* * He is running a public house for the common man

Public property: *Property belonging to the people in general* * A true citizen would never damage public property under any circumstances

Public purse: *The nation's*

*finances** Some politicians are alleged to have wasted money from the public purse

Public spirit: *Urge for social service* * We must have public spirit to make our lives worthwhile

Public wrong: *A crime which affects the community* * The agitated crowd was engaged in doing public wrong

Public-spirited: *Having regard for public interest* * A public-spirited man is devoted to public good

Pudding-faced: *Stupid* * If you give him half a chance, he can make you look pudding-faced

Pudding-hearted: *Coward* * She accused her husband of being a pudding-hearted man

Puff and blow: *Breathe hard* * The poor old man began to puff and blow after some physical exercise

Puff out: *Utter while panting; make something bigger and rounder* * A lot of exercise made him puff out for a moment * He puffed out the bladder to make the football bigger

Puff up: *Swell or make something to swell; to inflate* * Her cheeks swelled up when she puffed up the balloons before releasing them

Puffed out: *Quit out of breath* * He puffed out his cheeks

Puffed up: *Swollen with pride* * He was too puffed up with his own performance

Pull a face: *To grimace* * He pulled a face when he passed by a stinking pond

Pull a long face: *Look dismal; look serious* * His wife pulled a long face when he refused to buy her a new dress * He pulled a long face for having lost a large sum of money

Pull a thing to pieces: *Separate its parts* * The watchmaker pulled my watch to pieces for repairs

Pull about: *Distort; to treat roughly* * The minister alleged that his remarks made in a public meeting had been pulled about by the media

Pull ahead: *Move in front of* * The cyclists were together until the bend when John pulled ahead of all

Pull apart: *Bring as under by pulling* * He stood still pulling his hair * The child pulled apart the parts of the toy

Pull away: *Start moving* * They waved as the bus pulled away

Pull back: *To obstruct; to draw back; withdraw from a place; decide not to do because of some unavoidable problems; improve a team's position* * Drivers who park their cars illegally and pull back the traffic deserve to be punished * The army has been pulled back from the war-front as a result of truce * The army had to pull back to dodge the enemy * Their sponsors pulled back at the last moment * They pulled back a goal just before half time

Pull caps: *To scuffle* * Some animals were pulling caps in the bushes

Pull devil, pull baker: *Do your best both sides* * One should adopt the policy of pull devil, pull baker in any argument

Pull down: *Take down or apart; demolish; bring down; reduce in health or vigour* * A small crowd attempted to pull down a statue * The building is now being pulled down to make way for a highway * They were threatening to pull down the government by withdrawing their support * He seems to have pulled down due to his long illness

Pull for: *Row for; to support* * A lot of officers here have been pulling for exerting their influence to help you * The national union of mineworkers pressed the party to pull for a total ban on the import of coal

Pull in: *Stop a vehicle somewhere; bring somebody to a police station for interrogation; earn the large amount of money mentioned* * The van pulled in to the side of the road and waited * He looked like a suspect and the policeman pulled him in * I reckon he is pulling in a substantial amount

Pull in one's horns: *Abate one's ardour or pretensions* * The customers are pulling in their horns at a time of high interest rates

Pull into: *Enter into a station* * There was a great hustle and bustle when the train pulled into the station

Pull off: *Carry through successfully* * It will be a very fine piece of mountaineering if they pull it off

Pull off one's hat: *Salute by taking off hat* * They pulled off their hats in honour of the distinguished guest

Pull one's leg: *Make playful attempt to impose upon one's credulity* * I won't tell them I was only pulling your leg

Pull one's weight: *Give full effect to one's weight in rowing; do one's full share of work, cooperate wholeheartedly* * The competitors in boat-rowing race pulled their weight to win the first position * He accused the team of not pulling their weight in the playfield

Pull oneself together: *Make efforts to become normal; collect one's faculties* * He pulled himself together by throwing himself back into his works * He, being under serious troubles, did not lose heart at all and pulled himself together

Pull out: *Bring out by pulling; drive away from the side of the road; leave a station; withdraw; stop being involved* * He pulled out a bucket full of water from the well * A car suddenly pulled out in front of me * The train pulled out of the station after a stay of 10 minutes * They are pulling their troops out of the war zone * The project became so expensive that we had to pull out

Pull out all the stops: *Do everything possible* * He is pulling out all the stops to acquit himself well in the test he is likely to face

Pull over: *Move (a vehicle) to a side of the road and stop it* * The police pulled over his vehicle near a village for reckless driving

Pull round: *Bring or come back to good health or condition or to consciousness* * He is pulling round well after having suffered serious heart attacks in a row

Pull strings: *Use influence to get an advantage for something* * He had to pull strings for getting his friend a nice job

Pull the long bow: *To lie or boast beyond measure* * He is in the habit of pulling the long bow of his ability to bluff others

Pull the plug on: *Have the power to stop something* * Banks have the power to pull the plug on the project

Pull the strings: *Influence behind the scenes, as if working puppets* * The party in power pulls the strings in running the government according to its political will

Pull the wires: *Manage political party or movement by secret influence* * The party in opposition always tries to pull the wires of the party in power in order to outdo the activities of the latter

Pull the wool over one's eyes/ Draw the wool over one's

eyes: *To hoodwink or deceive* * You cannot pull the wool over my eyes by telling me lies about the work you have done

Pull through: *Bring or get to the end of something difficult or dangerous with some success; get better after a serious illness, operation, etc.; succeed in doing something very difficult* * Our troops were able to pull through despite heavy firing from the enemy camp * It is going to be tough but we will pull through together * The doctors think that the patient will pull through * I relied on my instincts to pull me through

Pull together: *Work together in a united manner* * They would be far better off, materially and emotionally, if they all pull together

Pull up: *Pull out of the ground; tighten the reins; bring to a stop; to halt; take to task; gain ground* * He pulled up his chair and sat beside me * He pulled up the restless horse to keep it under control * The driver had to pull up the vehicle at the petrol station for fuelling the engine * Nothing could pull him up from achieving his goal * The boss pulled up the clerk for neglect of duty * Sterling continues to pull up against the dollar * There is a strong feeling that his views are pulling up

Pull up one's socks: *Brace one's self for doing better* * You will have to pull your socks if you want to succeed in your career

Pull up stakes: *Prepare to leave a place* * He was obliged to think seriously to pull up stakes when he found it difficult to make his both ends meet

Pull-on: *Requiring only to be pulled on without fastening* * Some people like to wear pull-on clothes

Pullover: *A jersey, jumper, a body garment put on over the head* * Clothes that you put on like a jersey, jumper, etc. by pulling it over your head are all called pullovers

Pull-through: *A cord with rag for cleaning a rifle barrel* * Soldiers have to make use of a pull-through to keep their rifles in perfect working order

Pull-up: *An act of pulling up; a sudden stoppage* * A pull-up is an exercise that may help you enlarge your stature *

The pull-up of his heart beat has been said to be the cause of his death

Pump bullets into: *Fire a lot of bullets into* * A gunman went berserk and pumped bullets into the body of a passerby

Pump into: *Pull a lot of money into; force into* * He pumped all his savings into the business * It is difficult to pump facts and figures into a dull mind

Pump somebody full of something: *Fill somebody with something especially drugs* * They pumped him full of painkillers

Pump up: *Increase value or volume; fill a tyre, etc. with air using a pump; feel excited* * Interest rates were pumped up last month * Before taking up a long journey, he pumped up tyres of his cycle * He was naturally pumped up when he won a jackpot

Punch-drunk: *Stupefied by blows* * The punch-drunk boxer is now under medical care

Punic apple: *Pomegranate* * Everybody cherishes the taste of punic apple

Punto reverso: *A back-handed stroke* * While rowing a boat backwards, the rower makes use of punto reverso * He is an expert tennis player who can very well return the ball with punto reverso

Pure and simple: *Real; clearly understandable* * It is blackmail, pure and simple * His views on the tough subject were pure and simple * Laziness was a pure and simple cause of his ruin * The pure and simple fact of his failure was only his laziness

Pure gold does not fear the flame: *Truth cannot be belied* * It has been rightly said that pure gold does not fear the flame

Pure reason: *Reason absolutely independent of experience* * The pure reason behind the mischief has yet to be discovered

Purple emperor: *One of the largest British butterflies, and one of the most richly coloured* * People feel charmed and attracted by a purple emperor

Purple patch: *A passage of fine or (often) over-ornate, writing; period of success or good luck* * The journalists presented a purple-patch description of the touring spots in the green valley * In the last five minutes Liverpool struck a purple patch which culminated in their goal * He was enjoying a purple patch and scored 14 goals in 10 games

Purse one's lips: *Show one's resentment by pressing one's lips* * The officer pressed his lips at the slackness of his subordinate

Purse-proud: *Proud of one's wealth; insolvent from wealth* * The vast property he has inherited has naturally made him a purse-proud man * The purse-proud people have scant sympathy towards the poor

Purse-strings: *The strings fastening a purse* * Who holds the purse-strings in your house? * The government has to tighten the purse-strings

Purse-taking: *Robbing* * For a loafer, purse-taking is an easier act than to do some honest work

Push afar: *Move far beyond from point* * Don't push afar the matter from the real facts

Push along: *Leave and go on one's way* * The traveller stayed at an inn for the night and then pushed along in the morning

Push around: *To bully* * We do not like anybody to push us around in a crowd

Push aside: *Avoid thinking about* * He pushed aside the feeling of fear

Push for: *Make strenuous efforts to achieve* * We seriously need a push for economic growth

Push forward: *Continue in a determined way; press one's way forward; make others think or notice about* * The government is pushing forward with its electoral reforms * In spite of various difficulties during the long journey, they kept pushing forward * He had to push himself forward to get a promotion

Push off: *a boat pushed off to leave the bank/shore* * The rower of the boat pushed it off to ferry the people across a narrow strip of sea

Push on: *Make one's way ahead* * He is pushing on well in his studies

Push one's fortune: *Busy oneself in seeking a fortune* * To make your life purposeful, you will have to push your fortune

Push one's luck: *Take a risk and try to achieve more* * Don't push your luck and get yourself involved in a fight

Push out: *Produce in large quantities; row or to be rowed out towards open water* * This factory is pushing out cheap cotton shirts * When the vessel was fully loaded, it was pushed out into the open waters towards its destination

Push over: *Make one fall down by pushing* * He pushed me over in the playground

Push the bottle: *Take one's liquor and pass the bottle round* * The drunkard in the inn pushed the bottle from one person to another

Push through: *Get a new law or plan officially accepted* * The amendments of old laws had to be pushed through Parliament

Push to the wall: *Force to give place* * The minister pushed his secretary to the wall to accommodate his favourite man

Pushed for time: *Have no much time to spare* * As I am pushed for time, I regret my inability to dwell on the subject

Pushed from pillar to post: *Be forced to go from one person or situation to another but all in vain* * I was pushed from pillar to post for seeking official help

Puss in the corner: *A children's game in which places are continually being changed, while the player who is out tries to secure one of them* * The jubilant children are playing the game of 'puss in the corner'

Pussyfoot about or around: *Be undecided* * He is still pussyfooting about the proposed engagement

Put a bullet through: *To shoot* * He put a bullet through his own head with a shotgun

Put a cheat upon: *Deceive* * He put a cheat upon her and decamped with all her savings * In my experience litigants nearly always put a cheat upon their solicitors

Put a dog out of its misery: *Kill a dog because it is in pain* * We thought it proper to put our dog out of its misery

Put a good face on: *Assume a bold or contented bearing as regards* * A brave man when surrounded by difficult situations always put a good face on it * It is no use grumbling and try to put a good face on your sorrows

Put a new face on: *Alter aspect of* * In order to save his skin, he tried to put a new face on his offensive remarks made earlier

Put a person's eye out: *To blind him; supplant him in favour* * You cannot put his eye out when the event that he saw took place in the broad daylight * He enticed the young man by putting his eye out for doing an ignoble deed

Put a premium: *Show that something is urgent or valuable* * They put a premium on prevention and primary health care

Put a price on: *Say how much money something valuable is worth* * They have not yet put a price on the business

Put a spoke in one's wheel: *Interfere* * They were so jealous of his progress that they did their best to put a spoke in his wheel

Put a stitch: *Sew up wound* * The doctor had to put a stitch on his wound

Put a stop to: *Stop* * The earlier you put a stop to smoking, the better for you

Put about: *Change the course, as of a ship; publish; circulate; discuss* * They had to put about the ship in the high sea to escape the strong storm * The pictures of the suspect were put about in all the daily papers * I was not prepared to put about this delicate matter on the phone

Put across: *Carry out successfully; bring off; to perform so as to carry the audience with one* * He has given a half-page advertisement in a local paper to put his point across * The goalie put across a superb save * He very skilfully put his idea across to his listeners

Put all one's eggs into basket: *Risk all on one enterprise* * To guard against losing everything, it is better not to put all your eggs in one basket * I have applied for several jobs, because I don't want to put all my eggs into one basket

Put an end: *Cause to discontinue* * The board of education has put an end to teaching of this book from this session

Put an end to: *Stop; abolish* * Let's put an end to this kind of bickering once and for all * The authority has put an end to the old rule

Put aside: *To place aloof or separate* * He decided to put our differences aside * They want to put aside teaching from research

Put at ease: *Make one comfortable* * I am sure this new sofa set will put you all at ease * As he was worried and nervous, I tried to put him at ease by being friendly to him

Put away: *Renounce; to divorce; to kill; stow away; pack up; set aside; to imprison; to eat* * The prince has put away his claim to the throne * The married couple have been legally put away * The king was put away through a military coup * He was put away on a ferry to be dropped on a far off isle * He began to put away the things that he needed during the course of his long journey * The committee decided to put away a substantial amount of money for opening more primary schools in the rural areas * The murderer was put away for life-term on charge of killing an innocent person * They began to put away cooked food to satiate their hunger

Put back: *Push backward; delay; repulse; turn and sail back; to reduce one's finances* * He put me back to a second position by a marginal success * The meeting has been put back to next week * The heavy attack by the enemy has been put back * The threatening sea-storm made the sailors put back their vessel * He has put back his investments in a risky business

Put blame on: *To censure* * They put blame on him for leaking information to the press

Put by: *Set aside; parry; store up; save* * We must put by some money for our old age * He knew how to put by the clever inquisitive questions * Investors put by a lot of cash in anticipation of a disaster * We must put some money by for a rainy day

Put down: *To crush; to quell; to write down on paper; to reckon; to attribute; to give up; to surpass; to outshine* * The military government is determined to put down all opposition * Extra police were called in to put down the demonstrators * I have put down some important points of his speech in my note-book * How do you put down his success to the new post? * The committee refused to put down the blame without further information * He put himself down without a fight * He is hopeful of putting down the world record in swimming * He is so brilliant as to put down the rest of the class

Put down roots: *Begin to feel at home in place; develop roots* * After having travelled many countries for many years, he thought of putting down roots somewhere * The seeds are putting down roots to sprout in the form of plants

Put for: *Make an attempt to gain* * He seems determined to put for new heights in life

Put forth: *To extend; to propose; to publish; display; lend at interest; to set out from port; produce; extrude* * I have put forth an invitation to him to be present at the party * He has put forth some conditions to settle the bargain * Police have put forth the description of the most wanted man in various daily papers * New agricultural implements have been put forth in a stall for exhibition * The national banks are willing to put forth financial aid to the needy farmers * The sailors have since put forth to sea * The scientists have now put forth a new engine for battery-driven cars * Lava is put forth by a volcano

Put in: *Introduce; insert; to lodge; deposit; hand in; make claim; enter; enter a harbour; interpose; to perform towards completing a total; spend; pass; fill up with some occupations; to appoint* * The government has put in a number of money-saving schemes * He put in another paragraph into his will * The police have put in a report against the accused * If you do not put in money, you will lose your investment * All the opposition members of Parliament have put in their resignation * The company has put in a claim for damages * He has put in a claim for compensation * His name has been put in the squad of hockey players * Nobody is allowed to put himself in harbour without proper permission * The police grilled him by putting in more and more questions during the course of interrogation * He had to put in a good deal of labour to arrive at an exact total * The students put in more time and energy in their studies when the date of the examination drew near * It is very difficult to put in the thread through the eye of the needle * There is a great need to put the unemployed in some purposeful vocation * We will have to put in a suitable date for the meeting after apprising the members of the agenda

Put in a false position: *Bring anyone into a position in which he must be understood* * An innocent person should never be put in a false position

Put in a good word for: *Recommend; speak in favour of* * He put in a good word for my further promotion * He expressed his gratitude to his boss for putting in a good word for my appointment as an excise inspector

Put in an appearance: *Appear in person; be present* * The fugitive suddenly put in an appearance before the court * He was required to put in an appearance before the judge as a witness

Put in cold storage: *Neglect* * For want of sufficient funds, most of our schemes have been put in cold storage

Put in for a job: *Apply* * Are you going to put in for that job?

Put in mind: *Remind* * Put in mind the date of the meeting one day before it takes place

Put in one's oar: *Interpose when not asked* * Don't put in your oar when I am advising someone in a serious case

Put in order: *To put serially* * It looks nice if the things are put in order

Put in remembrance: *Remind* * I had to put in remembrance myself that being confident is not the same as being perfect * Your loving photos will always put me in remembrance about your sweet and affectionate nature

Put in the picture: *Give information to understand a situation* * Just to put you in the picture, there have been a number of changes here

Put in the wrong: *Cause to appear in error or guilty of injustice* * He did not press the charges because he was in the wrong

Put into one's hands: *Entrust* * The authority has put a new task into his hands

Put it across: *Make acceptable; bring to a successful issue* * He had the skill to put new ideas across * If you find any fault in the working system of the firm, you must put it across * He was sure of putting a business deal across

Put it mildly: *Not to say anything rude* * I was, to put it mildly, annoyed at his accusation

Put it past one: *Judge it inconsistent with one's character* * The charge of accusation cannot put it past his natural instincts

Put it to you: *To suggest you to do something* * I put it to you that you are the only person who has a motive for crime

Put off: *Lay aside; take off; lay aside the character of; palm off; dismiss; turn aside with evasions, excuses or unsatisfying substitutes; divert; postpone; idle away; spend in vain; to push from shore; an excuse; a makeshift; evasion; a postponement* * The Sessions Court has put off the decision of the lower court * He put off his clothes and began to swim in the lake * We must put off our doubts and fears * Make sure he does not try to put you off with faulty goods * I think we can safely put off their objection * The company is putting off the genuine demands of the employees on false pretexts * The war put off people's attention away from the economic situation * He put off his departure for a week * He put off his time and energy in idle pursuits of a luxurious life * The sailors have put off the vessel towards high water for fishing * You cannot save your skin on that lame put-off * He has been charged of tax put-off * Riots led to put-off of the local elections

Put on: *To don or clothe with; assume, especially deceptively; superimpose; impose; mislead or deceive; to affix, attach, apply; to add; to stake or wager; move forward; move faster; set to work; set in operation; incite; to turn on the supply of; to score* * He put on his clothes and set out hunting * Stop putting me on an act and behave yourself * The features of different faces were put on over another * A new tax has been put on fuel * Putting on the court in a trial is a serious offence * The label should be firmly put on the packages * They have put on a number of conditions to the agreement * She is putting on her make-up * I have nothing to put on to my earlier statement * They have put on handsome money in the horse race * He put his step on to shake hands with me * The doping put him on to win the race by defeating the athlete ahead of him * The mechanic managed to put the defunct machine on * It is time to put our plan on to serve the interest of man in the street * The party agreed not to put its supporters on to violence * He asked them why they had not put the lights on * The president's team has put on 350 runs in the first innings

Put on the foil: *To overcome; bring to nought* * You will have to find some way to put your difficulties on the foil * All their attempts to score a goal were put on the foil by the rival team

Put on the market: *Offer for sale* * That house is put on the market

Put on the screw: *Apply pressure progressively; to extract payment* * The truck operators are threatening to blockade so as to put the screw on the government * The mafia has put the screw on some people and collected large sums of money from them

Put on the spot: *Doom to assassination* * Most of the persons who have been put on the spot by the terrorists are given full security * Even clever people are not terribly clever when put on the spot

Put on weight: *Get fatter or heavier* * I am really lucky as I never put on weight

Put one in mind: *Remind one* * This puts me in mind of an amusing incident

Put one on one's mettle: *Rouse one to do one's best* * This unexpected new difficulty put me on my mettle

Put one over somebody: *Persuade to believe that is not true* * Don't try to put one over me

Put one through one's paces: *See him to show what he can do* * An acid test is given to put him through his paces

Put one wise: *Put one in possession of information* * He put him wise about the imminent danger looming large

Put one's back into: *Do with might and main* * They have put their backs into the tough task of fighting against heavy odds

Put one's back up: *Show or arouse resentment* * This sort of attitude really puts my back up

Put one's best foot forward: *Make one's best effort* * He put his best foot forward that enabled him to reach his coveted goal

Put one's cards on the table: *Reveal one's views with frankness* * He put his cards on the table to be very clear about his complaint

Put one's faith to: *Place full reliance upon* * He puts his faith to acquisition of technical education

Put one's finger on: *To identify* * The victim at once put her finger on the rapist

Put one's foot down: *Take a firm stand; take a resolute stand* * You will have to put your foot down to stop him from making a fuss * Where discipline is concerned I do put my foot down

Put one's foot in it: *Spoil anything by some indiscretion or rashness; to blunder, to get into a scrape* * Don't put your foot into it when you do not know the real picture * You are sure to put your foot in it if you meddle in his affairs

Put one's hand in one's pocket: *Give money in charity* * I admit that he pleaded the cause of the poor very eloquently, but will he put his hand in his pocket?

Put one's hand to the plough: *Begin an undertaking* * He will certainly prove his worth in the new assignment once he puts his hand to the plough

Put one's mind to: *Give one's attention or mental energy to* * If you really put your mind to it, you can make a mark in mathematics

Put one's nose out of joint: *To supplant in another's love or confidence; to disconcert; to rebuff* * He had his nose put out of joint by her sophistication * His wry smile put her nose out of joint * She did not understand that her rejection of his proposal had put his nose out of joint

Put one's shirt on: *Bet all one has on* * The union put its shirt on the success of the venture

Put one's shoulder to the wheel: *Set to work in earnest as if to get a coach out of the mine* * Let us put our shoulders to the wheel instead of seeking help from others

Put out: *Dismiss from a game and innings; to send forth; stretch forth; extinguish; annoy; to place in an interest; to expand; publish; to disconcert; put to inconvenience; to offend; dislocate; exert; produce; place with others or at a distance; go out to sea, leave port; remove bodily or blind (an eye); to expel* * One of the cricketers was put out of the field on disciplinary grounds * The pilot put out wrong signals that resulted delay in landing * The vulture put out its wings before taking flight * Put out the candle before you go to bed * Firefighters tried to put the flames out * He was put out when I refused his request for a loan * I cannot put myself out to that kind of venture * He had to put out a large sum in pursuing his claim through the court * Pictures of the suspect have been put out in all the daily papers * His threatening tone put me out of answers * The plaintiff was put out when the suit was dismissed * Do not put me out by making a nuisance of yourself * I do not want to put anybody out with my jokes * He put out his shoulder in the accident * He fell off his horse and put his elbow out * He tried to put out all his authority to make them accept the plan * The finance director put out the figures of the previous year before the house * The sweeper put the rubbish out of the house to be placed out of sight * The fishermen have put their boats out for fishing in the open sea * The injured persons were put out by the police before getting admitted to the hospital * He was put out of examination hall for using unfair means

Put out of sight: *Remove from view; to eat or drink up* * The offensive posters were put out of sight wherever they were pasted * The hungry men put all the eatables and drinks out of sight

Put over: *To refer; carry through successfully; impress an audience, spectators, the public favourable with; impose; pass off* * The matter has been put over for further consideration * We hope that the UN will put over a sustained programme * He had the skill to put over his ideas convincingly before the people * New taxes are likely to be put over luxury items * The main demonstration has been planned to be put over peacefully

Put paid to: *End; stop; destroy* * They decided to put paid to their relationship * He was put paid to by the police for speeding * You have put paid to all the evidence

Put pen to paper: *Begin writing* * He is guiding the children to put pen to paper

Put pressure on: *Force to persuade somebody to do something* * Advertisements put pressure on girls to be thin

Put right: *Make amends for* * The sooner we put ourselves right, the better it would be for us

Put somebody on the spot: *Make somebody feel awkward*

by asking difficult questions * The interviewer's questions really put him on the spot

Put somebody through it: *Force somebody to experience something difficult or unpleasant* * They really put me through it (asked me difficult questions) at the interview

Put someone out of his misery: *Tell someone the result or not to keep someone any longer* * The doctor put him out of his misery by informing that the delivery of his wife had been quite successful

Put someone through paces: *You get someone to show you how well he can do something* * The boxers are in the hands of the British coach who is putting them through their paces

Put someone up to something: *Encourage someone* * He was very kind to put me up to carry on with my studies

Put something into practice: *Apply something* * It is easy to say something than putting it into practice * He is determined to put his new ideas into practice

Put the cart before the horse: *To reverse the natural order of things* * To carry coal to Newcastle is something like putting the cart before the horse * This puts the cart before the horse if we say that elections should follow, not precede any agreement * Holding the feast before marriage is like putting the cart before the horse

Put the change on: *To delude; trick* * I put the change on myself into believing that all would come right in the end * We are trying to put the change on a man who keeps bothering everyone here

Put the dead wood on: *Gain a great advantage over* * Repeated good shots in his game put dead wood on his opponent

Put the finger in the eye: *To weep* * The man who witnessed the tragic incident could not help putting the finger in the eye

Put the kibosh on something: *Stop something finally from happening* * They have after all decided to bury the hatchet and put the kibosh on an even keel

Put the last hand to: *To finish or put the finishing touch to* * The painter has yet to put the last hand to his new painting

Put the lid on: *Make impossible* * His impudence has put the lid on it

Put the saddle on the right horse: *Impute where it is deserved* * By appointing him as an ambassador, the government has put the saddle on the right horse

Put the screw on: *Put pressure* * The employee's association has put the screws on the company by threatening to go on a strike if its demands are not met

Put the shot: *Throw the weight in a competition* * He won a gold medal in the put the shot event at the Olympic Games

Put the wind up somebody: *Frighten somebody* * He is so bold that nobody can put the wind up him by way of funny tricks

Put their heads together: *Consult one another* * The directors of the company put their heads together to formulate a new scheme

Put things in perspective: *Show things in an objective way* * He tried his best to put things in the right perspective and the audience praised his efforts

Put through: *Bring to an end; accomplish; put in telephonic communication; pass* * They have managed to put the deal through * The first part of the project has been safely put through * Would you please be good enough to put me through to your boss? * The proposal was put through without opposition

Put through the mill: *Make a difficult time* * They really put me through the mill in my interview

Put to: *To apply; to add to; connect to' harness; to shut; set to; give* * The new technology was put to use in farming * Extra load of work would put him to more trouble * There was nothing to put him to crime * We have a good scope of putting our rivers to produce hydro-electric power in abundance * The hardened criminal has been put to a dark cell * We must be on the alert if put to face any ugly situation * I am sorry to put you to so much inconvenience

Put to a question: *Interrogate* * He is being put to a question for hoarding a large amount of money beyond his own means

Put to a stand: *Stop* * The agitators put the vehicular traffic to a stand

Put to death: *To kill; cause to be killed* * He put his wife to death by strangulating her

* The murderer has been put to death for killing an innocent man in cold blood.

Put to hard: *Be hard pressed* * He was put to hard in running his business smoothly due to paucity of funds

Put to it: *Press hard; to distress* * The trade unions are putting him to it to stand firm * I did not want to frighten him or put him to it

Put to rights/set to rights: *Set in order* * He is doing his best to put the misguided youth to rights

Put to sea: *Begin a voyage* * Many explorers in the days of yore put to see for discovering unknown parts of world

Put to shame: *To disgrace* * Our sportsmen should acquit themselves well in international games so that our country is not put to shame

Put to sleep: *Kill; make unconscious with drugs* * Our pet dog suffering from an incurable disease was put to sleep on the advice of the vet * The patient was put to sleep by drugs before his operation

Put to sword: *To kill* * In Saudi Arabia, a person guilty of a heinous crime is put to sword instead of getting him hanged

Put to the hammer: *To auction* * Plots of various sizes will be put to hammer by the Housing Board next week

Put to the proof: *To test* * Printed matter is being put to the proof

Put to the test: *Find out usefulness or effeciiveness of* * His theories have never been put to the test

Put to the vote: *Ask people to vote on* * The issue was put to the vote in the house for final approval

Put to the worse: *To defeat* * He put the champion to the worse in three sets

Put together: *Consider in totality; perform something successfully; get something well organized; establish in good relationship* * Your department spent more last year than all the others put together * He took it apart brick by brick and put it back together into its original shape * He is trying to put a team together for next season * We got to work on putting all the books together subject wise in different racks

Put two and two together: *Draw a conclusion from various facts* * Putting two and two together, I assumed that his car was used for committing the crime

Put up: *Start from cover (as a horse); stow away; put aside; to parcel up; to sheathe; to compound; endure tamely; accommodate with lodging; to take lodgings; to nominate or stand for election; to offer for sale; to present (a good fight, etc.); to compound; pre-concert* * The hare and tortoise put up the race towards the winning post * He put himself up on a ferry and landed in an unknown place * Children put up some of their pocket money to buy Diwali presents * He has put up many articles to be mailed to his bosom friend * The television was put up in a snug coverlet * The problem is put up by the medical system here * I left the meeting room because I could not put up a long wait for the chairman * All the delegates invited from abroad were put up in the Mount View Hotel * We can put you up for the night * You can put up in the inn for the night * The new party is putting up 20 candidates for 25 seats in the coming elections * The old paintings have been put up to be disposed of through auction * The ch-ampion put up a good fight in boxing by defeating his rival in the last round * The famine has put up many problems for the poor farmers * Some additional preconditions about filling the new post have been put up through an advertisement in the newspaper

Put up the hair: *Dress the hair upon the head instead of wearing it hanging* * She put her hair up not to let them fall free

Put up the shutter: *Stop business for day* * Shopkeepers in the city have put up the shutters very early today

Put up to: *Incite to; make conversant with; supply with useful information or tips about* * Some of the older boys will have to put up to tease him * They were accused of putting up the crowd to violence * We have to put the new generation up to new scientific principles * Some educational magazines put us up to understand many valuable tips for leading a happy and purposeful life * He put up the file to his boss for his signatures

Put up with: *To endure; tolerate* * I a not going to put up with his smoking any longer * I cannot put up with his insolence

Put upon: *Take undue advantage of; impose upon* * Don't try to put upon the weakness of others * Restrictions must be put upon the trespassers

Put upon point: *To ration by points* * The distribution of kerosene oil has been put upon points through a ration card

Putter around: *Not to do something in particular* * I spent the morning puttering around the house

Putter-on: *An instigator* * He was accused of being the main putter-on of the coup

Put-up: *Speciously pre-concerted* * It was mere a put-up show to bluff the spectators

Puzzle over/about: *Think hard to understand or explain* * He puzzled over the question all evening

Q

Qualify as: *Study for and obtain a diploma or a degree for a certain type of work* * He qualified as an electrician last year

Qualify for: *Pass a test and so proceed to the next step* * This training will qualify you for a better job or for higher studies

Quantity surveyor: *A person who estimates how much material is required for a building* * Construction of a hospital building was taken up after consulting the quantity surveyor

Quantum leap or quantum jump: *Considerable progress* * This discovery marks a quantum leap forward in the fight against cancer

Quarrel about: *Angry argument about* * They had a quarrel about money

Quarrel between: *Angry argument* * There was a quarrel between the two contestants

Quarrel over: *Involve in angry argument or disagreement* * She quarrelled with her mother over their father's will

Quarrel with: *Disagree with* – Nobody can quarrel with your conclusion

Quarrel with one's bread and butter: *Act in a way prejudicial to one's means of subsistence* * You would certainly be a stupid fellow to quarrel with your bread and butter

Quarter-bound: *Having leather or cloth on the back only* * In the olden era, man used to move about quarter-bound while hunting for meat

Queen ant/bee: *Leading ant; bee in a colony* * It is only a queen ant/bee that lays eggs

Queer fish: *A person of odd habits or nature with which one is not in sympathy* * He is really a queer fish as he displays eccentric behaviour * Our new officer is a queer fish and as a result nobody likes his officious attitude

Queer street: *The feigned abode of person in debt or difficulties* * Keep away from him as he looks like a pretender belonging to the queer street

Queer the pitch: *Make the place of performance unavailable; to spoil one's chance* * They queered the pitch of a promising career in life

Quench one's thirst: *Drink so much that one no longer feels thirsty* * He stopped to quench his thirst at a stream

Question mark: *Over; against* * A big question mark hangs over his future with the team

Question of privileges: *Any question arising out of the rights of an assembly or of its members* * Since this involves the question of privileges, it must be given due consideration

Queue up for: *Wait in a line of people* * We had to queue up for an hour for the tickets

Queuing up: *Gathering in a line for some cause* * People are queuing up to help the victims of a car accident

Quick as a flash: *Very quickly* * Quick as a flash he jumped into the pool to save the drowning boy

Quick at: *Prompt at* * She is quick at understanding

Quick in: *Ready in* * He is quick in his answers

Quick on the draw: *Quick in understanding or reacting; quick at pulling out a gun to shoot* * You cannot fool him as he is very quick on the draw * He is quick on the draw when hunting for animals

Quick sand: *Dangerous area of soft sand where you can sink in easily* * You should be very careful not to tread in a quick sand area

Quick-tempered: *Become angry very quickly* * As he is a quick-tempered person it is advisable for you to refrain from provoking him with your words

Quick-witted: *Having ready wit* * Every one admires him for his quick-witted answers

Quid's in: *Have more money left than expected* * Since I am quid's in, I can afford to spend more money on luxury goods

Quit cost: *Pay expenses* * You will have to quit cost for the damage done to his car by your negligent driving

Quit not certainty for hope: *We must make most of certainty rather than to hang on hopes* * Keep safely the artifact that you already have instead of hoping for another because you should quit not certainty for hope

Quit one's self: *Behave* * He does not know how to quit himself in public

Quit scores: *Balance accounts* * Both the opposing parties now stand at quit scores

Quit-claim: *A deed of release* * He was offered a job after having signed a document on quit-claim

Quite a bit of: *A large number or amount of* * In the course of the investigation, quite a bit of stolen articles were found in his possession

Quite a few: *A considerable number; several* * Quite a few people were standing there to watch the puppet show * I have a support of quite a few persons in this case

Quite a lot of: *A large number or amount of* * We drank quite a lot of wine

Quite a something: *Impressive or unusual in some way* * She is quite a beauty

Quite another: *Very different* * To preach is easy but quite another to put the same into practice

Quite so: *Exactly so; exactly, just as you have said* * It is quite so to feel inactive during the hot season * From her appearance it seemed she was quite so in her teens

Quite some time: *Sufficient time* * He has not been seen for quite some time

Quite something: *Impressive or unusual in some way* * You find he is quite something when you get to know him better * The car that he has purchased is quite something

Quixotic project: *One which is considered foolish or extravagant* * The quixotic project on exploration of gas has been rejected by the audit committee

R

Rabbit on: *Keep talking for a long time (on matters not important or interesting)* * Why must you rabbit on the same topic for hours endlessly?

Race against time: *An effort to do before time or possible event* * It was a race against time to carry out rescue operations to save the lives of the people caught in the floods

Rack and manger: *Wasteful abundance; waste and destruction* * It is of no use to live at rack and manger * Natural disasters create problems in dealing with rack and manger

Rack and pinion: *A means of turning rotation into linear motion or linear into rotation by a toothed wheel engaged in a rack* * I have yet to see the working of rack and pinion and its usefulness in the system

Rack and ruin: *A state of neglect or collapse* * Many ancient temples and idols are going to rack and ruin due to public neglect and awareness

Rack one's brains: *Strain one's memory* * I am still racking my brains to remember as to where I had seen her earlier

Rack rent: *A rent stretched to the utmost annual value of the thing rented; an exorbitant rent* * Rake company has been paying rack-rent for that building keeping in view its central location

Rack up something: *Collect something as profit or loss in business or point in a competition* * The company has racked up a huge profit in two years * In five years of boxing, he has racked up a record of 90 wins

Rack-rent: *Highest rent* * The rack-rent of this building has been fixed at 500 rupees per month

Ragged school: *A voluntary school for destitute children* * It is a good thing to run a ragged school for educating poor children

Rags to riches: *From being extremely poor to being very rich* * His was a classic tale of rags to riches

Raid the market: *Derange prices artificially for future gain* * The businessmen have raided the market purposefully to serve their personal interests

Rail at/against: *Use abusive language to* * Never rail at anybody * He railed against the injustice meted out to him

Rail something in/off: *Separate an area or an object placing rails around it* * The machine was railed in/off as a safety precaution

Rain cats and dogs: *Pour down heavily* * The match was held up because it began to rain cats and dogs * Yesterday it rained cats and dogs preventing us from reaching college on time

Rain in torrents: *Rain in violent showers* * It rained in torrents and the streets were flooded with water

Rain or shine: *Under all circumstances* * Rain or shine, I must support him in this election

Rained off: *Cancelled or stopped because of rain* * The game of cricket has been rained off again

Rainy day: *Bad times* * A prudent person would certainly save something for a rainy day

Raise a siege: *Abandon or put an end to a siege; relinquish besieging* * At last the Mughal army had to raise a siege of the fort which was defended by brave Rajputs * After capturing the fort, the Mughal army raised a siege of it

Raise Cain/Raise the roof: *Make determined or angry fuss* * The juvenile delinquents were raising Cain by hooting with laughter and creating a din

Raise money on: *Get money by pawning* * He is raising money on articles pawned by the owners who failed to pay back the money to him

Raise one's hat: *Take one's hat off in salutation* * He raised his hat to the boss as a mark of respect

Raise the devil: *Create riots* * Those who create the devil were soon overpowered by the troops

Raise the dust: *Cause uproar* * The opposition raised the dust over the provocative comments made by a member of the Treasury Bench in the Upper House

Raise the market: *Bring about a raise in prices* * Persistent demand and short supply of articles/goods have raised the market

Raise the roof: *Make a prodigious din* * Their shouts and cheers raised the roof.

Raise to the ground: *Demolish completely* * Many buildings were raised to the ground due to consistent bombardment

Raised the wind: *Obtain ready money; collect money by any means* * They are raising the wind through trade in jewellery

Rake in: *Earn a lot easily* * The privatisation of public enterprises has helped them rake in huge profits

Rake it in: *Earn a lot of money quickly* * His coffee shop is a great success and he is raking in it

Rake-off: *Illegal payment paid as a commission* * He got a rake-off from the income-tax payer for concealing his true income

Rake over: *Examine past happenings and keep on talking about the same and which other people would like to forget* * He had no desire to rake over the past

Rake up: *Recall unnecessarily* * Raking the past up will only make things worse

Rally round: *Be together in difficult or unpleasant situating* * The whole family rallied round when grandmother fell seriously ill

Ram home: *Emphasise strongly and convincingly* * Railway lines are dangerous places and it is up to parents to ram home the danger to their children

Ram into: *Hit against with force* * He rammed his truck into the back of a standing car in front

Range against: *Join to oppose* * The whole family seemed ranged against him

Ranging fancy: *Inconsistent affection* * There still prevails a ranging fancy between the two friends

Rank and file: *Common soldiers; ordinary people (masses)* * The rank and file in the army fought bravely against the enemy * The rank and file will be greatly benefited by the new Act * The rank and file are definitely influenced by a party's pre-election promises

Rant and rave: *Speak or complain in a loud or angry way* * He ranted and raved about the way he was befooled

Rap over the knuckles: *Criticise for* * The company was rapped over the knuckles for broadcasting the interview

Raring to go: *Eager to go* * The new recruit arrived all dressed up and was raring to go

Rat on somebody: *Tell somebody in authority about something wrong that somebody has done* * Where I come from, you don't rat on your friends

Rat on something: *Not do something that you have agreed or promised to do* * The government is accused of ratting on its promises to the unemployed

Rat race: *Competition for success in the business world* * There is a brisk rat race going on in the production of weapons of mass destruction overtly and covertly

Rather than: *Instead of* * I think I will have a cold drink rather than coffee * Why don't you ask for help rather than trying to do it on your own?

Rather you than me: *Used for saying that you would not like to do something that another person is going to do* * I will do the work because I feel it is rather you than me!

Rattle along: *Move with rattling sound* * The loaded cart rattled along the road

Rattle around: *Be living or working in a room or building that is too big* * He spent the last few years alone rattling around the old family home

Rattle off: *Speak rapidly* * He can rattle off the names of all the countries in the world

Rattle on: *Talk continuously on things not important or interesting in an annoying way* * I listened in silence as he rattled on about his unflinching determination on any issue

Rattle one's cage: *Annoy one* * Who rattled your cage?

Rattle the sabre or sword: *To threaten war* * Pakistan has rattled sabre or sword many a times over the Kashmir issue

Rave about: *Speak enthusiastically* * They were raving about the latest singer

Rave at: *Address in wild, uncontrolled language to* * For fully five minutes she stood there raving at us

Raving mad: *Completely crazy* * I am afraid he has gone raving mad over that girl

Raw deal: *Harsh, inequitable treatment; unfair treatment* * Old workers often get a raw deal * I think women are getting a raw deal in the matter of their political representation * My brother has certainly had a raw deal from his boss for getting dismissed so soon

Ray of sunshine: *A person or thing that makes life better, brighter and more cheerful* * The prestigious job has now brought a ray of sunshine in his life

Reach for: *Reach in order to get whatever is named* * He reached for the match-box before lighting a fire

Reach for the stars: *Try to be successful at something that is difficult* * He wants to reach for the stars by wanting to become a billionaire without putting in hard labour

Reach out: *Stretch out* * He reached out his hand for the knife but it was too far away

Reach out to: *Show interest in or want to help to* * Some charitable institutions are reaching out to poverty-stricken people in various parts of the country

Reach to: *Reach as far as* * He wore a coat that reached (down) to his knees * On one wall there was a book-case that reached (up) to the ceiling

React against: *Act in opposition or move in an opposed or contrary direction* * People will not endure oppression forever because there comes a time when even a worm reacts against unpleasant treatment meted out to it

React to: *Respond* * If you pester them needlessly they are bound to react to your behaviour

Read about: *Read the details concerning* * For our homework we have to read about the Industrial Revolution

Read between the lines: *Infer what is not explicitly stated* * If we read this statement between the lines, we will easily understand it * On reading between the lines of his letter it seems he needs money

Read for: *Study* * I must read for I have to prepare for my examination

Read into: *Find in a person's writing, words, behaviour, etc.; give an interpretation of one's own to what is written or spoken* * It would be wrong to try to read too much into a light-hearted play * I think you are reading into his statement more than is intended

Read of: *Learn of through a printed source* * I have read of people living several weeks on nothing but a glass of water a day

Read off: *Take as a reading from an instrument* * I have read off the quantity of water consumed as per the water-meter

Read one's palm: *Interpret from the lines on a hand about one's future happenings* * I saw a palmist reading her hand and assuring her of a suitable match in her life.

Read out: *Read aloud* * He is obliged to take his turn at reading out the announcement

Read over/through: *Read carefully from beginning to end to look for mistakes or check details* * I have read over your petition and find its contents satisfactory

Read person's hand: *Tell fortune as per lines of palm* * A palmist read my hand and told me many unbelievable things

Read someone the riot act: *Warn someone to stop being disorderly* * The headmaster read all the students the riot act in order to maintain discipline

Read through: *Read from beginning to end* * I have read through this interesting novel twice

Read up: *Amass knowledge by reading; become informed by readings* * I will need to read up on the case before the meeting * I have read up on the dangers of all these drugs

Ready at: *Quick at* * The new clerk is ready at figures

Ready at hand: *Easily available when needed* * I keep my pistol ready at hand

Ready for: *Willing or in condition for* * We are ready for departure * I am ready for work

Ready for the fray: *Ready to fight; ready to take part in the action* * They are ready for the fray on the controversial issue

Ready in: *Prepared beforehand* * The little scholar is ready in his replies to the queries

Ready money: *Money ready at hand; cash* * I have sufficient ready money to meet any emergency * I bought this house on payment of ready money to its owner

Ready wit: *Prompt to answer* * I have always envied people with a ready wit as they know just what to say and when

Ready-made: *Ready for immediate use* * He generally puts on ready-made garments

Real estate: *Immovable property* * He is intent on investing in real estate

Reap the fruits of one's deeds: *Benefit or suffer as a direct result of one has done* * He committed many crimes and is now reaping the fruits of his deeds in jail

Rear on something: *Give a particular type of food or entertainment* * He was the son of sailors and reared on the stories of the sea

Rear-view mirror: *Mirror in a car to see what is behind without turning round* * Every car or truck has a rear-view mirror

Rears its head/Ugly head: *Become visible or noticeable* * The threat of strikes rears its head every now and then

Reason out: *Try to find the answer to a problem in a logical way* * Reason it out for yourself!

Reason with: *Persuade someone to be more sensible* * I tried to reason with him, but he wouldn't listen

Recharge your batteries: *Get back strength and energy by resting for a while* * The proper way to recharge your batteries is to have a cup of tea coupled with a walk in the open

Reckon on: *Expect to happen or rely on happening* * They hadn't reckoned on a rebellion

Reckon up: *Calculate the total amount or number of* * He reckoned up the cost of everything in his mind

Reckon with: *Treat with seriously* * They are already a political force to reckon with

Reckon without one's host/Count without one's host: *Count up one's bill without reference to the landlord; fail to take account of some important possibility* * I reckoned without my host the cost of the building to be about a few million * He counted without his host the unexpected expenditure involved for undertaking the long journey

Reconcile oneself to: *Make agree* * He could not reconcile himself to the prospect of giving up his studies.

Reconcile to: *Be content* * At last he became reconciled to his lot

Reconcile with: *Be friendly* * He was persuaded to be reconciled with his opponent

Reconnaissance in force: *An attack by a large body to discover the enemy position and strength* * Reconnaissance in force is also one of the most important tactics exercised in any war

Recoup your losses: *Get back money which you have lost* * We hope to recoup our losses through the purchase of new bonds

Recourse to: *Option to an emergency* * The public believes its only recourse is to take to the street.

Recover from: *Become well; get back to a former position of prosperity; get back to former state or mental condition* * He is slowly recovering from his illness * Has the country recovered from the effects of the war? * I have yet not recovered from my astonishment

Rector Magnificus: *The head of a German University* * The Vice-Chancellor of the Punjab University met his counterpart, the Rector Magnificus of a German university to discuss some important academic issues

Red carpet: *Official welcome* * The chief guest invited by the government on the occasion of the Republic Day was given a red carpet welcome

Red flag: *Signal of danger* * At the sight of a red flag shown by a boy, the railway driver stopped the train and thus saved the lives of many passengers

Red game: *Grouse* * The boss gave a patient hearing to his red game

Red herring: *Irrelevant matter introduced to distract attention* * They were using the issue as a red herring

Red in tooth and claw: *Opposition or competition that is violent and without pity* * The boxers who locked their horns with each other were red in tooth and claw

Red letter day: *A day of rejoicing* * 15th of August is a red letter day in the history of India because we acquired freedom on this day

Red rag: *Anything that excites anger* * Don't show a red rag to a bull if you want to remain safe

Red rag to a bull: *Cause for irritation or anger* * Communism to a socialist is like a red rag to a bull * Telling him that he did not know philosophy was akin to showing a red rag to a bull

Red tapism: *Office formality involving delay due to office routine* * The delay in reply to his petition was due to red tapism

Red-handed: *In the act of committing crime* * The thief was caught red-handed with the stolen good in his hand

Red hot: *Extremely excited* * He got red hot when he was abused in public

Reduce to powder: *Crush into dust* * Various roots of dried herbs were reduced to powder for making medicines

Reduce to system: *Restore to systematic condition* * It was not an easy task to reduce to system the disorganised management

Reduced circumstances: *Impoverished* * They are descendants of the royal family and are now living in reduced circumstances

Reduced in body: *Lean and thin* * He looked quite reduced in body as a result of some serious ailment

Reduce the balance: *Make things equal again* * They needed only one goal to reduce the balance in the second half of the hockey match

Reduced to: *Force into a particular state or condition; usually a worse one* * He is reduced almost to a skeleton * The authority reduced the rebels to submission * They were reduced to starving * She was reduced to tears by their criticism

Reduced to ashes: *Turn into ashes* * The hut that caught fire was reduced to ashes in no time

Reduced to the ranks: *Demote* * Some non-commissioned officers were reduced to the ranks by the brigadier for neglect of duties

Reel in: *Pull by winding around a reel* * I slowly reeled the fish in

Reel off: *Utter rapidly fluently* * She reeled off a long verse to the surprise of her listeners

Refer to: *Assign to; impute to; attribute to; mention about; be connected to; look at or consult; send for help or advice; submit for decision; hand over for consideration; direct for information* * The teacher referred a difficult task to each of the students * I denied the motive that my employer was referring to * He referred his success to hard work and a bit of luck * In his speech, he referred to a recent trip to Canada * The word 'art' usually refers to humanities and social sciences * You may refer to your notes if you want * My doctor referred me to a specialist * Your case has been referred to the court of appeal * The proposed plan was referred to the committee * In this connection, you may kindly refer to my statement already sent to you

Reflect on/upon: *Credit or discredit; be a criticism of; consider or think on* * The results reflect the amount of effort put in by him to earn credit * Such behaviour can only reflect on your upbringing * I do not wish to reflect on your sincerity * I must reflect on what answer to give to his query

Refrain from: *Hold back; stop from or not to do something* * Do refrain from spitting in public * Let us hope they will refrain from hostile action * They appealed to the protesters to refrain from violence

Regale with: *Amuse or entertain with* * He regaled us with tales of fairyland

Regard for: *Respect for* * I have every regard for my elders

Regardless of: *Without caring for* * He openly insulted the old man regardless of hurting his feelings

Register at a hotel: *Write your name or address when you arrive at the hotel* * It is compulsory for everybody to register himself at a hotel for his stay there

Regular army: *Permanent, professional army* * It is known that China has a largest regular army in comparison to any other country in the world

Regular officer: *Professional officer* * India is still deficient in providing a regular officer in the army

Reign of terror: *Period when law and order have broken down* * The reign of terror has taken deep roots in some countries

Rein in: *Pull on the rein to control (a horse); start to control or be strict* * A new rider must be careful to rein in a shaky horse * We must rein ourselves in public spending

Reinvent the wheel: *Waste time in creating something that already exists and is working well* * There is no point in reinventing the wheel

Rejoice in the name of: *Have a name that sounds funny* * He rejoiced in the name of Pitcher Fitcher

Relate to: *Connected with* * We shall discuss the problem as it relates to our specific interest * It does not matter even if the information given by you relates to a secret sex-scandal

Relatively speaking: *Comparing something with all similar things* * Relatively speaking, these jobs provide good salaries

Relief fund: *Money raised for helping the needy* * The general public is always alive to making contribution towards the relief fund

Relief works: *Construction undertaken to give work to unemployed* * Our government has provided many avenues of relief works for those who are unemployed

Relieve one of: *Take from one's possession; steal from someone; free one from* * Let me relieve you of some of your bags * The thief relieved me of my purse while boarding a train in a rush * He has been relieved of his night duty

Relieve yourself: *Urinate* * I had to relieve myself behind the bush

Rely on/upon: *Trust or have faith; depend on* * You can rely on me to keep your secret * He cannot be relied on to tell the truth * You may safely rely upon my word * They relied on heavily on the advice of their professional advisers

Remarkable for: *Noted for* * The juggler is remarkable for his uncommon skill

Remedial class: *Class of special instruction for students who are weak in a subject* * This school has arranged remedial classes for weak students in different subjects after school hours

Remember one in a will: *Leave something in a will* * He remembered me in his will

Remember one to: *Commend one to* * After reading my letter, kindly remember me to your parents

Remembered for: *Famous or known for* * That gentleman is remembered for his generosity and philanthropy

Remind of: *Remember or think about* * This smell reminds me of France * You remind me of your father when you say that * The Taj reminds us of the Mughal Emperor, Shahjahan

Remit something to somebody: *Take or send (a question to be decided) (to somebody)* * The matter has been remitted to a higher tribunal

Remonstrate with: *Make a protest* * I had to remonstrate with him upon his unpardonable negligence

Render an account of oneself: *Explain; justify oneself* * He has been served with a notice to render an account of himself for his false statement

Render down: *Melt (fat)* * He rendered down the fat liquid by heating it

Renege on: *Break a promise* * They had to return a large sum of money because they had reneged on the deal

Reopen old wounds: *Remind of unpleasant past happening* * We do not like to reopen old wounds of the past two wars with Pakistan

Repair to: *Go to (especially go frequently, go in large number to)* * Many tourists repair to seaside resorts for the summer

Report back: *Return to a place to work again* * Take an hour for lunch and report back at 2.00 p.m.

Report back to: *Give information about* * Find out as much as you can about him and report back to me

Report for work: *Inform personally that you have arrived for work* * The mason has reported .to the landlord for work

Report oneself: *Give information about oneself* * He reported himself to the Head of the Department about his appointment as an assistant

Report to: *Be responsible to* * You will be reporting to John for your daily progress as wanted by him

Repose in: *Trust in* * We repose in him our faith because of his honesty

Repose on: *Lay on* * As he reposed on his bed, the picture hung on the wall mesmerised him

Reproach someone with something: *Blame someone for something* * The head of the department is bound to reproach him for his carelessness

Reproach with: *Find fault with* * He reproached me with neglect of duty

Republic of letters: *The world of books and authors* * The present era is a republic of letters

Reside in: *Be in or caused by* * In America the supreme authority resides in the president * The source of the problem resides in the fact that the currency is too strong

Resign one's claim: *Give up one's claim* * A selfless person is always ready to resign his claim if he finds that something has gone wrong under his stewardship

Resign to fate: *Surrender to fate* * We have no alternative but to resign to our fate when anything takes place beyond our control

Resign yourself to: *Accept the unpleasant that cannot be*

avoided * We have to resign ourselves to our fate

Resolve into: *Separate or separated into; gradually turn into a different form; gradually become or be understood* * They were able to resolve a complex argument into its basic elements * The orange light resolved itself into four lanterns * The discussion eventually resolved itself into two main issues

Resolve on/upon: *Decide or determine* * He resolved on making an early start

Resolve to do: *Strong determination to achieve* * The government reiterated its resolve to uncover the truth

Resonate with: *Be filled with sound; be full of particular quality or feeling; be similar to what somebody thinks or believes* * The room resonated with the chatter of many voices * He makes a simple story resonate with complex themes and emotions* These issues resonate with the demands of the voters

Resort to: *Make use of for help or to gain one's purpose; frequently visit* * If other means fails, we shall resort to force * I am sorry you have resorted to deception * The police watched the cafes where the wanted man was known to resort to violence

Rest assured: *Emphasise what you say is true will definitely happen* * Rest assured that we will do all we can to find him

Rest in peace: *Express one's wish towards a dead person to rest in peace* * Pray for the soul of the departed person to rest in peace

Rest on one's laurels: *Do nothing further after earning honor or distinction; be content with one's success and rest* * He is now resting on his laurels after having served his country in good faith * The government cannot afford to rest on its laurels but must press ahead with major policy changes

Rest on one's oars: *Rest after hard work* * After the examinations, I am thinking of going to Shimla to rest on my oars

Rest on or upon: *Depend or rely on* * All our hopes rest on you * Look at those clouds resting upon the mountain top * His fame rests upon his plays more than upon his novels * The whole argument rests on a false assumption

Rest with: *Be left in hands or*

charge of * It rests with you to take a decision on the matter

Restaurant car: *Carriage on a train where you can have a meal* * Many of the passenger trains have restaurant cars

Restraint of princes: *Embargo* * The government has imposed restraint of princes on supply of weapons of mass destruction to rogue countries

Result from: *Happen because of* * Job losses resulted from low production * Any damage resulting from negligence must be paid by the borrower

Result in something: *Make something happen* * The cyclone has resulted in deaths of thousands of victims

Retail at: *Sell for (a certain price)* * These shoes normally retail at a very low price

Retail outlet: *Shop which sells goods direct to the customer* * We purchase our ration and other goods from retail outlets

Retain a lawyer: *Agree with a lawyer that he will act for you (and pay him in advance)* * We have retained a lawyer to represent us when our case comes up before the court for hearing

Retire from something: *Stop doing one's usual work as a result of age factor, etc.* * He has now retired from active service

Retire into: *Become unsociable* * The old philosopher decided to retire into loneliness

Retire one's steps: *Go back over the same path again* * On half way market, I retired my steps to collect my purse at home

Retire to bed: *Go to bed* * I usually retire to bed at 10 o'clock at night

Retroactive to: *Which takes effect from* * This rule would be retroactive from the month of April

Retrograde step: *Step which makes things worse than they were before* * The closure of the factory is a retrograde step

Revel in something: *Enjoy something very much* * He is revelling in his freedom * They revel in gossip

Revenge yourself on: *Get satisfaction by deliberately inflicting injury in return for injury on yourself* * He was determined to revenge himself on the man who betrayed him

Revert to: *Return to a former state; return to an earlier topic*

or subject; return to original condition * His manner seems to have reverted to normal * The conversation kept reverting to the events of last Monday * The fields have reverted to moorland

Revolve around/round: *Move around in a circle; have as the main interest or subject; go around in a circle* * The earth revolves around the sun * His whole life revolves around surfing * The discussion revolved around the question of changing the club's name * The wheel revolves around its axis

Rhetoric question: *Question to which you do not expect an answer* * It seems to be a rhetoric question motivated politically

Ribbon development: *Line of buildings extended along the main road* * The haphazard ribbon development in the outskirts of any large town or city is on the increase day by day

Rich in: *With many resources* * This area is rich in lush green vegetation * The hilly region here is rich in minerals

Riches have wings: *Wealth would never stick itself permanently anywhere* * It could not be farther from the truth to say that riches have wings

Richly deserve: *Deserve very much* * He richly deserved his promotion to a higher rank

Rid of: *Make free* * He had to put in hard labour to rid himself of debt * Efforts are afoot to rid the world of terrorism

Riddle with: *Make many holes in; full of* * The dead body of the dacoit was riddled with bullets * His typing was slow and riddled with mistakes

Ride a wave of: *Enjoy or be supported by the particular situation or quality mentioned* * The schools are riding a wave of renewed public interest

Ride at anchor: *To float* * The ship is riding at anchor for loading and unloading goods

Ride down: *Overtake by riding; charge and overthrow or trample* * The rider of the horse rode down all the competitors in the horse race * The cavalry had to ride down the rowdy crowd that had gone violent

Ride for a fall: *Court disaster* * The driver of the speeding truck was riding for a fall any time anywhere

Ride herd on: *Keep watch or control over* * The police will need to ride herd on the crowds of youth on the streets

Ride of the ring: *Practice the sport of riding rapidly and catching a hanging ring on a spear* * The people felt astonished to watch the ride of the ring on an official ceremonial day

Ride on something: *Depend on something; sit or be on something especially astride* * My whole future is riding on this interview * The boy was riding on his father's shoulders

Ride one down: *Overtake one by riding* * I rode him down in the horse race by a very narrow margin and won the gold medal

Ride out: *Keep afloat throughout; cut out from a herd by riding* * The ruling party thinks it can ride out the political storm * He was successful in riding out the herds of elephants and rhinos

Ride roughshod: *Not to take consideration of other people's feelings* * We should never ride roughshod over the genuine demands of poor people * These laws allow the security forces to ride roughshod over the human rights of the people

Ride the crest of: *Enjoy great success or support because of a particular situation or event* * The band is riding the crest of its last tour

Ride the high horse: *Be proud and arrogant* * Some officers of the top echelons in the civil services do ride the high horse * After his promotion, the executive engineer has begun to ride the high horse

Ride to hounds: *Take part in fox hunting* * They have chalked out a programme to ride to hounds tomorrow

Ride up: *Work up out of position* * Short skirts tend to ride up when you sit down

Riding habit: *Special dress for horse riding* * He bought a horse and got a riding habit in the bargain

Riding the fair: *The ceremony of opening a fair by procession* * Arrangements are underway for riding the fair

Riff-raff: *Worthless members of society* * As a matter of fact, the riff-raff carry no weight in any society

Rig out: *An outfit; furnish with complete dress* * He was wearing a smart rig out bought the previous day *

I was accepted for the job and rigged out in uniform

Rig up: *Make or build quickly* * We manage to rig up a shelter for the night

Right a wrong: *Correct an unfair situation or something bad* * You should have tendered an apology to him to right a wrong

Right and left: *Everywhere* * He owes money right and left

Right arm: *The main support* * Without his right arm I would not have been able to complete my higher education

Right as a trivet/Right as rain: *Perfectly right* * You need not worry about his health as I found him as right as trivet yesterday

Right away: *Straightaway* * He wants to see you right away for consultation on some critical issue

Right down: *Plainly* * He was very tall and dressed right down

Right mind: *Sane* * He seems to be in his right mind now

Right of way: *The right of public to pass over a piece of ground* * No restriction could be imposed on the right of way here * Is there a right of way across the fields?

Right off: *Without delay* * As soon as I saw the dirty man entering the house I drove away right off

Right out: *Outright* * No one party is expected to gain a right out majority

Right to the bottom: *Exactly up to the bottom* * You will have to go right to the bottom of this case to unearth true facts

Right up my street: *I know a lot about; I am very interested in* * This job seems right up my street

Right, wrong side: *The side intended to be turned outward or inward* * People should know right, wrong side at a particular place to avoid any scope of accident

Right-down: *Out-and-out* * Whatever he said was right-down a tissue of lies

Right-hand man: *Chief helper, assistant or supporter* * Our vice-principal is the right-hand man of our principal

Right-minded: *Of right (correct) mind or idea* * A right-minded person earns respect everywhere

Right-of-way: *A track over which there is such a right* * At railway crossings, the right of way should be given to the train by the public vehicles

Rigor mortis: *Stiffening of the body after death* * Rigor mortis is a natural process which occurs two to four hours of a person's death

Ring a bell: *Begin to arouse a memory* * His name did ring a bell in my mind yet I could not recall who it was and where we had met

Ring off: *Signal the ending of a telephone conversation* * He rang off before I could explain

Ring out: *Sound clearly, loudly and suddenly* * A number of shots rang out at a short distance

Ring the bell: *Achieve a great success; make a sound of signal through an electric device* * He rang the bell by winning the gold medal in an international shooting event * Ring the bell to see if they are inside the house

Ring the bells backward: *Reverse the order of chime* * In the temple, they ring the bells backward, that is, from a high tone to a lower one

Ring the changes: *Proceed through all the permutations in ringing a chime of bells; do a number of things repeatedly in varying order* * The children liked the chime of bells ring the changes for a play * Ring the changes by adding spice, dried fruit or olives

Ring the shed: *Win a sheep-shearing competition* * It was really a treat to watch the agility of shearers who ring the shed

Ring true: *Sound genuine* * The account of the event he gave rings true

Ring up: *Summon by bell; communicate by telephone* * There was a ring up for you by the boss just a short while back * I will ring you up by this evening

Ringside seat: *Position from which one can observe or experience what is happening* * He is being transferred to headquarters for six months for management training

Rinse out: *Make clean* * Rinse out the dishes before use

Rip at: *Attack violently by tearing or cutting* * He will have to rip at the belly of his enemy with a bayonet to kill him

Rip into: *Go very quickly and violently into or through* * A bullet ripped into his shoulders

Rip off: *Cheat or defraud* * The taxi driver looks like a crook and may rip off the tourists by charging high rates

Rip up: *Tear into small pieces* *

He ripped up all the old invalid documents and threw them into a dustbin

Rip up old scores: *Revive past quarrels* * It would be foolish on your part to try to rip up old scores

Rip-roaring: *Noisy; great success; wild and noisy* * The protesters raised rip-roaring slogans against their employers * He will achieve a rip-roaring success in his new enterprise * There were rip-roaring cries in the inn by some drunkards

Rise above: *Not be affected or limited by problems, etc.; morally good; be of higher standard* * He had the courage and determination to rise above his physical disability * I try to rise above all prejudice * His work rarely rises above the mediocre

Rise against: *Rebel* * All the people rose against the tyranny of the dictator

Rise bedtimes: *Rise early in the morning* * It is good fobr the health to rise bedtimes and breathe fresh air

Rise from the ranks: *Work one's way up from private soldier to commissioned officer; become a self-made man* * Our new officer knows his job well despite having risen from the ranks * He deserves all praise for his rising from the rank

Rise in revolt: *To riot or rebel* * The peasants rose in revolt against the tyranny of the new dictator

Rise to the occasion: *Prove equal to emergency* * The mill-owner rose to the occasion by fulfilling the demands of the labourers to avert the strike

Rise up against: *Rebel or fight against* * He called on the people to rise up against the invaders

Rise with the sun: *Be out of bed at sunrise* * He rises with the sun every day

Rising forty: *Nearly 40-years old* * From his looks he seems rising forty

Rising generation: *The young* * We do look up to the rising generation for all round development in the health of our country

Risk life and limb/Risk your neck: *To risk being killed or injured* * Our brave soldiers are always ready to risk their lives and limbs to save the honour and integrity of the country

Risk money: *Allowance to a cashier to compensate for ordinary errors* * The small errors in the accounts are covered as risk money in favour of the cashier

Riveted to the spot/ground: *Shocked or frightened that one cannot move* * Hearing the unbearable news of her only son being killed, she was riveted to the ground

Road house: *Hotel by a main road* * We had our meals at a road house on our way to Kulu

Road to success: *Path which leads to success* * Hard work is the only road to success

Roaring business: *Profitable business* * They have been running a roaring business for the last three years.

Rob Peter to pay Paul: *To satisfy one by depriving another* * It is not at all justifiable to rob Peter to pay Paul

Rock the boat: *Disturb or cause problem* * He was told to keep his mouth shut and not rock the boat

Rock-bottom: *Lowest: possible* * Prices hit rock-bottom during recession

Rogue elephant: *Savage elephant driven out of the herd by other elephants; person who does not behave in the same way as others* * Have you ever seen a rogue elephant? * The society has condemned him as a rogue elephant

Rogue's gallery: *A police collection of photographs of criminals* * When he looked at the rogue's gallery, he at once identified the real murderer

Rogue's march: *Music played in derision of a person expelled* * The corrupt colonel was greeted with rogue's march

Roll back: *Reduce or end; force back* * Most major political reforms of the past five years will need to be rolled back * Some provisions of the law were to roll back taxes to the earlier level of 1980 * He rolled back the cuffs of the shirt

Roll down: *Open by turning a handle* * He rolled down the window of his car and started to shout at them

Roll in: *Arrive, in large numbers or quantities* * Offers of help are rolling in from various quarters to save the victims of tsunami tragedy

Roll of honour: *List of soldiers who have died during a war/ List of prize-winners* * His name exists in the roll of honour for having shot down as many as 10 war planes of the enemy

Roll on: *Pass steadily* * Time is rolling on and we are growing older

Roll one's R's: *When speaking the letter 'R' to make tip of the tongue vibrate* * You will have to roll your R's while making use of this letter in English language

Roll up: *Assemble; arrive; close by turning a handle* * People were rolling up there to watch the tricks of the magician * He finally rolled up two hours late * He rolled up the window of the car on seeing the beggar

Roll up one's sleeves: *Prepare to work or fight* * He is rolling up his sleeves to clean the used utensils * From hot words they began to roll up their sleeves for a violent fight

Roll with the punches: *Adapt yourself to a difficult situation* * The boxer knows how to roll with the punches to counter any hard blows from the opponent

Roll-call: *Taking attendance by calling out names* * All the students in the class were present at the roll-call

Rolled gold: *Metal coated with gold and rolled very thin* * Some people deal in rolled-gold ornaments which are sold at a very low price

Rolling in money: *Having a lot of money* * Most of the enterprising people in America are rolling in money

Rolling in the aisles: *Laughing a lot* * The joker soon had us rolling in the aisles with his antics

Rolling stone: *A person who never sticks to one place* * He is going on changing jobs like a rolling stone which can never stay in one place

Rolling-pin: *A cylinder of wood or glass, usually a foot long* * We make use of the rolling-pin to roll out dough for making *chapattis*

Rolling-stock: *Railway coaches, wagons, etc. or all the stock that is on the wheels* * All the rolling-stock is easily driven by a railway engine, irrespective of the heavy load

Rome was not built in a day: *A complicated task will take a long time and needs patience* * Seeing the huge monuments and buildings, it is obvious that Rome could not have been built in a day

Romp away/Romp ahead/ Romp home: *Make progress or win quickly and easily* * In the final heat of the race, he romped away, leaving behind all other competitors

Romp through: *Do easily and quickly* * He romped through the examination questions

Roof rack: *Grid fixed to the roof of a car for carrying luggage* * Many of the cars have roof racks for carrying luggage

Roof of the mouth: *Palate* * The upper bridge of our teeth is supported by the roof of the mouth at its edge

Room for: *Scope for* * There is room for more improvement * There could be no room for doubt

Room to swing a cat: *A minimum of space; confined space* * Even the room to swing a cat would serve my purpose * I am surprised how you manage to live here when there is no room to swing a cat!

Root about: *Turn up the ground with snout in search of food* * The pigs rooted about for food

Root and branch: *Every part; completely or entirely* * The Second World War destroyed the hold of Nazism root and branch * There can be no just rule unless we eradicate corruption root and branch at all levels of our administrative set-up

Root for: *Support or encourage in a sport competition or in a difficult situation* * I am here to root for you

Root for a team: *Cheer a team on* * Spectators rooted for a team that won the match against a very tough team

Root out: *Find by searching; exterminate* * I managed to root out a copy of the document * A huge effort was made to root out the rats

Root through: *Search for by moving things or turning them over* * It must be somewhere as she rooted through the suitcase

Rooted to the spot: *Frightened or shocked that you can not move* * I was rooted to the spot when a speeding truck from opposite side moved within a hair's breadth of me

Rope in: *Bring in; enlist* * Visitors were roped in for potato picking and harvesting * They hoped to rope in the public to solve the problems of the poor

Rope off: *Separate an area using ropes to stop people from entering therein* * Police roped off the street to investigate the accident

Rope's end: *The end of a rope used for flogging* * The rogues can understand the language of rope's end only

Ropes of sands: *Bond with no cohesion; delusive security* * The oral promises made by him to return the borrowed money within a day have proved ropes of sands * To think life to be a bed of roses would be tantamount to believing in ropes of sand

Rose without thorn: *Impossible happiness* * There is no rose without thorn

Rose-coloured spectacles: *A way of looking at a situation as being better or more positive than it really is* * He tends to view the world through rose-coloured spectacles

Rot has set in: *Things are beginning to go badly* * The rot has set in the organisation with the appointment of an inexperienced manager

Rotation of crops: *Growing different crops in turn* * Rotation of crops keeps the farmers busy throughout the year in tilling the land

Rotten apple: *Bad person who has bad effect on others in a group* * A rotten apple injures its companions

Rotten to the core: *Extremely bad* * The organisation is rotten to the core.

Rough and ready: *Unpolished, not elaborate* * This carpenter makes rough and ready boxes * His manners are rough and ready, but he is good at heart

Rough diamond: *An uncut diamond; a person possibly of great worth but of rude exterior and unpolished manners* * He came across as a rough diamond near a coal mine * He lacks social graces as he is a rough diamond which needs to be polished

Rough estimate: *Approximate calculation* * According to a rough estimate the project is likely to cost an enormous amount of money

Rough it: *Live in a primitive manner; take whatever hardships* * The backward tribes are habitual to rough it out * The explorers had to rough it when they reached the jungle

Rough justice: *Punishment that does not seem fair; treatment that is fair but not expected* * It was rough justice that they lost in the closing seconds of the game * There was a certain amount of rough justice in his downfall

Rough music: *Uproar* * The announcement caused rough music in the crowd

Rough on: *Hard luck for; pressing hard upon* * It was rather rough on her to have lost her husband soon after her marriage * Adversity is roughing on him to do extra labour day and night

Rough out: *Shape out roughly* * I have roughed out some ideas about my next plan

* They have roughed out a possible framework for the next play

Rough passage: *Difficult time* * We had better prepare for a rough passage when we start up the business

Rough patch: *Time of personal or financial difficulty or trouble* * Their marriage is going through a rough patch

Rough ride: *Painful or unpleasant experience* * The managing director sent for him and apparently gave him a rough ride for losing the contract

Rough- spoken: *Rough in speech* * Though he is a rough-spoken man, yet he is kind at heart

Rough up: *Beat or attack someone* * He complained against the cop who had roughed him up at the police post

Rough in: *Sketch in roughly* * You need to rough in his character for finally giving it a nice shape

Rough-and-tumble: *Haphazard and scrambling;* a scuffle * It is rather difficult to understand rough-and-tumble game of politics * He was involved in a rough-and-tumble with a photographer

Rough-hewn: *Roughly shaped* * It is a rough-hewn carving of a horse's head

Rough-wrought: *Shaped out or done roughly or in a preliminary way* * It is yet a rough-wrought sketch to be given proper shape

Round a number up: *Increase it to the nearest whole number above* * He rounded a number up to make the value of his item from 699 rupees to 700 rupees

Round about: *An emphatic form of round; approximately; using shortest or most direct way* * I had been to Shimla and the villages round about * He is ready to pay somewhere round about 10 million for the vintage car * We came here by going around a roundabout * I heard the news in a roundabout way

Round here: *Near where you are now or where you live* * There are no descent schools round here

Round of applause: *A short period of cheers by clapping* * There was a great round of applause when the dance ended

Round of golf: *Going round all the holes in golf course* * I want to play a round of golf

Round off: *Complete or finish off*

neatly * He rounded off by proposing a toast to the attendant * The celebrated musician rounded off his tour with a concert at Chandigarh

Round on: *Assail in speed; turn on; suddenly speak angrily to* * It is a usual for politicians of different parties to round on each other * He really knows how to round on the charm * He rounded on the journalists, calling them 'a pack of vultures'

Round out: *Fill out to roundness* * Don't let your body round out by eating fats * Her figure is beginning to round out

Round peg in a square hole: *He occupies a position to which he is not suited* * He is not in a position to run the factory as successfully as his father as he is a round peg in a square table

Round to: *Turn the head of a ship to the wind* * As a strong wind blew, the sailors had to round it to the wind to avoid any risk to the ship

Round trip: *Trip to destination and back* * I completed my round trip only yesterday * I have purchased my round-trip ticket

Round up: *Bring to a whole number; bring together; ride round and collect; gather in; summary of most important points* * The price had been rounded up from 558 to 560 rupees * The cowboy rounded up the cattle * I rounded up a few friends for a party * The police has been able to round up the proclaimed offender * We will be back after the break with a round up of today's other programmes

Roundabout: *A place where two or more roads meet forming a circle so that all traffic must go round in the same direction* * Take the second exit at the roundabout

Round-up: *Driving together as of all the cattle on a ranch; a set of people wanted by the police; a collection of facts or information, etc.* * It was rather fascinating to watch the round-up of a herd of cattle on the ranch * The police is on a round-up task of all bad elements involved in the crime * He gave us the much needed round-up of secret information dealing with the case

Rout somebody out: *To pull somebody out from where he is hidden* * We were routed out of our cabins before breakfast for passport examination

Route march: *Training march by the soldiers* * The recruits are on route march for two hours

Rowing boat: *Small boat for rowing* * We hired a rowing boat and kept rowing it in a lake for about an hour

Royal road: *Easy road* * Hard work is the royal road to success in life * Practice is the royal road to success when learning a language

Rub down: *Rub vigorously; make smooth by rubbing* * I came out of the water and rubbed myself down with a towel * I saw the carpenter rubbing down the woodwork with sandpaper

Rub in: *Massage on* * He rubbed in some sort of oily substance to get rid of the pain in his legs * Rub in a little oil to make you hair smooth and glossy when it is dry

Rub it in: *Keep reminding repeatedly of a fault* * I knew, I behaved foolishly, but you need not rub it in

Rub off: *Become part of a person's character resulting in spending time with those having the same quality; remove or be removed by rubbing* * His sense of fun has rubbed off on her children also * If you write on the blackboard, rub it off at the end of the lesson * The gold colouring had begun to rub off

Rub one's nose in it: *Keep reminding one in an unkind way about past mistakes* * I have already regretted my mistake, so it is impertinent on your part to rub my nose in it

Rub salt into the wound: *Make a difficult thing more difficult or unpleasant* * I had no intention of rubbing salt into the wounds of my friend

Rub shoulders: *Come into social contact* * I had to rub shoulders with many people during the course of my long journey abroad

Rub the wrong way: *Irritate by tactless handling* * She did have a way of rubbing people up the wrong way

Rub up: *Polish; freshen one's memory* * Rub up the silver spoons * I have joined the evening classes to rub up my English * Let me rub up the cause that created a rift between them resulting in a divorce

Rub up the wrong way: *Annoy or Irritate without intending to* * What are you going to get out of him if you rub him up the wrong way

Rubbing alcohol: *Pure alcohol used as an antiseptic* * He has been advised to make use of rubbing alcohol to cure his skin disease

Rubbish tip: *Public place where rubbish can be dumped* * People must be careful to take the garbage to a rubbish tip

Rubble work: *Coarse masonry* * He is still earning his living by doing rubble work

Rub out: *Erase* * He has to rub out the pencil marks in his exercise book

Ruck up: *Make untidy folds* * Your dress is rucked up at the back

Ruffle feathers: *Annoy or upset* * Politicians are usually careful not to ruffle the feathers of their constituents * The senator's speech ruffled a few feathers in the business world

Ruin agate/Ruin marble: *One with marking like ruins* * This old building represents signs of its ruin agate

Rule of the road: *The regulation to be observed in traffic by road, water, etc.* * It would keep us safe if we abide by the rules of the road

Rule of thumb: *Any rough and ready practical method* * A good rule of thumb for a salesman is to generate sales of ten times his salary for his employer to make a profit * Are there any rules of thumb for English prepositions?

Rule out: *Exclude* * The player has been ruled out of today's match on account of his injury * Local detectives have ruled out foul play

Rule the roost: *Lord it or predominate* * These days the republicans are ruling the roost in America and pursuing its own manifesto

Rule with a rod of iron: *Autocratic rule* * The black days have since gone when the people were ruled with a rod of iron * In dictatorship, one who is at the helm of affairs rules with a rod of iron

Ruled paper: *Paper with lines on it* * He uses only ruled paper for writing purposes

Ruling party: *Party which forms the government* * A ruling party is responsible to run its internal and external administrative affairs in the best interest of the public at large

Ruling passion: *Passion or motive which dominates; the chief incentive* * His ruling passion is his ambition to be the best in everything * Writing novels is his ruling passion these days

Rumble on: *Continue slowly and*

steadily for a long time * Discussions are still rumbling on over the construction of a new railway-track

Run a rig: *Play a trick on* * He is very adept in running a rig to the amusement of the company

Run a test: *Do a test* * The doctors decided to run some more tests on the blood samples

Run across: *Come upon by accident; cross quickly on foot* * He ran across some old friends in the village * He ran across to his neighbour's flat to borrow some sugar

Run after: *Try to catch; go after in order to get attention of* * The dog was running after a rabbit * She runs after every good-looking man in the village

Run against: *Collide; compete with* * As he fell, his head ran against the table * I am willing to run against him in the forthcoming race

Run along: *Be off* * Now, children, run along!

Run amuck: *Run forth murderously assailing all who come on the way* * The elephant suddenly ran amuck and trampled many people on its way

Run around with: *Usually disapproving** He is always running around with unruly elements

Run at: *Run towards somebody to attack* * He ran at me with a knife in his hand

Run away: *Leave rapidly or rapidly flee; escape* * I want your advice, so don't run away, * The boy ran away and went to sea (became a sailor)

Run away with the idea: *Assume hastily* * Don't run away with the idea that all that glitters is gold

Run back: *Consider again* * I will run back over the procedure once again

Run cold: *Be scared* * His blood ran cold at the sight of a lion

Run counter: *Go contrary* * The result of his plan ran contrary to his expectations

Run down: *Speak ill of; pursue to exhaustion; captured also; collide with and knocked over or sink; disparage; become exhausted; be weak from overwork* * He is always running me down in front of other people * At long last he managed to run down the escaped prisoner * The liner ran down a fishing-boat during the dense fog * That man does not like me since he is always running me down * The battery has run down; it needs recharging * He is looking run down as a result of overworking

Run errands: *Be sent to convey messages, etc. or perform small pieces of business* * He often runs errands for his master

Run for: *Continue for a particular period of time; be valid for a particular period of time; be a candidate for* * Her training as a nurse ran for a full year * This permit to sell alcohol runs for a year only * Who do you think will be running for presidentship during the next elections?

Run for it: *Run suddenly and fast in order to get out of danger* * We got caught in a heavy thunderstorm, so we had to run for it

Run foul of: *Strike against* * He felt that they had run foul of democracy

Run hard: *Press hard behind* * He ran hard to catch hold of the fugitive

Run high: *Become excited or heated* * He ran high when they did not obey his orders * You better take complete rest as your temperature is still running high

Run in: *Go in; arrest and take to a lock up; bring new machinery into good condition by preliminary working; take part in a race* * The sun ran in behind the thick clouds and the breeze became cold * The drunken men were run in for creating a public disturbance * He is still running in his new car and does not exceed 50 miles an hour * There are only five horses running in the first race

Run in the blood: *Be a hereditary character* * The same aristocratic temper is running in the blood of this family

Run into: *Meet by chance; enter an area of bad weather; experience difficulties; reach a particular level; crash into* * Guess who I ran into today? * We ran into thick fog on the way home * Be careful not to run into a debt * His income runs into six figures * The bus went out of control and ran into an electric pole

Run into debt: *Get into debt* * It is easier to run into debt than to get out of it

Run in fine: *Allow very little margin of time, etc.* * I wonder if paucity of time and space may even run in fine for further improvement

Run of the house: *Go anywhere in the house* * He has the run of the house

Run off: *Cause to flow out; to take*

impression of or to print; repeat; to recount; elope with; cause a race to be run * The refugees had to run off from the troubled regions for their safety * He wants to run off 20 copies of this document on the duplicating machine * The opposition have been running off their calls for the resignation of the alleged corrupt minister * The witness began to run off details of the case to the court * She has run off with her bank manager * The 200-metres race is scheduled to be run off tomorrow

Run off with: *Steal and run away* * The treasurer has run off with the club's funds

Run on: *Continue in the same line and not in a new paragraph; talk continuously; elapse; join; be joined together (of written letters of alphabet); sudden demand by a lot of people* * He can run on trifling matters without an end to them * He will run on for an hour if you don't stop him * Time is running on, whether you do something or do nothing * When children are learning to write, they should let the letters run on and not write them separately * When the new currency measures were announced, there was a run on the bank

Run on the pound: *Sudden selling of the pound on foreign exchange* * At occasions, there had been a run on the pound for its sterling value

Run one's face: *Obtain things on credit by sheer impudence* * He has become unpopular for running his face

Run out: *Run short; terminate; expire; leak; a batsman running between the wickets fails to reach his crease before the ball; go out; come to an end; be exhausted; reach an end of (stocks, supplies); abandon* * Our provisions are running out * When does the lease of the house run out? * The validity of my driving licence runs out on 30th of this month * The drum has run out a small amount of water * He was run out before he had scored * The tide is running out * When does the lease of the house run out? * His patience is running out * We are just running out of beer * Her husband has run out on her for adultery

Run out of: *Be short of* * He has run out of money to expand his business

Run over: *To overflow; overthrow;*

go over curiously; knock down and drive over; review; run across * He kept on pouring milk till my tea cup ran over * The democratic regime was run over through a military coup * He ran over his notes before starting his lecture * Two children were run over and killed * Let us run over our part again before the drama starts * I ran over an old friend of mine at a village fair

Run rings around someone: *Do things more efficiently than someone* * That stenographer runs rings around his colleagues in the same trade

Run riot: *Behave in a disorderly way or undisciplined manner or be beyond control* * They let their kids run riot * The three prisoners who ran riot were shot down by the guards

Run risks: *Put oneself to risks* * One must be prepared to run risks to succeed in business

Run short: *Come to the short; lacking; exhausted; not have enough of something* * The enemy's forces are running short of ammunition * He is running short of courage * They have run short of fuel as also necessary ration * As we are rather running short of time, we had better discuss the last item of the agenda in the next meeting

Run somebody ragged: *Make somebody do a lot of work so that they become tired* * The jailor ran the criminal ragged for creating trouble inside the jail

Run someone to earth: *Find someone after a difficult search* * He went off to meet his stranded friend who he had run to earth

Run the gauntlet: *Be expected to unpleasant remark or treatment* * He ran the gauntlet of their criticism * They had to run the gauntlet of many news correspondents

Run the guard: *Get past the guard without detection* * The prisoner ran guard on the gate and made good his escape

Run the risk of doing something: *Do something which may involve risk* * He was ready to run the risk of being taken prisoner by the enemy * They run the risk of being caught

Run through: *Exhaust; transfix; to read or perform quickly; pass quickly; be present; discuss, repeat or read quickly; perform, act or practice; spend money* * Don't give up until you have run through all possibilities * We were all running at the cruel image of the war * The examiner is busy in running through the answer sheets * An angry murmur ran through the crowd * Thoughts of revenge kept running through his mind * A deep melancholy runs through his poetry * He ran through the names on the list * Can we run through Scene III again? * He ran through the entire amount within a brief period of time

Run to/run up to: *Amount to; be of a particular size or amount* * The expenditure on various events of the games runs to millions of dollars every year * The book runs to nearly 300 pages

Run to earth: *Go into its hole* * When the cat chased a rat, it soon managed to run to earth

Run to seed: *Shoot up too rapidly in preparation for seeding instead of producing the vegetative growth desired by the grower; to disappoint the expectation of development; become exhausted; go waste* * If unused, winter radishes run to seed in spring * My all hopes and efforts to become a chess-champion are likely to run to seed * When he was young and sturdy, he had a lot of muscle, but now he is running to seed * Don't let your valuable time run to seed

Run to waste: *Be wasted or lost* * What a pity to see that entire water running to waste!

Run together: *Mingle or blend* * The sound of laughter and singing ran together in the evening air

Run up: *Make or mend hastily; build hurriedly; to spring up; hang; allow to reach a large total* * While on my way to school, I asked the shoemaker to run up my torn shoe * They ran up a hut to live in close to a jungle * If I ever know who did this, I will run him up * How had he managed to run up so many debts?

Run up a score: *Run with a debt* * He had run up a score on account of his prodigal habit

Run up against: *To experience (difficulties)* * The government is running up against considerable opposition to its tax-reforms * He ran up against a solid wall of opposition on the sensitive issue raised by him

Run upon: *Be considered with (of thoughts); strike (of ship)* * His thoughts were running upon the past events of his life * The ship ran upon the rock

Runabout: *A vagabond; a small vehicle or aeroplane* * We should be watchful about the activities of the runabouts * They do make use of a runabout when they are out for a game in the icy tracks of North or South Pole

Runaway: *An animal or a vehicle under the control of the owner; happening very easily or quickly and not be able to control; fugitive; quick or immediate; of a person who left without telling anyone* * It was very difficult to bridle a runaway horse * The driver of the runaway car got confused on how to make it stop without any kind of damage * The runaway success of the player was applauded by one and all * The rebel leader was a runaway from justice * There was a runaway inflation after the war * Some protection measures have to be taken for the runaway children

Run-down: *In weakened health* * In his youth he started to feel run-down and failed to consult a doctor for tuberculosis

Run-in: *An arrangement or fight* * The player has had numerous run-ins with the referee

Runner-up: *Person who comes after the winner in a race* * The runner-up was the recipient of a silver medal in the 100-metre race

Running commentary: *A commentary accompanying a text; a broadcast description of a game or any other event in progress* * My younger son kept up a running commentary for the whole trip * We kept on listening the running commentary of the cricket match

Running fight: *A fight between pursuer and the pursued* * There was a running fight in the street between the two rival parties

Running fire: *Rapid succession of fire* * Our Jawans gave a befitting reply to the running fire of the enemy

Running low: *Becoming scarce* * For want of raw material, the supply of many items are running low

Running title: *The title of a book, continued from page to page on the upper margin* * This particular book has a running title throughout

Run-off: *A race to decide a dead heat; urinate* * It will be a treat to watch the final heat of 200-metre run-off tomorrow * He has gone out to get rid of run-off

Run-on: *In verse, carrying the sense on beyond the end of the line* * He is moved to write a run-on about the brave fighting tactics of Marathas

Rush at: *Make an attack* * The brave soldiers rushed at the enemy with their rifle bayonets when they ran short of ammunition

Rush hours: *Day's time of maximum activity* * During the evening rush hours, the road is often congested with vehicles

Rush into print: *Publish quickly* * He wants to rush his new article on health into print

Rush out: *Produce very quickly* * The editors rushed out an item on the crash for the late news

Rush through: *Deal with official business very quickly* * The members wanted to rush a Bill through Parliament

Russian tea: *Tea with lemon and no milk, usually served in a glass* * Many people like to have Russian tea instead of other kinds of refreshments

Rust away: *Affected by rust and gradually losing strength* * The ploughs were not in use and were rusting away

Rustle up: *Get ready quickly; make or find quickly without planning* * They have been busy rustling up a new business * I am sure I can rustle up a sandwich for you

Rust-proof: *Which will not rust* * Rust-proof metal has a substance or chemical that saves it from rusting

S

Saddle up: *To saddle a horse* * He saddled up and rode off

Safe and sound: *Safely; secure and uninjured* * They turned up safe and sound from the space flight * The doctor found him safe and sound though he met with a nasty accident

Safety valve: *A valve that opens when the pressure becomes too great; any outlet that gives relief* * Residents heard an enormous bang as a safety valve on the boiler failed * Exercise is a good safety valve for the tension that builds up at work

Sail close to the wind: *Keep the boat's head so near to the wind as to fill but not shake the sail; be in danger of transgressing an approved limit* * There was no way out for the sailor but to sail close to the wind * I warned him he was sailing dangerously close to the wind and risked prosecution

Sales-talk: *Boasting talk to effect sale* * The owners of the factory have already had sales-talk for their new product

Sales work: *Work or things (made) for sale; work carelessly done* * All that we see in the exhibition here is meant for sales work * This sales work of yours won't bring you the expected price

Salt down: *Preserve with salt; to lay by; store up* * The dead body of the martyr had to be salted down for three days to enable the people to offer their homage * A prudent person would salt down some money for his old age * I got all the emotion out of me which had been salted down

Salt of sorrel: *Acid potassium carbonate, a solvent for ink-stains* * Salt of sorrel can help you remove the ink-stains

Salt of tarter: *A commercial name for purified potassium carbonate* * A chemist or a physicist must know the value of salt of tarter

Salt of the earth: *The choice of the highest excellence* * They think of themselves as the salt of the earth and quite rightly too

Salt of vitriol: *Sulphate of zinc* * The salt of vitriol is used in preparation of some medicines

Salt of wisdom: *Wisdom gained by experience* * This complicated matter needed salt of wisdom to come to some meaningful conclusion

Salt of wormwood: *Potassium carbonate* * Do you know the person who first discovered the salt of wormwood?

Salt out: *To obtain a precipitate by adding a salt* * Through chemical processes a particular substance can be salted out from a liquid

Saucer eye: *A large round eye* * When I presented her a diamond ring as a surprise gift she stood there to gaze it with her saucer eyes

Save (your) reverence/Saving (your) reverence: *With all due respect to you* * Save your reverence, I wish you a very happy and long life

Save one's face: *Avoid humiliation or appearance of climbing down** He could not save his face from the biting criticism for his misdeeds and had to resign his post

Save you: *A greeting (God save you)* * During his departure on a risky mission, his friends raised their hands saying, 'Save you!'

Say: *For example; suppose* * Let's take any writer, say Kalidas, who wrote many masterpieces in Sanskrit * There is no reason to say that he is a liar

Scale and Platt: *Stairs with straight flights and landings* * The passengers travelling by air make use of Scale and Platt while boarding or alighting from an aeroplane

Score off: *Achieve a success against; get the better of* * He was always trying to score off his teachers in arguments * No one can score off him in an argument * His shyness scored off him

Scot and lot: *An old legal phrase embracing all forms of tax, hence all forms of responsibility, duty, etc.; an old legal tax entitling all the paid to vote in parliamentary elections* * Every citizen is bound to act within the purview of Scot and lot * Those who paid Scot and lot only got the right to vote in the days of yore

Scrape acquaintance with: *Contrive somehow to get on terms of acquaintance* * I managed to scrape acquaintance with some top musicians

Screaming force: *One highly ludicrous* * The prisoner's trial as shown on the play-stage was a screaming force

Seamy side: *The wrong side of a garment; the disreputable, sordid or unpleasant side or aspect of life* * It looked ludicrous to see him clothed in the seamy side of his underwear * We were surprised to know the seamy side of his character

Second childhood: *Mental weakness in extreme old age; the childishness of old age* * One generally becomes forgetful at the stage of second childhood * Second childhood is a time in the life of an adult person when he tends to behave in a childish manner

Second nature: *A deeply ingrained habit* * Diplomacy was second nature to him

Second storey: *The first floor* * They are living in the second storey of that building

Second thoughts: *Reconsideration* * These delicate matters need second thoughts

Second wind: *Power of respiration recovered after breathlessness; recovery of breath in prolonged exertion* * Finding a second wind, he rode away from his pursuers * After running a 1,500 metre-race, she was out of breath and lay down flat on the ground to have a second wind

Second-hand: *Derived from another; not original; already used by previous owner; dealing in a second-hand goods; indirectly; a hand that indicates second-hand* * The news I have got is a second-hand one * I think you should go back to your second-hand plan * He could purchase a second-hand car * Buying a second-hand car can be a risky business * A second-hand shop sells second-hand goods * The second hand of any watch shows the seconds only

Secret service: *A department of government whose operations are not disclosed; espionage* * Maintaining secret service by a government is very essential in the interest of a nation to save it from any evil designs of the enemy * The authorities have arrested several people suspected of doing secret service for their respective countries

Secular arm: *Civil power or authority, opposite to spiritual or ecclesiastical one* * Secular arm has all along been rendering an important role in uniting the people of different castes and creeds

Secular games: *Games held at long intervals* * The modern Olympic Games and other international sports can , in a sense, be called secular games

Secularism: *The belief that the state, morals, education, etc. should be independent of religion* * Our political leaders always profess that they are committed to secularism

See a wolf: *Be tongue-tied (in allusion to an old superstition)* * We saw a wolf when the magician put a dagger into his mouth and passed it down to his belly before pulling it out to the surprise of one and all

See about: *Consider; do whatever is done about; attend to* * I will see about the legal aspect of the case if a suit can be filed against him * My father went to the station to see about my ticket * It will not be possible for me to see about all his demands * I have some urgent piece of work to see about today

See daylight: *Arrive at some comprehension, illumination or prospect of a solution* * The publication of his new novel has yet to see daylight * It was a long time before he finally saw daylight and realised what was going on

See eye to eye: *Think alike* * I do not see eye to eye with my parents on my future career

See eye to eye with: *Agree* * They seem to see eye to eye with each other on various promising aspects of the new plan

See life: *See how other people live especially the disreputable* * It would be a fantastic experience if you go out and see life for yourself * He has certainly seen a bit of life

See off: *A company at one's departure* * I went to the airport to see my friend off * I was seen off at the railway station by many of my friends

See one further: *See one hanged, or the like* * The hangman saw him further but remained unmoved * We could not gather the courage and strength to see those dying further

See out: *Conduct to the door; see to the end; outlast* * My secretary will see you out soon after the business is over * They have enough fuel to see the winter out * People should listen to his music as it will see us all out * He can see out anyone on the dance floor

See over: *Be conducted all through* * We need to see over the house before we can make you an offer

See the light: *Come into the view or being; be converted* * I think he has finally seen the light and is going to retire, while he is still able to enjoy * He was an atheist but now he says he has seen the light * Some of the men wanted to strike but when the leader of the union convinced them that the time was not ripe to do so, they saw the light

See through: *Participate in to the end; back up till difficulties end; understand the hidden nature of* * He is determined to see the job through * His courage and good humour saw him through * I can see through his scheme and he cannot cheat me so easily

See through a millstone: *See for into or through difficult questions* * He was clever enough to see through a millstone during the course of his interview

See to: *Look after; make sure about* * Who is going to see to the house while you are away? * Can you see to it that this important message is conveyed to him before this afternoon?

See what I can do: *Do what I can do* * Rest assured, I will see what I can do for you

See which way the cat jumps: *Watch how things are going to turn before committing oneself* * Let's see which way the cat jumps so that we can take an appropriate step in the matter

See with half an eye: *See without difficulty* * I could see with half an eye his deceitful tactics

Seek after: *Go in quest of* * The police is quite active and will seek after the abducted child

Seek for: *Look for* * We seek for politeness from all our employees * We have been seeking for our missing dog for the last three days

Seek out: *Look for and find; bring out from hidden place* * The detectives had to work hard in seeking out the real culprit * The police raided the house on a tip and now plan to seek out the fugitive prisoner

Sell a pup: *Involve one into a specious bad bargain; swindle* * It is his profession to live on by selling a pup to any credulous person * He made off by selling a pup in the form of a gold-coated iron necklace to an old lady for 1200 rupees

Sell by the candle: *Offer for sale by auction as long as small piece of candle burns; the bid made just before it goes out being successful* * The antique jewellery fetched an enormous amount from the highest bidder through the sell by the candle

Sell one's life dearly: *Injure the enemy before one is killed* * Thousands of brave soldiers sold their lives dearly in the war so that we could live in freedom

Sell out: *Dispose of entirely; seek one's commission* * He sold all his property out and left the country to settle in Canada for good * He is a prospective salesman and would never sell it out

Sell smoke: *To swindle* * They have prospered through tactics of selling smoke only

Sell up: *Sell the goods of, for debts; to sell all* * He advised his friend to sell up a part of his property to get rid of the debts * He sold up all his possessions before leaving the country to settle abroad

Selling-price: *Price at which a thing is sold* * The selling-price of each item has been mentioned on the board placed in front of the counter of this shop

Send about one's business: *Dismiss promptly; send someone away or stop from doing things that do not concern him* * The authorities concerned sent him about his business for his corrupt dealings * The teacher sent the student about his business when he was found listening to private conversation in the staff room

Send down: *Rusticate or expel* * The examinee has been sent down for three years for using unfair means in the examination hall

Send for: *Require by message to come or be brought* * I have sent for the doctor to see my ailing mother * I wil send for your free catalogue today

Send off: *A demonstration at starting or at departing; dispatch* * Many of his friends went to the airport to send him off * See that these parcels are sent off at once

Send one away with flea in one's ear: *Tell one some home truths* * I had to send him away with a flea in his ear for his lame excuses

Send one packing: *Dismiss summarily since the time he betrayed me* * I always send him packing whenever he comes to extend his hand of friendship towards me * If he comes here again asking for money, send him packing * The incompetent typist was sent packing

Send to Coventry: *Exclude from social intercourse* * He being a wolf in sheep's clothing has been condemned to be sent to Coventry

Send to the right about: *Dismiss summarily or force to retreat* * Instead of hearing his plea, the boss not only warned him but sent him to the right about

Send word: *Send an intimation* * He sent word that he would not be able to dine with us

Senior service: *The navy* * This young man prefers joining senior services to land forces

Sensation novel: *One dealing in violent effects and strained emotion* * Reading of a sensation novel turned him into a notorious bandit

Sensible horizon: *The visible horizon* * I see no sensible horizon to solve this knotty riddle

Sensible note: *Leading note* * The sensible note of his preaching was to live and let others live

Sensitive flame: *A flame that rises or falls in response to sound* * He is a man of sensitive flame, so you will have to be careful while dealing with him

Separate maintenance: *A provision made by a husband for his wife* * After being deserted by her husband, she is living on a separate maintenance

Serve a writ on: *Deliver a summon to* * The appellate court has ordered to serve a writ on the dependant

Serve one a trick: *Play a trick on one* * The magician served him a trick by surprising the latter for depriving him of his purse

Serve one right: *Be no worse than one deserves* * It serves him right for being so stubborn

Serve one's time: *Pass through an apprenticeship* * He served his time of two years in learning the trade of carpentry

Serve out: *To deal or distribute; punish; retaliate on* * The cook himself served out the meal to the special guests * Those responsible for this crime will be severely served out * The boy hit his sister, who served him out by kicking on his shin

Serve the turn/Serve one's turn: *Answer one the purpose; to do well enough* * If you lend me your motorcycle it will serve my turn and come back in time * This pesticide will serve us the turn in getting rid of harmful insects

Serve time: *Undergo a term of imprisonment* * These days he is serving time in jail for having picked the pocket of a passenger

Serve up: *To bring to table; give or offer* * He served up a delicious meal * He served up the usual excuse

Set about: *To begin take in hand; attack; spread, as a rumour* * We need to set about finding a solution * The servant set about the business of cleaning the house * Most dogs will not set about unless provoked * The guerrillas usually set about at night * He was set about to be involved in a crime

Set against: *Assail* * The case has set a neighbour against neighbour in the village * A small provocative remark set the two friends against each other for a long time

Set a going: *Put in motion* * They set the machinery at a going

Set apart: *Put aside; ignore or forgive; make different from* * They decided to set apart some money every month as a contribution for opening a school in the village * Let's set apart our differences and do something meaningful * His elegant and clear writing sets him apart from other journalists

Set aside: *Put away; to reject; annul; lay by* * The government has set aside a handsome money for opening new schools in rural areas * The appellate court has set aside the decision of the lower court for fresh hearing * The proposal put up for consideration of the committee has been set aside on practical grounds * It would be prudent to set aside some money for old age

Set at defiance: *Challenge* * If you set the country law at defiance, you will get into trouble

Set at naught: *Treat as if no account; despise; disregard; flout* * Had he not set at naught my advice, he would not have suffered at all * How I set at naught myself for my cowardice! * He set at naught the orders of his boss and the result was his instant dismissal *

Those who set at naught the traffic laws are prone to fall victims to accidents

Set by: *Lay up; put aside; to value; to care* * A thousand pieces of data are set by in a computer's memory * We have set by sufficient fuel for the winter * The property has been set by at over a million rupees * She did not set by the fact that he has been married two times before

Set by the ears: *Set at strife* * He set the two fast friends by the ears and kept laughing in his sleeves whenever some quarrel arose between them

Set down: *Lay on the ground; put in writing; appoint a time for; to judge; esteem; to pitch; attribute charges; lay down authority* * He set down his heavy bag for a breather * They were asked to set down a summary of their views * He has set down an hour for a walk every morning * He deserves to be set down for his simplicity and straightforwardness * I tried to be friendly but he set me down completely * A regiment has been set down near the border * The judge refused to set down the blame without further information * You cannot set down hard and fast rules to be observed in every aspect of life

Set eye on: *See or catch sight of* * I would never like to set my eye on that rascal

Set fair: *Steadily fair* * He seems set fair to win the championship

Set fire to: *Ignite* * He set fire to a haystack of his neighbour due to an old feud

Set forth: *Exhibit or display; expound or declare; praise or recommend; punish; start on a journey; explain views or facts in a clear way* * They will be setting forth new designs at the trade fair this spring * The president set forth his views in a television interview * The new restaurant is set forth to the sight of the visitors * Those responsible for this crime will be severally set forth * They are now ready to set forth on their epic journey to pilgrimage centres * The teacher set forth the basis of his approach to the teaching staff

Set free: *Release; put at liberty* * During the course of rescue operations many prisoners were set free from wreckages of the old buildings caused by a minor earthquake * The magistrate set the captive free for lack of sound evidence

Set hand to: *Set to work on* * Scientists have now set their hands to finding out the possibility of life on Mars

Set in: *Begin; become prevalent; run landwards* * Rain seemed to have set in for the day * After the Second World War, a peaceful atmosphere has set in throughout the peace-loving countries * Due to some technical snags in the ship, the sailors had to set it in

Set in hand: *Undertake; set someone about doing* * University professors both teach and set in hand research * The research scholar has been asked to set in hand a new project

Set in order: *Adjust* * The mechanic was able to set my radio in order

Set little by: *Regard or esteem little* * That quack is set little by the people

Set much by: *Regard or esteem much* * The new surgeon is set much by the people for his great skill in surgery

Set off: *Mark off; lay off; start off; send off; to show in relief or to advantage; counterbalance; balance or compensate for; start* * The playing area was set off with a white line * Read this book through and set off such points as could be helpful in the forthcoming examination * My mother set me off on the piano when I was five * I am setting the files off to my boss * This gold frame sets off the painting very well * He knows how to set off gains against losses * He has to set off his small salary by living economically * They have set off on a journey round the world

Set on: *Move on; incite to attack; instigate; bend upon* * Can we set on to the next item of the agenda? * The farmer threatened to set his dog on us * The government has set on a programme of economic reforms * He is set on mastering the English language

Set on edge: *Excite* * Agitators were setting the people on edge to rebel against their rulers

Set on fire: *Ignite* * The bomb blast set on fire many of the houses * A young man has been accused of setting the house on fire

Set on foot: *To originate; set a going; start* * The scientist has set on foot a new theory on prolongation of human life * His sharp aggressive tone set on foot the events that led to his downfall * The heated discussion set on foot an ugly situation in the form of a brawl among them

Set one's cap at: *Try to attract a suitor* * He has set his cap at that beautiful young girl

Set one's face against: *Oppose strenuously* * They set their faces against the amendment of some basic fundamental articles of the Constitution which guarantee freedom of speech

Set one's hand to: *Engage in; wider take; to sign* * He has set his hand to trade in drugs * The agency concerned has announced that it will set its hand to investigate into the accident * He has set his hand to the written agreement dealing with the execution of the intended project

Set one's mind on: *Fix a settled desire upon* * I have set my mind on becoming a lawyer

Set one's seal to: *Give one's authority or assent to* * Her election to the premiership will set her seal to a remarkable political career

Set one's teeth: *Clench the teeth as in a strong resolution* * He seems to have set his teeth to teach a lesson to his opponent

Set one's teeth on edge: *Irritate; to cause a strange grating feeling in teeth; to make eager or stimulate desire* * That vulgar noise is really setting my teeth on edge * His unseemly murmurs sets my teeth on edge * Erotic images often set young man's teeth on edge

Set oneself: *Bend one's energies* * He set himself as if he was determined to defeat his opponent in a wrestling bout * I have to plan my academic work rather carefully and set myself clear objectives

Set oneself against: *Oppose* * I never feel bitterness towards those who set themselves against me

Set out: *To mark off; equip and send forth; to start or go forth; begin with an intention; adore; expound* * He used a rope to set out the circle * A party has already been set out on an exploration mission * They have set out on a global journey (odyssey) via sea routes * He reached his goal that he has set out for himself * I deeply set out my teachers and guides who enabled me to attain the present distinguished position * He is well known for setting out his views on diplomatic matters

Set speech: *A studied oration* * The set speech that he made in the seminar was applauded by all the participants

Set spur to: *Apply the spurs and ride off quickly* * In the olden days, the cavalry would set spur to their horses from one quarter to another

Set store by: *To value greatly; attach importance* * He sets store by his wisdom * Many of us set store by high moral character

Set terms: *Deliberately picked, usually outspoken language* * They have agreed to do the work on set terms

Set the heart at rest: *Render easy in mind* * We cannot set our hearts at rest so long as we are unable to make our both ends meet

Set the heart upon: *To come to desire earnestly* * He has set his heart upon pursuing higher studies abroad

Set the heather on fire: *Create a disturbance or a sensation* * A slight tremor set the heather on fire throughout the neighbouring villages

Set to: *Affix; apply oneself; to set as a bone* * The labels should be firmly set to all the parcels to be dispatched tomorrow * I am set to finish the job in hand within a week * Doctors have decided to set to my broken arm

Set to work: *To employ in, or engage energetically in a piece of work* * The carpenter has set to work to pepare wooden furniture

Set up: *To erect; put up; arrange; begin; enable to begin; begin a career; place in view; put in type; make pretensions; arrange matters so as to implicate, incriminate, embarrass or make fool of; establish* * The soldiers have set up barricades to protect themselves against the agitators * Posters advertising the release of a new film have been set up all over the town * The government has agreed to set up a public enquiry * He has set up a new independent business. * With the increasing trade, the company has set up more branches of business dealings in various parts of the country * After he left college, his father set him up in the family business * They have set up various articles of domestic use in an open stall * The compositor has set up the whole matter for final printing * The Australian cricket team was set up to win the World Cup but had to eat humble pie in the final match * They are clever enough to set up a snare to humiliate anybody who oppose them * It is expected from our budding athletes that they would set up new records in the Olympic Games

Set up one's bristle: *Show resistance* * The citizens have every right to set up their bristles against unjust laws

Set up one's rest: *Make one's find stake; take a resolution; take up abode* * He set up his rest to win the race but all in vain * The gambler set up his rest to stake all that he had in anticipation of getting back the lost money * In the long run, he was left with no option but to set up his rest all alone

Set upon: *Set on* * The security guards set their dogs upon the intruders * He was set upon by a vicious dog

Set you up: *Set up deceived* * They claimed that they were not selling drugs but that they had been set up by the police

Set-back: *A check; reverse or relapse* * He has suffered a serious set-back in his political career * His malaria has again set back though he was treated properly

Set-down: *An unexpected rebuff; a snub; a rating* * He felt humiliated to have received a set-down from his boss in the presence of the staff * His comments were clearly intended as a set-down * New public opinion polls show the president's approval set-down at its lowest point since he took office

Set-out: *An outfit; preparations; a display of dishes, etc.; company or clique* * The army personnel wear a particular set-out that distinguishes them from the civilians * To achieve any successful progress one has to undergo a great deal of set-out * People were astonished to see a set-out of plenty of delicious dishes arranged for the guests at a marriage party * A set-out of people may be working together for common good

Settle in: *Prepare to remain indoor for the night; move into a new house, flat, etc. and adapt to live in a new environment* * As a result of our late arrival, we managed to settle in an inn for the night * If I get that job in the rural school, I would find no difficulty in getting myself settled in there with my family

Set-to: *A bout; a fight or argument; a hot contest* * A heavy weight set-to is likely to take place some time next week * It is not easy to guess who will be the winner in the set-to between the adversaries * Preparations are afoot to organise a set-to for participants at the open stadium

Seven principal virtues: *Faith, hope, charity, justice, prudence, temperance, fortitude; the first three the theological, the last four the moral virtues* * There may or may not be a rare person endowed with seven principal virtues

Seven Works of Spiritual Mercy: *Convert sinners; instruct the ignorant; council the doubtful; console the afflicted; bear wrongs patiently; forgive injuries and pray for the living and the dead* * A person certainly deserves to be adored if he/she has the attributes of the Seven Works of Spiritual Mercy

Seventh heaven: *A state of great delight* * Since they got married, they have been in seventh heaven

Sew up: *Enclose or close up by sewing; complete satisfactorily; tire out; bring to a standstill; nonplus, make drunk* * The tailor has sewn up the torn coat * The election campaign has been sewn up progressively * We got sewn up after having covered a long journey * Continued attacks by the terrorists has sewn up normal life * I was completely sewn up by his rebuff to my suggestion * Having had too much alcohol, he got sewn up and kept staggering

Shack away: *Ease off freely* * How could he shack away under the strict vigilance of his master?

Shake (off) the dust (of) from one's feet: *To renounce all intercourse* * He, being deserted by his near and dear ones, has shaken the dust from his feet in order to keep aloof of any social contacts

Shake down: *Cheat of one's money at one stroke; extort money by threats or blackmail; search thoroughly; to frisk (a person); go to bed; get into harmony, become adjusted to a new environment or new conditions, etc.;* * The bandits shook him down at the point of pistol and made good their escape * The magistrate ordered the dismantling of police check-posts on the highway used to shake down motorists for bribes * We can't shake down the whole building except for the suspect's apartment * We were all shaken down at the airport by the searching personnel before we were allowed to go out * You can shake down at my place for tonight * The new teaching staff is shaking down here nicely

Shake hands: *Salute by grasping the hand moving it up and down* * He nodded greetings to my sister and shook hands with me when we met by chance at the dinner party

Shake the head: *Turn the head from side to side in token of reluctance, disapproval, etc.* * She shook her head in disbelief

Shake up: *To rouse; mix; disturb; loosen by shaking* * He was still in sleep so I had to shake him up * You will have to shake up the sugar in your cup of tea * What could possibly shake up such tranquillity? * You can get rid of this trap by shaking up the two ends of the string

Shame-proof: *Insensible to shame* * He is a shame-proof jailbird

Shape one's course: *Direct one's way* * Like it or not, our families shape our course of life and make us what we are

Share and share alike: *In equal share* * The two friends are running a new business on the basis of share and share alike investments

Share bone: *The pubis* * Share bone is a protective frame of one's kidney

Shark's manners: *Rapacity* * The shark's manners of landowners seeking greater profit are on the increase day by day

Sharp practices: *Knavish ways, verging on dishonesty* * The building industry brought in rules to protect the customers from sharp practices

Sharp-cut: *Well-defined; clear-cut* * In our Constitution, there are sharp-cut articles that guarantee the civil liberties of the citizens * There is no sharp-cut reply to the knotty question

Sharper: *A cheat* *A sharper would be disqualified from candidature

Sharp-eyed: *Good at noticing or observing things* * A sharp-eyed shopkeeper at once spotted the fake currency

Sharp-looking: *Hungry-looking* * His sharp-looking features rang the bell of alarm in the ear of the landlord

Sharp-nosed: *Having a pointed nose; keen of scent* * She looks pretty beautiful with her sharp-nosed face * We do utilise the service of sharp-nosed dogs in tracing the culprits

Sharp-set: *Hungry; keen in appetite for anything* * Both the parties are sharp-set for power * Generally, all people have a sharp-set desire for all round development in life

Sharp-sighted: *Having acute sight; shrewd* * A hawk, being a sharp-sighted bird, can locate its prey while hovering in the air * He is a sharp-sighted politician who avoids offending the electorate unnecessarily

Sharp-visage: *Thin faced* * That sharp-visage girl regaled the audience with her melodious songs

Sheath the sword: *End war* * The two warring countries had ultimately to sheathe the sword and agree to a compromise

Shed crocodile tears: *Show false grief* * The sight of his shedding crocodile tears made me sick

Sheep-scoring: *The counting of sheep* * The shepherd completed his sheep-scoring in the sheep-shed at the fall of the evening to ensure that none of them were missing

Sheer off: *Move aside; take oneself odd* * I thought the boats were going to collide, but one sheered off at the last moment * When he saw me, he took himself off in the other direction

Shell out: *Pay up; disburse* * Eventually they shelled out, but only after receiving several reminders * The authority concerned has been ordered to shell out aid even in the form of money to the victims of the earthquake

Shield of brawn: *The thick skin of a pig's side especially when stuffed with meat* * He is rearing many pigs having shield of brawn to be sold to the butcher at high prices

Shield-hand: *The left hand* * He, habitually, uses his shield-hand while writing anything

Shift about: *Vacillate; turn quite round to the opposite point* * We cannot shift about on the question of the party's leadership * The swing of the voters is still shifting about the side of his political adversary

Shift for oneself: *Depend on one's own resources* * He was left with no other alternative but to shift for himself in his life's struggle

Shiver on the brink: *Hesitate to plunge* * He shivered on the brink before he dived into the icy water of the river

Shoot the works: *At games of chance, to risk one's all on one play, hence to make one's maximum effort* * After having lost a large sum of money in gambling, he was blindly ready to shoot the works but his friend forced him not to do so

Short cut: *A shorter way than the usual one* * To save time, you can take a short cut across the field to reach there

Short measure: *Less than the due and professed amount* * He was willing to give short measure in this bargain

Short of: *Less than; without going as far as; insufficient supply of* * I will not sell my watch short of 5,000 rupees * Short of a miracle, we are certain to lose * Short of asking her to leave, there is not a lot we can do about the situation * We are short of provision to feed the platoon for a week or so

Short-clog: *One who is good for nothing but paying the bill* * Even a short-clog is a part and parcel of society

Shorten sail: *To reduce its extent* * They planned to undertake a voyage to Australia but due to some emergency they had to shorten sail to an Indian port only

Short-sighted: *Having clear sight only of near objects; lacking foresight* * Testing showed him to be very short-sighted * The short-sighted policy of the government in not boosting technological research

Short-spoken: *Curt in speech* * People avoid conversing with him for his being a short-spoken fellow

Short-tempered: *Easily put into a rage* * I am a bit short-tempered sometimes

Short-winded: *Soon becoming breathless* * A person suffering from heart trouble gets short-winded even after a little exertion

Shot-free/Scot-free: *Safe from shot* * In the absence of evidence, the magistrate let the accused off shot-free

Shoulder-high: *As high as the shoulder* * We managed to succeed in wading across the shoulder-high water stream

Show (one's) face: *Appear* * Don't show me your face if you fail to mend yourself * How dare you show your face in here after saying all those dreadful things?

Show a clean pair of heels: *Escape by running or run off* * The thief showed a clean pair of heels when pursued by the police

Show a leg: *Make an appearance; get up* * The proclaimed offender at last showed a leg before the trial court * At sun-rise, I am rather particular to show a leg to carry on with my daily routine

Show cause: *Argue against the confirmation of a provisional order of judgment* * He has been served with a show cause notice for contempt of court * He has been asked to show cause why he should not be expelled from the party membership

Show fight: *Show a readiness to resist* * He was keen to show fight about the charges levelled against him

Show forth: *Manifest; proclaim* * He showed forth a pleasing personality on stage * He confidently showed forth that he is offering the best value in the market

Show of hands: *A vote by holding hands up; a vote indicated by raising hands* * The resolution was passed by a show of hands by the members of the academic council

Show off: *Display ostentatiously* * He only bought this sports car to show off and prove that he can afford one * Our new professor cannot teach well though he tries to show off his knowledge

Show one the door: *Turn out of the house; expel* * When I told my bank manager that I wanted to borrow some money, he showed me the door * Would they forget and forgive or show him the door? * Those who indulged in unfair means in the examination hall were shown the door by the invigilator

Show one's cards: *Expose one's secrets or designs* * He showed his cards to one of his friends on how he became rich by cheating others

Show one's colours: *Show one's party or character* * The company he keeps clearly shows his colours

Show one's hand: *Expose one's purpose* * Some day he will show his hand as to why he became a notorious criminal

Show one's head: *Allow oneself to be seen* * The queen

showed her head in an open car to the people standing alongside the road

Show one's teeth: *Show anger* * When I challenged him to a bout, he accepted it with a show of his teeth

Show the white feather: *Show the signs of cowardice* * Brave men do not show the white feather in danger

Showmanship: *Skilful display* * The showmanship by the magician was really a wonderful treat for the lookers on

Show up: *To expose; be conspicuous or easily visible; be present; appear to advantage or disadvantage; show clearly by contrast; embarrass or put to shame; arrive; appear; to lodge; hand in* * I wish you would not show me up before my parents for the blunder I have made * Her wrinkles showed up in the strong sunlight * Only three of the people we invited to the party did not show up * The dark clouds show up the imminence of a heavy downpour * The amount spent on defence shows up to that spent on housing and health * The speech was deliberately designed to show up the prime minister * By the time I showed up on the scene, it was all over * He shows up as a perfect gentleman * He shows up to be in his late thirties * They have shown up the compensation against the factory * He has four weeks in which to show up an appeal * My advice to anyone who finds anything on a bus is to show it up to the police

Shut down: *Stop working* * The company plans to shut down four factories and cut 10,000 jobs

Shut in: *Enclose; confine; settle down* * The park that shuts in the monument has recently been enlarged * The hostages had been shut in for so long that they could not cope with the outside world * Eventually I would like to shut in and have a family, but not yet

Shut off: *Exclude; switch off* * The academy shut off women from its classes * He shut off the coffee machine

Shut out: *Prevent from entering* * Don't forget to shut out the cat when you leave for work

Shut up: *Close finally or completely; confine; cease speaking; reduce to silence* * Having suffered a great loss in the business, he had to shut it up * By the time we got there all the market traders were shutting up their shops * It was a time of yore when women were shut up within the four walls * I wish you would shut up for a moment and listen to what the rest of us have to say * The cinema fans in the hall were shut up when the film started on the screen

Sick and tired of: *Wearied to the point of disgust* * I am sick and tired of hearing all these people moaning

Sicken for: *Show early symptoms of* * It seems that he is sickening for a bout of flu

Sick-thought Ted: *Lovesick* * He was moping around like a sick-thought Ted teenager

Sick-tired: *Be sick to vomit* * After taking his meals, he is feeling sick-tired

Side by side: *Close together; abreast* * All the members of the family sat side by side on the sofa to watch television * The motorcyclist came side by side of her car and abused her

Sigh of relief: *Relaxation* * He heaved a sigh of relief after having climbed a steep hill

Sight for sore eyes: *A most welcome sight* * The lush green valley was really a sight for sore eyes

Sight seeing: *Going around to see objects of interest* * We had plenty of time to go sightseeing in and around Delhi

Sight worthy: *Worth looking at* * We had chalked out a programme to visit sight-worthy places in Kashmir

Sign away: *Transfer by signing* * Under the treaty, both sides will sign away a third of their nuclear weapons

Sign in: *Sign one's name on coming in* * Every visitor staying in a hotel is required to sign in at the reception counter and wear a visitor's badge

Sign on: *Engage* * We are signing on the services of a professional administrator

Sign out: *Sign one's name on going out* * Don't forget to sign out before you leave the hotel * You have to sign books out when you borrow them from the library

Significant figures or significant digits: *The figures 1 to 9, or ciphers occurring medially* * The following numbers are expressed to three significant figures: 3.15, 0.0127, 1.01

Silver- tongued: *Plausible; eloquent* * He is a famous silver-tongued lawyer in the city * Her silver-tongued speech won the hearts of one and all

Sing another song/Sing another time: *To change to a humbler tone; express an opinion different from someone else or one's own earlier one; to change one's mind* * It is hard to believe a politician as he tends to sing another song to please his voters from time to time * He is now singing another tune to harass his opponent on one ground or other

Sing out: *Call out distinctly; shout; assume a humble tone* * A voice suddenly sang out above the rest * I sang out for help but nobody came * I had to sing small before my boss to relieve me of my night duty

Singed cat: *One who is burned slightly without bursting into flames* * A singed cat could not help but moan and groan out of pain

Single file/Indian file: *One behind other* * It became easy to distribute sweetmeats to all the school boys who stood in a single file

Single-eyed: *One-eyed; devoted; unselfish* * A single-eyed person should make for a good marksman * I have personally been single-eyed to this cause for many years * He started to earn the reputation of a single-eyed boy with a heart of gold

Single-foot: *A brisk walking with each foot striking the ground separately, a rack or amble* * A single-foot walk in the morning is one of the best physical exercises

Single-handed: *By oneself; unassisted; with or for one hand* * He was successful in completing that arduous job single-handedly * How could you manage to do this all single-handed? * Having lost his left hand in an accident, he is doing everything single-handed

Single-hearted: *Sincere; without duplicity* * We are all the praise for his being so single-hearted

Single-minded: *Ingenuous; bent upon one sole purpose* * He had a single-minded desire to win the race * He has a single-minded approach for becoming a promising lawyer

Singly: *One by one; alone* * The wooden bridge over the rivulet was so narrow that we had to go across singly * I am afraid of going out singly at night

Sink into oblivion: *Become forgotten* * These toys will be around for a year or two before sinking into oblivion

Sinking fund: *A fund formed by setting aside income to accumulate at interest to pay off debt* * The company wisely created a sinking fund to clear off its debts in the future

Sin-offering: *A sacrifice in expiation of sin* * He gave a large sum of money in charity as sin-offering for having done sinful acts in his youth

Sisters of mercy: *Member of a female religious communities who tend the sick* * The role played by sisters of mercy was really laudable

Sit at: *To live at the rate of expense of* * The skilled workers won't accept less than 200 rupees each per day to sit at the workplace

Sit back: *Take no active part, or no further active part* * He is not the kind of person who can sit back and let others do all the work

Sit by: *Look on without taking any action* * We cannot sit by and watch the tragedy take place

Sit down: *Take a seat; pause; rest; take up position prior to beginning a siege; accept meekly* * Please sit down and have a cup of tea * He sat down for a while before continuing his climb up the steep hill * He loves to sit down with his chin in his hands * The soldiers managed to sit down in the vicinity of the town to ensure further action * We cannot sit down with the type of threat issued to us unless our genuine demands are met

Sit in judgement: *Criticise* * How dare you sit in judgement on me?

Sit on the fence: *Not to take sides; be neutral* * He is not afraid of making decisions and is a man who never sits on the fence * He tends to sit on the fence at meetings

Sit on the splice (cricket): *Play a defensive game* * In order to avoid defeat in the second innings, the players kept sitting on the splice

Sit on/upon: *Hold an official enquiry regarding; repress; check or delay dealing with* * The government has decided to sit on/upon the stamp paper scam * The police is determined to sit on the bad elements and maintain law and order * They have still been sitting on my application

Sit tight: *Maintain one's seat; keep one's position quietly and unobtrusively* * We sat tight and waited to be rescued * Shareholders are advised to sit tight until the crises pass

Sit under: *Be in the habit of hearing the preaching of* * Those who sit on the priest or minister in a church regularly benefit spiritually

Sit up: *Rise from a recumbent to a sitting position or from a relaxed to an erect seat; become alert or startled; remain up instead of going to bed; keep watch during the night* * Let me sit you up in the bed, so you will be more comfortable * The telephone ring at the dead of night sat me up from my sound sleep * I shall be late getting back, so please don't sit up for me * Our dog sits up attentively to see that nothing goes wrong at night

Sit out: *Sit apart without participating; sit to the end of; outstay* * I am feeling tired, so I think I will sit it out the next dance * The company is willing to sit out the strike of its employees and not yield to their demands * As a guest I did not like to sit out to the discomfort of my host

Sitting pretty: *In an advantageous position* * They bought their house while the prices were low, so now they are sitting pretty

Skeleton in the house/Skeleton in the closet/Skeleton in the cupboard: *A hidden domestic sorrow or shame* * A family having any skeleton in the cupboard will never reveal it to any outsider

Skeleton key: *A key for picking locks, without the inner bits* * A skeleton key also called as master key can open several doors or locking systems

Skin-tight: *Fitting close to the skin* * We prefer putting on skin-tight dresses in winter

Skin-wool: *Wool from a dead sheep* * Skin-wool can be as good as wool obtained from an alive sheep for making woollen garments

Skipper's daughters: *White-topped waves* * The skipper's daughters followed the ship like a cavalcade of white horses

Slack away: *To ease off freely* * It is a common trend with our hockey team to slacken away in the last minutes of the game

Slack in stays: *Slow in going about (of a ship)* * The ship is slacking in stays because of bad weather

Slack off: *Ease off* * We waited until the traffic had slacked off * Don't slack off in your studies

Slack up: *Ease off; to slow* * The tense situation has since slacked up * Slack up before you reach the crossroads

Slap-up: *Superlatively fine* * It was really a slap-up feast that we had on his birthday party

Sleep in: *To oversleep* * I kept working very late at night resulting in sleeping in late

Sleep like a top: *Sleep very soundly* * The fatigue made me sleep like a top throughout the night

Sleeping partner: *A partner who does not take active interest* * He has invested money in the business as a sleeping partner

Sleepy-head: *A lazy person* * We can't expect any progress out of a sleepy-head

Slight off: *Put off; set aside with contempt* * The meeting had to be slighted off for lack of quorum * The appellate court has slighted off conviction of the arrested on framed charges

Slight over: *Ignore* * If you slight over my advice, you may meet with some disappointment

Sling ink: *Write for the press* * The correspondent is slinging ink on the events of the day

Slip of the pen: *A light mistake made unintentionally by a writer* * By a slip of the pen he wrote that Keats was a great novelist

Slip of tongue: *A slight mistake made unknowingly by a speaker* * By a slip of the tongue, Ramesh said that Bernard Shaw was a great poet

Slip on: *Put on loosely or in haste* * He slipped on his torn coat and made for the wedding party

Slip one's ways: *Make one's way quickly* * He slipped his ways fearing fall of night

Slip-up: *An error or failure* * There seems to be some slip-up somewhere in his performance

Slow-footed: *Slow of pace* * A slow-footed person would take at least 10 hours to cover a long distance of 30 miles * He has always been a slow-footed walker

Slowcoach: *A laggard; a sluggish person* * A slowcoach cannot finish a small job even in one whole day * I can't afford employing that slowcoach in any field work.

Slow-gaited: *Accustomed to walk slowly* * If I accompany that slow-gaited man, I will certainly be too late to reach my office in time

Slug-a-bed/slugabed: *One who*

lies long abed * Go and wake up that slug-a-bed for breakfast

Small and small: *Little by little* * The thick layer of the snow turned small and small into water till it disappeared completely

Small capitals or small caps: *Capital letter of the height of lower case* * The letter I received from my friend was addressed to me in small capitals

Small change: *Small coin* * If you stand in need of small change, you can have it from the bank in exchange of your five-rupee note

Small fry: *Small things collectively; person or thing of little importance* * The packet containing gifts that I presented seemed like a small fry to him * He is a haughty person and looks upon me as a small fry * A small fry has no voice in the society

Small hours: *Hours immediately after midnight* * The robbers looted the landlord during the small hours

Small potatoes: *Anything of no great worth* * People who suffered as a result of the earthquake had to be content with small potatoes

Small-time: *Unimportant; insignificant* * He has been given a role of a small-time actor for the time being * Before the development of Chandigarh into a beautiful city, it was a cluster of small-time villages

Small-tooth comb: *A comb with a row of teeth on both sides; an arrangement for minute investigation* * The use of small-tooth comb may help brushing out lice from thick hair * They had to apply a small-tooth comb to unearth true facts of the case

Smash up: *A serious smash or accident* * The windscreen of my car was smashed up when the truck hit it in a head on collision

Smell a rat: *To have a suspicion of something afoot* * I am smelling a rat in his proposal, hence better watch out before accepting

Smell at: *Sniff at; take smell at* * I never smelled at it suspiciously * We stopped there for a while to smell at the scented pine woods

Smell of: *Have the smell of; to savour of* * I don't like the smell of onion * His recent comments smell of hypocrisy

Smell of the lamp: *Show signs of great elaboration or study* * His vast knowledge of the particular subject smells of the lamp

Smell out: *Find out by sniffing* * At Customs, dogs are used to smell out narcotics in passengers' luggage

Smell-trap: *Drain-trap* * Shut the smell-trap to avoid the foul smell

Smile at: *Show amusement at; disregard of* * Everybody smiled at his foolish behaviour

Smile on: *Show favour to; be propitious to* * Luck generally smiles on those who are hardworking and honest * The stars are smiling on him by bringing in good returns in the form of dividends on several shares owned by him

Smokescreen: *A cloud of smoke raised to conceal movement* * The dense fog created a smokescreen and brought the traffic to a halt

Smoke-room story: *Story unsuitable for telling elsewhere* * The disturbing happening that took place in the family last night is a smoke-room story

Smooth spoken/Smooth tongued: *Conciliatory; plausible; flattering; soft in speech* * The dispute was settled through a smooth-spoken approach within the party * She is a smooth-spoken lawyer * Through his smooth-spoken remarks he has earned a good reputation and status in the office * A smooth-spoken person can never irritate his listeners

Smooth-faced: *Having a smooth face or surface; pleasant-looking* * After having trudged through rough and hilly tracks, we at last entered a smooth-faced plain * Our hungry eyes feasted on the smooth-faced scenes in the valley

Smoothing plane: *A small fine plane used for finishing* * A smoothing plane was introduced by the Air Force at the end of the air show

Smooth-paced: *Having a regular easy pace* * It won't take us more than an hour to reach there even if our movement is smooth-paced

Snake in the grass: *One who injures furtively; a lurking danger* * Beware of robbers as they are snakes in the grass * Our commandos are vigilant enough to confront a snake in the grass

Snap one's fingers at: *Treat with contempt* * They always snap their fingers at those who oppose them

Snap one's nose off/Snap one's head off: *Speak snappily or answer in an irritated and rude manner* * I dislike him for snapping his nose off even on small matters or over trifles

Snapshot: *A hasty shot; instantaneous photograph* * Mediapersons took snapshots of the scenes at the war front * You will have to pay some more charges to the photographer for getting a snapshot

Snatch-purse/Snatch thief: *A thief who snatches* * An old lady was deprived of her purse by a snatch-purse riding a motorcycle

Snip-snap: *The action or sound of scissors; quick, snappy dialogue* * The haircutter set my hair right after some snip-snap * He amused us with his snip-snap soon after he appeared on the stage

Snowed up: *Blocked or isolated by snow* * The road leading to Rohtang Pass is snowed up for most part of the winter

So and so: *This or that person or thing; such-and-such person or thing* * I can't remember so and so as there was such a crowd at the meeting

So as: *In such a manner as or that; in order; if only; on condition that* * Treat them so as to become your true friends * Work hard so as to pass the exam creditably * His candidature will be accepted so as to make him get through the interview

So as to: *With the purpose or consequences* * We went early so as to get good seats in the front row * Keep the fruits and vegetables in the fridge so as to keep them fresh

So far: *To that extent or degree or point or such an extent; a degree; a point* * Now that we have come so far we may as well go all the way * Everything is in order so far * They are proud of their achievements so far

So help me [God]: *A form of solemn oath* * I swear to be honest and truthful, so help me God to stick to my words

So long as: *Provided only that* * You may borrow the book so long as you keep it clean

So many: *Such and such a number of* * He is involved in so many cases of crime that they warrant serious investigations

So mote I thee – *So may it be; the assent of God to the aspiration of man* * The church resounded with the sound of so mote I thee at the end of the pastor's sermon

So much: *Such-and-such an amount; in such a degree; to*

such an amount; that amount of; an equal amount * He has so much of money to last for his life * He is so much in debt that he can hardly repay * How could you afford to meet so much burden all alone? * So much help would enable you to stand on your own feet * He contributed so much as his friend did for this noble cause

So much as: *As much as; even* * Eat only so much as one can digest easily * He did so much work as was necessary * He does not sleep so much as four hours a night * So much as a B.A. pass could not handle the office work to meet our expectations

So much for: *That disposes of; that is the end of; no more of* * So much for the present business but now take up the next item of (on) the agenda to deal with * So much for the story and I will tell you another one when we meet here again.* I have so much of contribution to offer to this cause

So that: *With the purpose that; with the result that; if only* * We have invited them also so that we could exchange our views on the matter for our common interest * We have so arranged matters that one of us is always on duty * I shall be there so that you are happy

So then: *Thus; then it is; therefore* * They plan to reduce the staff and so then to cut costs * Since you had signed the bond, so then it is your responsibility * They could not afford sufficient funding, so then they had to abandon the scheme

So to speak: *As one might put it; as it were; if one may use that expression* * If there is any unavoidable difficulty, so to speak, we have other options also * The trouble, so to speak, could not be brought under control * The expression 'cry over spilt milk', so to speak, makes us understand that one is bemoaning an irreparable loss

So-and-so: *This or that person or thing; such-or-such a person or thing** So-and-so person will stand by you in case you are questioned by the police * So-and-so book will help you increase your general knowledge * So-and-so person will not be allowed to enter without a pass or ticket * So-and-so book will not serve my purpose

So-called: *Styled thus [usually implying doubt or denial]* * So-called recipes would not stand the test of time

Soft mark: *An easy dupe; one easy way to cope with* * A credulous person becomes a soft mark for any trickster * Increase in commercial activities between India and Pakistan can create a soft mark towards friendly relations between the two nations

Soft thing: *An easy task; a snug job* * It is a soft thing to preach morals but rather hard to observe * He is very happy to have had a soft thing at last

Solar salt: *Salt got by evaporation of sea-water by the sun* * Fortified solar salt is commonly used in salty food

Soldier of fortune: *One ready to serve anywhere for pay or his own advancement* * If opportunity offers itself, he will be happy to be a soldier of fortune

Solid with: *On a firm footing of understanding with; packed tight with; supporting fully* * They remained solid with one another in the implementation of the scheme in the teeth of opposition * The bus, solid with passengers, accidentally plunged into the river * They were solid with the party in getting the Bill passed

Some deal: *In some degree; somewhat* * Some deal it is that you have finalised with him * The situation has changed some deal now

Some few: *An inconsiderable number* * All were agreeable but for some few who looked plain angry

Some gate: *Somewhere; somehow* * By this time the plane must be some gate near its destination * He, some gate, managed to please his superiors

Some when: *Sometime or other* * I will see him some when I want to seek his opinion on this particular issue

Some while: *Sometimes* * You see the farmers are some while busy cultivating their land

Somebody: *Some person; a person of importance* * Somebody stole my bicycle when I was inside the post-office to buy some postage stamps * People are gathering there to greet somebody coming to address them

Someone else's: *Some other person* * As this is someone else's job, why should I be expected to do it?

Something like a fine specimen: *A model of what the thing should be; around; approximately* * He fought in the battle-field something like a fine specimen of the past * China has the largest number of army men amounting to two million something like a fine specimen

Sometime: *At a time not fix; at one time or other; formerly* * The visitor is expected to be here sometime in the evening * I will see if I can come sometime to seek your advice on some matters * Have you met Sourav Ganguly personally sometime during the day? * I learnt that the house had sometime served as an inn

Sometimes: *At times; now and then* * He can be really bad-tempered sometimes * Such natural events like this one may take place sometimes

Someway/Someways/Some wise: *In some way; somehow* * He is manoeuvring someway[s] to get the better of his opponent in the bout * The prisoner managed someway to scale the jail wall and escape

Somewhat: *In some degree; an unfixed quantity or degree* * The distance between these two places is somewhat very long * He is down with fever somewhat reaching 103 degree Fahrenheit * He told me somewhat in a whisper about his trip abroad

Somewhere: *In or to some place* * His annual income from the sale of crops is somewhere around one lakh rupees * He might have lost his Parker pen somewhere else * I thought he was in a hurry to go somewhere

Son of a gun: *Soldier's bastard son; a rogue; a rascal* * People call him 'son of a gun' whenever he does something expected of a dare-devil * He is somewhat a son of a gun, but very charming

Soothe to say: *In truth; if truth must be told* * He has been falsely implicated in a robbery case, but, soothe to say, he has no hand in it * Though he looks to be a thorough gentleman yet, soothe to say, he is a wolf in sheep's clothing

Sore throat: *An inflamed and uncomfortable condition of the tonsils and neighbouring parts* * The doctor is treating him for a sore throat

Sort of: *As it were; rather* * Teachers must put the brakes on, sort of, when they noticed students looking puzzled * The patient has responded to the treatment sort of better than expected

SOS: *An appeal for help or rescue* * We have received an SOS from the area asking for food parcels

So-so (so so): *Neither very good nor very bad; tolerable; indifferent* * The condition of the patient is still so-so * At times, the heat was barely so-so * The festival has the usual mixture of films — good, bad and so-so

Sought after: *In demand* * Good and fast stenographers are always most sought after

Source-book: *A book of original documents for study* * A source-book helps the writers to elaborate on the true events of the past

Sow one's wild oats: *Indulge in youthful dissipation or excesses or commit the usual follies especially of youth* * Those who begin to sow their wild oats are likely to fall prey to some disease or other

Sow the wind and reap the whirlwind: *Act wrongly and receive a crushing retribution* * The man troubled the girl so much that a time came when he was arrested and that is he discovered that if you sow the wind you reap the whirlwind

Spacious times: *Days of expansion (in knowledge, trade, etc.) and scope (for discovery, adventure) as in the reign of Queen Elizabeth* * People have since long been witnessing amazing spacious times of advancement covering all progressive aspects of human life

Spare room: *A parlour; a bedroom for visitors* * After having our dinner, we went to sit in the spare room to discuss some important matters * There is a spare room almost in every home for stay of a casual guest

Speak a ship: *To hail and speak to someone on board her* * When on a voyage by sea, every passenger would like to speak a ship to kill time

Speak by the card: *Speak with precision and to the point* * A wise and sensible person would always speak by the card in a considerate manner

Speak evil of: *To slander* * We should not speak evil of others behind their back

Speak fair: *Address one in conciliatory terms* * He spoke fair in uniting the disgruntled persons in the political party

Speak for: *Speak on behalf of or in favour of; be proof of; to witness to; to engage* * The deputy minister had to speak for the prime minister on some issues raised in Parliament in the absence of the latter * He spoke for joint efforts of the people to face the natural calamity * His ability to get through the acid test speaks for his intrinsic qualiaty * His good health speaks for the success of the treatment * It is a movie that speaks for both the mind and the eye

Speak for itself: *Needs no explanation* * The candid view expressed in this book speaks for itself about the intellectual acumen of the author

Speak one's conscience: *Give one's opinion; speak frankly* * At last, he rose to speak out his conscience concerning the true picture of the case * He firmly spoke his conscience not to tolerate the kind of threat given to him

Speak one's mind: *Say plainly what one thinks* * A true statesman would always speak his mind without any doubt, fear or care

Speak out: *Speak boldly, freely, unreservedly, so as to be easily heard* * He spoke out strongly at all the rallies around the country during the election campaign

Speak to: *Converse with; address; reprove; attest; testify to; comment on; discuss* * The two friends were engaged in speaking to each other on some personal matters * I did speak to him for telling a lie * His bold defiance spoke of his courage and determination * He refused to speak to me until after the journey

Speak to the heart: *To comfort, encourage* * When in distress, he always speaks to the heart with the thought that life is beset with ups and downs

Speak up: *Speak as to be easily heard* * I am a bit hard of hearing, so please be good enough to speak up whatever you want to say to me

Speak volumes: *Convey much* * His simple living and high thinking speak volumes of his personality

Special pleading: *Unfair or one-sided argument aiming rather at victory than that truth* * It is a part of diplomacy to accept special pleading of any rogue country

Speed up: *Quicken the rate of working* * We should not show complacency at the present state of development but continue to speed up its progress instead * Soon after leaving the station, the train speeded up

Spell backward: *Spell in reverse order; perversely to misrepresent or misconstrue the qualities* * We can spell backward the word 'raw' as 'war' * It is quite wrong to spell backward regarding disadvantages of smoking which would become advantages of smoking

Spell baker: *Do something difficult* * He, no doubt, spelled baker by saving the child at the risk of his own life from the rising flames that had engulfed the whole house * People were dumbfounded when he successfully spelled baker by scaling the highest skyscraper in the city without any aid

Spend one's breath: *Spend one's time in profitless talk* * I am very particular about spending my breath on convincing him about the advantages of exercise

Spending money: *Pocket money* * Everybody needs some spending money to meet his casual or unpredicted requirements

Spendthrift: *One who spends the savings of thrifts; excessively lavish* * A spendthrift would never utilise money for any good cause * We are all surprised at his squandering money like a spendthrift

Spick and span: *Very neat and clean; tidy* * Our principal wants the college building to be spick and span

Spill the beans: *To cause embarrassment by letting out a secret* * Some people are such loudmouths that they do not mind spilling the beans on some personal matters

Spin a yarn: *Tell a story* * They spun a yarn about being in desperate need of money

Spin out: *To prolong; protract* * We are having such a good time that we decided to spin out our stay by another week * I have no desire to spin out the process

Spirit of wine: *Alcohol* * I could smell the spirit of wine from his breath

Spit and polish: *Cleaning up of uniform and equipment, especially to excess* * The car needs some spit and polish

Splice the main brace: *Serve out an allowance of spirits; fall to drinking; partake of alcoholic spirit* * They spliced the main brace amongst us before launching a new campaign * After having spliced the main race, the guests began to dance in gay abandon

Split hairs: *Make superfine distinction* * They are bent upon splitting hairs on a controversial issue

Split mind: *Schizophrenia* * He is suffering from a split mind as he cannot decide anything one way or the other

Split on a rock: *To meet some unforeseen and disastrous difficulty* * After having done away with the dictatorial regime in Iraq, the Americans are bound to split on a rock to bring about law and order in Iraq

Split one's vote: *Divide one's votes among two or more candidates* * His willingness to split his vote has made it difficult to gauge as to who will rule the roost

Split personality: *A tendency towards schizophrenia* * His split personality has made him oddly rough and tough in his dealings with others * He is a split personality that may change from time to time

Split second: *A fraction of a second* * The driver of the bus avoided a head on collision with the speeding car by a split second

Split the difference: *Divide equally the sum on matter in dispute; take the mean* * The arbitrator made them agree to split the difference in distribution of ancestral property amongst the four brothers * They had to split the difference to come to an understanding

Split the vote: *Injure a cause by influencing a possible supporter to vote in some other way* * The arch rivals split the vote that marred the due representation to be given to women

Spoil man: *One who looks for profit out of politics* * He is supporting the Republican Party as a spoil man

Spoil sport: *One who stops or interferes with sport* * A spoilsport bent on disturbing the proceedings was weeded out and the play continued peacefully

Spoiling for: *More than ripe or ready for; intent on* * Local councilors are spoiling for a fight over the running of the two village schools * They are spoiling for murder

Sponge on: *Be a parasite* * He spent his whole life sponging on his relatives * There are certain elements who sponge on society

Spontaneous generation: *Production of living organism from dead matter* * It is a natural phenomenon that we think it to be a spontaneous generation

Sport one's oak: *Keep one's outer door shut to keep away visitors* * A miser sports his oak when he thinks that a visitor would be an unnecessary burden on him

Sporting chance: *A very doubtful chance, such as a good sportsman might risk* * A good sportsman would never miss a sporting chance even if given an opportunity

Spot cash: *Money down* * I purchased this rare piece of antique jewellery on payment of spot cash

Spring a leak: *Begin to leak; become leaky* * The yacht has sprung a leak in the hall * The roof of our old house has sprung a leak and needs to be plugged before the rainy season

Spring a mine: *Cause it to explode* * The terrorists sprang a mine through a remote system that destroyed the bridge completely

Spring fever: *To spring lassitude* * He is being treated for spring fever

Square a man: *Bribe a person* * If you are thinking of getting this job done by squaring me, you are totally mistaken

Square a man: *Bribe a person* * They squared the waiter to find a better table

Square deal: *A fair bargain* * I struck a square deal with a foreign company and got a good order to export the leather goods

Square deal: *Fair bargain* * They expressed their satisfaction over the square deal

Square up to: *Face up to and tackle* * I think he squared up to the problematic situation boldly

Squire of dames: *One who devotes himself to ladies* * It would not be an unusual thing if someone likes to be a squire of dames even today

Stable equilibrium: *Condition in which a body will return to its old position after a slight displacement* * As the toy is rounded at the base, it can never stay in stable equilibrium but keeps on swinging right and left

Stair work: *Book stairs intriguing* * There are persons who rose to a high position through a stair work

Stamp out: *Put out by tramping; extirpate; put out; extinguish; make by stamping from a sheet*

with a cutter * The rebellion was stamped out with an iron hand * The heavy bombardment stamped out the entire population in the city * Firefighters took an hour to stamp out the flames * A die or a cutter is used to stamp coins of various denominations

Stand a good chance: *Have a reasonable expectation* * He is a hard worker and therefore stands a good chance to top the list of successful candidates

Stand against: *Resist* * People stood against the highhandedness of the police in detaining an innocent man for a long time

Stand at ease: *Used of soldiers, when freed from attention* * The company commander ordered the soldiers to stand at ease for some time

Stand by: *Support; adhere to; abide by; be at hand; hold oneself in readiness; prepare to work at* * Majority of the voters stood by the Congress Party in the general elections * He is committed to stand by truth and honesty * The parties concerned have agreed to stand by the agreement * The fighter planes have to stand by to meet any emergency * True friends stand by to help one another in the lurch * We are all set to stand by the assignments entrusted to us

Stand confessed: *Be revealed* * It stood confessed that they were intent on creating trouble

Stand down: *Leave the witness box; go off duty; withdraw from a contest* * After having been cross-examined, the witness in the court stood down * A sentry standing down is replaced by another * He thought it proper to stand down and not enter the political fray

Stand easy: *Used of a still easier position* * A carefree person has nothing to worry about but to stand easy

Stand fair with: *Be in the good graces of* * He stands fair with the people for being square in his dealings with one and all

Stand fast: *Be unmoved* * The rebels are standing fast and refuse to be defeated

Stand fire: *Remain steady under the fire of enemy* * The brave soldiers stood fire in the thick of the fight

Stand for: *Be a candidate for; direct the course towards; be a sponsored for; represent; to champion; put up for; endure* * Who do you think would be standing for presidentship of America during the next election? * The present government stands for rural development * Will you stand me for a charity I am doing? * The association was formed to stand for the weaker class in the community * He has always stood for reforms in our educational set-up * How can you stand for their rude behaviour?

Stand from: *Direct the course from* * You stand to make a lot from this deal

Stand good: *Be lastingly good; remain* * The old adage still stands good in any language

Stand in: *Do the usual activities of someone else* * As the worker did not turn up, we had to find a stand-in * Can someone be found to stand in while the sweeper is away on leave?—This entire meaning and sentences have had to be changed because the author has given wrong usage

Stand in one's own light: *Hinder one's own advantage* * He stood in his own light when he refused the lucrative appointment

Stand in the breach: *Bear brunt of attack* * The soldiers in the front line had to stand in the breach before arrival of the reinforcements

Stand in the gate: *Occupy a position of defence* * In the face of continuous air-raids, the army had to stand in the gate

Stand low: *Fall short of standard height* * Some of the young men stood low for recruitment in the army

Stand off: *Keep at a distance; direct the course from; forbear compliance or intimacy; suspend temporarily from employment* * It is in one's own interest to stand off bad company * How could you stand off your underhand activities so openly? * In spite of pressure from high-ups, he stood off tactfully without annoying them * The mill-owners had to stand off some workers as a result of power cut

Stand off and on: *Sail away from shore and then towards it* * It is a usual routine of the commercial vessels to stand off and on, i.e. to and fro

Stand on: *Continue on the same track or course; insist on; set store by; found upon* * He has always been standing on orthodox views to be followed up sincerely * Why do you stand on avenging yourself on him?

* There are many persons who stand on traditional values * For a person of your stature, it does not stand on you to speak so rudely * The case standing on insufficient evidence can give an advantage to the accused person in the court

Stand on one's own bottom: *Be independent* * Humanity demands that every citizen stands on his own bottom instead of being a burden upon anyone * As soon as he gets a job, he can stand on his own bottom for betterment of his life

Stand on terms: *Insist on conditions* * They will stand on terms in the agreement to make it acceptable without any prejudice

Stand on the defensive: *Be in the attitude of self-defence* * He had to stand on the defensive against the false allegations

Stand one in good: *Prove of good service* * His vast general knowledge stood him in good when he was personally interviewed for the job

Stand one's ground: *Maintain one's position* * He managed to stand his ground in the face of objections from many quarters

Stand one's hand/Stand shot/Stand treat: *To pay for a drink to another or treat especially to drink* * After having won the game, he offered to stand his hand to his fast friend at a pub

Stand out: *To project; be prominent; not to comply; refuse to yield* * India's assertion in standing out further expansion of the UN Security Council is in the interest of world community at large * The Taj Mahal stands out as one of the most wonderful monuments of the world * Some of the leaders were keen to stand out with the general consensus of giving due representation to women in Parliament * They were determined to stand out against any undue pressures

Stand pad: *Beg by the roadside* * The aged man was left with no other means but to stand pad

Stand shot: *Pay the bill* * He willingly stood shot at a party dinner arranged in a deluxe hotel

Stand to: *A precautionary parade or taking of post; fall to; backup; uphold; take up a position in readiness for orders; set to work* * A stand to march was taken by the soldiers in the disturbed areas of the town

* He stood to brooding about what had happened to him * I will certainly stand to your genuine demands * The rebels stood to their demands with threats * We have the duty to stand to the law of the country * The platoon stood to receive the necessary orders for further action from the concerned commander * After having taken a little rest, I again stood to carry on the job

Stand to one's guns/Stick to one's guns: *Maintain one's position staunchly* * He is a man of high moral character and always stands to his guns in any argument

Stand to/Fall to: *Set to work; to back up; uphold; be likely to* * After getting necessary instructions from the commanding officer, the battalion stood to march towards the war front * The man denied his involvement in the fray and the witness stood to confirm his statement * Our policy has been to stand to the law * This old vehicle stands to be completely unserviceable and needs to be disposed of

Stand up: *Get to one's feet; take position for a dance; be clad; fail to keep an appointment with* * The whole class stood up to pay respect to the teacher when he entered the class-room * When the band master nodded to start playing the tune, all the couples stood up for the dance * She stood up in blue velvet * I was in a bad mood for I had been stood up

Stand up for: *Support to attempt to depend* * You must stand up for your rights

Stand up to: *Meet face to face; fulfil manfully* * It was brave to her to stand up to those bullies * He was able to stand up to all difficult trial periods

Stand upon: *Stand on; to attack* * Where do you stand upon the existing set up of education? * They stood upon him for betraying the party's secrets

Stand upon points: *Be punctilious* * People have all regard for him on the very basis that he always stands upon points

Stand well: *Be in favour* * The new project stands well to bring in large dividends

Stand with: *To be consistent* * The results are standing with our earlier research

Standing orders: *Permanent rules for conduct of proceedings* * A worker in an organisation has to abide by its standing orders so long these remain in force

Stand-offish: *Conceited; haughty* * His stand-offish attitude has deprived him of friends * I was surprised to hear him talk in a stand-offish manner

Stand-up: *Erect; a fight in earnest* * The soldier saluted his officer in a stand-up position * We joined them in a stand-up argument

Star and stripes: *The flag of the United States of America with 13 red and white stripes and a blue field containing as many stars as there are states* * The American national flag has a distinctive marking of stars and stripes on it

Star turn: *The chief item in an entertainment; a pre-eminent performer* * What was the star turn in the show you watched yesterday? * Amitabh Bachchan has acquired a prominent place as a star turn in the Indian film world

State of siege: *A condition of suspension of civil law or its subordination to military law* * In a dangerous situation, like war, a government may declare a state of siege to limit the freedom of its citizens

Stave and tail: *In bear-baiting, to intervene with stave and by grasping the dog's tail* * In early days, people used to make use of stave and tail by setting dogs to attack a bear ina sport

Stay out: *To outstay; stay to the end of* * After the kindness that had been shown to him, he didn't want to stay out his welcome * He had to stay out on field duty till the task assigned to him was over

Stay put: *Remain where one or as it is put* * Just stay put with the luggage while I go and find a cab

Stay the stomach: *To alley cravings of hunger for the time* * They had to stay the stomach by taking tea with biscuits

Steady-going: *A steady habit or action* * A steady-going person is sure to march ahead in life

Steal a march on: *Gain an advantage secretly* * The company is looking at ways to steal a march on its foreign competitors

Steal a marriage: *Marry secretly* * He is thinking of stealing a marriage with a girl of his choice

Steal one's thunder: *Make use of another's invention against him or her* * He had no intention of letting the foreign secretary steal any of his thunder

Steer clear of: *Avoid* * We must steer clear of bad company

Steering committee: *A group who decide what measure shall be brought forward and when* * A steering committee has been appointed to apprise the government of the utility of the proposed new project

Step by step: *Gradually; little by little or slowly* * Step by step, the children began to understand the process* His English is improving step by step

Step in/Step into: *Enter easily or unexpectedly* * He stepped straight into a job as soon as he left college

Step on it: *To hurry* * Since I was too late for my office, I had to step on it

Step on the juice: *Accelerate a motor car* * The car coming from behind stepped on the juice to overtake me

Step out: *Go out a little way; increase the length of the step and so the speed* * He was about to step out of the house when a car skidded to a halt in front of him * He had to step out more and more to win the race

Step short: *Shorten the length of one's step* * The more you get tired by walking the smaller you would step short

Step up: *Come forward; build up into steps; raise by a step; increase the voltage of; increase the rate of production* * Nobody has so far stepped up to give clues on the abducted girl * He stepped up to receive his prize * The minaret has been stepped up in stone from the bottom upwards * A temporary platform has been stepped up in order to enable the prime minister to make a public speech * They had to step up the voltage to meet the requirements of city dwellers * The various factories are running in full swing to step up production with the role purpose of improving the economic health of the country

Step-wise: *In the manner of steps* * Through step-wise promotion, the soldier rose to the rank of a captain

Stick at: *To hesitate or scruple at; persist at* * He sticks at nothing * Morally he always sticks at his stand * He sticks at his work ten hours a day

Stick by: *To be firm in supporting; adhere closely to* * Her husband was charged with fraud but she stuck by him * They stick by their decision

Stick in: *Persevere assiduously; adhere to a wound* * Even in adverse situations he sticks in his studies and may get through the civil service examination * The waterproof bandage was made to stick in the small wound

Stick it into: *To over charge systematically; gain victory* * He is clever enough to stick it to anybody even for disposal of material of a little value * The champion boxer stuck it to his opponent in the third round of the fight

Stick out: *To project; continue to resist* * Many buildings in the old town are sticking out over the street * He is determined to stick out against the pressure put on him by the party leader * They plan to stick out for higher wages

Stick to: *Preserve in holding to* * Be bold enough to stick to your stand even under odd circumstances

Stick up for: *To speak or act in defence of* * One should not be afraid to tell the truth and to stick up for the oppressed

Stick them up: *Hold up your hands* * If in trouble, just stick them up and we will understand the signal

Stick-in-the-mud: *A person who lacks ambition; an old fogy* * My father is a real stick-in-the-mud * The party is run by a bunch of sticks-in-the-mud who resist progress

Stick up: *A stand-up collar; to stand up; to waylay and plunder* * The stuck-up-collar shirt and a new suit added to the personality of the charming man * Please stick up and be firm in explaining your viewpoint * The robbers stuck up the passengers of the night bus

Sticky end: *An unpleasant end; disaster* * The match was won by our team but had a sticky end as one of the key players was injured badly

Sticky wicket: *A difficult situation to cope with* * The management is on a sticky wicket on the issue of releasing higher bonus this year

Stiff-necked: *Obstinate* * His stiff-necked attitude has landed him in trouble

Still and anon: *From time to time* * I ask you to go back to the office and seek an apology from him for your rude behaviour still and anon but you are adamant

Still and on: *Nevertheless* * He continued to walk still and on during the stormy weather

Still stand: *A standstill; an armistice* * The negotiations between both the foreign secretaries have come to still stand * The still stand will continue between two warring tribal groups for long

Still waters run deep: *A quiet exterior often conceals strong emotions, resolution, cunning, etc.* * Do not provoke the quiet girl as she may shout at you for you must remember that still waters run deep

Stir abroad/forth/out: *To go out of doors* * Please stir out for the moment as we have to discuss a family issue

Stir up: *To excite; to incite; to arouse; to mix by stirring* * Every sane human being will be stirred up at the plight of poor children dying of hunger in underdeveloped countries * Do not try to stir up his emotions * The feelings were stirred up of the workers with anger when they saw the dead body of their leader * Please stir up sugar in the tea

Stock company: *A permanent repertory company attached to a theatre* * I am planning to start an independent stock company

Stock exchange: *A building for the buying or selling of stocks and shares; an association of persons transacting such business* * The stock exchange will remain closed tomorrow because of a holiday

Stone's throw: *At a short distance* * Please visit my place when you go for a walk as I reside at stone's throw from the bus stand

Stony-hearted: *Hard hearted* * The stony-hearted father showed no mercy when his daughter returned home late in the rain

Stool of repentance: *A place in church where delinquents especially fornicators were exposed* * I am going to confess my crime in the evening when I visit the stool of repentance in the church

Stop off/stop over: *To break one's journey* * I will definitely stop over to meet you next time when I go home

Stop press: *Late news inserted in a newspaper after printing has begun; a space for it* * The stop press did mention of the appointment of my favourite leader as the new prime minster of our country * Make two columns of news available for stop press

Stop short: *To come to a sudden standstill* * The speedy bus came to a stop short of the boy who was sleeping on the pavement

Stop the mouth of: *To silence* * One cannot stop the mouth of those who want to criticize everything just for the sake of criticism

Stop thief: *A cry for help to catch the thief* * The sharp cries of the old man to stop thief alerted the security guard of the bank

Stop watch: *An accurate watch readily started and stopped; used in timing a race, etc.* * We require a stop watch for tomorrow's athletic meet to record the timings

Store teeth: *False teeth* * He lost his store teeth and was unable to chew food

Storm in a tea cup: *Get excited over a trifling* * There was a storm in a tea cup when the minister announced his resignation at the press conference

Straddle-legged: *Having the legs wide apart* * The straddle-legged dead body of the horse was a gory scene to watch

Straight play: *One without music* * The performance of all the actors was appreciable but overall the show was boring as it was a straight play

Straight talk: *A candid outspoken talk* * Let us have a straight talk and not try to sidetrack the main issue

Straight ticket: *All the nominees of a political party and no others* * The straight ticket means a complete domination of the ruling party since the opposition has boycotted the election

Straight tip: *A racing tip that comes straight from the owner; inside information that can be relied on* * The straight tip helped me to put money on the lucky winner * This straight tip is from a very reliable source

Straightway: *Directly; immediately; without loss of time* * You go straightway to the director and explain your problem * Don't waste time but go straightway to the hospital for the treatment * Call the surgeon straightway as the condition of the patient is deteriorating

Strain a point: *To waive a scruple* * Don't strain the point further as it has been understood already

Strain courtesy: *To deal with scant courtesy* * I felt very bad as my uncle treated me with strain courtesy

Strange woman: *A whore* * The life of a strange woman is full of misery and mental torture

Strategic position: *A position that gives its holder a decisive advantage* * Our forces occupied a very strategic position after a fierce battle

Stream of consciousness: *The continuous succession of thoughts, emotions, both vague and well-defined, that forms an individual's experience* * While sitting alone, a stream of consiousness prevails over one's thoughts and imagination

Stress of weather: *Violent and unfavourable winds* * Stress of weather forced the pilot to turn the plane back

Stretch a point: *To go further than strict rule follows* * It was not possible for the broker to stretch a point in his offer

Stricken battle: *A pitched battle* * A stricken battle took place in the desert and our forces won

Strike a bargain: *To come to terms* * I did strike a good bargain after surveying the market when I went to buy a new sofa-set

Strike a match: *To light it by friction or a grazing stock* * Please strike a match so that the unwanted grass is razed to the ground

Strike at: *To attempt to strike; aim a blow at* * The enemy was planning to strike at midnight but our forces were already ready to repulse the attack * The robber tried to strike at the bus passenger but was overpowered

Strike back: *To return to blow; to back fire; to burn within the burner* * The boxer will strike back hard in the second round to emerge victorious in the bout * The army struck back with full might on the enemy and destroyed them completely * The whole material was struck out just by sheer negligence of the technician

Strike bottom: *To reach the bottom with the leads* * The industrial growth rate has struck bottom during the last six months

Strike hands: *To make a contract* * I could strike hands ultimately in favour of my company

Strike home: *To strike right to the pint aimed at* * The shooter struck home so accurately that the spectators were dumbstruck

Strike in: *Interpose; agree; fit* * Please strike in correct words in this line as I am not able to structure it properly * Both the companies have decided to strike in for a joint venture abroad * The trouser was so tight that I could not strike in myself in it

Strike into: *To enter upon suddenly; to break into* * The robbers will strike into the house to commit robbery * Cholera has struck into in the town

Strike off: *To erase from an account; to deduct; to print; to separate by a blow* * Please strike off the wrong entries of my account in the ledger * Can't you strike off the debit entries from the account book? * Please strike off the interview of the chairman on the front page * I had to strike off heavy blows to separate the fighting brothers

Strike oil: *To find petroleum when boring for it* * Reliance company has struck oil in Bombay High

Strike out: *To bring into light; to direct one's course boldly outwards; to strike from the shoulder; to swim away; to efface* * Please strike out the misdeeds of the corrupt officers in the newspaper * The statement struck out by the minister shows a firm response to the corrupt officials * The gunner struck out the stringer missile directly on the target * To strike out against the tide might result in disaster only * To strike out the meaningful out of nothing is the real test of a skilful man

Strike root: *To take root or become established* * Communism had struck roots in East European countries

Strike sail: *To lower the sail; to abate one's pretension* * The captain ordered to strike sail the moment he was satisfied with the arrangements * I cannot strike sail if you continue to argue unnecessarily

Strike terror: *Terrify* * The dacoits struck terror in the night and killed all the members of a house after looting the valuables

Strike up: *To begin to beat; sing or play* * The miscreants started striking up the innocent * Let us go out and strike up merrily

Strike while the iron is hot: *To act while the occasion is favourable* * A person who knows when to strike while the iron is hot will never face failure in life

Strike work: *Cease work* * The workers decided to strike work as the news spread of cuts in their wages by the management

Strong suit: *One's forte* * You cannot enter the tiger's den as it is his strong suit

Struck on: *Inclined to be enamoured of* * I have been struck on with Russian literature and classical Russian authors emotionally

Strung up: *Nervously tensed* * I was highly strung up when the manager asked me to bring the confidential report

Stuck up: *Vain; rude* * My proposal has been considered by the production manager but stuck up because of the cost involved * The stuck-up attitude of the director resulted in serious confrontation with the workers

Such as: *For example* * Please buy for me a shirt such as the one worn by you

Such as it is: *Being what it is (and no better)* * You will have to accept the matter such as it is

Such like: *Of that kind* * The grapes such like from Afghanistan are full of juice

Suchwise: *In such a manner* * Please give the example suchwise that every layman can understand the meaning

Suck in: *A disconcerting disappointment* * His poor grade in the examination was a suck in

Suck the monkey: *To drink from a cask through an inserted tube; to drink rum, etc. from a coconut* * The boys were so excited that they started sucking the monkey the moment they entered the pub * Have you ever sucked the monkey?

Sum and substance: *The gist; essence* * The sum and substance of the story is that we have lost the election

Sum total: *Complete or final total* * Please do the sum total and let me know the exact profit or loss in this deal

Summer friends: *Friends in prosperity* * You will get many summer friends but remember a friend in need is a friend in deed

Sure card: *A sure means to succeed* * The sure card to success is hard work

Sure enough: *No doubt; in very fact; accordingly* * I am sure enough to reach there well on time * The circumstantial evidence was sure enough proof of his involvement in the crime * You need not worry as I will get the job done sure enough

Sure thing: *A certainty; beyond doubt* * I bet your winning the election is a sure thing * It is a sure thing that our team will win the World Cricket Cup

Surrender at discretion: *To surrender unconditionally* * The forces were made to surrender at discretion as they had no other choice

Swear the peace: *To take oath before a magistrate that a certain person ought to be put under bond to keep the peace* * So many people came forward to swear peace against the criminal

Sweep the board: *To win everything* * Our athletes swept the board in the long distance race in the Asian Games

Swing the lead: *To invent specious excuses to evade duties* * I think the reasons put forth by you are nothing but an attempt to swing the lead * My friend is a master in swinging the lead, especially during the peak-hours of work

Swollen headed: *Self-conceit, especially in one carried away by success* * That swollen headed man is despised by all because of his arrogant attitude

Sword of Damocles: *Any disaster which is likely to occur* * The sword of Damocles is hanging on the fate of the ousted ruler's family

T

Tag, rag and bobtail: *All sorts of riff-raff* * Let us stop all this tag, rag and bobtail forever and concentrate on our respective duties

Tail of the eye: *The outer corner of the eye; the margin of the field of vision* * I am having pain in the tail of my eye since yesterday * I could see from the tail of my eye a bull raging towards me

Take a back seat: *To sink into obscurity or subordination* * The minister was asked to take a back seat by the prime minister

Take a brief: *To undertake a case* * The client asked the lawyer to take a brief of the whole case and study it properly

Take a class: *To take honours in an examination* * I am taking a class this session

Take a fancy for: *To like* * I have developed a fancy for your new office

Take a leaf out of another's book: *To profit by his example* * I have not taken any leaf out of another's book while handling the new project

Take a name in vain: *To use a name lightly or profanely* * Why must you take his name in vain because he is a very famous leader and has nothing to do with the issue?

Take a pride in: *Make a thing an object in which one's pride is concerned* * I take a pride in declaring openly that this book has been written by me

Take a rise out of: *To lure into reacting to provocation* * You are simply trying to take a rise out of him by making remarks that will annoy him unnecessarily

Take a telling: *To do as one is told without having to be told again* * He will take a telling once you make him listen to your point of view

Take advantage of: *To profit* * Do not try to take any undue advantage of my simplicity

Take after: *To follow in resemblance* * You take after the same model as is displayed here

Take aim: *To aim deliberately* *

If you take aim and fire, you will definitely hit the target

Take air: *To get wind; become known* * He took air of my intention and left my premises immediately * You will have to take air in the new locality before starting any new venture

Take amiss: *Take offence at* * Don't take it amiss as my intention was not to offend you

Take an oath: *To have an oath administered to one* * The accused was asked to take an oath before submitting his defence

Take breath: *To recover freedom of breathing* * I stopped to take a breath and started running again as a wild dog was chasing me

Take by storm: *Conquer or capture by a violent attack* * The security forces launched an attack at night and took by storm the key post

Take care of: *To look after with care* * You must take care of the child as I will be out of the house for a few hours

Take charge of: *To assume the care of* * I have been asked to take charge of new branch office for a short time

Take down: *To reduce; to lower; to go above in class; to demolish; pull down; to report or write down to dictation; to escort to the dining room* * You will need to take down the sail as the wind has started blowing * The teacher asked the student to take down the front row * The unauthorised structure was ordered by the municipal authorities to be taken down within a week * You must take down the dictation and show me the draft immediately * I request you to give me the honour to take you down to the dining hall

Take down a peg: *To humiliate in some degree; to snub* * I had to take down a peg in the presence of the whole class when the teacher rebuked me * He was forced to take down a peg because of his stubborn attitude

Take effect: *To come into force* * The new tax slabs will take effect from next year only

Take eggs for money: *To be put off with mere promises of payment* * My tenant is a crooked man as he tries to give eggs for money every time I demand rent

Take exception to: *To object to* * The opposition party has taken strong exception to the remarks of the senior Member of Parliament

Take for: *To suppose to be, especially wrongly* * What did you take me for that you made such a derogatory statement about me?

Take for granted: *Assume* * Do not take me for granted because it is not necessary that I will support you in the next election

Take French leave: *To depart without notice or permission; to disappear suspiciously* * I am taking French leave today just to see that everything is alright in the office * A good number of students took French leave and went for a movie

Take hair of dog that hit you: *Drink more to cure the effect of drink* * If you are having a hangover from last night's session then take hair of dog that hit you

Take heart: *To be encouraged* * Just take heart and come prepared for the next round of the meeting

Take heart of grace: *To take courage from a favour shown* * I took heart of grace from you and will show more positive results in the final examination

Take heed: *To be careful* * You must take heed of your father's advice before coming to any final decision regarding your marriage

Take horse: *To mount on horseback* * Let us take horse and bet in a race

Take in: *Deception; fraud; to cheat; to enclose; to comprise; to annex; to receive; to conduct to the dining room; to subscribe for* * I have been taken in by his trap * One should not take in every word that a fraud says * The fort was taken in by the British forces after a fierce battle * Have you taken in your salary? * Take in the guests to the dining room for the meal * I want to take in membership of the new club

Take in hand: *To undertake* * I have been asked to take in hand this new project which was under your control

Take in vain: *To use with unbecoming levity* * I request you not to take in vain my advice but be serious abut it

Take into account: *To take into consideration* * Take into account all the possibilities before coming to a final decision about running the factory or not

Take into one's head: *To be*

seized with a motion * Do not take into your head the fact that you have been turned down for the job

Take it easy: *To avoid exertion; to be in no hurry* * You have been running here and there in connection with your work but now you must take it easy, else you will affect your health * There is enough time to catch the train, so take it easy

Take it ill: *To be offended* * He took it ill to be overlooked in the party by the host

Take it in snuff: *To take offence* * You should not take my statement in snuff as I had made it in a light vein and had no intention of insulting you

Take it kindly: *Feel it as a kindness* * I take it kindly the gesture shown by you

Take it lying down: *To make no resistance or protest* * The agitators took the lying down attitude in their stride as they knew that there was not much force in their demands

Take it out of: *To exhaust the strength or energy of* * The stiff competition shown by the other competitors took it out of me by the time the race ended

Take leave of: *To bid farewell* * The guests took leave of their host as the dinner was well over and the weather was bad

Take liberties with: *To treat with undue freedom or familiarity* * Do not try to take liberties with me as I do not like it and may hit back at you

Take me with you: *Let me understand what you mean* * Narrate the incident again and try to take me with you

Take measures: *To adopt means to gain an end* * Take all measures to end the strike at the earliest

Take no account of: *To overlook* * Just avoid him and take no account of his presence in the meeting

Take notice: *To observe; to show that observation is made; to remark upon* * I have taken notice of your remarks on the file and will reply soon * The teacher has taken notice of our activities in the class * Take proper notice of all the statistics duly flagged

Take occasion: *To take advantage of an opportunity* * Unless one takes occasion at the proper time and place, one cannot be sure of success

Take off: *To remove; to mimic; to leave the ground for a jump*

or flight * Do not take off your clothes as the mosquitoes will bite you * Don't try to take off my style * The aeroplane had already taken off when we reached the airport

Take off one's hands: *To relieve one of* * I have been asked by the management to completely take my hands off this project with immediate effect

Take offence: *To feel displeasure* * Why are you taking offence at my remarks when all I did was to raise my doubts about the success of the new scheme

Take on: *To receive abroad; to undertake; to take into employment* * I will take you on when you visit me, but not in India * Will you take on this boxer in the next round? * Can you ask your boss to take me on in his factory?

Take on trust: *To believe without proof or evidence* * Can you take on trust my statement as it is?

Take one's adieu: *Say goodbye* * Let us take his adieu and march off at the earliest

Take one's change: *To accept what happens; to risk an undertaking* * You will have to take a change if you want any business scheme to be successful * Do not take any changes as you might be in trouble

Take one's chance out of: *Avenge oneself on* * I cannot let the opportunity go by but will take my chance out of it

Take one's choice of: *To take what one wishes; decide between possibilities* * You are lucky to be offered the chance to take as per your choice whatever you want in this departmental store * There is no other alternative but to take your choice out of these options only

Take one's courage in both hands: *To pluck up courage; to gather boldness* * He had to take his courage in both hands before speaking out his mind in front of the gathering

Take one's ease: *To make oneself comfortable* * Take it easy and wait for me because I shall be back shortly

Take one's life: *To kill him* * He was so frustrated with his failure that he took his life by consuming poison

Take one's measure: *To estimate one's character and abilities* * I can take anybody's measure the way one speaks

Take one's tap in one's lap: *To*

bundle up and go home * The athletes were asked to take their tap into their laps by the coach because of their dismal performance

Take one's turn: *To participate in rotation* * Don't rush through the crowd but take your turn to get the food packed

Take one's way: *To set out; proceed; to follow one's own inclination or plan* * Take your way and start moving forward towards the entry gate * Everybody has to take one's way in life and decide what he or she wants to do

Take order: *To take measure* * Please take order well in time so that everything is ready on time

Take out: *To remove from within; to extract; to go out with; to receive an equivalent for; to copy* * Take out that stuff out of my room * The dentist advised me to get one of the ailing tooth to be taken out * Please take out my pet also when you go out for a walk * I have taken out the job in another firm * Kindly take out five more copies of this document

Take over: *To receive by transfer* * I got my posting orders yesterday and I will take over the new assignment today itself

Take over a new leaf: *Reform; change* * The new CEO has taken over a new leaf with an aim to increase production

Take part in: *To share; to assist in* * To take part in another person's sorrow gives you immense satisfaction * Help me and take part in the post-production process of this film

Take part with: *To take the side of* * The umpire was alleged to take part with men in blue

Take place: *To come to pass; to take precedence* * The accident took place in front of my eyes and the pillion-rider died on the spot * The welcome address has to take place before the speech of the chief guest

Take rank of: *To take precedence of* * The troops have fallen in to take rank of promotion orders followed by transfer orders

Take rise: *To incite* * He tried to take a rise out of me but I remained cool and calm

Take shape: *To assume a definite form or plan; to be embodied or worked out in practice* * Things are taking proper shape after so many months of hard work * Let this model take a shape before honing it

Take ship or shipping: *To embark* * Rush and take ship if you want to reach your destination on time

Take sides: *To range oneself with one party or another* * The leaders who continue to take sides have no political future in the long run

Take stock in: *To trust to; to attach importance to* * I take full stock in of your version of the story and believe it to be completely true * Please don't take stock in of his tall stories

Take stock of: *To make an inventory of goods on hand; to make an estimate of; examine in detail* * Kindly take stock of all the items and update the registers * Can you take a stock of these goods for me as I have to go early?

Take the bit in one's teeth: *To throw off control* * The sudden jerk forced the driver to take the bit in his teeth and he lost control completely

Take the bread out of one's mouth: *To deprive of the means of living* * By announcing a lockout in the factory the management has taken the bread out of worker's mouth

Take the bull by the nose/horn: *To grapple boldly with a danger or difficulty; not evade difficulty* * There is no point in postponing the issue because some time or other you will have to take the bull by the horn

Take the chill off: *To warm slightly; to make lukewarm* * Ask the cook to take the chill off the soup and serve it

Take the field: *To begin war-like operations* * Let us not waste time but take the field immediately

Take the gilt off the gingerbread: *To destroy the glamour* * The model slipped on the ramp and this incident took the gilt off the gingerbread

Take the liberty: *To presume* * Why must you take the liberty of approaching her with your demands when she does not like you?

Take the pledge: *To give a written promise to shun intoxicating liquor* * I have taken a firm and strong pledge to help the poor

Take the plunge: *To commit oneself definitely after hesitation* * Better study all the pros and cons before taking the plunge

Take the reins: *To take control* * The new captain has taken over the reins of the team

Take the road: *To set off; depart* * Let us take the road as it is getting dark

Take the shine out of: *To outshine; eclipse; cause to appear inferior* * The hard hitting by the batsman took the shine out of the new ball * My performance has taken the shine out of his hands

Take the veil: *To become a nun* * She has decided to take the veil for the rest of her life

Take the wind out of one's sail: *To deprive one of an advantage* * The new policy guidelines issued by the management are likely to take the wind out of worker's sail

Take thought: *To conceive a purpose; to be anxious or grieved* * To take thought is necessary before embarking on any new project * Taking thought is one of the prerequisites of a good manager * There is no point now taking thought once you have missed the golden opportunity to earn a good salary

Take time by the forelock: *Act at once; to seize an opportunity* * You will have to take time by the forelock if you do not want to miss a golden opportunity

Take to: *To adapt oneself to; to become fond of* * Unless one takes to one's heart to do a job, no proper implementation can take place * He has taken to her simplicity and likes her very much

Take to heart: *To come to feel in earnest* * It appears he has taken to heart the death of his neighbour

Take to one's heels: *To run away* * All children took to their heels and ram surrounded the teacher to catch his attention off

Take to pieces: *To separate into components* * The machine will have to be taken to pieces for loading it on to the truck

Take to task: *To call to account* * Please call the salesman and take him to task for not doing as told

Take to the heather: *To become an outlaw* * He has fallen into bad company and taken to the heather

Take to the road: *To become a highwayman* * You decide to take to the road and your life will be full of risks

Take to wife: *To marry* * The time has come for me to take to wife

Take up: *To lift; to raise; to pick up for use; to interrupt sharply; to adopt the practice; to resume* * Please help me in taking up this box * Please take up my promotion case with the next higher authority * Take up that ladder and bring it near the wall * Do not try to take up this issue at this time with the boss since he is in thick of a discussion * It is not easy to take up a new system or custom * Let us take up this project afresh

Take up a quarrel: *To settle a dispute* * Instead of paying a heavy fee to the advocate, why don't you try to take up a quarrel with your neighbour amicably?

Take (up) arms: *To resort to fighting* * The rebels have decided to take up arms since the peace negotiations have failed with the government

Take up short: *To take by surprise* * The adverse remarks passed during the conference by some of the members were taken up short by the chairman

Take up the cudgels: *Defend vigorously* * The minister took up the cudgels in support of new taxation policy announced by the government department

Take up the word: *Continue a discourse begun by someone else* * The disciple took up the word as he found his master gasping for breath in the middle of his talk

Take up with: *To begin to associate with; from a connection with* * We cannot finish the work on our own but will have to take up with some big player * My firm has taken up with a reputed company abroad for our overseer administrative arrangements

Take upon oneself: *To take responsibility for; to undertake* * Why don't you take upon yourself the responsibility instead of giving it to the new manager? * The director has taken upon himself to make sure that the production targets are met by the due date

Take warrant on oneself: *To make oneself responsible* * I realise my folly and take warrant on myself for the loss

Take with a grain of salt: *To be cautious while accepting a statement; to believe with some reserve* * I have my doubts about what he is saying and hence I take with a grain of salt his words

Taken aback: *Surprised* * I was taken aback by the reverse stand taken by my friend in the meeting

Taking a long view: *Planning over a long period* * I was taking a long view so that no stones are left unturned to make this project a grand success

Taking off: *Removal; assassination* * The chairman has been taken off from his post * The rebel leader was taken off by one of his comrades

Talk against time: *To keep on talking merely to fill up time* * The man on the other side of the phone was merely talking against time and harassing the girl

Talk as a Dutch uncle: *To rebuke* * Don't try to talk as a Dutch uncle to me

Talk big: *To talk boastfully* * It is easy to talk big but difficult to implement

Talk down: *To argue down; to talk as to inferiors in intellect or education* * There is no point in talking down to him as he is adamant on his stand * He talked down to me and it humiliated me considerably

Talk like a book: *To talk pedantically or with precision and readiness* * On the subject of philosophy, he can talk like a book as he has spent his life on reading about the subject

Talk like a pen-gun: *To chatter volubly* * Two girls were talking like a pen-gun in the library and disturbing others

Talk of the devil: *Here comes the person we were talking of* * You talk of the devil and you find him there

Talk over: *To persuade; convince; to discuss; consider together* * I am hopeful that I shall be able to talk over my teacher on this issue * Let us talk over the problem and try to find a solution amicably

Talk round: *To talk of all sorts of related matters without coming to the point; to bring to one's way of thinking by persuasive talk* * The meeting continued for two hours and the management and union leaders were talking round only * Some people have the ability to talk round over each and every issue

Talk through one's hat: *To talk wildly or at random* * I don't believe him because I feel that he is just talking through his hat

Talk through the back of one's

neck: *To talk utter nonsense* * You are talking through the back of your neck, hence better go out of the room

Talk to: *To address; to rebuke* * The principal wants to talk to the students today * My father talked to me for coming home late in the night

Talk up: *To speak boldly; to praise or boost* * I am not afraid to talk up this issue of rights * A small talk up with the boy will pep him up

Talk you down: *An apparatus by means of which instructions are given to the pilot of an aircraft to help him to land* * The air-traffic controller talked him down and the pilot immediately understood the technical problem

Talking of: *Apropos of; now that mention has been made of* * Do carry on the conversation when talking of the new doctrine * Since you were talking of his character, I shall give you the real picture which is shocking

Tall copy: *A book with ample margin above and below* * Can you lend me your tall copy for a day?

Tall hat: *A top hat* * The lady with a tall hat was looking very pretty at the party

Tall story: *Exaggerate on improbable account* * My friend is in the habit of telling tall stories

Tar and feather: *To smear with tar and then cover with feathers* * A man suddenly jumped in front of me in the jungle with tar and feather and frightened me

Teach school: *To be a teacher in a school* * I want to teach school when I grow up

Teach your grandmother to such eggs: *Speak contemptuously to one who would teach those older and wiser than himself* * There are certain people who after reading a little consider themselves to be clever enough to teach their grandmother to such eggs

Team spirit: *The spirit of self suppression in cooperation* * Our cricket team is having very good players but it lacks team spirit

Team work: *Work done by organised divisions of labour; regard to success of the whole rather than personal exploits* * Any task can be completed with ease if done with good teamwork * The captain attributed the success of his team to team spirit

Teamster: *One who drives a team*

* John Smith is a great teamster and is likely to take his team to victory

Tear a cat: *To rant (angry outburst)* * He tore a cat against his opponents when they started making personal and insulting remarks against him

Tear of a strip: *To reprimand* * The sergeant ordered to tear of a strip of the policeman for negligence of duty

Tear one's hair: *To pull the hair in a frenzy of grief or rage* * The old man was tearing his hair when he lost all his money in the lottery

Tear oneself away: *To go off with great unwillingness* * I had no choice except to tear myself away from the party as I was not feeling well

Tear sheet: *A page torn out for reference* * Please tear a sheet from the dictionary and pass it on to me

Tear to tatters: *Tear into small pieces* * The chairman is likely to tear to tatters my application for the post of a treasurer

Tear up: *To remove from a fixed state by violence; to pull to pieces* * The police was called up by the municipal authorities to tear up the illegal structure * You will have to tear up the top storey of the building

Tee up: *Tee off; to start quickly* * The four-ball was asked to tee off at five in the morning * Please tee up so that we can finish the game on time

Tell one's beads: *To say one's prayers* * The speeding bus so terrified my father that he started telling his beads

Tell one's own tale: *To speak for oneself* * He is fond of telling his own tale whether one is willing to hear it or not

Tell tale: *One who tells the private concerns or misdeeds of others; to play the informer* * The police could find important clues from the person who used to tell tales to them in the past

Tell tales out of school: *To reveal confidential matters* * I don't believe him as he is in the habit of telling tales out of school

Tell the truth and shame the devil: *Put the devil to disgraceful defeat by boldly telling the truth* * I feel the time has come to tell the truth and shame the devil

Tenant at will: *One who holds land only so long as the owner pleases* * I am not the owner of this building but a tenant at will

Tend out an: *To attend* * You are

bound to tend out an emergency meeting tomorrow

Terms of reference: *A guiding statement defining the scope of an investigation or similar piece of work* * The terms of reference of the fact-finding tribunal were laid down clearly in the notification

Textural criticism: *Critical study directed towards determining the true reading of a text* * The textual criticism of an old script has to be done very meticulously by a person having a sound knowledge of the subject

Thank one's stars: *Be grateful* * I really thank my stars that I was not asked to speak in front of so many persons

Thanks to: *Owing to* * It is thanks to you that I could repay my debt

That is to say: *In other words* * That is to say, the teacher asked the student to obey his instructions

That's flat: *I tell you plainly* * Why not tell him flat that you cannot go to the movie with him?

That's your sort: *That's right; well done; go on* * I know you can handle this tricky issue because that's your sort * It was well done by you as that's your sort

The acid test: *A decisive test* * Tomorrow's match will be the acid test for our hockey team

The back of beyond: *A place of extreme remoteness* * We trekked to the back of beyond and lost our way

The ball at one's feet: *He has nothing to do but seize the opportunity* * When the ball is at your feet, why are you waiting for it to come to you?

The bishop has put his foot in it: *Burnt while cooking* * Since it was his first day, the bishop put his foot in it

The boot is on the other leg: *The tables are turned; the responsibility is now the other way; the reverse is the truth* * The prosecutor can easily prove that the boot is on the other leg with his strong arguments

The brief and the long: *All-sided view; the long and the short* * The hotel room where we stayed during our holidays gave a picturesque brief and the long

The cap fits: *Person feels that general remark is true of him; the illusion is felt to apply* * He will be persuaded by the teacher that the cap fits him as he is suitable to play the role of Shylock in the play * The applause by the crowd was misunderstood by the artist as the cap that fitted him

The case: *The fact; the reality* * The case in detail was explained to the advocate by the defendant * Unless you explain the case in detail to the advocate, he won't be in a position to defend you

The clean potato: *The right thing* * Can anyone tell me what is the clean potato to handle this naughty class?

The coast is clear: *There is no obstacle or danger in the way* * This is the time to increase the speed of the boat as the coast is clear

The common: *That is common or usual* * To smoke in public is very common these days

The common good: *The interest of the community at large* * The common good of the general public cannot be sidelined by any government

The common people: *The people in general* * The government should focus its attention on the welfare of the common people

The courage of one's conviction: *Courage to act up to; consistently with* * Unless one has the courage of one's conviction, one cannot speak boldly in front of the public * Are you having enough courage of your conviction to stand firmly on this sensitive issue?

The Creator: *The Supreme Being; God* * Has anybody ever seen the Creator of this universe? * Nothing moves without the will of the Creator

The cut of one's jib: *Appearance* * You cannot judge from the cut of one's jib about one's real character

The day: *The end of work* * Let us call it the day

The defects of one's qualities: *Virtues carried to excess; the faults apt to accompany or flow from good qualities* * One cannot take the defects of one's qualities to prove oneself right * It is but natural that the defects of one's qualities will be revealed

The departed: *The deceased* * May the soul of the departed rest in peace

The depths: *The lowest pitch of humiliation and misery* * The shameful act of the boy has landed the name and fame of the family into the depths

The devil and all: *Much ado; turmoil* * There was devil and all by the members at the meeting * The discussion started rationally but soon it was devil and all

The devil's tattoo: *Drumming with the fingers on a table; in the absence of mind or impatience* * While sitting on a chair and playing the devil's tattoo, I was trying to entertain myself * The devil's tattoo means that one's thoughts are wandering

The die is cast: *An irrevocable step has been taken; there is no turning back now* * The die is cast now and we have no other option except to attack

The dismal science: *Political economy* * The dismal science is a new subject being discussed and debated

The enemy: *The devil* * The enemy was at our doorsteps and our forces were caught unaware

The estates of realm: *Lords spiritual, Lords Temporal, and Commons, often misused for the legislature* * The estates of realm were observed in ancient times

The evil one: *Devil* * Have you ever seen the evil one?

The exception proves the rule: *The existence of some exception shows a rule exists* * The exception proves that the rule otherwise holds good

The fact of the matter: *The plain truth about the matter in question* * The fact of the matter was put forth to the judge by the advocate clearly and with solid evidence

The fair sex: *The female sex* * One has to be generous and kind towards the fair sex

The fat is in the fire: *A critical act has precipitated the trouble* * The provocative speech by the leader started the riots proving that fat is in the fire

The few: *The minority* * The government is responsible for ensuring the safety and security of the few in this country

The fine wits: *The fine senses* * The fine wits prevailed and the boy replied sensibly during the interview

The first thing: *Before doing anything else* * The first thing a person should do after getting up in the morning is to brush one's teeth

The fiscal questions: *Free trade or protection* * The finance minister explained the fiscal questions during an answer-question session

The flowery land: *China* * Have you ever visited the flowery land?

The four seats: *To sit down* * Please take four seats and wait for your turn

The fourth estate: *The press* * The fourth estate has become very powerful nowadays

The game is not worth the candle: *The thing is not worth the labour or expense of it; result not justifying the cost or trouble* * I think we are wasting too much of our energy in haggling with the shopkeeper when the game is not worth the candle

The game is up: *The game has started; the scheme has failed* * The game is up and we are late * The game is up, declared the chairman gloomily and decided to wind up the company

The goods: *The real thing* * Unless the goods are delivered to us we cannot believe that they are true to the samples

The household: *The royal domestic establishment* * The whole household was waiting eagerly for the Crown Prince

The how and the why: *The manner and the cause* * Unless one understands the how and the why, there is no point in fiddling with the system

The last day: *The day of judgement* * All sins will be accounted for on the last day of our lives as believed by all Christians

The last enemy: *Death* * Every human being has to face the last enemy

The last extreme: *The utmost pitch of misfortune* * Poverty has driven him to the last extreme

The last gasp: *The point of death* * I was present with my mother when she took the last gasp

The last straw: *Any final event which cannot be endured* * We will fight till the last straw to regain our property

The last trump: *The trumpet that will sound on the last day* * The trumpet major began the last trump and all were silent immediately

The last word: *The closing remark in an argument especially if having an appearance of conclusiveness; the exclusive statement; the ultimate authority* * The last word of the chairman was sufficient enough for the members to understand the outcome of the meeting * The principal had the last word in taking disciplinary action against the students * The President of India has the last word in announcing capital punishment

The long and short of it: *The*

sum of the matter in a few words * Instead of narrating the whole incident in detail, can you tell me the long and short of it?

The long robe: *The legal profession* * I had dreamed to be in the long robe

The Lord's token: *Plague spots* * The people saw the Lord's token on his whole body and were terrified

The New World: *The Western Hemisphere; America* * Have you ever visited the New World? * The New World continues to dominate the world economy

The odour of sanctity: *A fragrance after death alleged to be evidence of saintship; facetiously applied to the living who have denied themselves the sensual indulgence of washing* * The odour of sanctity brought a sense of peaceful calm in the room and the people were overwhelmed with emotions * The spiritual glow on the face of the head priest gave a glimpse of total peace as well as the odour of sanctity

The Old World: *The Eastern Hemisphere comprising Europe, Africa and Asia* * A visit to the Old World always brings us close to history and educates us about its past glory

The other day: *Not long ago; on an unspecified day* * I visited the market the other day and realised that there was a steep price rise in consumer goods

The other world: *The spiritual world* * Can anyone tell anything about the other world? * The other world is a matter of belief as well research

The period: *The current age* * The period has transformed itself into a period of computers and mobiles

The powers that be: *The existing ruling authorities* * It depends on the powers that be to take a final policy decision regarding the problem of unemployment in our country

The preacher: *The author or spokesman of the Book of Ecclesiastes* * The preacher started the discourse and all became too engrossed in it

The press: *Printed matter, especially newspapers* * Please send this news to the press so that even a common man gets information about AIDS

The primrose path: *Easygoing*

way of living * The primrose path is nothing but an illusion as life is full of struggle and misery

The public weal: *The well-being, interest and prosperity of the country* * To ensure that public weal is not compromised is the foremost duty of every leader of repute

The short and the long: *Same as the long and short* * The short and the long part of the story were equally interesting

The small hours: *Early hours of the morning* * Have you ever enjoyed the chirping of the birds during the small hours?

The thin end of the wedge: *A small beginning that is bound to be followed by a large or significant development* * Every mega project remains at the thin end of the wedge in the beginning

The thing: *That which is conventional* * The thing as it is has to be accepted otherwise we will not be able to understand the concept

The three R's: *Reading, writing and arithmetic* * A person who is not well versed in the three R's is like an illiterate

The whole world: *The sum of what is contained in the world* * The whole world is watching the economic development taking place in our country

The why and wherefore: *The whole reason* * Unless one knows the why and wherefore of the whole situation, it is not correct to pass any remark

The (wooden) wedge: *The student lowest on the classical Tripos list* * There is no point in wasting your time with that (wooden) wedge

The world's end: *The most distant point possible* * I have a dream to go to the world's end in my life

Their name is legion: *They are too many* * Their name is legion and we are bound to be beaten by them in the match

Then and there: *At once and on the spot* * The constable started thrashing the pickpocket then and there

There and then: *Forthwith* * The teacher asked the students to finish their homework there and then

There is no love lost between them: *They have no liking for each other* * It is better they take divorce since there is no love lost between them

There or thereabouts: *Somewhere near* * The knife with

which the boy was murdered was lying there or thereabouts on the ground

There's many a slip between the cup and the lip: *Failure is possible at the last moment* * One cannot be sure of anything since there's many a slip between the cup and the lip

Thin skinned: *Having a thin skin; sensitive* * The thin-skinned person is likely to fall sick frequently * My younger daughter is very thin skinned and gets hurt very easily

Think aloud: *To utter one's thoughts unintentionally* * It was a casual remark thought aloud which created a stir amongst the devotees

Think better of: *To revise one's decision; to have the better opinion of* * After considering all the pros and cons, the chairman started thinking better of his earlier decision * It is always advisable to think better of getting an expert view

Think for: *To expect* * I cannot think for a better result in the examination than this one

Think good: *To be disposed* * I am thinking good to annul the agreement with the new company

Think little of: *To have poor opinion of* * My boss thinks little of my friend who is working directly under him

Think much of: *To have good opinion of* * My boss thinks much of me I feel

Think out: *To devise; project completely; to solve by a process of thought* * Let us think out some ways and means to sort out this problem * It is better to think out in detail before starting any new venture * Unless we sit together and think out a workable solution, the situation will not improve

Think over: *To reconsider at leisure* * I will think over this proposal and communicate to you my decision

Think scorn: *To disdain or think beneath one* * To think scorn about him is not a proper view to take

Think shame: *To be ashamed* * The teacher told the student to think shame on his bad behaviour

Think up: *To find by thinking; devise* * You will have to think up and come forward with a possible solution

This day week: *A week from today* * I will report back the completion of this task by this day week

Thorn in the flesh: *Any cause of constant irritation* * His presence was felt like a thorn in the flesh by some members of the committee

Thorough paced: *Thoroughly or perfectly paced or trained* * One has to be thoroughly paced before one is ready for any international athletic meet

Thoroughfare: *A passage or way through; a road open at both ends; a public way or street; right of passing through* * This is not a thoroughfare and all trespassers will be prosecuted * As this is a very narrow thoroughfare, the car cannot pass through it

Thoroughgoing: *Going through or to the end; going all lengths* * I like to be thoroughgoing in all my work so that nobody can find a fault in it

Thread and thrum: *The good and bad together* * The thread and thrum have to be taken along in life

Thread of life: *The thread imagined to be spun and cut by fate* * Living by the thread of life lies in the hands of the Creator and over which we have no control

Three time three: *Three cheers thrice repeated* * Three times three were repeated to encourage both the teams at the stadium

Three went way: *A meeting place of three roads* * Unless proper signboards are displayed, travellers cannot find the correct route at three went way

Throttle down: *To slow down by closing the throttle* * I throttled down on the accelerator as the road became very narrow

Through and through: *Through the whole thickness; completely* * The bullet hit the thief in the leg and went through and through * The teacher clearly told the students to complete their home-work through and through

Through the day: *In the day time* * It becomes very refreshing if one takes a nap through the day

Through the night: *In the night time* * One feels very tired the whole day if one does not get proper sleep through the night

Through the nose: *Exorbitantly* * I had to pay through the nose for the gas cylinder because the stock was almost exhausted

Through thick and thin: *In good and bad times* * We should stand by our friends through thick and thin and not leave them in the lurch

Through train: *A train that goes the whole length of a long journey* * I prefer to travel through train if the journey is very long

Throw a fit: *To have a fit; behave wildly* * The lady tends to throw a fit at the mildest of provocations * The lady threw a fit when challenged by the traffic constable

Throw a party: *To give a party* * I want to throw a party to celebrate my success in the final examination

Throw about: *To cast about or try expedient* * It is better to throw about all possible ways and means before accepting defeat

Throw away: *To reject; toss aside; to fail to take advantage of* * My application for leave was thrown away in the dustbin by the boss * The chairman threw away the idea given by me to increase production * Our team simply threw away the easy chances of converting the goals and lost the match

Throw back: *To refuse; to revert to some ancestral character* * The patient simply threw back the medicine in protest * His attitude threw back the memories of a royal king

Throw cold water on: *To discourage* * The boss simply threw cold water on my proposal to open another branch of the office

Throw dirt: *To besmirch a reputation* * The opposition party got the opportunity to throw dirt on our leader by making a mole out of a mountain

Throw down: *To demolish* * We will have to throw down the illegal structure as it is against the municipal laws

Throw down the gauntlet: *To accept a challenge* * The new police inspector threw down the gauntlet openly to the criminals and was not frightened to face even death

Throw dust in one's eyes: *To deceive* * The financer has thrown dust in the eyes of the investors and has simply vanished with the money

Throw in: *An act of throwing in from the touchline to put the ball back into play (in football)* * The throw in was so accurate that the striker sent the ball rolling in the goal

Throw into the discard: *To throw on the scrap heap* * The chairman threw into the discard my suggestions

Throw off: *To divest oneself of; to disengage or release oneself from* * I want to throw off myself away from this irresponsible team * The moment I came to know about the real character of my friend, I threw off myself completely from his company

Throw on: *To put on heartily* * My feelings were thrown on by me in front of the gathering as I could not control my emotions

Throw oneself into: *To engage heartily in* * You will have to throw yourself into the project completely to complete it on time

Throw oneself on: *To assail; to entrust oneself to the power of* * The big boy threw himself on when he entered the pub * The new don has thrown himself on the gang members by sheer terror

Throw open: *To cause to swing wide open; to make freely accessible* * Please just throw open the window to let the fresh air come in * The government has decided to throw open its policies to the public

Throw out: *An act of throwing out; to reject; to expel; to leave behind* * Just throw out that man out of this meeting as he is a menace * The key batsman was thrown out of the team because of poor fielding

Throw over: *To discard or desert* * I have thrown over our servant as he had started stealing the valuables

Throw sheep's eyes at: *To ogle sheepishly* * Young boys tend to throw sheep's eyes at girls during an exhibition

Throw stones: *To find fault with others* * One should not try to throw stones at others but rather look into one's own performance

Throw to the dogs: *To throw away* * The economic policies of the previous government have been thrown to the dogs by the new government

Throw up: *To erect hastily; to show prominently; to give up; to resign; to vomit* * The structure was thrown up to accommodate all the members on the stage * A lavish party was thrown up by my father to celebrate my success in the competition * The captain admitted the failure of his team and threw up the captaincy * The girl just threw up as the car moved on the hilly track

Throw up the sponge: *To acknowledge defeat by throw-*

ing into the air the sponge with which a boxer is rubbed down between rounds; to give up any struggle * The match was not over but the writing on the wall was clear as the team had thrown up the sponge

Thrust one's nose into: *To meddle officiously with* * Don't try to thrust your nose into the private life of the husband and wife

Thrust one's throat: *To assert or force upon one insistently without listening to an answer* * The chairman continued to thrust his throat while the journalist was trying to question him

Tick off: *To reprimand* * The teacher ticked off the student for being late every day

Tick over: *Of an engine* * Please just tick over as I am tightening the screws

Ticket of leave: *A licence to be at large before the expiry of sentence* * The jailor reluctantly agreed to give ticket of leave to the prisoner

Tickle one's fancy: *Amuse* * The clown was trying unsuccessfully to tickle the spectator's fancy

Tickle the ear of: *Flatter* * Don't try to tickle the ear of your boss by praising him unnecessarily

Tie up: *To parcel up; to tie so as to remain up; restrict the use of; by conditions* * Tie up all the items in a packet * The thieves tied up the landlord after looting the valuables * The new economic package has been tied up with lot of conditions

Tied to a woman's apron strings: *Bound as a child to its mother* * Though he is married he continues to be tied to a woman's apron strings

Time about: *In turns; alternately* * Both the boys went out off the class to time about frequently to play

Time and again: *Repeatedly* * I have told my son time and again to concentrate on his studies since the examinations are drawing near

Time and tide: *Chances* * Time and tide wait for no one; so do good whenever you can

Time immemorial: *For a very long time* * I have not visited my home town since time immemorial

Time of day: *The time by the clock; the point of time reached; a greeting; salutation* * The time of day reminded us to move fast as it was getting dark in the forest * All the athletes completed the race by the time of day * The soldier raised his hand to the head to gesture the time of day

Time out of mind: *During the entire time within human memory* * I don't remember such a catastrophe hitting the planet earth in the time out of mind

Tip off liquor: *To turn up the vessel till quite empty* * The bartender tipped off liquor from the last bottle and declared that the stocks had finished

Tip one the wink: *To convey a secret hint* * My friend tip me the wink in the meeting and I understood that I was giving wrong information

Tip the scale: *To depress the one end of the scale* * The shopkeeper tipped the scale so cleverly that nobody could foresee the undue gain he was making

Tip-top: *Excellent* * The new departmental store is well maintained and tip-top

Tire woman: *A lady's maid* * One cannot finish the dressing up and make up without the help of a tire woman

Tit for tat: *Blow for blow* * My befitting reply was a solid tit for tat for the critical remarks against my research paper

To a degree: *To some extent* * I agree with your statement to a degree

To a hair: *Exactly; with perfect nicety* * The batsman executed the cover drive to a hair and all appreciated it

To a man: *Without exception* * Please distribute the pamphlets to a man present in the meeting

To a nicety: *With a great exactness* * The text was corrected by the professor to a nicety and handed over to the publisher

To a T: *With perfect exactness* * The function was organised by the managing committee to a T

To a tee: *Exactly* * The road turns left and goes straight to a tee where my house is located

To a wonder: *Marvellously; extremely well* * The new principal has taken this institution to a wonder during his tenure

To all appearances: *So far as it appears to anyone* * It is all right if the new structure looks aesthetically elegant to all appearances

To all intents and purpose: *In every important respect* * The design of a building has to be perfect to all intents and purpose

To and from: *From one spot to*

another and back again * The teacher was taking a round of the class to and from to ensure that the students took their examination without resorting to any malpractice

To bale out: *To escape from an aeroplane by parachute* * The pilot baled himself out immediately after the engine caught fire

To be awake to: *To be fully aware of* * One should be awake to all recent technological advances

To be brief: *To speak in a few words* * The presiding officers asked the guest speaker to deliver his keynote address while trying to be brief

To be sure: *A certainty; beyond doubt* * Try to be sure about your departure so that all preparations are done well in time * One has to be sure before raising any finger towards any person

To blow the gaff: *To disclose a secret* * One of the gang members was quick enough to blow the gaff as he could not withstand the police pressure

To boot: *In addition* * Another box was added to the boot and the truck was loaded fully

To bowl over: *To knock down; to overwhelm; to overspread and crush by something heavy or strong; to reduce to helplessness* * My friend was bowled over by a beautiful girl at the party * He was so bowled over by her beauty that he could not speak a single word to her * The car parked near the tree was bowled over by a road-roller * He has been bowled over by his poverty and is unable to attend the function

To burn one's faggot: *To recant a heresy* * You may try hard but you can't burn one's faggot

To come: *Future* * The times to come will be very different as well difficult for the new generation

To cudgel one's brains: *To take mental pains* * This riddle is so complicated that one will have to cudgel his brains for a solution

To death: *Extremely* * I am tired to death of your endless bitter criticism

To do to wit: *To cause to know* * I want to do to wit so that my quest for truth is satisfied

To express oneself: *To give expression to one's thoughts* * The speaker told the audience that they were free to express themselves one by one

To have not to: *To be obliged to* * I have decided to have not to attend the wedding reception

To have two strings to one's bow: *To have an alternative device* * My scheme was planned in detail and I chose to have two strings to my bow to avoid any chances of failure

To hold at bay: *To prevent an enemy from coming close or a problem* * He is trying to keep his creditors at bay * She bit her lips to hold her tears at bay

To hold the baby: *To be left in lurch with a responsibility* * Everybody in the office simply left and I alone was left to hold the baby during the rush hours

To levy war: *To make war* * Perhaps the government will have to levy war against the increasing terrorist activities across the boarder

To make the best of one's way: *To go as well as one can* * One should try to make the best of one's way with the ultimate aim to succeed in life

To match: *In accordance; as in colour* * Do ensure that to match both the chairs, they are of the same quality and size * This shade has to match with the existing one for a better look in contrast

To my mind: *To my thinking; in my opinion; to my liking* * To my mind, this piece of art is not so good and appealing * The colour of the wall does not appeal to my mind

To one's face: *In one's presence* * I rebuked her to her face for being late to office

To one's hand: *In readiness* * It is better to have a bird in one's hand than two in the bush

To one's taste: *To one's liking* * One would like to eat as per one's taste only

To order: *According to; an order* * The boys were asked to fall in to order of height * We have yet to order the dinner

To pieces: *Into a state of disruption* * Our plan was thrown to pieces by the head of the department

To play possum: *To feign death* * I played possum to deceive the lion and was lucky enough to escape alive

To point: *To the smallest detail* * One will have to go to point to make sure that there are no loopholes which can mar the chances of its success

To put an earmark on: *To set aside for a particular purpose* * I have put an earmark on this point and will ponder over it leisurely at the appropriate time

To range oneself: *Take sides; to settle down to reputable ways especially on marrying* * I am not supposed to range myself with either of the teams as I am a referee today * The time has come now for me to range myself decently

To row up the cards: *To give in; to confess defeat* * The boxer decided to row up the cards in the first round itself

To say nothing of: *Not to mention* * It is better to say nothing of this misadventure to anybody as people will make fun of us

To scale: *In proportion to actual dimensions* * All the pieces of wood were cut to scale by the carpenter to make a fine quality window

To seek: *Not to be found; wanting; at a loss to know* * I was trying to seek my lost dog but could not find it * Nobody knows what your are trying to seek from you life * The tragedy may force me to seek help from my family

To sell: *For sale* * I am ready to sell my old car at a discount

To serve apprenticeship: *To undergo the training of an apprentice* * You will have to serve apprenticeship initially before you are promoted

To shuttle off: *To thrust aside; wriggle out of* * The police shuttled off the unwanted load from the train and started a thorough search * Somehow I could shuttle off from the complicated situation and save my money

To spare: *Over and above what is required* * Do you have a pen to spare for me?

To speak of: *Worth mentioning* * The guest speaker considered it worth to speak of organising a meeting

To speak to: *So as to have conversation with* * I wanted to speak to one of the panelists on the stage to get the answers to my queries

To stand at bay: *To face the dogs at close quarters* * We were standing at bay and praying that someone would come to our help

To the backbone: *Thoroughly or absolutely* * Brian Lara plays to his full potential to the backbone

To the bad: *In a bad condition; in deficit* * The bike was put to the bad by sheer carelessness * The factory was put to the bad before I took over

To the bone: *To the utmost part* * My friend did help me to the bone to help me finish my class-work

To the contrary: *To the opposite effect* * My sincere advice was taken to the contrary by the students

To the end of chapter: *Throughout* * The child listened carefully and sat to the end of the chapter

To the fore: *At hand; prominent* * The alternative plan was at the fore which helped in solving the problem * The prime minister was at the fore during the last summit of developing countries

To the full: *In full measure; completely* * I was satisfied with the performance of the child to the full

To the last: *To the end; till death* * The brave Jawans fought to the last to defend their post

To the life: *Very closely like the original; exactly drawn* * This painting is really a masterpiece and appears to the life

To the manner born: *Accustomed from birth* * He is habitual to the manner born to fall asleep immediately after having his meal at night

To the nines: *To perfection; elaborately* * The move was so planned to the nines that the defence of the other team was mesmerised by our forwards scoring the winning goal * The reception was held to the nines by the organisers and pleased the guests no end

To the nth: *To any power; to the highest degree* * I shall not hesitate to approach the nth to get full justice for the poor farmers * I can go to the nth to defend the honour of my family

To the point: *Apposite* * Better narrate the incident to the point and quickly at that

To the top of one's bent: *To the full measure of one's inclination* * He has already given enough hint to the top of his bent to buy this car at any cost

To the tune of: *To the amount of* * I presented to my wife a diamond ring costing to the tune of 10,000 rupees

To wit: *That is to say; namely* * It is just adding to wit what has been already communicated in writing

Toad in the hole: *Meat baked in batter* * Have you ever tried toad in the hole?

Toe the lines: *Stand with toes against a marked line, as in*

starting a race * All the players were standing with toes the lines and ready for the game

Tom, Dick and Harry: *Anybody; people in general* * Any Tom, Dick and Harry cannot do this job as it requires expertise * How can I invite every Tom, Dick and Harry to the small party that I am organising?

Tom-noddy: *The puffin; a fool* * Tom-noddy was the character who was always called on by the villagers for help and he never said 'no' * You try to be a simple man and the people will behave as if you are Tom-noddy

Tom Tiddler's ground: *A place where wealth is to be had for the picking up; no man's land (from a children's game so called)* * The Tom Tiddler's ground has remained a mystery and fairytale, yet people of my town believe in its existence * Playing Tom Tidler's ground was my favourite game when I was a child

Tone down: *To give a lower tone to; to moderate; to soften; to harmonise the colours of as to light and shade* * The moment I apologised, the shouting by the old man toned down * Can you please tone down a bit as I am a heart patient * The artist had tried to tone down the colours but the painting has not come up as expected

Tongue tied: *Silent through confusion or fear* * The passengers were tongue tied as the dacoits threatened them with death

Tongue work: *Babble; chatter* * The tongue work was so annoying that the chief guest ordered to throw the disturbing girls out of the concert * The girls continued to tongue work and the whole class was disturbed

Too many irons in the fire: *Too many things on hand at once* * If you have too many irons in the fire, you will put yourself to great tension only

Tooth and nail: *With all possible vigor and fury; with great fierceness* * Our Jawans fought tooth and nail and won the battle ultimately

Top dog: *The winner or dominant person* * Bravo has been acknowledged as a top dog by his teammates

Top one's part: *To surpass oneself in playing it* * He topped his part and his teammates were jubilant as well proud of him

Topsy-turvy: *Top side down* * The topsy-turvy policies of the government only resulted in confusion and chaos

Toss off: *To drink off* * Let us toss off to commemorate your victory

Toss out: *To prank up (trick, joke)* * He tossed out a funny story and the gathering burst into peals of laughter

Toss up: *To throw up a coin in order to decide; to cook and serve up hastily* * Both the captains were in the middle of the ground and ready for the toss up when we reached in the stadium * The new cook was trying to toss up pizza but he burnt his fingers

Total abstainer: *One who abstains altogether from all forms of alcohol* * I am a total abstainer as I have taken a vow not to touch tea, coffee or alcohol

Total war: *War with every weapon at the combatant's disposal; sticking at nothing and sparing no one* * The troops were at total war since the mission was to be achieved at any cost

Touch and go: *Extremely doubtful* * The race was so competitive that it was a matter of touch and go in deciding the winner

Touch bottom: *To reach the lowest point* * Our economic growth has touched bottom this year

Touch of the tar brush: *An infusion of Negro, Indian or coloured blood* * The touch of the tar brush has created its own problems

Touch up: *To improve by a series of small touches* * I want to touch up my drawing room during this festival

Touch upon: *To say something about; to verge* * I wanted to touch upon the downward trend in the economy but hesitated as the statistics were not available

Lousy tea: *High tea* * A lousy tea was arranged by the mayor in the evening since the guest list comprised big guns of the town

Town and gown: *The general community and the members of the university* * The town and gown were present to felicitate the new chancellor

Trail of pike: *To serve as a soldier* * To be a trail of pike is my mission in life

Trail one's coat: *To invite a quarrel* * By giving a provocative speech, the speaker was trailing his coat only with the opposition party

Trailing edge: *The rear edge* *

The boy was sitting on the trailing edge of the balcony and just fell down

Train fine: *To bring body or mind to a high pitch of efficiency* * The aim of this workshop is to train fine the management trainees

Tread a measure: *To go through a dance* * Let us tread a measure and enjoy the evening

Tread on one's corner: *To hurt one's feelings* * You don't know your remarks have tread on my corner badly

Tread on the neck of: *To oppress or tyrannise over* * You are unnecessarily trying to tread on the neck of my brother who is a simple man

Tread upon eggs: *To walk wearily; to steer one's way carefully in a delicate situation* * In the mine-laid areas, the soldiers were walking as if treading upon eggs * The negotiations with the bride's parents were carried by my father as if treading upon eggs

Treaty port: *A port open by treaty to foreign trade* * The treaty port has helped both the nations and the business is growing fast

Trip up one's heels: *To trip up or overthrow* * He was running so fast that he could not control the momentum and tripped up his heels

Triple time: *Three beats; three times three beats* * The bugler sounded triple time and everybody fell silent * The hooter was timed to sound triple time to make the public aware about the air attack

Troops break: *Disperse in confusion* * The troops were asked to break and to wait for further orders

Trot out: *To exhibit the paces of; to be forward; produce for show; to walk out with* * The horse was trying to trot out with the drum beat * Let us try to trot out the carts moving slowly and forcing us to be late * I want to trot out the best item for the chief guest * Would you like to trot out with me in the evening?

Trouble one for: *Ask one to pass* * Will you please take the trouble to allow us to go fast?

True colours: *To appear in one's real character* * Some people show their true colours once their selfish ends are achieved

Try a fall: *To participate in a wrestling bout* * He will try a fall and is likely to win also

Try and: *Try to* * You try and I am sure you will be successful

Try back: *To revert; hark back* * Let us try back to the earlier plan and rectify our mistakes * Don't try back too much on him

Try conclusions: *To engage in a contest* * The Lions Club is likely to try conclusions to decide who is the best singer in this town

Try for: *Make an attempt to reach or gain* * Let us try for the best with full sincerity

Try on: *To put on for trial; as a garment; to attempt* * My best friend has been charged of murder and is being tried on * Let me try on this new necklace * Let us try on again and push the truck down

Try out: *A test performance* * Let me try out this new car by taking a test drive

Tuck in: *A hearty feed* * I have tucked in a hearty meal to last me for the rest of the journey

Tuck out: *To take out* * Tuck out enough materials for the long journey

Tuck shop: *A confectioner's shop* * Let us go to the tuck shop during the recess period

Tuck up: *To gather up; to contract; to hang* * Let me tuck up enough courage to go the principal * I could not tuck up with him as his ideas are totally different to mine * The prisoner was tucked up as per the orders of the court

Tug of war: *A laborious contest; a contest in which opposing teams tug at a rope and strive to pull one another over a line* * A tug of war competition is really very entertaining

Tumble in/Tumble upon: *To incline inward above the extreme breadth; of a ship's side; to fit; as a piece of timber into other work; to go to bed* * The boat tumbled in because of the excess load and started submerging in the water * The passengers started tumbling in as the raging storm started tilting the balance * This piece of wood will not tumble in this space, hence better replace it * This wooden trunk will definitely tumble upon this heavy drum * As it is too late to go out, we had better tumble in and go to sleep.

Tumble over: *To toss about carelessly; to upset; to fall over* * He tumbled over the bottle of beer to the man sitting next to me * I was completely tumbled over at the decision of my son to quit studies and start business * He just tumbled over and broke his leg

Tumble to: *To comprehend* * I could not tumble to the plan thoroughly at first glance

Tumble up: *To get out of bed; to throw into confusion* * It is very difficult to tumble up in the winter * Your ideas are more likely to tumble up than solve the issue

Tune in: *To adjust a wireless receiver for reception* * Let us tune in and listen to the running commentary on the cricket match

Tune up: *To put instruments into tune for beginning; to begin to perform* * Once the violinist tuned up his instrument, he was ready for the concert * The artists were all ready and tuned up for the performance when one artist suddenly fell down

Turk's head: *A kind of knot; a long broom; a figure set up for practice in swordsmanship* * I shall make a Turk's head and you try to unwind it * I do require a Turk's head to clean that shaft * The person hitting the Turk's head with maximum speed was declared the best

Turn a blind eye to: *Feign not to see* * The teacher turned a blind eye to the student who was cheating in the examination

Turn a deaf ear to: *To ignore* * He turned a deaf ear to my suggestion and the result was total failure of the project

Turn about: *Alternately; in rotation; to face round to the opposite quarter; to spin; to rotate* * The security guards will turn about for the next shift * The wheel of cycle has turned about fully * The commander ordered the platoon to turn about and wait for the next order * Can you turn about the ball in the air?

Turn adrift: *To unmoor and let float away; to cast off* * With the intention to deceive the guards, the pirates turned adrift as if they were going away * If the weather permits, we shall turn adrift tomorrow itself

Turn again: *To turn back; to revert* * If you lose wealth you will see that people generally turn against you * My suggestions have been turned again by the board of directors

Turn against: *To render hostile; to rebel against* * The key witness turned against and the case of the prosecution became weak * The failed negotiations with the government gave a setback to peace and the rebel leaders turned against the government

Turn an enemy's flank/line: *To manoeuvre so as to attack on the rear; to outwit* * The plan prepared by the CEO was to turn an enemy's flank and surprise them * You cannot match him as he can turn an enemy's flank in any situation

Turn around one's little finger: *To be able to persuade to anything* * That old man can turn his boss around his little finger with his wit and humour

Turn aside: *To avert; to deviate; to avert the face* * The boy tried to turn aside but the teacher caught hold of him and brought him into the class- room * There is no point turning aside the main road and get caught in a traffic jam * My friend turned aside as he did not want to face me

Turn away: *To dismiss from service; to discharge; to avert; to look in another direction; to deviate* * The manager turned away the employee from service as he was involved in a fraud * The heavy smoke is being turned away from the cylinder of my bike * I tried to turn away but the principal saw me and called out to me * I shouted for help when a stranger snatched my purse but the passengers in the bus just turned away * We completely turned away from the main route and were lost

Turn back: *To cause to retreat; to return* * The heavy firing by the police forced them to turn back * We have gone far from our house and now we should turn back immediately

Turn colour: *To change colours* * Some leaders tend to turn colour and switch their parties

Turn down: *To bend; double; fold down; as a light; to reject* * By turning down and stretching one feels very relaxed * The production has turned down this year * Just turn down all the papers neatly and put in my briefcase * My application for leave has been turned down by the teacher * My car's colour has turned down with time and it requires a fresh coating

Turn forth: *To expel* * My proposal to turn forth the inefficient worker was rejected by the manager without giving any reason

Turn in: * *To bend inward; to enter; to go to bed* * I tried to turn in the key in the hole in the darkness but failed * Let us turn in as it has started raining * The mother told the children that it was time to turn in

Turn into: *To become something else by a process of change* * Silver crockery turns into black or green colour with time

Turn loose: *To set at liberty* * The ferocious dog was turned loose by its owner and he attacked the thief

Turn off: *To deviate; to dismiss; to divert; to complete; achieve by labour; to shut off; to hang* * Do not try to turn off at this stage else the whole plan will crumble * The employee was turned off from service by the management as he was involved in a fraud case * The teacher asked the students to turn off the project and leave

Turn on: *To set running; to depend on* * All the athletes were on their mark and well set to turn on * I was turning on my friend for a loan and he obliged me very kindly

Turn on one's heels: *To turn sharply round; to turn back or away* * The soldier smartly saluted, turned on his heels and marched away * He turned on his heels and walked away without even bidding farewell to her

Turn one's back upon: *Ignore* * He turned his back upon me at the party since I was not well dressed

Turn one's coat: *To change one's principles; to turn from one party to another* * The man who turns his coat is not considered dependable by anyone

Turn one's hand to: *To apply oneself to* * You will have to turn your hand to studies if you want to be successful in your life

Turn one's head: *To make one giddy; to get infatuated with success* * The hilly journey normally turns one's head * The instant flow of wealth in his new business has turned his head

Turn out: *To adjust it so as to eliminate; to bend outwards; to drive out; to expel; to put to pasture; to produce and put forth; to prove in the result; to muster; to go on a strike; to get out of bed* * Please turn out and let the others move ahead * Don't turn out this file unnecessarily * He turned out and sped away very fast * The teacher turned out the noisy students out of his class * The new machines have turned out to be more productive than the old ones * The students have decided to turn out against the poor quality of food in the hostel * Don't turn out suddenly as it is dark in the room and you will be hurt

Turn over: *To roll over; to set the other way up; to change sides; to hand over; pass on; to handle or do business to the amount of; to examine by turning the leaves* * Just turn over so that I could put ointment on your back * This is the time to take a stock of the situation and turn over things * The politicians usually turn over the parties as per their calculative gains * Please turn over the key of my house to my servant * The baton was successfully turned over by the athlete to the next runner in the relay race * The turn over in the current financial year shall hopefully will be double of the previous year * Let me turn over the contents of the box before I can tell what is inside

Turn over a new leaf: *To begin a new and better course of conduct* * The boy decided to turn over a new life once he came out of the reform home

Turn penny: *One who is eager for profit* * He has to be patient and wait for his enterprise to run well and not turn penny

Turn tail: *To turn away* * The horse turned its tail away and refused to budge from its spot

Turn the cat in the pan: *To change sides with dexterity* * He is so cunning that when he would next turn the cat in the pan cannot be told beforehand

Turn the corner: *To go round the corner; to get past a difficulty or danger* * I will just turn the corner and will be back shortly * With great difficulty and a bit of luck we could turn the corner in our mountain-climbing expedition

Turn the scale: *To decide; determine* * You will have to turn the scale if you want things to happen as per your wish * It is for every individual to turn the scale

Turn the stomach: *To nauseate* * I usually turn the stomach on hilly road journeys

Turn the tables: *To bring about a complete reversal of circumstances; to change sides as in backgammon* * The master stroke by the forwards in the dying moments turned the tables on the opposition team * The teams had to turn the tables as per the rules of the game

Turn the wind: *To go; cause to move; from side to side or on a winding course* * Let us turn the wind and be away from the madding crowd * It was the nasty remark of the chairman which caused the members to turn the wind * He has turned the wind due to sheer determination and courage

Turn to: *To have recourse to; to point to; to result in; to change or be changed into* * I had to turn to my best friend when all doors were closed

Turn to account: *Turn to advantage* * The mistakes of our opponents turned to account for our team and we won the match

Turn Turk: *To become Mohammedan; to be completely reversed* * After visiting Saudi Arabia, my friend has decided to turn Turk * He turned Turk completely from his earlier statement

Turn turtle: *To render a turtle helpless by turning it on its back; to turn bottom up* * If you turn turtle, the poor animal will be in a lot of trouble * I was banking on financial support from my friend but he turned turtle at the last moment

Turn up: *To point upwards; to fold upwards; to come or bring; to light; to appear by chance; to disturb; to make lighter* * The boy turned his hands up in a silent prayer * Please turn up all the loose sheets and keep them securely in the locker * The manager has still not turned up for the meeting * Please turn up the lamp as it is getting dark * The principal turned up in our class-room and checked the attendance * Some hooligans turned up during the cultural programme and spoiled the evening * Your sincere advice has turned up my problems to a large extent

Turn up one's nose at: *To refuse or receive contemptuously* * The director turned up his nose at the new transfer policy rules framed by the technical committee

Turn up trumps: *To behave in a very helpful or generous way especially unexpectedly* * He turned up trumps at my request and went out of the way to make sure that my work was completed in time

Turn upon: *To cast back upon; retort* * I never believed that my friend will turn upon me when I needed him most * He turned up angrily to his friend at his insulting remarks

Twiddle one's fingers: *To be idle* * I am just twiddling my fingers and waiting for my friend since last one hour

Twin one's head: *To make one giddy; to get infatuated with success* * The hilly journey usually makes my head twin * The high success in the early years has made his head twin

Twinkling of an eye: *Very quickly* * He was so fast that he reached the roof-top in the twinkling of an eye

Twist the lions' tail: *To irritate Britain* * Our new economic policy is likely to twist the lion's tail

Two faced: *Having two faces; double dealing* * The new mask I purchased at the fair is two faced * His two-faced attitude had an ulterior motive to cheat us

Two or three: *A few* * There were just two or three spectators to watch the first show of our play

Two strings to one's bow: *An alternative in reserve* * One should have always two strings in one's bow for unforeseen circumstances

U

Under a cloud: *In trouble; disgrace* * I need financial help from you as I am seriously under a cloud * The shameful attitude of the boy brought the whole family under a cloud

Under-age: *Too young* * You are under-age to see this movie

Underarm: *Armpit* * Use deodorant to kill the bacteria which form underarm

Under-bare poles: *With all sails furled* * The boat moved very fast in the open sea under-bare poles

Under command of: *Authority commanded by* * The troops marched ahead victoriously under the command of General Patton during the war

Underdog: *Anyone in adversity* * The West Indies cricket team is the underdog in the forthcoming World Cup Cricket tournament as they have not been in form since the past two years

Under-fire: *Exposed to the enemy's fire* * The troops faced heavy casualties as they were suddenly under-fire

Under-hatches: *Under arrest; in confinement* * The convict was taken under-hatches the moment the verdict was announced against him

Under one's hand: *With one's proper signature attached* * The document was sealed safely under the hand of the principal and dispatched

Under-one's hat: *In confidence* * You should have taken me under your hat before taking such a crucial decision

Under-one's own steam: *By one's own unaided efforts* * The team ultimately won the crucial match under the captain's own steam

Under one's thumb: *Under one's domination* * The manager has managed to keep the whole staff under his thumb

Under-one's very nose: *In full view* * The purse was stolen from the suitcase by the thief under everybody's very nose

Under-one's wing: *Under one's*

protection * The king vowed to take the rebels of neighbouring country under his wings

Under penalty of: *With liability in case of infraction to the penalty of* * He has been put under a heavy penalty of a few thousand rupees for evasion of taxes

Under sail: *Having the sails spread* * The ship is already under sail and you have come late

Under seal: *Authenticated* * The document handed over to you is under seal and be careful to carry it

Under the auspices of: *Under the prosperous lead or patronage of* * The troops marched ahead victoriously under the auspices of the able general

Under the counter: *Reserved for the favoured; secret* * Do keep a few tickets for the next show of this movie under the counter * The operation was kept under the counter till the commandos busted the enemy's den completely

Under the eye of: *Under the observation of* * You are under the eye of a hidden camera, hence resist from playing any tricks

Under the heel: *Crushed* * The rebels were handled firmly and put under the heel by the army

Under the knife: *Undergoing a surgical operation* * He had to be under the knife for removal of the cyst on his skin

Under the rose: *In confidence* * Better to take all the members under the rose before moving the resolution

Under the sun: *On earth* * Peaceful co-existence is the law of Nature under the sun

Under the weather: *Indisposed; drunk* * I cannot attend office today as I am feeling under the weather * Don't believe his statement as he is under the weather

Under-the-counter: *Hidden from the customer's sight* * The salesman tried to cheat me by keeping the better quality items under-the-counter

Under-water: *Below the surface* * A different and unexplored world lies underwater

Under-way: *In motion; as a vessel* * The train is already under-way so do not try to climb on to it now * The boat was under-way when the storm struck

Up and doing: *Active* * He is very up and doing even after a prolonged illness

Up and down: *Often to and fro* * I have to make frequent trips up and down from my residence to the office

Up hill and down dale: *Vigorously and persistently* * He pursued the plan up hill and down dale before receiving approval from the authorities

Up in arms: *In readiness to resist* * The criminal was up in arms but the police overpowered him immediately

Up one's sleeve: *In secret reserve* * Always keep something up your sleeve for difficult times

Up the pole: *Drunk; in favour* * I don't believe him as he is up the pole at the moment * I am not up the pole with your idea regarding going out at night in this deserted town

Up to date: *Abreast of the times; adapted or corrected to the present time* * This piece of information is not up to date * Your watch is not up to date at all

Up to snuff: *Knowing; not likely to be taken in* * He is already up to snuff and will not hesitate to come forward * He is trying his best but not up to snuff in the final squad participating in the Asian Games

Up to the elbows: *Completely engrossed* * He is up to the elbows in his studies because the exam starts next Monday

Up to the eyes: *Deeply involved* * I am up to the eyes on this project, so do not disturb me

Up to the knocker: *Up to the required standard of excellence or fashion* * She tried hard but could not come up to the knocker in the beauty contest

Up to the mark: *Satisfactory* * The performance of the male actor in the drama was not up to the mark

Up to time: *Punctual; not later than the due time* * He will not be late for the show, he is always up to time

Up-a-gum tree: *In straits* * Do help me financially as I am up-a-gum tree these days

Upon a thought: *In a moment; with the speed of thought* * He responded upon a thought to the interviewer and was declared successful * He answered all the questions of the quiz master upon a thought

Upon conscience: *On my conscience; truly* * I swear upon my conscience that I am telling you the truth

Upon my honour: *An appeal to*

one's honour in support of a statement * The statement made by the minister in Parliament was upon his honour, as he clarified

Upon one's legs: *In an independent position* * You are not upon your legs to take such an important decision without consulting your parents

Upon the gad: *Upon the spur of the moment* * He became so agitated during the discussion that he slapped his friend upon the gad

Upon the shun: *Bent on evading notice* * The revenue authorities pasted the notice on the door of the residence since the landlord was bent upon the shun

Upon the whole: *Generally speaking; all things considered* * This is not such a serious issue upon the whole on which you should be too annoyed * The dispute stands resolved ultimately upon the whole

Upper ten: *The richest; the most influential class* * To be in the upper ten, you require hard work

Ups and downs: *Good times and bad times* * The ups and downs in the life should be treated as passing reflections of one's *karma* (fate)

Upset the apple-cart: *To throw all plans into confusion* * The sudden decision of the director to postpone the exams has upset the apple-cart completely as we were thinking of going abroad

Upside down: *In complete confusion* * The whole plan was turned upside down

Use and wont: *The customary practice* * The use and wont of any society have to be followed strictly to maintain originality

Use up: *To consume* * To use up any medicine after its expiry date is very dangerous

Used-up: *Exhausted* * All the resources have been completely used up and there has been no progress in this case

V

V-day: *Victory day; specific May 8, 1945, when Germany surrendered unconditionally* * V-day will be remembered as a turning point in world history

Very well: *Phrase signifying acceptance of facts or a situation* * The facts of the case were received very well by the jury

Vested interest(s): *Interests already established; the class of persons who have acquired rights or powers in any sphere of a country's activities* * I have vested interests in wanting to visit my home town * A certain category of people having vested interests have managed to get the rules modified in their favour

Vexed question: *A question which cannot be decided easily* * This being a vexed question requires detailed deliberations

View away: *To see break in cover* * Do take a view away and assess the situation properly

Virgin honey: *Honey that flows from the comb* * Virgin honey is difficult to find

Visible means: *Means or resources which are apparent to or ascertainable by others* * All visible means were adopted to resolve the tangle

Visit with: *Be a guest with; chat with* * Please visit with me our village * Please go and visit with the concerned man to know the details of the project

Vote down: *To defeat or suppress by vote* * He was voted down and forced to resign

Vote in: *To elect* * The vote in is going in full swing right from the word go

Vote of no confidence: *The legal method of forcing the resignation of a government or governing body* * He was ousted from the post of chairman as a vote of no confidence was passed against him by an absolute majority

Votive offering/Votive picture/Votive tablet: *One dedicated in fulfilment of vow* * I am in complete votive offering and committed to fulfil the mission

Vouch to warrant: *To cite as authority; to assert; declare; to testify; to support by evidence* * You can vouch to warrant his statement as an authority * Please try to vouch to warrant from him the exact facts * The emergency has been vouched to warrant with immediate effect by the government * Do not worry, I will vouch to warrant for you if need be

W

Wade in: *To make a vigorous attack* * The army had to wade in with full preparation in the battle-field

Wage-earner: *One who works for wages; one who earns the money that supports* * A sole wage-earner can hardly feed a big family

Waif and stray: *Strayed properly* * A waif and stray attitude will result in utter confusion only

Wails and wisdom: *The homeless* * The government was forced to evacuate the wails and wisdom to a safer place well before the typhoon struck

Waist-deep: *As deep as to reach the waist* * I had to cross waist-deep water to reach my house

Waist high: *As high as to reach up to the waist* * As the rainy water was waist high, it became very difficult to cross the road

Wait about: *To delay action; to be in attendance or in readiness to carry out orders; to bring food to the table and clear away used dishes; lie in ambush for; await* * Just wait about till we get the green signal from the boss * Do not be lax but just wait about and execute the job assigned in a professional manner * The waiter waited about till we were ready for the meal * The troops were just waiting about in the bushes and were ready to attack * Just wait about for me till I am back

Wait attendance: *To remain in attendance* * Please remain outside and wait attendance

Wait for: *To stay in expectation* * Please wait for further communication

Wait off: *To allow oneself to be temporarily outdistanced by other competitors; reserving one's energies for the final stretch* * The defending champion allowed himself to wait off to let the juniors a chance * The athlete in the last lane was waiting off and won the race by making a fast dash in the last lap

Wait on: *To continue to wait* *

Don't be in a hurry but just wait on as I shall be back shortly

Wait table: *To wait at table during a meal* * We will join you shortly while you just wait table

Wait up: *To stay out of bed waiting* * I was waiting up for you so that we could go for a walk

Wait upon: *To call upon; visit formally; to accompany; to attend and serve; to be connected with or follow as a consequence; to carry out the duties of; to gaze at* * Please wait upon him till I rejoin you shortly * Don't hesitate to wait upon the chairman * I can't wait upon you in the evening as I am already committed * Please wait upon the guests personally and make them comfortable * You will have to wait upon sincerely as it is an important task * Don't keep on waiting upon that lady as it is not proper

Wake a night: *To remain awake* * You will have to wake a night completely to catch the thief

Waken to: *To become conscious of; alive to* * He was waken to his senses the moment proper care was ensured by the hospital * He was waken to abruptly by his father at midnight

Walk away from: *To outdistance or undo easily* * The parcel lying there appears to be suspicious, so just walk away from it immediately

Walk into: *To beat; to storm at* * The big man walked into the next round of the boxing match by knocking down his opponent in the first round * The manager walked into the conference room in an agitated manner

Walk off: *To leave; to depart; to get rid of by walking as disagreeable feelings or effects* * He walked off the meeting in protest * I was ready to walk off for the airport when I got the news about the cancellation of the flight * The meeting lasted long and I had to walk off as nobody was serious about the agenda

Walk off with: *To take surreptitiously; to win easily* * The moment he hit the bull's eye, he walked off with the winning amount * The West Indies cricket team walked off with an easy victory in the opening tie of the tournament

Walk on: *To walk ahead; to continue to walk* * He walked on speedily and I could not keep pace with him

Walk on air: *To be exultant or light-hearted* * I felt as if I was walking on air the moment I came out of the examination hall

Walk one's chalks: *To quit; go away without ceremony* * The secretary had to walk with his chalks as the majority of the members were against him * The president was thrown out of the post and he had to walk with his chalks

Walk the chalk: *To keep a correct course in manners or morals* * If you cannot walk the chalk, you will not be accepted as a respectful member of our society

Walk the hospitals: *To be a student under clinical instruction at a general hospital or infirmary* * I am walking the hospitals these days

Walker on: *One who plays parts in which he has nothing to say* * In this play, my role is like a walker on the street

Walking case: *A patient but not confined to bed* * Though he has recovered, yet he is a walking case

Walking orders: *Dismissal* * The manager passed immediately the walking orders to his peon for being late

Walk-on: *One in which the actor has nothing to say* * I was given initially only a walk-on part in the play

Walk-out: *To leave as a gesture of disapproval* * The agitated employees staged a walk-out in protest against the stubborn attitude of the chairman during the meeting

Walk out on: *To desert; leave in the lurch* * The workers were so disgusted with their leader that they decided to walk out on him * The accountant abruptly walked out on the job and everybody was shocked to know the mess he has created in the accounts

Walk-over: *A race where only one competitor appears and has merely to cover the course to win* * The basketball team got a walk-over their opponent as the team failed to report on time * I got a walk-over in the first round as my opponent did not turn up

Wall up: *To block with a wall; to entomb in a wall* * The street was walled up in the end and we had to come back * The children of Guru Gobind Singh were walled up by the enemy

Walls have ears: *There may be*

listeners * Avoid speaking loudly as they say that even the walls have ears

Want wit: *A fool; one without sense* * He proved himself to be a want wit and made a mockery of himself in the meeting * He is a want wit and cannot survive in this business

War baby: *A baby born during a war; a soldier's illegitimate baby* * He was a war baby who lost his father immediately after his birth * The war baby gets social stigma by birth

War neurosis: *A better term for shell shock* * The tragic news of the accident of her husband left her as a war neurosis

War of nerves: *Systematic attempts to undermine morale by means of threats, rumours and counter rumours, etc.* * The enemy was diplomatically defeated in the war of nerves which was a big moral victory for our forces

War to the knife: *Unrelenting conflict* * The problem in West Asia is like war to the knife between Arabs and Jews

War wearied: *Wearied with; tired of war* * War-weary soldiers were too shattered to even think of another movement towards the border * The regiment was so war wearied that they wished it would end soon

Warm up: *To become or make warm; to heat; as cooked food; eager* * Better warm up so that your body is toned up to play the crucial match * Do warm up the stove * Warm up the food for me as I am too tired * He was too warmed up to listen the outcome of the match of his favourite team

Warrant of attachment: *A writ authorising the seizure of property* * A warrant of attachment was issued by the court in my favour ultimately

Wash down: *To help the swallowing or digestion of a solid food* * Just gulp some beer to wash down the food

Wash one's brain: *To drink copiously* * Don't try to wash your brain as you will be in trouble

Wash one's dirty linen at home: *To keep secret sordid family affairs* * Try to wash your dirty linen at home only to save your family from embarrassment

Wash one's hands of: *To disclaim responsibility* * He washed completely his hands of the crime committed by his son and disowned him

Wash one's hands off: *Have no further connection* * He completely washed his hands off from his friends who were members of a thief-gang

Wash out: *To remove by washing; to wash free from dirt; to disappear or become fainter as a result of washing; to cancel* * Please try to wash out the stains from my shirt * The crockery has to be washed out before using it since it is full of dirt * The colour of my shirt has been almost washed out * The match was washed out due to bad light

Wash up: *To wash one's hands and face; to wash the dishes and cutlery after a meal; to sweep up on to the shore* * Please wash up quickly and come to the dining table * You will have to help in washing up before we retire * The waves washed us up completely as we approached the sea-shore

Wassail bowl: *A cup from which health is drunk* * Let us pray for you and have a drink from the Wassail bowl

Waste product: *Material produced in a process that is discarded on the completion of that process* * The industrial waste products being dumped in the rivers are polluting the water

Watch after: *To follow the movements of* * Just try to watch after that boy who is roaming in front of your house since long

Watch and ward: *The old custom of watching by night and by day in towns and cities; uninterrupted vigilance* * Watch and ward schemes are becoming very popular in residential colonies to prevent thefts * Watch and ward staff was not alert when the security officer paid a surprise visit

Watch in: *To keep awake to welcome* * Please watch in and receive the guest properly as he will be coming late at night

Watch one's step: *To step with care; to act warily; be careful not to arouse opposition* * Please watch your steps as it is too dark outside * Watch your steps before you move the resolution in the meeting * You will have to watch your steps to avoid any problems during the meeting

Watch up: *To sit up at night* * Watch up the security

guards by making surprise visits at night

Watching brief: *Instructions to a counsel to watch a legal case* * The watching brief was given to the advocate but he failed to comply with the instructions

Watch out: *A look out* * Watch out your son's company

Water of life: *Spiritual refreshment; whisky, etc.* * Water of life was given to the dying man to give him final solace * Let's have water of life to celebrate your promotion in office

Water on the brain: *Hydrocephalus* * The water on the brain proved fatal for him

Water on the knee: *An accumulation of serious fluid in the knee-point* * With old age approaching, one has to be careful about water on the knees

Ways and means: *Resources; methods* * You have to devise ways and means to get this project cleared as per schedule * The ways and means adopted to carry on a particular job are as crucial as planning

Weak side: *That side or point in which a person is most easily influenced or most liable to temptation* * Since we are on the weaker side, we cannot take a final stand on this policy issue

Weaker sex: *Woman* * Special laws have been promulgated by the government to protect the weaker sex from cruelty

Weal and woe: *Prosperity and adversity* * Weal and woe are shadows of each other as they occur one after another

Wear and tear: *Loss by wear or use* * My brand new shoes were condemned to the dustbin because of excessive wear and tear

Wear away: *Consume; to decay or fade out; to pass off* * The whole stock was worn away by the troops before the next supplies could reach in time of scarcity * Every living thing ultimately wears away with passage of time * The clothes tend to wear away due to frequent washing

Wear down: *To diminish; overcome* * The demand for the new high-speed server may wear down by next year very fast * I could wear down the urge to buy the new dress ultimately

Wear off: *To pass away by degrees* * Every new object tends to wear off with repeated usage

Wear on you: *A curse* * Illiteracy

is a wear on you poor people

Wear one's heart on one's sleeve: *To show feelings openly* * The girl wears her heart on her sleeve because she seems to fall for any guy that she meets

Wear out: *Become useless by decay; to harass* * My new shoes have worn out very fast since I started playing cricket every day * The advocate was grilling the accused to wear him out so that the truth would come out

Wear the breeches: *To be master; of wife ruling her husband* * Who wears the breeches in the house – the wife or the husband? * The wife who wears breeches dominates her household

Weather a point: *To gain an advantage or accomplish a purpose against opposition* * I could ultimately weather a point after putting all the statistics on the table in the conference

Weather alone: *To make headway against adverse weather* * Last winter, I had to travel early morning by car to Delhi and had to weather alone because of thick fog

Weather anchor: *The anchor lying to windward* * The ship has just weather-anchored

Weather on: *To gain on in a windward direction* * We will have to weather on before the storm starts

Weather out: *To hold out against till the end* * Try to weather out and make sure that the task is completed in time

Weather the storm: *Outlive the trouble* * I could weather the storm the moment my friend offered his free services at my factory

Week about: *In alternate periods of seven days* * I have to travel almost week about as my job profile demands it

Week in week out: *Continuously without a break* * I want a break very badly as I have been week in week out for long

Weigh anchor: *To take up the anchor* * The ship will need to weigh anchor to drop the passengers ashore

Weigh down: *To force down; to preponderate over* * Don't try to weigh down unnecessarily * I am not trying to weigh you down but am explaining the true facts only

Weigh in: *To ascertain one's weight before a fight or after a horse race; to join in a project* * Just weigh in the competitors properly so that there is no mismatch * Do weigh in with me and we both will finish the task well before schedule

Weigh in with: *To produce in a discussion* * Please weigh in with the statistical information so that your case is well accepted

Weigh out: *To weigh and dispense in portions accordingly; to ascertain one's weight before a horse race* * Don't be in a hurry but weigh out all the options before taking a final decision * Let's weigh out the running mares well in time

Weigh to the beam: *To outweigh completely* * His arguments were weighed to the beam and he won the case

Weigh up: *To force up; to consider carefully and assess the quality of; as a person* * Why are you weighing up the issue without any conviction? * Please weigh up all the pros and cons carefully * Shall we weigh you up again after the medical test?

Weight with: *To influence* * You will have to put your weight with the manager so that he settles the case in your favour

Weighed in the balance and found wanting: *To be found incomplete* * The proposal was well prepared by the enthusiastic engineer to increase the production capacity but it was weighed in the balance and found wanting

Well-acquainted: *Having intimate personal knowledge* * My boss is very well-acquainted with the art of designing

Well advised: *Prudent; in one's right mind* * A well-advised man will never be hasty in decision-making * I was well advised by my secretary not to travel at night as the area was not safe

Well and good: *Phrase signifying assent* * Your views are taken well and good

Well-appointed: *Well equipped* * The fire brigade team was well-appointed to tackle any mishap during the fire outbreak

Well-balanced: *Having the parts properly adjusted for smooth working; sane and sensible* * The software and hardware has to be compatible and well-balanced so that a computer operates properly * A well-balanced person can look after the financial health of a company

Well-becoming: *Proper or suitable* * The building project is taking shape of a well-becoming monument

Well-behaved: *Behaving or acting in accordance with propriety or with requirements* * My son is a very well-behaved child

Well-being: *Welfare* * To look after the well-being of the troops is the foremost duty of every commanding officer

Well-beloved: *Very dear* * A wife is a well-beloved of the husband

Well-be seen: *Showy in appearance* * To be well-be seen among peers is becoming common nowadays

Well-born: *Born of a good family; not of mean birth* * He was well-born, hence he was given good education also * He is a well-born man and very polished too

Well-breathed: *Strong of lung; not out of breath* * Even after running five rounds of the ground, he was well-breathed

Well-bred: *Educated to polished manners; of good stock* * I have got my son admitted in a posh school so that he is well-bred to move in a cultured society * As we are well-bred for the rainy days we need not worry

Well-conditioned: *In a desirable condition* * My old car is still well-conditioned to run smoothly

Well-conducted: *Properly managed; acting properly* * The show was well conducted by the master of the ceremonies * The play was well conducted by the artists though it was their first attempt

Well-connected: *Having influential relations* * In your case, I shall advise you to contact some well-connected person who may help you in getting a job

Well-derived: *Of good stock or antecedents* * One can earn a lot by taking a leaf from one's well-derived past

Well-desired: *Much sought after* * This new model of the car is well-desired by me since long

Well directed: *Skilfully aimed* * The play was well directed and appreciated by the audience

Well-disposed: *Healthy; well placed; inclined to be friendly* * I am well-disposed now after the treatment I received * He is now well-disposed after the initial struggle in the new company * That man appears to be well-disposed towards me

Well-doer: *One who thrives and is prosperous* * As he is performing well in business he is a well-doer

Well-done: *Bravely; nobly* * It was a well-done acting on your part * To help the down-trodden is a well-done task

Well-earned: *Thoroughly deserved* * The hockey team was successful in winning a well-earned victory

Well enough: *In a moderate but sufficient degree* * I cleared my entrance examination well enough to step in further

Well-famed: *Very famous* * A well-famed musician is going to play tonight and I want to enjoy it

Well-fed: *Plump* * The well-fed kid could not run at all and came last in the race

Well-founded: *Built on secure foundation; based on solid evidence or sound reasoning* * The multistoreyed building has to be well-founded and earthquake-proof to avoid any disaster * The arguments put forth by the prosecution were so well-founded that they sealed the fate of the culprit

Well given: *Well disposed* * The patients were well given by the medical specialist in spite of being less experienced

Well-gotten: *Obtained honestly* * The deal was well-gotten by my friend in spite of stiff competition

Well-graced: *Popular* * The well-graced and charming actor was cheered by the crowd the moment he entered the auditorium

Well-grounded: *Firmly founded* * The pillars have been well-grounded to make the structure solid

Well informed: *Having sound and sufficient information on a particular subject* * Just keep me well informed about the step-by-step developments in the crucial case

Well intentional: *Having or arising from good intentions* * My move is absolutely well intentional and favours you

Well-judged: *Correctly calculated* * The captain took a well-judged decision and declared the innings to put pressure on the opposite team

Well knit: *Closely and firmly connected* * All the members of the team are well knit under the new captain

Well known: *Fully known; celebrated; notorious* * The chairman is well known to me and I shall put a word in your favour before the interview * Well-known artists gathered together to participate in a charity show * The well-known gangster was killed by the police in an encounter

Well-liking: *In good condition* * I am feeling well-liking after the fever

Well-lined: *Full of money* * The well-lined suitcase remained unclaimed at the police station for months

Well-looking: *Good looking* * A well-looking personality looks appealing to everybody

Well-mannered: *Polite* * The well-mannered child pleased the gathering by his overall behaviour

Well-meant: *Rightly* * The argument was very appropriate and well meant as per the occasion

Well-met: *An old complimentary greeting* * He was well met by the hosts at the party at the entrance itself

Well-minded: *Favourably inclined* * All well-minded person approved the funds to be spent on his workers

Well-nigh: *Nearly; almost* * The pilot with his sharp reflexes avoided the mishap well-nigh

Well-off: *In good circumstances; fortunate* * I am well-off now and can repay the debts easily * I am lucky and well-off to have an obedient son, faithful wife and a charming daughter

Well-pleasing: *Acceptable* * A well-pleasing personality is a delight and pleases everyone

Well-probed: *Correctly governed; properly arranged* * The well-probed report included all the details of the case * The portfolio was well probed

Well proportionate: *Having correct proportions* * The distribution of his property is well proportionate amongst all his children

Well-read: *Of wide reading* * He is a well-read man and has a very good collection of books

Well-regulated: *Well ordered* * The proceedings of the meeting were well-regulated by the coordinator

Well-respected: *Highly esteemed; given due consideration* * Our college principal is a well-respected man amongst all the students * Your views are well-respected but cannot be accepted

Well-rounded: *Symmetrical; well constructed and complete* * The building has been beautifully designed and well-rounded also

Well-seen: *Experienced; skilful* * The new overseer is well seen and very efficient * A well-seen surgeon cannot fail

Well set: *Properly arranged; firmly fixed* * Everything is well set for the show, so let us go immediately * The broken pieces of the toy were well set by affixing with a good solution

Well-set up: *Well built* * The proposal has been well-set up as it is backed by solid statistical inputs

Well-spoken: *Spoken well or fittingly; graceful or courteous in speech* * His well-spoken reply gave a shock to the arrogant clerk * The president delivered a well-spoken address and the gathering was flattered

Well-tempered: *Having a good bodily or mental constitution; of steel/mortar* * He is a very well-tempered politician who plans his campaign systematically * A well-tempered structure will last any strong tremor

Well-the-wed: *Well-mannered; abounding in moral wisdom* * The well-the-wed kid charmed the gathering with his manners * Can we say that the well-the-wed are bygone in the present times?

Well thought of: *Reasoned soundly and arranged with skill* * Your plan is really well thought of but cannot be implemented practically

Well-thumbed: *Showing marks of much handling* * The book received today appears to be well-thumbed

Well-timbered: *Strongly built of wood/Furnished with much growing timber* * The new furniture which we purchased for our house is well-timbered

Well-timed: *Opportune* * Your well-timed remarks really made me confident and gave the much required support

Well-to-do: *Well-off; prosperous* * He belongs to a well-to-do family

Well-turned: *Accurately rounded; shapely* * A well-turned piece of art was sold at a high price during the auction

Well-up for: *Well prepared for* * I am well-up for any test or cross-examination in the court

Well up in: *Well versed in; well acquainted with* * He is well up in his trade and can be relied upon to complete the job

Well warranted: *Having good credit* * I am dependent on my friend who is well warranted and will definitely help me

Well-wilier: *A well-wisher* * I am your well-wilier and will not do anything to discredit you

Well-wish: *Act of wishing well* * We all pray and well-wish you for a speedy recovery

Well-won: *Gained honestly or by hard endeavour* * A well-won effort is always a result of hard work and dedication

Well-worked out: *Thoroughly or logically planned or developed* * The plan was well-worked out by the commander before the troops marched out for the attack

Well-worn: *Much worn; trite* * The well-worn dress ultimately lost its colour and texture with time

Wend one's way: *To make one's way; follow the road especially in a leisurely fashion* * He will need to wend his way though the large crowd that has gathered in the hall to see him * Let us just wend our way as there is neither any hurry nor are we late

Wet blanket: *A damper of spirit* * The injury to the star player put a wet blanket on the cheerful mood of the winning team

Wet one's clay: *To drink* * Let's go out and just wet our clay to chill out

What a plague: *What the devil* * What a plague has struck this town this monsoon!

What a vengeance: *What a mischief* * With what a vengeance the kids hit out at their opponents in the game of hockey

What do you say to: *How about; are you inclined towards* * What do you say about my new project? * What do you say to this pay package that we have offered you?

What price: *What about now; what do you think of* * Shall we go back later to the hotel, but at what price? * Can you give some idea about what price will it be to board this flight?

What reek: *What does it matter* * What reek it is at this stage to support him since the council has already dismissed him from chairmanship?

What though: *Notwithstanding the fact that* * He continued to propose her name for two years what though she did not respond at all

What time: *When* * By what time will you reach here?

What with: *By reason of* * Can you explain what with you have entered my premises?

What's to do: *What is the matter* * What's to do which brings you here at this odd time?

What's what: *The true position of affairs; the proper, conventional, profitable way to behave or proceed* * The chairman could not explain what's what of the financial plan during the meeting * Unless one knows what's what, one cannot succeed in any project

Wheels within wheels: *A situation in which a complication of influence are at work* * There are so many wheels within wheels that I am thoroughly confused and can't make out head or tail out of it

When all's said and done: *Considering all facts* * When all's said and done, the verdict might be in favour of our cousin

When as: *At what time* * When as you reach home, give me a ring immediately

Wherewithal: *Resources* * They could not open a shop because they do not have the wherewithal

Whet: *Stimulate* * The tasty snacks served before the dinner whetted the guest's appetite for the dinner that was to follow

Whether or not: *Whether so or not so; in any case; in any event* * You will have to report on duty today itself whether or not you like it * You cannot leave things as they are because you have to finish the job whether you like it or not

Which is which: *Which is the one, which is the other?* * Can you tell me which is which from these packages so that I could pick up the right one?

Whip and spur: *With great haste* * We could barely manage to reach before the show started with whip and spur * The forces moved with whip and spur to spring a surprise on the enemy

Whip the cat: *To practice small economies; to work by the day as a dressmaker, tailor, etc.; going from house to house; to idle; to play a practical joke* * Let us try to whip the cat at first before planning for the mega event later on * He is whipping the cat along with his father after finishing his school level education * He goes out early in the morning from one village to another and whips the cat till evening to sell the handicrafts * There is no point in whipping the cat and wasting precious time for the results to come out * The friends whipped the cat and made fun of me to enjoy themselves

White flag: *An emblem of truce or surrender* * The enemy raised the white flag and it was all over

White lie: *A conventional phrase not strictly true; a well meant falsehood* * The witness gave his statement in the court full of white lies to save the accused * A white lie told frequently appears to be half truth

White livered: *Cowardly* * The white-livered action of yours cast a slur on your name and fame

Whited sepulchre: *One who is not what he seems to be* * He is a whited sepulchre and cannot be trusted

Who but he: *Who else? He only* * This daring stunt in the movie could have been performed by who but he, our famous action hero.

Why not: *A challenge for reason* * Why not fight a boxing bout with me?

Why on earth did you say that: *What evermade you say that* * Why on earth did you say that when you could have kept quiet?

Why, so: *So let it be* * If you wish the designing of the house will be as per my taste, why, so!

Wide awake: *Fully awake* * I was wide awake when I heard some noise in the backyard of my house in the dead of the night

Wide of: *Indifferent to; far from deserving* * The wide of attitude towards life can result in frustration * The idea is wide of planning, hence it can't be discussed further.

Wide of the mark: *Far out; astray from the truth* * The wide of the mark throw by the fielder helped the batsman to reach the crease easily * There is no point giving a statement wide of the mark without proper back up by facts and figures

Widespread: *Diffused* * The widespread rumours created tension in the city and the police was called on the streets

Widow's cruse: *A source of supply that never fails* * We are thriving on the widow's cruse though we don't know for how long

Widow's mite: *A small offering generously given* * I cannot donate more than a widow's mite as I am financially tight these days

Widow's weed: *The mourning*

dress formerly worn by all widows * The ladies in the widow's weed were looking very sad and serious

Wigs on the green: *A fray* * What we will gain to have wigs on the green on minor matters?

Wild goose chase: *A hopeless search or adventure* * A wild goose chase ultimately resulted in frustration only as we could not find the hidden treasure in the garden

Wild honey: *Honey made by wild bees* * The wild honey is of the finest quality and pure as well

Will and pleasure: *Wishes* * The wills and pleasure, if fulfilled easily, can bring immense pleasure to all

Willy-nilly: *Whether one wishes or not* * Being a social animal one has to follow certain customs and rituals willy-nilly

Win and wear: *To enjoy possession of* * Just relax and win and wear the jackpot items as you have been lucky to win it

Win by a head: *To win very narrowly* * Our candidate won the election by a head in the assembly polls

Win in a centre: *To win easily* * My friend won in a centre the election to the post of president of students' council

Win of: *To get the better of* * Our team could finally manage to win of the last league match in the tournament

Win on: *To gain on; to obtain favour with* * Try to win on his favour for me since you know the chairman * He has won on his boss and now he is trying to get himself posted out

Win one's spurs: *To earn knighthood; to gain distinction by achievement* * The Lord of Essex won his spurs from the Queen because of his bravery in the battle-field * To win on one's spurs gives real satisfaction

Win out: *To get out; to be successful* * The batsman was actually trying to win himself out by hitting wide balls * To win out with one's hard work is not that easy as it appears because one has to be really dedicated to the cause

Win over: *To bring over one's opinion o party* * I was able to win over the union leaders after a long discussion with them

Wind a ship: *To turn the ship about end for end* * Please wind the ship at the earliest if you want to avoid serious trouble

Wind up: *The close; to finish; to come to a conclusion; to adjust for final* * Please wind up the game immediately as it has started raining heavily * Better wind up your speech as we have overshot the time schedule * Let us wind up the preliminaries and be ready for the gala event

Wind up and down: *To resolve in the mind* * I am winding up and down in mind to reassess the position and come to a final conclusion

Wink at: *Ignore* * Don't wink at me unnecessarily

Wipe out old scores: *To take revenge on* * As I have to wipe out some old scores with him I will not vote in his favour in the forthcoming senate election

Wire away: *To act or work with vigour* * The workers were fully wired up with the resolve to increase the production

Wire into: *To eat vigorously and assiduously* * Have patience and don't try to wire into the food as it will affect you adversely in the long run

Wise to: *Aware of* * I am fully wise to your viewpoint and you can rest assured that I will support you

Wise women: *A witch; a midwife* * A wise woman can create havoc if she is offended * In rural areas, people still depend on wise women as the basic medical facilities are not readily available

Wish fulfilment: *The satisfaction of a desire in dreams* * At least I had my wish fulfilment in buying a car which is not possible for a poor man

Wish one further: *To wish one was in some other place* * I wish my daughter one further in USA on her birthday

Wishful thinking: *A type of thinking in which the individual substitutes the particular thing will happen or is so; engendered by desire that it should happen; thinking about and wishing for an event or turn of fortune that may not take place* * Everyone makes some wishful thinking for something or other in their life

Wishing/wish bone: *Wish bone; the merry thought* * The wishing bone might be a good boon for our family * Merely having wishing bones does not mean success unless you do hard work for fulfilling your wish

Wit and wisdom: *Cleverness and wisdom* * The wit and wisdom of the speaker was at its best when he handled all kinds of questions with aplomb

With a bad grace: *Ungraciously* * The chairman left the meeting midway with a bad grace as he was being grilled by the media

With a grain of salt: *With reservation; as of a story that cannot be admitted* * I accept your version of the incident with a grain of salt * The narration submitted by the correspondent should be taken with a grain of salt as it does not sound plausible

With a siserary: *Suddenly; on the spot* * The boy jumped in front of a speeding car with a siserary and was killed

With a view to: *Having in mind* * It is better to consider all pros and cons with a view to achieve your targets successfully

With a will: *Heartily and energetically* * I am with you on this new project and with a will to achieve it as per the target

With all one's heart: *Most willingly* * My services are at your disposal with all my heart

With an eye to: *For the purpose of* * My friend wants to settle down abroad with an eye to better career prospects there than in India

With bated breath: *With breath restrained from reverence or fear* * I saw with bated breath the robbers strike my servant with a rod

With child: *Pregnant* * Please take care of her as she is with child

With closed doors: *In private; the public being excluded* * Let us discuss the issue with closed doors * The court ordered to start the proceedings of the case with closed doors

With empty hands: *Idle* * The leaders came back from the meeting with empty hands

With flying colours: *Triumphantly* * West Indies won the World Cricket Cup with flying colours

With good grace: *In amiable fashion* * The players accepted their defeat with good grace

With might and main: *With great energy* * The forwards pushed the ball with might and main in the dying minutes of the match

With one accord/consent: *Unanimously* * The resolution was passed by the executive committee with one accord/consent

With one foot in the grave: *On the brink of death* * That old man is getting married with one foot in the grave

With one voice: *Unanimously* * The resolution was passed by the cabinet against the recent terrorist attacks with one voice

With one's back to the wall: *In desperate straits* * With my back to the wall, I decided ultimately to fight to the end

With one's own accord: *With spontaneous unanimity* * All political parties have resolved to fight terrorism with their own accord

With open arms: *With affection and pleasure* * The delegation was welcomed by the management with open arms

With reference to: *Concerning* * This paragraph is with reference to the text only and should not be excluded in the speech by the manager

With respect/regard to: *Concerning* * This special economic package by the government is with regard to alleviating the problems of the tribals

With that: *Thereupon* * With that gesture, I could make up what the boss was trying to hint

With the tail between the legs: *Like a beaten cur* * The dog ran away with the tail between the legs when I fired a gun-shot

With vengeance: *To an excessive degree* * The enemy gathered the forces to strike with a vengeance

With whole skin: *Safe* * The whole family was lucky enough to survive with whole skin in the car accident

Withdrawing room: *A room used to retire into; detached* * Let us sit and relax in the withdrawing room * He turned to the withdrawing room out of anger

Within cry of: *Within hearing distance* * I could rush to the request for help in the street as I was within the cry of her call

Within doors: *In the house* * Most of the women are confined within doors in summer

Within measure: *Moderately* * One should spend money within measures to avoid landing in a debt

Within the four corners of: *Contained in* * Keep this proposal within the four corners of this room for the time being

Without book: *From memory* * I can reiterate without book whatever I have learnt

Without distinction: *Indiscriminately* * Is it worthwhile to pass the entrance examination with distinction! * The grant given by the government to the flood-hit areas was distributed without distinction

Without doors: *Out of doors; outside the family* * The boy was thrown without doors because of his bad behaviour * Any ceremony without doors is not appreciated by the community

Without measure: *Immoderately* * The plan was bound to fail as it was executed without measure

Without prejudice: *A phrase used to require an understanding that nothing detracts from one's claims if the negotiation fails* * Sweets were distributed to one and all without prejudice to anyone

Without price: *Priceless; without anything to pay* * The diamond ring is without price for me since my wife gifted it to me * This book is without price as the author himself has gifted it to me

Without rhyme or reason: *Without any cause* * The workers suddenly stopped work in the factory without rhyme or reason

Woe into: *Calamity will befall; may calamity befall* * I pray to God that the killer of the children be woe into

Woe is me: *Unhappy that I am; cursed am I!* * Woe is me that I was not present at the time of her illness to help her

Wolf in sheep's clothing: *A deceiver* * Please don't trust him at all as he is a wolf in sheep's clothing

Woman child: *A female child* * We have been blessed with a woman child after many years

Woman culler: *A killer of women* * The woman culler was ultimately nabbed by the police after he had murdered many

Woman grown: *Grown to womanhood* * Once a female attains woman grown, her overall personality changes

Woman of the town: *A whore* * After the death of her husband, she had no means of livelihood except to be a woman of the town

Woman of the world: *A woman of fashion; a married woman*

* A woman of the world likes to lead a glamorous life * A female becomes a complete lady after becoming a woman of the world

Woman post: *A female messenger* * The postal department appoints woman post also nowadays

Woman tired: *Henpecked* * The woman tired attitude of his irritated everybody

Woman vested: *Wearing women's clothes* * Can you believe that some male likes to be woman vested?

Wonderstruck: *Struck with astonishment* * I was wonderstruck at the phenomenal and unexpected outcome of the match

Wooden-headed: *Stupid* * That wooden-headed servant knows nothing except to sit and watch TV porgrammes

Word for word: *Literally; verbatim* * I have memorised the Holy Book word for word

Word of honour: *A promise which cannot be broken without disgrace* * To keep my word of honour, I will have to support my friend whether I like it or not

Work against: *To exert oneself in opposition to* * He was with me all the time but working against me in the election campaign

Work double tides: *To work night and day* * You will have to work double tides if you want to save money in a short span

Work for: *To exert oneself in support of* * We all must work for her in the next election to make her win

Work in: *To intermix; to introduce carefully and deliberately* * Don't try to work on two to three issues in the deliberations to create confusion * Please work in the issue after studying all the pros and cons

Work into: *To make way gradually into; to change; alter* * He has worked into the top hierarchy of the party after many years of dedicated work * Can you work into the system to improve it?

Work like a nigger: *To toil hard like a slave* * I require a complete break as I have been working like a nigger since last December

Work of art: *A production in one of the fine arts* * My first work of art was appreciated by the crowd at the exhibition

Work off: *To separate and throw off; to get rid of gradually; to print ready for circulation; to dispose of by handling* *

Please work off the family and business woes * Just work off from that man's company as he will ditch you one day as per my observations * The article is final and edited for work off * Just work off the plan and move forward

Work on: *To act or operate upon; to influence; try to do so* * Let us work on together and finish the job well in time * Can you work on the manager for me, please? * Why don't you work on and see the trend?

Work one's passage: *To earn one's passage one has to work hard* * I had to work my passage while going abroad since I had no finances to clear my debts

Work one's will: *To do exactly what one chooses* * Unless you work your will, you can neither enjoy nor be satisfied with your work

Work out: *To effect by continued labour; to make by cutting, digging etc.; to exhaust; to solve or calculate; to study fully* * Unless you work out with vigour, you cannot achieve the desired results * Please work out as per the design and as per the directions of the engineer * Don't work out too much that you get fatigued * Let us work out the proposal in detail before proceeding further * The plan has worked out well because I could complete the project as desired

Work the oracle: *To achieve the desired results by manipulation, intrigue, wire pulling, etc. to raise money* * I will be happy to see positive growth for which you will have to work the oracle

Work up: *To excite; to create by slow degree; elaborate* * The boxer was completely worked up before the start of the bout * The athlete was slowly working up the tempo of his run in the last leg of the race * Do try to work up the plan in detail * Don't try to work up the issue

Work upon: *Exert influence on* * Please try to work upon the manager and get my file moved up at the earliest

Work with: *To strive to influence by appeals* * You will have to work with some influential person to get your case move in your favour

Working majority: *A majority sufficient to enable the party in office to carry on without accidental defeats* * The government is just continuing with a working majority and may fall any time

Working to the rule: *Observing all the regulations scrupulously for the express purpose of slowing down work* * The agitated employees decided to work to the rule to register their protest

World old: *Exceedingly ancient* * The world-old fossils excavated recently will reveal many secrets relating to ancient civilisations

World power: *Strong enough to make the influence felt in world politics* * USA continues to be a world power

World war: *A war of world wide scope* * The Second World war was more destructive than the first one

World-wearied: *Weary or tired of the world* * Poverty, illiteracy and chaos make me world-wearied

Worldwide: *Extending over; found everywhere in the world* * Reliance Industry is expanding its core business worldwide

World without end: *Eternal* * Who knows where is the world without end?

Worldly wise: *Having the wisdom of those experienced in* * A worldly wise man can lead us to salvation

Worn out: *Much injured or rendered uselessly wear; past; gone* * The worn out soldiers have been transferred to the base hospital * The worn out days cannot come back again * A new thing bought today becomes worn out with passage of time

Worry down: *To swallow with a strong effort* * The quality of food was so bad in the hotel that we had to worry it down

Worry out: *To find a solution by intense or anxious effort* * You will have to worry out and solve this issue today only

Worse luck: *More's the pity* * It is nothing but never-ending worse luck with me that my business continues to run in loss

Worth one's salt: *Good for anything at all* * An accountant worth his salt would know the latest changes in the taxation laws

Worth the whistle: *Worth the trouble of calling for* * It was worth the whistle to shout for help in the darkness when feeling frightened

Worthwhile: *Worth the time and pain* * It is worthwhile to take a chance and try to find our way in this jungle

Worthiest of blood: *In questions of succession; male as opposed to female* * The worthiest of blood was crowned the next king * The worthiest of blood gets legal rights

Wound up: *To coil completely; to wind the spring; to furl; to tighten; to hoist* * We must wind up the watch completely * Unless you wind up fully, the machine won't work at all * Let us wind up the flag on the rooftop * The screws have to be wound up accurately so that the nuts and bolts fit into each other * The caretaker wound up the national flag unfurled earlier in the day

Wrapped up in: *Bound up in; engrossed in* * The child was wrapped up in warm clothes before being taken out * The ladies are all wrapped up in during the winter months

Wring from: *To extort from* * There are umpteen methods to wring any confession from the innocent

Wring off: *To force off by wringing* * One may try to wring off from bad company but the deeds will haunt one forever

Wring out: *To squeeze out by twisting* * Just wring out and the juice will come out automatically

Writ of privilege: *An order for the release of a privileged person from custody* * The writ of privilege was accepted by the court and our leader was released immediately

Write down: *To put down in written characters* * Please write down your resume on a piece of paper and submit immediately

Write off: *As an irredeemable loss* * The spoiled postage stamps have to be written off

Write out: *To transcribe; to write in full; to exhaust one's mental resources by too much writing* * Please help me in writing out this stuff as I am too occupied with some other work * Don't cut short the text but write it out without any modifications * I think I will be a complete write out after I have finished writing this book

Write up: *Excite; to create by slow degrees; elaborate; to achieve by effort and gradually* * The boy is sure to write up on finding his name in the list of awardees * Do not feel frustrated, just keep writing up * Can you write up completely so that everybody understands the plan comprehensively * You will have to write up all the points in your thesis before submitting it for approval

Writing on the wall: *A happening foreshowing downfall and disaster* * The writing on the wall was clearly visible for the Mughal army the moment their commander died in the battle-field

Wrong-timed: *Importunate* * The wrong-timed statement put the chairman in an embarrassing position during the meeting

Wry mouthed: *Having a crooked mouth; unflattering* * The witness went wry mouthed when he could not reply during the cross examination

X

X factor: *The designs for people in military that civilians do not face, for which they receive payment* * It is only defence experiments also are entitled for X factor

X marks the spot: *Where something is located or hidden* * Follow the X marks the spot and you will find the treasure

X-rated: *Not suitable for children sections of the society* * X-rated films are meant only for adults

Y

Year after year: *Every year for many years* * My family goes to the same place during summer vacations year after year

Year book: *A book published for a year* * A year book is a must for every company

Year by year: *As the years pass* * The love between husband and wife becomes more affectionate year by year

Year long: *Lasting for a year* * Year-long festivals were held in the village to celebrate the victory of good over ill

Year of grace: *Year of Christian era; A.D.* * Year of grace is synonymous with the year of Christian era

Year's mind: *A commemorative service on the anniversary of a death or burial* * The year's mind of President was well attended by every sections of the society

Year of discretion: *The age when a man can distinguish between right and wrong* * The year of discretion at a later stage of life are full of wisdom

Yellow press: *Newspapers engaged in sensational news and prone to reckless exaggeration* * Yellow press is supposed to play a vigilant role

Yeomen's service: *Powerful aid* * To help the famine-affected people is a yeoman's service.

Yield their palm: *To confess one's inferiority* * There is no harm in yielding to one's palm instead of boasting

Yield up the ghost: *Give up the ghost* * One should not be superstitious and yield up the ghost

Young hand: *Inexperienced* * Indian hockey team participating in the Olympic consists of mostly young hand

Z

Zero hour: *The time when something important is to begin* * Any member of the house is free to ask any question during the zero hour

Zip it: *To tell someone to be quiet* * The chairman asked the Secretary to zip it any plan to the media before the project is formally launched

Zip your lip: *To shut up; keep quiet* * Zip your lip, any utterance will annoy the speaker

Zero tolerance: *Policy of applying laws very strictly wherein people are punished even for minor offences* * The administration of the newly set up factory was based on zero tolerance

Zigzag: *A line or pattern that looks like a series of letter W's as it bends to the left and then to the right again* * The path from the hill to my cottage descends in a series of zigzags

Zero gravity: *A state in which there is no gravity, or where gravity has no effect* * An astronaut experiences a state of weightlessness in space due to zero gravity

Zero-rated: *Of goods and services, etc. on which you do not need to pay VAT* * Medical, accountancy and education are categorised as zero-rated under the new policy of finance ministry

Zebra crossing: *An area of road marked with broad black and white lines where vehicles must stop for people to walk across* * We should always cross the road at zebra crossing

❑❑❑